MANAGING FRONT OFFICE OPERATIONS

Educational Institute Courses

Introductory

INTRODUCTION TO THE HOSPITALITY INDUSTRY
Fourth Edition
Gerald W. Lattin

AN INTRODUCTION TO HOSPITALITY TODAY
Third Edition
Rocco M. Angelo, Andrew N. Vladimir

TOURISM AND THE HOSPITALITY INDUSTRY
Joseph D. Fridgen

Rooms Division

FRONT OFFICE PROCEDURES
Fifth Edition
Michael L. Kasavana, Richard M. Brooks

HOUSEKEEPING MANAGEMENT
Second Edition
Margaret M. Kappa, Aleta Nitschke, Patricia B. Schappert

Human Resources

HOSPITALITY SUPERVISION
Second Edition
Raphael R. Kavanaugh, Jack D. Ninemeier

HOSPITALITY INDUSTRY TRAINING
Second Edition
Lewis C. Forrest, Jr.

HUMAN RESOURCES MANAGEMENT
Second Edition
Robert H. Woods

Marketing and Sales

MARKETING OF HOSPITALITY SERVICES
William Lazer, Roger Layton

HOSPITALITY SALES AND MARKETING
Third Edition
James R. Abbey

CONVENTION MANAGEMENT AND SERVICE
Fifth Edition
Milton T. Astroff, James R. Abbey

MARKETING IN THE HOSPITALITY INDUSTRY
Third Edition
Ronald A. Nykiel

Accounting

UNDERSTANDING HOSPITALITY ACCOUNTING I
Fourth Edition
Raymond Cote

UNDERSTANDING HOSPITALITY ACCOUNTING II
Third Edition
Raymond Cote

BASIC FINANCIAL ACCOUNTING FOR THE HOSPITALITY INDUSTRY
Second Edition
Raymond S. Schmidgall, James W. Damitio

MANAGERIAL ACCOUNTING FOR THE HOSPITALITY INDUSTRY
Fourth Edition
Raymond S. Schmidgall

Food and Beverage

FOOD AND BEVERAGE MANAGEMENT
Third Edition
Jack D. Ninemeier

QUALITY SANITATION MANAGEMENT
Ronald F. Cichy

FOOD PRODUCTION PRINCIPLES
Jerald W. Chesser

FOOD AND BEVERAGE SERVICE
Second Edition
Ronald F. Cichy, Paul E. Wise

HOSPITALITY PURCHASING MANAGEMENT
William P. Virts

BAR AND BEVERAGE MANAGEMENT
Lendal H. Kotschevar, Mary L. Tanke

FOOD AND BEVERAGE CONTROLS
Fourth Edition
Jack D. Ninemeier

General Hospitality Management

HOTEL/MOTEL SECURITY MANAGEMENT
Second Edition
Raymond C. Ellis, Jr., David M. Stipanuk

HOSPITALITY LAW
Third Edition
Jack P. Jefferies

RESORT MANAGEMENT
Second Edition
Chuck Y. Gee

INTERNATIONAL HOTEL MANAGEMENT
Chuck Y. Gee

HOSPITALITY INDUSTRY COMPUTER SYSTEMS
Third Edition
Michael L. Kasavana, John J. Cahill

MANAGING FOR QUALITY IN THE HOSPITALITY INDUSTRY
Robert H. Woods, Judy Z. King

CONTEMPORARY CLUB MANAGEMENT
Edited by Joe Perdue for the Club Managers Association of America

Engineering and Facilities Management

FACILITIES MANAGEMENT
David M. Stipanuk, Harold Roffman

HOSPITALITY INDUSTRY ENGINEERING SYSTEMS
Michael H. Redlin, David M. Stipanuk

HOSPITALITY ENERGY AND WATER MANAGEMENT
Second Edition
Robert E. Aulbach

7/99

MANAGING FRONT OFFICE OPERATIONS

Fifth Edition

Michael L. Kasavana, Ph.D.
Richard M. Brooks, CHA

Disclaimer

This publication is designed to provide accurate and authoritative information in regard to the subject matter covered. It is sold with the understanding that the publisher is not engaged in rendering legal, accounting, or other professional service. If legal advice or other expert assistance is required, the services of a competent professional person should be sought.

—From the Declaration of Principles jointly adopted by the American Bar Association and a Committee of Publishers and Associations

The authors, Michael L. Kasavana and Richard M. Brooks, are solely responsible for the contents of this publication. All views expressed herein are solely those of the authors and do not necessarily reflect the views of the Educational Institute of the American Hotel & Motel Association (the Institute) or the American Hotel & Motel Association (AH&MA).

Nothing contained in this publication shall constitute a standard, an endorsement, or a recommendation of the Institute or AH&MA. The Institute and AH&MA disclaim any liability with respect to the use of any information, procedure, or product, or reliance thereon by any member of the hospitality industry.

2113 N. High Street
Lansing, Michigan 48906-4221

The Educational Institute of the American Hotel & Motel Association is a nonprofit educational foundation.

Printed in the United States of America
3 4 5 6 7 8 9 10 00 01 02 99

Library of Congress Cataloging-in-Publication Data
Kasavana, Michael L., 1947–
Managing front office operations / Michael L. Kasavana, Richard M. Brooks. — 5th ed.
p. cm.
Includes bibliographical references and index.
ISBN 0-86612-179-X (pbk.)
1. Hotel management. I. Brooks, Richard M. II. Title.
TX911.3.M27K385 1998
647.94'068—dc21 98–29129
CIP

Editor: George Glazer

Contents

About the Authors

Michael L. Kasavana, Ph.D., is a Professor in *The* School of Hospitality Business at Michigan State University, where he is considered the School's resident computer expert. Dr. Kasavana did both his undergraduate and graduate work at the University of Massachusetts—Amherst. He received a bachelor's degree in hotel, restaurant, and travel administration; a master of business administration in finance; and a doctorate in management information systems. He has written several books, instructional software packages, and a host of research journal and trade industry magazine articles.

Dr. Kasavana's teaching and research efforts have been sharply focused on computers in hotels, restaurants, casinos, and clubs. He is an active consultant and a recipient of the MSU Distinguished Faculty Award, MSU Teacher–Scholar Award, and the Eli Broad College of Business Withrow Teacher/Scholar Award. He has presented numerous seminars on a variety of topics in the United States, Canada, Hong Kong, and other areas of the world. Dr. Kasavana is also a member of the International Technology Hall of Fame sponsored by Hospitality Financial and Technology Professionals (HFTP) and a recipient of the Distinguished Achievements Award from the Food Service Technology Consortium (FS/TEC).

In addition to his responsibilities at the MSU hospitality school, Dr. Kasavana serves as the university's Faculty Athletic Representative to the NCAA, Big Ten, and CCHA athletic conferences. He also chairs the MSU Athletic Council.

Richard M. Brooks, CHA, currently serves as Vice President—Operations for BridgeStreet Accommodations, Inc., and is responsible for day-to-day management of the company's lodging and information operations as well as its central reservation system. Prior to joining BridgeStreet Accommodations, Mr. Brooks was Vice President of Rooms Management for Renaissance Hotels and Resorts, and Stouffer Hotels and Resorts. Mr. Brooks was also Resident Manager at the Boca Beach Club in Boca Raton, Florida, and has held positions with Hyatt Hotel Company, NCR Corporation, and Purdue University.

Mr. Brooks received B.A. and M.B.A. degrees in lodging management from Michigan State University. He has also been designated a Certified Hotel Administrator by the Educational Institute of the American Hotel & Motel Association and is a member of the International Technology Hall of Fame sponsored by Hospitality Financial and Technology Professionals (HFTP). Mr. Brooks is a member and past co–chairperson of the AH&MA Technology Committee and a past member of the AH&MA Strategic Planning Committee. In addition, Mr. Brooks has been a guest speaker at recent International Hotel and Motel Expositions in New York and many International Hospitality Technology Expositions and Conferences.

Chapter 1 Outline

The Hospitality Industry
- Defining the Term Hotel
- Classifying Hotels

Size

Target Markets
- Commercial Hotels
- Airport Hotels
- Suite Hotels
- Extended Stay Hotels
- Residential Hotels
- Resort Hotels
- Bed and Breakfast Hotels
- Timeshare and Condominium Hotels
- Casino Hotels
- Conference Centers
- Convention Hotels
- Alternative Lodging Properties

Levels of Service
- The Intangibility of Service
- Quality Assurance
- Rating Services
- World-Class Service
- Mid-Range Service
- Economy/Limited Service

Ownership and Affiliation
- Independent Hotels
- Chain Hotels

Reasons for Traveling
- Business Travel
- Pleasure Travel
- Group Travel
- Buying Influences

Multicultural Awareness

Summary

Case Studies

1

The Lodging Industry

Ellsworth M. Statler—the Henry Ford of the modern hotel—once said, "The guest is *always* right."[1] Some might counter this turn-of-the-century hotelier by saying, "Guests are *not* always right—but they are always *guests*." Either way, these statements reflect the ultimate challenge facing hospitality professionals: to provide service that meets the ever-changing needs and demands of guests.

For many, the hospitality industry holds a certain glamour and sophistication. This is partly due to the image most hotels choose, refine, and project to the public. Much of this image is created through architecture and design. Yet a building is really only bricks, mortar, steel, glass, and furnishings. The property's architecture and style may be important in setting the theme, but it is the hotel's staff that is essential to the creation of its ambience.

Front office personnel are literally on the front line in creating that image. Front desk agents, concierge, bell attendants, and door attendants are among the first employees guests see upon arriving at a hotel. The variety of talents and skills needed to satisfy guest needs makes front office work interesting and rewarding. And since no two guests, two hotels, or—for that matter—two days are ever the same, front office work can't help but be exciting and challenging.

This chapter will outline some basics about the hospitality industry, as well as show how hotels can be classified by size, market, level of service, and ownership and affiliation. A discussion on the reasons people travel will also be presented. Finally, the chapter will touch on some of the challenges the industry faces when accommodating the increasing number of guests from different cultures and nations.

The Hospitality Industry

The hospitality industry is part of a larger enterprise known as the travel and tourism industry. The travel and tourism industry is a vast group of businesses with one goal in common: providing necessary or desired products and services to travelers. Since 1992, travel and tourism has been recognized as the largest civilian industry in the world, employing one out of every ten persons worldwide.[2] It includes everything arising from the interaction of travelers with the businesses, governments, and people who make that travel possible. In the United States alone, more than 4 million miles of roads, 16,000 airports, and 47,000 lodging properties serve tourists. Travel and tourism is second only to health services in providing the most jobs. And it is the third largest industry, with travel spending contributing $1.24 billion *each day* to the U.S. economy.[3]

Exhibit 1 Overview of the Travel and Tourism Industry

Travel and Tourism Industry

Lodging Operations	Transportation Services	Food and Beverage Operations	Retail Stores	Activities
Hotels	Ships	Restaurants	Gift Shops	Recreation
Motels	Airplanes	Lodging Properties	Souvenir Shops	Business
Resorts	Autos	Retail Stores	Arts/Crafts Shops	Entertainment
Timeshare Hotels	Buses	Vending	Shopping Malls	Meetings
Condominiums	Trains	Catering	Markets	Study Trips
Conference Centers	Bikes	Snack Bars	Miscellaneous Stores	Sporting Events
Camps	Limousines	Cruise Ships		Ethnic Festivals
Parks		Bars/Taverns		Cultural Events
Extended Stay		Banquets		Seasonal Festivals
Bed and Breakfast		Contract Food Services		Gaming
Casinos				
Convention Hotels				
Cruise Ships				

Exhibit 1 divides the travel and tourism industry into five parts, and shows some of the components of each part. The hospitality industry consists of lodging and food and beverage operations—plus institutional food and beverage services, which do not cater to the traveling public. Lodging operations stand apart from other travel and tourism businesses since they offer overnight accommodations to their guests. Many lodging properties provide food and beverage service, recreational activities, and more.

An organization that addresses travel and tourism issues in the United States—particularly those affecting the hospitality industry—is the *American Hotel & Motel Association (AH&MA)*. Other countries have similar trade associations. These national trade associations work together through the International Hotel and Restaurant Association (IHRA) for common purposes. IHRA is based in Paris. As the trade association of the American lodging industry, AH&MA is a federation of hotel and motel associations located in the 50 states, the District of Columbia, Puerto Rico, and the U.S. Virgin Islands. AH&MA represents nearly 1.4 million hotel and motel rooms constituting more than 11,000 industry hotels, motels, and resorts—or 45% of the total rooms inventory in the United States. Canada and most other countries with many lodging establishments have national organizations as well.

A leading service of AH&MA is its *Educational Institute.* Since its founding in 1952, more than two million individuals have benefited from its programs and services—making it one of the largest hospitality industry educational centers in the world. This non-profit foundation provides essential educational and training resources for the expanding hospitality industry, and helps prepare dedicated individuals for careers and career advancement within the industry.

Defining the Term Hotel

With so many properties offering so many services in such a huge industry, it is easy to see why people get confused about the differences between hotels, motels, inns, and other lodging establishments. The fact is that the distinctions are not always clear. The confusion is compounded because owners can classify their properties as they deem appropriate—making it even more apparent why universally agreed-upon definitions are difficult to create. Still, despite the numerous exceptions, some general property distinctions do exist and are widely accepted.

A *hotel* or *inn* may be defined as an establishment whose primary business is providing lodging facilities for the general public, and which furnishes one or more of the following services: food and beverage service, room attendant (housekeeping) service, concierge, bell and door attendant service (sometimes called uniformed service), laundry or dry cleaning, and use of furniture and fixtures. Hotels range from 50 to 2,000 rooms, and sometimes more—some new hotels in Las Vegas have over 5,000 rooms. Inns usually average between 5 to 50 rooms and provide a higher level of personalized service.

The term *motel* is a contraction of *motor hotel*. It is a lodging facility that caters primarily to guests arriving by automobile. Early motels often provided parking spaces near guestrooms, but that has changed in recent years as motel owners and franchisors have become more aware of guest security. Motels may be located in any setting, but are usually found in suburban or roadside areas. They became especially successful in the 1950s and 1960s with the development of the interstate highway system in the United States. Many motels are two-story or low-rise buildings located near major highways. Pool areas with shrubbery, trees, and children's playgrounds are familiar "trademarks" for many motels. In most cases, motels do not offer the full range of services and facilities available in a hotel.

Unless otherwise indicated, this text will use the term **hotel** as a general term for motels, hotels, inns, suite hotels, conference centers, and other lodging properties.

Classifying Hotels

Placing a hotel in a particular grouping is not easy. Because of the industry's diversity, many hotels do not fit into any single well-defined category. Nonetheless, several general classifications do exist. The categories discussed in this chapter are based on hotel size, target markets, levels of service, and ownership and affiliation. It is important to note that a particular property may fit into several categories.

Size

Size—or the number of guestrooms in a property—gives us one common way to categorize hotels. Hotels are typically grouped in four size categories:

- Under 150 rooms
- 150 to 299 rooms
- 300 to 600 rooms
- More than 600 rooms

These categories enable hotels of similar size to compare operating procedures and statistical results. Unless otherwise specified, hotels in the classifications discussed in the remainder of this chapter may be of any size.

Target Markets

One of the most important marketing questions facing a hospitality operation is: "Who stays at our property and whom else can we attract?" Through marketing research, tools, and strategies, lodging properties seek to identify **target markets.** Target markets are distinctly defined groups of people that the hotel hopes to retain or attract as guests.

A recent trend in the hospitality industry is to define or identify smaller, distinct groups or "segments" within larger target markets, and to develop products and services aimed specifically at satisfying these groups or segments. This process of **market segmentation** has contributed to substantial growth, particularly within hotel chains (see Exhibit 2). For example, Marriott Hotels and Resorts now has many different brand names: Marriott Marquis, Marriott Hotels, Marriott Inns, Courtyard by Marriott, Fairfield Inn by Marriott, and Residence Inn by Marriott. Each brand is directed toward a specific type of guest—or *market segment*—that Marriott identified as having potential. The advantage to this approach is that a variety of properties can be located in a particular geographical market, thereby attracting a variety of guests. The disadvantage is that guests may become confused when trying to differentiate between the facilities and services of each brand in a chain.

Hotels target many markets and can be classified according to the markets they attempt to attract and serve. The most common types of properties based on target markets include commercial, airport, suite, residential, resort, bed and breakfast, timeshare, casino, conference center, and convention hotels. There are also several alternative types of lodging operations that directly compete with hotels and these are discussed at the end of this section.

Commercial Hotels

The first hotels and inns were usually located in the towns and villages they primarily served. It was not until the age of railroads that the hotel business began to

Exhibit 2 The Holiday Inn Family of Hotels

Holiday Inn® Family of Hotels

Holiday Inn Express®: With more than 600 hotels located around the world, Holiday Inn Express® hotels and Holiday Inn Express® Hotel & Suites are the right choice for travelers seeking a comfortable place to sleep, without frills, at an attractive rate. Providing a complimentary continental breakfast bar and free local phone calls in the US, Holiday Inn Express® hotels offer no-frills lodging, at a reasonable rate, with the reassurance of the Holiday Inn® reputation.

Holiday Inn Select®: Designed with business travelers in mind, all Holiday Inn Select® hotels provide free local phone calls; a large, well-lit work area with a phone and voicemail service; easy dataport access, weekday newspaper delivery and more in every room. In addition, they offer a range of meeting facilities and business support services. With more than 70 locations in the Americas, Holiday Inn Select® is the right place for travelers who need a better place to do business. Holiday Inn Select® -- where every room, at every location, is business class.

Holiday Inn

Holiday Inn®: Holiday Inn® hotels and Holiday Inn® Hotel and Suites are the right choice for today's business and leisure travelers providing up-to-date products and features, value for money and friendly service. With more than 1,500 convenient locations around the world, most hotels provide a restaurant and lounge, swimming pool and a range of meeting facilities.

Holiday Inn® hotels -- for the traveler seeking service and value with the reassurance of the Holiday Inn® reputation.

(continued)

Exhibit 2 *(continued)*

Holiday Inn SunSpree® Resorts:
Providing a fun, affordable resort experience, Holiday Inn SunSpree® Resorts also known as Holiday Inn® Resorts®, are located in a wide variety of leisure destinations. Enhanced swimming pools, in-room refrigerators and coffee makers, and full-service restaurants are just a few of the benefits.
From snorkeling to mountain biking, volleyball to basketball, each Holiday Inn SunSpree Resort® offers a unique experience for the traveler seeking a fun, affordable resort experience with the reassurance of the Holiday Inn® reputation.

Holiday Inn Garden Court®: Located in Europe and South Africa, each Holiday Inn Garden Court® hotel have a style and character unique to its location. Offering quality guest rooms, meeting and leisure facilities as well as the services and amenities appropriate in each unique location with the reassurance of the Holiday Inn® name.

Information at the Internet site of Holiday Hospitality Corporation (http://www.holiday-inn.com) describes features of Holiday Inn brands in relation to the major target markets they attempt to attract.

expand in the United States. Traveling by railroad was faster, easier, and safer than traveling by horse-drawn carriage or even by the first automobiles. Railroads connected the country; railroad stations were generally located near the center of each town. Travelers getting off trains usually needed a place to stay. As more people traveled, the demand for hotels grew. In turn, more hotels were built, many conveniently located near railroad stations. When it was originally built, the Waldorf-Astoria Hotel in New York City had its own underground railroad entrance for important persons arriving by rail. In time, hotels located in the city center catered not only to travelers but also became the social centers of the community.

Like their historic counterparts, today's commercial hotels are usually located in downtown or business districts—areas that are convenient and of interest to their target markets. These hotels are the largest group of hotel types and cater primarily to business travelers. Although commercial hotels primarily serve business travelers, many tour groups, individual tourists, and small conference groups find these hotels attractive. In the past, commercial hotels were referred to as *transient hotels* because of the relatively short length of guest stays compared with other hotels.

Guest amenities at commercial hotels may include complimentary newspapers, morning coffee, free local telephone calls, cable television, and access to VCRs and videos, personal computers, and fax machines. Car rental arrangements, airport

The famed Plaza Hotel has both a historic and business flair, located in the heart of New York City. (Courtesy of the New York Convention & Visitors Bureau, Inc., Two Columbus Circle, New York, New York. ©John Calabrese)

pick-up services, coffee shops, semi-formal dining rooms, and cocktail lounges are usually provided. Most commercial hotels have conference rooms, guestroom suites, room service, and banquet meal service. Commercial hotels may offer laundry-valet service, uniformed services including concierge service, in-room refreshment centers, complimentary local transportation, and retail stores. Swimming pools, health clubs, tennis courts, saunas, and jogging areas may also be among the property's features.

Airport Hotels

Just as railroads spurred the first expansion of hotels in the United States in the late 1800s and early 1900s, air travel encouraged a distinct type of hotel growth in the

1950s through the 1970s. Air travel did not really exist in its current form until modern commercial jet aircraft were introduced in the late 1950s. These jets traveled much faster and were much larger than earlier aircraft, and prompted dramatic economic growth in the United States. Demand skyrocketed for lodging facilities located near airports—especially international airports. Similar to the way hotels appeared near downtown railroad stations, hotels appeared near airports across the United States.

Airport hotels are popular because of their proximity to major travel centers. More than any other type of hotel, airport hotels vary widely in size and level of services. Typical target markets include business clientele, airline passengers with overnight travel layovers or canceled flights, and airline personnel. Hotel-owned limousines or courtesy vans often transport guests between the hotel and the airport. Signs announcing direct telephone service to nearby hotels for reservations and pick-up service are a common sight in most airports. Many airport hotels feature conference rooms to attract a particular market: those guests who travel to a meeting by air and wish to minimize ground travel. Guests who stay at airport hotels often enjoy significant cost savings and convenience from such arrangements.

Suite Hotels

Suite hotels are among the newest and fastest-growing segments of the lodging industry. These hotels feature guestrooms with a living room or parlor area and a separate bedroom. Some guest suites include a compact kitchenette with a refrigerator and in-room beverage service. In exchange for more complete living quarters, suite hotels generally have fewer and more limited public areas and guest services than other hotels. This helps keep suite hotels' guestroom prices competitive in the marketplace.

Suite hotels appeal to several different market segments. People who are relocating transform suites into temporary living quarters; frequent travelers enjoy the comforts of a "home-away-from-home"; and vacationing families discover the privacy and convenience of non-standard hotel accommodations designed with a family in mind. Professionals such as accountants, lawyers, and executives find suite hotels particularly attractive since they can work or entertain in an area besides the bedroom. Some suite hotels offer complimentary evening receptions, breakfasts, or hors d'oeuvre or snack service. Such gatherings give guests an opportunity to socialize, which may be important for guests staying at the property for extended periods.

Extended Stay Hotels

Extended stay hotels are similar to suite hotels, but usually offer kitchen amenities in the room, which suite hotels usually do not. They are designed for travelers who intend to stay five days or longer and require reduced hotel services. Extended stay hotels usually do not provide uniformed services, and often do not provide food, beverage, or guest laundry service. Like suite and residential hotels, they attempt to bring more of a homelike feeling to the interior and exterior designs. In

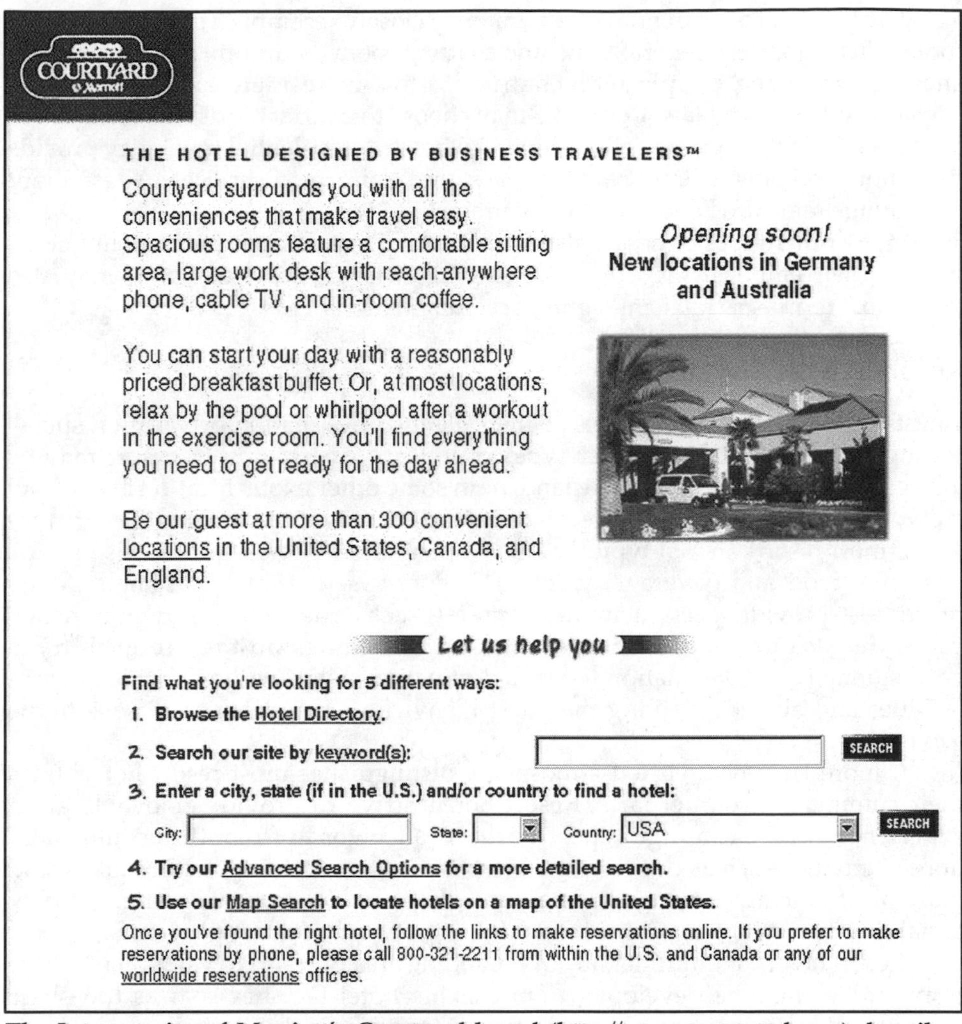

COURTYARD
Marriott
THE HOTEL DESIGNED BY BUSINESS TRAVELERS™
Courtyard surrounds you with all the conveniences that make travel easy. Spacious rooms feature a comfortable sitting area, large work desk with reach-anywhere phone, cable TV, and in-room coffee.
You can start your day with a reasonably priced breakfast buffet. Or, at most locations, relax by the pool or whirlpool after a workout in the exercise room. You'll find everything you need to get ready for the day ahead.
Be our guest at more than 300 convenient locations in the United States, Canada, and England.
Opening soon!
New locations in Germany and Australia
Let us help you
Find what you're looking for 5 different ways:
1. Browse the Hotel Directory.
2. Search our site by keyword(s):
SEARCH
3. Enter a city, state (if in the U.S.) and/or country to find a hotel:
City:
State:
Country: USA
SEARCH
4. Try our Advanced Search Options for a more detailed search.
5. Use our Map Search to locate hotels on a map of the United States.
Once you've found the right hotel, follow the links to make reservations online. If you prefer to make reservations by phone, please call 800-321-2211 from within the U.S. and Canada or any of our worldwide reservations offices.

The Internet site of Marriott's Courtyard brand (http://www.courtyard.com) describes benefits for business travelers and provides several ways for potential guests to gather more information about properties in specific locations.

addition, unlike most types of hotels, room rates are often determined by the length of stay.

Residential Hotels

Residential hotels provide long-term or permanent accommodations for people in urban or suburban areas. Located primarily in the United States, these properties house residents who want and can afford daily, limited hotel services. Residential hotels are not nearly as popular and prevalent as they once were. They have been replaced in part by condominium and suite hotel properties.

The layout of a residential guest unit may closely resemble a suite hotel guestroom. Guest quarters generally include a sitting room, bedroom, and small kitchenette. Sometimes, people who contract to live in residential hotels may be considered tenants by law. Residents may choose to contract for some or all of the services provided to guests in a commercial hotel. A residential hotel may provide daily housekeeping, telephone, front desk, and uniformed services. A restaurant and lounge may also be located on the premises.

Many other types of hotels also house semi-permanent or permanent guests, despite their emphasis on other markets. Likewise, residential hotels may also offer short-term—or transient—guest accommodations.

Resort Hotels

Guests often choose resort hotels as their planned destination or vacation spot—setting resorts apart from other types of lodging operations. A resort may be located in the mountains, on an island, or in some other exotic location away from crowded residential areas. The recreational facilities and breathtaking scenery typical of most resorts are not typical of most other hotels. Most resort hotels provide extensive food and beverage, valet, and room services for vacationers. Many resorts also provide special activities for guests such as dancing, golf, tennis, horseback riding, nature hikes, sailing, skiing, and swimming. Most resort hotels try to be positioned as a "destination within a destination" by providing a wide range of facilities and activities, giving the guest many choices and fewer reasons to the leave the property.

A more leisurely, relaxed atmosphere distinguishes most resort hotels from their commercial counterparts. Resort hotels strive to provide enjoyable guest experiences that encourage repeat business and word-of-mouth recommendations. Activities such as dancing, golf, tennis, horseback riding, nature hikes, and more are frequently arranged for groups of guests. Resort hotels often employ social directors who plan, organize, and direct a range of guest programs.

Resort hotel communities are an expanding area of resort development. These communities may be developed from existing hotel facilities sold as timeshare units or condominiums, or as new destination properties developed specifically as resort communities.

Bed and Breakfast Hotels

Bed and breakfast hotels, sometimes called B&Bs, are an often forgotten group of lodging properties. B&Bs range from houses with a few rooms converted to overnight facilities, to small commercial buildings with 20 to 30 guestrooms. The owner of a B&B—the host or hostess—usually lives on the premises and is responsible for serving breakfast to guests. Breakfast service may range from a simple continental breakfast to a full-course meal. Thousands of B&Bs are in operation today, deriving popularity from intimate, personal service for leisure travelers. Most B&Bs offer only lodging and limited food service or—as the name implies—breakfast only. Meeting rooms, laundry and dry-cleaning services, lunch and dinner, and

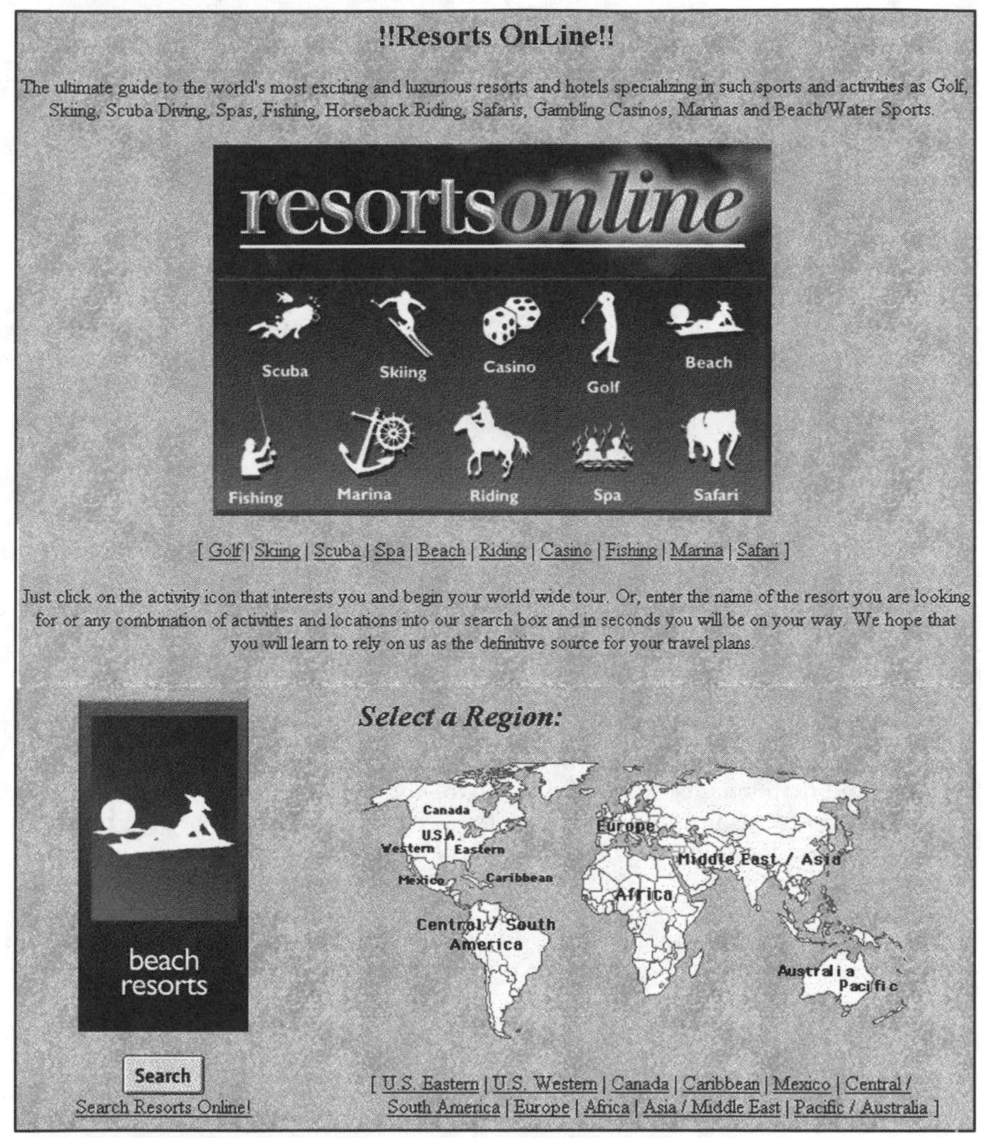
!!Resorts OnLine!!
The ultimate guide to the world's most exciting and luxurious resorts and hotels specializing in such sports and activities as Golf, Skiing, Scuba Diving, Spas, Fishing, Horseback Riding, Safaris, Gambling Casinos, Marinas and Beach/Water Sports.
resortsonline
Scuba
Skiing
Casino
Golf
Beach
Fishing
Marina
Riding
Spa
Safari
[Golf | Skiing | Scuba | Spa | Beach | Riding | Casino | Fishing | Marina | Safari]
Just click on the activity icon that interests you and begin your world wide tour. Or, enter the name of the resort you are looking for or any combination of activities and locations into our search box and in seconds you will be on your way. We hope that you will learn to rely on us as the definitive source for your travel plans.
Select a Region:
Canada
U.S.A.
Western
Eastern
Mexico
Caribbean
Central / South America
Europe
Middle East / Asia
Africa
Australia Pacific
beach resorts
Search
Search Resorts Online!
[U.S. Eastern | U.S. Western | Canada | Caribbean | Mexico | Central / South America | Europe | Africa | Asia / Middle East | Pacific / Australia]

The Internet site of Resorts OnLine (http://www.resortsonline.com) enables leisure travelers to search an extensive database of resort properties by desired activities and by geographical region.

recreational facilities are usually not offered. Due to limited services, the price for a room at a B&B is generally lower than at a full-service hotel.

Timeshare and Condominium Hotels

Another expanding segment of the hospitality industry is the *timeshare hotel.* These are sometimes referred to as *"vacation-interval"* hotels. Timeshare properties typically involve individuals who purchase the ownership of accommodations for a specific period of time—usually one or two weeks a year. These owners then occupy the unit—usually a condominium—during that time. Owners may also have the unit rented out by the management company that operates the hotel. Since the property functions as a hotel in many respects, travelers renting the unit may not realize it is actually part of a timeshare hotel. These hotels are becoming especially popular in resort areas. Owners may not be able to afford owning a condominium year-round, but can afford fractional ownership (ownership of a unit for a few weeks a year). One popular feature of timeshare hotels is the ability to trade ownership time with another owner in another location. For example, an owner of a beach-front timeshare unit may want to trade time in the unit for time in a winter ski unit. Often, the management company can work with the owner to find someone who wants to trade. This allows both owners the opportunity to vary their vacations each year, without giving up the benefits of ownership. Two major timeshare exchange companies are Interval International and Resort Condominiums International (see Exhibit 3).

Condominium hotels are similar to timeshare hotels. The difference between the two lies in the type of ownership. Units in condominium hotels only have one owner instead of multiple owners, each for a limited amount of time each year. In a condominium hotel, an owner informs the management company of when he or she wants to occupy the unit. That way, the management company is free to rent the unit for the remainder of the year. When the management company rents the unit, the revenue goes to the owner.

Timeshare and condominium owners receive the revenue from the rental of their units and pay the management company a fee for advertising, rental, housekeeping, and maintenance services. Timeshare and condominium owners are also responsible for furnishing and paying for the general maintenance of their units. In many cases, condominium and timeshare hotels were actually built as apartment or condominium buildings and converted to lodging use. Normally, these units consist of a living room, dining area, kitchen, bathroom, and one or more bedrooms. Guests of condominium hotels usually rent a unit for at least one week. It is not uncommon for guests to contract for a specific unit at a specific time each year.

Casino Hotels

Hotels with gambling facilities may be categorized as a distinct group: casino hotels. Although the guestrooms and food and beverage operations in casino hotels may be quite luxurious, their function is secondary to and supportive of casino operations. Until recently, casino hotel guestrooms and food and beverage facilities were not expected to earn a profit. Today, most casino hotels expect all their operations to be profitable. Similar to resort hotels, casino hotels tend to cater to leisure, vacation travelers.

Casino hotels attract guests by promoting gaming and headliner entertainment. A recent trend in casino hotels is to provide a broad range of entertainment opportunities, including golf courses, tennis courts, spas, and theme recreational activities. Casino hotels frequently provide specialty restaurants and extravagant floor shows, and may offer charter flights for guests planning to use the casino

Exhibit 3 Resort Condominiums International (RCI)

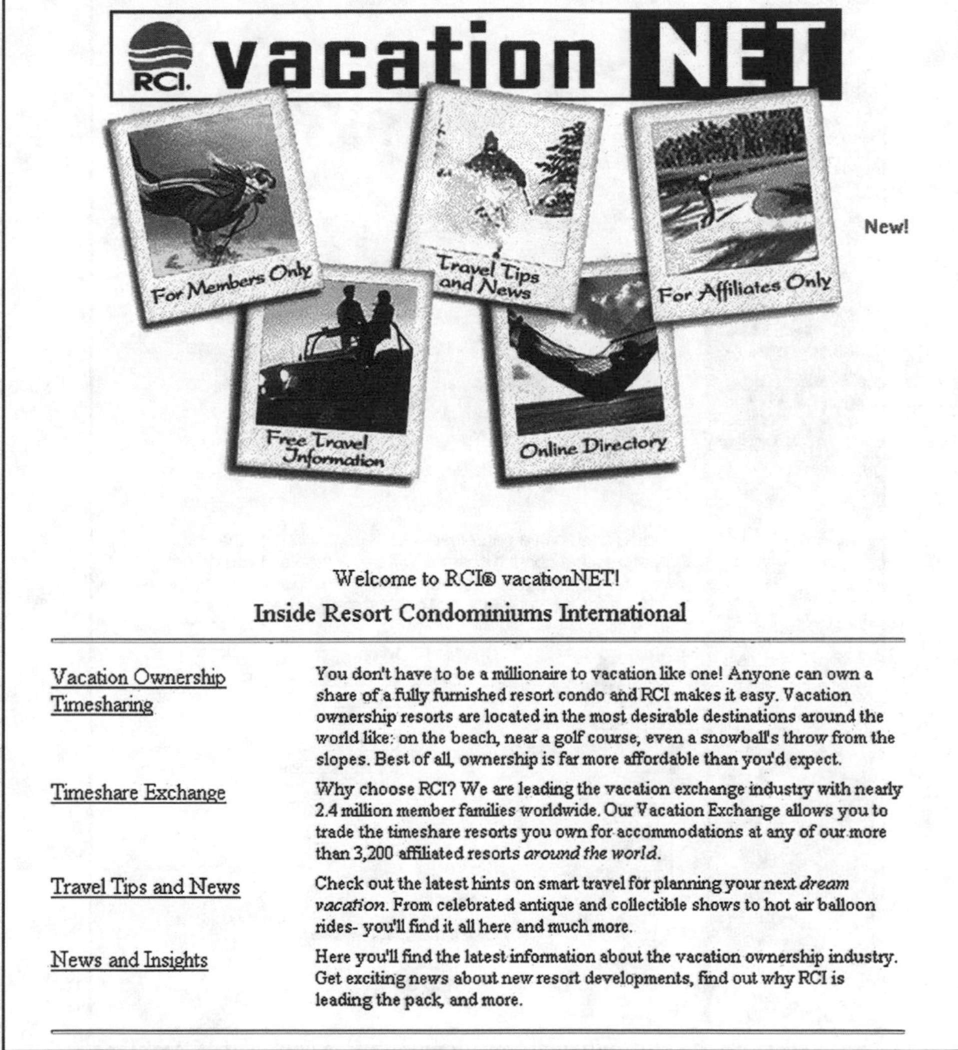

RCI.
vacation NET
For Members Only
Travel Tips and News
For Affiliates Only
New!
Free Travel Information
Online Directory
Welcome to RCI® vacationNET!
Inside Resort Condominiums International
Vacation Ownership Timesharing
You don't have to be a millionaire to vacation like one! Anyone can own a share of a fully furnished resort condo and RCI makes it easy. Vacation ownership resorts are located in the most desirable destinations around the world like: on the beach, near a golf course, even a snowball's throw from the slopes. Best of all, ownership is far more affordable than you'd expect.
Timeshare Exchange
Why choose RCI? We are leading the vacation exchange industry with nearly 2.4 million member families worldwide. Our Vacation Exchange allows you to trade the timeshare resorts you own for accommodations at any of our more than 3,200 affiliated resorts *around the world*.
Travel Tips and News
Check out the latest hints on smart travel for planning your next *dream vacation*. From celebrated antique and collectible shows to hot air balloon rides- you'll find it all here and much more.
News and Insights
Here you'll find the latest information about the vacation ownership industry. Get exciting news about new resort developments, find out why RCI is leading the pack, and more.

The Internet site of Resort Condominiums International (http://www.rci.com) provides information about vacation ownership and timesharing. RCI is the inventor of vacation exchange and the world's largest provider of exchange services for more than 2.2 million timeshare owners from more than 3,100 resorts around the world.

facilities. Gambling activities at some casino hotels operate 24 hours a day, 365 days a year; this may significantly affect the operation of the rooms and food and beverage divisions. Some casino hotels are very large, housing as many as 4,000 guestrooms under one roof.

Another recent trend is riverboat gambling. Because most riverboats do not provide lodging accommodations, hotels are often located where the riverboats

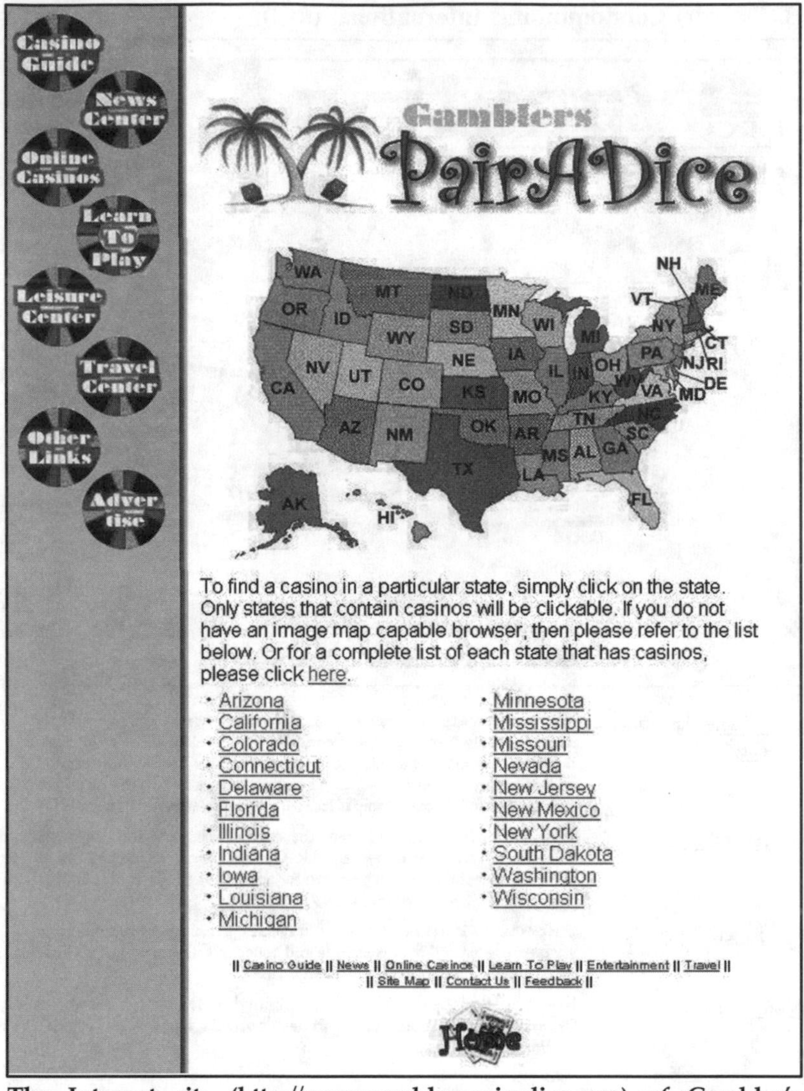

The Internet site (http://www.gamblerspairadice.com) of Gambler's PairADice provides links to casino hotels in the United States.

dock to accommodate gamblers. These hotels are not considered casino hotels because they do not have gaming as part of their facilities. However, they do contribute to the economy through jobs, revenue, and taxes paid for by the guests gambling on the boats.

Conference Centers

While many hotels provide meeting space, conference centers are specifically designed to handle group meetings. Most full-service conference centers offer

Las Vegas is home to several large convention facilities, being a favorite convention spot for many state, regional, and national associations. (Courtesy of the Las Vegas News Bureau and the Las Vegas Convention Center, Las Vegas, Nevada)

overnight accommodations for meeting attendees. Because meetings are their focal point, conference centers typically place great emphasis on providing all the services and equipment necessary to ensure a meeting's success—for example, technical production assistance, high-quality audiovisual equipment, business service centers, flexible seating arrangements, flipcharts and display screens, and so forth.

Conference centers are often located outside metropolitan areas and may provide extensive leisure facilities: golf courses, indoor and outdoor swimming pools, tennis courts, fitness centers, spas, jogging and hiking trails, and more. Conference centers typically charge meeting planners a single price, which includes attendee guestrooms, meals, meeting rooms, audiovisual equipment, and other related services. Guest amenities may not be as plentiful at conference centers since these centers concentrate more on fulfilling the needs of meeting planners and organizers than on meeting the needs of program attendees.

Convention Hotels

Convention hotels are another segment of the lodging industry that has grown significantly in recent years; the demand for the convention market has nearly doubled in the past 20 years. While most commercial hotels have fewer than 600 rooms, convention hotels—designed to accommodate large conventions—offer as many as 2,000 rooms or more.

Convention hotels have a sufficient number of guestrooms to house all the attendees of most conventions. Convention hotels often have 50,000 square feet or more of exhibit hall space—plus ballrooms and an assortment of meeting rooms. Most properties offer dining facilities ranging from self-serve restaurants or cafeterias to elaborate formal dining rooms. Convention hotels are primarily directed toward business travelers with a common interest. A full line of business services is generally available, including teleconferencing, secretarial assistance, language translation, and facsimile (fax) machines. Examples of convention hotels are the Opryland Hotel in Nashville, Tennessee; the Wyndham Anatole Hotel in Dallas, Texas; and the Hyatt Regency in Chicago. Often casino hotels offer similar facilities.

Convention hotels usually attract the convention market for state, regional, national, and international associations. They also attract regional, national, or international corporate meetings. While most hotels book the majority of their group business within two years of the meeting date, it is not uncommon for convention hotels to book their business up to 10 years in advance. Many groups are so large that they have to book space that far in advance to assure adequate facilities and housing for their attendees.

In some cases, convention hotels do not have all the facilities needed, but are affiliated with a local *convention center.* The convention center is usually owned by the local community, and often has its own sales force. Convention centers not only have space for meetings and conferences, they also have more than adequate space for exhibits and booths. Some convention centers have more than 500,000 square feet of floor space in one building. Convention centers normally coordinate efforts with nearby hotels to ensure that guestrooms are available for convention attendees. Hotels, in turn, sell the convention center to appropriate markets to garner rooms business.

Alternative Lodging Properties

Besides hotels, there are several other types of lodging establishments which compete for business and leisure travelers. Recreational vehicle parks, campgrounds, and mobile home parks are somewhat like hotels since they involve the rental of space for overnight accommodations. But although similarities exist, these alternatives stand apart from other facilities, sometimes vigorously competing for overnight accommodation revenues. In some resort areas, parks and campgrounds are strong competitors with traditional lodging operations because they appeal to a broader range of travelers. For example, many state and national parks offer campgrounds and lodges that compete directly with hotels. These facilities may have an advantage over local hotels since they are located on park land, are usually competitively priced, and may be subsidized.

Still another form of alternative lodging is the corporate lodging business. Corporate lodging is designed for guests wishing to stay longer periods of time, often up to six months, or longer. While hotels are usually designed for guests staying from one to ten nights, corporate lodging is better suited to guests with very long stay requirements. Guests often include business executives moving from one city to another, consultants on temporary assignments, corporate training programs, and special projects connected with movie or sporting events. Instead of using hotels or hotel-type buildings, corporate lodging usually provides fully furnished apartments for guests. In many cases, the apartments are provided by the building owners. In other cases, the apartments are provided to the guest by a service provider. The provider rents the apartment, rents the furniture and housewares and provides housekeeping and other services to guests. Since apartments are used instead of hotel buildings, corporate lodging can be provided in many locations by a single provider in a community, allowing greater flexibility in location to the guest. Corporate lodging is usually cost-competitive with hotels, since apartments can be rented and furnished by the owner or service provider for a lower daily cost than that incurred by hotels.

Another example of alternative lodging is the cruise ship industry. Cruise ships have become major competition for resorts, especially in the Caribbean region, and are primary competitors of resort hotels. They offer many amenities similar to those offered at island resorts, while having the unique advantage of moving from island to island as part of the experience. Modern cruise ships offer all the advantages of resort hotels. Staterooms come equipped with many modern conveniences, such as ship-to-shore telephones, satellite television, fitness centers, movie theaters, multiple dining and cocktail lounge facilities, spas, casinos, shopping and, of course, the novelty of waking up in a different location each morning. Cruise ships may be as small as 20 cabins or as large as 800 cabins or more. Some cruise ships now even offer small conference facilities for corporate or association meetings.

Levels of Service

Another way to classify lodging properties is by level of guest service. Service level is a measure of the benefits provided to the guest. The level of guest service offered in a hotel varies without regard to hotel size or type, and some hotels offer more than one level of service. The level of service is usually reflected in a guest's room rate. Before specific levels of service are discussed, some basic issues surrounding service must be presented.

The Intangibility of Service

Hotels are not simply in the business of selling *tangible* products such as comfortable beds and wholesome food. In fact, it is the *intangible* services a hotel provides that contribute most to the guest's hospitality experience. These services are not physical things, but rather actions, deeds, performances, or efforts. For example, a meal served in a hotel dining room is certainly a tangible element of a guest's experience. However, hospitality means more than just a good meal—it means surrounding the meal with a particular ambience, including the dining room's decor and the attitude of its staff. These intangible elements can be just as important as the tangible elements to the guest.

The difficulty is that after a service has been delivered, the purchaser generally has nothing tangible to show for it. Services cannot be touched, tasted, or tried on for size—and are virtually impossible to "return." For the most part, guests leave a hotel with only the memories of their experiences. To counteract this, many hotels try to create an image of their services that is powerful, clear, and precise. The hotel's service becomes an instantly recognizable standard, signature, or trademark of the hotel—almost like a tangible product. The hotel's employees must then sustain that image through their commitment to service.

Every service provided by a hotel must be appropriate to the market the property wishes to attract and satisfy. For example, guests at a small lodging property probably would be surprised if someone attempted to escort them to their rooms after registration. However, in a hotel with an appropriately defined market and level of service, escorting guests to rooms is an expected, important part of the image of the hotel.

Quality Assurance

The intangible services that a hotel delivers tend to be less standardized than the tangible objects produced by a manufacturer. One of the greatest challenges facing the hospitality industry today is controlling service variability. The consistent delivery of services is the result of a program of **quality assurance.**

The traditional quality control techniques of manufacturing industries may not be appropriate for the hospitality industry. In manufacturing industries, consumers are normally isolated from the production processes, and products are tested and inspected before they are sold. In hotels, some quality control techniques used in manufacturing industries may apply: guestrooms are inspected after they are cleaned, and the recipes of menu items are tested before the items appear on a restaurant's menu. However, in many instances, guests are not isolated from the hotel's production processes. For example, registration is a service that is produced, delivered, and consumed simultaneously in the presence of the guest.

Consistency is the key to quality service. And the ingredients of consistency are the standards that a lodging property develops. But, while standards establish and define quality, only the hotel's staff can make quality a reality. It is the consistency of a particular hotel or chain of hotels that often creates or sustains customer loyalty and preferences, as well as a unique market niche.

Rating Services

Several groups in the United States provide hotel evaluation and rating services for travelers. The best known of these services are provided by the *American Automobile Association (AAA)* and the *Mobil Travel Guide.* The finest hotels rated by AAA have earned either a five- or four-*diamond* rating. *Mobil Travel Guide* awards either five or four *stars* to the hotels earning its highest ratings.

It is extremely difficult for a hotel to earn either five diamonds or five stars. Standards are very strict and include consistency in the quality of facilities and services from year to year. While there are hundreds of four-diamond and four-star hotels in the United States, there are fewer than 50 five-diamond or five-star hotels.

In other parts of the world, similar rating services are provided by private organizations and by governments. For example, the Mexican government provides ratings of hotels from one star to five stars, plus an additional category of

Gran Turismo for the finest hotels. In Europe, one of the best-known and respected rating services is provided by Michlin.

For the sake of simplicity, lodging properties can be discussed in terms of three different levels of service: world-class, mid-range, and economy/limited. In many cases, a subclass of world-class hotels—first class—refers to hotels earning either four diamonds or four stars under the AAA or *Mobil Travel Guide* rating services.

World-Class Service

Hotels offering **world-class service**—sometimes called luxury service—target top business executives, entertainment celebrities, high-ranking political figures, and wealthy clientele as their primary markets. World-class hotels provide upscale restaurants and lounges, exquisite decor, concierge service, and opulent meeting and private dining facilities. Guests may find oversized guestrooms, heated and plush bath towels, large soap bars, shampoo, shower caps, clock radios, refreshment centers, and more expensive furnishings, decor, and artwork in the hotel's guestrooms. Housekeeping services are typically provided twice daily including a nightly bedroom turn-down service. Magazines and daily newspapers may be delivered to each guestroom.

The public areas of a world-class hotel may be large and elaborately decorated and furnished. Several food and beverage outlets are frequently available to cater to the tastes of the hotel's guests and visitors. There may also be a variety of retail outlets, such as gift shops, clothing and jewelry stores, specialty retail shops, and international newsstands.

Above all, world-class hotels stress personalized guest services and maintain a relatively high ratio of staff members to guests. This ratio enables the hotel to offer an extensive variety of amenities and unique services and to respond quickly to guest requests. Some of the finest hotels in Asia boast a ratio of two or more employees per guest. Many of the world-class hotels in North America have more than one employee per guest. World-class hotels frequently employ a multilingual concierge who provides extra assistance for guests. Among their many activities, concierges may help guests register, obtain tickets for transportation or entertainment, provide travel directions and sightseeing information, or arrange for secretarial or business services.

Executive Floors. In some hotels, certain floors are designated to provide some of the hotel's guests with world-class attention. Properties offering *executive floors* (sometimes known as *tower, concierge,* or *club floors*) provide non-standard guestroom furnishings and additional guest services in these areas of the hotel. Executive floors usually are designed with larger, deluxe guestrooms that may contain a number of unique amenities. Recent trends for these floors include in-room fax machines, videotape players, large televisions, and even computers. Executive-level guestrooms or suites might also feature an in-room refreshment center and may be stocked with signature bathrobes, fresh fruit, and fresh-cut flowers.

Usually, the luxury services offered on executive floors are not confined to the guestroom. A concierge, or personal butler, may be stationed on each executive

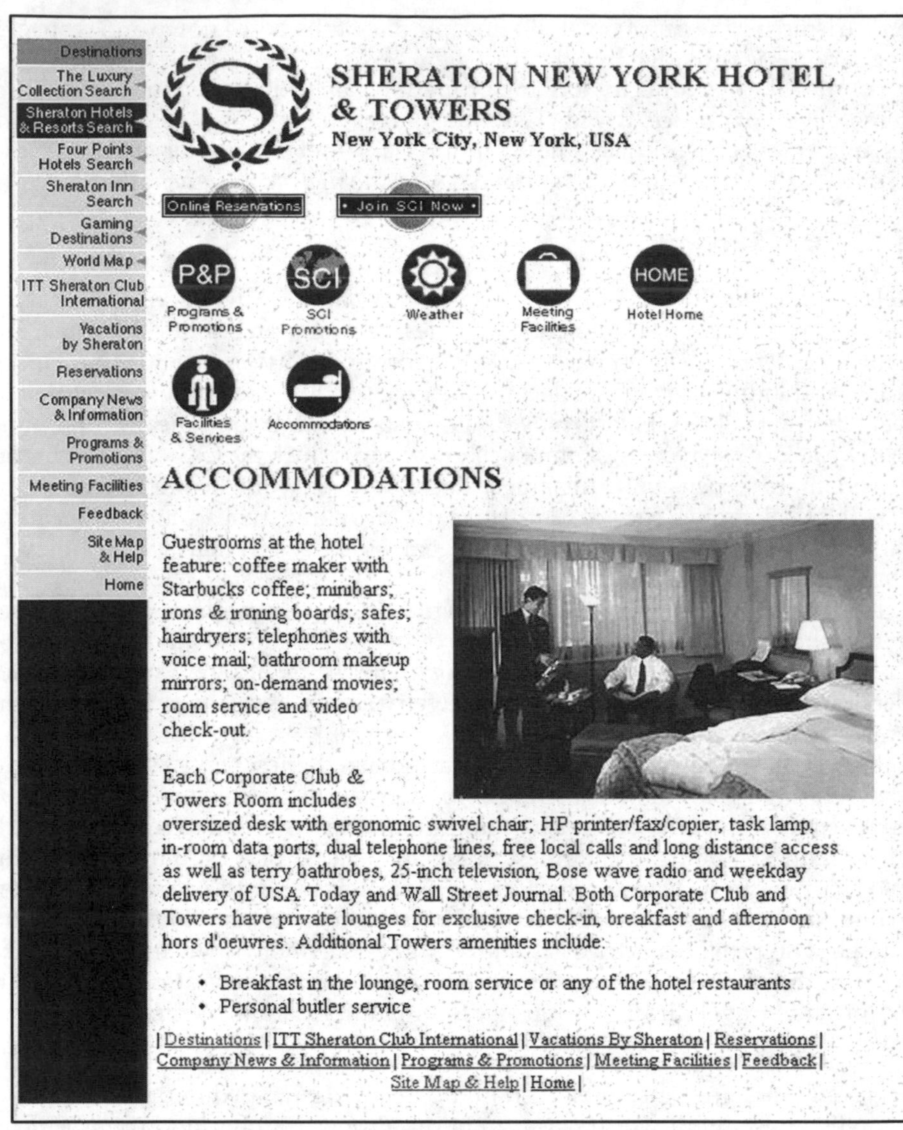

The Internet site of the Sheraton New York Hotel & Towers, accessed through Sheraton's main site (http://www.sheraton.com), describes the special guestroom features and amenities of the executive floors at the hotel.

floor. Access to these floors may be restricted by the use of special elevator keys that allow only authorized guests to enter. In many cases, the executive or tower floors contain a private lounge. Special complimentary food and beverage services may be offered in the evening, and a continental breakfast may be served in the morning. Conveniences such as secretarial services or special check-in and check-out arrangements may also be available.

Mid-Range Service

Hotels offering **mid-range service** appeal to the largest segment of the traveling public. Mid-range service is often modest but sufficient. Although the staffing level is adequate, the mid-range property does not try to provide elaborate services. A mid-range property may offer uniformed guest services, airport limousine service, and food and beverage room service. Like world-class and first-class hotels, mid-range properties range in size from small to large. The typical hotel offering mid-range service is of medium size—roughly 150 to 299 rooms.

The property may offer a specialty restaurant, coffee shop, and lounge that cater to visitors as well as hotel guests. The lounge may feature entertainment on the evenings when the hotel is expected to be most busy. Guests likely to stay at a mid-range hotel include businesspeople, individual travelers, and families. Rates are lower than world-class or first-class hotels since the properties offer fewer services, smaller rooms, and a smaller range of facilities and recreational activities. Such factors often make mid-range hotel properties appealing to those travelers desiring some hotel services, but not the full range of luxuries of world-class or first-class properties. Since meeting rooms are usually available at mid-range hotels, people planning small conferences, group meetings, and conventions may also find mid-range hotels attractive.

Economy/Limited Service

Economy/limited service hotels are also a growing segment of the hospitality industry. These properties provide clean, comfortable, inexpensive rooms and meet the basic needs of guests. Economy hotels appeal primarily to budget-minded travelers who want rooms with the minimal amenities required for a comfortable stay, without unnecessary, often costly, extra services. Since a large proportion of the population travels on limited funds, economy lodging properties have a potentially large market from which to attract clientele. The clientele of economy properties may include families with children, bus tour groups, traveling businesspeople, vacationers, retirees, and groups of conventioneers.

In the early 1970s, the only amenities offered by many economy properties were an in-room telephone, a bar of soap, and a television set with local channels. Most economy properties now offer cable or satellite television, swimming pools, limited food and beverage service, playgrounds, small meeting rooms, and other special features. What most economy properties *do not* usually offer is room service, uniformed guest services, large group meeting rooms, laundry or dry-cleaning services, banquet rooms, health clubs, or any of the more elaborate amenities found at mid-range and world-class properties.

An economy property generally does not provide full food and beverage service, which means guests may need to eat at a nearby restaurant. Many economy hotels do, however, provide a free continental breakfast in the lobby area.

Ownership and Affiliation

Ownership and affiliation provide another means by which to classify hotel properties. Two basic equity structures exist: independent hotels and chain hotels. An

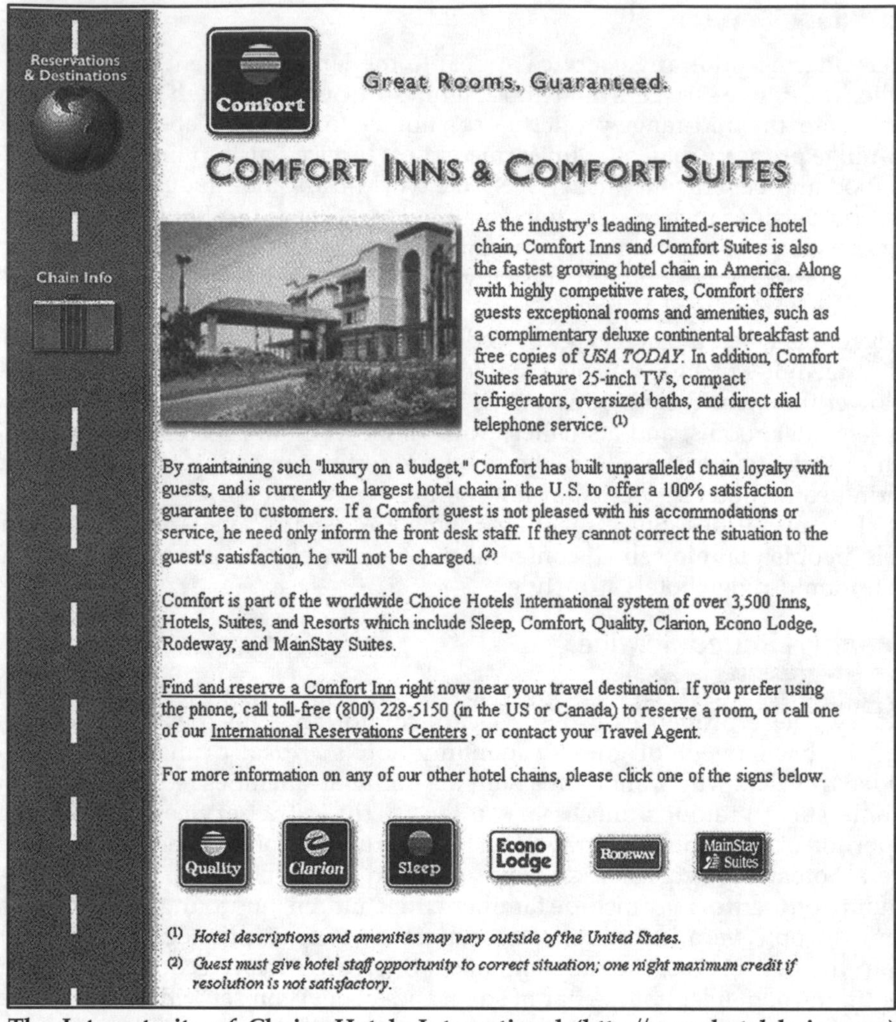

The Internet site of Choice Hotels International (http://www.hotelchoice.com) identifies benefits for market segments targeted by each brand within the chain.

independent hotel has no affiliation with other properties. **Chain hotel** ownership may take a number of forms, depending on the association that the chain organization has with each property. This chapter points out several distinct forms of chain ownership, including management contracts, franchises, and referral groups. Many chain hotel companies tend to be a mixture of several types of ownership.

Independent Hotels

Independent hotels have no identifiable ownership or management affiliation with other properties. In other words, independent hotels have no relationship to other hotels regarding policies, procedures, marketing, or financial obligations. A typical example of an independent property is a family-owned-and-operated hotel that is not required to conform to any corporate policy or procedure. From a business perspective, some independent properties are organized as sole proprietorships or partnerships, while others are incorporated by their owners to restrict insurance risk and personal liability.

The unique advantage of an independent hotel is its autonomy. Since there is no need to adhere to a particular image, an independent operator can offer a level of service geared toward attracting a specific target market. Moreover, the flexibility inherent in a smaller organization often allows the independent hotel to quickly adapt to changing market conditions. An independent hotel, however, may not enjoy the broad advertising exposure or management insight and consultancy of an affiliated property, and is unable to take advantage of the volume purchasing power of a chain hotel. Examples of well known independent hotels include The Breakers in Palm Beach, Florida, The Carlysle Hotel in New York, and the Del Coronado in San Diego.

Chain Hotels

Chain ownership usually imposes certain minimum standards, rules, policies, and procedures to restrict affiliate activities. In general, the more centralized the organization, the stronger the control over the individual property. Chains with less dominant central organizations typically allow individual hotel managers to exercise more creativity and decision-making autonomy.

Several different structures exist for chain hotels. Some chains own affiliated properties, but many do not. Some chains have strong control over the architecture, management, and standards of affiliate properties. Other chains only concentrate on advertising, marketing, and purchasing. Some chains may have only a small corporate structure and minimum membership standards and therefore would not be equipped to provide a high level of assistance to local ownership.

A chain is usually classified as operating under a management contract or as a franchise or referral group. The following discussion highlights how each type of chain operates, and how each type differs from the other.

Management Contracts. Management companies are organizations that operate properties owned by other entities. These entities range from individual businesspeople and partnerships to large insurance companies. Here's an example of how a management company might be hired to run a hotel. A group of businesspeople may decide that a hotel would enhance local business conditions. If the group's preliminary business feasibility study was favorable, the group might attempt to obtain financing to build the hotel. Many lending institutions, however, would require professional hotel management, and possibly chain affiliation, before they would approve a loan. At this point, the group could contract with a professional hotel management company to operate the proposed property, probably on a long-term basis. Assuming the hotel management company was acceptable to the lenders, a **management contract** would be signed by the developers and the management company.

Under this type of contract, the owner or developer usually retains the financial and legal responsibility for the property. The management company usually operates the hotel, pays its expenses and, in turn, receives an agreed-upon fee from the owner or developer. After operating expenses and management fees have been paid, any remaining cash usually goes to the owners, who may use this cash to pay debts, insurance, taxes, and so forth.

Management contracts have proven successful for many major hotel chains. Some management contract companies do not have a brand name. These companies usually operate franchises or independents for property owners. The franchising company provides the purchasing power, advertising, and central reservation system, while the management company provides the management expertise.

Management contracting is usually a means of rapidly expanding a hotel company's operations with far less investment per property than direct ownership requires. Hotel management companies are sometimes established just to manage hotels for other investors. These companies appear to offer a unique advantage to property owners and managers because of their expertise in operations, financial management, staffing, marketing and sales, and reservation services.

Franchise and Referral Groups. Some of the best-known U.S. hotels belong to franchise and referral groups. These properties can be found in most cities and towns, along interstate highways, and in resort areas. Franchise and referral groups have enjoyed the majority of growth in the world-wide lodging business in recent years because travelers prefer to stay with brands they recognize and owners trust in brand names to attract business. There is, however, an organizational distinction between these two types of chain hotels.

Franchising is simply a method of distribution whereby one entity that has developed a particular pattern or format for doing business—the *franchisor*—grants to other entities—*franchisees*—the right to conduct such a business provided the franchisee follows the established pattern. In the lodging industry, most organizations offering franchises have first established the quality of their product and expertise in operations by developing parent-company (franchisor-owned) hotels. Franchise organizations typically have established standards for design, decor, equipment, and operating procedures to which all franchised properties must adhere. This standardization is what enables franchise chains to expand while maintaining a consistent, established product and level of service.

The franchisor usually provides the franchisee with other reasons for purchasing a franchise aside from a strong brand name. These include national or international central reservation networking, national advertising campaigns, management training programs, advanced technology, and central purchasing services. Some franchisors also provide architectural, construction, and interior design consulting services. Some of the better-known franchising companies are Holiday Inn; Choice International (Quality Hotels and Inns); Ramada, Inc.; and Days Inns. In some cases, a company may provide management contract services as well as sell franchises. For example, most Sheraton Inns are franchises, while most Sheraton brand hotels are either owned by Sheraton or have Sheraton management contracts.

A franchise arrangement is not necessarily right for all lodging properties. Some operations are so distinct that belonging to a franchise system and conforming to a set of standards may be perceived as harmful. For these operations, a referral group might be more appropriate. **Referral groups** consist of independent hotels which have banded together for some common purpose. While each property in a referral system is not an exact replica of the others, there is sufficient consistency in the quality of service to consistently satisfy guest expectations. Hotels within the group refer their guests to other affiliated properties. Through this approach, an independent hotel may gain a much broader level of exposure. Best Western International—one of the largest hotel systems in the world—is an example of a referral group. Preferred Hotels and Leading Hotels are referral groups serving generally upscale hotels.

Belonging to a franchise or referral group provides several benefits, the most obvious being a more extensive reservation system and expanded advertising through pooled resources. These advantages are so important that lending institutions may often be reluctant to loan money to potential investors unless the investors have established an affiliation with a franchise group or referral organization.

As with franchise organizations, referral groups provide central purchasing services. These services reduce expenses to the individual hotels since items are purchased in larger quantities. Owners can purchase interior furnishings, bath amenities, linen and towels, and restaurant items at quantity prices. Referral groups do require members to maintain certain operating standards, so that their quality can be consistently experienced by guests.

Reasons for Traveling

Guests, like hotels, can be placed in categories. These categories—some quite elaborate—are typically most useful to a property's marketing function. Classifying guests by their reasons for traveling offers some useful general insights into the different wants and needs of guests. According to one survey, the reasons for guest travel today are as follows: [4]

- 30% are transient business travelers.
- 26% are attending a conference or group meeting.
- 24% are on vacation.
- 20% are traveling for other reasons (personal, family, special event, etc.).

The more information a hotel has about its guests, the better it can anticipate their needs and serve them. Although industry-wide statistics can provide an overview of the typical hotel guest, the guest mix for a particular hotel can vary tremendously by hotel location and type. Individual hotels may develop specific profiles of their guests' characteristics through research questionnaires. A wide variety of guest characteristics and habits can be surveyed to provide a better understanding of specific guest wants and needs.

But generally, the market for the lodging industry can be segmented into three major categories, based on reasons for travel: business, pleasure, and group.

Business Travel

The business travel market is important to many lodging properties. Historically, business travelers were the first and primary markets for hotels, dating back to the railroad age. In the United States, more than 35 million people take business trips each year. Business travelers average about five trips per year, and because business travelers are less likely to share rooms or stay with friends or relatives, they account for a significant portion of lodging demand. Regular business travel is that segment of the business travel market not related to meetings and conventions.

Regular business travel is an important source of business for many lodging properties. Within the last few years, hotels and airlines have designed specific products and services for the traveling business executive. Increased attention has also been given to traveling businesswomen. A special segment of business travelers is predisposed to stay at luxury hotels. Frequent business travelers generally provide their travel agent with broad parameters outlining the type of hotel in which they wish to stay. The growing number of suite hotels directed specifically toward the business traveler has influenced growth within this market segment. Business hotels usually have amenities and facilities specifically directed at business travelers. Examples include meeting space, offices in the building which can be rented by travelers, secretarial or computer services, in-room safes, and twenty-four hour room service. In addition, one of the latest trends is to provide Internet access, either through computers or the guestroom television.

Pleasure Travel

While business travel generally rates as an important source of business for hotels, pleasure travel is also very important. More and more people are experiencing an increase in discretionary income and leisure time; as a result, more and more people are traveling. Travelers find motels located at almost every interstate highway exit, as well as airport hotels near almost every major airport.

The segments of the pleasure travel market often overlap. The specific segmentation of the pleasure travel market often depends on the attractions, products, and services offered by the destination area of a lodging property. Typical market segments include specialized resort travel (for example, those seeking health spa facilities or instruction in such sports as tennis and golf), family pleasure travel, travel by the elderly, and travel by singles or couples.

Of all the travel industry market segments, pleasure travelers are among the most difficult to understand. In contrast with business travelers, who consider the cost of travel a necessary expense, pleasure travelers are generally price-sensitive. Income is an important factor in shaping the demand for pleasure travel. Vacation activities and lodging accommodations compete for the traveler's discretionary income as well as leisure time. The amount of discretionary income directly affects pleasure travel because it is the source for supporting leisure-related activities.

There are two hybrids of business and pleasure travel. One hybrid occurs when a business finances an employee's pleasure travel as an incentive; the intent being for the employee to rest, relax, and have a pleasant trip. Another hybrid form occurs when a business traveler adds vacation travel at the end or beginning of a scheduled business trip.

Group Travel

Group travel is considered different from business travel because some groups, such as organized tours, travel for pleasure.

Business travel related to meetings and conventions is commonly classified into two markets: *institutional* and *corporate/government*. Gatherings held by the institutional market are usually open to the public. Examples of institutional gatherings include the national conventions held by various trade associations. Gatherings held by the corporate/government market are usually closed to the public because they often deal with private corporate or government business matters. Examples of corporate gatherings include management meetings, sales meetings, new product introductions, training seminars, professional and technical meetings, and stockholder meetings.

Conventions and smaller meetings are critically important to much of the lodging industry. They result in the sale of guestrooms, as well as banquet and meeting room facilities. Meetings and conventions can attract hundreds or thousands of people, but the decision of where and when to have a meeting is typically made by a single meeting planner. The hotel's sales and marketing department often focuses its efforts on meeting planners. In some cases, sales and marketing personnel can persuade meeting planners to hold meetings at a property during the off-season, thereby generating revenue during a slow time.

Buying Influences

Many things affect a traveler's selection of overnight accommodations. Buying influences may include satisfactory experiences with a hotel, advertisements by a hotel or a chain organization, recommendations by others, a hotel's location, and preconceptions of a hotel based on its name or affiliation. To persuade guests to choose one hotel over others, many hotels develop a marketing plan that may include the use of billboards, newspaper and radio advertisements, printed publications, personal and telephone sales efforts, public relations activities, and direct mail pieces. Travel agents may also influence a consumer's hotel selection. Consumers often depend on travel agents to select a hotel that is appropriate to their needs. This is becoming more important as more businesses are using **travel management companies** (large travel agencies with significant room rate negotiating power) to control travel expenses. American Express, Rosenbluth Travel, and Carlson Wagon Lits are the best-known examples of travel management companies.

A potential guest's buying decision may also be influenced by the ease of making reservations and the reservations agent's description of the hotel and its rooms. The agent's tone of voice, helpfulness, efficiency, and knowledge are all factors that may contribute to a caller's decision to stay at a particular hotel. Sometimes the potential guest may call several hotels in the destination area to compare room rates, services, and amenities.

What influences repeat business? Many guests say that the most important factors that bring them back to a hotel are the quality of service and the property's

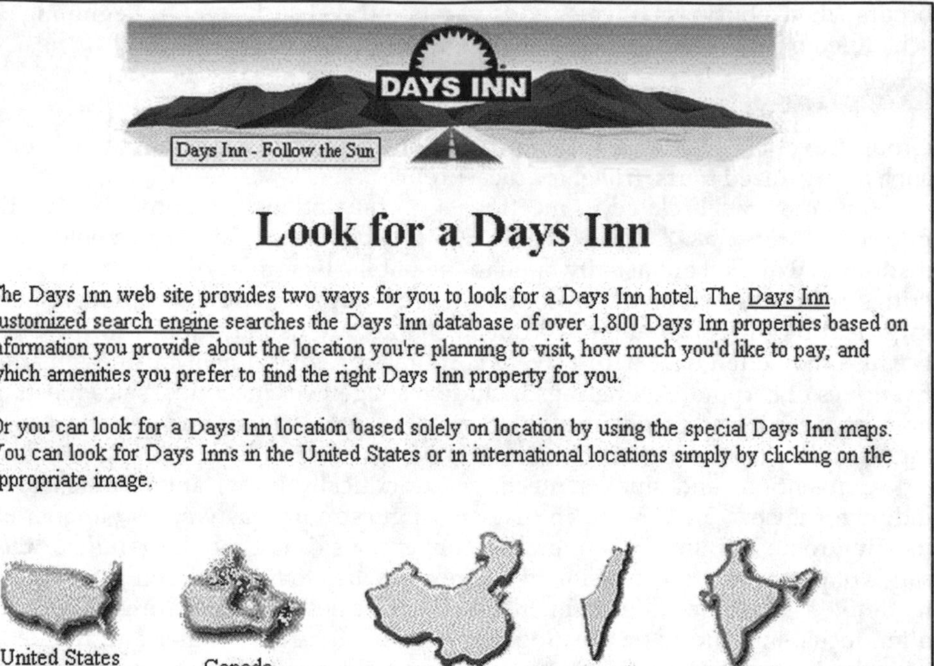

DAYS INN
Days Inn - Follow the Sun
Look for a Days Inn
The Days Inn web site provides two ways for you to look for a Days Inn hotel. The Days Inn customized search engine searches the Days Inn database of over 1,800 Days Inn properties based on information you provide about the location you're planning to visit, how much you'd like to pay, and which amenities you prefer to find the right Days Inn property for you.
Or you can look for a Days Inn location based solely on location by using the special Days Inn maps. You can look for Days Inns in the United States or in international locations simply by clicking on the appropriate image.
United States
Canada
China
Israel
India
Mexico
Philippines
Netherlands
South Africa

The Internet site of Days Inn of America, Inc. (http://www.daysinn.com), enables travelers to search for properties by geographical location or, as shown on the facing page, by a more targeted search based on location, room rates, and desired amenities.

overall cleanliness and appearance. Good service is good business. Front office staff are among the most visible hotel representatives in this regard. The challenge facing the front office is to obtain repeat business by providing a level of service that meets and exceeds guest expectations.

Business travelers offer a tremendous opportunity for attracting repeat business. Satisfied business travelers may not only return for the same business purposes, but may also bring other business acquaintances, family members, guests, or even revisit the property for a personal vacation.

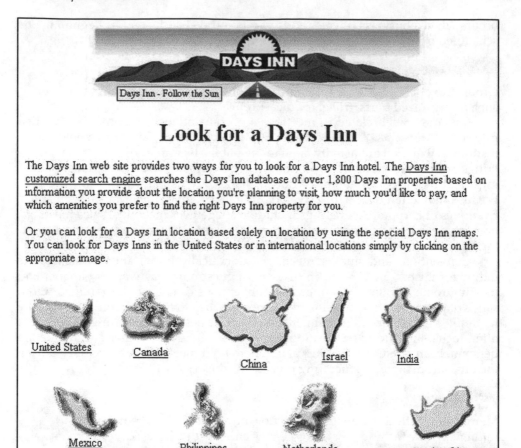

Guests often become loyal to particular chains or properties. Chain or brand loyalty can be a matter of habit, maximization of value to price, or past satisfaction with the hotel's products or services. Since it is difficult to obtain reliable prepurchase information about services, consumers may be reluctant to change hotels because they are unsure whether the change will actually increase satisfaction. In

Finding the Right Days Inn for You

If you need help, please see Instructions on How to Search for Days Inn Properties.

Enter Your Travel Destination:

City: [ ]

State or Province: All

Country: All

Zip or Postal Code: [ ]

Sort Results By: ◉ Random Order ○ Alphabetical Order

[Start Search] [Clear All Fields]

For a more specific search, complete the following fields. Otherwise, press START SEARCH above.

Enter the Hotel Property Name: [ ]

Room Price Range: All

Property Features and Amenities Search
Note: Select REQUIRED hotel amenities:

☐ 24 Hour Front Desk	☐ AM/FM Alarm Clock	☐ Babysitting/Child Services
☐ Bar/Lounge	☐ Barber/Beauty Shop	☐ Beach
☐ Business Center	☐ Casino	☐ Coffee Maker in Room
☐ Concierge	☐ Express Checkout	☐ Fishing
☐ Fitness Center or Spa	☐ Free Local Telephone Calls	☐ Free Newspaper
☐ Free Parking	☐ Golf	☐ Hairdryer in Room
☐ Handicapped Rooms/Facilities	☐ Laundry/Valet Services	☐ Meeting/Banquet Facilities
☐ Mini Bar	☐ Modem Lines in Room	☐ No Smoking Rooms/Facilities
☐ Pets Allowed	☐ Pool	☐ RV or Truck Parking
☐ Restaurant	☐ Room Service	☐ Safe Deposit Box
☐ Shops/Commercial Services	☐ Skiing	☐ Television with Cable
☐ Tennis	☐ VIP Rooms/Services	

[Start Search] [Clear All Fields]

order to "comparison shop" for services, consumers must visit various hotel properties in person. Also, consumers often perceive greater risks in purchasing services than they do in purchasing manufactured products. This increases the likelihood of brand loyalty when a lodging property succeeds in satisfying its guests.

Frequent traveler and electronic marketing programs are a recent development in creating and sustaining brand loyalty for hotels, restaurants, and airlines. Programs such as Marriott Honored Guest, Hyatt Gold Passport (see Exhibit 4), and Holiday Inn Priority Club are designed to give guests an added incentive to stay at one brand of hotel over another. Many such programs are affiliated with airline and car rental programs and offer rewards for flying a specific airline, staying at a specific hotel chain, and renting a specific company's car. Rewards can be free airline trips, free hotel stays, free car rentals, free amenities, discount food and beverage services, guestroom upgrades, and even entire vacations to customers who accumulate a large number of credits.

Since many hotel companies offer similar frequent traveler programs, the original intention of these programs to increase brand loyalty has been somewhat diluted. Many frequent travelers have actually come to expect frequent guest programs, thereby devaluing such programs and making them less enticing. Although frequent guest programs are expensive to operate, most hotel companies perceive them as worthwhile in retaining some valued repeat guests whose business might otherwise be lost.

Another reason guests may become brand-loyal is their own recognition that repeat patronage may lead to greater satisfaction of their needs. This can be an especially important factor in the luxury sector of the lodging industry. The hotel staff and management may learn the tastes and preferences of regular guests and therefore be better able to provide the types of services these guests expect. The Ritz-Carlton chain has developed an extensive guest history system to communicate guest preferences to each hotel, even though a guest has never stayed at a particular property before.

One factor affecting brand loyalty in the lodging industry is the unavailability of some brands in certain locations. If a consumer prefers to stay in hotels belonging to a specific chain, but is unable to locate an affiliate at a particular destination, he or she may decide to stay at a property belonging to a different chain. This is one way the consumer learns about competing brands. If the competing brand offers roughly the same quality level or higher, loyalty to the former hotel chain may diminish.

Multicultural Awareness

Hotels face an interesting and enormous challenge as international travel continues to expand. International guests bring a different set of needs and expectations. For example, hotels lacking translation services may be severely disadvantaged in a city where a Japanese company has just opened a manufacturing plant. Multicultural factors are also important considerations in staffing, interior design, food and beverage services, and recreational facilities. To meet this multicultural challenge,

Exhibit 4 Hyatt's Gold Passport Program

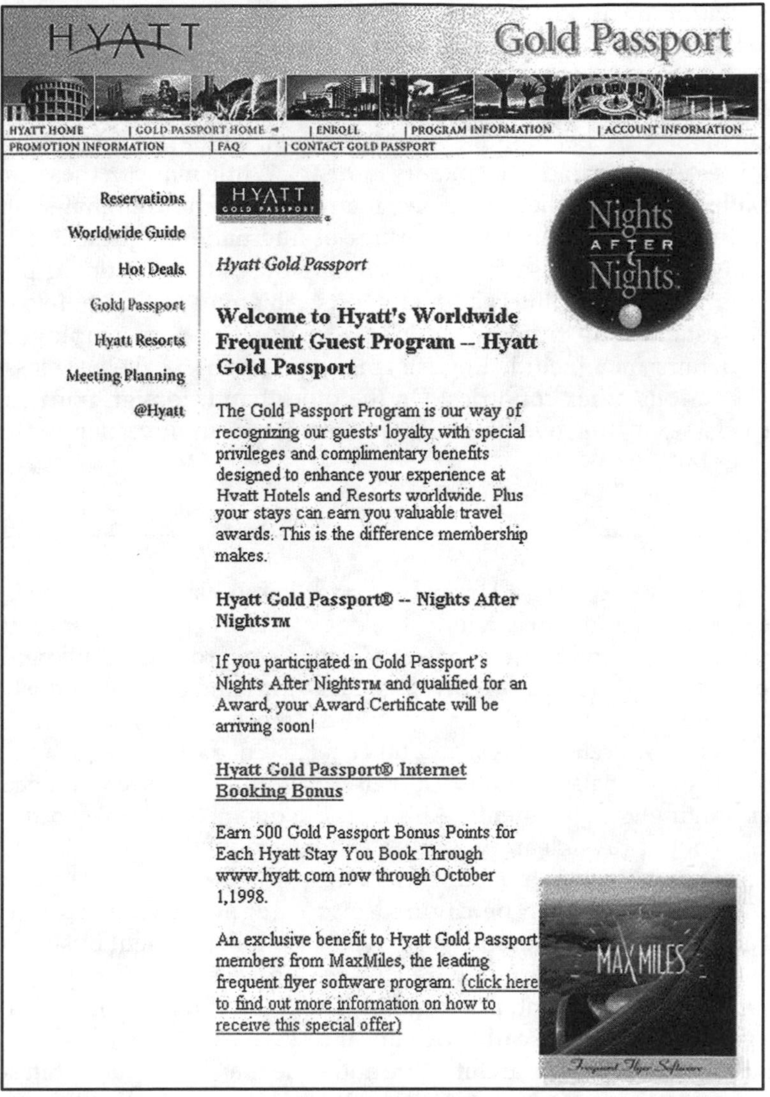

The Internet site of Hyatt Hotels Corporation (http://www.hyatt.com) describes its frequent guest program. Note that the company offers program points for members who book their stays over the Hyatt's Internet reservations system.

hotel managers must decide what markets they want to serve and establish a program to accommodate those markets.

Consider how Japanese guests would appreciate a traditional Japanese breakfast of miso soup, fish, and rice, while guests from Great Britain would enjoy a familiar breakfast of fried eggs and breakfast meats. The expression of cultural differences is not limited to differences between nations. Differences are also expressed within a nation's borders. For example, a traditional breakfast in the American South includes grits, while fried potatoes are often served in other parts of the country.

A large portion of the labor force in U.S. hotels today is foreign-born. People from Mexico, the Caribbean, India, Pakistan, Japan, China, and Africa are among the employees working in the hospitality industry. While many of these employees hold unskilled or semi-skilled positions, many possess multilingual skills and an understanding of the customs and cultures of international guests. The enlightened manager looks to these foreign-born employees for additional proficiency and versatility in serving international guests. This means that hotels may find themselves establishing training programs for foreign-born employees. These training programs may include English language lessons, as well as classes in the customs of various other countries. On the other hand, foreign-born employees may teach classes to improve the skills of native-born employees in serving international guests.

Summary

The hotel industry is part of a larger enterprise known as the travel and tourism industry. The travel and tourism industry, one of the world's largest industries, is composed of a vast group of businesses oriented toward providing necessary or desired products and services to travelers. The travel and tourism industry can be segmented into five parts: lodging operations; transportation services; food and beverage operations; retail stores; and other related activities. The lodging operations classification consists of hotels, motels, inns, suite hotels, conference centers, and other lodging establishments. Although the distinction between these property types is not always clear, properties can be grouped by size, target market, level of service, and ownership and affiliation.

Like hotels, guests can be divided into categories. Guests are typically grouped according to their reasons for travel: vacation, transient business, conference attendance, personal or family-related reason, weekend trip, government or military business, or residential relocation. The more information a hotel knows about its guests, the better it can anticipate and service their needs.

While a hotel property's architecture and style may be important in setting its theme, front office personnel play an integral role in defining its image. The variety of talents and skills needed to satisfy guest needs makes front office work interesting and rewarding.

Given the increasing multicultural challenge facing hotel management, properties need to decide which markets they want to serve and establish a program to accommodate those markets. A key to guest service and satisfaction appears to be multilingual skills and an understanding of foreign customs and cultures. The enlightened manager may seek out foreign-born employees for added proficiency in serving international guests. In essence, hotels may find themselves establishing unique training programs for foreign-born employees.

Endnotes

1. Floyd Miller, *Statler—America's Extraordinary Hotelman* (New York: Statler Foundation, 1968), p. 36.
2. *Travel and Tourism: The World's Largest Industry,* World Travel and Tourism Council Report, 1992.
3. *Lodging Industry Profile* (Washington, D.C.: American Hotel & Motel Association, 1996). Pamphlet prepared each year by AH&MA's Communications Department.
4. *Lodging Industry Profile.*

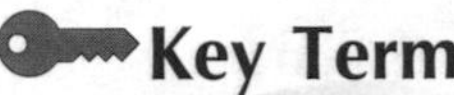

Key Terms

chain hotel—a hotel owned by or affiliated with other properties.

economy/limited service—a level of service emphasizing clean, comfortable, inexpensive rooms that meet the most basic needs of guests. Economy or limited service hotels appeal primarily to budget-minded travelers.

franchising—a method of distribution whereby one entity that has developed a particular pattern or format for doing business (the franchisor) grants to other entities (franchisees) the right to conduct such a business provided they follow the established pattern.

hotel—a general term used to describe motels, motor hotels, inns, suite hotels, conference centers, and other operations providing lodging facilities, various services, and conveniences to the traveling public.

independent hotel—a hotel with no ownership or management affiliation with other properties.

management contract—an agreement between the owner/developer of a property and a professional hotel management company. The owner/developer usually retains the financial and legal responsibility for the property, and the management company receives an agreed-upon fee for operating the hotel.

market segmentation—the process of defining or identifying smaller, distinct groups or "segments" within larger markets; "corporate business travelers," for instance, as a segment of "business travelers."

mid-range service—a modest but sufficient level of service that appeals to the largest segment of the traveling public. A mid-range property may offer uniformed service, airport limousine service, and food and beverage room service; a specialty restaurant, coffee shop, and lounge; and special rates for certain guests.

quality assurance—an approach to ensuring the consistent delivery of services.

referral group—a group of independent hotels that have banded together for their common good. Hotels within the group refer their departing guests or those guests they cannot accommodate to other properties in the referral group.

target markets—distinctly defined groupings of potential buyers (market segments) at which sellers aim or "target" their marketing efforts.

travel management company—a large travel agency with significant room rate negotiating power.

world-class service—a level of guest service that stresses personal attention. Hotels offering world-class service provide upscale restaurants and lounges, exquisite decor, concierge services, opulent rooms, and abundant amenities.

Review Questions

1. What do all travel and tourism businesses have in common? How does the hospitality industry relate to the travel and tourism industry?
2. What are four general ways of classifying hotels? Why can hotels fit into more than one category?
3. What are some distinctions between resort hotels and commercial hotels?
4. For what purpose are conference centers specifically designed? How do they serve their target market?
5. What are some basic issues surrounding the concept of service? How can a hotel help ensure consistency in an intangible product?
6. What is world-class service? What personnel are common in a world-class hotel? What is an executive floor?
7. What is a unique advantage of an independent hotel? How might independent hotels be at a disadvantage?
8. How might a management contract be involved in the development of a hotel? What are the differences between a franchise and a referral group?
9. What are three chief categories of travelers, in terms of the purpose for traveling? How can a hotel influence a traveler's decision to visit or return to the hotel?
10. Why is international travel becoming so important to the hospitality industry? What major challenges do hotel managers face in this area?

Internet Sites

For more information, visit the following Internet sites. Remember that Internet addresses can change without notice.

Travel and Lodging Associations

American Hotel & Motel Association (AH&MA)
http://www.ahma.com

Council on Hotel, Restaurant and Institutional Education (CHRIE)
http://www.chrie.org

The Educational Institute of AH&MA
http://www.ei-ahma.org

Hospitality Financial & Technology Professionals
http://www.hftp.org

Hospitality Sales and Marketing Association International (HSMAI)
http://www.hsmai.org

International Hotel & Restaurant Association (IHRA)
http://www.ih-ra.com

Travel and Tourism Research Association (TTRA)
http://www.ttra.com

Travel Industry Association of America (TIA)
http://www.tia.org

World Tourism Organization (WTO)
http://www.world-tourism.org

Hotels and Hotel Companies

Best Western
http://www.bestwestern.com

Choice Hotels International
http://www.hotelchoice.com

Canadian Pacific Hotels
http://www.cphotels.ca

Days Inn of America, Inc.
http://www.daysinn.com

Hilton Hotels
http://www.hilton.com

Holiday Hospitality Corporation
http://www.holiday-inn.com

Hyatt Hotels Corporation
http://www.hyatt.com

Inter-Continental Hotels
http://www.interconti.com

ITT Sheraton Corporation
http://www.sheraton.com

Marriott Hotels, Resorts, and Suites
http://www.marriott.com/lodging

Opryland Hotel
http://www.opryhotel.com

Radisson Hotels Worldwide
http://www.radisson.com

Ritz Carlton Hotels
http://www.ritzcarlton.com

Walt Disney World Resorts
http://www.disneyworld.com/vacation

Westin Hotels and Resorts
http://www.westin.com

Condominium and Timeshare Organizations

American Resort Development Association
http://www.arda.org

Community Associations Institute
http://www.caionline.org

Disney Vacation Club
http://www.disney.com/DisneyVacationClub/index.html

Hilton Grand Vacations Company
http://www.hgvc.com

Hyatt Vacation Club
http://www.hyatt.com/athyatt/vacation/index.html

Interval International
http://www.interval-intl.com

Marriott Vacation Club
http://www.marriott.com/vacationclub

Resort Condominiums International, Inc.
http://www.rci.com

Casino Hotels

Ballys Casinos
http://www.ballys.com

Caesar's Palace
http://www.caesars.com

Casinos
http://www.ct-casinos.com

Harrahs Casino
http://www.harrahs.com

Trump Castle Casino
http://www.trumpcastle.com

Case Study

A Big Fish in a Small Pond Flounders in the Great Lakes

Jeff Marlin took down his hospitality management diploma from his office wall and packed it on top of a nearly full box of books and papers. It was Jeff's last day as assistant general manager of the Fairmeadows Inn in suburban Lake Zurich, Illinois. Tomorrow he started a new job as front office manager at the Merrimack, an 800-room convention hotel in downtown Chicago.

Not bad for someone just three years out of school, he thought to himself as he finished packing. *After this job, there's nothing I can't handle*. It was true, the assistant GM's job had taught him to be a jack of all trades. He had hired many of the property's 20 employees and knew them all by name. He had a good relationship with the head of housekeeping; he knew he could count on a quick response to special requests like readying a handicap-accessible room on short notice. He was proud that during his tenure at the Fairmeadows Inn, his property had consistently had the highest average daily rate and highest occupancy of all the Fairmeadows properties in his region.

With no full-time sales department, Jeff had become quite skilled at drumming up business among local groups. The Chamber of Commerce and the Kiwanis held monthly luncheon meetings (catered by the restaurant across the street) at the Fairmeadows and always put up visiting guests at the property. During the summer softball season, the 124-room property was "hopping" as softball teams of 15 or 20 players from neighboring regions stayed overnight at the Fairmeadows when they played the Lake Zurich team. Even then, Jeff was pleased with the front desk's ability to handle check-in and check-out procedures smoothly. At other times of the year, front desk traffic was easier, with only two or three people checking in or out at any given time.

Jeff knew that he could handle anything his new job would throw at him. Hadn't he learned the Fairmeadows' new computer system faster than anyone on staff—and trained the front desk staff how to use the programs? Reservations, sales, check-in/check-out, training, daily reports—*yeah, I'm ready to move up*, Jeff thought.

Jeff's confidence got its first jolt as he strolled through the front doors of the Merrimack the next morning at 8 o'clock. Over 200 people jostled one another in the lobby as four front desk agents worked non-stop to get them checked out. *What's going on here?* Jeff wondered. A bell attendant asked the dazed young man if he could be of assistance then gave Jeff directions to the general manager's office.

"Welcome aboard, Jeff," said Al Grayling, as Jeff entered the G.M.'s office. "Hope you didn't have any trouble finding me."

"Who are all those people in the lobby?" Jeff asked. "I've never seen such a crowd before."

Al laughed. "Get used to it, Jeff. That's actually one of our smaller groups checking out this morning. There'll be lots of days when you and your staff will be checking out one group of 400 people and checking in another 400."

"Of course," Jeff laughed weakly. "It's a convention hotel. I knew that. Well, where do I start?"

Al took Jeff out to the front desk, where he was introduced to the morning shift—Carole, Franklin, Ashari, and Dean. They greeted him briefly, then turned their attention back to the guests who were checking out. At the Fairmeadows Inn, Jeff often pulled a shift at the front desk when things got busy. Glancing over Franklin's shoulder, though, Jeff realized that the computer system the Merrimack used was completely different from what he was used to, and the check-out methods performed so efficiently by his new staff were also unfamiliar. *Better let them do what they do best until I pick up the routines,* he decided.

The phone rang. Jeff knew he could handle that. "Merrimack Hotel, Jeff Marlin. How may I help you?"

"Jeff? This is Nancy Troutman, director of sales. You're the new front office manager, right? Al Grayling said you'd be starting today," said the voice on the other end of the line. "Jeff, I need you to let me know when the cosmetics sales convention group checks in. I want to meet with Sheila Watkins as soon as she arrives to go over plans for their awards banquet. I'm at extension 805. Got it? The information should be in the group résumé book at the front desk. Bye."

Jeff had to ask Ashari for the group résumé book; they didn't even have one at the Fairmeadows Inn. She also showed him the daily report, which was three pages longer than the reports he was used to. He tried to figure out the different set-up and the unfamiliar items—F&B, banquets, groups in and out, VIP list, out of order rooms. *I need a report to explain this report,* Jeff thought.

As long as he was looking at reports, he decided to ask Ashari for a copy of the night audit.

"Oh, that goes right to accounting," she explained.

"Not to me?" he asked. She shook her head, then pointed out the number for accounting on the staff phone list.

The list itself overwhelmed Jeff. So many departments, so many managers. PBX, reservations, sales, front office—he'd handled all of that at his last job. Here at the Merrimack, there was a separate department for each function. Would he ever find his way around this organization?

Maybe I'd have been better off as a big fish in my small pond, he thought.

After lunch, Jeff was back at the front desk. Working with Dean, he was getting oriented to the Merrimack's room management software and feeling his confidence rebound a little. It was still a couple of hours until the cosmetics convention group came in, so traffic at the front desk was fairly slow.

A couple, the woman in a wheelchair, came to the front desk. The Armbrusters had reservations for a handicap-accessible room, but when Jeff checked the room status, he discovered that no such rooms were clean and ready for occupancy. He asked Dean to continue taking the Armbrusters' registration information while he attempted to resolve the situation with their room.

Jeff searched the phone list until he found the housekeeping manager, Dolores Manta. "Dolores, this is Jeff at the front desk. I need a handicap accessible room prepared for immediate occupancy. How quickly do you think you could have one ready?"

"Just who are you?" asked Dolores. "We do have procedures around here. Don't you know you can't order a room like you order a pizza? No one informed me that an accessible room was a priority. Why did you wait until 1:30 to tell me this? Didn't you know they were coming in? Isn't it in the log?"

The head housekeeper at the Fairmeadows Inn had never responded to any of Jeff's requests like this; he was taken aback. What was the big deal, anyway?

"I'm the new front office manager; it's my first day," he explained. "No, I didn't know they were coming in. The log? Uh, I don't know about…oh, wait, here it is. I guess I didn't know…" He tried to recover. "I apologize for not following the right procedure; but I still have two guests here who need a room. Do you have any suggestions for me?"

"Well, my staff is pretty tied up getting rooms ready for those 500 cosmetics salespeople coming in at 4 p.m., but I'll see if I can take someone away from that and prepare Room 167 for you," said Dolores. "But Jeff, don't let it happen again."

The cosmetics convention group was late arriving, but Jeff stayed on to make sure that Nancy Troutman was notified about their arrival. He didn't want to start that relationship off as badly as he had with the housekeeping manager. She was surprised, though, when he called.

"Why didn't you just assign the task to one of the front desk agents?" she asked. "I didn't mean that you personally needed to take care of this, just as long as I got the word. Thanks, though."

By the end of his first long day, Jeff wasn't at all certain he wanted to come back for a second day. This was supposed to be a career move up, but it sure didn't feel that way. He decided to call Gavin Albacore, a college buddy who was reservations manager at a convention hotel in St. Louis. *Maybe he would have some good advice,* Jeff thought.

Discussion Questions

1. How could the general manager at the Merrimack have made Jeff's transition into his new job easier?
2. What steps could Jeff have taken to make a smoother transition to the new job?

3. What advice might Jeff's friend have to help him make this a successful career move?

Case Number: 3321CA

The following industry experts helped generate and develop this case: Richard M. Brooks, CHA, Vice President—Operations, Bridgestreet Accommodations, Inc., Cleveland, Ohio; and S. Kenneth Hiller, CHA, Director of Transition and Owner Relations, Marriott Hotels International.

This case also appears in *Case Studies in Lodging Management* (Lansing, Mich.: Educational Institute of the American Hotel & Motel Association, 1998), ISBN 0-86612-184-6.

Choosing the Right Person for the Job

Alan Christoff looked up from the report on his desk as his assistant brought in the morning mail. He flipped through the stack until he came to a large envelope bearing the unmistakable logo of the prominent hotel chain for which he was senior vice president of development. Christoff was in the process of finding someone to head up the hotel company's new interval ownership business unit. Construction was already underway on phase one of the company's first venture—a 200-unit timeshare resort on the South Carolina coast. The plan called for the resort to be built in phases with an anticipated five-year sellout and a 12-month building cycle—two buildings a year for five years. When it was finished, the resort would feature 20 two-bedroom units in each building, along with tennis courts, swimming pools, and a central facilities building. Selling one-week intervals per unit and closing a sale with one out of every ten prospects on site visits, the sales effort might have to attract over 100,000 prospects to reach the sellout goal.

Christoff's immediate concern was finding a manager for the hotel chain's interval ownership business unit. The human resources manager had forwarded him the resumes of the three applicants she felt were best qualified for the position. Christoff slid the résumés out of the envelope and sat back to review them.

The first résumé was that of Micah Thompson. Christoff recognized the name as one of the hotel chain's rising stars. He held a hospitality degree from Cornell and had earned his CHA designation. His career had begun in operations; his résumé listed experience with reservations and yield management. Currently the general manager of the company's Daytona Beach hotel, Thompson's impressive sales and marketing skills had earned him a reputation for success in opening new properties and turning around troubled properties.

In his cover letter, he cited his pre-opening experience, marketing skills, familiarity with resort destinations, and his desire to grow with the company. "I am certain that being general manager of this timeshare operation will not be significantly different from managing a hotel," he wrote.

Christoff chuckled at that statement. He wondered if Thompson had ever tried to run a property as it was being built around him, or dealt with the logistics of conducting site inspections for literally tens of thousands of prospective timeshare customers. Still, Thompson did have a strong track record with the hotel company and was well-regarded by the hotel company's executive team. With the company's history of internal promotions, Thompson ought to be a shoo-in for the job, thought Christoff.

Christoff turned to the next résumé. Elena Ramirez was currently the assistant general manager at a 400-unit resort condominium property in Colorado. She had formerly been an owners' relations manager with another resort condominium. Ramirez had strong knowledge of the real estate product and a proven track record in dealing with a rental program and property resales. From her job descriptions, it appeared that all of her experience had been with whole ownership condominiums, rather than with interval ownership.

"In addition to my experience with onsite sales and condominium rental programs, I have developed a strong working relationship with our owners' association and feel confident in dealing with individual owners and understanding their unique needs," Ramirez wrote in her cover letter. She also made a point of noting that her current property had twice the number of units as the hotel chain's planned 200-unit resort, so she felt confident of her abilities to succeed in the new environment.

Let's see, mused Christoff. Four hundred units; that's 400 owners. I wonder if she realizes she would be managing 10,000 owners? Still, she probably had a better idea of what she would be facing than someone who had never worked in the condominium business before.

The final résumé was from Earl Jackson. He was a timeshare industry veteran with nearly 10 years of experience at interval ownership properties. Before that, he had been in the real estate industry for 12 years. Christoff noted that Jackson had even included his real estate license number on his resume. Jackson's timeshare experience included operations, marketing, and sales. Christoff looked for evidence of hotel experience, but found none.

"I look forward to the opportunity to work with a branded chain," Jackson wrote. "I believe my experience in vacation-ownership management will enable me to work effectively with the sales staff to sell inventory and to communicate with both owners and hotel company management."

Discussion Questions

1. What criteria should Christoff consider when selecting a manager to head up the interval ownership business unit?
2. Based on criteria developed in Discussion Question #1, what are the strengths and weaknesses of each applicant?
3. Which applicant should Christoff hire and why?

Case Number: 604CJ

The following industry experts helped generate and develop this case: Jerry Hewey, CHA, Condominium Consultant, Aspen, Colorado; Larry B. Gildersleeve, Senior Vice President, Interval International, Miami, Florida; Pedro Mandoki,

CHA, President, Plantation Resort Management Inc., Gulf Shores, Alabama; Jack Rush, CHA, General Manager and Managing Agent of the Port Royal Ocean Resort Condominium Association in Port Aransas, Texas.

This case also appears in *Case Studies in Condominium and Vacation Ownership Management* (Lansing, Mich.: Educational Institute of the American Hotel & Motel Association, 1998), ISBN 0-86612-176-5.

Chapter 2 Outline

Organizational Missions
- Goals
- Strategies and Tactics

Hotel Organization
- Organization Charts
- Classifying Functional Areas
- Rooms Division
- Food and Beverage Division
- Sales and Marketing Division
- Accounting Division
- Engineering and Maintenance Division
- Security Division
- Human Resources Division
- Other Divisions

Front Office Operations
- Organization
- Goals and Strategies
- Workshifts
- Job Descriptions
- Job Specifications

Summary

Case Study

Appendix: Model Job Descriptions

2

Hotel Organization

A PERSON ENTERING A HOTEL LOBBY for the first time might never guess the complexities underlying the day-to-day operation of the property. He or she might not recognize that the courtesy of the door attendant, the competent and friendly manner of the front desk agent, and the tidiness of the guestroom reflect the workings of an efficient organization. The actual network of a hotel's divisions, departments, and personnel in a smoothly operating hotel should be invisible to the casual observer. But the services that result from a hotel's smooth operation are highly visible and present the hotel with a unique challenge.

For a hotel to run effectively and efficiently, every employee must understand, and work to achieve, the property's mission. Every employee must ensure that guests are so impressed by the property's facilities and services that they will want to come back and will enthusiastically recommend the property to others.

Teamwork is the key to success. All employees must have a spirit of cooperation both within and between their departmental areas. While every department and division should strive to offer and improve quality guest service, it is especially important that good service be emphasized in high profile locations such as the front office. The ability of front office employees to answer questions, coordinate services, offer choices, and satisfy guest requests is critical to the hotel's mission.

This chapter examines the relationship of hotel employees, departments, and divisions to each other, as well as how each contributes to achieving the property's mission. Several sample job descriptions for front office staff positions are presented in the Appendix to this chapter.

Organizational Missions

Every organization has a reason or purpose to exist. Its purpose forms the basis for the organization's mission. An organization's mission can be expressed in a **mission statement,** which defines the unique purpose that sets one hotel or hotel company apart from others. It expresses the underlying philosophy that gives meaning and direction to hotel policies. Hotel employees may derive a sense of purpose from a well-conceived mission statement. For example, a hotel's mission may be to provide the finest facilities and services in the market while providing a good place to work for its employees and a reasonable return on investment to the owners.

A hotel's mission statement should address the interests of its three main constituent groups: guests, management, and employees. First, a hotel's mission statement should address the basic needs and expectations of the hotel's guests.

Regardless of a hotel's size or service level, it is safe to assume all guests have the following basic expectations:

- Safe, secure accommodations
- A clean, comfortable guestroom
- Courteous, professional, and friendly service
- Well-maintained facilities and equipment

Hotel guests generally anticipate a particular level of service at a given property. If a hotel clearly defines its markets and consistently delivers the level of service those markets expect, it can successfully satisfy its guests, encourage repeat business, and improve its reputation.

Second, a hotel's mission statement should reflect its management philosophy. Since styles of operation differ, mission statements often vary from property to property. In fact, a hotel's mission is one of the principal means it uses to distinguish itself from other hotels. A mission statement guides managers in their jobs by identifying the property's basic values.

Third, the mission statement should help the hotel's employees meet or exceed the expectations of both guests and management. A mission statement can also serve as a basis for job descriptions and performance standards and as an introduction to the property for new employees. The property's mission statement should appear in employee handbooks and training manuals, and should accompany job descriptions.

Consider this example of a hotel mission statement:

> The mission of our hotel is to provide outstanding lodging facilities and services to our guests. Our hotel focuses on individual business and leisure travel, as well as travel associated with group meetings. We emphasize high quality standards in our rooms and food and beverage divisions. We provide a fair return on investment for our owners and recognize that this cannot be done without well-trained, motivated, and enthusiastic employees.

Goals

Once the hotel has defined and formulated its mission statement, the next step is to set goals. **Goals** are those activities and standards an organization must successfully perform or achieve to effectively carry out its mission. A goal is more specific than a mission; it requires a certain level of achievement that can be observed and measured. Measurable goals encourage hotel employees to perform effectively while enabling management to monitor employee progress. Management and staff should be periodically evaluated on their progress toward meeting the goals. Management can determine whether goals are being achieved or whether corrective action is necessary. A properly written goal includes an action verb followed by a specific form of measurement such as a time interval or a level of quality, quantity, or cost.

Examples of measurable front office goals might be:

- Increase the hotel's average occupancy level by two percent above the previous year's level.
- Increase the volume of repeat guest business by 10 percent.
- Reduce average check-in and check-out times by two minutes.
- Reduce the number of guest complaints by 20 percent.

Other hotel departments and divisions, such as sales or housekeeping, may be counted on to help the front office achieve many of its goals. For this reason, some hotel goals are stated as property-wide goals, not simply as departmental or divisional goals.

Strategies and Tactics

By establishing property-wide, measurable goals, a hotel enables its managers and employees to concentrate on specific strategies that will help the property achieve its goals. Goals define the purpose of a department or division; they direct the actions of managers and employees and the functions of the department or division toward fulfilling the hotel's mission. To achieve its goals, a department or division establishes **strategies.** Strategies are the methods a department or division uses to achieve its goals. **Tactics** further define how goals will be achieved. They are the day-to-day operating procedures that implement successful strategies. It is important that goals and strategies set at the departmental and divisional levels correspond to the property's mission and its property-wide goals.

Examples of goals, strategies, and tactics involving areas within the front office are:

- Registration—*Goal:* Operate the front desk efficiently and courteously so that guests may register within two minutes of arrival. *Strategy:* Preregister all expected guests with reservation guarantees as rooms become available from Housekeeping. *Tactic:* Preprint registration cards for arriving guests and separate the cards of all guests with a reservation guarantee.
- Guest Cashiering—*Goal:* Post all charges reaching the front desk within thirty minutes. *Strategy:* Provide sufficient staffing to enable rapid and accurate posting of guest charges when they are received. *Tactic:* Review occupancy forecasts weekly to develop proper staffing guidelines.
- Bell Stand—*Goal:* Respond to every check-out luggage request within ten minutes. *Strategy:* Keep a log of when bell attendants are dispatched and when they return from each guest call. *Tactic:* Enter guest name, room number, bell attendant assigned, and time out and time in for each luggage request.
- Telephone Department—*Goal:* Answer every telephone call within three rings of the telephone, no matter whether it is an inside call or an outside call. *Strategy:* Perform telephone traffic studies periodically, reviewing the number of calls received, to ensure the proper number of telephone lines are available for both incoming and outgoing telephone calls. *Tactic:* Print traffic report from telephone switch daily and record volume by time on a spreadsheet.

Hotel Organization

The people authorized by a hotel's owner to represent his or her interests are called hotel management. In small properties, hotel management may be represented by one person. Management guides the operation of the hotel and regularly reports the general state of the hotel's financial health to its owner. The major duties of a hotel management team include planning, organizing, coordinating, staffing, directing, controlling, and evaluating hotel activities and/or personnel. Management performs its duties to reach specific objectives and goals. These duties involve the activities of various hotel divisions and departments.

The top executive of a property is usually called the general manager or managing director. The general manager of an independent hotel normally reports directly to the owner or the owner's representative. The general manager supervises all hotel divisions, either through a resident or assistant manager, or through division heads. Chain organizations usually have a district, area, or regional executive supervising the general managers located at the properties within his or her jurisdiction.

While the general manager is responsible for supervising all hotel divisions, he or she may delegate responsibility for specific divisions or departments to a resident manager or director of operations. When the general manager is absent, the resident manager usually serves as the acting general manager. And when both the general manager and resident manager are off the premises, a manager-on-duty is often appointed to assume overall managerial responsibility.

Historically, resident managers actually *lived* in the hotel. Essentially, it was the resident manager's job to be available 24 hours a day, seven days a week. Over time, more authority has been delegated to other managers. While many resident managers are still responsible for the rooms division, it is rare for a property to require its resident manager to live on the premises.

To qualify for a department head position, an individual must thoroughly understand the functions, goals, and practices of a particular department. Despite the many variations in management structure, front office managers are usually considered department heads, and typically are the preferred candidate for manager-on-duty responsibility.

Organization Charts

An organization requires a formal structure to carry out its mission and goals. A common way to represent that structure is the **organization chart.** An organization chart is a schematic representation of the relationships between positions within an organization. It shows where each position fits in the overall organization, as well as where divisions of responsibility and lines of authority lie. Solid lines on the chart indicate direct-line accountability. Dotted lines indicate relationships that involve a high degree of cooperation and communication, but not a direct reporting relationship.

An organization chart should be flexible. It should be reviewed and revised yearly, or more often if business conditions significantly change. Employee responsibilities may change as individuals assume more duties, depending on their qualifications and strengths. Some organizations list each employee's name on the chart along with his or her title. A copy of the property's organization chart should be included in the employee handbook distributed to all employees.

Since no two hotels are exactly alike, organizational structures must be tailored to fit the needs of each individual property. The charts in this chapter illustrate several organizational possibilities: a full-service property; a property with separately owned food and beverage operations; and a rooms-only hotel.

A full-service property that offers both lodging and food and beverage service will probably have an extensive organizational structure. Exhibit 1 shows an organization chart outlining the management-level positions in a large full-service property. All but two of the lines on the chart are solid, indicating reporting relationships. The dotted lines connecting the sales director to the catering director and the reservations manager represent the close working relationship needed among these positions.

Some hotels may lease food and beverage outlets to another company. This means that the food and beverage operations and guestroom operations are separately owned and managed, which also means there is potential for conflict. Exhibit 2 shows a typical organization chart for a hotel with leased food and beverage operations. In this example, informal consulting relationships exist between the managers and owners of the two businesses. The restaurant manager and the hotel's sales department manager must also work closely together. These relationships are indicated by dotted lines.

Exhibit 3 presents a possible organizational structure for a hotel without a restaurant. These organization charts illustrate some of the many organizational variations that are possible among lodging properties.

Classifying Functional Areas

A hotel's divisions and departments (its *functional areas*) can be classified in almost as many ways as the hotel itself. One method involves classifying an operating division or department as either a **revenue center** or **support center.** A revenue center sells goods or services to guests, thereby generating revenue for the hotel. Typical revenue centers include the front office, food and beverage outlets, room service, and telephone. Even if a revenue center is not operated by the hotel itself (as is often the case with retail stores), the money the revenue center pays to lease the hotel space contributes to the hotel's income.

Support centers, also referred to as cost centers, include the housekeeping, accounting, engineering and maintenance, and human resources divisions. These divisions do not generate direct revenue, but provide important support for the hotel's revenue centers. Designers of accounting and information systems often find it useful to segment a hotel by revenue and support centers.

The terms **front of the house** and **back of the house** may also be used to classify hotel departments, divisions, and personnel. Front-of-the-house areas are areas where guests interact with employees. Such areas include the front office, restaurants, and lounges. In back-of-the-house areas, interaction between guests and employees is less common. Such areas include housekeeping, engineering and maintenance, accounting, and human resources. Housekeeping staff do

Exhibit 1 Organization Chart: Management Positions in a Full-Service Hotel

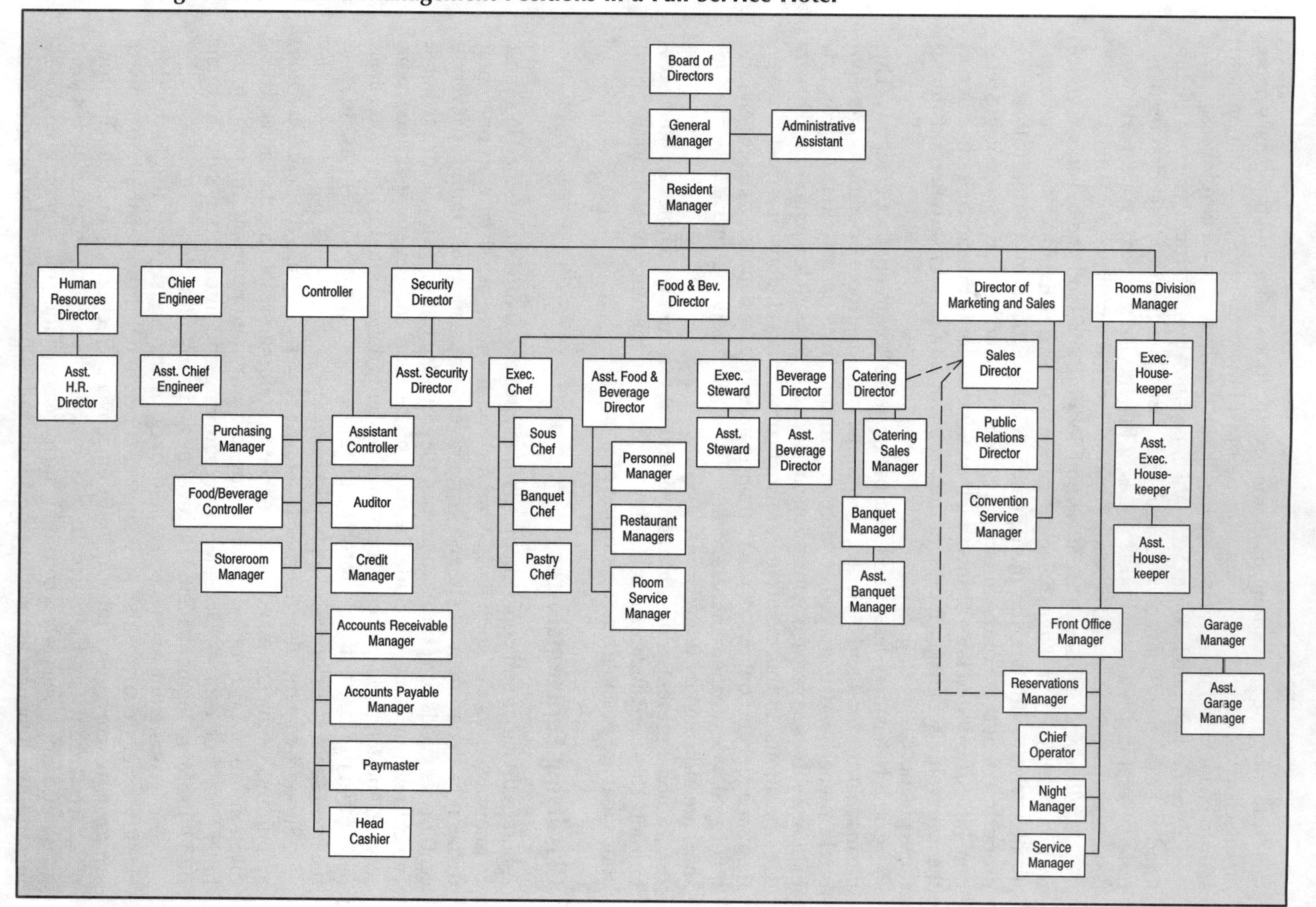

Exhibit 2 Organization Chart: Hotel with a Leased Food and Beverage Operation

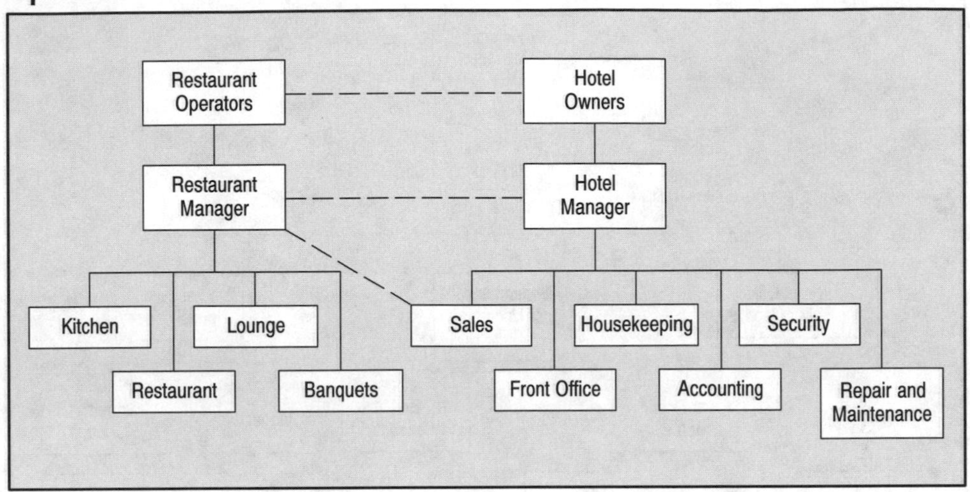

Exhibit 3 Organization Chart: Rooms-Only Hotel

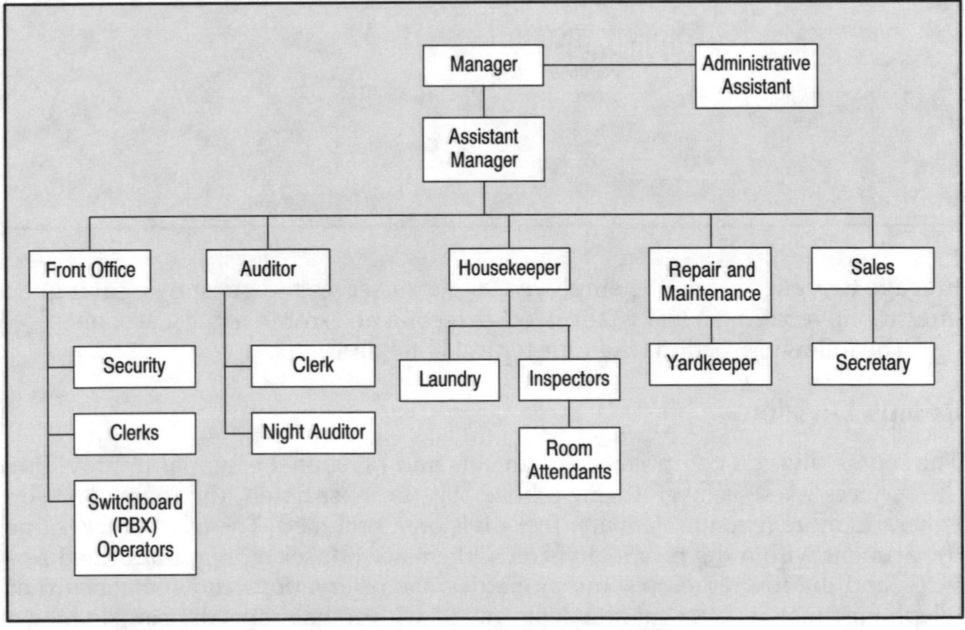

occasionally interact with guests, but it is not part of their primary duties as it is for front desk and bell staff. Although back-of-the-house employees may not *directly* serve the guest by taking an order, assisting with registration, or delivering

Exhibit 4 Organization Chart: Rooms Division of a Large Hotel

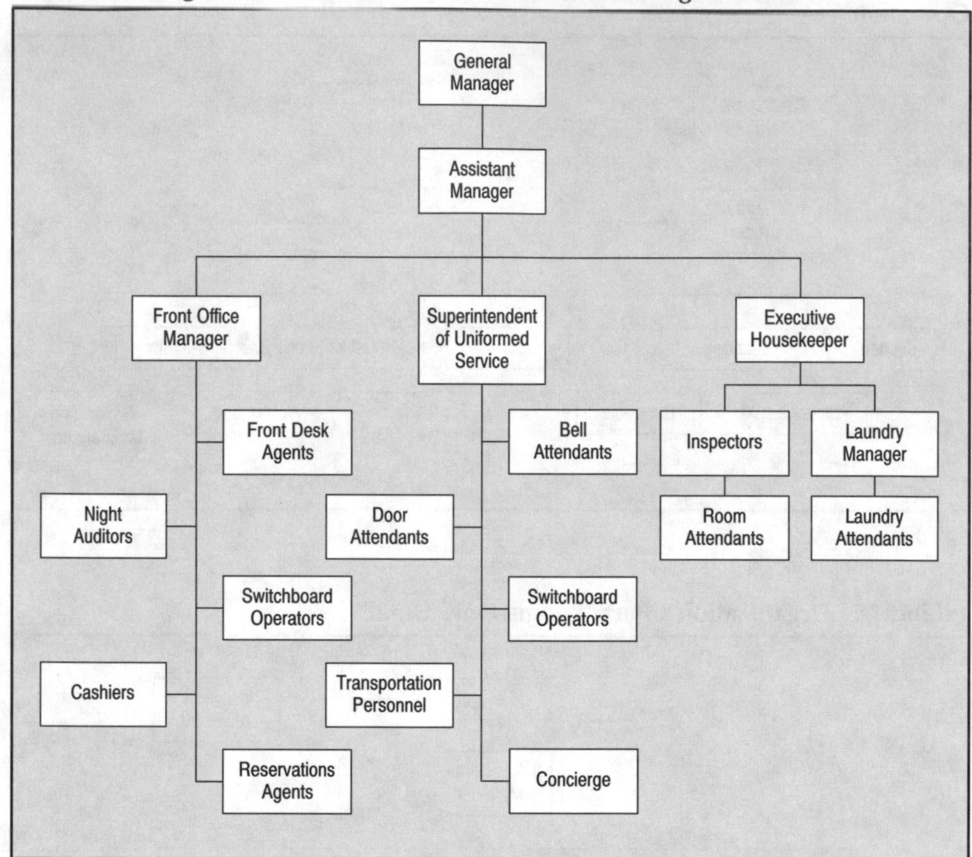

luggage to a guestroom, the employee *indirectly* serves the guest by cleaning the guestroom, repairing a leaky faucet, or correcting an error in a guest account.

The following sections examine typical hotel divisions.

Rooms Division

The rooms division comprises departments and personnel essential to providing the services guests expect during a hotel stay. In most hotels, the rooms division generates more revenue than all other divisions combined. The front office is one department within the rooms division. Others are housekeeping, uniformed services, and the concierge. In some properties, the reservations and switchboard or telephone functions are separate departments within the rooms division. Exhibit 4 shows a sample organization chart for the rooms division of a large hotel.

The Front Office. The front office is the most visible department in a hotel. Front office personnel have more contact with guests than do staff in most other departments. The front desk is usually the focal point of activity for the front office and is prominently located in the hotel's lobby. Guests come to the front desk to register; to receive room assignments; to inquire about available services, facilities, and the city or surrounding area; and to check out. The front desk often serves as the hotel control center for guest requests concerning housekeeping or engineering issues. Foreign guests use the front desk to exchange currency, find a translator, or request other special assistance. In addition, it may also be a base of operations during an emergency, such as a fire or a guest injury.

Other front office functions include receiving and distributing mail, messages, and facsimiles (faxes), as well as guest cashiering. Cashiers post charges and payments to guest accounts, all of which are later verified during an account auditing procedure (often called the *night audit*). Front desk personnel also may verify outstanding accounts receivable, and produce daily reports for management. Some hotels have added concierge services to their list of front office functions. In a sense, concierge services are simply an extension of the guest services provided by front office personnel.

The functions of the front office are to:

- Sell guestrooms, register guests, and assign guestrooms.
- Process future room reservations, when there is no reservation department or when the reservation department is closed.
- Coordinate guest services.
- Provide information about the hotel, the surrounding community, and any attractions or events of interest to guests.
- Maintain accurate room status information.
- Maintain guest accounts and monitor credit limits.
- Produce guest account statements and complete proper financial settlement.

Reservations. More than half of all hotel guests make reservations. These individuals arrange for hotel accommodations through such means as toll-free telephone numbers; direct telephone lines; hotel sales representatives; travel agencies; property-to-property networks; postal delivery; telex and fax; e-mail; and other communications services.

Every lodging property has its own way of monitoring and managing its reservations function. The reservations department is responsible for receiving and processing reservation requests for future overnight accommodations. Although procedures may differ from hotel to hotel with regard to reservations handling, maintenance, processing, and confirmation, the purpose is still the same: to accommodate guest requests in a manner that maximizes hotel occupancy and room revenue.

In the past, the reservations department basically took orders. Potential guests called or wrote the hotel, and reservations were made or denied based upon room availability. No real sales efforts were made since responsibility for room sales rested with the front desk. Most guests were satisfied to know they had a room; they did not want to know such specifics as bed type, rate, location, or amenities.

Guests will often find several employees on hand at the front desk to assist with their lodging needs. (Courtesy of Best Western Midway Motor Lodge, Grand Rapids, Michigan)

In fact, most reservations departments would not have had such information available when responding to caller questions.

Computers have corrected this information shortage. Computers can be programmed to provide reservations agents with information on the types of rooms available (including room rate, view, furnishings, amenities, and bed size) for a given day. Some computer systems can even provide agents with the exact room number if necessary. Such technology has shifted responsibility for room sales from the front desk to the reservations department. More recent technology even alerts the reservation agent automatically when the caller is a returning guest. Computers can provide reservations agents with a great deal of information on the hotel, some of which should be provided to the guest on request.

Computers have helped transform reservations agents into true salespeople. Reservations agents should convey the desirability, features, and benefits of staying at the hotel, rather than simply processing an accommodation request. It is no longer satisfactory for a reservations agent to defer to the front desk to determine a room's rate at registration. This shift in responsibility away from the front desk to the reservations department is important because it allows management to accurately forecast not only occupancy but revenue as well. Reservations agents should confirm the rate over the telephone at the time the guest makes the reservation. In fact, most guests requesting a reservation will not book a room without receiving a confirmed rate. The agent should reinforce the guest's decision to stay at the property and thank the guest for his or her business.

It is essential for reservations department personnel to work closely with the hotel's sales and marketing division when large group reservations are being solicited or processed. In fact, some hotel companies now place the reservations functions in the sales department instead of the front office. In any case, sales department representatives must be kept informed of room availability to ensure they know how many rooms they can sell on any given day. On a day-to-day basis, reservations agents must maintain accurate reservation records and closely track room availabilities in order to avoid *overbooking*. Overbooking can create bad feelings and contribute to lost business in the future. The management of reservations is further complicated by the fact that several states have enacted legislation prohibiting overbooking.

Communications. The telephone switchboard area or department maintains a complex communications network similar to that of any large company. The telephone department may also be referred to as a **private branch exchange** or **PBX**. Hotel switchboard or PBX operators may have responsibilities that extend beyond answering and distributing calls to the appropriate extension. When long-distance calls are routed and priced through the switchboard, charges must be relayed to a front office cashier for posting to the proper guest account. Switchboard operators may also place wake-up calls, monitor automated systems (such as door alarms and fire alarms), and coordinate emergency communications. Operators also protect guests' privacy, and thereby contribute to the hotel's security program by not divulging guestroom numbers. Some hotels now instruct guests to call the hotel operator for all service requests, including housekeeping, room service, and even bell service. Another recent trend involving guest safety with telephone systems is to have all house phones (telephones in public areas of the hotel used for calling within the hotel) ring the operator for call processing. This reduces the risk of unwanted or mistaken telephone calls. Many hotels also provide guest paging services over a public address system.

Recent technological advances have considerably decreased the responsibilities and workload of telephone switchboard operators. Hotels have placed telephones in each guestroom, thereby allowing guests to place their own room-to-room or outgoing phone calls. Most guestroom phones offer touchtone convenience and many feature a message-waiting light. Another recent innovation is guest voice mail, reducing the reliance on hotel operations to record messages for guests and turn on message waiting lights in guestrooms. Call accounting computer systems make it possible for guests to place calls without operator intervention. In addition, call accounting systems can place direct distance dialed calls over the least costly route available. Call accounting systems, which automatically price calls, also enable hotels to add surcharges and access charges to local and long-distance calls. In many cases, call accounting systems communicate with the front desk computer to automatically post the telephone charges to the guest's account. Another recent technological development is answer detection equipment, which permits the call accounting computer to identify when an outgoing telephone call is actually answered. This reduces disputes at the front desk over charges for calls that were not actually completed.

Computers can also be used to automatically place wake-up calls to guestrooms at preprogrammed times. When a front desk agent or switchboard operator receives a request for a wake-up call, the room number and the desired time are entered into the computer system. The computer can then place the wake-up call as specified, and play a recorded message once the phone is answered. This can be especially helpful in large hotels where hundreds of wake-up call requests can be received for the same time. In world-class hotels, the wake-up call may be placed by the hotel operator, while the computer alerts the operator to make the call at the requested time.

Uniformed Service. Employees who work in the uniformed service department of the hotel generally provide the most personalized guest service. Given the high degree of attention awarded guests by this department, some properties refer to uniformed service simply as *guest service.* Among the primary positions within the uniformed service department are:

- *Bell attendants*—persons who provide baggage service between the lobby area and the guestroom
- *Door attendants*—persons who provide curb-side baggage service and traffic control at the hotel entrance
- *Valet parking attendants*—persons who provide parking service for guests' automobiles
- *Transportation personnel*—persons who provide transportation services for guests
- *Concierges*—persons who assist guests by making restaurant reservations, arranging for transportation, and getting tickets for theater, sporting, or other special events, and so on

While personnel in reservations, front desk, and communications areas affect guest perceptions, it is often personnel in uniformed service who make a lasting impression. This is especially true in properties such as world-class or luxury hotels that offer a broad range of guest services. Uniformed service staff are usually classified as "tipped employees," since a portion of their income is derived from guests' gratuities. To some degree, uniformed service personnel can affect their income through the quality and frequency of service they provide.

While uniformed service jobs may not appear complex, they are critical to the smooth operation of a hotel. Quite often it is the ability of uniformed service staff to properly anticipate guest needs and communicate effectively with guests that makes the difference in the hotel's service quality. In many hotels in the United States, implementation of accommodations for guests identified in the American with Disabilities Act (ADA) comes under the uniformed services department.

Among the major challenges facing the manager of the uniformed service department are: setting the proper service standards, training employees, and ensuring that employees successfully provide quality service. Since uniformed

Bell staff can make guests feel welcome by using their professional communications skills.

service employees generally receive among the lowest hotel wages, keeping them trained and motivated can be an enormous job. Without a doubt, well-motivated uniformed service employees can enhance the hotel's image while earning good income through a combination of wages and tips and producing personal rewards.

Bell attendants. Many guests arrive at a hotel with heavy baggage or several pieces of luggage. Guests receive help handling this luggage from probably the best-known employee among the uniformed service staff: the bell attendant.

Bell attendants should be carefully selected. Since most hotels have carts for transporting baggage, the physical ability to actually *carry* the baggage is not a critical job qualification. More important, bell attendants should have strong oral communication skills and display genuine interest in each guest. Depending on the size and complexity of the hotel, bell attendants may be counted on to:

- Transport guest luggage to and from guestrooms.
- Familiarize guests with the hotel's facilities and services, safety features, as well as the guestroom and any in-room amenities.
- Provide a secure area for guests requiring temporary luggage storage.
- Provide information on hotel services and facilities.
- Deliver mail, packages, messages, and special amenities to guestrooms.
- Pick up and deliver guest laundry and dry cleaning.
- Perform light housekeeping services in lobby and entry areas.
- Help guests load and unload their luggage in the absence of a door attendant.

While many of these tasks appear simple, they all require a degree of professionalism. For example, to assist a guest with his or her luggage, the bell attendant must know how to properly load a luggage cart. Fragile items must not be placed below heavy items. The cart must also be properly balanced so that it does not tip over or become difficult to steer.

Due to their direct contact with guests, bell attendants have an opportunity to communicate vital information to guests and help them feel welcome at the hotel. A bell attendant who consistently and clearly communicates a warm welcome and proper information to each guest is a very valued employee. One of a hotel's best marketing opportunities occurs when the bell attendant escorts the guest to his or her room. Being familiar with the area outside the hotel as well as the hotel's restaurants, entertainment lounges, recreational activities, meeting rooms, and safety and security measures is an important part of the job. It is through informal conversation that bell attendants become key players in the hotel's sales and marketing efforts. Bell attendants should make an extra effort to learn guests' names. This makes guests feel more welcome and allows the bell attendant to provide more personal service.

Door attendants. Door attendants play a role similar to bell attendants: they are dedicated to welcoming the guest to the hotel. These employees are generally found in hotels offering world-class or luxury service. Some of the duties door attendants perform include:

- Opening hotel doors and assisting guests upon arrival.
- Helping guests load and unload luggage from vehicles.
- Escorting guests to the hotel registration area.
- Controlling vehicle traffic flow and safety at the hotel entrance.
- Hailing taxis, upon request.
- Assisting with valet parking services.
- Performing light housekeeping services in the lobby and entry areas.

Like bell attendants, door attendants must be well informed about hotel facilities and the local community. Guests frequently ask door attendants for directions to businesses, government offices, transportation centers, restaurants, and local landmarks and attractions. One of the most challenging responsibilities for a door attendant is controlling vehicle traffic at the hotel entrance. Controlling vehicle traffic can be a very demanding job, especially when the hotel is busy.

Experienced door attendants are capable of handling all these tasks with aplomb. A skilled and experienced door attendant learns the names of frequent guests. When these guests return to the hotel, the door attendant is able to greet them *by name* and can introduce them to other front office staff. Such personal service enhances the reputation of the hotel and provides the guest with a unique experience.

Valet parking attendants. Valet parking is generally available at hotels offering world-class or luxury service. Specially trained employees park guest and visitor automobiles. The personal attention and security of valet parking service is considered both a luxury and a convenience. Guests do not have to worry about finding a parking space, walking to the hotel in inclement weather, or finding their vehicles in the parking lot. Hotels generally charge a higher fee for valet parking than for self-service parking. In addition to paying the higher fee for valet parking, guests are also likely to tip the valet parking attendant.

Valet parking attendants are also responsible for the security of vehicles being moved to and from the hotel entrance. Attendants should not take a car into their care without issuing a receipt to the guest or visitor, usually in the form of a ticket. On the hotel portion of the ticket the attendant should note any existing damage to the vehicle. Vehicle keys must be kept in a secure area, and issued only by qualified personnel. Cars should not be issued to guests or visitors without proper documentation; in most cases, guests or visitors must return the receipt or ticket issued by the attendant before they can receive their keys. If a key is lost or given to the wrong person, the vehicle can be rendered inoperable or considered stolen and the hotel may be held financially responsible.

The uniformed service department is responsible for all vehicles under its care and reports information to the front desk each night so that parking charges can be posted to guest accounts. In addition, when the vehicle entrance to the hotel is busy, valet parking attendants should help keep the area running smoothly by providing traffic control assistance.

Transportation personnel. Already common to most airport hotels, transportation services and departments are gaining in popularity at other types of properties. Many airport hotels offer complimentary bus service between the airport and the hotel on a regular schedule. In some cases, a guest can simply step from an airport's baggage claim section to a conveniently located courtesy van area. In other cases, the guest must telephone the hotel to be picked up. Some hotels provide direct connect phone lines through a courtesy board at the airport for guest convenience.

Bus or courtesy van drivers must be well trained and properly licensed to operate the vehicle. Since these drivers are sometimes the first contact the guest will have with the hotel, it is important for them to be polite, efficient, and knowledgeable about the property. It is generally customary for drivers to provide some information about the hotel while in transit, either through a live spoken presentation or a pre-recorded audio tape. Drivers should also help guests entering and exiting the vehicle. An experienced driver efficiently and carefully loads guest luggage into the van. As a result of such assistance, guests won't have to wrestle with heavy bags while getting on and off the vehicle. Recently, many hotels have equipped vans with two-way radios. While these radios are provided primarily for safety and scheduling reasons, drivers may ask guests for their names and relay the information to the hotel. This allows the hotel to prepare for guests before their actual arrival.

Another recent addition at many hotels is providing courtesy transportation service to local business, shopping, entertainment, sporting, and dining establishments. At some properties, limousines may be made available to VIP guests. Transportation personnel may be classified as either tipped or non-tipped employees.

A concierge's knowledge of local businesses and attractions can be an asset to guests seeking recreation outside the hotel. (Courtesy of Renaissance Orlando Resort, Orlando, Florida)

In all cases, drivers must present the proper image of the hotel. Guest privacy must be maintained, especially in limousines. Any conversations among guests must be considered confidential and should not be discussed with hotel employees, family, or friends. Traffic safety is a critical concern. Drivers must be licensed according to state and federal laws. In addition, drivers must know how to check their vehicles to ensure that all equipment is working correctly. Safety equipment, such as flares and fire extinguishers, must be checked regularly and drivers must be familiar with their use.

Concierges. Even though this guest service position has existed for quite some time, the concierge is perhaps the least understood position in the uniformed service area. In the distant past, the concierge was the castle doorkeeper. A concierge's job was to ensure that all the castle occupants were secure in their rooms at night. Traveling royalty often were accompanied by a concierge who provided security and traveled ahead of the royal party to finalize food and lodging arrangements. As hotels became more common in Europe, the concierge eventually became part of the staff that provided personalized guest services. It is not uncommon to find a concierge at a world-class or luxury hotel.

Certified concierges may be identified by the prominent gold crossed keys displayed on their jacket lapel. To earn these keys, a concierge must be certified by the international association of concierges, known as ***Les Clefs d'Or*** (Golden Keys). This concierge association has established high standards for its members. While many hotels employ experienced staff to assist guests with special needs, the title *concierge* technically applies *only* to members of *Les Clefs d'Or.*

Concierges may provide custom services to hotel guests. Duties include making reservations for dining; securing tickets for theater and sporting events; arranging for transportation; and providing information on cultural events and local attractions. Concierges are known for their resourcefulness. Getting tickets to sold-out concerts or making last-minute dinner reservations at a crowded restaurant are part of a concierge's responsibility and reputation. Most successful concierges have developed an extensive network of local, regional, and national contacts for a variety of services. Especially important, however, are the local contacts the concierge has established at restaurants, box offices, car rental offices, airlines, printers, and other businesses. Some hotels actually encourage concierges to visit appropriate businesses and organizations to establish and strengthen such relationships. Finally, a highly successful concierge should speak several languages.

The concierge position is generally a salaried position, but gratuities from guests are common expressions of gratitude for exemplary service. In some hotels, the head concierge is the manager of the uniformed services department. When this is the case, the head concierge assumes additional responsibilities for supervising all uniformed service personnel. In large hotels, the head concierge is often too busy to undertake such tasks and supervises employees in the concierge department only.

As mentioned in the introduction to this chapter, service is becoming more important in attracting and holding a hotel's guests. In many hotels offering world-class and mid-range accommodations and services, the role of the full service concierge is becoming a key to establishing the reputation of the hotel.

Housekeeping. Housekeeping is perhaps the most important support department for the front office. Like the front office, housekeeping usually is part of the rooms division of the hotel. In some hotels, however, the housekeeping function is considered an independent hotel division. Effective communication among housekeeping and front office personnel can contribute to guest satisfaction while helping the front office to effectively monitor guestroom status. Housekeeping employees inspect rooms before they are available for sale, clean occupied and vacated rooms, and communicate the status of guestrooms to the front office. At most properties, a front desk agent cannot assign a guestroom until the room has been cleaned, inspected, and released by the housekeeping department.

The housekeeping department often employs a larger staff than other departments in the rooms division. Normally, an executive housekeeper is in charge of the department, aided by an assistant housekeeper. The department also includes inspectors, room attendants, lobby and general cleaners, and laundry personnel. Room attendants are assigned to specific sections of the hotel. Depending on the hotel's service level, average guestroom size, and cleaning tasks, room attendants may clean from 8 to 18 rooms per shift. If the hotel has its own laundry, housekeeping department staff may be charged with cleaning and pressing the property's linens, towels, uniforms, and guest clothing.

Housekeeping personnel (usually executive housekeepers) are responsible for maintaining two types of inventories: recycled and non-recycled. Recycled inventories are those items that have a relatively limited useful life but are used repeatedly in housekeeping operations. These inventories include such items as linens, uniforms, and guest amenities like irons and hair dryers. Non-recycled inventories are those items that are consumed or worn out during the course of routine housekeeping operations. Non-recycled inventories include cleaning supplies, small equipment items, and guest supplies and personal grooming items. Guest amenities and linens are among the items and conveniences most often requested by guests.

To ensure the speedy, efficient rooming of guests in vacant and inspected rooms, the housekeeping and front office departments must promptly inform each other of any change in a room's status or availability. Teamwork between housekeeping and the front office is essential to effective hotel operations. The more familiar housekeeping and front office personnel are with each other's departmental procedures, the smoother the relationship.

Food and Beverage Division

The hotel's food and beverage division generally ranks second to the rooms division in terms of total revenue. Many hotels support more than one food and beverage outlet. There are almost as many varieties of hotel food and beverage operations as there are hotels. Possible outlets include quick service, table service, and specialty restaurants, coffee shops, bars, lounges, and clubs. The food and beverage division also typically supports other hotel functions such as room service, catering, and banquet planning. Banquets, normally held in the hotel's function rooms, may represent tremendous sales and profit opportunities for the food and beverage division. Hotels that appeal to group and convention business typically generate large amounts of banquet and catering revenues. Catered functions, such as weddings and anniversaries, may also provide significant revenue opportunities for the food and beverage division.

Sales and Marketing Division

The size of a hotel's sales and marketing staff can vary from one part-time person to more than a dozen full-time employees. Sales and marketing responsibilities are typically divided into four functions: sales, convention services, advertising, and public relations. The primary goal of the division is to promote the sale of hotel products and services. To this end, sales and marketing staff need to coordinate their efforts with the front office and other hotel divisions to effectively assess and communicate guest needs.

Marketing employees strive to attract guests to the hotel. Marketing staff research the marketplace, competing products, guest needs and expectations, and future demand. These employees then develop advertising and public relations programs for the hotel based on their findings. Sales staff, on the other hand, strive to create revenue through the sale of hotel products to guests and groups. Front desk agents also may act as salespersons, especially when negotiating with and registering walk-in guests.

Accounting Division

A hotel's accounting division monitors the financial activities of the property. Some hotels use off-premises accounting services to complement the work of their internal accounting division. In this case, the hotel's staff collects and transmits data to a service bureau or chain headquarters. A hotel that performs its accounting work on the premises will employ a larger accounting staff with a higher level of responsibility.

Accounting activities include paying outstanding invoices, distributing unpaid statements, collecting amounts owed, processing payroll, accumulating operating data, and compiling financial reports. In addition, the accounting staff may be responsible for making bank deposits, securing cash loans, and performing other control and processing functions as required by hotel management. In many hotels, the night audit and the food and beverage audit are considered accounting division activities.

The accounting division's success depends on close coordination with the front office. The front office cashiering and guest accounting functions include monitoring cash, checks, credit cards, and other methods of guest account settlement. The most common financial transactions handled by front office staff members are receiving cash payments, verifying personal checks, imprinting credit cards, making change, and monitoring guest account statements. In small hotels, the front office is also responsible for monitoring the credit status of registered guests.

Engineering and Maintenance Division

A hotel's engineering and maintenance division is responsible for maintaining the property's structure and grounds, as well as its electrical and mechanical equipment. This division may also be charged with swimming pool sanitation, parking lot cleanliness and fountain operations. Quite often, the operation of the hotel's safety equipment comes under this division as well. Some hotels, however, may have a separate grounds department or an outdoor and recreation department for these tasks. Not all engineering and maintenance work is handled by the hotel's staff. Often, problems or projects require outside contracting. For example, special skills may be needed to calibrate building controls, charge fire extinguishers, and test and adjust building fire alarms. The special equipment needed to clean kitchen duct work, dispose of grease and other refuse, or remove snow from parking lots may require that these tasks be contracted.

The front office must efficiently exchange information with a representative of the engineering and maintenance division to ensure guest satisfaction. A guest complaint about a leaky faucet, malfunctioning lamp, or sticking lock should not rest with a front desk agent but should be written up and quickly relayed to engineering and maintenance staff for corrective action. Conversely, front desk staff must be informed quickly about maintenance problems that render a room unsuitable for sale. They also must be informed when the room becomes ready for sale again.

Security Division

All employees should be concerned about the safety and security of hotel guests, visitors, and employees. Security staff may include in-house personnel, contract security officers, or retired police officers. Security responsibilities may include patrolling the property; monitoring surveillance equipment; and, in general, ensuring that guests, visitors, and employees are safe and secure. Critical to the effectiveness of the security division is the cooperation and assistance of local law enforcement officials.

A hotel's security program is strongest when employees outside the security division participate in security efforts. For example, front desk agents play a critical part in key control by issuing room keys to registered guests *only*. Room attendants practice security when they verify a guest's room key *before* allowing that guest to enter a room they are cleaning. All employees should be wary of suspicious activities anywhere on the premises, and report such activities to a member of the security staff. A key role of the security divison is to maintain a strong awareness in the hotel's staff of safety issues through training and enforcement of standards.

Human Resources Division

Hotels have increased their investment in and dependence on human resources management. The size and budgets of human resources divisions have grown steadily, along with their responsibility and influence. This expanded role is mirrored by the growing preference for the broader term *human resources management* over *personnel management*. In properties that are not large enough to justify a separate human resources office or division, the hotel's general manager often supervises the human resources function.

Recently, the scope of the human resources division has changed in response to new government legislation, a shrinking labor pool, and growing pressures from competition. Although techniques have changed, the basic functions of the human resources division remain the same: employment (including external recruiting and internal reassignment), training, employee relations (including quality assurance), compensation, benefits, administration (including employee policies), labor relations, and safety.

Other Divisions

Many hotels staff a variety of other divisions to serve the needs of their guests. The range of possibilities reflects the diversity of hotels.

Retail Outlets. Lodging properties often establish gift shops, newsstands, or other retail outlets in their lobbies or public areas. These outlets generate revenue for the hotel based on a percentage of sales or a fixed space rental fee.

Recreation. Some hotels—primarily resorts—staff a division dedicated to providing group and individual recreational activities for guests. Some recreation divisions also undertake landscaping the grounds and maintaining the pool. Golf, tennis, bowling, snorkeling, sailing, walking tours, bicycle trips, horseback riding, hikes, and other activities may be arranged by recreation division staff. The division may also plan and direct activities such as arts and crafts shows or children's programs. Typically, recreation employees collect fees for organized activities or arrange for charges to be posted to guest accounts.

Casino. Casino hotels will have a casino division that operates games of chance for guests and protects the property's gambling interests. The casino division may offer various forms of entertainment and other attractions to draw customers into the property and its gambling facilities. For casino hotels, revenues derived from gambling are usually larger than revenues from hotel operations. Therefore, casino priorities may take precedence over hotel priorities.

Front Office Operations

Traditional front office functions include reservations, registration, room and rate assignment, guest services, room status, maintenance and settlement of guest accounts, and creation of guest history records. The front office develops and maintains a comprehensive data base of guest information, coordinates guest services, and ensures guest satisfaction. These functions are accomplished by personnel in diverse areas of the front office department.

While no industry standards exist for front office positions, front office organization charts can be used to define departmental reporting and working relationships. The highest level of employee and guest satisfaction can be attained through a carefully designed front office organization, together with comprehensive goals and strategies, workshifts, job descriptions, and job specifications.

Organization

Large hotels often organize the front office according to functions, with different employees handling separate areas. This division of duties can enhance the control the front office has over its own operations. Front office personnel can provide more specialized attention if each area is responsible for only one segment of the guest's stay. Such a separation of duties may not be practical in a small hotel, where it is common for one or two individuals to handle all front desk operations.

The front office in a large hotel supports many positions with a considerable separation of duties. These positions typically include, but are not limited to:

- A front desk agent who registers guests and maintains room availability information.
- A cashier who handles money, posts charges, and oversees guest account settlement.
- A mail and information clerk who takes messages, provides directions to guests, and maintains mail.
- A telephone operator who manages the switchboard and coordinates wake-up calls.

- A reservations agent who responds to reservation requests and creates reservation records.
- A uniformed service agent who handles guest luggage and escorts guests to their rooms.

If a hotel property is computerized, each employee may be restricted to accessing only those computer records pertinent to his or her function.

The front office of a mid-size hotel performs the same functions, but with fewer employees. Staff are often cross-trained and job duties are typically combined. For example, a front desk agent may also serve as a cashier and mail and information clerk. He or she may also be trained to assume the duties of a switchboard operator and a reservations agent in their absence. During busy periods, several desk agents may be working at the same time. Although each staff member may be assigned identical duties, the desk agents may informally divide the functions among themselves. For example, one person may decide to register guests and handle the switchboard, another may function as a cashier, and a third may handle reservations and information requests.

Small hotels may have a single front desk agent who performs nearly all the functions with little assistance. If the front desk agent becomes overwhelmed by the workload, the general manager or accountant, if properly trained, may help relieve the burden. In a small property, the general manager and accountant often become more directly involved with front office operations.

Goals and Strategies

The goals and strategies of the front office are based on the hotel's mission statement and overall goals. For example, one front office goal might be to encourage more **walk-ins** (guests who arrive at the hotel desiring a room but having no reservations) to stay at the property. This front office goal contributes to helping the hotel meet its goal of increasing occupancy percentage. A strategy to accomplish this goal could be for front desk agents to improve their sales presentation by more thoroughly describing the available guestrooms and hotel services. Another hotel goal might be to reduce the time necessary for guests to complete registration. A related front office goal might be to eliminate distractions at the front desk; a strategy for achieving this goal might be to ensure that front desk agents engaged in assisting guests are not interrupted by telephone calls. Simply stated, the front office should base its goals on the hotel's goals and create strategies to meet those goals.

Workshifts

A 40-hour workweek is the typical workload for front office employees in most hotels. Federal and state wage and hour laws apply to the front office, and, in addition, some properties may be bound by union contracts and rules. A front office employee may be assigned to any one of the property's workshifts, depending on the needs of the front office and the staff member's availability. Traditional front office workshifts are:

- Day shift 7 A.M.–3 P.M.
- Evening shift 3 P.M.–11 P.M.
- Night shift 11 P.M.–7 A.M.

A recent trend in front office operations is to provide a limited level of guest service during late night hours, thereby reducing the number of employees required on the night shift. The front office is likely to offer only limited services during these hours.

Front office workshifts may vary with guest business patterns. A program of flexible work hours, or **flextime,** allows employees to vary the time they start and end work. Certain busy hours during a work shift, however, may require the presence of a majority of the staff. For example, one front desk agent may work from 6 A.M. to 2 P.M. so that wake-up calls and check-outs can be handled more efficiently through the 7 A.M. shift change. On the other hand, scheduling a front desk agent to work from 10 A.M. to 6 P.M. may allow for smooth processing of guest arrivals during the time evening shift personnel are scheduled for a meal break.

Other types of alternative scheduling include variations on the traditional workweek of five 8-hour days. A **compressed work schedule** occurs when an employee works 40 hours in fewer than five days (for instance, four 10-hour days). **Job sharing** is an arrangement by which two or more part-time employees share the responsibilities of one full-time position. Each worker may perform all aspects of the position on alternate days, or the duties may be divided while both work simultaneously.

Part-time employees are an increasingly important source of labor for the hospitality industry. Many potential workers, such as students, parents of young children, and retirees, may not be available to work full time. Part-time workers give the front office the flexibility to respond to fluctuating guest demands while reducing overall labor costs. Alternative scheduling programs, however, require careful planning and evaluation before implementation.

Job Descriptions

A **job description** lists all the tasks that compose a work position. A job description may also outline reporting relationships, responsibilities, working conditions, equipment and materials to be used, and other important information specific to the place of employment. To be most effective, job descriptions should be customized to the operational procedures of a specific lodging property. Job descriptions should be task-oriented; they should be written for a position, not for a particular employee. Job descriptions will become dated and inappropriate as work assignments change, so they should be reviewed at least once a year for possible revision. Employees should be involved in writing and revising their job descriptions. Properly written job descriptions can minimize employee anxiety by specifying the chain of command and the responsibilities of the job.

Well-written job descriptions can also be used:

- In evaluating job performance.
- As an aid in training or retraining employees.

- To prevent unnecessary duplication of duties.
- To help ensure that each job task is performed.
- To help determine appropriate staffing levels.

Each front office employee should be given a copy of the job description for his or her position. Final job candidates may also be given a copy of a job description, even before an employment offer is made. This is preferable to having someone accept a job and then decide it is unsuitable because he or she was unaware of the job's requirements.

A word of caution about job descriptions is appropriate. The Americans with Disabilities Act (ADA) states that people with disabilities are considered qualifed for a position if they can perform the position's **essential functions** with or without **reasonable accommodation.** Job descriptions should be created before an open position is advertised and they should list essential functions. Management must not discriminate against an applicant with a disability merely because the applicant cannot perform a non-essential function. Improper job descriptions may not only lead to improper hiring decisions, they may also expose the hotel to liability for illegal discrimination. At the same time, proper job descriptions may open opportunities for qualified applicants who have disabilities covered under the ADA.

The Appendix to this chapter presents a sampling of model front office job descriptions.

Job Specifications

Job specifications list the personal qualities, skills, and traits a person needs to successfully perform the tasks outlined in a job description. Basically, front office job specifications spell out front office management's expectations for current and prospective employees. Job specifications are usually developed after job descriptions since a particular job may require special skills and traits. Factors considered for a job specification are: formal education, work experience, general knowledge, previous training, physical requirements, communication ability, and equipment skills. Job specifications are often the basis for advertising job opportunities and for identifying eligible applicants; they may also be used to identify current employees for promotion. A sample job specification for a generic front office staff member is shown in Exhibit 5.

Although standardized job specifications do not exist throughout the industry, certain traits and skills can be expected to appear in job specifications of most hotels. Because of their high degree of guest and visitor contact, front office positions often require extraordinary interpersonal skills. Evaluating an applicant on the basis of these traits may be highly subjective. Nonetheless, traits important to front office work include:

- Professional demeanor
- Congenial personality
- Helpful attitude
- Flexibility

Exhibit 5 Sample Job Specification: Front Office Positions

Job Specification
Front Office Personnel

Our property considers the following traits important for the successful performance of front office work.

1. *Professional Demeanor*
   - Reports to work on time
   - Has a positive attitude toward the job and the hotel
   - Recognizes positive and negative aspects of the job
   - Possesses maturity in judgment
   - Appears businesslike
   - Maintains control and composure in difficult situations
2. *Congenial Nature*
   - Smiles readily
   - Exhibits cordial and pleasant behavior
   - Is a people person
3. *Helpful Attitude*
   - Is sensitive to the guests' needs
   - Possesses a sense of humor
   - Responds and speaks intelligently
   - Demonstrates creativity
   - Practices good listening skills
4. *Flexibility*
   - Willing and able to accept a different workshift if necessary
   - Understands others' points of view
   - Willing to try new ways of doing things; innovative
   - Works well with guests and hotel staff; a team player
5. *Well-Groomed Appearance*
   - Dresses appropriately; meets property standards for wear and care of uniform, jewelry, and personal grooming

- Well-groomed appearance
- Detail-oriented

Successful performance of front office procedures usually requires general skills acquired through education and experience. Valuable employees possess practical skills, knowledge, and aptitude. Two specific skills often needed for front office work are mathematical abilities (for cashiering and accounting tasks) and keyboarding (for recordkeeping and computer operation).

Finally, an outgoing personality and a willingness to learn are especially important qualities for a front office employee. Front office personnel must be team players. They must be willing to work together for the benefit of the entire operation. Front office job descriptions, as well as job specifications, are typically prepared by the front office manager with input from front office employees.

Summary

The services that result from a hotel's smooth operation are highly visible and appreciated. Guests are more likely to return to or recommend a lodging property if they had an enjoyable stay. For a hotel to run effectively and efficiently, every employee must understand and work to achieve the property's mission. The hotel's mission statement expresses the underlying philosophy that gives meaning and direction to hotel policies. The hotel's mission statement should address the interests of three diverse groups: guests, management, and employees. A sound mission statement should address guests' expectations, reflect management's philosophy, and provide hotel employees with a sense of purpose.

The front office is typically responsible for developing and maintaining a comprehensive data base of guest information, coordinating guest services, and ensuring guest satisfaction. Larger hotels tend to organize the front office by functional areas in order to enhance control over operations. In a computerized property, each employee may be restricted to accessing only those electronic records pertinent to his or her function.

A hotel operating department can be classified as either a revenue center or a support center. By definition, a revenue center sells goods or services to guests, thereby generating its own revenues. A support center does not generate direct revenue, but instead provides important backing for the hotel's revenue centers. The terms front of the house and back of the house may also be used to classify hotel operational areas. Front-of-the-house areas are those zones of the hotel in which guests and employees directly interact. In back-of-the-house areas, there is little direct connection between guests and support staff. Although back-of-the-house employees may not directly serve the guest by taking an order, assisting with registration, or delivering luggage to a guestroom, the employee indirectly serves the guest by cleaning the guestroom, repairing a leaky faucet, or correcting an error in a guest account. Typical hotel operating divisions and departments include rooms, reservations, food and beverage, sales and marketing, accounting, engineering and maintenance, security, and human resources.

A job description lists a majority of the tasks composing a position. A job description may also outline reporting relationships, responsibilities, working conditions, equipment and materials to be used, and other important information specific to the property. To be most effective, job descriptions should be customized to the operational procedures of a specific lodging property. Job specifications list the personal qualities, skills, and traits a person needs to successfully perform the tasks outlined in a job description. Several sample front office area job descriptions are presented in the Appendix to this chapter.

Key Terms

back of the house—the functional areas of a hotel in which staff have little or no direct guest contact, such as the engineering, accounting, and human resources divisions.

Clefs d'Or—the international association of concierges; the title *concierge* technically applies only to members of *Les Clefs d'Or.*

compressed work schedule—an adaptation of full-time work hours that enables an employee to work the equivalent of a standard workweek in fewer than the traditional five days.

essential functions—a term used in the Americans with Disabilities Act; according to EEOC guidelines, the essential functions of a job are those functions or fundamental job duties that the individual who holds the position must be able to perform unaided or with the assistance of a reasonable accommodation.

flextime—a program of flexible work hours that allows employees to vary their times of starting and ending work.

front of the house—the functional areas of a hotel in which staff have extensive guest contact, such as the food and beverage facilities and the front office.

goal—a definition of the purpose of a department or division that directs the actions of employees and the functions of the department or division toward the hotel's mission.

job description—a detailed list identifying all the key duties of a job as well as reporting relationships, additional responsibilities, working conditions, and any necessary equipment and materials.

job sharing—an arrangement by which two or more part-time employees share the responsibilities of one full-time position.

job specification—a list of the personal qualities, skills, and traits needed to successfully perform the tasks outlined by a job description.

mission statement—a document that states the unique purpose that sets a hotel apart from other hotels; a mission statement expresses the underlying philosophy that gives meaning and direction to the hotel's actions, and addresses the interests of guests, management, and employees.

organization chart—a schematic representation of the relationships among positions within an organization, showing where each position fits into the overall organization and illustrating the divisions of responsibility and lines of authority.

private branch exchange (PBX)—a hotel's telephone switchboard equipment.

reasonable accommodation—a term used in the Americans with Disabilities Act; making a change in the usual way of doing a job so that a qualified person with a disability can participate, as long as making this change does not impose "undue hardship" on the employer.

revenue center—a hotel division or department that sells products or services to guests and thereby directly generates revenue for the hotel; the front office, food and beverage outlets, room service, and retail stores are typical hotel revenue centers.

strategy—a method by which a department or division plans to achieve its goals.

support center—a hotel division or department that does not generate revenue directly, but supports the hotel's revenue centers; support centers include the housekeeping, accounting, engineering and maintenance, and human resources divisions.

tactics—the day-to-day operating procedures that implement strategies.

walk-in—a person who arrives at a hotel without a reservation and requests a room.

Review Questions

1. What is the purpose of a hotel's mission statement? What are the three groups of people whose interests should be addressed in a mission statement?
2. How do a hotel's goals relate to its mission statement and to departmental and divisional goals and strategies?
3. How does an organization chart show employee reporting and consulting relationships? Why should an organization chart be flexible?
4. Which hotel departments and divisions are typically classified as revenue centers? Why?
5. Which hotel departments and divisions are typically classified as support centers? Why?
6. What main divisions are typically found in the organization of a full-service hotel?
7. How may a limited-service hotel differ in its organization from a full-service hotel?
8. How does the front office interact with the rest of the rooms division and the other main divisions in a full-service hotel?
9. Why is it impossible for some front offices to divide employee duties according to function?
10. What are the three traditional front office workshifts? What variations on the traditional workweek might a hotel adopt?
11. How can job descriptions be used? How do they differ from job specifications?

Internet Sites

For more information, visit the following Internet sites. Remember that Internet addresses can change without notice.

Associations

American Culinary Federation (ACF)
http://www.acfchefs.org

American Hotel & Motel Association (AH&MA)
http://www.ahma.com

The American Society of Travel Agents (ASTA)
http://www.astanet.com

The Educational Institute of AH&MA
http://www.ei-ahma.org

Hospitality Financial & Technology Professionals
http://www.hftp.org

Hospitality Sales and Marketing Association International (HSMAI)
http://www.hsmai.org

International Hotel & Restaurant Association (IHRA)
http://www.ih-ra.com

International Society of Meeting Planners
http://www.iami.org/ismp.html

Meeting Professionals International (MPI)
http://www.mpiweb.org

National Restaurant Association (NRA)
http://www.restaurant.org

Professional Convention Management Association (PCMA)
http://www.pcma.org

Publications—Online and Printed

Electronic Gourmet Guide
http://www.foodwine.com

Food Network: Cyber Kitchen
http://www.foodtv.com

Food Magazine
http://www.penton.com/corp/mags/fm.html

Internet Food Channel
http://www.foodchannel.com

Lodging Hospitality
http://www.penton.com/corp/mags/lh.html

Lodging Online
http://www.ei-ahma.org/webs/lodging/index.html

Nation's Restaurant News Online
http://www.nrn.com

Meetings and Conventions
http://www.meetings-conventions.com

Meetings and Travel Online
http://www.mtonline.com

Meetings Industry Mall
http://www.mim.com

On the Rail—News for Food Professionals
http://www.ontherail.com

Restaurant Hospitality
http://www.penton.com/corp/mags/rh.html

Restaurants and Institutions
http://www.rimag.com

Successful Meetings
http://www.successmtgs.com

Tradeshow Week
http://www.tradeshowweek.com

The Virtual Clubhouse
http://www.club-mgmt.com

Case Study

Dark Days at Sunnyvale: Can Teamwork Part the Clouds?

The Sunnyvale Resort is a 300-room luxury property with a lake on one side and a golf course, riding stables, and tennis courts on the other. Once considered the premier resort of the South, the rich (both old and new money) considered it fashionable to winter at Sunnyvale back in the twenties and thirties. However, by the sixties its glory had begun to fade and so had its revenues. In 1978, the resort added 50 suites and 20,000 square feet of meeting space in an effort to attract group business. This helped for a time, but in the last five years both occupancy and room rates were caught in a seemingly unstoppable decline. Recently, the resort lost a star and was now listed in the guides as a three-star property.

Losing a star spurred Thomas Redgrave to take action. Mr. Redgrave was the resort's owner, and he was not happy that a property that should be making $15 to $16 million a year in revenue had grossed less than $12 million in each of the last two years. He gave the general manager, who had been with the resort since 1977, a nice farewell dinner and a gold watch, then hired Ken Richards, an experienced general manager from a convention hotel in Richmond, to come in and turn things around.

At a meeting with Ken, Mr. Redgrave summed up the situation as he saw it. "I'd like to renovate Sunnyvale and really bring it back to where it ought to be. As a businessman, I know sometimes you have to spend money to make money. But I'd have to put several million dollars into the place to do it right. The way things are going at Sunnyvale right now, I'm not sure I'd get the kind of return on investment that I should.

"The last general manager was here long before I bought the place and he didn't communicate with me very much. I try to be a 'hands-off' owner and I gave him plenty of room, but for the last few years the numbers have been bad and getting worse, and he didn't seem to know what to do about it. I'll be honest—I don't know that much about the hotel business. But that's why I hired you. I want you to find out what's wrong and get the revenues back up to where they should be. If I see signs that you've got Sunnyvale back on track, I'll open the purse strings. It'll take some time, but we'll make everything at Sunnyvale first-class again. That'll make me happy, and down the road it'll make your job a whole lot easier."

From his experience at other properties, Ken knew that low occupancy and low rates were not the resort's real problems, only the symptoms. His first inspections of the property revealed quite a few minor blemishes—walls that needed painting, leaky showerheads, thin carpets, and so on. In fact, the entire resort, even the relatively new suites and meeting spaces, had an air of genteel shabbiness. But, more importantly, Ken took time during his first week to meet one-on-one with all of Sunnyvale's managers. He especially wanted to learn all he could about his department heads before calling his first executive staff meeting next Monday morning.

Skip Keener, the resort's director of sales, had been with Sunnyvale for over 40 years and fondly remembered the resort's glory days. "When I first got here, the property sold itself," he told Ken. "Never had a problem filling the place up. We were featured in *Southern Living* magazine practically every year. But all of a sudden we fell out of fashion, and then in the seventies they put in all that meeting space that I have to sell to groups like vacuum-cleaner salesmen, the Kentucky Aluminum Siding Association, and the North Carolina Association of Used Car Dealers. This is the kind of business that keeps us going now. I tell you, the place sure isn't what it used to be."

The resort's executive housekeeper, Ruth Harless, had been with the property for almost 30 years and she missed the glory days, too. "It was a slower pace back then," she said. "Guests stayed longer—ten days, two weeks, even a month or more. You got to know them and they got to know you. Now, most guests are here for a big meeting and are out in two or three nights. It's 'rush, rush, rush.'" Ken learned that Ruth's reputation for upholding cleaning standards was not what it used to be. The comments he heard were: "She used to be a real stickler for detail—every room was spotless, but there's no denying that the rooms just aren't as clean anymore." Ken also learned that Ruth had stopped attending executive staff meetings years ago. "I don't have time" was her excuse.

Bob Ruggles was the resort's chief engineer. Since he had been with the property for "only" 11 years, Skip and Ruth still considered him "the new guy." "I don't know why, but I just never hit it off with them," he lamented to Ken. He also lamented the fact that, because the resort was old, he was faced every day with a large number of minor maintenance problems. "If it's not the plumbing, it's the electrical. If it's not the electrical, it's the HVAC system acting up. It's always something. I run to put out one 'fire' and two more take its place. I can't catch up."

The reservations manager, Teresa Mansfield, had been with the resort for three years but she was also considered a "newcomer," and no one on the executive staff went out of the way to talk to her. One assistant manager from another department told Ken that "she seems angry about something all the time, but she never says much." Her complaint was that she was left out of the decision-making at the resort and was expected to just do as she was told. Skip frequently sold more rooms than were allocated to group sales, for example, without telling her. "I don't know exactly what rooms I can sell from one day to the next."

The last, and newest, member of the executive staff was Jon Younger, the resort's food and beverage director. He had arrived at the property just six months ago, after the previous F&B director of 28 years, Abe Williams, had retired. Unfortunately, Abe had chosen to coast into retirement, and the department's performance had declined during the last three years of his tenure. Smart and ambitious, Jon had tried to whip the food and beverage staff back into shape and restore the resort's reputation for F&B excellence, but his opportunities to shine had been few. Skip, the director of sales, had received so many F&B complaints from clients during Abe's last years that he had begun to book most of the big F&B group functions off-site, and "comp" a lot of the minor ones he allowed the resort's F&B department to handle (a complimentary cocktail party for a group's first night was a favorite giveaway). Jon had asked Skip to book more F&B functions in-house and had lobbied the previous general manager for support, but had made no headway.

In his early thirties and feeling the pressure of his first job as a department head, Jon had become defensive and abrasive in his dealings with Skip and the others.

By Friday of Ken's first week, Sunnyvale's major difficulties were coming into focus. The sales department was so busy bringing in business that it wasn't communicating with the rest of the staff like it should. The result was confusion, poor service, and dissatisfied guests. To entice dissatisfied guests back to the resort, the sales staff was constantly lowering room rates. It was a downward spiral that Ken had to find a way to stop.

Next Monday morning, Ken began his first staff meeting by reassuring his department heads that the owner was committed to the resort's long-term health. "Mr. Redgrave wants to put a lot of money into the place and make it a four-star property again, but first he wants to see that we can turn the rates and occupancy around and beef up the bottom line. I'm committed to taking action quickly and I know all of you want to makes things better, too." Ken picked up a pen and a legal pad and surveyed the managers gathered around the table. "I've looked at the reports," he nodded toward a stack of papers on the table in front of him, "but I'm interested in hearing what all of you think. Does anyone have any ideas about why the revenue's been down the past few years?"

Silence hung over the room while the department heads looked at the table or shot sidelong glances at each other. Finally, Jon Younger spoke up. "I think a big problem is that we're giving too much food and beverage business away." Another silence descended on the group.

"Yes," Ken agreed after a while, trying to prompt more comments, "I noticed in the financial statements that the F&B lines seem very low for a resort of this size. What's going on there?"

"Well, I hate to say it," Skip said, "but I got so many complaints from clients that I finally decided I'd better send them off-site for F&B. I've lined up a few outside caterers that do a good job for me, and just up the road there's the Mountainview Gourmet Steakhouse. I send groups up there and they get steaks bigger than their plates, servers in Wild West costumes, skits and 'gunfights' and other entertainment while they eat—they love it."

"The problem with that," Jon said sharply, "is that Skip's not giving me a chance to show what I can do. Those complaints he's talking about happened back when Abe was here. And we're getting killed with all the comps he's giving away. Every group that comes in gets a comp cocktail party the first night, which wipes out the restaurant's dinner sales because everybody goes to the party and scarfs down the heavy hors d'oeuvres and free booze. Why not a banquet the first night? That's high-profit business that we really need."

"What about that, Skip?" Ken asked.

"Well, all I can say is that it's hard when a client looks you in the eye and says 'Last time we booked here, the banquet was terrible—eight of my people stood around embarrassed because you under-set by eight places, you forgot the ice sculpture, the soup was cold, the entrées were late and most of them were cold, too, and I had to listen to my people griping about it the entire time I was here. So if you want me back you're gonna have to do something different.' A lot of my clients come back every year or two, and they remember the things that went wrong the last time."

Ken made a note on his pad. "But the problems your clients refer to didn't happen on Jon's watch, is that right?"

"True," Skip said. "But I still have to fight the perception that we can't deliver quality F&B."

Another silence descended on the group. Ken turned to Teresa. "What problems do you see in the reservations area?"

Teresa swallowed hard. It wasn't her usual style to speak up, but this might be the best time to get things out in the open with the new general manager. "Well, one thing that could be better," she began, "is that I'm never sure how many rooms Skip has sold, so occasionally I've had to turn guests away because of overbookings. But much more often we've suffered from 'underbookings.' That's when Skip asks for more rooms than he really needs, rooms I could have sold, but they stand empty because he blocked them off and then didn't need them for his groups. That happens a lot more than it should.

"It's also hard to have to sell the less-desirable rooms all the time," Teresa continued. "Skip tends to use up the suites and the nicer guestrooms—even the ones allocated to me—with his groups. To make it worse, I'm under pressure to sell those less-desirable rooms at a premium. The budget calls for a group rate of $150, but a lot of the time Skip gives groups a $120 rate. This pressures me to sell my allotment of rooms at an even higher rate than my budgeted target of $170 per room. That's hard to do when all the rooms that are left are at the end of the hall, or next to the laundry, or the ones with no view."

Skip crossed his arms over his chest. "Groups should get a break, especially with the kind of service they usually get around here. And part of your paycheck isn't riding on how many rooms you sell, like mine is. If you think it's easy selling ten thousand rooms a year, try it sometime!"

Ken turned to Skip. "You had to meet a 'rooms sold' target, not a revenue target?"

"Correct. No bonus unless I sold ten thousand rooms. It's not easy, especially when there's problems—VIPs standing in the lobby because their suites aren't ready, for example. Do you have any idea how hard it is to sell somebody the next time, when the first thing that happens to Mr. Bigshot is that he has to cool his heels in the lobby while his room is cleaned? Instead of getting ushered up to his nice suite and feeling pampered, he gets ticked off."

"Wait a minute," Ruth interrupted. "Whenever that happens, I always pull room attendants off their regular rooms so they can blitz through the suites and get them ready."

"Ready?" Skip snorted. "They're never as 'ready' as they should be! If I had a nickel for every time the fresh flowers and fruit baskets weren't placed in the suites like they're supposed to be—"

"I get them in the rooms every time I'm notified," Jon interjected.

"You're right, Jon, sometimes I forget to tell you," Ruth said defensively, "but I have my hands full just trying to 'rush rush rush' to get everything clean and get my crew back on their regular duties. It disrupts the entire day."

"What about the cleaning problems?" Skip asked Ruth. "It's embarrassing when the president of a state association comes to me—this happened just two weeks ago—and tells me his wife found a hairball in the bathtub drain and is afraid to take a shower now."

"What do you expect when you tell people they can check in at noon, when check-out time is noon, too?" Ruth said. "We're not given time to do a proper job."

"Does that happen a lot?" Ken asked. "I mean, people wanting to check into suites that people have just checked out of?"

"All the time," Ruth said.

"So you have to do these 'cleaning blitzes' pretty often?" Ken laid a hand on the reports in front of him. "I noticed that housekeeping's labor costs are pretty high—all those blitzes helps explain it."

"They certainly happen more often than they should," Ruth replied. "And you're right, it's costly, because my crew has to stay later to finish their regular assignments. The overtime adds up."

"The guest complaints add up, too," Teresa said. "When Ruth pulls her crew from their regular assignments to blitz the suites, the regular guestrooms aren't getting done. So they get cleaned late, and those guests end up inconvenienced and unhappy. So the guest dissatisfaction ripples down through the entire resort."

"Also," Ruth added, "when you have ten minutes to try to whip a room into shape, you intentionally skip over some things and miss others, so the constant blitzing doesn't do my housekeepers any good, either. They start to get sloppy even when they aren't rushed. Some of them figure if a quick touch-up is okay for a VIP suite, it's okay for a regular guestroom, too. I really have to fight that attitude with some of my crew."

"We've got to plan a little better in the future," Ken said, scribbling in his legal pad.

"It's hard to plan when you don't get much advance notice about groups coming in or what their needs are," Teresa said pointedly, looking at Skip.

"It's one of the reasons I can never catch up," Bob chimed in. "I never know what's going on, either. I just get calls all the time: 'Leaky toilet in Room 113.' 'The guest in Suite 27 turned on the air conditioning and nothing happened.' Fine. I ask for the rooms for five days, then suddenly they have to be sold because a big group's coming in. The repairs aren't made, guests complain, and I get chewed out."

"And I have to lower the rates next time for that group," Skip said. "I call the client and he says a bunch of my people were unhappy last time, why should I come back? So I give him a break on the rates, comp the coffee breaks, breakfasts, what have you, to try to get him to come back for another year. Sometimes it works, and sometimes I lose a group."

"And my housekeepers are unhappy because they keep reporting maintenance problems that never get fixed," Ruth said. "They ask me why, and I don't know what to tell them, because I'm never told why either."

"If you would talk to me once in a while, I'd be glad to tell you," Bob said. "It's not all my fault. I can't get any cooperation out of anybody."

"Do you really need five days every time?" Teresa asked. "Cooperation is a two-way street, you know. Sometimes it's hard to keep a room 'out of order' that long."

"I'd like to have five days. I don't see why it's such a big deal."

"One room out for five days is not a big deal," Skip said, "but you keep adding rooms to your list, so eventually it gets to be a big deal."

Ken held up his hands to signal a halt to the discussion, then surveyed the group over steepled fingers. "Obviously there's a lot of frustration in this room. You're frustrated because you want to get your jobs done, but your co-workers—instead of helping you—are sometimes getting in the way. This not only frustrates you, but frustrates our guests as well, because they're not receiving the service they should." Ken paused. "You're not getting in each other's way on purpose, or because you want to make someone else's life miserable," Ken smiled. "I just think you're all too focused on your own areas and aren't seeing the big picture.

"From what I've heard today, I'd say our biggest problem is that we're not talking to each other. We've got to learn to communicate better so we can serve each other and our guests better. More communication will help bring the bigger picture into focus for everybody.

"I want to show Mr. Redgrave some positive changes within 90 days," Ken continued. "With that in mind, I'd like all of you to come to next Monday's staff meeting with ideas on how you can improve communication and work together better as a team. I'll think about it as well, and come to the meeting prepared with recommendations for each of you. I think teamwork will be the key to doing a better job of satisfying our guests and moving revenues in a positive direction."

Discussion Questions

1. What are the problems that each department experiences because of poor communication among the executive staff?
2. What recommendations can Ken make to each of the resort's department heads to help them work together as a team?
3. What actions should Ken take if his department heads, after a suitable period of time, don't seem to be coming together as a team?
4. What can Ken show Sunnyvale's owner in the next 90 days to demonstrate that the resort is making progress?

Case Number: 3322CA

The following industry experts helped generate and develop this case: Richard M. Brooks, CHA, Vice President—Operations, Bridgestreet Accommodations, Inc., Cleveland, Ohio; and S. Kenneth Hiller, CHA, Director of Transition and Owner Relations, Marriott Hotels International.

This case also appears in *Case Studies in Lodging Management* (Lansing, Mich.: Educational Institute of the American Hotel & Motel Association, 1998), ISBN 0-86612-184-6.

Appendix
Selected Front Office Model Job Descriptions

Cross-training front office employees has helped standardize procedures in many hotels. In a small hotel, for instance, one employee may handle reservations, registration, switchboard, and check-out tasks. Lines of responsibility have also blurred as more and more properties adopt computerized front office recordkeeping systems. These systems can combine information required for most front office tasks in a common data base that can be accessed by many front office employees.

Many hotels refer to front office employees as *front office agents, guest service representatives,* or something similar. Even in hotels with a traditional division of duties, the titles for each position may change over time. These changes may reflect a reevaluation of the tasks involved or an attempt to avoid the negativity associated with certain titles. The position titles used in this text represent trends in the lodging industry. This Appendix presents generic model job descriptions for typical front office positions found in a mid-size hotel.

JOB DESCRIPTION

POSITION TITLE: FRONT OFFICE MANAGER

REPORTS TO: Assistant Manager or General Manager

POSITION SUMMARY: Directly supervises all front office personnel and ensures proper completion of all front office duties. Directs and coordinates the activities of the front desk, reservations, guest services, and telephone areas.

DUTIES AND RESPONSIBILITIES:

1. Participates in the selection of front office personnel.
2. Trains, cross-trains, and retrains all front office personnel.
3. Schedules the front office staff.
4. Supervises workloads during shifts.
5. Evaluates the job performance of each front office employee.
6. Maintains working relationships and communicates with all departments.
7. Maintains master key control.
8. Verifies that accurate room status information is maintained and properly communicated.
9. Resolves guest problems quickly, efficiently, and courteously.
10. Updates group information. Maintains, monitors, and prepares group requirements. Relays information to appropriate personnel.
11. Reviews and completes credit limit report.
12. Works within the allotted budget for the front office.
13. Receives information from the previous shift manager and passes on pertinent details to the oncoming manager.
14. Checks cashiers in and out and verifies banks and deposits at the end of each shift.
15. Enforces all cash-handling, check-cashing, and credit policies.
16. Conducts regularly scheduled meetings of front office personnel.
17. Wears the proper uniform at all times. Requires all front office employees to wear proper uniforms at all times.
18. Upholds the hotel's commitment to hospitality.

PREREQUISITES:

Education: Minimum of two-year college degree. Must be able to speak, read, write, and understand the primary language(s) used in the workplace. Must be able to speak and understand the primary language(s) used by guests who visit the workplace.

Experience: Minimum of one year of hotel front-desk supervisory experience, experience handling cash, accounting procedures, and general administrative tasks.

Physical: Requires fingering, grasping, writing, standing, sitting, walking, repetitive motions, verbal communications, and visual acuity.

JOB DESCRIPTION

POSITION TITLE: FRONT DESK AGENT

REPORTS TO: Front Office Manager

POSITION SUMMARY: Represents the hotel to the guest throughout all stages of the guest's stay. Determines a guest's reservation status and identifies how long the guest will stay. Helps guests complete registration cards and then assigns rooms, accommodating special requests whenever possible. Verifies the guest's method of payment and follows established credit-checking procedures. Places guest and room information in the appropriate front desk racks and communicates this information to the appropriate hotel personnel. Works closely with the housekeeping department in keeping room status reports up to date and coordinates requests for maintenance and repair work. Maintains guest room key storage, and maintains and supervises access to safe deposit boxes. Must be sales-minded. Presents options and alternatives to guests and offers assistance in making choices. Knows the location and types of available rooms as well as the activities and services of the property.

DUTIES AND RESPONSIBILITIES:

1. Registers guests and assigns rooms. Accommodates special requests whenever possible.
2. Assists in preregistration and blocking of rooms for reservations.
3. Thoroughly understands and adheres to proper credit, check-cashing, and cash-handling policies and procedures.
4. Understands room status and room status tracking.
5. Knows room locations, types of rooms available, and room rates.
6. Uses suggestive selling techniques to sell rooms and to promote other services of the hotel.
7. Coordinates room status updates with the housekeeping department by notifying housekeeping of all check-outs, late check-outs, early check-ins, special requests, and part-day rooms.
8. Possesses a working knowledge of the reservations department. Takes same day reservations and future reservations when necessary. Knows cancellation procedures.
9. Files room keys.
10. Knows how to use front office equipment.
11. Processes guest check-outs.
12. Posts and files all charges to guest, master, and city ledger accounts.
13. Follows procedures for issuing and closing safe deposit boxes used by guests.
14. Uses proper telephone etiquette.
15. Uses proper mail, package, and message handling procedures.
16. Reads and initials the pass-on log and bulletin board daily. Is aware of daily activities and meetings taking place in the hotel.

(continued)

FRONT DESK AGENT *(continued)*

17. Attends department meetings.
18. Coordinates guest room maintenance work with the engineering and maintenance division.
19. Reports any unusual occurrences or requests to the manager or assistant manager.
20. Knows all safety and emergency procedures. Is aware of accident prevention policies.
21. Maintains the cleanliness and neatness of the front desk area.
22. Understands that business demands sometimes make it necessary to move employees from their accustomed shift to other shifts.

PREREQUISITES:

Education: High school graduate or equivalent. Must be able to speak, read, write, and understand the primary language(s) used in the workplace. Must be able to speak and understand the primary language(s) used by guests who visit the workplace.

Experience: Previous hotel-related experience desired.

Physical: Requires fingering, grasping, writing, standing, sitting, walking, repetitive motions, hearing, visual acuity, and may on occasion have to lift and carry up to 40 pounds.

JOB DESCRIPTION

POSITION TITLE: RESERVATIONS AGENT

REPORTS TO: Front Office Manager

POSITION SUMMARY: Responds to communications from guests, travel agents, and referral networks concerning reservations arriving by mail, telephone, telex, cable, fax, or through a central reservation system. Creates and maintains reservation records—usually by date of arrival and alphabetical listing. Prepares letters of confirmation and promptly processes any cancellations and modifications. Tracks future room availabilities on the basis of reservations, and helps develop forecasts for room revenue and occupancy. Additional duties may include preparing the list of expected arrivals for the front office, assisting in preregistration activities when appropriate, and processing advance reservation deposits. Knows the types of rooms the hotel has as well as their location and layout. Knows of all hotel package plans—meaning status, rates, and benefits.

DUTIES AND RESPONSIBILITIES:

1. Processes reservations by mail, telephone, telex, cable, fax, or central reservation systems referral.
2. Processes reservations from the sales office, other hotel departments, and travel agents.
3. Knows the types of rooms available as well as their location and layout.
4. Knows the selling status, rates, and benefits of all package plans.
5. Knows the credit policy of the hotel and how to code each reservation.
6. Creates and maintains reservation records by date of arrival and alphabetical listing.
7. Determines room rates based on the selling tactics of the hotel.
8. Prepares letters of confirmation.
9. Communicates reservation information to the front desk.
10. Processes cancellations and modifications and promptly relays this information to the front desk.
11. Understands the hotel's policy on guaranteed reservations and no-shows.
12. Processes advance deposits on reservations.
13. Tracks future room availabilities on the basis of reservations.
14. Helps develop room revenue and occupancy forecasts.
15. Prepares expected arrival lists for front office use.
16. Assists in preregistration activities when appropriate.
17. Monitors advance deposit requirements.
18. Handles daily correspondence. Responds to inquiries and makes reservations as needed.
19. Makes sure that files are kept up to date.

(continued)

RESERVATIONS AGENT *(continued)*

20. Maintains a clean and neat appearance and work area at all times.
21. Promotes goodwill by being courteous, friendly, and helpful to guests, managers, and fellow employees.

PREREQUISITES:

Education: High school graduate or equivalent. Must be able to speak, read, write, and understand the primary language(s) used in the workplace. Must be able to speak and understand the primary language(s) used by guests who visit the workplace.

Experience: Previous hotel-related experience desirable.

Physical: Requires fingering, grasping, writing, standing, sitting, walking, repetitive motions, hearing, visual acuity, and good speaking skills.

JOB DESCRIPTION

POSITION TITLE: FRONT OFFICE CASHIER

REPORTS TO: Front Office Manager

POSITION SUMMARY: Posts revenue center charges to guest accounts. Receives payment from guests at check-out. Coordinates the billing of credit card and direct-billed guest accounts with the accounting division. All guest accounts are balanced by the cashier at the close of each shift. Front office cashiers assume responsibility for any cash used in processing front desk transactions. May also perform a variety of banking services for guests, such as check cashing and foreign currency exchange.

DUTIES AND RESPONSIBILITIES:

1. Operates front office posting equipment.
2. Obtains the house bank and keeps it balanced.
3. Completes cashier pre-shift supply checklist.
4. Takes departmental machine readings at the beginning of the shift.
5. Completes guest check-in procedures.
6. Post charges to guest accounts.
7. Handles paid-outs.
8. Transfers guest balances to other accounts as required.
9. Cashes checks for guests following the approval policy.
10. Completes guest check-out procedures.
11. Settles guest accounts.
12. Handles cash, traveler's checks, personal checks, credit cards, and direct billing requests properly.
13. Posts non-guest ledger payments.
14. Makes account adjustments.
15. Disperses guest records upon check-out.
16. Transfers folios paid by credit card to each credit card's master file.
17. Transfers folios charged to the non-guest ledger to each company's master file.
18. Balances department totals at the close of the shift.
19. Balances cash at the close of the shift.
20. Manages safe deposit boxes.

PREREQUISITES:

Education: High school graduate or equivalent desired. Must be able to speak, read, write, and understand the primary language(s) used in the workplace.

Experience: Previous hotel-related experience beneficial.

Physical: Requires fingering, grasping, writing, standing, sitting, walking, repetitive motions, hearing, and visual acuity. Must possess basic computational ability.

JOB DESCRIPTION

POSITION TITLE: HOTEL SWITCHBOARD OPERATOR

REPORTS TO: Front Office Manager

POSITION SUMMARY: Speaks clearly, distinctly, and with a friendly, courteous tone. Uses listening skills to put callers at ease and obtains accurate, complete information. Answers incoming calls and directs them to guest rooms through the switchboard (PBX) system or to hotel personnel or departments. Takes and distributes messages for guests, provides information on guest services, and answers inquiries about public hotel events. Provides a paging service for hotel guests and employees. Processes guest wake-up calls.

DUTIES AND RESPONSIBILITIES:

1. Answers incoming calls.
2. Directs call to guest rooms, staff, or departments through the switchboard or PBX system.
3. Places outgoing calls.
4. Receives telephone charges from the telephone company and forwards charges to the front desk for posting.
5. Takes and distributes messages for guests.
6. Logs all wake-up call requests and performs wake-up call services.
7. Provides information about guest services to guests.
8. Answers questions about hotel events and activities.
9. Understands PBX switchboard operations.
10. Provides paging services for hotel guests and employees.
11. Knows what action to take when an emergency call is requested or received.
12. Monitors automated systems including fire alarms and telephone equipment when the engineering and maintenance department is closed.

PREREQUISITES:

Education: High school graduate or equivalent. Must be able to speak and understand the primary language(s) used by guests who visit the workplace.

Experience: Previous hotel-related experience desirable.

Physical: Requires fingering, grasping, writing, standing, sitting, walking, repetitive motions, hearing, visual acuity, and good verbal skills.

JOB DESCRIPTION

POSITION TITLE: NIGHT AUDITOR

REPORTS TO: Front Office Manager or Accounting Department

POSITION SUMMARY: Checks front office accounting records for accuracy and, on a daily basis, summarizes and compiles information for the hotel's financial records. Tracks room revenues, occupancy percentages, and other front office operating statistics. Prepares a summary of cash, check, and credit card activities, reflecting the hotel's financial performance for the day. Posts room charges and room taxes to guest accounts including guest transactions not posted during the day by the front office cashier. Processes guest charge vouchers and credit card vouchers. Verifies all account postings and balances made during the day by front desk cashiers and agents. Monitors the current status of coupon, discount, and other promotional programs. Is able to function as a front desk agent especially in terms of check-in and check-out procedures.

DUTIES AND RESPONSIBILITIES:

1. Posts room charges and taxes to guest accounts.
2. Processes guest charge vouchers and credit card vouchers.
3. Posts guest charge purchase transactions not posted by the front office cashier.
4. Transfers charges and deposits to master accounts.
5. Verifies all account postings and balances.
6. Monitors the current status of coupon, discount, and other promotional programs.
7. Tracks room revenues, occupancy percentages, and other front office statistics.
8. Prepares a summary of cash, check, and credit card activities.
9. Summarizes results of operations for management.
10. Understands principles of auditing, balancing, and closing out accounts.
11. Knows how to operate posting machines, typewriters, and other front office equipment and computers.
12. Understands and knows how to perform check-in and check-out procedures.

PREREQUISITES:

Education: Minimum of a two-year college degree. Must be able to speak, read, write, and understand the primary language(s) used in the workplace. Must be able to speak and understand the primary language(s) used by guests who visit the workplace.

Experience: Minimum of one year of hotel front desk supervisory experience, experience handling cash, accounting procedures, and general administrative tasks.

Physical: Requires fingering, grasping, writing, standing, sitting, walking, repetitive motions, verbal communications, and visual acuity.

JOB DESCRIPTION

POSITION TITLE: GUEST SERVICES MANAGER

REPORTS TO: General Manager/Front Office Manager

POSITION SUMMARY: Oversees all guest services operations, including front desk, reservations, PBX, bell staff, and transportation services to ensure quality and guest satisfaction.

DUTIES AND RESPONSIBILITIES:

1. Answers letters of inquiry regarding rates and availability.
2. Trains new Guest Services department personnel.
3. Maintains a thorough knowledge of the room rack locations, types of rooms, room rack operations, package plans, and discounts.
4. Maintains a detailed knowledge about the hotel's services and hours of operations.
5. Oversees servicing and security of the safe deposit boxes.
6. Knows all safety and understands emergency procedures and how to act upon them. Understands accident prevention policies.
7. Knows cash handling procedures. Files and posts all changes to guest master and city ledger account.
8. Possesses a thorough knowledge of credit and check-cashing policies and procedures and adheres to them.
9. Anticipates and intervenes in all incidents of guest dissatisfaction and attempts to satisfy all such guests, within hotel policy.
10. Develops and maintains all aspects of the hotel's reservations system directed toward the maximization of profit.

PREREQUISITES:

Education: Minimum of a two year college degree. Ability to speak and understand the primary language(s) used by guests who visit the workplace. Ability to speak, read, write, and understand the primary language(s) used in the workplace.

Experience: Minimum one year of hotel front-desk supervisory experience, experience handling cash, account procedures, and general administrative tasks.

Physical: Requires fingering, grasping, writing, standing, sitting, walking, repetitive motions, verbal communications, and visual acuity.

JOB DESCRIPTION

POSITION TITLE: CONCIERGE

REPORTS TO: Front Office Manager

POSITION SUMMARY: Serves as the guest's liaison for both hotel and non-hotel services. Functions are an extension of front desk agent duties. Assists the guest—regardless of whether inquiries concern in-hotel or off-premises attractions, facilities, services, or activities. Knows how to provide concise and accurate directions. Makes reservations and obtains tickets for flights, the theater, or special events. Organizes special functions such as VIP cocktail receptions. Arranges for secretarial services.

DUTIES AND RESPONSIBILITIES:

1. Develops a strong knowledge of the hotel's facilities and services and of the surrounding community.
2. Provides guests with directions to attractions or facilities in or outside the property.
3. Provides guests with information about attractions, facilities, services, and activities in or outside the property.
4. Makes guest reservations for air or other forms of transportation when requested. Obtains necessary itinerary and tickets.
5. Makes guest reservations for the theater and other forms of entertainment when requested. Obtains necessary tickets and provides directions to facilities.
6. Organizes special functions as directed by management.
7. Arranges secretarial and other office services.
8. Coordinates guest requests for special services or equipment with the appropriate department.
9. Contacts roomed guests periodically to ascertain any special needs.
10. Handles guest complaints and solves problems to the degree possible.

PREREQUISITES:

Education: Minimum of two years college education with emphasis in business, sales, or marketing. Must be able to speak, read, write, and understand the primary language(s) used in the workplace and by guests who visit the workplace

Experience: Minimum of two years sales experience with a minimum of one year supervisory experience.

Physical: Requires bending, stooping, climbing, standing, walking, sitting, fingering, reaching, grasping, lifting, carrying, repetitive motions, visual acuity, hearing, writing, and speaking. Must exert well-paced mobility to reach other departments of the hotel on a timely basis.

Chapter 3 Outline

The Guest Cycle
- Pre-Arrival
- Arrival
- Occupancy
- Departure

Front Office Systems
- Non-Automated
- Semi-Automated
- Fully Automated

Front Office Forms
- Pre-Arrival
- Arrival
- Occupancy
- Departure

The Front Desk
- Functional Organization
- Design Alternatives

Front Office Equipment
- Room Rack
- Mail, Message, and Key Rack
- Reservation Racks
- Information Rack
- Folio Trays
- Account Posting Machine
- Voucher Rack
- Cash Register
- Support Devices

Telecommunications
- Telecommunications Equipment

Property Management Systems
- Reservations Management Software
- Rooms Management Software
- Guest Account Management Software
- General Management Software
- Back Office Interfaces
- System Interfaces

Summary

Case Study

3

Front Office Operations

All the functions, activities, and areas of the front office are geared toward supporting guest transactions and services. Critical to the success of the department and the hotel are appropriately designed and used front office work areas, equipment, and forms. Also paramount is the accurate planning and monitoring of front office transactions.

To many guests, the front office *is* the hotel. It is the main contact point for nearly every guest service the hotel provides. This chapter will examine front office operations in terms of the various stages of a guest's stay, referred to as the guest cycle. Discussion will focus on the various forms, work space designs, equipment, related tasks, and computer applications appropriate to each stage.

The Guest Cycle

The financial transactions a guest makes while staying at a hotel determine the flow of business through the property. Traditionally, the flow of business can be divided into a four-stage **guest cycle.** Exhibit 1 diagrams these four stages: pre-arrival, arrival, occupancy, and departure. Within each stage, important tasks related to guest services and guest accounting can be identified and analyzed.

The guest cycle in Exhibit 1 is not an inflexible standard. Since activities and functions tend to overlap between stages, some properties have revised this traditional guest cycle into a sequence of pre-sale, point-of-sale, and post-sale events. For computerized properties, this revised sequence may improve coordination among hotel operating departments. However, the traditional guest cycle is still widely used in the industry.

Front office employees need to be aware of guest services and guest accounting activities at all stages of the guest stay. Front office employees can efficiently serve guest needs when they clearly understand the flow of business through the hotel. Exhibit 2 indicates which front office personnel are most likely to serve the guest during each stage of the guest cycle. The guest cycle also suggests a systematic approach to managing front office operations.

Pre-Arrival

The guest chooses a hotel during the *pre-arrival stage* of the guest cycle. The guest's choice can be affected by many factors, including previous experiences with the hotel; advertisements; company travel policy; recommendations from travel agents, friends, or business associates; the hotel's location or reputation; frequent traveler programs; and preconceptions based upon the hotel's name or chain affiliation. The

Exhibit 1 The Guest Cycle and Related Front Office Functions

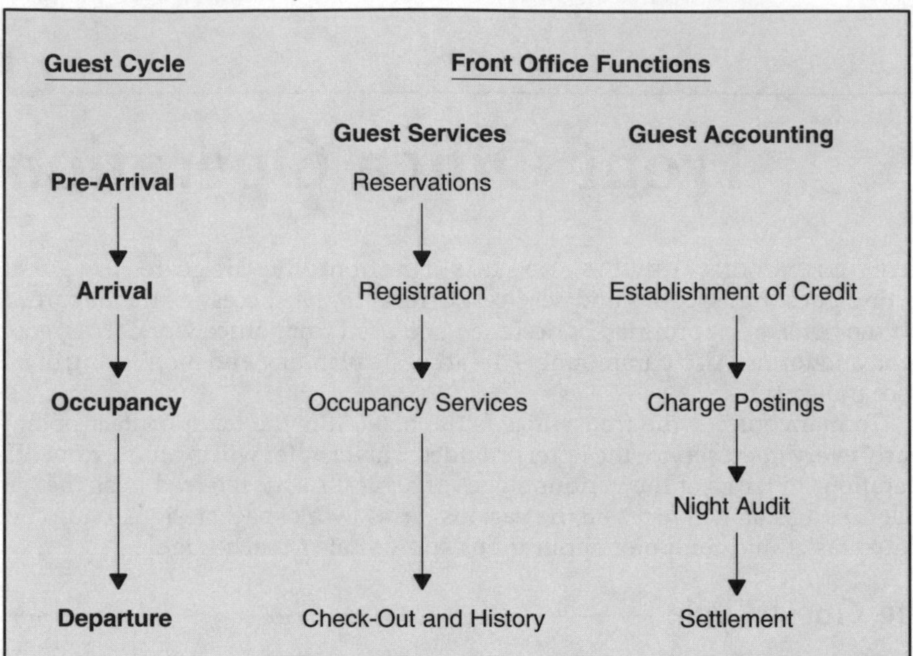

guest's decision may also be influenced by the ease of making reservations and how the reservations agent describes the hotel and its facilities, room rates, and amenities. In reality, the reservations area is the sales office for the hotel's non-group business. Its employees must be "sales-oriented" and present a positive, strong image of the hotel. The attitude, efficiency, and knowledge of the front office staff may influence a caller's decision to stay at a particular hotel.

A reservations agent must be able to respond quickly and accurately to requests for future accommodations. The proper handling of reservation information can be critical to the success of a lodging property. Efficient procedures will also allow more time for the reservations agent to capture needed information and to market hotel services.

If a reservation can be accepted as requested, the reservations agent creates a reservation record. The creation of a reservation record initiates the hotel guest cycle. This record enables the hotel to personalize guest service and appropriately schedule needed staff and facilities. By confirming a reservation, the hotel verifies a guest's room request and personal information, and assures the guest that his or her needs will be addressed. Using the information collected during the reservations process, a hotel may also be able to complete pre-registration activities. Such activities include assigning a specific room and rate to guests who have not yet registered, and preparing a **guest folio.** A guest folio is a record of the charges incurred and credits acquired by the guest during occupancy.

Exhibit 2 Interaction During the Guest Cycle

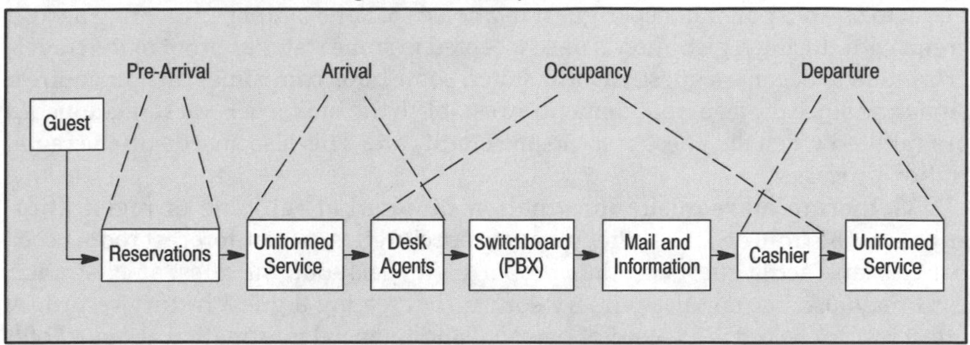

An effective reservation system helps maximize room sales by accurately monitoring room availabilities and forecasting rooms revenue. By analyzing reservation information, front office management can develop an understanding of the hotel's reservation patterns. Data collected during the reservations process become especially useful in subsequent front office functions. But, without a doubt, the most important outcome of an effective reservations process is having a room available when the guest arrives.

Arrival

The *arrival stage* of the guest cycle includes registration and rooming functions. After the guest arrives, he or she establishes a business relationship with the hotel through the front office. It is the front office staff's responsibility to clarify the nature of the guest-hotel relationship and to monitor the financial transactions between the hotel and the guest.

The front desk agent should determine the guest's reservation status before beginning the registration process. Guests with reservations may have already undergone pre-registration activities. Guests without reservations, termed walk-in guests, present an opportunity for front desk agents to sell guestrooms. To sell successfully, the front desk agent must be very familiar with the hotel's room types, rates, and guest services and be able to describe them in a positive manner. A guest is not likely to register if he or she is not convinced of the value of renting a particular hotel room.

A registration record, completed either as part of pre-registration activity or at the time of check-in, is essential to efficient front office operation. A registration record should include information about the guest's intended method of payment, the planned length of stay, and any special guest needs such as a rollaway bed, a child's crib, or a preferred room location. It should also include the guest's billing address, telephone number, and his or her signature.

Most states require a guest's signature on the registration record to establish the person's intention of becoming a hotel guest. Since both the hotel and the traveler gain certain legal benefits when the traveler is a guest rather than simply a visitor, obtaining the guest's signature can be a very important part of the registration process. A recent trend is to allow other forms of identification to serve as proof of intent to establish an innkeeper-guest relationship. For example, presenting a valid credit card during registration is now accepted in some states as proof of the traveler's intent to become a guest. In these states, some hotel companies do not require a signature since the legal requirements to establish the innkeeper-guest relationship are fulfilled when the guest presents the credit card. This also speeds up the registration process.

Gathering all requisite information in detail at the time of registration enhances the front office's ability to satisfy special guest needs, forecast room occupancies, and settle guest accounts properly. At check-out, the guest's registration card may also become the primary source for creating a guest history record. A guest history record is a record of personal and financial information about a hotel guest that can help the hotel in its marketing and sales efforts. It can also help the hotel in registering and serving the guest upon his or her return stay.

The front desk agent uses registration information to assign a room type and a room rate for each guest. Room and rate assignment also depends on reservation information (long-run availability) and room status (short-run availability) information. The housekeeping status of a room must be relayed to the front desk as soon as possible in order for the front desk to maximize room sales. Some common room status terminology is defined in Exhibit 3.

When assigning guestrooms, the front desk agent must also be aware of guestroom characteristics for each room type. Hotel room types may range from a standard single guestroom to a luxurious suite. Exhibit 4 contains the definitions of some typical hotel room types. Furnishings, amenities, and location within the property will tend to differentiate rooms within the same room type.

Front desk agents must also be sensitive to accessibility issues for guests with physical impairments. The Americans with Disabilities Act now requires new and renovated properties to be barrier-free in design. The term *barrier-free* means that facilities and accommodations must be designed with the disabled in mind. Some of the more prevalent features of barrier-free guestrooms are extra-wide doorways for wheelchairs (both entry doors and bathroom doors), extra-large bathrooms, grab bars beside the toilet and inside the bathtub area, roll-in showers for wheelchairs, lowered vanity countertops and extra knee space under the sink, handles on doors and bathroom fixtures instead of knobs, and strobe lights and pillow shakers as part of the smoke and fire detection systems (for the deaf). Other aspects of barrier-free design are addressed later in this chapter.

Once the guest decides to rent a room, the front desk agent turns his or her attention to identifying the guest's method of payment. The hotel guest accounting cycle depends on registration information to ensure deferred payment for rendered services. Whether the guest uses cash, personal check, credit card, or some alternative method of payment, the front office must take measures to ensure eventual payment. A proper credit check at the outset of a transaction greatly reduces the potential for subsequent settlement problems. If a guest has not secured management approval of credit before arriving at the property, the hotel may deny the guest's request for credit at the time of check-in.

Exhibit 3 Room Status Terminology

During the guest's stay, the housekeeping status of the guestroom changes several times. The various terms defined are typical of the room status terminology of the lodging industry. Not every room status will occur for each guestroom during every stay.

Occupied: A guest is currently registered to the room.

Complimentary: The room is occupied, but the guest is assessed no charge for its use.

Stayover: The guest is not expected to check out today and will remain at least one more night.

On-change: The guest has departed, but the room has not yet been cleaned and readied for resale.

Do not disturb: The guest has requested not to be disturbed.

Sleep-out: A guest is registered to the room, but the bed has not been used.

Skipper: The guest has left the hotel without making arrangements to settle his or her account.

Sleeper: The guest has settled his or her account and left the hotel, but the front office staff has failed to properly update the room's status.

Vacant and ready: The room has been cleaned and inspected and is ready for an arriving guest.

Out-of-order: The room cannot be assigned to a guest. A room may be out-of-order for a variety of reasons, including the need for maintenance, refurbishing, and extensive cleaning.

Lock-out: The room has been locked so that the guest cannot re-enter until he or she is cleared by a hotel official.

DNCO (did not check out): The guest made arrangements to settle his or her account (and thus is not a skipper), but has left without informing the front office.

Due out: The room is expected to become vacant after the following day's check-out time.

Check-out: The guest has settled his or her account, returned the room keys, and left the hotel.

Late check-out: The guest has requested and is being allowed to check out later than the hotel's standard check-out time.

Registration is complete once a method of payment and the guest's departure date have been established. The guest may be given a room key and a map of the property and allowed to proceed to the room without assistance, or a uniformed service person may escort the guest to the room. When the guest arrives at the room, the occupancy stage of the guest cycle begins.

Occupancy

The manner in which the front office staff represents the hotel is important throughout the guest cycle, particularly during the *occupancy stage.* As the center

Exhibit 4 Room Type Definitions

The following room type definitions are common throughout the lodging industry.

Single: A room assigned to one person. May have one or more beds.

Double: A room assigned to two people. May have one or more beds.

Triple: A room assigned to three people. May have two or more beds.

Quad: A room assigned to four people. May have two or more beds.

Queen: A room with a queen-size bed. May be occupied by one or more people.

King: A room with a king-size bed. May be occupied by one or more people.

Twin: A room with two twin beds. May be occupied by one or more people.

Double-double: A room with two double (or perhaps queen) beds. May be occupied by one or more persons.

Studio: A room with a studio bed—a couch which can be converted into a bed. May also have an additional bed.

Mini-suite or junior suite: A single room with a bed and a sitting area. Sometimes the sleeping area is in a bedroom separate from the parlor or living room.

Suite: A parlor or living room connected to one or more bedrooms.

Connecting rooms: Rooms with individual entrance doors from the outside and a connecting door between. Guests can move between rooms without going through the hallway.

Adjoining rooms: Rooms with a common wall but no connecting door.

Adjacent rooms: Rooms close to each other, perhaps across the hall.

of hotel activity, the front desk is responsible for coordinating guest services. Among many services, the front desk provides the guest with information and supplies. The front office should respond to requests in a timely and accurate way to maximize guest satisfaction. A concierge may also be on staff to provide special guest services.

A major front office objective throughout the guest cycle is to encourage repeat visits. Sound guest relations are essential to this objective. Guest relations depend on clear, constructive communications between the front office, other hotel departments and divisions, and the guest. The hotel must be aware of a guest complaint in order to resolve it. Front desk agents should carefully attend to guest concerns and try to seek a satisfactory resolution as quickly as possible.

Security is another primary front office concern during occupancy and, to some extent, throughout all stages of the guest cycle. Security issues likely to apply to front office employees include the protection of funds and valuables. Procedures for hotel and guest key control, property surveillance, safe deposit boxes, guests' personal property, and emergencies are also important.

A variety of transactions during the occupancy stage affect guest and hotel financial accounts. Most of these transactions will be processed according to front office account posting and auditing procedures.

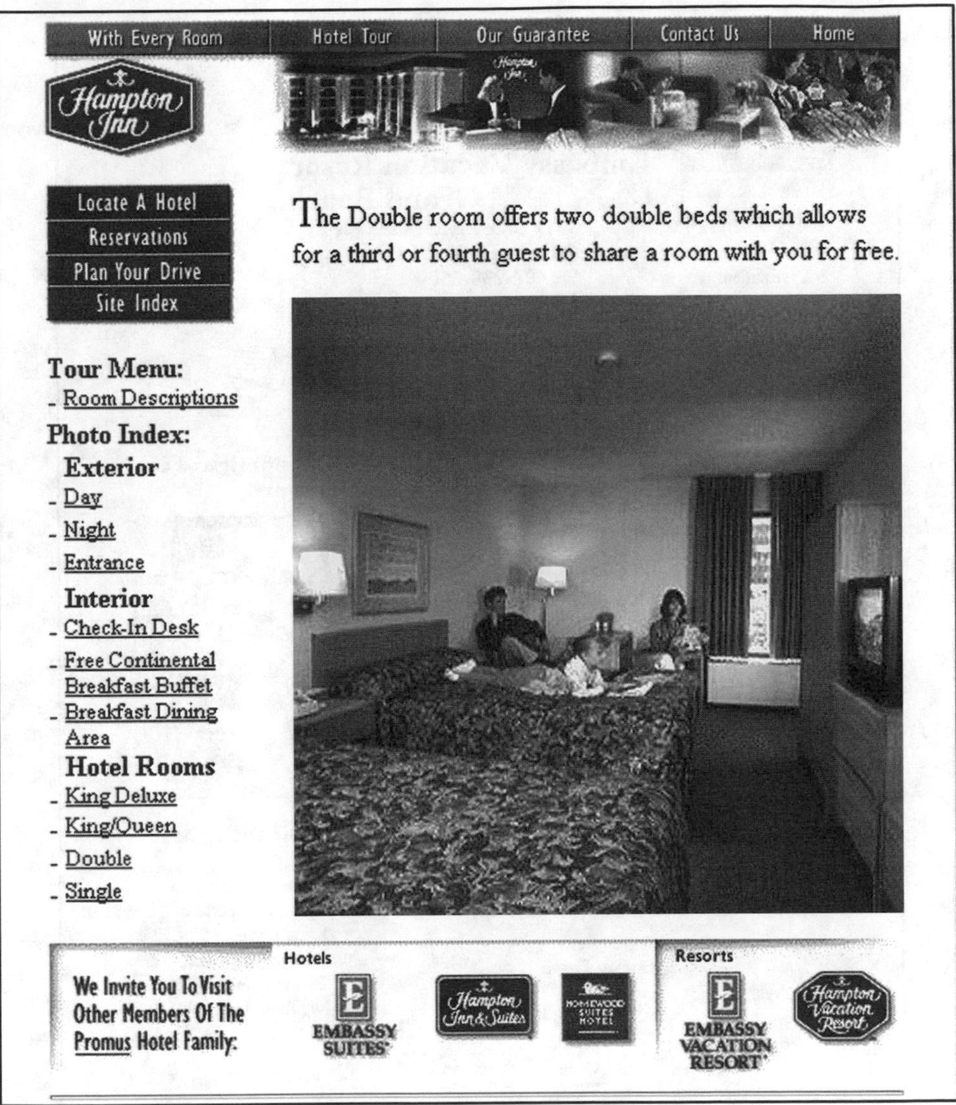

Room types offered by Hampton Inns include: King Deluxe, King Study, King/Queen, Double, and Single. The company's Internet site (http://www.hampton-inn.com) provides detailed descriptions of each room type as well as photographs of the different types of rooms.

The room rate of the guestroom is usually the largest single charge on the guest's folio. Additional expenses can be charged to a guest's account if he or she established acceptable credit at the front desk during registration. Goods or services purchased from the hotel's restaurant, lounge, room service department, telephone department, transportation areas, gift shop, and other revenue outlets may be charged to guest accounts. Many hotels set a high balance on the amount which

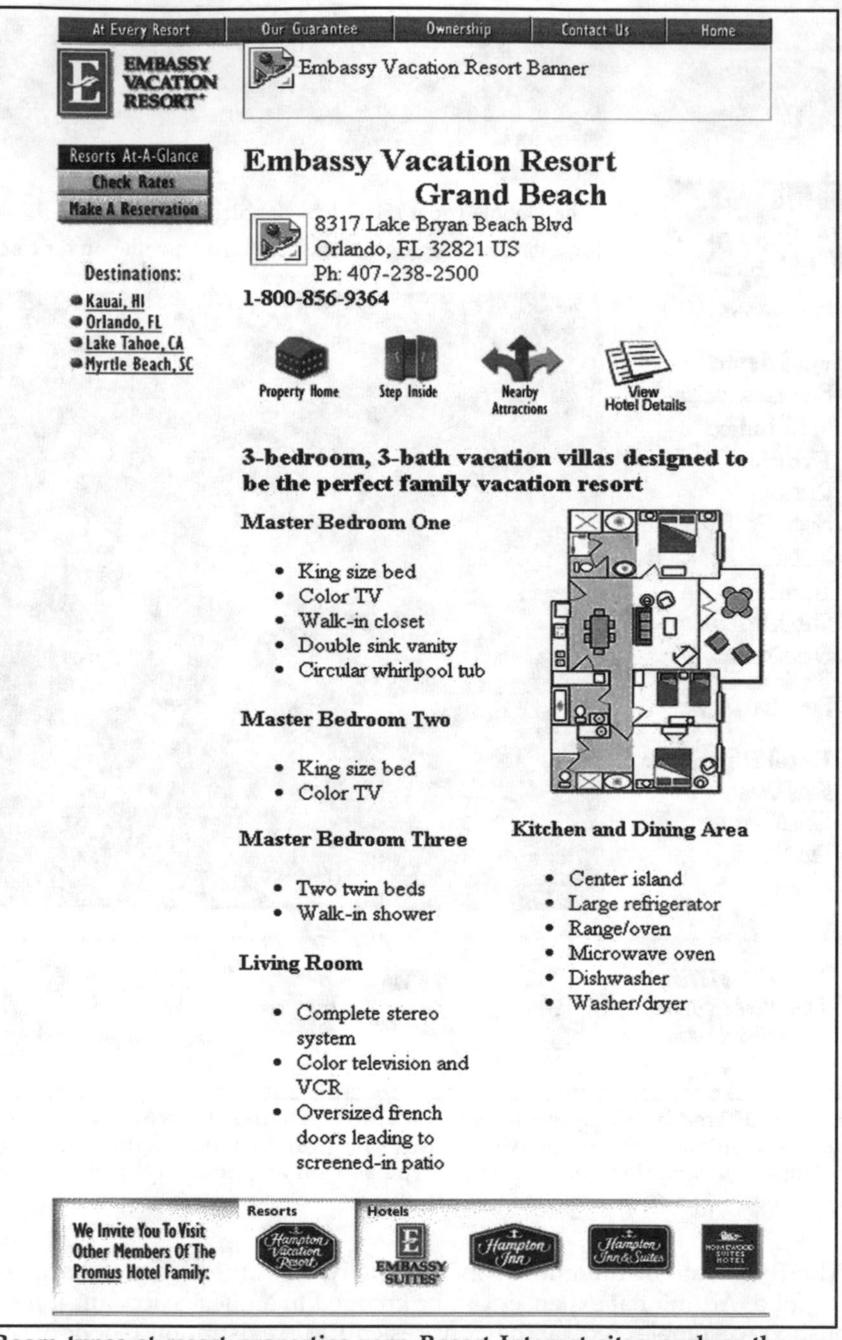

Room types at resort properties vary. Resort Internet sites, such as the one for the Embassy Vacation Resort of Grand Beach in Orlando, Florida (http://www.embassyvacationresorts.com), provide details, including photographs and floor plans.

guests can charge to their accounts without partial settlement. This amount is usually referred to as the **house limit.** Guest accounts must be carefully and continually monitored by the front office to ensure that this house limit is not exceeded.

Front desk accounting records must be periodically reviewed for accuracy and completeness. This need is met through the night audit. Although the name implies that this process takes place in the evening, this is not necessarily the case. In hotels with computerized front office accounting systems, the audit can be conducted at any time during the day. Some computerized properties choose to call the audit the *front office audit* or *system update.* Even though computerized properties *can* perform the audit at any time, they almost invariably follow the nighttime tradition since transaction volumes tend to be lower during the late evening hours.

Regardless of how or when the audit process takes place, room charges (room rates and room tax) are posted to guest accounts as part of the audit routine. Other audit tasks usually include: verifying charges posted to guest accounts, balancing and checking accounts against credit limits, resolving discrepancies in room status, verifying front desk cashier balances, and producing operating reports.

Departure

Guest services and guest accounting aspects of the guest cycle are completed during the cycle's fourth phase: *departure.* The final element of guest service is processing the guest out of the hotel and creating a guest history record. The final element of guest accounting is settlement of the guest's account (that is, bringing the account to a zero balance).

At check-out, the guest vacates the room, receives an accurate statement of the settled account, returns the room keys, and leaves the hotel. Once the guest has checked out, the front office updates the room's availability status and notifies the housekeeping department.

During check-out, the front office staff should determine whether the guest was satisfied with the stay and encourage the guest to return to the hotel (or another property in the chain). The more information the hotel has about its guests, the better it can anticipate and serve their needs and develop marketing strategies to increase business. Hotels often use expired registration records to construct a **guest history file.** These records can be either registration cards or electronic files. A guest history file is a collection of guest history records. Information in a guest history file allows the hotel to better understand its clientele and provides a solid base for strategic marketing. The hotel can also develop a profile of guest characteristics through the use of a research questionnaire. A wide variety of guest characteristics and habits can be surveyed to assess guests' wants and needs.

The purpose of account settlement is to collect money due the hotel prior to guest departure. Depending on the guest's credit arrangements, the guest will pay cash, use a credit card, or verify pre-established direct billing instructions. Account balances should be verified and errors corrected before the guest leaves the hotel. Problems may occur in guest account settlement when charges are not posted to the guest's account until *after* the guest checks out. These charges are called **late charges.** Even if the charges are eventually collected, the hotel usually incurs additional costs through billing the guest. Settling accounts with outstanding balances for departed guests is generally handled by the accounting department, not the front office. However, the front office is responsible for providing complete and accurate billing information to assist the accounting department in its collection efforts.

Once the guest has checked out, the front office can analyze data related to the guest's stay. Front office reports can be used to review operations, isolate problem areas, indicate where corrective action may be needed, and highlight business trends. Daily reports typically contain information about cash and charge sales, accounts receivable, and front office operating statistics. Operational analysis can help managers establish a standard of performance which can be used to evaluate the effectiveness of front office operations.

Front Office Systems

The technology used for front office recordkeeping and equipment has evolved in three stages:

- Non-automated (manual)
- Semi-automated (electro-mechanical)
- Fully automated (computer-based)

Before the 1920s, technology in the front office was almost non-existent and manual operations were the rule in lodging operations. The semi-automated operations through the early 1970s laid much of the groundwork for the development of automated operations in the late 1970s. The following overviews, based on the phases of the traditional guest cycle, represent the evolution of front office recordkeeping systems. In practice, many properties combine elements of each approach to produce an effective and comprehensive system.

Non-Automated

Non-automated front office recordkeeping systems rely solely on handwritten forms. Some small hotels may still find this method of recordkeeping sufficient to meet their information needs. The elements of handwritten systems have determined the structure of many front office processes. Techniques common to non-automated systems can be found in even the most advanced automated systems.

Pre-arrival activities. Reservations agents enter requests into a loose-leaf notebook or onto index cards. Non-automated hotels typically accept reservations for six months into the future (called a six-month reservation horizon) and are unlikely to commit space beyond that time. Reservation confirmations, pre-registration activities, and occupancy forecasts are not common in non-automated hotels. Reservation information may also be placed on a density chart or graph to illustrate future room availabilities and help managers identify high and low room demand periods. A density board is usually set up as a matrix, with days of the month for rows and number of available rooms for columns. As rooms are blocked or booked, the matrix cells that correspond to the dates of stay and number of rooms are colored in. These colored squares reflect the density or concentration of rooms reserved.

Arrival activities. Upon arrival, guests are asked to sign a page in a registration book or complete a registration card. Room assignments are made using a manual card replacement technique involving a **room rack** and, sometimes, color-coded flags indicating the housekeeping status for each room in the property. A room rack is an array of metal file pockets that displays guest and room status information in room number order. The registration card is often time-stamped during check-in and may be placed in the room rack to indicate occupancy.

Occupancy activities. Multiple-copy registration slips, which may be part of the registration card, allow copies of the guest's personal data to be distributed to the room rack, switchboard operators, and uniformed service personnel. The original registration card often doubles as a guest account folio. Revenue outlets send documentation (vouchers) of charges to the front desk for posting to guest folios. The revenue outlet also maintains a sales record of all charged transactions so that guest account postings can be cross-checked as part of the night audit routine. Although adding machines may be used to facilitate accounting procedures, monitoring guest activities within a manual process may become repetitive, cumbersome, and tedious.

Departure activities. At check-out, guests settle their accounts and return their room keys; the cashier notifies the housekeeping department of departures. Registration cards or rack slips are removed from the room rack and marked to indicate departure. The registration card or rack slip may then be filed in a cardboard box and serve as the hotel's guest history file. If the registration card was time-stamped at check-in, it should also be time-stamped at check-out.

Semi-Automated

A semi-automated, or electro-mechanical, front office system relies upon both handwritten and machine-produced forms. Semi-automated systems and equipment are becoming less common in small and mid-size hotels. Advantages of a semi-automated system over a non-automated system include automatically generated and easy-to-read documents that detail the steps of a transaction. These documents represent what is known as an audit trail. The disadvantages of semi-automated equipment include the complexities of operating and controlling devices that are not integrated with other systems and that are subject to frequent maintenance problems.

Pre-arrival activities. Guests making reservations may call a national reservations network or contact the hotel directly. When reservation requests grow beyond the front desk's ability to handle them efficiently, many hotels create a reservations department. Pre-registration activities include preparation of registration cards, guest folios, and information slips. Room assignments are usually made based on room rack status, as in a non-automated process. As in non-automated hotels, semi-automated properties may also opt to maintain a manual reservation density board.

Arrival activities. When guests with reservations arrive at the hotel, they simply verify the previously recorded registration information and sign a pre-printed registration card. Walk-in guests generally complete a multiple-copy registration card. Copies are distributed to the room rack, the switchboard operator, and the information rack.

Occupancy activities. The use of semi-automated systems may not significantly reduce the paperwork needed to chart the hotel guest cycle. Vouchers are used to communicate charge purchases to the front desk, and revenue outlets rely on sales record entries to prove transactions. Mechanical and electronic cash registers and front office posting machines are used to process many of the records formerly processed by hand. The use of this equipment enables the front office to handle guest accounting transactions more accurately and rapidly. A night audit procedure based on posting machine records is used to verify account entries and balances.

Departure activities. A more thorough audit routine, made possible by a semi-automated system, leads to faster and smoother guest check-outs. Front desk agents experience fewer discrepancies in guest accounts and are able to efficiently reconcile guest accounts. They are also able to relay room status information to housekeeping much more quickly than they could in a non-automated system. Registration cards may be collected and placed in the property's guest history files for future reference.

Fully Automated

Front office recordkeeping is computer-based in fully automated hotels. Computer systems designed for use in the hospitality industry were first introduced in the early 1970s, but were not considered viable until the late 1970s. These initial systems tended to be expensive, making them attractive to only the largest hotel properties. During the 1980s, computer equipment became less expensive, more compact, and easier to operate. User-friendly software packages evolved for various hotel functions and applications which did not require the sophisticated technical training demanded by earlier computer systems. The development of versatile personal computers encouraged system vendors to approach smaller lodging properties. By the late 1980s, computer systems were cost-effective for hotels of all sizes.

Pre-arrival activities. The reservations software of an in-house computer system may directly interface with a central reservations network and automatically quote rates and reserve rooms according to a pre-determined pattern. The reservations software may also automatically generate letters of confirmation, produce requests for guest deposits, and handle pre-registration activities. Electronic folios can be established and pre-registration transactions can be processed for guests with confirmed reservations. A reservations software package may also generate an expected arrivals list, occupancy and revenue forecasts, and a variety of informative reports.

Arrival activities. Guest information collected during the reservation process may be automatically transferred from the computer's reservation record to the front desk. For walk-in guests, guest information is entered manually into the computer by a front desk agent. The agent may then present a computer-prepared registration card to the guest for verification and signature. The installation of on-line credit card authorization terminals enables front desk personnel to receive timely credit card approval. Registration data, stored electronically in the computer, can be retrieved whenever necessary, thereby making a room rack unnecessary. Electronic guest folios are also maintained and accessed through the computer's memory.

A recent innovation in technology is the self check-in/check-out terminal. In fact, these terminals have been in existence for many years, but they either have been too expensive or have not had strong customer acceptance. This has changed recently, as the cost of technology has been significantly reduced. In addition, the acceptance of automated teller machines (ATMs) used by most banks has had a direct impact on guests, who are now more willing to accept self-help equipment in lodging establishments.

To use one of these terminals, the guest inserts a credit card into the machine, which reads the magnetic strip on the credit card and communicates with the central property management system. The central system locates the guest's reservation and returns the information to the terminal. The guest is asked to verify name, departure date, rate, and room type on the display. Some systems allow changes to this information and some require that the guest go to the front desk if any changes are necessary. If the information is correct, the system assigns a room with the property management system and prints out a rooming slip with the room number. Guests then take the slip to a special line at the front desk and receive a key. The most advanced systems provide electronic room keys that are individually created when the guest checks in.

Most world-class service hotels do not use self check-in/check-out terminals because they want to keep personal contact between the hotel staff and the guest. Self check-in terminals are being accepted in large convention hotels where long check-in and check-out lines can diminish a guest's experience. These terminals are used to reduce these long lines and get guests to their rooms faster. The need for personal service is not as high in these hotels. Other hotels, such as economy-priced hotels and some mid-range hotels that do not provide a lot of personal service, also are using these systems. One additional advantage of these systems in economy and mid-range hotels is that they may eliminate the need for a night shift at the front desk. The equipment can handle all check-ins and check-outs.

Occupancy activities. With a fully automated front office system, non-automated room racks and electro-mechanical or electronic posting machines are replaced by computer terminals throughout the front office. As guests charge purchases at revenue outlets, the charged amounts are electronically transferred to the front office computer from the point-of-sale location. These charges are then automatically posted to the proper electronic guest folio. Instantaneous postings, simultaneous guest account and departmental entries, and continuous trial balances free the night auditor to spend time on auditing, rather than focusing primarily on guest account balancing.

Departure activities. A neatly printed electronic folio helps assure the guest that the statement is complete and accurate. Depending on the method of settlement, the computer system may automatically post the transactions to appropriate accounts. For a guest account that requires billing, the system is capable of producing a bill to be sent to the guest. Once the guest's account is settled and the postings are considered complete, departed guest information is used to create an electronic guest history record.

Off-premises service bureaus may enable hotel operations to enjoy some of the benefits of automation without having to support an in-house computer system. A service bureau requires the hotel to provide the bureau's offices with data for processing. A popular application has been payroll accounting. Employee time records are sent to the service bureau to convert into paychecks and payroll reports for management. However, service bureaus, which focus primarily on back office functions, are not a feasible option for front office activities.

Front Office Forms

The front office relies on various forms to monitor the guest's stay. This section discusses front office documents employed in the four stages of the traditional guest cycle. The number and nature of documents will vary with the degree of automation in a hotel.

Pre-Arrival

Since reservations initiate the guest cycle, capturing and maintaining reservation data is critical to effective front office operations. Reservations are recorded on a **reservation record** or entered into a computer-based **reservation file.** The guest may be sent a letter of confirmation to verify that a reservation has been made and that its specifications are accurate. The confirmation process permits errors in communication to be corrected before the guest arrives and verifies the guest's correct mailing address for future correspondence. Using an automated interface between the reservation system and a word processor, world-class hotels often provide confirmations in the form of letters, making the process seem more personal.

Non-automated and semi-automated front offices usually rely on a reservation rack to monitor reservations with reservation rack slips. The information contained on a reservation rack slip represents only a portion of a complete reservation record. Reservation rack slips are often color coded to indicate the characteristics of the reservation.

Arrival

The front office may use a **registration card** or a computer-based equivalent to check in guests. The registration card may contain blank spaces for the guest to fill in (as often found in non-automated or semi-automated hotels), or may be preprinted with guest information from the computer file (as often found in automated hotels). Registration cards require the guest to furnish personal data and to indicate length of stay and method of settlement. As mentioned before, many states require the guest's signature on the registration card before the relationship between the hotel and the guest is considered legal. Registration cards may also be required by law to contain printed statements relating to the availability of safe storage for guest valuables. Finally, registration cards usually show the room rate, allowing the guest to confirm it. This reduces questions about the price of the room at check-out.

Front offices that use room racks depend on the creation of room rack slips during the arrival stage. A room rack slip may contain personal guest data and a declaration of the room rate, expected departure date, and room number. The presence of room rate data simplifies the preparation of a rooms revenue report, while the verification of the guest's expected departure date helps the front office develop accurate future room availability schedules. Completed room rack slips are placed in the room rack in such a manner as to indicate room status. The presence of a rack slip in an assigned room slot indicates that the room is occupied. Rack slips are also sent to the telephone department and are filed alphabetically in the information rack.

Credit must be established or verified during check-in as well. In non-automated or semi-automated hotels, credit card numbers are often recorded as a form of payment guarantee during the reservation process. Payment guarantees are used in case the guest does not arrive at the hotel. However, they are seldom used to establish credit. Most credit card companies require an actual swipe of the credit card in an electronic recording device or imprint on a credit card voucher in order to establish credit. During check-in, the credit card information is recorded. In non-automated and semi-automated hotels, the front desk agent will usually request credit approval on the credit card for a pre-established amount. Should the balance go over that amount during the stay, additional requests are made to the credit card company. In automated hotels, the front office computer automatically requests the credit approval during check-in and, when the balance goes above the approved level, the system automatically requests additional approvals from the credit card company.

Occupancy

Once the guest is registered, the front office creates a guest folio to serve as a statement of the charges and credits incurred by the guest. While folio information is comparable across front office recordkeeping systems, folio formats tend to vary. In nearly all recordkeeping systems, information from the guest registration card is transferred to a folio during folio creation. Folios should be pre-numbered for control purposes since the folio number can also be entered onto the guest's registration card for cross-indexing. Folios may have several duplicate pages, depending on the hotel's needs. A minimum of two folio copies is normally required. One copy of the guest folio is used by the front office as a record of the guest's stay, and one copy is given to the guest during check-out as account documentation. Additional folio copies are used by the hotel for such purposes as assistance in direct billing after departure, and to reconcile departmental sales reports.

In a non-automated system, a folio card contains a series of columns for recording debit entries (charges), credit entries (payments and adjustments), and a perpetual (current) account balance. At the end of the business day, each column of the folio is reviewed and the ending account balance is carried forward as the opening guest account balance for the following day.

In a semi-automated system, guest transactions are posted sequentially on a folio card by a front office posting machine. The transaction date, the originating revenue center, the transaction amount, and the resulting account balance are printed. Mechanical posting machines do not store folio balances, so they must be re-entered each time a charge or credit requires posting. The front desk cashier enters the last balance of the folio into the machine and it prints as a *pick-up balance.* The previous balance and the pick-up balance must be the same, or the system will be out of balance. This is where the majority of folio balancing problems occur in a semi-automated system.

In a fully automated system, electronic folios simplify transaction posting and handling. For a guest with a reservation, personal data already stored in the computer are verified at registration or as part of pre-registration activities. Walk-in guest accounts require the front desk agent to enter guest information during the registration process. Once the information is entered, an account number is assigned by the system and an electronic folio is automatically created and available for immediate transaction posting. Electronic folios are stored internally and can be printed on demand.

A **voucher** is a support document detailing the facts of a transaction. Non-automated and semi-automated properties depend on vouchers to communicate information from remote revenue centers to the front desk. A voucher is a *support document* and does not replace the *source document* created at the point of purchase. Common types of vouchers include charge vouchers, allowance vouchers, transfer vouchers, and paid-out vouchers. During a night audit routine, vouchers help ensure that all transactions requiring account posting have been processed correctly. Fully automated properties may require few vouchers, or, in some cases, no vouchers at all. This is because remote revenue centers can be electronically connected (interfaced) with the front office computer system, thus reducing the need for support documentation.

In non-automated and semi-automated systems, an information rack slip may be prepared to enable switchboard operators and guest services personnel to quickly locate a specific guest in the hotel. When a telephone caller asks to be connected with a guest, the switchboard operator can search the alphabetical information rack to identify the guest's room number and complete the connection. Fully automated front office systems replace traditional information racks with a computer terminal, thereby eliminating the need for information racks and rack slips. These terminals can be used to quickly access the guest's record and display the comprehensive information it contains. Because they can be electronically connected, other electronic equipment such as point-of-sale terminals and telephone switchboards can also display guest information.

Departure

Guest folios should be kept current throughout occupancy to ensure an accurate account balance for settlement at departure. In addition to the guest folio, other forms may be required for account settlement. A credit card voucher, for example, may be needed if the guest elects to pay by credit card. In some hotels, a cash voucher is used to document a cash settlement. A transfer voucher will be needed if the guest's account is direct billed—that is, transferred from a guest receivable to a non-guest receivable account. Even in a fully automated system, several documents may be produced to prove transactions and provide a basis for comprehensive auditing.

During the departure stage, front desk agents may need to create a guest history record for inclusion in the guest history files. As stated earlier, a guest history record contains information helpful to marketing and sales efforts, and can be helpful in registering and serving the guest during a return visit. In addition, state law may require that certain guest data be retained for a specified period. Most fully automated systems automatically create an electronic guest history record as part of the check-out process. A computerized guest history file is a data base of invaluable information.

The Front Desk

Most front office functions are performed at the front desk. The front desk is where guests register, request information and services, relate complaints, settle their accounts, and check out.

Most front desks are prominently located in the hotel lobby. A typical front desk surface is a counter approximately three-and-a-half feet high and two-and-a-half feet deep. Its length may vary according to the number of rooms in the hotel, the duties performed at the front desk, and the physical design of the hotel lobby. Signs may be placed on or above the desk to direct guests to the proper activity center for registration, cashier, check-out, information and mail handling, and other guest services. Front desk designs usually screen front office forms and equipment from guests or visitors standing at the desk, since much front office information is considered confidential and proprietary.

Functional Organization

The functional efficiency of a front desk depends on the organization of the work stations located at the desk. The design and layout of the desk should provide each front desk employee with easy access to the equipment, forms, and supplies necessary for his or her assigned tasks. Ideally, the front desk layout is planned and its furniture and fixtures situated according to the functions performed at designated activity centers along the desk. However, as lines of responsibility overlap among front desk personnel, largely because of cross-training and computerization, more front desks are being designed with position flexibility in mind.

Efficiency is an important concern in front office design. Whenever front office employees have to turn their backs to guests, leave guests unattended, or take too long to complete a process, front desk design could be improved. Studies which examine how front office personnel interact with guests and equipment often suggest changes in front desk design.

Design Alternatives

Various hotel supply companies have researched industry needs and redesigned front desk areas to make them more aesthetically appealing. For instance, there is general agreement that traditional mail, message, and key racks are unnecessary at the front desk. Mail, messages, and keys can be stored in drawers or slots located under or away from the front desk, thereby making the front desk area appear more streamlined. This also improves guest security by hiding keys and mail, thereby preventing unauthorized individuals from knowing the occupancy status of a room.

Some hotels have circular or semicircular front desk structures. The circular desk encloses the front desk staff with its counter. In a semicircular arrangement, there is normally a straight wall at the back of the desk with a door leading to front office support services. Circular and semicircular desks allow greater service to more guests at the same time; they also tend to appear more modern and innovative than the traditional straight desk. This design, however, presents potential problems in the sense that guests can approach the desk from all angles, even though front office work stations and equipment are situated in specific spots. Extra care may be necessary to ensure the success of these and other innovative desk designs.

Some hotels have experimented with a lobby arrangement which includes no front desk at all. In a deskless environment, registration and room assignment may be handled at a small table or personal desk in a low-traffic area of the lobby. A concierge, receptionist, or special guest service employee may serve as guest host. Although a guest host may perform many of the same functions as a front desk agent, the service is intended to be more personal and informal. Guests often enjoy a casual, seated registration instead of a long wait standing in line at a front desk counter.

Accessibility. The traditional standards for front desk design may not satisfy the physical needs of all hotel guests. Accessibility is an important consideration in the general design of a hotel, especially its front office area. The Americans with Disabilities Act of 1990 stipulates that companies which serve the general public must make public areas and services readily accessible to the disabled. This means that public areas and accommodations in new and renovated lodging properties must be barrier-free, including front desk areas. According to the law, existing businesses will be required to make architectural and physical changes that are "readily achievable" given the company's size and financial resources. This may require the removal of architectural barriers such as curbs and steps, and changes in the size and setup of doorways. The law may also require that a portion of the front desk be of a more accessible height and design to accommodate people using wheelchairs or people with other special needs.

Front Office Equipment

In non-automated and semi-automated properties, the layout of the front desk is centered on a collection of mechanical racks and specialty equipment designed to produce, store, or display front office forms. In a semi-automated system, these racks are positioned beside posting machines, cash register devices, and other pieces of equipment that facilitate front office tasks. Exhibits 5 and 6 show possible layouts of front office equipment in semi-automated and automated hotels.

Exhibit 5 Sample Layout of a Semi-Automated Front Desk

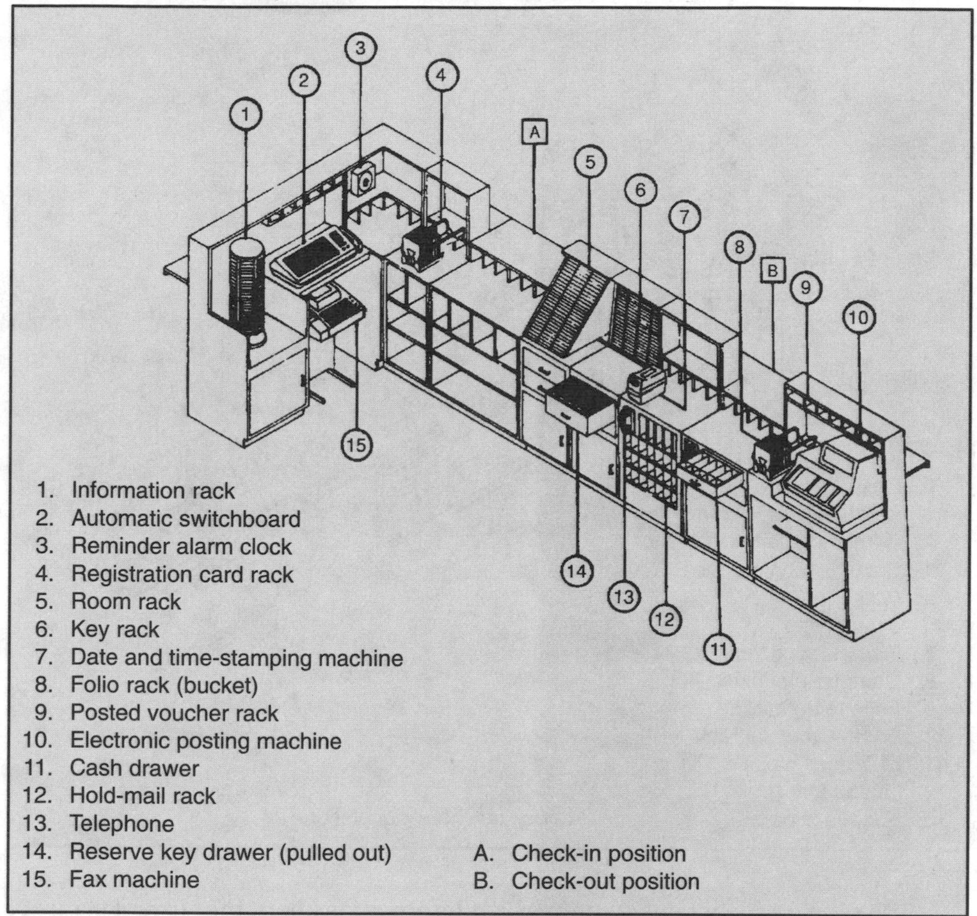

1. Information rack
2. Automatic switchboard
3. Reminder alarm clock
4. Registration card rack
5. Room rack
6. Key rack
7. Date and time-stamping machine
8. Folio rack (bucket)
9. Posted voucher rack
10. Electronic posting machine
11. Cash drawer
12. Hold-mail rack
13. Telephone
14. Reserve key drawer (pulled out)
15. Fax machine

A. Check-in position
B. Check-out position

Most of the machinery described in the following sections will not appear in a hotel which uses a non-automated recordkeeping system. In a fully automated hotel, most of the machinery and other equipment is replaced by a front office computer system. The following discussion of front office equipment applies chiefly to semi-automated properties.

Room Rack

The room rack has traditionally been considered the most important piece of front office equipment in non-automated and semi-automated hotels. As pointed out earlier, a room rack is an array of metal file pockets designed to hold room rack slips that display guest and room status information. The room rack is normally recessed into the front desk counter, tilted against the desk, or mounted below or behind the desk. When key slots are added to the room rack, it can serve as a combination room and key rack.

Exhibit 6 Sample Layout of a Fully Automated Front Desk

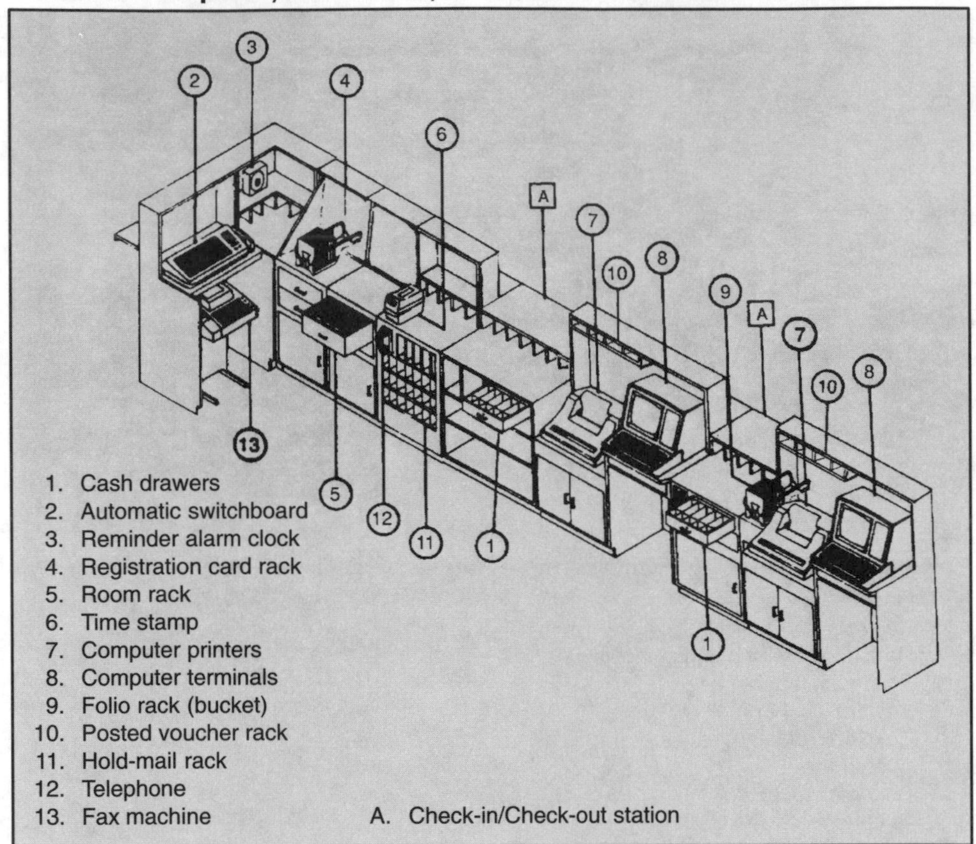

The room rack contains a summary of information about the current status of all rooms in the hotel. A room rack slip or, in some hotels, the guest registration card itself can be inserted into the room rack to display guest information, room number, and room rate. The intent is that one glance at the room rack should immediately inform the front desk agent of the occupancy and housekeeping status of all rooms. The room rack may also contain information about room types, features, and rates. Front desk agents normally use this information to match available rooms with guest requests during the registration process.

In a fully automated property, the need for a room rack is eliminated. Equivalent information can be stored in a computer system and displayed on a front desk terminal whenever needed.

Mail, Message, and Key Rack

A key rack is an array of numbered compartments used to store guestroom keys. Historically, key racks were positioned so as to be visible to front desk agents and guests alike. This arrangement permitted guests and front office staff to know the occupancy status of a room by the number of keys present in its assigned slot. Key racks no longer are prominently featured at the front desk. Instead, they are often placed in front desk drawers to help ensure the safety and security of guests by not disclosing occupancy information.

To minimize the number of racks in the front desk area, hotels may combine the key rack with either the room rack or the mail and message rack. A combination mail, message, and key rack can be either a freestanding wall unit, an under-the-counter row of compartments, or a set of drawers. Some front offices use this rack as a room divider by placing it between the front desk and the switchboard areas of the front office. When the mail and message compartments of the rack are open from both sides, telephone operators (who are positioned on one side of the rack) and front desk agents (who are positioned on the other side of the rack) have equal access to rack contents. Operators who record telephone messages for guests can insert them into the rack from the back side; front desk agents can retrieve the messages from the front side for guest presentation.

If guestroom telephones are equipped with message lights, they can be used to notify guests when they have messages at the desk. In-room message lights may be activated with a control switch beside each room's slot in the mail, message, and key rack.

In a fully automated lodging property, a mail rack may be all that is necessary. The function of a key rack may be performed by the master console of an electronic locking system. State-of-the-art voice mail messaging systems can record and store messages for guests in the voice of the caller. The message light is automatically turned on in the room when the message is recorded. To retrieve a message, the guest simply dials the electronic message center from a room or house phone and retrieves the message.

Reservation Racks

Front offices of non-automated and semi-automated hotels often use both advance and current reservation racks. In an *advance reservation rack,* reservation rack slips or registration cards are arranged by the guests' scheduled dates of arrival and, within each day's grouping, alphabetically by the guests' or groups' names. A *current reservation rack* is a portable subset of the advance reservation rack. Early each morning, the advance reservation rack slips or registration cards for that day's expected arrivals are loaded into the current reservation rack and taken to the front desk. The current reservation rack is used by front desk agents to assist in processing guests during registration.

In a fully automated property, both advance and current reservation racks may be eliminated. The equivalent information may be internally managed by the computer's reservation software and be accessible upon demand.

Information Rack

An **information rack** is composed of two index listings of in-house guests, one by the guest's last name and one by assigned room number. An information rack is commonly used to assist front office employees with proper routing of telephone calls, mail, messages, and visitor inquiries. The information rack normally consists of aluminum slots designed to hold guest information slips. These slots can be easily arranged and rearranged to fit the immediate needs of the hotel. Front office computer systems eliminate the need for an information rack since guest name and room number data are easily retrievable through a computer system terminal.

Folio Trays

In non-automated and semi-automated properties, guest folios are stored in a front office folio tray (or folio bucket) and arranged in ascending order by guestroom number. Guest folios remain in the tray throughout the occupancy stage of the guest cycle, except when they are used in posting transactions. Both the front office cashier and front desk agent are likely to require access to folios stored in the tray.

A second folio tray is normally located in the hotel's accounting office. This tray contains the folios of departed guests being direct-billed or of guests who paid by credit card. Once these accounts are settled, the folios are moved to a permanent storage location.

In a computerized front office, the folio tray does not really *hold* the folio since it is held electronically in the computer. The folio tray may, however, hold the completed registration card, if appropriate, and imprinted credit card voucher for each registered guest. To facilitate check-out, folios may be printed in advance for those guests expected to depart and filed in the folio tray along with other documentation.

Account Posting Machine

Semi-automated hotels that allow guests to charge purchases to their rooms use an account posting machine to post, monitor, and balance these charges. A posting machine normally provides:

- A standardized means of recording transactions.
- A legible guest account statement.
- A basis for cash and deferred payment management.
- An analysis of departmental sales activity.
- An audit trail of charge purchase transactions.

In a semi-automated operation, the account posting machine should be located near the front office folio tray and voucher rack.

Historically, posting machines have presented several advantages and disadvantages to front office operations. One of the main advantages is that the guest's copy of the folio is printed—not handwritten. These machines also have built-in tabulation devices that allow management to systematically audit current charge postings. As a third advantage, posting machines update account balances after each posting. On the other hand, posting machines may be cumbersome, prone to error, and difficult to operate. Although a semi-automated posting procedure is more efficient than a manual posting procedure, it still may not be responsive or comprehensive enough.

Products	Services
ADVERTISING & PROMOTION	ASSOCIATIONS & INSTITUTIONS
APPAREL	CLEANING SERVICES
BATHROOMS	CONSULTANTS, CONSULTING
BEDDING, LINEN & UNIFORMS	FOOD SERVICES
BEVERAGE EQUIPMENT/SERVICES	FRANCHISING
BEVERAGES	GUEST SERVICES
CLEANING	MAINTENANCE SERVICES
CONSTRUCTION, BUILDING MATERIALS	PROFESSIONAL SERVICES
DRAPES, TEXTILES	REAL ESTATE
ENTERTAINMENT	
ENVIRONMENT CONTROL/CLEANING	
EQUIPMENT	
FITNESS/HEALTH CLUB	
FLOOR COVERINGS	
FOOD SUPPLIES	
FOOD/KITCHEN EQUIPMENT	
FRONT DESK	
FURNITURES	
GUEST AMENITIES	
LIGHTING	
OUTDOOR & GARDEN	
PLUMBING	
SECURITY AND SAFETY	
TABLE TOP	
TECHNOLOGY	
VEHICLES	
WALLS/WALL COVERINGS	

The Internet site of hotelsupplies.com (http://www.hotelsupplies.com) provides access to numerous vendors supplying hotels with products and services.

Fully automated hotels do not use account posting machines since their system relies on electronic folios, not printed copies. The increasing popularity of competitively priced, computer-based front office computer systems is signaling the demise of account posting machinery.

Voucher Rack

For front desks that use an account posting machine, or in cases where no electronic linkage exists between a point-of-sale terminal and the front desk, a voucher may be used to support the posting of a transaction. Once the transaction is posted, the voucher may be stored for verification during the audit process. Vouchers may be filed for future reference in a voucher rack located near the account posting machine.

Cash Register

A front desk cash register is used to record cash transactions and maintain cash balances. The front office cashier is primarily responsible for its operation and contents. Historically, cash registers have been mechanical or electromechanical in design. In many cases, a cash posting function was built into the account posting machine to eliminate the need for the cash register. Today, computerized cash registers dominate the marketplace. Many specialized functions can be built into a computerized cash register to facilitate close monitoring of transactions. The cash register may also be connected with a front office computer system to provide more complete control over financial transactions and folio handling.

Most computer-based cash registers also include printing devices for producing transaction tapes, sales receipts, imprinted vouchers, and inventory and price control reports. Keys on a cash register may be used to record the:

- Amount of a transaction.
- Purpose of the transaction.
- Affected departments.
- Type of transaction.
- Identity of the cashier.
- Amount tendered.
- Method of payment.

The guest and the cashier can follow the progress of a transaction through the register's operator display. The cash drawer may be divided into several money compartments, or may have removable drawers for individual cashier cash banks.

Support Devices

The front office may have numerous pieces of support equipment in addition to its racks, registers, and machines. These devices can make cumbersome functions straightforward, facilitate information handling, and provide additional storage for data, files, and reports used in the front office area.

A *credit card imprinter* presses a credit card voucher against a guest's credit card. The impact causes the raised card number, expiration date, and name on the card to be recorded on the voucher for use in credit card billing and collection procedures. Imprinters may be manual or electric and may be connected to an automatic call-out authorization terminal.

A *magnetic strip reader* reads data that is magnetically encoded and stored on the magnetic stripe on the back of a credit card and transmits this data to a credit card authorization service. On the basis of the transaction data and the cardholder's account status, the credit card authorization service either approves or disapproves the transaction. The most recent technology integrates the magnetic strip reader and the front office computer. This allows more information to be transmitted to the credit card authorization service and more information to be stored in the guest's electronic record.

The operator of a *telewriter* writes with a pen-like stylus on a specially designed surface. The handwritten message written on this surface is displayed on a similar device located elsewhere. Similar to a fax machine, the telewriter is used to transmit written communication from one location to another (for example, from the front desk to housekeeping). One of the differences between fax and telewriter communication is that the telewriter requires point-to-point wiring; it doesn't use telecommunications technology.

Folios, mail, and other front office paperwork are inserted into a *time stamp device* to record the current time and date. This recording can be very important in establishing a chronology of events and transactions.

Security monitors, such as closed-circuit television monitors, allow front office or security personnel to monitor certain areas of the hotel from a central location.

A non-automated *wake-up device* is usually a specially designed clock with multiple alarm settings to remind front desk agents or telephone operators to place wake-up calls. A wake-up call log kept beside the clock informs the agents or operators which room numbers are to be called at what times. This clock is usually known as the *hotel clock.* Since wake-up calls are among the hotel's most important guest services, it is important that this clock always have the correct time. Many other services revolve around wake-up times, such as delivery of room service. Therefore, the hotel clock keeps the official hotel time for all departments.

International travelers are likely to make hotel reservations by a *telex* network connection. The caller directs a message from a local telex machine to the hotel's telex machine. A return telex may be used to confirm the reservation. Telex communication is faster than the postal service and more reliable than telephone networking since the hotel receives a written message. In many cases, fax machines have replaced telex machines.

Fully automated hotels may provide self check-in and check-out terminals for guests. These terminals do not eliminate front desk agents, but can free them to attend to other hotel duties which can enhance and expand guest service.

Telecommunications

Hotels must be able to support a broad range of telephone calls with adequate equipment to ensure an efficient and effective telecommunications system. There are many types of calls a guest may place during a hotel stay:

- Local calls
- Direct-dial long-distance calls
- Calling card calls
- Credit card calls
- Collect calls
- Third-party calls
- Person-to-person calls
- Billed-to-room calls
- International calls
- 800 or 888 toll-free calls
- 900 premium-price calls

Some of these types of calls require operator assistance while others are completed by the guest independently of an operator. In addition, a single call often fits into more than one category of call. For example, a direct-dial long-distance call could also be a credit card call; a person-to-person call could also be a collect call; and an international call could be a person-to-person credit card call. For many of these types of calls, the hotel can charge guests a surcharge for use of its telephone equipment.

A local call terminates within a local calling area and typically is billed on a per-call basis rather than on a per-minute basis. Local telephone calls are handled by the local phone company. Hotels may charge guests on a per-call basis or offer unlimited local calling for a flat daily charge. Some hotels do not charge guests at all for local calls. Each hotel determines its own local call policy.

Direct-dial long-distance calls are the most common calls placed by hotel guests. A long-distance call terminates outside the local calling area. Once a long-distance number is dialed, it is distributed over the hotel's telephone lines through the local phone company office, which routes the call to whatever long-distance carrier the hotel selected to handle its long-distance traffic. Direct-dial long-distance calls are also referred to as "1 + " calls since guests are typically required to first dial a "1" after accessing an outside line, then dial the area code and the telephone number they are attempting to reach. Together, this string of numbers eliminates the need for operator involvement.

Calling card calls are typically billed to a code number on a calling card issued by either a local phone company or by a long-distance company. Calling card codes may be a combination of the cardholder's area code and telephone number plus a four-digit personal identification number (PIN), or it may be a scrambled set of numbers unrelated to the cardholder's telephone number. Calling cards are not credit cards; phone companies, not financial institutions, issue them. Call placement with a calling card is accomplished by a "0+" procedure. The guest dials "0" plus the number he or she is trying to reach. Then, the guest hears a "bong" or tone signaling him or her to input the calling card number. An operator is not required. Whenever a calling card is used, the hotel does not bill the guest for telephone charges. The long-distance company bills the call to the calling card account. Many telephone companies accept credit card calls such as Visa, MasterCard, and American Express as valid phone-charge cards. Call placement is similar to calling card procedures.

With collect calls, a guest first dials "0" and then the full telephone number, then waits several seconds for an operator. The guest informs the operator that the call is collect—the call is to be billed to the receiving party. The operator stays on the line and verifies that the receiving party accepts the charge. Most telephone companies pay a commission to the hotel for collect calls placed by guests. Third-party calls are similar to collect calls, except that the billed number is not the called number. In most cases, the operator may require that someone at the third-party number accept the charge before putting through the call. The hotel's telephone company bills the third party and the amount does not appear on the guest's folio.

Person-to-person calls are not connected unless a specific party, named by the caller, verifies that he or she is on the line. This is an expensive call, but has no cost if the requested party is not available. Unlike credit card, collect, or third-party calls, a person-to-person call is charged to the number initiating the call.

Billed-to-room calls are operator-assisted calls. An operator places the call for a guest and later informs the hotel of the amount of the charge. Billed-to-room calls can also be handled automatically by a call accounting system (described in a later section).

International calls can be direct-dialed or placed with operator assistance. To direct-dial an international call, the guest typically dials an international access code, a country code, city code, and the telephone number. Similar to long-distance calls, the hotel bills the guest for direct-dialed international calls, while the phone company bills the guest for calling card or credit card calls.

Toll-free calls can be direct-dialed from a guestroom as either local calls or long-distance calls. In either case, the guest receives access to an outside line and dials "1" plus the 800 or 888 number. Calls made to businesses that charge callers a fee for the call (a fee separate from the one the telephone company charges for placing the call) are 900 or premium-price calls. Problems can arise when these types of calls are made from guestrooms. Guests may be shocked and mistakenly blame the hotel upon receiving their charges. The businesses involved in 900 telephone services charge widely varying rates. One business might charge $1.50 per minute; another might charge $3.50 for the first minute and $2.00 for each additional minute; a third business might charge a flat rate of $9.00 a call. Another problem that arises is that the hotel's telephone system may be able to track only the costs involved in placing the call and not the premium charged by the 900 service company. A guest could settle a phone charge of $2.50 at check-out and the hotel could later receive a bill of $39.50 for the same call.

Telecommunications Equipment

To serve guests efficiently and price calls properly, hotels need the right mix of telephone equipment and lines. There are many types of telephone lines or *trunks*. Each type of line is designed to carry certain types of calls. There are lines dedicated to incoming calls, lines dedicated to outbound calls, and two-way lines as well. Based on the level of guest service, each hotel must determine the types and number of lines to have installed. Systems and equipment that hotels use for placing and pricing calls include:

- PBX system
- HOBIC system
- Call accounting system
- Guestroom phones
- Pay phones
- Pagers and cellular phones

PBX Systems. Historically, an important piece of equipment controlling phone service at hotels with more than forty rooms was the switchboard or private branch exchange (PBX). This equipment takes inbound calls to the hotel's PBX operator's console. The hotel's operator sends these calls on to particular extensions or station lines. These might be at the front desk, guestrooms, offices, the kitchen, or other areas. This arrangement allows the hotel to have a large number of telephones share a limited number of telephone lines. Outbound calls are usually placed without the hotel operator's help. Some hotel PBX systems have advanced features enabling them to handle data as well as voice communications. Room attendants can update the status of guestrooms by dialing a code from guestroom phones.

HOBIC Systems. Before hotels began pricing their own calls, their telephone companies priced them. The system used to process these calls was called the Hotel Billing Information Center (HOBIC). Guest calls went out over special hotel telephone lines called HOBIC lines. When a guest placed a call, an operator at the local telephone company would intercept the call, break onto the line, and arrange for the call to be billed to a collect number, a third-party number, a telephone company calling card, or the caller's hotel room. If the call was billed to the guestroom, the operator would inform the hotel of its duration and cost. The operator would either phone the hotel the time and charges of the call or send the information to the hotel's teletype or fax machine at the front desk where the charge would be posted to the appropriate guest folio. HOBIC systems still exist today and are used as backup systems for more sophisticated call accounting systems.

Call Accounting Systems. These systems enable hotels to place and price telephone calls without assistance from phone company operators or front desk staff. A **call accounting system (CAS)** is a set of software programs that initiate the placement, pricing, and posting of calls. The CAS may interface with a hotel's computer system and electronically post charges to guest folios, or it may simply print charge slips for the front desk staff to post appropriately. Some CASs have a least-cost-routing component that routes a dialed call to the type of line that can carry the call at the lowest cost.

Guestroom Phones. Along with other telecommunications equipment, guestroom phones are increasing in sophistication and capabilities. For example, guests can plug personal computers or portable fax machines into some guestroom phones.

These phones have an input jack for standard computer or fax machines. An increasing number of hotels are providing two-line guestroom phones, so one line can accommodate a computer while the guest talks on the other line. Other features of some guestroom phones include: conference calling, speed dialing, hold buttons, call-waiting, hands-free speakers, and a message-waiting alert. Some phones combine voice, mail, fax, and other technologies so guests can retrieve messages, order room service, receive written documents, and place wake-up call requests.

Pay Phones. Hotels rarely purchase their own pay phones due to the potentially high maintenance costs. These phones generally take a lot of abuse and are placed in public areas such as in or near the hotel lobby, meeting rooms, conference areas, banquet rooms, and restaurants. Many hotels have their pay phones supplied and maintained by a company other than their local phone company. Pay phones are not connected to the hotel's PBX system or CAS system and so the hotel receives no direct revenue from their operation. Instead, most telephone carriers contract to pay the hotel a commission on operator-assisted long-distance calls placed from the pay phones. The carrier sets the rates, bills the guest directly, and sends the hotel an agreed-upon commission.

Pagers and Cellular Phones. Some hotels offer a pager or cellular phone rental service to guests at check-in. In the case of cellular phones, the hotel bills the guest for the number of minutes of recorded use, as indicated by the phone's usage meter. Calls placed through cellular phones do not go through the hotel's CAS and therefore are priced outside the system and posted manually to the appropriate guest folios.

Other Technology. Often, hotels install telephone systems with sophisticated features for reasons other than just cost effectiveness. Examples of these features include automatic call dispensing systems, telephone/room status systems, facsimile (fax) machines, and call detection equipment.

In many cases, *automatic call dispensing* is limited to wake-up services. The operator enters the room number and time for each wake-up call into the computer. At the scheduled time, a telephone call is automatically placed to the guest's room. Once the guest answers the call, the computer may activate a synthesized voice that reports the current time, temperature, and weather conditions. Another variation on automatic call dispensing allows the hotel to call rooms in case of an emergency or to call all guests with a specific group to remind them of a meeting.

Telephone/room status systems can assist with rooms management and prohibit the unauthorized use of telephones in vacant rooms. Housekeeping or room service employees can use guestroom telephones to enter data concerning room service charges (for example, what was consumed from an in-room bar), maintenance information, or current room status information. Since these features improve communication, they also contribute to lower payroll costs and help ensure a more efficient in-room bar restocking system for guestrooms.

Hotels catering to business travelers will offer facsimile (fax) services. A fax machine makes it possible to transmit or receive full-page documents. The process involves an exchange of information via telecommunication between two photocopy machines.

The industry is also reaping dramatic benefits from another new technology: *call detection.* Call detection equipment works with the hotel's telephone equipment and call accounting systems. Call detection equipment has the ability to pinpoint the exact moment when a telephone call is connected. This helps improve billing accuracy and reduces guest account discrepancies since only answered calls will be billed.

Property Management Systems

All front office computer systems do not operate identically. However, some generalizations about **property management systems (PMSs)** may illustrate the nature of front office computer applications. A property management system contains sets of computer software packages capable of supporting a variety of activities in front and back office areas. The four most common front office software packages are designed to help front office employees perform functions related to:

- Reservations management
- Rooms management
- Guest account management
- General management

Exhibit 7 summarizes front office computer system applications.

Reservations Management Software

A computer-based reservations package enables a hotel to rapidly process room requests and generate timely and accurate rooms, revenue, and forecasting reports. Most lodging chains participate in computer-based global distribution systems and central reservation systems. Global distribution systems (including Internet operations) capture, process, and forward reservation information. Central reservation systems typically store reservations data, track rooms reserved, control reservations by room type and room rate, and monitor the number of reservations received.

A property using a front office computer system can receive data sent directly from a remote reservations network. Computerized in-house reservations records, files, and revenue forecasts are immediately updated as reservation data are received at the hotel. It is through electronic file updating that the computer system remains current and in control of reservations activities. The most modern systems allow real time, two-way communication between remote reservations networks and hotel computers, enabling instantaneous updates of inventory and guest information. This way, accurate hotel guestroom inventories and pricing are communicated between both systems.

In addition, previously received reservation data can be automatically reformatted into pre-registration materials, and a current expected arrivals list can be produced. Various reservation management reports, containing a summary of

Exhibit 7 Front Office Computer Applications

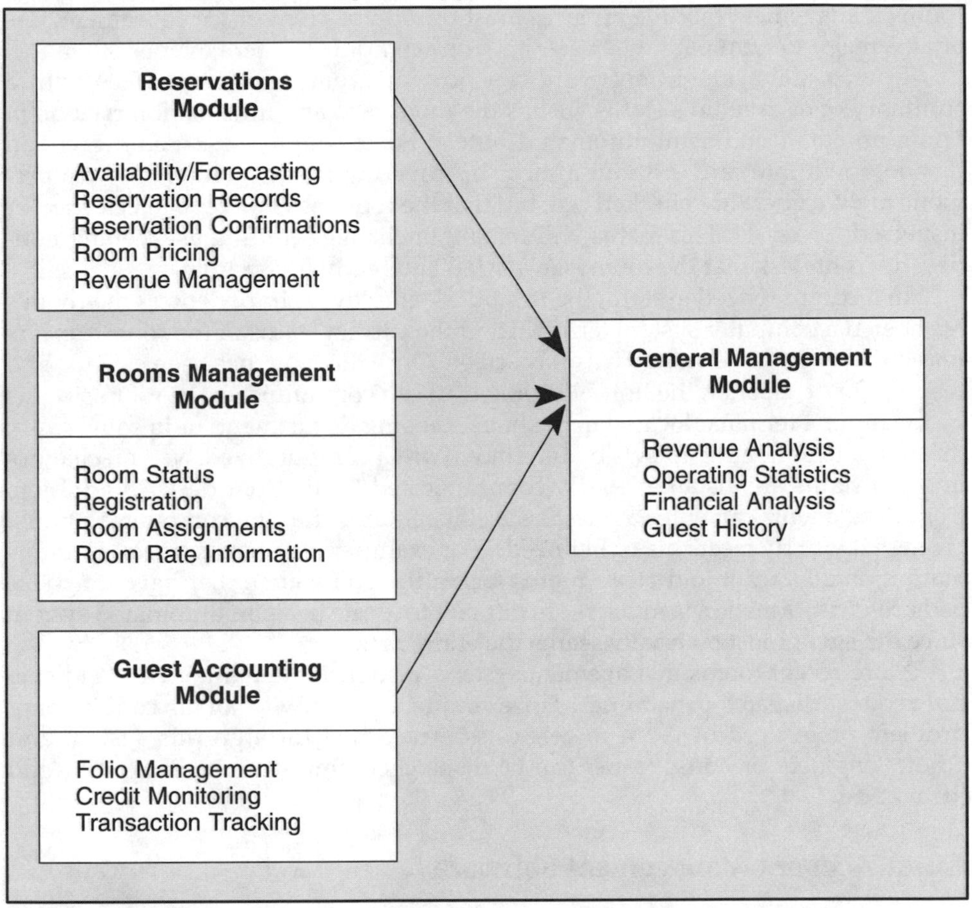

reservation data and guest account status information, can also be generated. Current reservations management software also includes upgraded rate control features, guest history modules, and more detailed property information such as bed types, guestroom views, and special features.

Reservation management software can also track deposits due, request deposits, and record deposit payments made. This is very important to resorts, which often require deposits in order to confirm reservation requests. Hotels may require deposits as well for special occasions, such as a local special events weekend.

Rooms Management Software

Rooms management software maintains current information on the status of rooms, provides information on room rates, assists in room assignment during registration, and helps front office personnel coordinate guest services. A rooms management module can also be used to provide rapid access to room availability data during the reservation process. This information can be especially useful in short-term reservation confirmation and rooms revenue forecasting. Since the rooms management module replaces most traditional front office equipment, it is often a major determinant when selecting one computer system over another.

Rooms management software can provide front desk employees with a summary of each room's status, just as the room rack and information rack do in non-automated and semi-automated hotels. For example, on a room rack, an upside-down rate card without a rack slip covering it may signify that the previous night's guest has checked out, but that the room has not yet been cleaned or inspected for resale. This status will remain unchanged until housekeeping notifies the front desk that the room is inspected and ready for occupancy.

In a computerized system, the front desk employee simply enters the room's number at a computer system terminal and the current status of the room appears immediately on the terminal's display screen. Once the room has been cleaned and readied for occupancy, the housekeeping staff can communicate the room's status by means of a terminal located in the housekeeping department, or in some cases, through a telephone or television interface. With a computerized system, changes in room status are instantaneously communicated to the front desk. In addition, front desk agents can enter a guest's specific requests into the computer to find a room that exactly meets his or her needs. For example, an agent can request information on all vacant and clean rooms facing the golf course that have king-size beds. Such information is much more difficult to locate in a non-automated system since the agent must manually search the entire rack.

More recent rooms management systems also include maintenance and special request dispatch capabilities. For example, a room with an air conditioning problem or in need of extra towels can be recorded through this system and a hotel engineer or housekeeper can be dispatched almost immediately to fulfill the request.

Guest Account Management Software

Guest account management software increases the hotel's control over guest accounts and significantly modifies the traditional night audit routine. Guest accounts are maintained electronically, thereby eliminating much of the need for folio cards, folio trays, and account posting machines. The guest accounting module monitors predetermined guest credit limits and provides flexibility through multiple folio formats. At check-out, previously approved outstanding account balances can be automatically transferred to an appropriate accounts receivable file for subsequent billing and collection. Account management capabilities represent some of the major benefits of a property management system; they are also among some of the system's major justifications. For example, a credit manager in a large convention hotel can save a great deal of time by having the computer monitor the credit limits of all guests and report all accounts which are approaching or have exceeded their limits.

When the hotel's revenue outlets are connected to the front office computer system, remote electronic cash registers can be used to communicate guest charges to the front office. These charges can then be automatically posted to appropriate

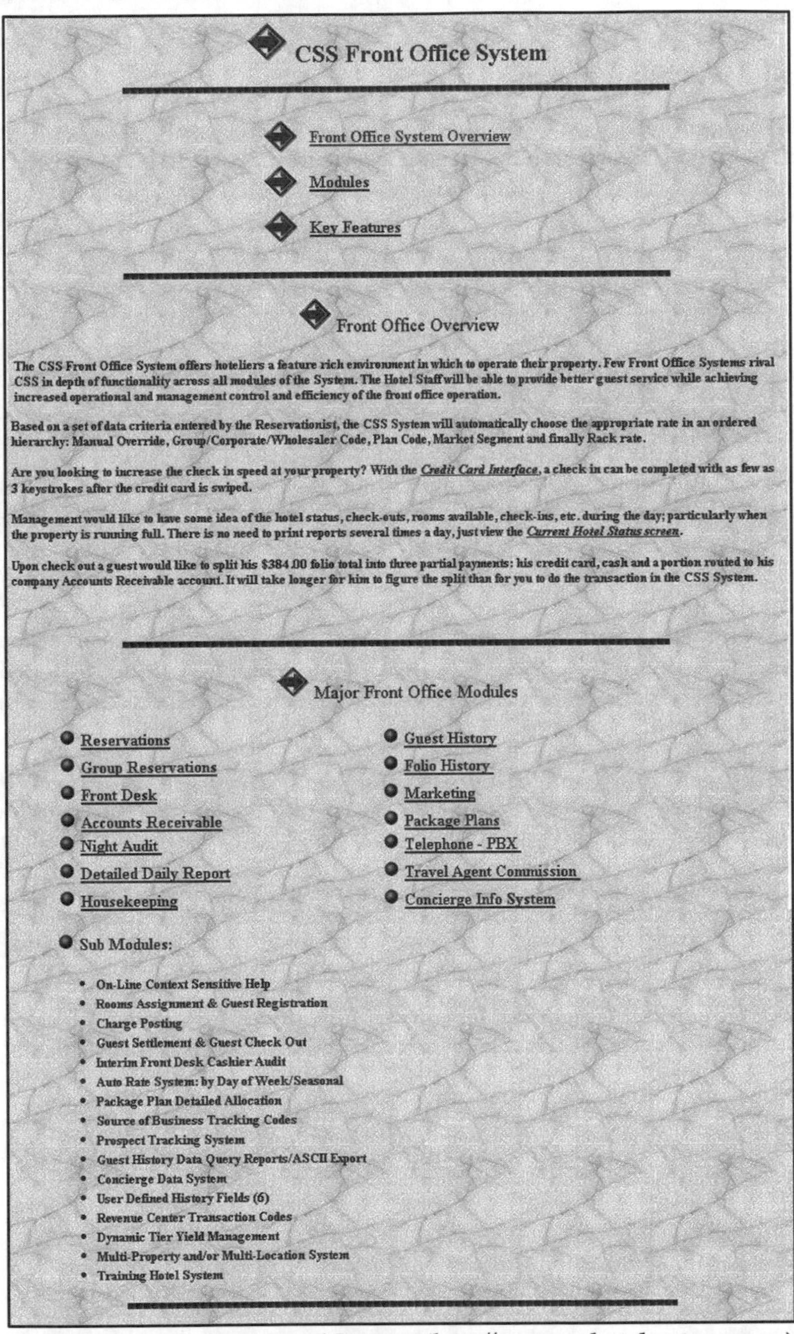

CSS Front Office System

- Front Office System Overview
- Modules
- Key Features

Front Office Overview

The CSS Front Office System offers hoteliers a feature rich environment in which to operate their property. Few Front Office Systems rival CSS in depth of functionality across all modules of the System. The Hotel Staff will be able to provide better guest service while achieving increased operational and management control and efficiency of the front office operation.

Based on a set of data criteria entered by the Reservationist, the CSS System will automatically choose the appropriate rate in an ordered hierarchy: Manual Override, Group/Corporate/Wholesaler Code, Plan Code, Market Segment and finally Rack rate.

Are you looking to increase the check in speed at your property? With the *Credit Card Interface*, a check in can be completed with as few as 3 keystrokes after the credit card is swiped.

Management would like to have some idea of the hotel status, check-outs, rooms available, check-ins, etc. during the day; particularly when the property is running full. There is no need to print reports several times a day, just view the *Current Hotel Status screen*.

Upon check out a guest would like to split his $384.00 folio total into three partial payments: his credit card, cash and a portion routed to his company Accounts Receivable account. It will take longer for him to figure the split than for you to do the transaction in the CSS System.

Major Front Office Modules

- Reservations
- Group Reservations
- Front Desk
- Accounts Receivable
- Night Audit
- Detailed Daily Report
- Housekeeping
- Guest History
- Folio History
- Marketing
- Package Plans
- Telephone - PBX
- Travel Agent Commission
- Concierge Info System
- Sub Modules:
  - On-Line Context Sensitive Help
  - Rooms Assignment & Guest Registration
  - Charge Posting
  - Guest Settlement & Guest Check Out
  - Interim Front Desk Cashier Audit
  - Auto Rate System: by Day of Week/Seasonal
  - Package Plan Detailed Allocation
  - Source of Business Tracking Codes
  - Prospect Tracking System
  - Guest History Data Query Reports/ASCII Export
  - Concierge Data System
  - User Defined History Fields (6)
  - Revenue Center Transaction Codes
  - Dynamic Tier Yield Management
  - Multi-Property and/or Multi-Location System
  - Training Hotel System

The Internet site of CSS Hotel Systems (http://www.csshotelsystems.com) provides detailed descriptions of the features and functions of software modules designed specifically for hotel front office operations.

electronic guest folios. Automatic posting reduces the number of late charges posted to the guest account after the guest has departed.

General Management Software

General management software cannot operate independently of other front office software packages. General management applications tend to be report-generating packages which depend on data collected through reservations management, rooms management, and guest account management programs. For example, general management software may be able to generate a report showing the day's expected arrivals and the number of rooms available for occupancy—a combination of reservations and rooms management data. In addition to generating reports, the general management module serves as the normal link between front and back office computer system interface applications.

Back Office Interfaces

A comprehensive property management system typically involves the hotel's back office. Although front and back office software packages can be independent of one another, integrated systems offer the hotel a full range of control over a variety of operational areas. Such areas include room sales, telephone call accounting, payroll, and account analysis. An integrated system cannot produce complete financial statements unless all the required data are stored in an accessible data base. Many reports generated by the back office system depend on the front office system's collection of data. Most vendors supply several back office application modules. The four most popular applications are:

- *General ledger accounting software,* consisting of accounts receivable and accounts payable software packages. Accounts receivable software monitors guest accounts and account billing and collection when integrated with the front office guest accounting module. Accounts payable software tracks hotel purchases and helps the hotel maintain sufficient cash flow to satisfy its debts.
- *Payroll accounting software* processes such data as time and attendance records, pay distribution, and tax withholdings.
- *Financial reporting software* helps the hotel develop a chart of accounts in order to produce balance sheets, income statements, and transactional analysis reports.
- *Inventory control software* monitors stocking levels, purchase ordering, and stock rotation. Additional computations include inventory usage, variance, and extensions.

System Interfaces

A variety of property management system (PMS) interface applications are available in a fully automated environment.

Non-Guest-Operated Interfaces. Common interfaces that are not initiated by guest activity include:

- A *point-of-sale (POS) system* allows guest account transactions to be quickly transmitted from remote revenue centers to the PMS for automatic posting to electronic folios.
- A *call accounting system (CAS)* directs, prices, and tracks guestroom telephone use for resale and automatic posting to electronic folios.
- An *electronic locking system (ELS)* may interface with the rooms management application to provide enhanced guest security and service.
- An *energy management system (EMS)* can automatically control the temperature, humidity, and air movement in both public spaces and guestrooms through a rooms management interface.

An EMS is a computer-based control system designed to automatically manage the operation of mechanical equipment in a lodging property. An EMS interfaced to a property management system offers a number of opportunities for energy control. For example, assume that on a particular night a 50 percent occupancy is forecasted for a 300-room hotel. Minimizing the hotel's energy consumption on this night becomes a factor in determining which rooms to sell. One approach would be to assign guests only to the lower floors and significantly reduce the energy demands of rooms on the upper floors. By interfacing an EMS to a front office rooms management system, it is possible to automatically control room assignments and achieve desired energy cost savings.

Guest-Operated Interfaces. Because the world's traveling public has become more computer-skilled, hotels can provide computer-based conveniences and services. Some hotels have gone beyond basic property management systems by installing a variety of automated devices that can be operated by guests. In some properties, guests may inquire about in-house events and local activities through automated information devices in public areas or the guestroom. When a printer is connected to a lobby information terminal, guests may receive individually prepared lists of events.

Recent technological advances allow guests to review their folios and check out of the hotel in the comfort and privacy of their guestrooms. In-room televisions or computers interfaced with a guest accounting module enable guests to simultaneously access folio data and to approve and settle their accounts by selecting a pre-approved method of settlement. Guestroom telephones interfaced with the hotel's computer system may also be used for this purpose. In-room computers linked to external computer information services can permit guests to access e-mail, the Internet, airline schedules, local restaurant guides, entertainment guides, stock market reports, news and sports updates, shopping catalogs, and video games.

An *in-room entertainment system* can be interfaced with a front office accounting module or can function as an independent system. In-room entertainment systems allow guests to pick various forms of entertainment from their guestroom televisions. If there is a charge for the service, such as a pay-per-view movie, video game, or Internet access, the charge is automatically calculated and reported to the front desk or posted to the guest folio. When interfaced with the accounting module, the system is capable of automatically posting charges to an electronic folio when the television is set on a pre-coded channel. To keep guests from inadvertently tuning to a pay channel, the housekeeping staff should be instructed to set the television on a non-pay channel, or preview channel, as part of their guestroom cleaning routine. Incorporating a preview channel can significantly reduce the number of pay TV or movie charges disputed by guests. Stand-alone in-room movie systems may even require the guest to dial an in-house department to request that the pay channel be turned on. The hotel staff member who loads the requested program may also trigger posting to the guest's folio.

There are two types of *in-room vending systems. Non-automated honor bars* consist of beverage and snack items in both dry and cold storage areas within a guestroom. The bar's beginning inventory level is recorded, and changes in inventory are noted by hotel employees on a daily basis. Appropriate charges for missing or consumed items are posted to the guest's folio. However, since honor bars are available at all times, this system may result in an unusually high volume of late charge postings. *Fully automated vending machines* contain fiber-optic sensors that record the removal of stored products from designated compartments. When a sensor is triggered, the vending machine sends appropriate information to a dedicated microprocessor and, in turn, to the front office accounting module for folio posting.

Another technology-based guest amenity is the *in-room fax machine.* Faxes can be sent and received directly from the guestroom without the need for anyone from the hotel staff to serve the guest. These are becoming popular in hotels serving meeting, convention, and business travelers. The latest models are connected to the hotel telephone system, which automatically calculates the cost of the fax and forwards the charge to the front desk computer. As the volume of faxes continues to grow, in-room fax machines and fax services provided by the hotel staff can become a significant revenue source. Guests can even receive a printed copy of their folio through the fax machine with this system.

Guest Services and Technology. As stated earlier, guest services are becoming a major tool for hotels to attract new guests. There is a new focus on how technology can be used to improve guest services, and some of them have already been mentioned above. Other services are now being introduced or developed to expand these services even further.

For example, in-room entertainment companies are developing systems to provide local information through guestroom televisions. Guests will be able to identify restaurants, museums, shops, and other points of interest through the guestroom television and receive detailed information on them. More advanced systems integrate with the Internet, shopping malls, e-mail, and other online services. In a similar way, hotels will be able to advertise their own services or other hotels in the chain. If a guest is interested in a particular hotel, the system will automatically connect to the chain's central reservation system.

Another emerging innovation in technology is the integration of the hotel telephone system with outside communications systems. Many hotels now provide each guest with a cellular telephone during his or her stay. When someone calls the guest, the hotel telephone system first rings the guest's room. If the guest does not answer, the phone system then tries to call the guest on the cellular telephone. If the guest does not answer the cellular phone, the system then forwards the caller to the voice mail system. All of this is done automatically through advanced interfaces and software in each system. Innovations of this kind will continue to grow in importance over the foreseeable future.

Perhaps just as exciting is the ability to connect the guest directly to the Internet through the guestroom television. Several companies are developing and testing high speed systems that allow guests to "surf the net" in the privacy of their own rooms.

These are just a few examples of current trends in applying technology to guest services. With a stronger emphasis on guest services, managers can expect more opportunities to apply guest service technology in many areas.

Summary

The functions, activities, and areas of the front office are geared toward supporting guest transactions and services. To many guests, the front office represents the hotel. It is the main source for nearly every guest service the hotel provides. The financial transactions a guest makes while staying at a hotel determine the flow of business through the property. This flow of business can be divided into four stages: pre-arrival, arrival, occupancy, and departure. Within each stage, important front office tasks related to guest services and guest accounting can be identified and analyzed. Front office employees need to be aware of guest services and guest accounting activities throughout the guest stay.

The guest chooses a hotel during the pre-arrival stage of the guest cycle. The arrival stage of the guest cycle includes registration and rooming functions. During the occupancy stage of the guest cycle, the front office provides the guest with services, information, and supplies. Other guest services and guest accounting aspects of the guest cycle are completed during the cycle's departure stage. Since activities and functions tend to overlap between stages, some properties have revised the traditional guest cycle into a sequence of pre-sale, point-of-sale, and post-sale events. For computerized properties, this revised sequence tends to improve coordination among hotel operating departments.

Non-automated front office recordkeeping systems rely solely on handwritten forms. A semi-automated front office system uses both handwritten and machine-produced forms. Advantages of a semi-automated system over a non-automated system include automatically generated, neatly printed documents that detail the steps of a transaction. Computer systems designed for use in the hospitality industry were first introduced in the early 1970s. Front office recordkeeping is computer-based in fully automated hotels.

Most front office functions are performed at the front desk. The front desk, prominently located in the lobby area, is where guests register, request information and services, relate complaints, settle their accounts, and check out. The functional efficiency of a front desk depends on its design and layout. The desk should provide each front desk employee with easy access to the equipment, forms, and supplies necessary for the performance of assigned tasks. Non-automated and semi-automated front offices typically rely upon a collection of mechanical racks and specialty devices designed to produce, store, or display front office forms. In a fully automated hotel, most traditional front office equipment has been replaced by a front office computer system. A hotel property management system contains sets of computer software packages capable of supporting a variety of activities in front and back office areas.

Key Terms

call accounting system (CAS)—a device linked to the hotel telephone system that accurately accounts for guest telephone calls by identifying each phone number dialed from guestroom telephones and tracking charges.

guest cycle—a division of the flow of business through a hotel that identifies the physical contacts and financial exchanges between guests and hotel employees.

guest folio—a form (paper or electronic) used to chart transactions on an account assigned to an individual person or guestroom.

guest history file—a collection of guest history records, constructed from expired registration cards or created through sophisticated computer-based systems, that automatically direct information about departing guests into a guest history database.

house limit—a credit limit established by the hotel.

information rack—an alphabetical index of registered guests, used in routing telephone calls, mail, messages, and visitor inquiries; normally consists of aluminum slots designed to hold information rack slips.

late charge—a transaction requiring posting to a guest account that does not reach the front desk for posting until after the guest has checked out and closed his or her account.

property management system (PMS)—a computer software package that supports a variety of applications related to front office and back office activities.

registration card—a printed form for a registration record.

reservation record—a manual record created by the reservationist as a result of the initial inquiry procedures. Typical data are: date of arrival, type and number of rooms requested, and number of persons in the party.

reservation file—a computer-based collection of reservation records.

room rack—an array of metal file pockets designed to hold room rack slips arranged by room number; the room rack summarizes the current status of all rooms in the hotel.

voucher—a document detailing a transaction to be posted to a front office account; used to communicate information from a point of sale to the front office.

Review Questions

1. What activities are involved in the four stages of the traditional guest cycle? Why have some properties replaced the traditional cycle with a three-stage sequence?
2. How does the departure stage of the guest cycle conclude both guest services and guest accounting activities? How can data about the guest stay be used by the front office?
3. How have front office recordkeeping systems evolved over the years?
4. How does a fully automated front office recordkeeping system enhance front office control over guest accounting data?
5. What forms and equipment are used in typical non- and semi-automated hotels during the pre-arrival stage of the guest cycle? Why are there two reservation racks?
6. What forms and equipment are used in typical non- and semi-automated hotels during the arrival stage of the guest cycle? How can mail, message, and key racks be adapted to the uses of a particular hotel?
7. What forms and equipment are used in typical non- and semi-automated hotels during the occupancy stage of the guest cycle? How do vouchers support front office accounting tasks?
8. What forms and equipment are used in typical non- and semi-automated hotels during the departure stage of the guest cycle? What are the uses of a guest history record?
9. What are some of the organizational concerns of front desk design? What criteria determine the appropriateness of a design?
10. What are the four most common front office software modules? How do they streamline front office recordkeeping? How does a general management module depend on the other three?

Internet Sites

For more information, visit the following Internet sites. Remember that Internet addresses can change without notice.

Equipment and Technology

AT&T
http://www.att.com

CMS Hospitality
http://www.cmshosp.com.au

CSS Hotel Systems
http://www.csshotelsystems.com

Executech Systems, Inc.
http://www.executech.com

Fidelio Products
http://www.micros.com/scripts/vertical.pl

Hitachi Telecom (USA), Inc.
http://hitel.com/lodge.htm

Hospitality Industry Technology Exposition and Conference
http://www.hitecshow.org

Hospitality Industry Technology Integration Standards
http://www.hitis.org

HOST Group
http://www.hostgroup.com

hotelsupplies.com, LLC
http://www.hotelsupplies.com

Lodging Touch International
http://www.lodgingtouch.com

MCI
http://www.mci.com

Sprint Biz
http://www.sprintbiz.com

Western Hospitality Systems
http://www.lodgingsystems.com

Case Study

Making the Most of Moments of Truth

#1—Gordon Sumner's Food for Thought

Freelance writer Gordon Sumner stepped off the hotel elevator and glanced at his watch. It was 10:00 A.M. on a Thursday and he was grateful to have had the chance to sleep in late after his 11:30 P.M. arrival the night before. Now the only thing he needed to start the day off right was a hearty breakfast. He headed to the front desk for directions to the hotel restaurant.

"Good morning," the man behind the desk said. "How can I help you?"

"You have a restaurant here, don't you?"

"Yes, we do. In fact, it just received a Golden Palate award from our city magazine."

"Well, I don't know if I'd recognize award-winning food if I ate it, but I would like a good breakfast," Gordon said.

"Then we have just the place for you, sir."

Gordon got directions from the agent and within two minutes he was sitting at a table in a bright, well-decorated restaurant. Looking around, he noticed half-a-dozen other people lingering over their breakfast and coffee at nearby tables. From what he could see, the food did look appetizing.

After several minutes passed without a visit from a wait person, Gordon finally noticed a waitress walking across the other side of the room. He caught her attention and asked to see a menu. Ten minutes later, he had to flag her down again. *Goodness,* he thought, *the food must be spectacular if this place can win awards despite such poor service.*

"Can I help you, sir?" she said as she approached his table.

"I'd like to order breakfast. Could I get a—"

"I'm sorry, sir, but we stopped serving breakfast at 9:45."

"Well, then, I guess an early lunch would be all right. I'm starving."

The waitress bit her lip. "Actually, we don't begin serving lunch until 11:15. That's about another hour from now."

It was frustrating to see people still enjoying their meal and to realize he wouldn't be able to join them. "All right," he said without enthusiasm, "could I get some coffee to go, then? Maybe I'll grab a newspaper from the gift shop and just—"

She was shaking her head. "I'm sorry, but the register is locked until lunch. We can't handle take-out orders."

"I see," he said, wondering why the man at the front desk hadn't bothered to explain any of this. "So tell me: where can a guy get something to eat around here?"

"You know, if I were you, I'd take the walkway over to the mall across the street. They have a pretty good food court."

Twenty minutes later, Gordon passed through the lobby on his way back from the mall and his fast-food meal.

The front desk agent called out to him, "And was your breakfast award winning, sir?"

"No, I can't say that it was," Gordon replied as he walked by.

The agent looked stricken. "Oh. I'm sorry to hear that. I hope you'll give us the chance to serve you again."

"Not likely," Gordon said under his breath as he stepped into the elevator.

#2—Freddie Bulsara: Dancers, with Wolves

Reservations Manager Freddie Bulsara was looking forward to a glorious Sunday, thanks to his booking prowess. This weekend marked a double coup. On Saturday, the hotel had hosted 230 young ballet dancers and their adult chaperones who were in town for a Sunday morning dance competition. Today, they would check out, opening up a large block of rooms that would match—almost to the room—the needs of a 200-member contingent of conventioneers from the Royal Fraternal Order of Wolves.

Freddie marveled at the perfection of his plan. The dancers would check out by 9:00 A.M., before leaving for their competition; the Wolves were to begin arriving at exactly 1:00 P.M. *Groups like this are really going to put this property on the map,* Freddie told himself.

But something wasn't right. When Freddie stopped at the front desk to ask how things went with the dancers, LeighAnne Crenshaw looked up from her work and said, "I can't really say. I'll let you know once they leave."

Freddie felt his heart skip a beat. "It's 11:45, LeighAnne. What are you talking about?"

"When I came in this morning, I found a note here that says the dancers asked to be allowed a late check-out, after their competition. I guess a lot of them wanted to be able to come back to their rooms and change their clothes before leaving. Their group leader had it all arranged."

"With *whom?*"

LeighAnne shrugged. "There's no name on the note, but it looks like Brian's handwriting. He would have been working the front desk when they all came in last night."

Brian. A new hire who hadn't been on the job for more than two months. His misguided need to do anything a guest asks is going to ruin everything I've worked for, Freddie thought. "Do you know when they'll actually be checking out, then?"

"Well, the competition started at 9:30, and they said it was about two hours' long. With travel time, I'd guess they'll be coming back within the next 30 minutes, if that tells you anything."

It tells me we won't have time for Housekeeping to finish with the rooms before the Wolves get here. We'll have to stall the conventioneers until their rooms are ready.

"I take that back," LeighAnne said, nodding toward the front entrance. "That looks like their bus now."

"Thank goodness!" Freddie said. "The sooner they get back to their rooms, the sooner we can clear them out and get Housekeeping started. It might be tight, but—"

Freddie stopped in mid-sentence. His mouth dropped open as the bus doors sprang open and the passengers made their way across the sidewalk to the revolving doors. He expected a stream of little girls in pink tutus. What he saw was a huge pack of middle-aged men wearing wolf ears and shouting, laughing, and punching each other in the arm.

"Oh no," Freddie whispered. He glanced at the clock as the first members of the Royal Fraternal Order of Wolves crossed the lobby toward the front desk.

The man in front—a tall, barrel-chested individual—tugged off his wolf ears and stuck out his hand. "You must be Freddie!" he said with a grin. "Darrell Drucker. We spoke on the phone!"

Freddie tried to return the man's energetic handshake, but his heart wasn't in it. The Wolves were quickly filling up every available space in the lobby. "Hello, Mr. Drucker," he managed to say. "We weren't expecting you until one o'clock."

Mr. Drucker looked taken aback. "Why, it's one o'clock right smack on the dot!"

Then surprise slowly spread across his face. "We musta forgot to turn our watches back when we crossed that time zone!" he said with a grin. "Well, Freddie, just point us to our rooms, and we'll get out of your hair."

"Actually, it's going to be—"

"Look at that!" one of the Wolves shouted across the lobby. He was smiling and pointing at the entrance, where dozens of pre-teen girls in tutus and pink and white tights were pressing their way through the doors and into the packed lobby.

"They're ba-a-ack," LeighAnne said dryly, quoting a haunted-house movie from the 1980s.

Freddie just hoped there was a ghost of a chance he would be able to keep everyone happy until the situation was straightened out.

#3—Reg Dwight: A Night to Remember

It had been a quiet Monday night until front desk agent Reg Dwight picked up the telephone at 3 A.M. On the other end of the line was a representative from an international airline. "About half an hour ago, we received a bomb threat concerning a flight to London that already was fueled, filled with passengers, and preparing for take-off," the woman began. "For their own safety, we have had to deplane those passengers, and now we have 260 people who need rooms until we can clear the plane, scan the baggage, and arrange for alternate transportation. Can we send them your way for the duration?"

Although Reg had worked many nights alone at the front desk, this was the first time he had ever faced a situation like this. He took a deep breath. "How many rooms would be involved?"

"With all the families and couples, we would need only about 175 rooms. The airline will of course cover the lodging costs, as well as one meal for everyone at your restaurant."

Reg checked availability. The passengers would have to spread out over most of the hotel, but the rooms were there. He was just about to calculate the financial windfall of 175 rooms at a rack rate of $84 when the woman added, "At 'distressed passenger' rates, of course." *Oh,* Reg thought. *That's $35 per room.* Reg wasn't aware of any existing hotel policies for handling a situation like this. Although it definitely would not be a money-making proposition—it actually cost $40 to deliver a guestroom—Reg thought the value of providing a needed service would outweigh any financial drawbacks. He hoped his supervisor would think so too.

He told the caller to send the passengers his way and he would take care of them. Reg then asked to be kept informed of the guests' new travel arrangements as soon as they were established. He figured the guests would arrive tired, anxious, and angry about having to get off a plane in the middle of the night and stay longer than expected. He hoped that, by being able to answer many of their questions, he could put them at ease.

"How soon will they arrive?" he asked.

"The buses should be leaving within 15 minutes, so they will reach your hotel around four o'clock. Just one more thing. You may want to let passengers know that their carry-on and checked baggage will be sent over as soon as it is thoroughly scanned, but that may not be until six. We will send all the shoes over then too."

Did she say "shoes"?

"I'm sorry, I must go," she hurried on. "I will ring back as soon as we have any news to share. Thanks so much for working with us during this emergency."

As soon as they hung up, Reg got on the phone. He knew he was going to need much more help than was normally available at 4 A.M. He called his supervisor at home, waking her to find out who he should contact. In addition to saying that she would come to work herself, she recommended that he call in kitchen, dining room, housekeeping, and front desk staff. Since she had also faced a similar situation before, she explained about the shoes.

"Before passengers can deplane using the inflatable slides, they have to take their shoes off. They usually collect them later on the runway. But in situations like this, the airline will just dump them all in boxes and send them over—unsorted, unpaired—along with a jumble of unidentified carry-on bags and checked luggage. We can put all the baggage in the Heritage Room. The shoes can go in the Carlton Room if Lorenzo hasn't already set up the A-V equipment for the noon meeting that's scheduled there. Hopefully, the shoes will be out in time to allow A-V setup just before the group has to have it."

"I'll make sure that happens."

"Tell you what. I'll be there as soon as I can to help with checking everyone in and covering whatever else needs to be covered. I'll give this some thought myself, but I'd like you to have a list ready for me of all the things you can think of that might be affected by having 260 possibly upset and worried guests arriving—and what those guests might want or need. We're just lucky we had the rooms to give them."

Reg took a deep breath. "*Lucky* wasn't the first word that came to mind."

Discussion Questions

1. What steps could the staff at Gordon Sumner's hotel have taken to improve their service?
2. What factors were out of Freddie Bulsara's control? How could he have prepared for problems?
3. What might Reg Dwight's list of affected areas and guest wants/needs include?

Case Number: 3323CA

The following industry experts helped generate and develop this case: Richard M. Brooks, CHA, Vice President—Operations, Bridgestreet Accommodations, Inc., Cleveland, Ohio; and S. Kenneth Hiller, CHA, Director of Transition and Owner Relations, Marriott Hotels International.

This case also appears in *Case Studies in Lodging Management* (Lansing, Mich.: Educational Institute of the American Hotel & Motel Association, 1998), ISBN 0-86612-184-6.

Chapter 4 Outline

- Reservations and Sales
- Types of Reservations
  - Guaranteed Reservations
  - Non-Guaranteed Reservations
- Reservation Inquiry
  - Central Reservation Systems
  - Global Distribution Systems
  - Intersell Agencies
  - Property Direct
  - Reservations Through the Internet
- Group Reservations
- Reservation Availability
  - Control Book
  - Computerized Systems
- The Reservation Record
- Reservation Confirmation
  - Confirmation/Cancellation Numbers
- Reservation Maintenance
  - Modifying Non-Guaranteed Reservations
  - Reservation Cancellation
- Reservation Reports
  - Expected Arrival and Departure Lists
  - Processing Deposits
  - Reservations Histories
- Reservation Considerations
  - Legal Implications
  - Waiting Lists
  - Packages
  - Potential Reservation Problems
- Summary
- Case Study

4

Reservations

THE MOST IMPORTANT OUTCOME of the reservations process is having a guestroom ready and waiting when the guest arrives. This guestroom should not be just *any* room, but *the* room that best meets the needs the guest expressed during the reservations process.

To achieve this outcome, hospitality operations must have efficient reservations procedures in place. Finely tuned methods allow reservations agents to record and act on reservation details, promote hotel services, and ensure accuracy. Reservations agents must be able to respond in a quick, accurate, and pleasant manner. The time they spend on paperwork, filing, and other clerical tasks should be held to a minimum.

Processing reservations involves matching room requests with room availabilities; recording, confirming, and maintaining reservations; and producing management reports. Reservation information is especially useful in other front office functions. For example, with the information gathered during the reservations process, front office personnel can finalize room assignments, initiate guest accounting and guest history files, and fulfill guest special requests.

This chapter describes typical activities associated with the reservations process. These activities include:

- Conducting the reservation inquiry
- Determining room and rate availability
- Creating the reservation record
- Confirming the reservation record
- Maintaining the reservation record
- Producing reservation reports

The nature of reservations will be examined before these activities are addressed in detail.

Reservations and Sales

Before computerization, reservations agents focused primarily on basic room availability information; they did not have an effective means by which to identify available rooms by room type. When a guest requested a room, the reservations agent could confirm that *a* room was available. The agent, however, could not be sure that a particular *type* of room or that specific furnishings or features were available. Reservations agents would note special requests on the reservation record, but it was up to the front desk to fulfill such requests at the time of check-in.

Such conditions continue to exist in non-automated properties. This is largely because the front desk controls room and rate assignments and performs many other tasks related to room sales. In non-automated hotels, reservations agents typically match requests for overnight accommodations against a simple inventory of available rooms.

By contrast, automation of the reservations process and front desk functions provides identical room and rate information to personnel in both areas. Since room features are normally categorized within the rooms management module, both front desk and reservations agents can review room and rate information for a specific date.

Given such data access capabilities, much of the responsibility for rooms sales has shifted from the front desk to the reservations department, especially in properties with front office computer systems. Requests for specific room types, locations, and special features can be immediately acknowledged and quickly confirmed as part of the reservations process. Many front office computer systems enable reservations agents to assign specific rooms. By shifting the selling function to the reservations department, much of the responsibility associated with projected room revenues and profitability analyses shifts as well. For these reasons, many lodging companies now view reservations as part of the sales department, even though the function has traditionally been part of the rooms division. Reservations agents are no longer simply order takers; they are trained in sales techniques. The telephone is the primary tool for selling rooms in the reservations office. Selling over the telephone is difficult, since the reservations agent must create an image of the hotel in the mind of the caller. Many hotel companies conduct extensive sales training programs with reservations agents, and use the position to identify staff members who would like to make sales their career. Many reservations offices have sales goals, including number of room nights, average room rate, and room revenue booked.

The ability of the reservations department to sell rooms, enhance inventory control, and improve guest satisfaction is often cited as an important justification for investing in a front office computer system. With proper emphasis on sales and marketing techniques, properties can more accurately forecast and better react to business volumes. Gathering forecasted sales information and using it to determine pricing or room rate strategies is often referred to as *revenue management.*

Types of Reservations

The majority of hotel guests make reservations. Reservations may take many forms. A brief discussion of the major types of reservations provides some important distinctions.

Guaranteed Reservations

A **guaranteed reservation** assures the guest that the hotel will hold a room until a specific time of the day following the guest's scheduled arrival date. This time may be check-out time, the start of the hotel day (that is, when the night audit has been completed and the books are closed for the day), or any time the lodging company chooses. The guest, in turn, guarantees to pay for the room, even if it is not used, unless the reservation is canceled according to the hotel's cancellation procedures. Guaranteed reservations provide some protection for the hotel's revenues even in the case of a **no-show,** a situation in which a guest makes a reservation but does not register or cancel the reservation. Variations of guaranteed reservations include the following.

Prepayment. A **prepayment guaranteed reservation** requires that a payment in full be received prior to the guest's day of arrival. From the perspective of the front office, this is generally the most desirable form of guaranteed reservation. This type of guaranteed reservation is commonly used at U.S. resorts and at hotels outside the United States.

Credit Card. Major credit card companies have developed systems to ensure that participating lodging properties receive payment for no-shows through **credit card guaranteed reservations.** Unless a credit card guaranteed reservation is properly canceled before a stated **cancellation hour,** the lodging property will charge the guest's credit card account for the amount of the room's rate; the card company will then bill the card holder. Credit card guaranteed reservations are the most common form of guaranteed reservation and are customary in commercial hotels. When billing for a no-show reservation, most hotels charge one night's rate plus tax. Resorts may charge more nights, since the length of stay at a resort is usually longer and it is more difficult to fill rooms due to advanced bookings.

Advance Deposit. An **advance deposit guaranteed reservation** (or partial prepayment) requires that the guest pay the hotel a specified amount of money before arrival. The amount of an advance deposit is typically large enough to cover one night's room rate and room tax. The pre-arrival amount will typically be larger if the reservation is for more than a one-night stay. If a guest holding an advance deposit guaranteed reservation fails to register or cancel, the hotel may retain the deposit and cancel the reservation for the guest's entire stay. This type of guaranteed reservation is more common at destination resorts and convention center hotels. A variation on this type of deposit applies the deposit received to the last night of the stay. This is intended to ensure resort revenue in case the guest decides to depart earlier than scheduled.

Travel Agent. Travel agent guaranteed reservations have become less common since both travel agents and hotels prefer the protection provided by credit card or advance deposit guarantees whenever possible. Under a travel agent guaranteed reservation, the travel agent guarantees the client's reservation. In the case of a no-show, the hotel generally bills the travel agency for payment and the travel agent must then collect from the guest.

Voucher or MCO. Another type of travel agent guarantee is the travel agency voucher or miscellaneous charge order (MCO). The MCO is a voucher issued by the Airline Reporting Corporation (ARC) and is controlled by many of the same travel agency regulations that control airline tickets. Many resorts prefer MCOs if they must accept vouchers because ARC guarantees payment if the travel agency defaults on the payment. With travel agency vouchers and MCOs, the guest has prepaid the amount of the deposit to the travel agent. The agent forwards a voucher or MCO to the hotel as proof of payment and a guarantee that the prepaid amount will be sent to the hotel when the voucher is returned to the travel agency for payment. Usually, with vouchers and MCOs, the travel agency deducts its commission before sending payment to the hotel. Travel agent vouchers and MCOs are less popular today because of major travel agencies who closed their doors, leaving hotels without payments due and guests with no recourse to collect what they had already paid.

Corporate. A corporation may sign a contractual agreement with the hotel which states that the corporation will accept financial responsibility for any no-show business travelers the corporation sponsors. A **corporate guaranteed reservation** involves a corporation entering into an agreement with a hotel. Such contracts are often popular in downtown or business center hotels with a large number of transient guests.

Non-Guaranteed Reservations

In the case of a **non-guaranteed reservation,** the hotel agrees to hold a room for the guest until a stated reservation cancellation hour (usually 4 P.M or 6 P.M.) on the day of arrival. This type of reservation does not guarantee that the property will receive payment for no-shows. If the guest does not arrive by the cancellation hour, the hotel is free to release the room, meaning that it can add the room to the list of other rooms available for sale. If the guest arrives after the cancellation hour, the hotel will accommodate the guest if a room is available.

It is common for hotels nearing full occupancy to accept only guaranteed reservations once a specified number of expected arrivals is achieved. The efficiency and accuracy of a hotel's reservations process is especially critical in full or nearly full occupancy conditions. The strategy here is to maximize hotel revenue by reducing the number of potential no-shows that the hotel cannot collect on. At the same time, it is important for hotel management to know the state law concerning guaranteed and non-guaranteed reservations. In some states, confirming a guaranteed reservation is considered a binding contract. If the hotel then fails to provide the room for a guaranteed reservation, legal penalties can be applied if the guest files a complaint with the state.

Reservation Inquiry

A property receives reservation inquiries in a variety of ways. Reservation requests may be made in person, over the telephone, in the mail, via facsimile or telex, through the Internet, through a central reservation system, through a global distribution system (airline reservation system), or through an intersell agency (see Exhibit 1). Hotel chains have come to realize that distribution of their product is critical to their success. The more channels of distribution they have, the more opportunities guests will have to inquire and book their rooms. Regardless of the source, the reservations agent will collect the following information about the

Exhibit 1 Sources of Reservations

Central Reservations System
- Affiliate Reservation Network (Hotel Chains)
- Non-Affiliate Reservation Network
  - Leading Hotels of the World
  - Preferred Hotels
  - Distinguished Hotels

Global Distribution Systems
- SABRE
- Galileo International
- Amadeus
- WorldSpan

Intersell Agencies

Property Direct

Internet

guest's stay through a process known as a reservation inquiry. The reservations agent should collect such information as the guest's name, address, and telephone number; company or travel agency name (if applicable); date of arrival and date of departure; and the type and number of rooms requested. The reservations agent should also try to establish the room rate, number of people in the party, method of payment or guarantee, and any special requests.

Most of the information gathered during the reservation inquiry will be used to create the **reservation record,** a process discussed later in this chapter. The reservations agent enters the gathered information onto a reservation form or into a computer terminal according to clearly defined procedures. Exhibit 2 contains a sample non-automated reservation form; Exhibit 3 shows a sample reservation display screen used in automated systems.

Reservations can be made for individuals, groups, tours, or conventions. A guest coming to the hotel as an individual and not part of a group is typically referred to as a free independent traveler, or FIT. Reservations of persons coming to the hotel as part of a group may be handled differently from those of FIT guests. For example, reservations for group members may be filed under the group's name rather than the guests' individual names. In addition, group reservations may receive special attention during pre-registration activities.

Central Reservation Systems

A majority of lodging properties belong to one or more **central reservation systems.** There are two basic types of central reservation systems: affiliate networks and non-affiliate networks.

An **affiliate reservation network** is a hotel chain's reservation system in which all participating properties are contractually related. Today, virtually every

Exhibit 2 Sample Non-Automated Reservation Form

THE EDUCATIONAL INN GUEST RESERVATION FORM

Date of Res ________________

Res. Clerk ________________

Please Print or Type

ARRIVAL DATE	DEPARTURE DATE	NO. NIGHTS	NO. PERSONS	RATE CONFIRMED
________	________	________	________	Adults $ ________
________ a.m.	________ a.m.		________	Children
________ p.m.	________ p.m.			

NO. ROOMS	ROOM TYPE:	QUEEN BED	2 DOUBLE BEDS	SUITE
________		(1 Qn. bed)	(2 Dbl. beds)	(2 bdrms.)

OTHER REQUESTS:	Crib	Connecting	Balcony	Other (Specify)
	Rollaway	Adjacent	Pool overlook	________

NAME RESERVATION WILL BE UNDER TEL: ( ) ________

Last ________ First ________ Mid. Init. ____ (Title, if one is offered) ________

STREET ADDRESS CITY STATE ZIP

____

REPRESENTING (where applicable) TEL: ( ) ________

____

STREET ADDRESS CITY STATE ZIP

____

IS RESERVATION GUARANTEED?* YES ______ NO ______

RESERVATION GUARANTEED BY

____

Credit Card No. (Specify) No. Exp. Date Deposit Other

RESERVATION MADE BY (if other than above) ________________

REMARKS ________________________________

____

____

- -

CHANGE OF RESERVATION

Original Reservation No. ________ Original Date of Arrival ________ Original Rate ________

Remarks ________________________________

____

*Reservations may or may not be guaranteed.

Exhibit 3 Sample Electronic Reservation Record

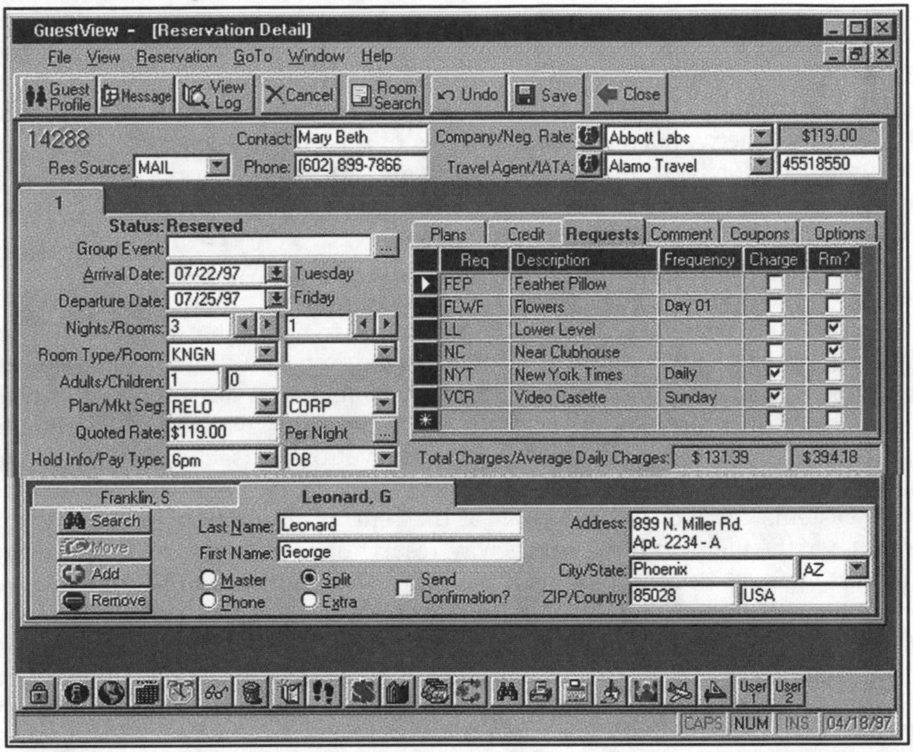

This electronic reservation record is from *GuestView,* a property management system offered by Anasazi, Inc., Phoenix, Arizona. The company's Internet site (http://www.anasazi.com) provides additional screen selections from its system.

chain operates its own reservation network or outsources the central reservation function and technology to a reservation service company.

Chain hotels link their reservations operations to streamline the processing of reservations and reduce overall system costs. Another intended outcome is that one chain property will attract business for or refer business to another chain property. In the case of group reservations, information may be shared among affiliate properties through an automated sales office program.

Reservations are often passed from one chain property to another through an automated reservation network. If one property is booked, the reservations agent handling the caller's transaction may suggest accommodations at a chain property in the same geographic area. Referrals may also be made to properties whose locations appear more convenient or suitable to the guest's needs. Affiliate reservation networks that allow non-chain properties to participate in the reservation system are able to represent themselves to a broader market. Non-chain properties in an affiliate reservation system are referred to as **overflow facilities.** Reservation requests may be routed to overflow facilities only after all the available rooms in chain properties (within a geographic area) have been booked.

A **non-affiliate reservation network** is a subscription system designed to connect independent or non-chain properties. Non-affiliate reservation networks enable independent hotel operators to enjoy many of the same benefits as chain-affiliated operators. Like an affiliate reservation network, a non-affiliate network usually assumes responsibility for advertising its service. Examples of non-affiliate reservation networks are Leading Hotels of the World, Preferred Hotels, and Distinguished Hotels. In many cases, these non-affiliate networks accept only a limited number of hotels in any geographical area to keep the value of their service high to the participating members.

A central reservations office (CRO) typically deals directly with the public by means of a toll-free telephone number. Most large lodging chains support two or more reservation centers, with calls being directed to the center nearest the caller. Reservation centers often operate 24 hours per day, most days of the year. At peak times, reservation centers have a large number of agents on duty at the same time.

Central reservations offices typically exchange room availability information with member properties and communicate reservation transactions as they occur. This is done through a terminal at the member hotel. More advanced central reservation systems connect the computer at the central reservations office with the computer at the member hotel. In this way, reservations information is transmitted immediately from the central reservations office to the hotel. Rapid-access reservation systems ensure that both the hotel and the central reservations office have accurate, up-to-date information on room availability. They also eliminate the need for reservations personnel to periodically update reservations data. Some central reservation systems also permit central reservations agents to transfer telephone calls directly to destination properties after a reservation record has been created.

Central reservation systems normally provide participating properties with the communications equipment necessary for handling reservation transactions. Communication equipment may take the form of a personal computer, a computer terminal, a teletype or telex machine, a facsimile machine, or TDD. The central reservation system typically charges a fee to participating hotels for the services and support equipment it supplies. Hotels may pay a flat fee for the communication equipment and an additional fee for each reservation transaction they receive through the system. Alternatively, some central reservation systems charge a flat percentage of room revenue to cover all CRO operational expenses. In turn, each property provides accurate and current room availability data to the central reservations office. Without such data, the central reservations office cannot effectively process reservation requests.

Affiliate and non-affiliate central reservation systems often provide a variety of services in addition to managing reservations processing and communications. A central reservation system may also serve as an inter-property communications network, an accounting transfer system, or a destination information center. For instance, a central reservation system is used as an accounting transfer system when a chain hotel communicates operating data to company headquarters for processing. When a central reservation system communicates reports on local weather, special events, and seasonal room rates, it serves as a destination information center.

Global Distribution Systems

Most modern hotel central reservation systems, whether they be an affiliate or a non-affiliate reservation network, connect with one of the **global distribution systems (GDS).** The largest and best known GDSs include SABRE, Galileo International, Amadeus, and WorldSpan. Each GDS is owned by an airline or consortium of airlines. GDSs provide worldwide distribution of hotel reservation information and allow selling of hotel reservations around the world.

This is usually accomplished by connecting the hotel company reservation system with an airline reservation system. Most travel agents around the world have terminals connected to one of the many airline reservation systems to book airline travel. By having hotel accommodations and automobile rentals available in the computer system at the same time, most airline systems provide single source access to most of the travel agent's selling requirements. In one transaction, a travel agent can sell an airline ticket, hotel room, and car rental.

Until recently, travel agents were reluctant to book hotel rooms through GDSs, because room availability and rates were not always accurate, and the confirmation process to the hotel was not always foolproof. Within the past few years, hotel companies have linked their central reservation systems to GDSs, which allows travel agents to look directly into hotel systems for availability and rates. Confirmations come from the hotel companies' systems, eliminating the concern about the inaccuracy of data or the unreliability of the confirmation process.

Since most airlines have leisure travel departments, airline reservations agents can also sell hotel rooms. With over 200,000 terminals around the world, GDSs have become a powerful force in hotel reservations. The volume continues to grow as more travel agents around the world begin to use these computer terminals.

Intersell Agencies

An intersell agency is a central reservation system that contracts to handle reservations for more than one product line. Intersell agencies typically handle reservation services for airline companies, car rental companies, and hotel properties—a "one call does it all" type of approach. Although intersell agencies typically channel room reservation requests to a hotel central reservation system, they may also communicate directly with a destination hotel. The fact that a hotel participates in an intersell arrangement does not preclude its participation in another form of central reservation system.

Property Direct

Hotels handle many of their reservation transactions directly. Depending on the volume of direct customer contact, a hotel may have a reservations department aside from the front desk. This arrangement is common in hotels of 250 rooms or more. A reservations department handles all direct requests for accommodations, monitors any communication links with central reservation systems and intersell agencies, and maintains updated room availability status information. Property direct reservation requests can reach a hotel in several ways:

Exhibit 4 Property Direct Reservations—FAX

Holiday Inn
CHESAPEAKE
FAX #: 804-523-0683

FAX YOUR REQUEST FOR RESERVATIONS
TO THE
LEAN, GREEN RESERVATION MACHINE
AT THE
HOLIDAY INN CHESAPEAKE

ROOM CODES

A. Standard Room (Two Double Beds)
B. Standard Room (Non-Smoking)
C. King Leisure Room (One King Bed)
D. King Leisure Room (Non-Smoking)
E. King Leisure Room (Handicap Room/1st Floor Only)
F. King Executive Room
G. King Executive Room (Non-Smoking)
H. King Parlor (Two-Room Suite)
I. King Parlor (Non-Smoking)

TODAY'S DATE ____________ TIME ______
COMPANY NAME OR GROUP ____________
CORPORATE # (If Applicable) ____________
ADDRESS ____________
CITY/ST./ZIP ____________
TELEPHONE & EXTENSION ____________
FAX # ____________

NAME ____________
ARRIVE ______ DEPART ______ ROOM CODE ______
Guarantee to Company ______ 6PM Hold ______
By Credit Card # ____________
Guest Pays Own Bill ____________
*Direct Bill to Company ______ Rm & Tax Only
Rm/Tax & Meals ______ All Charges ______
Comments ____________

NAME ____________
ARRIVE ______ DEPART ______ ROOM CODE ______
Guarantee to Company ______ 6PM Hold ______
By Credit Card # ____________
Guest Pays Own Bill ____________
*Direct Bill to Company ______ Rm & Tax Only
Rm/Tax & Meals ______ All Charges ______
Comments ____________

REQUESTS FOR RESERVATIONS RECEIVED BY FAX ARE SUBJECT TO ROOM AVAILABILITY. WE WILL CONTACT YOU WITHIN ONE HOUR WITH-CONFIRMATION NUMBER OR ALTERNATE ROOM TYPE/LOCATION CHOICES.

*Direct Billing arranged with approved credit application.

This faxable reservation form was developed by the Holiday Inn at Chesapeake, Virginia. The form is distributed to major clients who book multiple reservations—a type of reservation that can be very time consuming to place over the telephone.

- *Telephone:* Prospective guests may telephone the hotel directly. This is the most common method of direct reservation communications.
- *Mail:* Written requests for reservations are common for group, tour, and convention business. Generally, mail requests are sent directly to the reservations department of the destination property.
- *Property-to-property:* Chain hotel properties typically encourage guests to plan their next hotel stay while in an affiliated property by offering direct communication between properties. This approach can significantly increase the overall number of reservations handled among affiliated properties.
- *Telex, cable, fax, e-mail, and other:* Telex is often used to communicate international reservation requests. Cable, fax, and other methods of communication account for a small proportion of total reservation transactions (see Exhibit 4). Another option involves communicating reservations through TDD equipment. This equipment is a specially designed teletype machine that allows people with hearing disabilities to communicate by telephone.

Reservations Through the Internet

Many airlines, hotel companies, and car rental firms offer online reservation services through their Internet sites (see Exhibits 5 and 6). This enables travelers from many different market segments to use their personal computers to book flights, reserve hotel rooms, and select rental cars. Vacation travelers, business travelers, corporate travel offices, international visitors—all are able to use the World Wide Web to arrange for their own travel and accommodation needs. The variety of potential guests accessing Internet sites to place reservations has prompted travel and hospitality companies to develop simple, user-friendly reservation procedures.

Large and small hotels alike have a presence on the Internet. Chains often have a web site focusing first on the brand and its features, then on the individual properties. Most chain Internet sites allow visitors to the site to book reservations. Independent hotels are also experimenting with web sites. While they may not be as sophisticated as chain sites, usually due to the cost of operating such sites, they normally provide similar information and allow visitors to make reservations, if only by e-mail.

Exhibit 7 presents a series of screens that walk prospective guests through the process of reserving rooms at the Internet site of the Holiday Inn hotel chain. In this particular reservation process, users first identify the area of the world relevant to their travel needs and then narrow down their destination, first by country and then by city. The city screen provides a listing and description of hotels. After selecting a hotel, users input the necessary reservation information. They can guarantee their reservations by providing personal or corporate credit card data.

The degree of privacy and security of financial transactions over the Internet has prompted concern, and, in many cases, this concern has limited the volume of Internet commerce. Security procedures exist today and will become even more sophisticated in the future. When users access online reservation systems, web browsers generally provide a security alert.

In addition to providing a user-friendly reservations process and securing transactions, online systems also perform important marketing functions for the hospitality company. Reservation features of many Internet sites enable users to access detailed pictures of individual hotels. Some enable users to download multimedia presentations of the features and benefits of the hotel chain and of individual hotels—complete with a "walk through" of the property and a detailed look inside the various rooms and services offered.

Group Reservations

Group reservations can involve a variety of contacts: guests, meeting planners, convention and visitor bureaus, tour operators, and travel agents. Group reservations typically involve intermediary agents and require special care. Usually, when a group selects a hotel, its representative deals with the hotel's sales or reservations department. If sufficient accommodations are available, an agreed-upon number of guestrooms, called a **block,** is set aside for the group's members. Group members may be given a special reservation identification code or reservation card to use to

Exhibit 5 TravelWeb

INFO DEALS NEW RESOURCES FEEDBACK

SEARCH THE HOTEL DATABASE! BROWSE THE LIST OF HOTEL CHAINS BROWSE THE LIST OF INDEPENDENT HOTELS

SEARCH THE HOTEL DATABASE

Enter Your Travel Destination:

City: [ ]
State or Province: All
Country: All
Zip or Postal Code: [ ]
Search: ◉ All hotels ○ Only hotels that accept on-line reservations.
Sort Results By: ◉ Random Order ○ Alphabetical Order

Start Search Clear All Fields

For a more specific search, complete the following fields. Otherwise, press START SEARCH above.

Enter the Hotel Property Name: [ ]
Your Favorite Hotel Chain: All
Room Price Range: All

Property Features and Amenities Search
Note: Select REQUIRED hotel amenities:

☐ 24 Hour Front Desk	☐ AM/FM Alarm Clock	☐ Babysitting/Child Services
☐ Bar/Lounge	☐ Barber/Beauty Shop	☐ Beach
☐ Business Center	☐ Casino	☐ Coffee Maker in Room
☐ Concierge	☐ Express Checkout	☐ Fishing
☐ Fitness Center or Spa	☐ Free Local Telephone Calls	☐ Free Newspaper
☐ Free Parking	☐ Golf	☐ Hairdryer in Room
☐ Handicapped Rooms/Facilities	☐ Laundry/Valet Services	☐ Meeting/Banquet Facilities
☐ Mini Bar	☐ Modem Lines in Room	☐ No Smoking Rooms/Facilities
☐ Pets Allowed	☐ Pool	☐ RV or Truck Parking
☐ Restaurant	☐ Room Service	☐ Safe Deposit Box
☐ Shops/Commercial Services	☐ Skiing	☐ Television with Cable
☐ Tennis	☐ VIP Rooms/Services	

Start Search Clear All Fields

TravelWeb's Internet booking service (at http://www.travelweb.com) enables travelers to directly access hotel's central reservations systems to check room availability and make online credit card guaranteed reservations. Other features on the site include airline flight reservations, hotel photos, maps, weather, and special discount programs.

Exhibit 6 Travelocity

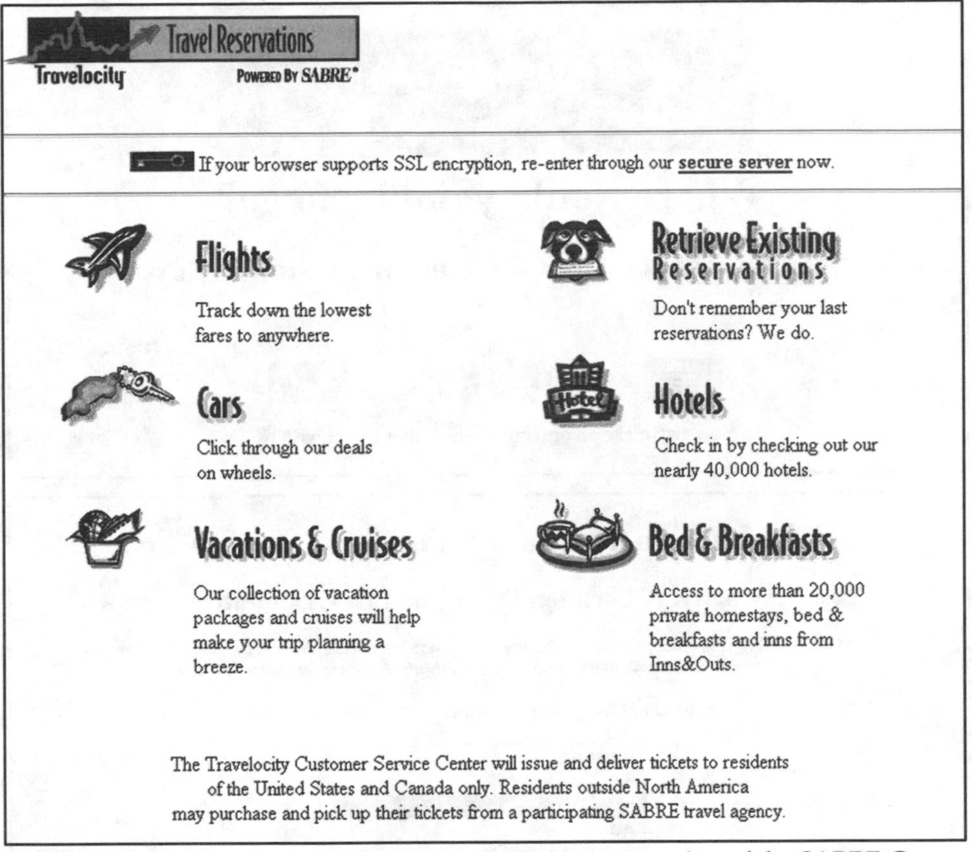

Travelocity (http://www.travelocity.com) is the Internet extension of the SABRE Group, Inc., an airline reservation system providing a global distribution system for hotels, car rental companies, bed and breakfast operations, and cruise lines.

reserve rooms within the group's assigned block. Reservations received from group members are applied against the rooms held in the group's block, thereby reducing the number of rooms available within the block. Rooms reserved for specific guests are referred to as **booked.** As group members reserve rooms, the room statuses change from *blocked* to *booked.* Normally, the hotel will establish progress chart dates to evaluate the progress of conversions from blocked to booked rooms. Unreserved rooms in the block may be released to the available room inventory at a predetermined date. This time frame is usually referred to as the group reservations **cut-off date.** Typically, the cut-off date is clearly stated in the contract the group or group's representative signs with the hotel. The hotel may honor reservation requests received after the cut-off date so long as rooms are available.

Although group reservation procedures appear simple, a number of potential problems may develop. The following sections consider possible solutions to some of these problems.

Exhibit 7 Holiday Inn—Internet Reservation Screens

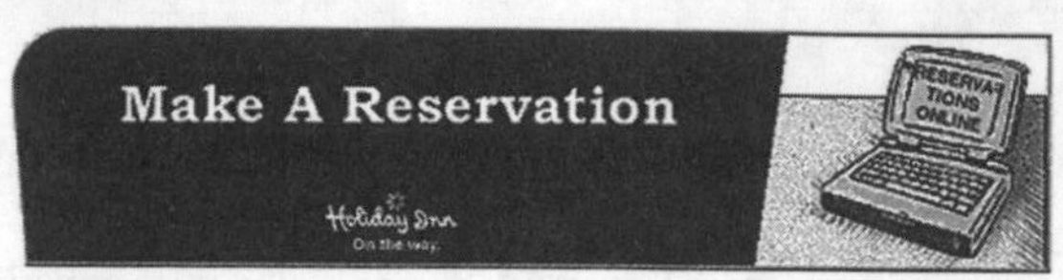

Where would you like to go?

Select a location from the flags or the links below:

You may make an unsecure reservation if you wish to.

Which Country Would You Like To Go To?

You May Select A Location From The List Of Countries Below

Find your Holiday Inn hotel by choosing the city you wish to visit, the highway on your travel route, or the attraction you wish to stay near *(usually only one hotel per attraction is listed)*.

• Select by City Select by Highway Select by Attraction

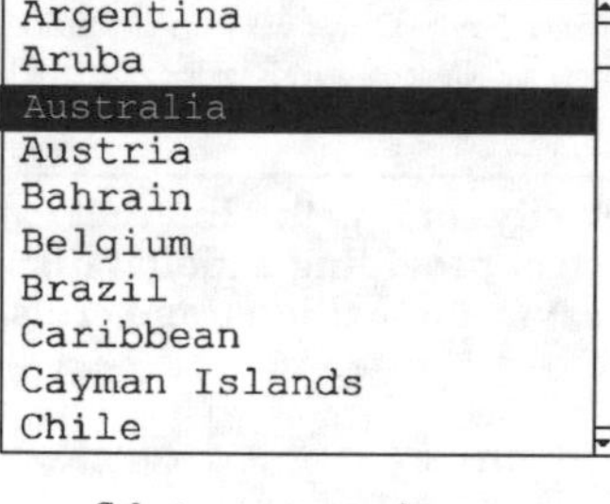

Select a country and press :

SEARCH COUNTRY

Holiday Inn's Reservation System can be found at their web site (http://www.holiday-inn.com).

Creating a Group Block. Group business is often highly desired by hotels. Yet, creating and controlling a group block has its pitfalls. When handling group blocks, the reservations manager should be aware of the following situations that can come into play.

- Group business demands that a contract be drawn up that specifies the exact number of rooms required and the quoted rates. The contract must also specify

Exhibit 7 *(continued)*

We make your trip easy.

[AUSTRALIA]

Choose a City you would like to visit:

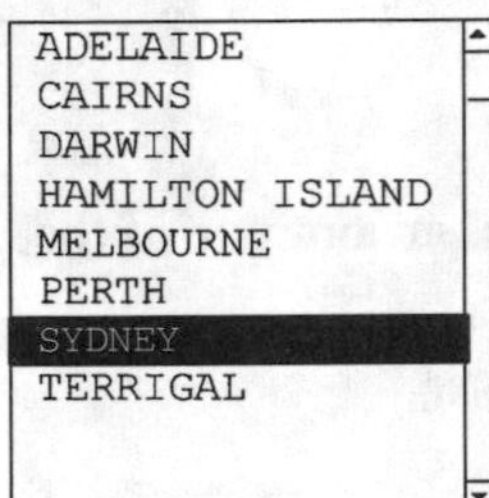

Search for hotels | Reset

Your Hotel Selections

We have 2 hotel(s) in the area you have selected:

SYDNEY-COOGEE BEACH, AUSTRALIA

```
Address                  -    242 ARDEN ST
                              SYDNEY COOGEE
                              AUSTRALIA
                              2034
Phone No                 -    61-2-315-7600
Fax No                   -    61-2-315-9100
```

Features of this hotel:

- **Whirlpool**
- **Suites Available**
- **Near A Beach**

```
Earliest check-in time -    2 PM
Check-out time         -    NOON
Nearest downtown       -    DOWNTOWN SYDNEY CBD
Distance from downtown -    9 MI
Nearest airport        -    SYDNEY INTL AIRPORT
Distance from airport  -    6 MI
```

Check Availability

(continued)

Exhibit 7 *(continued)*

What Are Your Availability Requirements?

SYDNEY-COOGEE BEACH, AUSTRALIA

Arrival date: [December ▾] [11 ▾]

(Only 50 weeks in advance booking is allowed)

Number of nights: ● 1 2 3 4 5 6 7 8 9

Number of rooms: ● 1 2 3 4

Number of adults: ● 1 2 3 4 5 6 7 8 9 10

Room Preference: ● Nonsmoking
Smoking

You may optionally enter a Priority Club number and one of the following two:

(Valid ID will be required at time of check-in)

Priority Club Membership Number [ ]

Worldwide Corporate Account Number [ ]

Alumni Mature Traveler Program [ ]

[Check Availability] [Reset]

Book Your Room Online

Booking Information

```
Hotel Selected        : SYDNEY-COOGEE BEACH,AUSTRALIA
Book from             : December  11
Number of Days        : 1
Room Preference       : Nonsmoking
Number of rooms       : 1
Number of adults      : 1
```

Rate and Availability Details

Rate is quoted for 1 person in DOLLAR (AUSTRALIA) per room no tax included.

Available Room Types:

Type of Room	Arrival Rate
● KNG LEISURE	215.00
2 DBL BEDS	215.00
2BD POOLSIDE	265.00
2BD VIEW	265.00

Extra person(s) charge: 35.00 DOLLAR (AUSTRALIA) for each adult over 2 person(s).
Persons 19 and under stay free.
Cancellation Policy: Must be cancelled prior to 6pm hotel time on December 11 or your credit card will be billed for 1 night.

Exhibit 7 *(continued)*

Please enter the following information :

First Name :

Last Name :

Address(Apt/Home/Street):

City :

District/State/Province :

Zip/Postal Code :

Country :

Phone Number :

Please choose Guarantee Method:

Guarantee to Travel Agency

Travel Agency IATA/ARC Number :

- American Express
- Master Card
- Carte Blanche
- Air Canada
- Visa
- Diners Club
- Discover
- JCB Card

Credit card # :

Expiration date : /

To make the Booking click =========> Book

To clear what you entered click ===> Reset

You can also call **1-800-HOLIDAY** if you are calling from the US, Canada, Puerto Rico or the US Virgin Islands. Elsewhere, call your nearest Holiday Inn Reservation Office.

the main group arrival and departure dates, any special considerations such as suites or complimentary rooms, and the group and individual billing arrangements. The contract should also note the group cut-off date for room availability.

- The reservations manager should verify the total number of rooms required for the group against what is available in the hotel. In automated hotels, the sales department often has access to a front office computer terminal to verify general availability before booking the group. However, the group block should always be verified by the reservations manager to be sure the system inventory is up-to-the-minute before confirming the block to the group leader.

If the group will take away rooms from transient (non-group) business, the reservations manager should notify the sales or general manager of the possible effect. This is called **non-group displacement.** Determining displacement is important, because the hotel may block rooms for group guests that it would normally sell to non-group guests, often at a higher rate. In addition, frequent guests of the hotel may have to be turned away and disappointed when a group takes these rooms.

- Before blocking the rooms, the reservations manager should check the group's history with the hotel, if available. For example, if the group requests a 50-room block and the record shows the group only picked up 40 rooms the year before, the reservations manager may wish to confer with the sales manager before finalizing the block. Reducing a block based on the group's history is called a **wash down** or a **wash.** If the group does not have a history at the hotel, it is sometimes possible to check with the hotel that last accommodated the group. By following these steps, the reservations manager helps control room inventories and ensures that as many rooms are available for sale as possible.

Conventions and Conferences. Problems can occur during a convention or conference if a close working relationship is not established between the hotel's sales staff and the group's meeting planner. If good communication and a spirit of cooperation are established early on, many problems can be avoided. Suggestions for hotels dealing with convention groups include:

- Know the convention group's profile, including its cancellation, no-show, and last-minute reservation history.
- Review all relevant hotel reservation policies with the convention planner.
- Be sure reservations agents are aware the convention has been scheduled.
- Produce regularly scheduled reports to update the status of the convention block.
- Generate an up-to-date list of registrants at regular intervals.
- Immediately correct any errors found by the convention planner.
- Confirm reservations from attendees as soon as possible.
- When group members cancel reservations properly, return the rooms to the group's block and inform the convention planner.
- Distribute the final rooming list to the convention planner and all hotel staff involved with the convention.

Convention and Visitor Bureaus. Large conventions sometimes require the use of rooms at more than one hotel to accommodate all the convention attendees. When conventions take many rooms at many hotels in a city, they are often called citywide conventions. Frequently, room requirements at several hotels are coordinated by a separate housing or convention bureau. Each hotel must determine the number and type of available rooms it is willing to set aside for convention use.

The objective of the bureau is to accommodate all attendees by coordinating hotel availabilities with reservation requests. The convention and visitor bureau will communicate reservation requests to the hotels involved on a daily basis. In return, each hotel informs the bureau of any requests or cancellations communicated directly to the property. Through such an exchange of information, the bureau should be able to help each hotel effectively manage its convention block.

Tour Groups. Tour groups are groups of people who have had their accommodations, transportation, and related travel activities arranged for them. Hotels should be especially careful to research the reliability and past performance of tour operators and travel agents. Once acquainted with a tour operator's history, reservations agents may feel more secure when blocking and booking reservations for a tour group. Suggestions for dealing with tour group reservations include:

- Specify the number and types of rooms to be held in a group block, including rooms for drivers and guides.
- Clearly state a cut-off date, after which unused rooms in the block will be released for other hotel use.
- State a date by which the organizer will provide a rooming list.
- Monitor the amount and due date of advance deposits required.
- Note on the reservation record any services and amenities the property will provide as part of the group package.
- Include the name and telephone number of the tour group's representative or agent.

Reservation Availability

When a property receives a reservation inquiry, it is important to compare the data with previously processed reservations. Processing a reservation request results in one of several responses. A property can:

- Accept the reservation as requested.
- Suggest alternative room types, dates, and/or rates.
- Suggest an alternative hotel.

In any reservation system, it is necessary to closely monitor the number of reservations in order to control **overbooking.** A hotel should use care when accepting reservations beyond the point where its rooms are expected to be occupied. As stated earlier, some states have laws concerning guests with guaranteed reservations who do not receive rooms when they arrive at a hotel.

Comparing historical reservation volumes against actual arrivals can produce an overbooking factor to serve as a booking guideline. Depending on the property's no-show reservation history, management may allow the reservations manager to overbook. Overbooking is a strategy aimed at helping the hotel to achieve 100 percent occupancy by hedging against no-shows, cancellations, and unexpected early

Exhibit 8 Reservations Control Book—Manual System

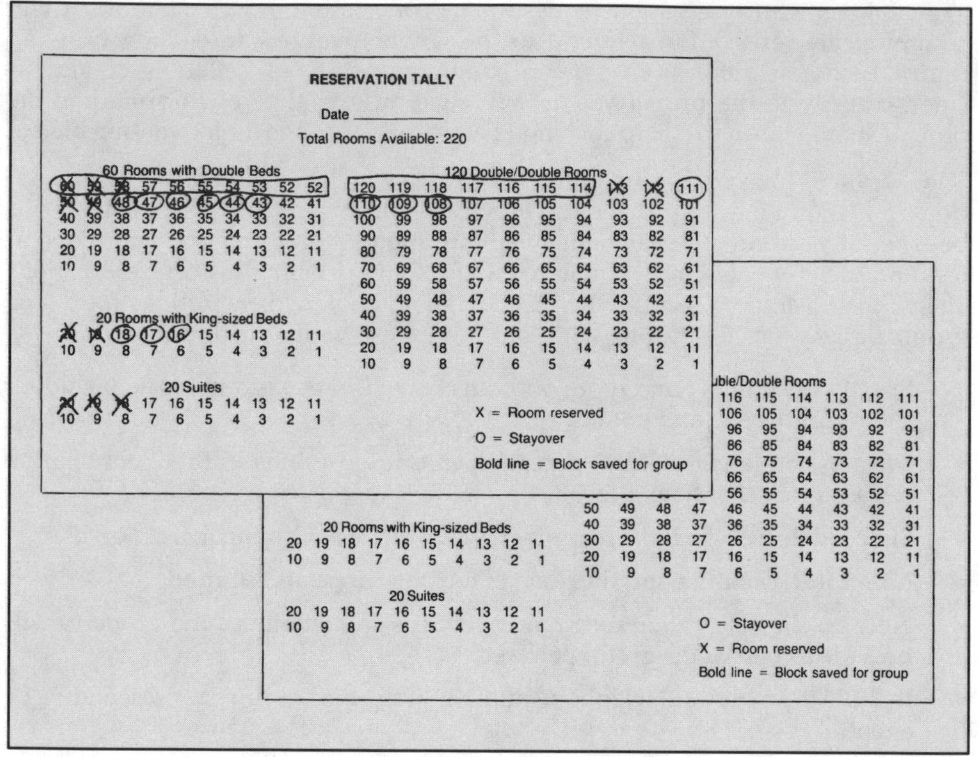

departures. Experienced reservations managers are able to forecast cancellations and no-shows with good accuracy. When booking a hotel slightly beyond its available room capacity, management attempts to ensure that as many rooms as possible are occupied.

Overbooking should be approached cautiously. If a reservations manager books too many rooms, guests with confirmed reservations may have to be turned away. This creates poor guest relations and discourages repeat business. To properly control overbooking, hotels must monitor room availability by coordinating booking, blocking, and cancellation information.

Control Book

A **reservations control book** is usually a standard three-ring, loose-leaf binder with a tally page assigned to each day of the year. Control books are used in non-automated hotels. Exhibit 8 shows two sample tally sheets from a reservations control book. On each page, the hotel's rooms and suites are divided into categories; each room or suite is assigned a number. For instance, if a hotel has 20 kings (that is, 20 rooms with king-size beds), the numbers 1 through 20 will be listed under that room category. When a reservation is received, an *X* is placed over the highest unmarked number for the requested room category on the expected arrival date. If the reservation is for more than one night, subsequent days are circled rather than *X*'d on the following pages. Circles denote stayover guests, rather than new guests expected to arrive on the day in question. A stayover guest is a guest who arrived at least one day before the day being examined.

Exhibit 8 shows that, within the category of 20 king-sized beds, two arrivals and 3 stayovers (that is, five occupied rooms) are expected, and fifteen rooms remain available for the date under scrutiny. For the 60 double-bed rooms, 2 individual arrivals, 3 group arrivals (from the 10 blocked), 6 stayovers, and 42 available rooms are expected. Some reservation tally sheets also track reservation activity by the number of guests as well as the number of rooms. Tracking guest data allows for the production of multiple occupancy statistics reports which detail the number of rooms occupied by more than one guest. These statistics are important sales mix data which can be useful in planning and forecasting the hotel's volume of business.

The hotel must update its reservations control book as cancellations or changes in reservations are received. A property may make an initial control book entry in pencil so that it can be easily changed; if initial entries are made in pen, a different color pen should be used to record reservation cancellations or changes. The use of a second color will help the hotel maintain a history of changes in control book transactions. Often, group blocks are noted in a different color to identify inventory separately from that available to the general public.

Computerized Systems

An in-house computerized reservation system can keep close track of reservations. Computer systems can tightly control room availability data and automatically generate many reservation-related reports (see Exhibit 9). Exhibit 10, for example, presents a daily expected arrival, stayover, and departure report. It shows that for January 19, 19 arrivals, 83 stayovers, and 4 departures are expected. In addition, this report projects estimated room revenue based on reported reservation information. Computerized systems can also generate reports summarizing reservations by room type, guest profile, and many other characteristics. The biggest advantage of a computerized reservation system is the improved accuracy of room availability information. As reservations agents input reservations and reservation modifications or cancellations into the system, the inventory of available rooms is immediately updated. In addition, if the front desk is part of the computer system, any front desk transaction involving no-shows, early departures, or walk-ins will immediately update the computer's room availability.

Exhibit 11 shows the screen of a guestroom control log from a Windows-based hotel sales program. For each day of the week, the screen shows the total number of rooms still available for sale, as well as the number of rooms allocated to definite and tentative group bookings and the number of rooms protected for front office sales to transient business. Room sales are coordinated in real time as salespeople, reservationists, and the front office manager have instant access to the most current information. The booking evaluator, also shown in Exhibit 11, enables everyone to assess the impact of individual group bookings on budgeted targets for rooms sales, average rate, and revenue per available room.

Exhibit 9 Room Availability—Computerized System

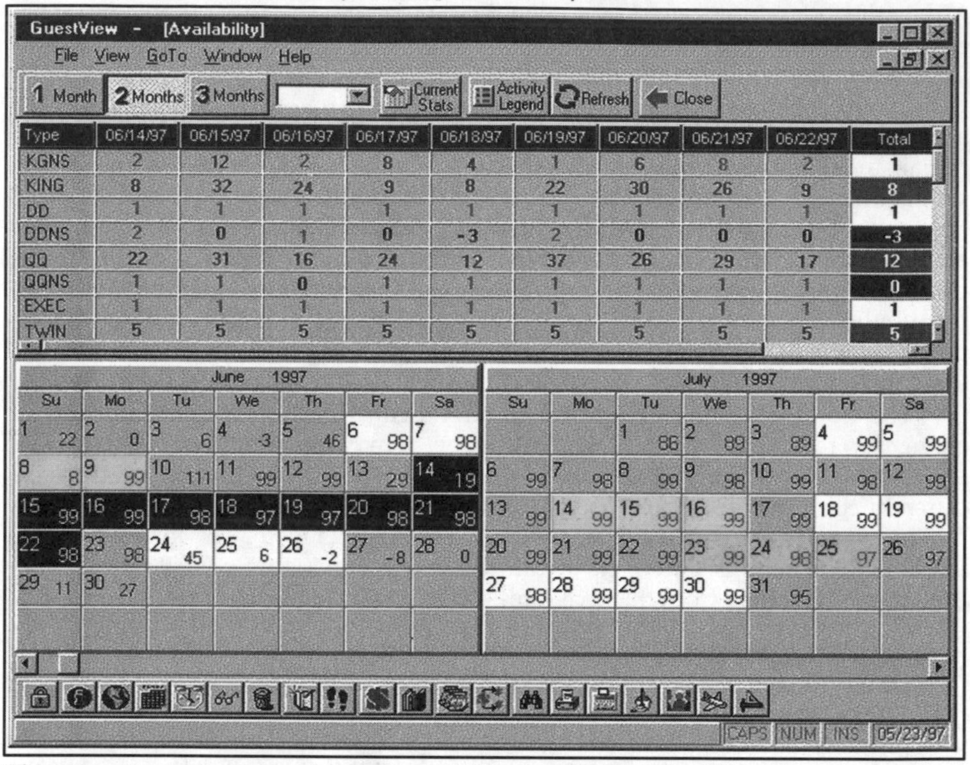

GuestView - [Availability]

File View GoTo Window Help

1 Month | 2 Months | 3 Months | Current Stats | Activity Legend | Refresh | Close

Type	06/14/97	06/15/97	06/16/97	06/17/97	06/18/97	06/19/97	06/20/97	06/21/97	06/22/97	Total
KGNS	2	12	2	8	4	1	6	8	2	1
KING	8	32	24	9	8	22	30	26	9	8
DD	1	1	1	1	1	1	1	1	1	1
DDNS	2	0	1	0	-3	2	0	0	0	-3
QQ	22	31	16	24	12	37	26	29	17	12
QQNS	1	1	0	1	1	1	1	1	1	0
EXEC	1	1	1	1	1	1	1	1	1	1
TWIN	5	5	5	5	5	5	5	5	5	5

June 1997

Su	Mo	Tu	We	Th	Fr	Sa
1 22	2 0	3 6	4 -3	5 46	6 98	7 98
8 8	9 99	10 111	11 99	12 99	13 29	14 19
15 99	16 99	17 98	18 97	19 97	20 98	21 98
22 98	23 98	24 45	25 6	26 -2	27 -8	28 0
29 11	30 27					

July 1997

Su	Mo	Tu	We	Th	Fr	Sa
		1 86	2 89	3 89	4 99	5 99
6 99	7 98	8 99	9 98	10 99	11 98	12 99
13 99	14 99	15 99	16 99	17 99	18 99	19 99
20 99	21 99	22 99	23 99	24 98	25 97	26 97
27 98	28 99	29 99	30 99	31 95		

CAPS NUM INS 05/23/97

This computer screen shows room availability information from *GuestView,* a property management system offered by Anasazi, Inc., Phoenix, Arizona. The company's Internet site (http://www.anasazi.com) provides additional screen selections from its system.

Exhibit 10 Daily Arrival, Stayover, Departure Report

ARRIVALS, STAYOVERS, DEPARTURES FOR KELLOGG CENTER
PAGE 001
01/19/XX 15:03

DATE	ARRIVE	STAYON	DEPART	GUESTS	SOLD	UNSOLD	REVENUE
01/19	19	83	4	135	102	43	5,185.00
01/20	34	57	45	131	91	54	4,604.00
01/21	37	55	36	130	92	53	4,495.50
01/22	15	6	86	29	21	124	1,116.00
01/23	12	14	7	36	26	127	1,252.00

Exhibit 11 Guest Rooms Control Log

Guest Rooms Control Log

Sunday, October 12, 19XX

8 Bookings			19XX	Sun 10/12	Mon 10/13	Tue 10/14	Wed 10/15	Thu 10/16	Fri 10/17	Sat 10/18	Sun 10/19
Total Available				210	25	-35	75	52	300	300	340
Grp Definite				130	190	150	40	45	15	15	0
Grp Tentative				0	0	0	0	68	75	75	0
Trans Protected				75	200	300	300	250	25	25	75
MAR				100	110	110	105	90	85	90	100
Court Report	D	IS	89	50	75	55					
Bose Corp.	D	CA	45	50	75	55					
UNH Alumni	D	CA	133	30	40	30	30	30			
U.S. Airforce	D	CA	92			10	10	15	15	15	
Int'l Dental	T	EMF	34					23	30	30	
IDS Board	T	DH	83					45	45	45	
Reader's Digest	P	CA	99						50	122	
Delphi User Grp	P	CA	113							50	50

Booking Evaluator

October, 19XX   Post As: Bose Speakers Audio Show

	Rooms	Avg. Rate	Revenue	Revenue PAR
Budget:	14280	102.00	1,456,560.00	78.31
Without Booking:	14107	101.75	1,435,387.25	77.17
With Booking:	14290	103.25	1,475,442.50	79.32

Dates: October, 19XX

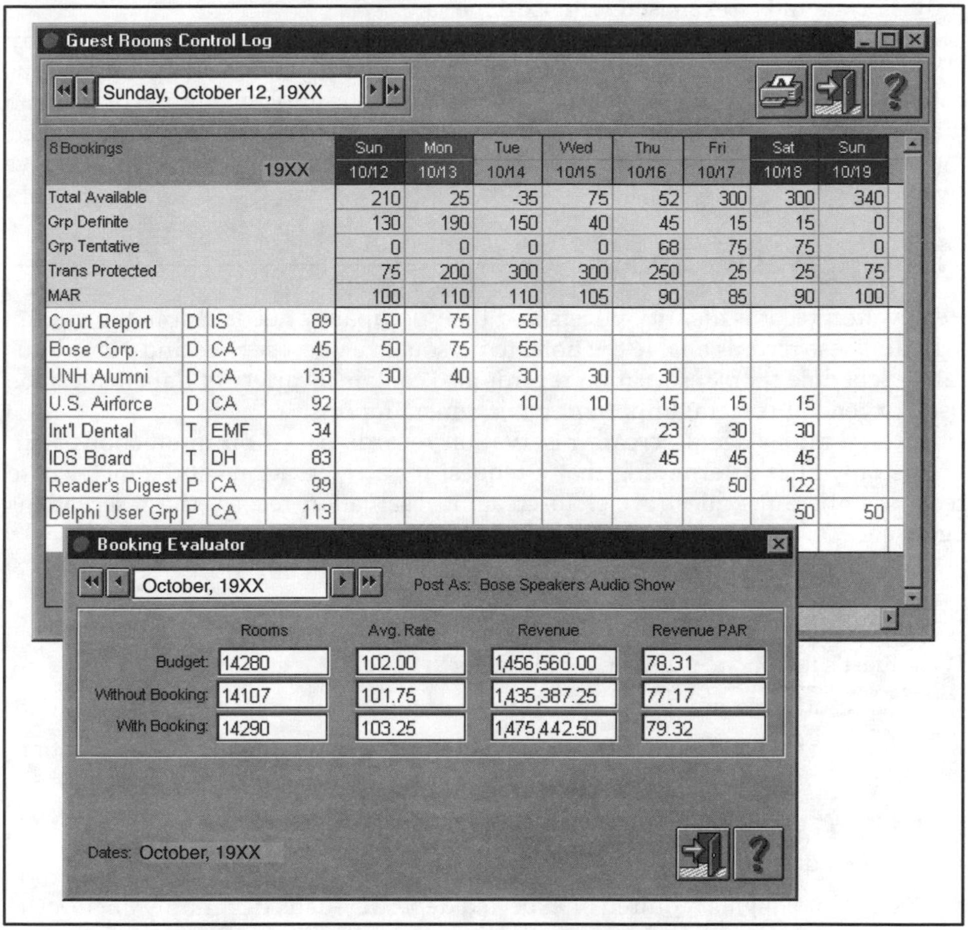

Source: Delphi 7/Newmarket Software Systems, Inc., Durham, New Hampshire. For more information, visit the company's Internet site at http://www.newsoft.com.

Once all rooms in a specific category are sold, the computer can be programmed to refuse any further reservations in that category. When checking availability in a closed category, a reservations agent may receive a message such as the following displayed on the screen: *The category of rooms requested is not available.* Some computerized reservation systems are programmed to automatically suggest alternative room types or rates, or even other nearby hotel properties. Computers can be programmed to itemize room availability for future periods. Systems may also display open, closed, and special event dates for an extended period of time. *Open dates* refer to available room days, while *closed dates* depict full-house forecasts. *Special event dates* can be programmed to alert reservations agents that a convention or large group is expected to occupy the hotel either before, during, or immediately following a caller's requested day of arrival. In addition, many hotel computer systems have a management override feature which enables overbooking. This override provision should be exercised with extreme care.

Hotel computer systems store reservation records electronically, thereby allowing the creation of waiting lists for high-demand periods. This feature contributes to the processing of group reservations and the implementation of revenue management strategies. The future time frame for tracking reservations is called the reservation horizon and most computer-based systems have horizons of two to five years.

The Reservation Record

Reservation records identify guests and their occupancy needs before the guests' arrival. These records enable the hotel to personalize guest service and more accurately schedule staff. Reservation records also contain a variety of data that can be used to generate several important management reports.

Reservations agents create reservation records based on interactions with guests only after determining that a request for a reservation can be met. These records initiate the guest cycle. To create a reservation record, the reservations agent collects and enters such guest data as:

- Guest name (and group name, if applicable)
- Guest's home or billing address
- Guest's telephone number, including area code
- Name, address, and telephone number of the guest's company, if appropriate
- Name of and pertinent information about the person making the reservation, if not the guest
- Number of people in the party, and perhaps the ages of any children
- Arrival date and time
- Number of nights required or expected departure date, depending on how the system is programmed
- Reservation type (guaranteed, non-guaranteed)
- Special requirements (infant, disabled guest, or no-smoking accommodations)
- Additional information as needed (method of transportation, late arrival, flight number, room preference, and so forth)

If a guest plans to arrive after the hotel's normal reservation cancellation hour, the reservations agent should inform the guest of the property's policy for non-guaranteed reservations. Once the agent has recorded the necessary information, some hotels immediately assign the guest a reservation confirmation number. Confirmation number assignment provides both the guest and the reservations department with a unique reference to the reservation record.

In the case of a guaranteed reservation, the reservations agent may need to obtain additional information for the reservation record. Depending on the guest's method of guarantee, an agent may be required to obtain:

- *Credit card information:* This information consists of the credit card type, number, expiration date, and the cardholder's name. A cancellation bulletin, listing numbers of invalid and expired cards, or a computer verification service should be consulted to ensure the credit card is valid. Some computerized reservation systems are connected to a transaction processing service which allows them to automatically verify credit card information.
- *Prepayment or deposit information:* This information comes in the form of an agreement from the guest to submit a required deposit to the hotel before a specified date. A proposed advance deposit or prepayment guarantee should be closely monitored to ensure the correct amount is paid by the designated date; if it is not, the reservation may need to be canceled or reclassified as non-guaranteed.
- *Corporate or travel agency account information:* This information includes the name and address of the booking company, the name of the person making the reservation, and the client's corporate or travel agency account number (if previously assigned by the hotel). For efficiency, the hotel may provide reservations agents with an approved list of corporate and travel agency account numbers to expedite the verification process.

Reservations agents should review the important aspects of guaranteeing a reservation with the guest. Guests must be aware that their accommodations will be held until a specific time following their scheduled arrival. Guests must also know that if they fail to cancel the reservation before a specified time, they may forfeit the deposit or the hotel may levy a charge against the guarantee.

Individual properties and chains may differ with respect to quoting and confirming room rates during the creation of a reservation record. Although published rates may be subject to change without notice, a rate quoted and confirmed during the reservations process must be honored. Reservations agents should be aware of several factors when quoting rates during the reservation recording process, including:

- Supplementary charges for extra services or amenities.
- Minimum stay requirements in effect for the dates requested, if any.
- Special promotions in effect for the dates requested, if any.
- Applicable currency exchange rates, if quoting rates to an international guest.
- Applicable room tax percentages.
- Applicable service charges or gratuities.

Reservation Confirmation

A reservation confirmation means that the hotel acknowledged and verified a guest's room request and personal information by telephoning, faxing, telexing, or mailing a letter of confirmation. A written confirmation states the intent of both parties and confirms important points of agreement: names, dates, rate, type of accommodation, number of rooms, deposit required or received, and number of guests. *Confirmed reservations may be either guaranteed or non-guaranteed.*

Reservation departments normally generate a letter of confirmation on the day the reservation request is received. Information can be retrieved from the reservation record and manually or electronically entered onto a specially designed form. While there are probably as many formats for confirmation letters as there are hotels, confirmation letters generally include:

- Name and address of guest
- Date and time of arrival
- Room type and rate
- Length of stay
- Number of persons in party
- Reservation classification: guaranteed or non-guaranteed
- Reservation confirmation number
- Special requests, if any

Depending on the nature of the reservation, a letter of confirmation may also include a request for a deposit or prepayment, or an update of the original reservation detailing reconfirmation, modification, or cancellation.

For guests requesting accommodations and services covered by the Americans with Disabilities Act, the confirmation letter is an important channel of communication. It lets them know that their special needs are understood and the accommodations will be ready. Hotels will often hold the rooms that are specially equipped for disabled guests in a separate inventory category to control them better.

Confirmation/Cancellation Numbers

As part of the reservation confirmation process, central reservation systems as well as individual properties may assign a reservation **confirmation number**. A confirmation number helps assure a guest that a reservation record exists. It can be especially useful to a hotel in referencing a specific reservation record requiring modification or cancellation. Similarly, hotels may issue a reservation **cancellation number** to guests properly canceling a reservation.

Issuing a reservation cancellation number protects both the guest and the hotel. In the event of any future misunderstanding, the assignment of a reservation cancellation number can prove that the hotel received the cancellation. In the case of a canceled guaranteed reservation, a reservation cancellation number may relieve the guest of an obligation to pay any charges posted against the guarantee. Without a reservation cancellation number, a guest may have trouble disputing a no-show billing made to a credit card account. Cancellation numbers are not normally assigned to guests who cancel their reservation after the hotel's stated cancellation hour. These reservations are considered canceled outside the available time frame. If the canceled reservation is non-guaranteed, the guest is not obligated to pay the hotel.

Each hotel's reservation system typically uses unique methods of generating cancellation and confirmation numbers. These numbers can include portions of the guest's scheduled arrival date, the reservations agent's initials, a property code and other relevant information. For example, under one system, the cancellation number 36014MR563 represents these facts:

360	=	guest's scheduled date of arrival (from consecutively numbered days of the year)
14	=	property code number
MR	=	initials of the reservations agent issuing the cancellation number
563	=	consecutive numbering of all cancellation numbers issued in the current year

Calendar dates can be expressed in three digits when the days of the year are numbered consecutively from 001 through 365 (366 in a leap year). These are often referred to as *Julian dates.* For example, the number 360 in the example corresponds to December 26 in a non-leap year.

Procedures for issuing cancellation numbers may be part of an established agreement between the hotel and a credit card company relative to no-show billing. Cancellation numbers should be recorded in a log or in an electronic file. Confirmation numbers can be recorded in a similarly formatted log. Cross-referencing reservation cancellation numbers by scheduled date of arrival can also help agents perform other related front office functions. For example, the cancellation of a reservation necessitates updating the reservation reports that assist management in staffing and facility planning.

Reservation Maintenance

No matter how thorough or attentive an agent may be during the reservations process, there is simply no way to avoid an occasional reservation change or cancellation. This fact does not make the care and proficiency of a reservations agent any less important. An agent's efficiency at organizing and retrieving reservation records and related files is vital to the reservations process. If a person contacts the hotel to change a reservation, for example, the reservations agent must be able to quickly access the correct record, verify its contents, and process the modification. The agent must also be able to promptly re-file the reservation record and update pertinent reservation reports. Automated reservation systems simplify these tasks, especially in the areas of reservation recording, filing, retrieving, and modifying.

Modifying Non-Guaranteed Reservations

Guests often make non-guaranteed rather than guaranteed reservations when they expect to arrive at the property before the hotel's reservation cancellation hour. However, situations can arise that make it impossible for a guest to arrive on time. For example, airline flights may be delayed, departure may be later than expected, or weather conditions may slow traffic. When delays are apparent, experienced travelers often contact the hotel to change their reservations from non-guaranteed to guaranteed since they know that non-guaranteed reservations may be canceled at the hotel's reservation cancellation hour. Reservations agents processing reservation status changes must carefully adhere to hotel policies. Typically, an agent would:

1. Obtain the guest's name and access the correct non-guaranteed reservation record.
2. Obtain the guest's credit card type, number, and expiration date and the cardholder's name, and verify the validity of the credit card.
3. Assign the guest a new reservation confirmation number, if it is hotel policy.
4. Complete the change from non-guaranteed to guaranteed reservation status according to additional property procedures, if any.

Reservation Cancellation

A prospective guest does the hotel a service when he or she takes the time to cancel a reservation. A reservation cancellation informs the hotel that a previously reserved room is once again available, and helps the front office more effectively manage its rooms inventory. Hotels should make processing reservation cancellations easy and efficient. Reservation cancellations, like any guest service, require the reservations or front office staff to be as polite, courteous, and effective as possible.

Non-Guaranteed. To cancel a non-guaranteed reservation, the reservations agent should obtain the guest's name and address, number of reserved rooms, scheduled arrival and departure dates, and reservation confirmation number, if available. This information will ensure that the correct reservation is accessed and canceled. After recording the cancellation, the agent will assign a cancellation number and may ask the caller whether he or she would like to make an alternate reservation. Reservations agents must ensure that the correct reservation record is canceled.

Credit Card Guaranteed. Most credit card companies will support no-show billings only if the hotel issues cancellation numbers for properly canceled reservations. Reservations agents may follow a cancellation procedure for credit card guaranteed reservations that involves the following steps:

1. Obtain information from the guest to access the correct reservation record. Be sure to verify that it is the correct reservation record. This information includes the guest's name and address, number of rooms, scheduled arrival and departure dates, and the reservation confirmation number. After processing, the guest should be assigned a reservation cancellation number. The agent should explain that the cancellation number should be retained by the guest as proof of cancellation in the event of an erroneous credit card billing.
2. Mark the reservation record as canceled, properly initial and date it, and add the cancellation number to the reservation record. If the cancellation is made by someone other than the guest, the reservations agent should add the caller's name to the canceled reservation record.
3. Log the reservation cancellation number.
4. Update room availability, returning the reserved room back to general inventory.

5. File canceled reservation documentation for future reference per hotel policy. Non-automated hotels commonly keep the reservation record until the expected date of arrival just in case the reservation was canceled by mistake. If necessary, the canceled reservation is given to the front desk for reference and research. In automated hotels, canceled reservations are stored electronically until after the expected arrival date. Should the reservation be cancelled in error, the front desk can easily recall the reservation from the electronic file and update it to a current status.

Advance Deposit. Policies related to the cancellation of advance deposit reservations vary greatly among hotel companies. The reservations agent should treat advance deposit cancellations with as much care as any other form of reservation cancellation. Deposits are normally returned to guests who properly cancel reservations. While reservations agents must always exercise care when assigning and recording reservation cancellation numbers, it is especially important when an advance deposit is involved.

Other Guaranteed Reservations. The person contacting the hotel to cancel a corporate account or travel agency guaranteed reservation is likely to be a representative of the corporation or travel agency, not the traveler. It is important to enter the name of the person canceling the reservation on the reservation record. A reservation cancellation number should be issued and logged similar to the way a credit card guaranteed reservation number is handled. In addition, a letter documenting the cancellation should also be sent to the guest's corporate or travel agency sponsor.

Reservation Reports

An effective reservation system helps maximize room sales by accurately monitoring room availabilities and forecasting rooms revenue. Regardless of the degree of automation, the number and type of management reports available through a reservation system are functions of the hotel's needs and the system's capability and contents. Popular reservations management reports include:

- *Reservation transactions report:* This report summarizes daily reservations activity in terms of reservation record creation, modification, and cancellation. Other possible reports include specialized summaries such as cancellation reports, blocked room reports, and no-show reports.

- *Commission agent report:* Agents with contractual agreements may be owed commissions for business booked at the property. This report tracks the amounts the hotel owes to each agent.

- *Turnaway report (or refusal report):* This report tracks the number of reservation requests refused because rooms were not available for the requested dates. The turnaway report is especially helpful to properties operating near full occupancy or hotels considering expansion.

- *Revenue forecast report:* This report projects future revenue by multiplying predicted occupancies by applicable room rates. This information can be especially important for long-range planning and cash management strategies.

Expected Arrival and Departure Lists

Expected arrival and departure lists are prepared daily to indicate the number and names of guests expected to arrive, depart, or stay over. In a non-automated or semi-automated system, the reservations department manually develops expected arrival data from a reservations control book, wall chart, or reservation rack. Hotels with high reservation volumes often load a reservation rack with guest information covering the next several days.

Each afternoon, reservations personnel review the data for the next day's expected check-in guests. Once verified, reservations are assembled alphabetically and either held in the reservations department overnight or brought to the front desk. In a computerized system, a list of expected arrivals may be automatically displayed or printed in the reservations department or at the front desk. Front desk agents depend on having expected arrival information to facilitate the guest registration process. Similarly, expected departure information can be used to expedite guest account settlement and check-out. Expected departure lists also help the front desk staff identify guests who may be staying beyond their expected departure date but have not told the hotel (overstays). This can be very important, especially when the hotel expects high occupancies and has already reserved the room for an incoming guest.

Computers can also produce preprinted registration cards for guests arriving with reservations. Some hotels preregister special guests, such as VIPs or those staying in specially prepared rooms. Depending on the amount of information collected during the reservations process, a guest may only need to sign a pre-arrival form or submit their credit card for processing to complete the registration process. By securing comprehensive information during the reservations process, the hotel can help ensure a more efficient guest registration process.

Processing Deposits

Advance deposits for reservations should be processed by employees who do not have access to reservation records. Reservations personnel should not directly handle checks or cash; a separation of duties provides better security. The general manager's secretary or the hotel's general cashier are two possible candidates for independent reviewer. These employees should endorse deposit checks with the hotel stamp immediately after receiving them and record the following information in a deposits received log: check number, check amount, date received, guest name, arrival date, and confirmation number, if known. The log should then be sent to the reservations department. Each reservation record should be updated with the status of its deposit information. A transaction report should be prepared that verifies the deposit log balances with the total reservation deposits entered for the day.

Generally speaking, advance deposits received from guests should be processed with special care. Most hotels discourage guests from sending cash through the mail; checks are preferred, since they are considered more secure.

Reservations Histories

Front office management can develop an understanding of the hotel's reservations patterns by analyzing reservation information. The hotel's sales and marketing division can use reservation data to identify trends, review available products and services, and assess the impact of its marketing strategies. Reservation histories include statistics on all aspects of the reservations process, including the number of guests, occupied rooms, reservations (by source), no-shows, walk-ins, overstays, and understays (people who checked out before a stated departure date). *Overstays* differ from *stayovers* in that a stayover is simply a guest who *continues to occupy* a room between his or her day of arrival and expected departure date. Knowing overstay and understay percentages, for example, can help management devise a plan for accommodating walk-ins or guests who request reservations at the last minute. Histories are also very helpful to track individual groups. Knowing the group booking pattern, arrivals before the start of the group block and departures after the end of the group block, is important to know for future bookings. In addition, tracking group guests who depart before their expected departure date is vital to be sure the hotel stays full when the group returns.

Reservation Considerations

The topics covered in this section are not part of the typical reservations process. Nonetheless, it is important for the reservations agent to understand the legal implications of a reservation and be familiar with waiting lists, packages, group reservations, and potential errors in the reservations process.

Legal Implications

The reservation agreement between the hotel and the guest begins at the time of guest contact. This agreement may be oral or written. Confirming a reservation to a prospective guest in language which states that the guest will be accommodated on a particular date may constitute a contract binding the hotel to provide accommodations on that date. If the confirmation is in response to a reservation request from the prospective guest, it may bind the prospective guest to fulfill the reservation.

Waiting Lists

Occasionally, a reservation request must be denied because the hotel is fully booked. However, with enough lead time, interested guests may be put on a waiting list for the proposed date. Hotels experiencing high-volume reservations may satisfy excess demand through this technique. A waiting list might be developed and used according to these guidelines:

- Advise the guest that no rooms are currently available for the requested dates.
- Offer to take the guest's name and telephone number.
- Agree to notify the prospective guest immediately if a room becomes available due to a cancellation or change.
- Help the guest find alternative dates or accommodations if no rooms become available.

Having a waiting list, when properly implemented and managed, is a good business practice that helps foster an atmosphere of good service.

Packages

Many hotels and resorts offer packages to guests. Packages always include the guestroom, plus features such as meals, golf, tennis, sports lessons, limousine service, sight-seeing, or other activities in or near the property. Generally, hotels and resorts provide guests with some sort of discount for purchasing the package. Guests often consider packages a convenience and a bargain since they don't have to arrange to purchase items and activities separately.

Reservations personnel must be very familiar with all the packages a property offers. Before buying a package, guests will usually ask the reservations agent to explain the package in detail. Reservations agents must know the package's features and all related prices. For example, if a guest wishes to stay at a resort for four nights, and the resort only offers a three-night package, the reservations agent must know the price of an extra night's stay. Packages can be very effective for hotels and resorts, especially when they are well designed and properly sold by the hotel staff.

Potential Reservation Problems

Some steps of the reservations process are more susceptible to error than others. If reservations agents are aware of these trouble spots and know how to successfully deal with them, mistakes will be less likely. The following sections discuss some common reservation problems.

Errors in the Reservation Record. Unfortunately, there are many opportunities for a reservations agent to make an error when creating a reservation record. For example:

- A reservations agent may record the wrong arrival or departure date, misspell the guest's name, or mistakenly reverse first and last names. For example, *Troy Thomas* might be recorded as *Thomas Troy.*
- A reservations agent may mistake a caller making a reservation for the guest and enter the caller's name on the reservation record; the caller may also inadvertently give his or her name rather than the guest's name.

To avoid such problems, the reservations agent should verify the information entered on the reservation record by reciting the information back to the caller. In addition, quoting the hotel's cancellation policy is appropriate at this time to avoid any issue of no-show billing or non-return of deposits. This communication technique can be especially important to hotels catering to international travelers. An error which prevents access to a reservation record can be disastrous to a hotel-guest relationship.

Misunderstandings Due to Industry Jargon. Sometimes, reservations agents are so accustomed to using industry jargon when speaking with other staff members that they use it when speaking with guests. This can lead to problems. For example:

- A family with a *confirmed reservation* may arrive two hours after the cancellation hour only to find that the hotel has no rooms available; the family thought a confirmed reservation was the same as a *guaranteed reservation.*
- Two business travelers book a *double room,* anticipating two beds; they are displeased to learn their room has only *one double bed.*
- Parents wishing to have their children stay in a *connecting room* mistakenly request an *adjacent room.* At check-in, the parents find that the children's room is across the hall or next door with no direct connection.

To avoid such problems, reservations agents should make every effort to understand what the guest needs and to explain what various terms mean at their particular property. After accepting a reservation, agents should repeat and confirm the exact nature of reserved accommodations. This should be done in addition to stating the hotel's general reservations policies and procedures.

Miscommunication with External Reservation Systems. There are some unique possibilities for miscommunication between guests and reservations agents at central reservation systems. For example:

- A central reservation system serving several hotels in the same city may book the guest into the wrong hotel; for instance, a chain's airport rather than its mid-city property.
- A system that handles hotels in similarly named cities may book the guest into a hotel in the wrong city or state (for example, Charleston, West Virginia, instead of Charleston, South Carolina; Pasadena, California, instead of Pasadena, Texas).

To avoid such problems, the reservations agent should furnish the guest with the full name and address of the property at which a reservation has been made. When a reservation system serves more than one hotel in the same city, a thorough description of the hotel's location can be extremely helpful to the guest. One new feature of electronic systems is a zip code check. Which this program, the reservation agent enters the zip code of the guest. The system identifies the city associated with the zip code, helping to minimize address errors.

Central Reservation System Failures. Unless communication between the hotel and the central reservation system is maintained effectively, problems can occur. For example:

- The hotel may fail to update the central reservation system about its room availabilities and rate changes in a timely fashion.
- The central reservation system may be delinquent in informing the property of reservations it has booked.
- Communications equipment, at either the central reservation system or the hotel, may become inoperable.
- The hotel may close reservations on a particular date with the central reservations system, but close too late to be effective.

- The reverse is also possible. The hotel may find rooms available at the last minute due to cancellations or early departures and fail to notify the central reservation system in time to gain last minute reservations.
- Global distribution systems also present problems. Hotel reservation systems without automated connections to the GDSs have to keep them constantly updated through a dedicated staff of employees. This can be time consuming and error prone.

To avoid such problems, reservations agents must be aware of the need for accurate and timely communication between the hotel and the central reservation system. When closing reservations for a certain date, the hotel must try to identify any reservations the central reservation system has confirmed but has not yet communicated. Faulty equipment at either end of the communication channel may impair the effectiveness of the central reservation process. Attention must be paid to ensuring a sound working relationship with the central reservation system. In addition, it is appropriate to double-check the global distribution systems to be sure hotel availability and rates are correctly displayed. This can be done by asking the central reservation system manager to forward copies of GDS listings on a regular basis. It can also be done by establishing a good relationship with a local travel agency and asking to look at what their GDS terminals show as an occasional spot check. Another way to check is to look at one of the many Internet sites which provide hotel availability and rates.

Summary

Effective hotel operations require an efficient reservations procedure. Reservations agents must be able to respond quickly, accurately, and pleasantly to requests for overnight accommodations. Processing reservations involves matching room requests with room availabilities; recording, confirming, and maintaining reservations; and producing management reports. Reservation information is especially useful in other front office functions.

In non-automated hotels, reservations agents typically match requests for overnight accommodations against a simple inventory of available rooms. Due to the limited availability of information, reservations agents focus primarily on equating inquiries with availabilities. In a semi- or fully-automated property, the reservation system typically contains more detailed and timely information covering room types and available rates. Given the capabilities of automation, much of the responsibility for room sales has shifted from the front desk to the reservations department. Requests for specific room types, locations, and special features can be acknowledged and confirmed as part of the reservations process.

The major types of hotel reservations are guaranteed and non-guaranteed. Hotels can draw reservations from various market sources within the hospitality industry, including central reservation systems, intersell agencies, and property direct reservations. There are two basic types of central reservation systems: affiliate networks and non-affiliate networks. Global distribution systems connect central reservation systems with airline computer systems and terminals around the world. The term intersell agency describes a central reservation system that contracts to handle more than just hotel rooms. A property direct system handles all requests for accommodations, monitors any communication links with central reservation systems and intersell agencies, and maintains updated room availability status reports for a single hotel.

Processing a reservation request can result in one of several responses: reservation acceptance; suggestion of alternative room types, dates, and/or rates; and suggestion of an alternative hotel property. In any reservation system, it is necessary to closely monitor the number of reservations accepted in order to avoid overbooking. A computerized reservation system can assist management in maintaining tight control over room availability data and can automatically generate many reservation-related reports.

Reservation records identify guests and their occupancy needs, prior to actual arrival. These records enable the hotel to personalize guest service and more accurately schedule staff. Reservation agents create reservation records based on interactions with potential guests. A reservation record initiates the hotel guest cycle. A reservation confirmation indicates the hotel's acknowledgment and verification of a guest's room request and personal information. A written confirmation states the intent of both parties and confirms important points of agreement, including the room type and rate for a specific date. Confirmed reservations may be guaranteed or non-guaranteed. As part of the reservation confirmation process, a reservation confirmation number may be assigned to each accepted reservation record. A confirmation number assures the guest that a reservation record exists. It can be especially useful to the hotel in retrieving a reservation record for updating, prior to registration. Similarly, hotels may issue a reservation cancellation number to guests properly canceling a reservation. Issuing a cancellation number to guests protects both the guest and hotel in the event of a no-show or a misunderstanding.

An effective reservation system helps maximize room sales by accurately monitoring room availabilities and forecasting rooms revenue. Regardless of the degree of automation, the number and type of management reports available through a reservation system are a function of the hotel's needs and the system's capability and contents. Typical reservations management reports include: reservation transactions report; commission agent report; turnaway report (or refusal report); and a revenue forecast report.

Key Terms

advance deposit guaranteed reservation—a type of reservation guarantee that requires the guest to pay a specified amount of money to the hotel in advance of arrival.

affiliate reservation network—a hotel chain's reservation system in which all participating properties are contractually related.

block—an agreed-upon number of rooms set aside for members of a group planning to stay at a hotel.

book—to sell or reserve rooms ahead of time.

cancellation hour—the hour after which a property may release for sale all unclaimed non-guaranteed reservations, according to property policy.

cancellation number—a number issued to a guest who has properly canceled a reservation, proving that a cancellation request was received.

central reservation system—a network for communicating reservations in which each participating property is represented in a computer system database and is required to provide room availability data to the central reservations center on a timely basis.

confirmation number—a code that provides a unique reference to a reservation record and assures the guest that the reservation record exists.

corporate guaranteed reservation—a type of reservation guarantee in which a corporation signs a contractual agreement with the hotel to accept financial responsibility for any no-show business travelers it sponsors.

credit card guaranteed reservation—a type of guarantee supported by credit card companies; these companies guarantee participating properties payment for reserved rooms that remain unoccupied.

cut-off date—the date agreed upon between a group and a hotel after which all unreserved rooms in the group's block will be released back to the general rooms inventory for sale.

global distribution system (GDS)—a distribution channel for reservations that provides worldwide distribution of hotel reservation information and allows selling of hotel reservations around the world; usually accomplished by connecting the hotel company reservation system with an airline reservation system.

guaranteed reservation—a reservation that assures the guest that a room will be held until check-out time of the day following the day of arrival; the guest guarantees payment for the room, even if it is not used, unless the reservation is properly canceled.

non-affiliate reservation network—a central reservation system that connects independent (non-chain) properties.

non-group displacement (or displacement)—the turning away of transient guests for lack of rooms due to the acceptance of group business.

non-guaranteed reservation—a reservation agreement in which the hotel agrees to hold a room for the guest until a stated reservation cancellation hour on the day of arrival; the property is not guaranteed payment in the case of a no-show.

no-show—a guest who made a room reservation but did not register or cancel.

overbooking—accepting more reservations than there are available rooms.

overflow facility—a property selected to receive central system reservation requests after room availabilities in the system's participating properties within a geographic region have been exhausted.

prepayment guaranteed reservation—a type of reservation guarantee that requires a payment in full before the day of arrival.

reservation record—a collection of data that identifies a guest and his or her anticipated occupancy needs before arrival at the property; enables the hotel to personalize guest service and accurately schedule staff.

reservations control book—a binder with a tally page for each day of the year, used in non-automated hotels to track reservations.

travel agent guaranteed reservation—a type of reservation guarantee under which the hotel generally bills the travel agency after a guaranteed reservation has been classified as a no-show.

wash down (or wash)—blocking fewer rooms than the number requested by a group, based on previous group history.

Review Questions

1. What are the major types of reservations? What are the responsibilities of the guest and the hotel in each case?
2. What information does a reservations agent need to create a reservation record?
3. How do non-affiliate reservation networks differ from affiliate reservation networks? How do central reservation systems differ from intersell agencies?
4. What methods can be used to guarantee a reservation? What is the difference between them?
5. What are common reservation control devices used by hotels? How is each used to monitor room availabilities?
6. What guest information is necessary for a reservations agent to guarantee a reservation?
7. What is the main purpose of a confirmation letter or telephone call?
8. How does proper cancellation of a reservation benefit the hotel? How can hotels make cancellations as easy as possible for guests?
9. What is the purpose of a cancellation number? How might a cancellation number be generated?
10. What management reports can be generated from reservations data? What are the uses of expected arrival lists and reservations histories?
11. How can reservation procedures for conferences, conventions, and tour groups be made more efficient? What precautions should a reservations manager take before creating a group block?

Internet Sites

For more information, visit the following Internet sites. Remember that Internet addresses can change without notice.

Internet Reservation Sites

Business Travel Net
http://www.business-travel-net.com

Biztravel.com—The Internet Company for the Frequent Business Travelers
http://www.biztravel.com

Hotels and Travel on the Net
http://www.hotelstravel.com

HotelsOnline
http://www.hotelsonline.net

Internet Travel Network
http://www.itn.net

Meetings Industry Mall
http://www.mim.com

Resorts Online
http://www.resortsonline.com

Travelocity
http://www.travelocity.com

TravelWeb
http://www.travelweb.com

Hotel Companies

Best Western International
http://www.bestwestern.com

Canadian Pacific Hotels
http://www.cphotels.ca

Hyatt Hotels & Resorts
http://www.hyatt.com

Inter-Continental Hotels & Resorts
http://www.interconti.com

ITT Sheraton Corporation
http://www.sheraton.com

Marriott Hotels, Resorts, & Suites
http://www.marriotthotels.com

Radisson Hotels Worldwide
http://www.radisson.com

Ritz-Carlton Hotels
http://www.ritzcarlton.com

Westin Hotels & Resorts
http://www.westin.com

Technology Sites

Anasazi, Inc.
http://www.anasazi.com

CSS Hotel Systems
http://www.csshotelsystems.com

Executech, Inc.
http://www.executech.com

Fidelio Products
http://www.micros.com/scripts/vertical.pl

Hospitality Industry Technology Exposition and Conference
http://www.hitecshow.org

Hospitality Industry Technology Integration Standards
http://www.hitis.org

HOST International
http://www.hostgroup.com

Lodging Touch International
http://www.lodgingtouch.com

Newmarket Software Systems, Inc.
http://www.newsoft.com

Western Hospitality Systems
http://www.lodgingsystems.com

Case Study

Sarah's Serious Reservations—Working with the CRO

Sarah Shepherd was visiting her hotel chain's Midwest central reservations office in Des Moines, Iowa, wondering why her general manager had wanted her to spend a day touring the facilities with other reservations managers. She had a lot of work to do back in Bloomington, and she didn't understand what good it could do her to see how a roomful of reservations agents took orders over the telephone. "Frankly, I don't know either," her GM had told her. "I just have the suspicion that we could make a lot better use of our central reservations system. We're currently booking 30 percent of our rooms with them. Maybe we could do better. I'd like you to find out if that's true and bring back some recommendations."

Right now, I'd recommend catching an early flight home, she thought as the tour leaders began dividing the large group into smaller teams. Recognizing Gabe Culberson, the reservations manager from her sister property in Bloomington, she went to join his team. "At least I'll have a friend to commiserate with," she said under her breath. Sarah and Gabe were joined by Gwen Hsu, a reservations manager from one of the chain's St Louis properties.

The tour began "on the floor," where Sarah, Gabe, and Gwen watched as 200 reservations agents answered an unending stream of telephone calls. "This is really the nerve center for the operation," their guide was telling them, trying hard to be heard without interrupting any of the ongoing phone conversations. "Every potential guest who picks up the phone and dials our toll-free number ends up talking to someone in this room. Using the information you've provided that appears on these monitors, agents answer guest questions about rates, availability, amenities, local attractions—the whole works. To the best of their ability, that is."

"What do you mean by that?" Gwen asked.

"Well, we can only pass along the information that managers like you provide. If it isn't in our reservations system, we don't know about it."

Gabe leaned toward Sarah. "That's for sure. You wouldn't believe the difference it made when we posted information about the new children's museum downtown." Then he chuckled. "What am I saying—you've probably noticed the healthy bump in family business, too, right?"

"What do you mean?" Sarah started to ask, but their tour guide was moving on.

The guide stopped behind a reservations agent who was telling a caller about one of the chain's downtown Chicago properties. "This is Michelle," the guide said, "and she's one of our most enthusiastic sales agents. I just wanted you to hear how she works her magic over the phone."

"—that's right, Mr. Davis," Michelle was telling the caller. "Now, I have you booked for a room with two double beds and a rollaway bed for five days. Since you mentioned that you and your wife will be traveling with three small children, though, I would personally encourage you to consider the benefits you would gain by staying in a suite instead. You're right. It is a more expensive room, but it will give your family substantially more room to spread out in during a long stay in the city. Plus, with the suite reservation I can also offer you a special family package price that includes reduced admission to the Field Museum of Natural History, the Museum of Science and Industry, and Shedd Aquarium. That will give your family something fun to do while you're at your conference." Michelle paused, scanning her terminal. "Yes, a hotel shuttle offers transportation to those attractions. Great, I'll reserve a suite in your name and make sure you get the family package price. You'll be able to pick up your museum and aquarium tickets at the concierge desk in the hotel lobby. Oh, and you might tell your wife that the hotel is just one block off of the Magnificent Mile, one of the best shopping districts in the nation. Thank you for calling, Mr. Davis. I hope you and your family will have a great stay."

Wow! Sarah thought with surprise. *She sounds just like one of my own sales agents. In fact, she might even be better than they are!*

The group started moving on when Michelle answered another call. Suddenly Sarah heard Michelle say the name of her own property in Bloomington.

"Wait a second," she called to their guide. "I'd love to hear this."

Michelle was studying her screen. "I'm sorry, sir. I do know that there's a new children's museum in Bloomington, but I don't have any information here about it. Other attractions? There is an annual Frontier Fest, but that's the only attraction I have a record of."

"What?" Sarah said, a bit too loudly. *The Frontier Fest died out two years ago. Why wasn't Michelle-the-Wonder-Agent telling this caller about the Worlds of Water Fun park that opened less than a mile away last year or the new mall and movie theaters? And why didn't she know anything about the children's museum?*

"It's five minutes from the airport and shuttle service is provided. One moment while I check. I'm sorry, I don't have any information about fees or whether that's a hotel shuttle or an airport shuttle. There may a charge."

But there isn't, Sarah thought, her heart sinking. *It's our own courtesy van. Why don't you know that?*

"I'm showing a rate of $105 for that room. Would you like me to reserve that for you, then, Ms. McQueen?" This time, Michelle paused for what felt like minutes to Sarah. "I understand. Well, thank you very much for your call. I hope we'll be able to serve you in the future."

Dejected, Sarah turned to her friend Gabe. "She just lost that sale for me."

Gabe peered at Michelle's monitor for a minute. "Actually, Sarah, I think *you* just lost that sale for your hotel." He explained what he meant over coffee during a break in their tour.

"Tell me how you work with central reservations," he said.

"I'm not sure I know what you mean. We tell them how many rooms they can sell, and usually they sell them. It's simple: people call in and the agents take orders."

"But it's not that simple—at least, it shouldn't be. You heard Michelle's conversation with that guy staying in Chicago. She definitely was not 'taking an order.' She was *selling*. She could do that because the Chicago property provided her with every piece of information she'd need in the selling process. That's what I try to do at our property. Anything that I'd normally tell our in-house sales staff I post to the central res system. If the pool is out for repair, if we've changed our menu, if we've added amenities or know of area attractions, if we offer special corporate discounts—all of that information gets added to the database here so it comes up on their screens when a guest calls in."

Sarah was suddenly thoughtful. "So you're saying Michelle didn't know about the children's museum or the defunct Frontier Fest or the courtesy van or our new rate structure because I didn't post the information."

Gabe nodded. "I also noticed that there wasn't any information about that renovation you guys did about a year and a half ago."

"Just rub it in, Gabe," Sarah said, starting to smile. "I admit I had no idea they could be such effective salespeople."

Just then Gwen Hsu walked up. "Oh, they're effective, all right. *Too* effective, if you ask me. My problem is that central res keeps overbooking my property, so I get a seemingly constant stream of guests—with confirmations—that I don't have any room for."

"So you walk them," Gabe said.

"Well, I sure don't walk the folks who've reserved with us directly. They're our regulars. The central res guests are usually one-timers who have to be in town for a meeting; odds are, I'll never see them again."

"Gwen, how often do you update your allocation of rooms with central reservations?" Sarah wondered.

"What do you mean?"

"Gabe's been telling me that central reservations can only work with the information we give them. I just wondered how often you changed their allocation or posted new occupancy information."

"I guess it's usually first-thing-in-the-morning, last-thing-at-night. In the morning, I post the allocation for the day; at night, I check in to see where they stand in relation to the reservations we've developed in-house. That's usually when I get the bad news."

"That may be the problem," Gabe interjected. "I'm on our system probably 12 times a day, updating information and adjusting the allocation. And we don't have a pattern of overbooking."

Gwen frowned, saying that sounded like a lot of work. She would have to evaluate it to decide whether the benefits warranted the extra effort. She then left to ask their guide a specific question before the second half of their tour began.

"That was a good question, Sarah," Gabe said. "You know, by the time the next trip to central res rolls around, I bet your property will be just as involved in and enthusiastic about the system as mine is."

"Actually, Gabe, I was thinking that, next time around, it'll be *your* property's turn to play catch-up," Sarah said, flashing a smile.

Discussion Questions

1. What kinds of information does Sarah need from other departments at her hotel that will enable her to work better with the central reservations office?
2. As the reservations manager, what might Sarah do to improve the effectiveness of her property's work with central reservations?

Case Number: 3324CA
The following industry experts helped generate and develop this case: Richard M. Brooks, CHA, Vice President—Operations, Bridgestreet Accommodations, Inc., Cleveland, Ohio; and S. Kenneth Hiller, CHA, Director of Transition and Owner Relations, Marriott Hotels International.

This case also appears in *Case Studies in Lodging Management* (Lansing, Mich.: Educational Institute of the American Hotel & Motel Association, 1998), ISBN 0-86612-184-6.

Chapter 5 Outline

5

Registration

REGISTRATION BEGINS when the front desk agent extends a sincere welcome to the guest. A warm greeting sets the tone for everything that follows. The front desk agent moves into the registration process after determining the guest's reservation status. To a great degree, registration relies on the information contained in a reservation record. Front office personnel will find registration simpler and smoother when accurate and complete information has been captured during the reservations process.

From a front desk agent's perspective, the registration process can be divided into six steps:

- Preregistration activity
- Creating the registration record
- Assigning the room and rate
- Establishing the method of payment
- Issuing the room key
- Fulfilling special requests

In addition to examining these steps, this chapter discusses creative registration options, the front office sales role, and strategies that can be used when guests cannot be accommodated.

Preregistration Activity

Through the reservations process, a guest provides nearly all the information needed to complete registration. In other words, guests who make reservations will likely experience a more rapid check-in.

Preregistration activities (registration activities that occur before the guest arrives at the property) help accelerate the registration process. Guests can be preregistered using the information collected by reservations agents during the reservations process. Typically, preregistered guests only need to verify information already entered onto a registration card and provide a valid signature in the appropriate place on the registration card.

Preregistration normally involves more than merely producing a registration card in advance of guest arrival. Room and rate assignment, creation of a guest folio, and other functions may also be part of the preregistration process. However, some front office managers may be reluctant to assign a specific room to a guest in advance of check-in since reservations are sometimes canceled or modified. Specific room assignments often become jumbled when last-minute changes in reservation status are made. In addition, assigning a large percentage of vacant rooms in advance of arrival may limit the number of rooms available to guests who are not preregistered. This imbalance can slow down the registration process and create a negative impression of the hotel. Hotels will tend to develop preregistration policies based on operational experience.

Preregistration tasks are performed manually in non-automated and semi-automated front office systems. Consequently, preregistration services may be limited to specially designated or VIP guests or groups. With a computerized system, preregistration activities can be conducted for all expected arrivals. Since data recorded during the reservations process serve as the basis for preregistration, computer systems can reformat a reservation record into a registration record. A sample computer-generated preregistration card is shown in Exhibit 1. Although a hotel may have to void some pre-arrival room assignments due to last-minute changes, the registration time saved by guests who register without complications usually compensates for the inconvenience caused by the small percentage of cancellations.

Preregistration helps plan for special requirements of guests as well as of the hotel. For example, frequent guests may have a special room they enjoy at the hotel and guests with disabilities may need rooms outfitted to their special needs. By preregistering these guests, the front desk agent can be sure to satisfy them. In addition, preregistration helps managers when they know that the hotel will be at full occupancy over the next several days. In order to fill the house properly, it may be necessary to match guest reservations of one or two nights with rooms that have been specially blocked for one or two nights in the future. In this way, rooms that are blocked will be available when the guests check in. In some hotels, this process is actually done one or two days in advance to be sure that the required rooms are available.

Preregistration lends itself to innovative registration options. For instance, a hotel courtesy van might pick up a guest arriving at the airport who has a hotel reservation. The driver of the van, equipped with appropriate information and forms, could request the guest's signature on a prepared registration card, imprint the guest's credit card, and give the guest a pre-assigned room key—all before the guest arrives at the hotel.

Another variation on preregistration for air travelers involves actual services at the airport. Some luxury hotels have arrangements with nearby airports to provide guests with convenient check-in services. The guest may leave an impression of a major credit card with an agent at an appropriate desk, frequently the airport transportation desk. Credit information is then transmitted through a specially interfaced communication device to the hotel's front desk. This arrangement allows the front office to approve the guest's credit, prepare and print guest registration records, ready room keys, and print any waiting messages. When the guest arrives at the front desk, the convenience of an abbreviated check-in process will be available.

Exhibit 1 Sample Computer-Generated Preregistration Card

NAME BUCKNER, LORIN — ROOM	NAME DONOVAN, JOHN — ROOM 727
FIRM — TYPE TB	FIRM ATLAS INC. — TYPE LD
ADD 777 RED CEDAR RD — # PTY 1	ADD 1299 MICHIGAN BLVD. — # PTY 2
CITY PLYMOUTH, MICHIGAN 48995 — DEP 05/24	CITY FLINT, MICHIGAN 48458 — DEP 05/24
RATE 47.00 — ARR 05/23	RATE 75.00 — ARR 05/23
TELE — CLERK 19	TELE 313-686-0099 — CLERK 19
MY ACCOUNT WILL BE SETTLED BY:	MY ACCOUNT WILL BE SETTLED BY
☐ AMEX ☐	☐ AMEX ☐
☐ VISA/M. CHG ☐	☐ VISA/M. CHG ☐
☐ CASH ☐	☐ CASH ☐
☐ CB ☐ OTHER	☐ CB ☐ OTHER
SPECIFY	SPECIFY
IF ABOVE INFORMATION IS NOT CORRECT, PLEASE SPECIFY IN AREA BELOW.	IF ABOVE INFORMATION IS NOT CORRECT, PLEASE SPECIFY IN AREA BELOW.
PLEASE PRINT (LAST) (FIRST) (INITIAL)	PLEASE PRINT (LAST) (FIRST) (INITIAL)
NAME	NAME
☐ HOME ☐ BUSINESS	☐ HOME ☐ BUSINESS
STREET	STREET
CITY STATE ZIP	CITY STATE ZIP
COMPANY	COMPANY
SIGNATURE	SIGNATURE
SS CODES: RESV#: 38923	SS CODES: UF SS RESV#: 38921
BC442300001569243	NGUAR
•• MSU IS AN AFFIRMATIVE ACTION/EQUAL OPPORTUNITY INSTITUTION••	•• MSU IS AN AFFIRMATIVE ACTION/EQUAL OPPORTUNITY INSTITUTION••
BUCKNER, LORIN 05/23	727 DONOVAN, JOHN 05/23
47.00	ATLAS INC. 75.00
777 RED CEDAR RD 05/24	1299 MICHIGAN BLVD. 05/24
PLYMOUTH, MICHIGAN 48995 #G 1	FLINT, MICHIGAN 48458 #G 2
	UF SS
BC442300001569243	NGUAR
ROOM: RATE: 47.00	ROOM: 727 RATE: 75.00
NAME: BUCKNER, LORIN	NAME: DONOVAN, JOHN
DEPARTING: 05/24	DEPARTING: 05/24
SS CODES:	SS CODES: UF SS
GNAME:	GNAME:

Courtesy of Kellogg Center, Michigan State University, East Lansing, Michigan

A less sophisticated approach to preregistration involves registering guests designated for VIP service at some place other than the front desk—for example, at the concierge desk. Some hotels arrange for VIP guests to be taken directly to their rooms, thereby avoiding possible delays which may be encountered at a busy front desk.

Exhibit 2 Sample Registration Card

ROOM | NAME | RATE | RESV. ID

ADDRESS

ARRIVAL | ETA | FLIGHT

GROUP

DEPARTURE | RATE | PERS.

CLERK INITIALS

ADULT | CHDRN. | RESV. CLERK | RESV. DATE

REGISTRATION

FOR SAFE KEEPING OF MONEY, JEWELRY AND OTHER VALUABLES INDIVIDUAL SAFE DEPOSIT BOXES ARE PROVIDED AT THE FRONT DESK AT NO CHARGE. THE SHERATON INN-LANSING WILL NOT BE LIABLE FOR ANY ITEMS NOT SECURED IN THIS MANNER.

HOTEL | TYPE | NR-ROOM | NIGHTS

ROOM DESCRIPTION

GUEST'S SIGNATURE X

HOME ADDRESS

DEPOSIT

CITY | STATE | ZIP

SPECIAL SERVICES

DR. LIC. # | STATE

D.O.B.

METHOD OF PAYMENT

☐ AMERICAN EXPRESS ☐ CASH ☐ DINERS CLUB ☐ CHECK
☐ VISA ☐ CARTE BLANCHE ☐ MASTER CARD

Sheraton Inn Lansing

S. Creyts Rd. at I-496
Lansing, MI 48917

95093 (4-82)

Courtesy of The Sheraton Inn, Lansing, Michigan

The Registration Record

After a guest arrives at the hotel, the front desk agent creates a **registration record,** a collection of important guest information.

Registration cards facilitate the registration process in non-automated and semi-automated hotels. The registration card requires a guest to provide his or her name, address, telephone number, company affiliation (if appropriate), and other personal data. Exhibit 2 shows a sample registration card. As this sample shows, some registration cards may include a printed statement about the hotel's responsibility for storing guest valuables. Such a statement may be required by state law. The registration card usually contains a space for the guest's signature. In some states, a guest's signature is a legal prerequisite to establishing a guest relationship with the hotel. In many states, however, this requirement has been replaced by other provisions, such as the intentional establishment of credit by the guest at the time of registration.

Even in automated properties, guests may be asked to sign a preprinted registration card either to comply with statutory requirements or to verify that the registration document is accurate. Although a state or local municipality may require a signed registration card, the electronic information record, not the registration card, establishes the basis for registration processing. Guests arriving without reservations (that is, walk-ins) will experience a different registration routine. Front desk agents will need to collect guest data and subsequently input those data into a

Exhibit 3 Flow of Guest Registration Information

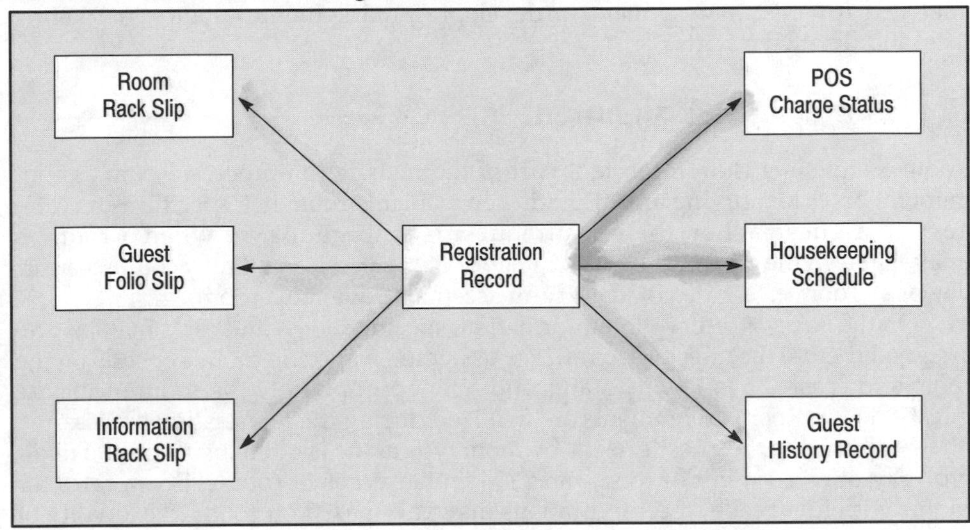

computer terminal at the front desk. Most registration information may be assembled from a registration card or from guest responses during check-in.

Registration cards, or their computer-generated equivalent, request guests to indicate their intended method of settlement for rooms and other hotel goods and services. In addition, front desk agents should confirm the guest's planned departure date and pre-assigned room rate. These elements are critical to rooms and revenue management. Clarifying the room rate at registration minimizes confusion and adjustments to the guest's folio at check-out. In non-automated and semi-automated hotels, the guest's registration card is either filed in the room rack or attached to the guest's folio and placed in a folio tray. Many registration cards also contain some form of acknowledgement on the part of the guest that he or she is personally responsible for payment in case the credit card or direct billing is not accepted. In a computerized hotel, the registration card is stored by itself in the folio tray and the information is electronically stored in a computer file.

Exhibit 3 diagrams the flow of guest registration information to other areas and functions of the hotel. The guest's intended method of payment may determine that guest's point-of-sale charge status. For example, a guest paying cash in advance at registration is likely to have a *no-post status* in the hotel's sales outlets. In other words, the guest may not be allowed to charge purchases to a room account. A guest presenting a valid credit card during registration may be allowed point-of-sale charge privileges. The decision to give charge privileges to a guest usually depends on the establishment of an acceptable method of credit at check-in.

At check-out, the information captured on a guest's registration card may be used as the primary source for creating a guest history record. This record may then become part of the data base to be used in the future by the hotel's sales and marketing efforts. The information contained in a guest history data base can be analyzed to assist management in developing marketing strategies, marketing lists, and detailed reports.

Room and Rate Assignment

Room assignment is an important part of the registration process. Room assignment involves identifying and allocating an available room in a specific room category to a guest. When the guest request is ambiguous, or when a room is unavailable in the guest's preferred category, a front desk agent may conduct a survey of all room categories to identify an acceptable available room.

On the basis of reservation information, specific rooms and rates may be pre-assigned (before the guest's arrival). Pre-assigning a specific room depends on the room's forecasted availability status and how appropriately the room meets the guest's needs. Room assignments are finalized during the registration process.

Determining the guest's needs by room type alone is often insufficient. Hotels typically offer a variety of room rates for similar types of rooms. Room rates for rooms with identical bed configurations may vary based on room size, quality of furnishings, location, amenities, and other factors. Front desk agents must be aware of each room's rate category, current occupancy status, furnishings, location, and amenities in order to best satisfy guest requests. Future reservation commitments must also be considered during room assignment so that rooms are not assigned in conflict with near-future reservation needs.

The front desk agent's ability to determine room status and an appropriate room rate is critical to an effective registration process. Each of these important topics is addressed separately.

Room Status

Effective room and rate assignment depends on accurate and timely room status information. Room status information is usually discussed along two time lines. In the long term (beyond the present night), a room's readiness is described by its **reservation status.** In the short term, a room's readiness is described by its housekeeping status, which refers to its availability for immediate assignment. Knowing whether the room is occupied, vacant, on-change, out-of-order, or in some other condition is important to rooms management.

Changes in a room's housekeeping status should be promptly communicated to the front desk in order to maximize room sales. Maintaining timely housekeeping status information requires close coordination and cooperation between the front desk and the housekeeping department. A **room status discrepancy** occurs when the housekeeping status information used by the housekeeping department differs from the room status information used by the front desk to assign rooms. Room status discrepancies can seriously affect a property's ability to satisfy guest needs and maximize rooms revenue. Room status discrepancies should be identified and resolved as quickly as possible.

A tremendous aid to the registration of early-arriving guests is the prompt relay of housekeeping information to the front desk. This is especially true during high-occupancy or full-occupancy (sold-out) periods. The more efficient the registration process, the more impressed with the hotel's efficiency of operation an incoming guest is likely to be. At most properties, the front desk agent is not authorized to assign a guestroom until the room has been cleaned, inspected, and released by the housekeeping department. Even though a guest arriving early may have to wait for a room, he or she will perceive the wait for a readied room as a better option than simply receiving a room key to a room that has not been properly prepared.

The two most common systems for tracking room status are mechanical room racks and computerized status systems.

Room Rack. The front desk may use a room rack to track the current housekeeping status of guestrooms. A room rack slip containing the guest's name, departure date, room rate, and other information is normally completed during the registration process and placed in the room rack slot corresponding to the room number assigned to the guest. The presence of a room rack slip indicates that the room is occupied. When the guest checks out, the rack slip is removed and the room's status shifts to on-change. An **on-change status** indicates that the room requires housekeeping services before it can be resold. As unoccupied rooms are cleaned and inspected, the housekeeping department notifies the front desk which, in turn, updates the room's status to available-for-sale.

Room status discrepancies can occur in non-automated front office systems for two reasons. First, the cumbersome nature of tracking and comparing housekeeping and front desk room status information often leads to mistakes. For example, if a room rack slip is mistakenly left in the rack even though the guest has checked out, front desk staff may falsely assume that a vacant room is still occupied. Potential revenue from the future sale of the room may be lost.

Room status discrepancies may also arise from delays in communicating housekeeping status information from the housekeeping department to the front desk. Communication between the front desk and the housekeeping department may be spoken, written, or conveyed through a communication device like a telewriter. Spoken communication, normally accomplished via the telephone, is used to relay status information quickly, but without supporting documentation. A written report has the advantage of documenting the information, but is time-consuming because it may require hand-delivery. A telewriter may be used to communicate and document information between two departments without requiring someone to be on the receiving end. Telewriters are especially helpful when front desk agents or housekeepers are busy with other responsibilities and do not have time to place a call or answer the telephone to update current room status.

Computer-based communication at automated properties can be accomplished in a number of ways. Some systems, for example, interface in-room telephones with the hotel's computer system so that housekeepers can enter room status information over the telephone system. Other systems may require housekeepers to use a computer terminal in the housekeeping department to update room status information. In any case, the electronic transmittal of information is quick and easy. Computerized systems are discussed in greater detail below.

In many properties, a front desk agent is responsible for producing a daily front office report called the **occupancy report.** The daily occupancy report lists rooms occupied for the night and indicates those guests expected to check out the following day. The executive housekeeper receives a copy of this report early in the morning and schedules occupied rooms for cleaning. The rooms occupied by guests expected to check out are usually scheduled to be cleaned last since guests tend to use their room until just prior to departure. If these rooms are cleaned early, they may have to be cleaned again. Checked-out rooms usually require more cleaning time than stayover rooms. If a guest checks out before the stated departure date, the front desk must notify housekeeping that the room should no longer be classified as a stayover. A special housekeeping routine coordinated with the front desk is often needed for cleaning and inspecting early check-out rooms.

At the end of a workshift, the housekeeping department prepares a **housekeeping status report** (see Exhibit 4) based on a physical check of all guestrooms. This report indicates the current housekeeping status of each room. It should be compared with the front desk occupancy report, and any room status discrepancies should be brought to the attention of the front office manager. This process helps ensure that front desk agents work with an accurate and up-to-date room rack, which is especially important when processing late check-ins.

Computerized System. In a computerized room status system, housekeeping and the front desk often have instantaneous access to room status information. For example, when a guest checks out, the process of settling the account in the computer automatically updates the room status to vacant and on-change. Housekeeping, in turn, is alerted that the room needs cleaning through a remote terminal located in the housekeeping department. A recent innovation connects a pager to the computerized room status system. The pager is worn by the room attendant and is activated automatically when the guest leaves. This allows even faster response by the housekeeping team. Room attendants then clean the room and notify the housekeeping department when it is ready for inspection. Housekeeping inspects the room and enters the room's status into the computer system via the housekeeping department's computer terminal or through the guestroom telephone if the hotel is properly equipped. This entry, in turn, updates rooms status information stored in the front office computer.

While room occupancy status within a computerized system is almost always current, housekeeping status may lag behind. The housekeeping supervisor may inspect several rooms at once, but may not update the computer's room status files until the end of an extended inspection round. Calling the housekeeping department after each room is inspected is generally inefficient in a large operation. Having to constantly answer the phone can be both an inconvenience and an interruption to the housekeeping department staff. Delays may also occur when a list of clean, inspected rooms is furnished to the housekeeping office but not immediately entered into the computer system.

Most problems associated with promptly relaying guestroom housekeeping status reports to the front office are eliminated when the computer system is directly connected to the guestroom telephone system. Such a network permits supervisors to inspect rooms, determine their readiness for sale, and change the

Exhibit 4 Housekeeping Status Report

Housekeeper's Report

Date ______________, 19 _____ **A.M. P.M.**

ROOM NUMBER	STATUS	ROOM NUMBER	STATUS	ROOM NUMBER	STATUS	ROOM NUMBER	STATUS
101		126		151		176	
102		127		152		177	
103		128		153		178	
104		129		154		179	
105		130		155		180	
106		131		156		181	
107		132		157		182	
108		133		158		183	
120						195	
121		146		171		196	
122		147		172		197	
123		148		173		198	
124		149		174		199	
125		150		175		200	

Remarks:

____

____

____

____

Housekeeper's Signature

Legend:
- ✓ - Occupied
- 000 - Out-of-Order
- — - Vacant
- B - Slept Out (Baggage Still in Room)
- X - Occupied No Baggage
- C.O. - Slept In but Checked Out Early A.M.
- E.A. - Early Arrival

room's housekeeping status in the hotel's computer system by entering a designated code through the guestroom telephone. Since the computer automatically receives the relay, no attendant needs to answer the phone. Such direct access helps minimize the possibility of a recording error. Within seconds, the room's updated status can be displayed on a computer terminal screen at the front desk. This interface can significantly reduce the number of guests waiting for room assignment, as well as the length of their wait. Most front office computer systems are also capable of producing a daily occupancy report at the end of the day.

Room Rates

A **room rate** is the price a hotel charges for overnight accommodations. The cost structure of the hotel dictates the minimum rate for a room, and competition helps the hotel establish its maximum rate. The room rate range is the range of values between the minimum and maximum rates. A hotel will usually designate a standard rate for each room. This rate is typically called the **rack rate** because traditionally the standard rate was the one posted on or near the room rack. The rack rate is considered the retail rate for the room. In most cases, rate discounts provided by the hotel are discounts to the rack rate.

Room rates are often confirmed as part of the reservations process. This is becoming the preferred way of doing business by most business travelers and travel agents. Assigning rates for walk-in guests is left to the front desk agent according to the hotel's policy guidelines. Front desk agents may sometimes be allowed to offer a room at a lower price than its standard rack rate. Normally, this occurs only when management deems it appropriate. For example, hotel management may be expecting low occupancy. In order to attract as much business as possible to the hotel, walk-in guests may be offered a rate below the rack rate to entice them to stay. Some hotels establish seasonal rate schedules in order to anticipate business fluctuations. The objective is to provide greater value during low demand periods and to maximize room revenue during high demand periods (a form of revenue management).

Other room rate schedules may reflect variations in the number of guests assigned to the room, service level, and room location. For example, room rates may cover billing arrangements for meals. Under the **American Plan (AP),** room charges include the cost of the guestroom and three meals per day. Under the **Modified American Plan (MAP),** the daily rate includes charges for the guestroom and two meals per day (typically breakfast and dinner). Sometimes, the phrase *full pension* is used in place of American Plan, and *semi-pension* in place of Modified American Plan. Under the **European Plan,** meals are priced separately from guestrooms. Resorts frequently use either the American Plan or the Modified American Plan. Most non-resort hotels in the United States set their rates according to the European Plan.

Room rates may also vary based on the type of guest. If authorized, front desk agents should know how and when to apply a special room rate during the registration process. Special room rates may include:

- *Commercial or corporate rates* for frequent guests.
- *Complimentary rates (no charge)* for business promotion.
- *Group rates* for a pre-determined number of affiliated guests.
- *Family rates* for parents and children sharing the same room.
- *Day rates* for less than an overnight stay (usually check-in and check-out on the same day).
- *Package-plan rates* for guestrooms sold in a package that includes special events or activities.
- *Frequent traveler rates* for guests earning discounts through the hotel's frequent traveler program.

Eligibility for special rates is generally contingent on management policy and the guest's profile.

Room Locations

When assigning guestrooms, a front desk agent must be aware of the characteristics of each room type. In most hotels built within the last fifty years, guestrooms within each room category tend to be approximately the same size. Older hotels, due to different construction techniques and materials, often had rooms varying significantly in size and configuration. Differences between two guestrooms generally lie in their furnishings, amenities, and location. Front desk agents should be familiar with various guestroom configurations, as well as the hotel's floor plan, in order to satisfy guest rooming requests. Exhibit 5 contains an example of a simplified hotel floor plan. Note the connecting rooms and handicapper-accessible rooms depicted in the floor plan.

The room rack or its computer equivalent should contain specific data about each room, such as its type, rate, and other pertinent information. Although the room rack primarily functions as a rooming control tool, it can also serve as a source of information for room location (so long as the rack's layout reflects the hotel's floor plan). For example, room racks may indicate connecting rooms, guestroom views, and the type of bed(s) in each guestroom. Front office computer systems can be programmed to provide similar types of guestroom information in an easy-to-reference format.

Individual guests or groups of guests may specify certain room locations in the hotel as part of their reservation requests. Groups may be promised their preferred rooms by the department that booked their business, usually the sales and marketing department or catering department. However, the booking department should be careful to check room availabilities with reservations before promising or committing specific facilities to an incoming group. Although the reservations department may block the desired rooms in advance, it is the responsibility of the front desk to assign guestrooms from the preferred block of rooms at registration.

Future Blocks

A primary concern in the room assignment phase of registration is knowing what rooms will be available in the near future based on reservation blocks. Usually, a reservations agent or the front office supervisor blocks reserved rooms on a calendar, wall chart, control book, room rack, or computer reservations file. If for any reason reserved rooms are incorrectly blocked or inadvertently overlooked, information discrepancies and/or rooming conflicts may result.

For instance, suppose a walk-in guest is assigned a room for a two-night stay. But if that room is booked for a guest arriving the next day—and the front desk agent is unaware of this commitment—rooming problems will likely arise when the second guest registers. Computer systems help reduce such booking errors because they can be designed to prohibit the front desk agent from selecting a preassigned, reserved room for a guest expected to check in at a later date.

Many guests believe that once they occupy a room, there is little that the hotel can do to change their status. Any attempt to move a registered guest to another room is often resisted; bad feelings may arise even if the guest agrees to move. Conversely, the incoming guest, who was promised a particular room, will

Exhibit 5 Simplified Hotel Floor Plan

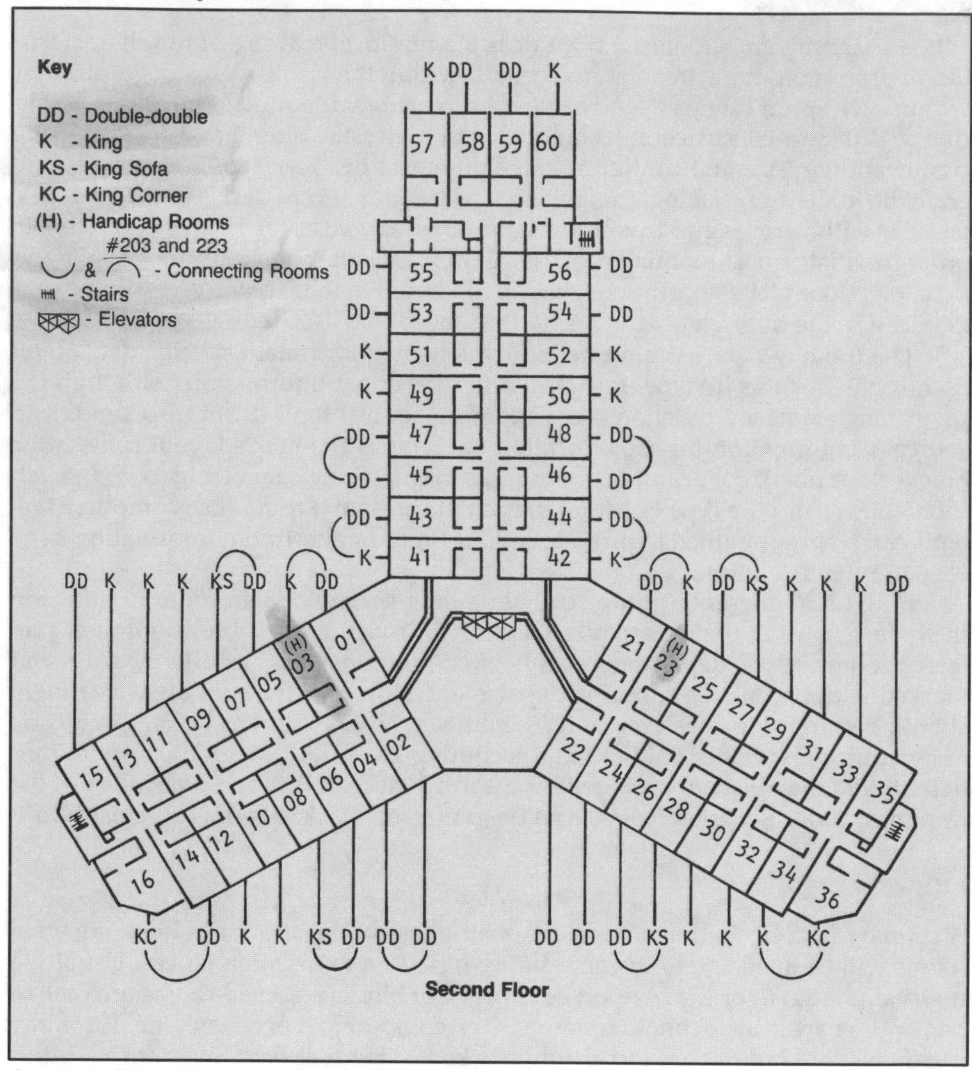

Courtesy of The Sheraton Inn, Lansing, Michigan

probably be inconvenienced and may be wary of the front desk's control over its room assignment process. These and related reasons make it imperative for the front office to be aware of all future guestroom commitments.

Method of Payment

Regardless of whether the guest intends to pay by cash, check, credit card, or other acceptable method, the hotel should take precautionary measures to ensure payment. Effective account settlement depends on the steps taken during registration to determine the guest's method of payment. The establishment of proper settlement or credit authorization at the time of registration will greatly reduce the potential for unauthorized settlement and subsequent collection problems.

Just as hotels vary in size, structure, and organization, so do the guidelines for establishing the guest's method of payment. The registration process plays an important role in front office guest accounting since front desk agents are responsible for gathering information at check-in on the intended method of payment. Common methods of room rate payment include: cash, personal checks, credit cards, direct billings, and special programs.

Cash

Some guests prefer to pay guestroom charges during registration, in advance of occupancy. As stated earlier, guests who pay cash for their accommodations at the time of registration are typically not extended in-house credit. Revenue outlets are usually given **PIA (paid-in-advance)** lists of cash-paying guests who are not authorized to have charge purchases posted to their guestroom accounts *(no post status).*

In some properties, PIA lists are replaced by a front office computerized system that interfaces the front desk to devices in the hotel's revenue outlets. Such systems won't allow outlet employees to post charges to guest accounts that are not authorized for in-house charges. Guests with no in-house charge privileges must settle their purchases at the point of sale. At check-in, front desk agents may require a cash-paying guest to leave an imprint of a credit card before extending in-house charge privileges to the guest.

Banks also consider cashier's checks, traveler's checks, and money orders equivalent to cash. A hotel that accepts such forms of legal tender should require proper guest identification. Front desk agents should compare the picture and signature on the guest's identification with the appearance and signature of the person presenting the tender. When there is doubt, the form of tender should be verified with the issuing bank or agency.

Personal Checks

Some lodging properties allow transactions to be paid by personal check, while others have a strict policy against accepting personal checks. Although a hotel has no obligation to accept personal checks, it cannot refuse to accept a personal check on the basis of sex, race, or other grounds that would warrant illegal discrimination. Individual properties must establish policies for accepting personal checks. Hotels must consider policies relative to payroll checks, personal checks written on out-of-state and foreign bank accounts, government checks, and second- and third-party checks.

Some hotels allow guests to cash personal checks as long as they have a credit card that provides a check-cashing guarantee, and as long as the amount of the check is within the credit card company's established credit limit. When this is the case, front desk agents should imprint the credit card onto the back side of the guest's personal check. Some hotels accept personal checks only during standard banking hours; this provision often allows the front office to obtain bank verification of the check, if necessary. Some hotels allow guests to write personal checks for the amount of the guestroom only. When this is the case, cash or credit card payment will be required for all other purchases.

Hotels that accept personal checks should require proper identification. The guest's driver's license number, address, and telephone number should be recorded on the *face* of a personal check. Bank stamps and clearing house imprints will often be recorded on the *back* of the check. In some hotels, the amounts and dates of cashed personal checks are recorded on the guest's registration card. This procedure helps ensure that guests do not exceed the property's pre-established check-cashing limits. If front office cashiers are not authorized to accept personal checks, they must be aware of what procedures to follow when a guest attempts to write a personal check.

Properties can also protect themselves against potential losses incurred through acceptance of fraudulent or bogus personal checks by following some basic guidelines:

- Do not refund cash if the original transaction was settled by personal check. If possible, return the guest's original personal check and, when appropriate, require an alternate form of payment. Some properties do not write a refund check, even if a refund is warranted, until the guest's bank verifies that the personal check in question has cleared.
- Do not accept undated or post-dated personal checks—that is, checks carrying no date or a future date instead of the current date.
- Require that personal checks written to settle an account be made payable to the hotel, not to "Cash." When a guest is allowed to write a personal check to obtain cash, not to pay a bill, that check should be made out to "Cash." This practice may prevent a non-paying guest (skipper) from later claiming that a personal check made out to "Cash" was used as payment against his or her hotel account.

Exhibit 6 suggests further steps to follow when accepting checks.

Second- and Third-Party Checks. In general, hotels will not accept second- or third-party checks. A *second-party check* is one made out to the guest presenting the check. A *third-party check* is one made out to someone who has in turn signed the check over to the guest presenting it. When accepting such checks, hotels may experience collection problems, especially if the maker of the check has registered a "stop payment" order on the check. If the hotel accepts a second-party check, the front desk agent should require the guest to endorse the check at the front desk, even if it has been previously endorsed. The agent can then compare the guest's two signatures (previous and current endorsements).

Check Guarantee Services. A personal check guarantee service can be a valuable asset for the hospitality industry. When such a service is available, a front desk agent usually telephones the service or uses a small, desktop terminal, and provides data from the tendered check and the amount of the transaction. The check guarantee service, in turn, determines the check writer's credit history and either guarantees or refuses to support payment. Since the hotel must pay a fee per check for this personal check guarantee service, its use is normally restricted to personal

Exhibit 6 Suggested Steps for Accepting Checks

Steps to Follow when Accepting Checks

1 Be cautious of new checking accounts

Of all the insufficient, "hot" checks, 90% are drawn on accounts less than a year old. The consecutive numbers in the upper right hand corner begin with 101 and you should be especially careful when taking low numbered checks. Because knowing the age of the account is so important, some banks now print a code of when the account was opened (for example, 0278 means February, 1978) on all checks.

2 Place all information on front of check

As described in Regulation CC, either write the information consecutively across the top of the front or use the cross method.

Driver's license number	Credit card number
Clerk's initials	Other ID or manager's approval

3 Examine driver's license carefully

After you have the license out of the customer's wallet and in your hand, quickly ask yourself the following questions: Is the person in the photo and in front of you the same person? Are the addresses on the check and license the same? When does the license expire? More than 60% of the forged checks last year were cashed with an expired driver's license. Also, the courts have ruled that licenses are legally worthless for identification as soon as they expire. Be sure you examine the driver's license carefully.

4 Other Negotiable Instrument Codes

On drafts issued by savings and loan institutions and mutual savings banks, magnetic bank routing numbers may start with the digit 2 or 3. Credit union drafts are honored by the bank on which they are drawn. International traveler's checks have routing numbers starting with 8000. U.S. Government checks contain the routing number 000000518.

5 Traveler's check identification

VISA—When held above eye level, a globe of the world will appear on the front left and a dove in the upper right.

MASTERCARD and THOMAS COOK—When held above eye level, on the right side of the check in a circle, a woman with short black hair will appear.

CITICORP—When held above eye level, a Greek god will appear on the right.

BANK OF AMERICA—No distinguishing watermarks.

AMERICAN EXPRESS—Turn check over. Moisten your finger tip and run it over the left denomination. If it smears it is good. Right side will not smear.

6 Be impressed with the check—not the person

Don't let a customer's appearance lull you into ignoring any of these steps. Frank Abagnale, the retired master forger, once cashed a $50 check written on a cocktail napkin, before a hidden camera for television, because the bank teller was more impressed by his appearance than by the item he presented. When you're in a hurry, or want to make an exception, think how you will defend your decision if the check is returned. Then, only the check will matter —not the circumstances in which you took it.

Developed by Frank W. Abagnale

Frank W. Abagnale & Associates/PO Box 701290, Tulsa, Oklahoma 74170/Telephone 918-492-6590

Courtesy of Frank W. Abagnale & Associates, Tulsa, Oklahoma

checks written to settle guest accounts. Check guarantee services usually do not guarantee checks drawn on foreign banks.

Credit Cards

Careful authorization and verification of credit cards are as important to front office cash flow as the precautions taken with any other method of payment. The front office usually compiles a set of steps for processing credit card transactions. In addition, credit card companies often require explicit procedures in order to ensure transaction settlement. As shown in Exhibit 7, credit card companies also provide helpful tips for avoiding fraud and implementing sound processing procedures. Hotels should have an attorney review their credit card procedures to be sure the hotel adheres to state and federal laws and to the specifications contained in credit card company contracts. Local banks may also provide procedural guidelines. Properties might also consider the following points when establishing a front desk policy for handling credit cards.

Expiration Date. When a guest presents a credit card, the front desk agent handling the transaction should immediately check the credit card's expiration date. If the date shows that the credit card has expired, the front desk agent should point this out to the guest and request an alternative method of payment. Since credit card companies are not required to honor transactions made with an expired card, the acceptance of an expired card places the hotel in an untenable position. If the hotel inadvertently accepts an expired credit card, it may not be able to collect payment for the guest's charged purchases.

On-Line Authorization. After checking a credit card's expiration date, the front desk agent should make sure the credit card isn't listed as stolen or otherwise invalid. Many hotels validate credit cards through an on-line computer service accomplished through a telephone interface. Once the telephone connection is complete, the required credit card and transaction data may be spoken, entered on a touch-tone key pad, or automatically captured through a magnetic strip reader. On the basis of the entered data, the credit card verification service consults an account data base and generates either an **authorization code** or a **denial code** for the guest's transaction.

On-line authorization services have the advantage of allowing the front desk agent to proceed with other tasks while the service verifies the transaction. The front desk agent can later check the authorization terminal to obtain and record the authorization or denial code number. It is important to note that on-line authorization services often charge a transaction processing fee.

Cancellation Bulletins. In properties without on-line credit card authorization, the front desk agent should validate a credit card by consulting the credit card company's current cancellation bulletin. Expired cancellation bulletins should also be retained and filed in case a dispute eventually arises between a credit card company and the hotel. The hotel can refer to previous cancellation bulletins to prove that a credit card number was valid at the time the credit card was accepted for payment. An attorney can advise the hotel on how long to retain such documentation.

Exhibit 7 Tips from Credit Card Companies

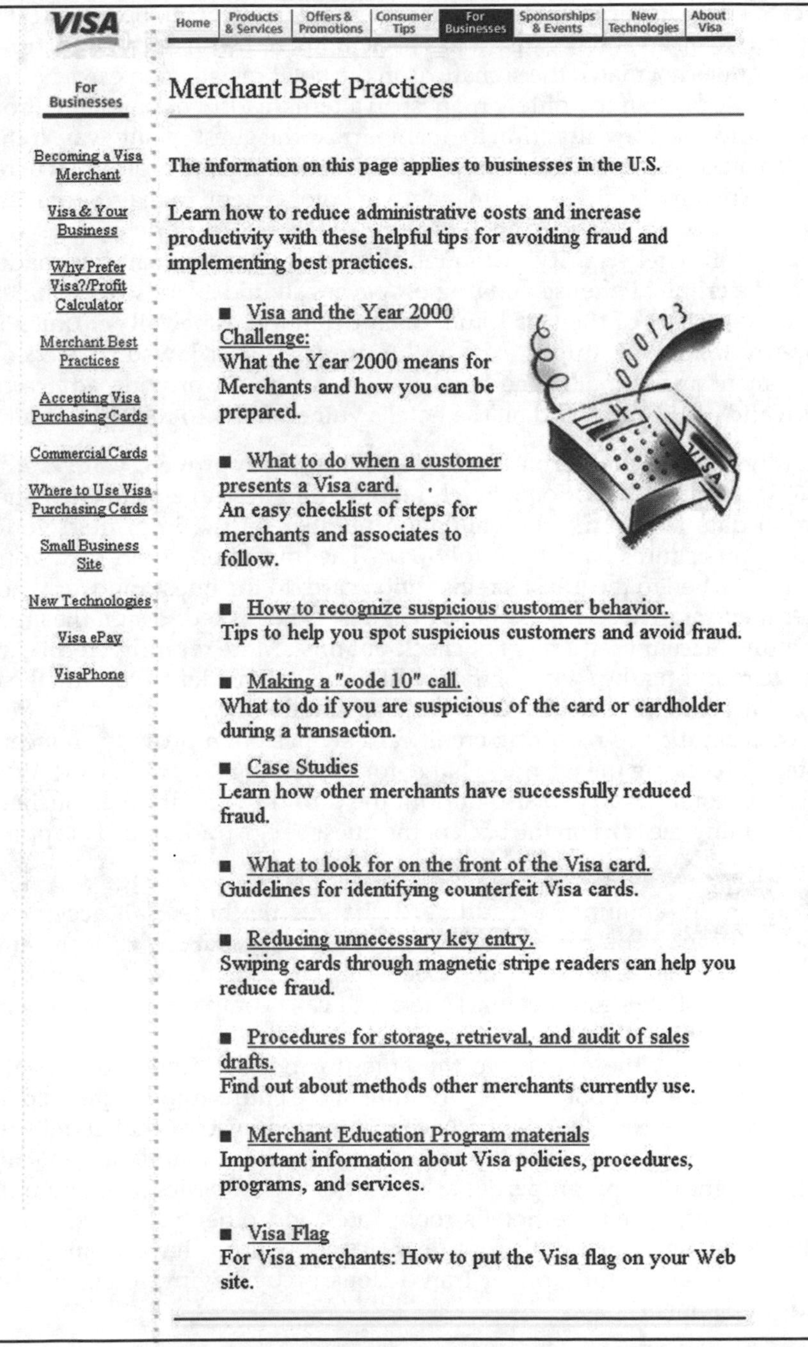
VISA

Home | Products & Services | Offers & Promotions | Consumer Tips | For Businesses | Sponsorships & Events | New Technologies | About Visa

For Businesses

Becoming a Visa Merchant

Visa & Your Business

Why Prefer Visa?/Profit Calculator

Merchant Best Practices

Accepting Visa Purchasing Cards

Commercial Cards

Where to Use Visa Purchasing Cards

Small Business Site

New Technologies

Visa ePay

VisaPhone

Merchant Best Practices

The information on this page applies to businesses in the U.S.

Learn how to reduce administrative costs and increase productivity with these helpful tips for avoiding fraud and implementing best practices.

- **Visa and the Year 2000 Challenge:**
  What the Year 2000 means for Merchants and how you can be prepared.
- **What to do when a customer presents a Visa card.**
  An easy checklist of steps for merchants and associates to follow.
- **How to recognize suspicious customer behavior.**
  Tips to help you spot suspicious customers and avoid fraud.
- **Making a "code 10" call.**
  What to do if you are suspicious of the card or cardholder during a transaction.
- **Case Studies**
  Learn how other merchants have successfully reduced fraud.
- **What to look for on the front of the Visa card.**
  Guidelines for identifying counterfeit Visa cards.
- **Reducing unnecessary key entry.**
  Swiping cards through magnetic stripe readers can help you reduce fraud.
- **Procedures for storage, retrieval, and audit of sales drafts.**
  Find out about methods other merchants currently use.
- **Merchant Education Program materials**
  Important information about Visa policies, procedures, programs, and services.
- **Visa Flag**
  For Visa merchants: How to put the Visa flag on your Web site.

The Internet site of Visa International (http://www.visa.com) provides hotels with practical information to guide credit card processing procedures.

Invalid Card. Front desk employees should follow established front office and credit card company procedures when a credit card appears to be invalid. The card may appear to be invalid because it has been tampered with or the signature on the credit card does not match the signature on the hotel registration card. Normally, it is appropriate for staff to politely request an alternate form of payment. Front desk agents should not draw attention to or embarrass the guest in any way. If the guest has no other acceptable means of payment, front desk agents typically will refer the situation to the front office credit manager or hotel general manager for resolution.

If a guest presents a card that appears stolen, the front desk agent might be advised to call hotel security. Although the federal government has made credit card fraud a criminal offense, lodging properties should exercise care in detaining guests they suspect of theft or fraud. Such detention, especially if unjustified or improperly instituted, might expose the property to a lawsuit based on false imprisonment and slander. The hotel's attorney should provide advice on handling invalid credit cards and on the hotel's vulnerability to related lawsuits.

Imprinting the Voucher. Front desk agents imprint approved, valid credit cards onto credit card vouchers. Some hotels require front desk agents to circle the card's expiration date and initial the validation number on the imprinted voucher as proof that procedures have been followed. The imprinted credit card voucher is normally attached to the guest's registration card, to the guest folio, or placed in a voucher file for safekeeping. Usually, the guest is not asked to sign the credit card voucher until account settlement or check-out time. More recently, credit card companies are requiring the swipe of the credit through a reader to capture the data. It is a more accurate process for them, as imprinted vouchers may be unreadable. Credit card companies requiring credit card swipes often provide an incentive to the hotel by reducing the fee they charge for processing the credit card. When this is done, it is not necessary to also imprint the card on a credit card voucher. However, imprinting the card on the back of the guest's registration card is appropriate.

Floor Limits. Credit card companies may assign hotels a **floor limit.** A floor limit is the maximum amount in credit card charges the hotel can accept without requesting special authorization on behalf of a credit card holder. If the amount a guest wants to charge to his or her credit card account exceeds the hotel's floor limit, the front office should contact the credit card company to request approval for the transaction.

In some cases, the penalty to the hotel for not obtaining authorization for charges exceeding the floor limit is forfeiture of the entire amount charged, not just the amount above the floor limit. A computerized system that monitors guest account balances can help identify guest credit card accounts approaching the floor limit. Some lodging properties ask credit card companies to assign unusually high floor limits, given the hotel's room rates and other pricing structures. By receiving a higher floor limit, front desk agents will not have to inconvenience guests by frequently authorizing transactions or by having to secure alternate methods of payment.

Reserving Credit. The front office may reserve a specified amount of preauthorized credit in a guest's credit card account to ensure payment for goods and services. For instance, a guest who arrives and plans to stay for several nights will be expected to incur room charges in excess of the hotel's floor limit. To avoid a potential credit authorization problem, the front office may want to reserve a credit line of *at least* an amount equal to the anticipated charges in the guest's credit card account.

Management must be aware of the laws that pertain to reserving credit, as well as related credit card problems. Consider the case of a guest who decides to leave earlier than planned, and tries to make a subsequent purchase, only to discover that his or her credit is tied up in a reserve created by the hotel. Laws related to reserving credit vary from state to state. In some states, the hotel would be obligated to notify the credit card company to release the unused portion of the reserved line of credit when the guest checks out. Also, some states stipulate that a hotel can only reserve an anticipated amount of credit if it informs the guest beforehand, and obtains the guest's consent. Hotels should consult legal counsel before establishing a front office policy for reserving credit against credit card accounts.

The Newest Technology to Establish Credit. The newest technology to establish credit combines many of the issues above. When a guest arrives to check in, the front desk agent asks for the credit card before looking into the computer system and retrieving the registration card. The agent then puts the card through a credit card reader, which is attached to the front desk computer system. The computer reads the card and attempts to identify the arriving guest by displaying the registration record to the agent or providing a list of possible matches. Once the agent has identified the proper guest, the computer automatically calculates the amount to be reserved and calls the credit card company without any additional action by the agent. By the time the registration is completed, the hotel has an approval code already on the guest record or a denial. In addition, most credit card companies do not require the imprint of the credit card on a voucher in this situation, so the speed of the check-in process is also improved.

Direct Billing

Some hotels extend credit to guests by agreeing to bill the guest or the guest's company for charges. **Direct billing** arrangements are normally established through correspondence between the guest or company and the front office in advance of the guest's arrival. A potential guest or a sponsoring company representative may be asked to complete the hotel's application for credit. The front office manager normally reviews and is responsible for approving a guest's credit application. A list of approved direct billing accounts is usually maintained at the front desk for reference during registration. At check-out, a guest with approved credit simply signs his or her folio after approving its contents, and a statement is direct-billed for collection. In a direct billing arrangement, the hotel, not a credit card company or third party, assumes full responsibility for account collection.

Special Programs and Groups

During registration, guests may present vouchers, coupons, or special incentive awards received from businesses, airlines, or other authorized agencies. Front desk agents must be aware of hotel agreements to honor such vouchers and know how to properly credit the bearer. Front desk agents, too, must use care when handling special program vouchers because such documents may differ in value, conditions, or terms. Since vouchers represent a form of payment and may be the actual documents the front office uses to bill the issuing company, careful handling is warranted. Since vouchers and coupons represent revenue to the hotel, the front desk should have a book containing samples of all vouchers and coupons currently being accepted. This book should be discussed in front desk agent training and should be readily available in case any questions arise.

Front desk agents must be careful when registering group guests to be sure that their special needs are handled. Registering guests associated with a group is different from registering individual guests. Guests arriving at the hotel to attend corporate meetings often have their billing arrangements pre-established. In some cases, the guest's room and tax charges are direct-billed to a group master account. Other charges, such as telephone, food, beverage, and laundry, are the responsibility of individual guests. In this case, credit must be established for each member of the group. However, when the group agrees to pay for all of the charges made by its guests, it is important that guests not be asked to establish credit. For example, VIPs or invited speakers for a group's meeting should sign their registration cards, verify their departure dates, and be issued their room keys. Also, in these cases, it may not be appropriate to print the room rates on the registration cards.

Denying a Credit Request

When a front desk agent discovers that a guest has a poor credit rating, he or she must exercise extreme care in denying the guest's credit request. A person's credit involves more than money; it often involves self-esteem. In discussing problematic credit issues, the agent must be as diplomatic as possible. The agent's tone of voice should remain friendly and subdued, no matter how belligerent the guest may become. While the property has certain rights to review and evaluate credit information, the guest also has the right to know why the front office will not accept his or her personal check, credit card, or direct-bill arrangement. Exhibit 8 lists some suggested procedures for resolving credit problems. These suggestions should be modified to fit the problem, the guest, and the hotel's policies.

Issuing the Room Key

By issuing a room key, the front desk agent completes the registration process. In some hotels, a newly registered guest is simply handed a map of the hotel and a guestroom key. For the security of both the guest and the property, room keys must be very carefully controlled. The theft, loss, or unauthorized duplication and use of guestroom keys threaten hotel security.

Hotels should have written policies governing guestroom key control. These policies should state who is authorized to issue guestroom keys, who receives such keys, and where and how guestroom keys are stored at the front desk.

For security reasons, the front desk agent should never announce the room number when handing a guestroom key to the guest. The front desk agent can,

Exhibit 8 Suggestions for Resolving Credit Problems

When a credit card issuer refuses to authorize a transaction:

- Discuss the matter with the guest in private.
- Use care when describing the guest's unauthorized transaction (for example, do not call the guest's credit card "bad" or "worthless").
- Offer the use of a telephone to help resolve the matter with a credit card company representative.
- Allow the guest a chance to provide alternate, acceptable means of payment.

When a guest's personal check cannot be accepted:

- Explain the hotel's check cashing policy.
- Remain friendly and cooperative.
- Discuss alternative methods of payment with the guest.
- If local banks are open, direct the guest to a nearby branch, or extend the use of a telephone.

however, draw the guest's attention to the room number on the key. Front offices that use a special code on keys instead of room numbers need to have the front desk agent discreetly explain to the guest how to interpret the code or write the room number for the guest.

If the hotel provides bell service, the front desk agent should ask whether the guest would like assistance from a bellperson. If so, the front desk agent should introduce the bellperson to the guest, hand the bellperson the guest's room key, and ask him or her to show the guest to the room. On the way to the room, the bellperson might explain the special features of the hotel and such things as restaurant locations, retail outlets' hours of operation, locations of ice and vending machines and emergency exits, emergency procedures, and other appropriate information. Once inside the guestroom, the bellperson can explain the features of the room and should make the guest comfortable, answer any questions, and hand the room key to the guest. If the guest is displeased with the room, the bellperson should listen attentively and bring the matter to the attention of the front desk agent for immediate action.

Fulfilling Special Requests

Part of registration is making sure that any special requests made by guests are acknowledged and acted on. For example, guests may have requested connecting rooms during the reservations process. These rooms should be blocked in advance to ensure that they are available when the guests arrive. If it appears that the guest's reservation requests were not properly handled, the front desk agent should strive to satisfy the guest's requests at registration, if possible. Other special requests may involve guestroom:

- Location
- View
- Bed type
- Amenities
- Special furnishings for disabled guests

A guest may request a room close to or far from an elevator; one that overlooks the ocean, pool, or city; one that has a king-size bed; or one that has a refreshment center or sitting area. In addition, guests may ask for special furnishings or arrangements in the guestroom. A couple arriving with a young child may request a crib. If the room was not pre-set with a crib, the front desk agent should contact housekeeping to arrange for prompt delivery of a crib. It is best to handle these types of requests during preregistration, however. Some guests may ask for other special items such as bed boards or ironing boards. Disabled guests may require rooms with certain design features such as grab bars in the bath tub or special lights attached to smoke and fire detection systems. The Americans with Disabilities Act requires most lodging establishments to have special accommodations for disabled guests. These rooms should be specially reserved whenever possible and not sold to anyone who is not disabled unless there are no other rooms left in the hotel.

Sometimes, special requests are made by another person on behalf of the guest. For example, the general manager may want to welcome a frequent guest by placing a fruit basket in the guest's room. Travel agents may order a bottle of champagne to be delivered to the guestroom of their client. Honeymooning couples may request that champagne and flowers be in their rooms when they arrive.

While many of the details surrounding special requests can be handled during preregistration, it is important for the front office to follow up on each request. Guests are quickly disappointed if, upon arrival at their room, they find that the hotel did not honor their requests. Front desk agents should mention the guest's special requests at check-in to make sure that the hotel has provided what the guest requested. In this way, guests are better assured that their requests have been met.

Creative Options

The registration process described in this chapter is typical of most hotels. Some hotels have experimented with different techniques to make registration more efficient and effective. Techniques tried, with varying degrees of success, include:

- *Eliminating the front desk.* Instead, a host waits in a reception area with a list of expected guests and their pre-assigned rooms. The host identifies guests, completes an abbreviated registration process, and sometimes escorts guests to their rooms. Marriott, Hilton, and several other hotel companies are currently using this procedure at selected hotels. Credit is established at the time the reservation is made through a special interface between the central reservation computer and the credit card company. With everything else in place, all the hotel has to do is preregister the guest and attach a room key to the registration card. When the guest arrives, a simple verification of the information on the registration card completes the process.

- *Having a hotel greeter register guests at a special lobby location.* The regular front desk is screened off and used only for sorting and filing records and, with the screen temporarily removed, for settlement at peak check-out time.
- *Creating a unique, separate registration area for VIP guests.* This approach is similar to the hotel greeter concept just mentioned, but is only available to VIPs.
- *Conbining the hotel registration with the meeting registration in a separate area of the building.* Separating non-group guests from groups enables the hotel to offer more personalized service.

The challenge is to make the hotel registration process innovative, while treating guests with expediency and care.

The rooming process can be further simplified for corporate gatherings, tour groups, and convention groups. The group's coordinator or the front desk computer can supply the staff with a rooming list that contains the names of members of an expected group. Room numbers can then be pre-assigned before the group arrives, and guestroom keys can be personally addressed and placed in envelopes with a welcoming note from the manager. A separate desk can be set up in the lobby, away from the front desk area, for the purpose of quickly distributing envelopes to arriving guests. Front desk agents still handle registration, but group representatives are nearby to welcome group members, provide convention information, or distribute meeting materials.

Some hotel front office services include temporary luggage storage for guests who arrive during heavy check-out periods. In addition, front desk agents may offer complimentary food or beverages to guests who may be inconvenienced. These guests may be directed to the hotel's lounge or restaurant to enjoy a more relaxed and leisurely wait while their guestrooms are being readied.

Self-Registration

A relatively new concept in front office registration is **self-registration.** Self-registration terminals are usually located in the lobbies of fully automated hotels. These terminals can vary in design: some resemble automated bank teller machines (ATM), while others possess both video and audio capability. Exhibit 9 shows one type of self-registration terminal. Recent technological advances allow hotels to place self-registration terminals at off-premises locations such as airports and car rental agencies. Regardless of which kind of guest-operated device is used, self-registration terminals can significantly reduce front office and guest registration time.

To use an advanced self-registration terminal, a guest generally must have made a reservation which led to the creation of a reservation record. At the time of self-registration, the guest may need to enter a reservation confirmation number or

Exhibit 9 Self-Registration Terminal

Courtesy of CAPDATA, Inc., Scottsdale, Arizona

insert a valid credit card into the machine. The terminal reads the magnetic strip on the back of the credit card and passes the name and credit card number to the hotel computer, which attempts to locate the reservation record. The terminal then prompts the guest to enter additional registration data using the terminal's keypad. Most terminals are interfaced with a computerized rooms management system, thereby enabling automatic room and rate assignment. Some terminals print out registration forms and request the guest to sign and deposit it into a drop box. Customized greetings or messages about special events or promotions can be added to system-generated forms or displayed on the terminal's screen. Some terminals then direct the guest to a guestroom key pickup area. In some cases, the terminal itself may dispense a guestroom key as a result of being interfaced with an electronic guestroom locking system.

Selling the Guestroom

Front desk agents will not have the chance to use efficient or innovative registration techniques if the guest is not convinced of the value of renting a hotel room. Part of the front desk agent's job is to create consumer acceptance of the hotel's products: guestrooms, facilities, and services. Front desk agents can take several approaches to selling guests on the value of staying at the hotel.

Front desk agents should practice sales techniques specific to their work. The registration process, for example, must move through certain stages to ensure quick and careful registration. But within these stages, front office staff frequently have the opportunity to make individual sales presentations. Properly trained front office staff can substantially improve room revenue by applying front office sales techniques, especially the technique of upselling.

Upselling refers to the efforts of reservations agents and front desk agents to convince guests to rent rooms in categories above standard rate accommodations. Hotels normally have several rate categories based on such factors as decor, size, location, view, and furnishings. Sometimes, the rack rate difference between two similar guestrooms can be substantial.

To upsell, front office and reservations staff must be trained to be more than simply order-takers. They must be trained to be professional salespeople. These personnel must see that they can upsell rooms in much the same way that a food server can sell an extra food item such as an appetizer or dessert. Front office staff should learn effective techniques for suggesting room options to guests. This involves knowing how and when to ask for a sale in a non-pressuring way and how to direct the sale from the guest's perspective.

Offering guestroom options is the key to the reservations and registration sales process, and it requires thoughtful planning and practice. Although the majority of upselling is conducted during the reservations process, front desk agents are likely to have similar sales opportunities with walk-in guests. Some hotels, as a matter of policy, offer registering guests more than one room option and then let them state their preferences. To create guest acceptance, the front desk agent must know how to describe the hotel's facilities and services in a positive manner.

A guest will probably provide several clues about what is acceptable for his or her stay; some information may already be available on a reservation record. Front desk agents should mention the physical features as well as the benefits and conveniences of alternative, available rooms. A guest may select a room immediately after it is described, or may wait until the front desk agent describes all the room options. Exhibit 10 lists some general suggestions for upselling guestrooms.

The front desk agent normally requests the guest to complete a registration card after selecting a room. As the guest is filling out the card, the front desk agent may

Exhibit 10 Suggestions for Upselling Guestrooms

- Always greet each guest with a smile in your voice as well as on your face. Be pleasant and businesslike. Remember: you are selling yourself as much as you are selling the hotel and its services.
- Establish and maintain eye contact with the guest.
- Find out the guest's name immediately and use it at least three times during the conversation. Always use courteous titles such as "Mr." or "Ms." when addressing the guest. Do not call a guest by his or her first name.
- Attempt to identify the needs of the guest since these needs may not have been identified during the reservations process. Match the guest's needs to the furnishings and/or amenities from among available rooms. For example, a guest staying at the hotel for three or four nights may appreciate and be more willing to pay for a larger or more isolated room than a guest staying only one night. Guests on a honeymoon or special vacation may be willing to pay for a room with a scenic view.
- Upsell rooms when possible. Offer an upgraded room by pointing out its features and benefits first, then mention its rate. If the guest has a reservation, describe the differences between the reserved and the upgraded room. Walk-in guests provide the best opportunity for upselling. If two different types of rooms are available, mention the features, benefits, and rates of both. Do not risk losing the sale by mentioning only the higher-priced room.
- Complete the registration process.
- Thank the guest and wish him or her a pleasant stay.

reinforce the guest's choice by recapping the room's special features. As registration draws to a close, the front desk agent should inform the guest about the hotel's revenue outlets, services, and facilities. Most guests appreciate this information.

Before the guest leaves the desk, the front desk agent should thank the guest for choosing the hotel and express a personal interest in making his or her stay as pleasant as possible. Some hotels have front desk agents place a personal call to the guest's room shortly after registration, to ensure that the guest's accommodations are satisfactory.

Upselling to walk-in guests often holds the best opportunity to create more revenue for the hotel. In some cases, only the highest rated rooms may be available. In other cases, a good selling effort, creating the impression of additional value, will convince a guest that the increased room rate is worth the expense. It is very common for hotels to offer incentive programs for reservations and front desk staff who successfully upsell rooms.

When Guests Cannot Be Accommodated

In general, a hotel is obligated to accommodate guests. Discrimination is prohibited in places of public accommodation on the basis of race, sex, religion, or national origin. Legitimate reasons for refusing to accommodate a guest may include a lack of available rooms, or the potential guest's disorderly conduct or unwillingness to pay for accommodations or services. In addition, state law may stipulate other reasons for guest denial. A front desk agent should not be the person who determines whether someone will be roomed or not. This is the responsibility of front office management. Management is also responsible for informing the person that he or she has to be turned away. Management, with the advice of legal counsel and the state hotel association, should instruct front office staff on policies and procedures concerning the acceptance or rejection of potential guests.

On occasion, a hotel may be short of available rooms and may not be able to accommodate guests. It is imperative that the hotel set policies for handling these situations. Seldom, if ever, should a hotel be unable to accommodate a guest with a reservation, especially a guaranteed reservation. When this happens, most hotels will make other arrangements for the guest. In the case of a guaranteed reservation, most full-service hotels will pay for the guest's room at another property. It is important to remember that the hotel may have no obligation to guests without guaranteed reservations, or to guests who arrive after the hotel's reservation cancellation hour (often 6 P.M.). Generally speaking, guests with reservations who arrive before the cancellation hour should be accommodated.

Walk-In Guests

The classic nightmare for the tired **walk-in** guest is to travel for miles and miles only to find that the hotel is fully occupied. Hotels have no obligation to accommodate guests who arrive without a reservation when no rooms are available for the night. If a walk-in guest cannot be accommodated, front desk agents can make the situation a little easier for the guest by suggesting and providing directions to alternative hotels nearby. The front desk agent may even offer to call another hotel to assist the guest.

Most of the time, guests who cannot be accommodated at the hotel would prefer to stay at a similar property. Hotels should keep a list, with phone numbers, of comparable properties in the area. Hotels can reap some significant benefits through mutual guest referrals as well as create goodwill. For one, guest referrals allow one hotel to compare how well it is doing on a given night with other area hotels. Competing properties, too, may reciprocate by sending overflow business to the hotel. But mainly, referrals should be viewed as part of the hotel's guest relations program. The extra care paid to turned away guests helps create an industry-wide atmosphere of concern and goodwill.

The situation may be more difficult when a walk-in guest believes he or she has a reservation. A hotel might take the following steps to clarify the situation:

- If the guest presents a letter of confirmation, verify the date and the name of the hotel; the guest may have arrived on a different date or at the wrong property. Most confirmation letters have a confirmation number which will help the front desk agent locate the reservation record.

- Ask whether another person might have made the reservation for the guest; the reservation may be at another property, or it may be misfiled under the caller's name, not the guest's name.

- Re-check the reservation file or computer system in view of the guest; perhaps the reservation was incorrectly filed or otherwise mishandled.
- Doublecheck the reservations file for another spelling of the guest's last name. For instance, B, P, and T may have been confused when the reservation was made during a telephone conversation. Also, check to see if the guest's first and last names were inadvertently reversed in the reservation file.
- If the reservation was made through a travel agency or representative, allow the guest to call the originating source for clarification.
- Ask the guest to confirm his or her arrival date; the guest may be arriving on a different day or a day late. Many hotels hold no-show registration cards from the previous day in the front of the registration file just in case a no-show arrives a day late.

If there seems to be no alternative to **walking** (turning away) the guest, a manager, not a front desk agent, should explain the matter in a private office. Registering one guest in view of another who cannot be accommodated can be extremely awkward and embarrassing.

Guests with Non-Guaranteed Reservations

A number of situations or circumstances can delay a guest's scheduled arrival. Guests frequently do not have the chance to change a non-guaranteed reservation to a guaranteed reservation by the time they realize they will arrive past the hotel's reservation cancellation hour. As a result, the hotel may not hold the room for the guest and may not have a room available when the guest arrives. If the hotel cannot provide a guestroom, front office management must be extremely tactful when informing the guest. Blame should not be placed on either party since the lack of accommodations is neither the guest's nor the hotel's fault.

Guests with Guaranteed Reservations

If reservations are carefully handled and sound forecasting procedures are followed, the property should not have to deny accommodations to a guest with a guaranteed reservation. Nonetheless, a property should have a policy for front desk staff to follow in such situations.

The front office manager should take charge and make necessary decisions when it appears the property will not have accommodations for a guest with a guaranteed reservation. The manager may:

- Review all front desk transactions to ensure full occupancy.
- Re-take an accurate count of rooms occupied, using all relevant data.
- Compare the room rack, housekeeper's report, and guest folios for any discrepancy in occupancy status.
- Telephone **due-outs** (guests expected to check out today) who have not yet checked out and confirm their departure time. If they do not answer the telephone, the rooms department should visit the guestroom to verify continued

occupancy. The guest may have left the hotel without stopping at the front desk or properly completing check-out. The guest may have expected to be billed, or may have paid in advance, or simply forgot to check out at the front desk. Finally, an early discovery of a **skipper** (a guest who leaves with no intention of paying for the room) will allow the guestroom to be assigned to another guest.

- Personally check the current status of rooms listed as out-of-order. Perhaps an out-of-order room might be readied for sale. If a guest is willing to occupy an out-of-order room, perhaps its rate could be appropriately adjusted. These decisions must be made by front office management.
- Identify rooms pre-blocked for one or two days in the future and preregister guests arriving today who will depart in time to honor the blocks.

Front desk staff should be consistent when discussing the lack of accommodations with arriving guests. Helpful suggestions include:

- Guests may be encouraged to return to the hotel at the earliest date of availability. Upon their return, they may be placed on a VIP list, provided a complimentary room upgrade, or be presented with a small gift as compensation for the inconvenience of being turned away.
- Management should prepare a follow-up letter to be sent to guests who arrived with a reservation but could not be accommodated, apologizing again for the inconvenience and encouraging the guest to consider returning to the hotel (with appropriate incentives).
- If a member of a convention block cannot be accommodated, the group's meeting planner should be notified. The planner may be able to solve the problem by arranging for some attendees to alter their current rooming status. In such situations, it is important for the front office staff to have a strong working relationship with the meeting planner.
- If a member of a tour group cannot be accommodated, the tour organizer should be notified immediately and the situation explained. This notification may better enable the organizer to properly deal with the problem and subsequent membership complaints.
- The hotel may pay the transportation expenses associated with having the guest travel to an alternative property. Financial considerations are especially important when walking a guest with a guaranteed reservation. The hotel may also notify its telephone department of the change to another hotel so that incoming calls and faxes can be redirected without confusion or concern on the part of the caller or the relocated guest.

Summary

Through the reservations process, a guest provides nearly all the information needed to complete registration. The focus of front office operations shifts to the registration process once the arriving guest's reservation status is known. Front office personnel will find registration smoother and simpler when the information contained in a reservation record is accurate and complete. The registration process can be divided into six steps: preregistration activity; creating the registration record; assigning the room and rate; establishing the method of payment; issuing the room key; and fulfilling special guest requests.

Preregistration activities occur before guest arrival and are intended to accelerate the registration process. Guests can be preregistered when reservations agents gather the proper information. Typically, preregistered guests only need to verify registration information and provide a valid signature to complete the registration process. In addition, room and rate assignment, creation of a guest folio, and other functions may also be part of a hotel's preregistration activities.

The registration record is a collection of important guest information, and is created at the time of check-in. Registration cards, or their computer-generated equivalent, should inquire about the guest's intentions relative to method of payment and planned date of departure. Front desk agents should always confirm the guest's departure date and pre-assigned room rate.

Room assignment involves identifying and allocating an available room in a specific room category. Based on reservation information, specific rooms and rates may be assigned before the guest arrives. Pre-assigning a specific room depends on the room's forecasted availability status and how appropriately the room meets the guest's needs. Room assignments are finalized during the registration process. Effective room and rate assignment depends on accurate and timely room status information (long-term "reservation status" and short-term "housekeeping status").

Effective account settlement depends on the steps taken during registration to determine the guest's method of payment. Proper settlement or credit authorization at the time of registration will greatly reduce the potential for subsequent collection problems. Just as hotels vary in size, structure, and organization, so do the guidelines for establishing the guest's method of payment. The registration process may also play an important role in guest accounting, since it deals directly with method of payment.

By issuing a room key, the front desk agent completes the registration process. Hotels should have written policies governing guestroom key control. If the hotel provides bell service, the front desk agent should ask whether the guest would like assistance from a bellperson and then communicate specific room information to the bellperson.

Part of registration is making sure that any special requests made by guests are acknowledged and dealt with. While many of the details surrounding special requests can be addressed during preregistration, it is important to follow up on each request. Guests are quickly disappointed if they arrive at their room and find that the hotel did not honor a request. Front desk agents should mention special guest requests during registration to assure the guest that the hotel will meet the guest's wants and needs.

A relatively new concept in front office registration is self-registration. Self-registration terminals are usually located in the lobbies of fully automated hotels.

These terminals can vary in design and may resemble an automated bank teller machine.

Upselling at the front desk is a common practice used to enhance the value of the lodging experience to the guest while increasing hotel revenues. Front desk agents should identify opportunities for offering better accommodations to guests and selling their value. For example, guests who travel regularly as part of their work may appreciate rooms with special business amenities at a small increase in the room rate they confirmed. Many hotels provide incentive programs for agents making the most of such opportunities.

Relocating (or walking) guests must be done with great care and concern. Guests who believe the hotel has not acted in their best interest will be very upset. They may cause a disturbance in the hotel and may refuse to return in the future. Further, they may criticize the hotel to friends and co-workers, creating an even larger negative image of the hotel. Walking a guest should be done by a manager, not a front desk agent. Hotels should pay for all the nights the guest is relocated, and attempt to bring the guest back as quickly as possible. Upscale hotels usually add transportation to and from the relocated hotel and advise their telephone departments to redirect incoming telephone calls and faxes to the other location.

Key Terms

American Plan (AP)—a billing arrangement under which room charges include the guestroom and three meals; also called full pension.

authorization code—a code generated by an online credit card verification service, indicating that the requested transaction has been approved.

denial code—a code generated by an online credit card verification service, indicating that the requested transaction has not been approved.

direct billing—a credit arrangement, normally established through correspondence between a guest or a company and the hotel, in which the hotel agrees to bill the guest or the company for charges incurred.

due-outs—guests expected to check out on a given day who have not yet done so.

European Plan—a billing arrangement under which meals are priced separately from rooms.

floor limit—a limit assigned to hotels by credit card companies indicating the maximum amount in credit card charges the hotel is permitted to accept from a card member without special authorization.

housekeeping status report—a report prepared by the housekeeping department indicating the current housekeeping status of each room, based on a physical check.

Modified American Plan (MAP)—a billing arrangement under which the daily rate includes charges for the guestroom and two meals—typically breakfast and dinner.

occupancy report—a report prepared each night by a front desk agent that lists the rooms occupied that night and indicates those guests expected to check out the following day.

on-change status—indicates that the room requires housekeeping services before it can be resold.

PIA (paid-in-advance)—a guest who pays his or her room charges in cash during registration; PIA guests are often denied in-house credit.

rack rate—the standard rate established by a hotel for a particular category of rooms.

registration card—a printed form for a registration record; in most states, the guest's signature on a registration card is required by law.

registration record—a collection of important guest information created by the front desk agent following the guest's arrival; includes the guest's name, address, telephone number, and company affiliation; method of payment; and date of departure.

reservation status—an indicator of a room's long-term availability for assignment.

room rate—the price a hotel charges for overnight accommodations.

room status discrepancy—a situation in which the housekeeping department's description of a room's status differs from the room status information which guides front desk employees in assigning rooms to guests.

self-registration—a computerized system that automatically registers a guest and dispenses a key, based on the guest's reservation and credit card information.

skipper—a guest who leaves with no intention of paying for the room.

upselling—a sales technique whereby a guest is offered a more expensive room than what he or she reserved or originally requested, and then persuaded to rent the room based on the room's features, benefits, and his or her needs.

walk-in—a guest who arrives at a hotel without a reservation.

walking—turning away a guest who has a reservation because of a lack of rooms.

Review Questions

1. What are the steps of the registration process from the viewpoint of the front desk agent?
2. What are the advantages of preregistering guests? What might limit the front office's ability to preregister guests?
3. What information is usually requested on a guest registration card? How is this information useful to the front office?
4. Why is current room status information essential to an effective guest registration process?
5. What are the advantages of a computerized room status system?
6. What are some examples of special room rates?
7. What major methods of payment are used by guests? What forms of tender are generally considered equivalent to cash?

8. What procedures do front desk agents use for accepting a credit card as a method of payment during registration?
9. How can front desk agents create acceptance of the hotel's rooms and facilities during the registration process?
10. What procedures should the front office consider when a guest cannot be accommodated?
11. What is upselling? When is it appropriate? What are some things a hotel can do to upsell a guest?

Internet Sites

For more information, visit the following Internet sites. Remember that Internet addresses can change without notice.

Credit Card Companies

American Express Company
http://www.americanexpress.com

Diners Club International
http://www.dinersclub.com

MasterCard International
http://www.mastercard.com

VISA International
http://www.visa.com

Hotel Companies

Best Western
http://www.bestwestern.com

Canadian Pacific Hotels
http://www.cphotels.ca

Hyatt Hotels & Resorts
http://www.hyatt.com

Inter-Continential Hotels
http://www.interconti.com

ITT Sheraton Corporation
http://www.sheraton.com

Marriott Hotels, Resorts, & Suites
http://www.marriotthotels.com

Radisson Hotels Worldwide
http://www.radisson.com

Ritz-Carlton Hotels
http://www.ritzcarlton.com

Westin Hotels and Resorts
http://www.westin.com

Technology Sites

Anasazi, Inc.
http://www.anasazi.com

CSS Hotel Systems
http://www.csshotelsystems.com

Executech Systems, Inc.
http://www.executech.com

Fidelio Products
http://www.micros.com/scripts/vertical.pl

Hospitality Industry Technology Exposition and Conference
http://www.hitecshow.org

Hospitality Industry Technology Integration Standards
http://www.hitis.org

HOST Group
http://www.hostgroup.com

Lodging Touch International
http://www.lodgingtouch.com

Newmarket Software Systems, Inc.
http://www.newsoft.com

Western Hospitality Systems—InnSure
http://www.lodgingsystems.com

Case Study

Everybody Sells: Turning Front Desk Agents into Salespeople

"Come in, come in!"

Ben, a slim, gray-haired figure in a dark three-piece suit, rose from his leather desk chair and waved Keith into one of the two chairs on the other side of the massive oak desk. Keith said "Thank you" and glanced around the general manager's office as Ben settled into the chair next to his. Keith had been in the office a few times before, but he was still impressed by the floor-to-ceiling bookshelves behind the desk, the lithographs of old hotels that lined the walls, the awards and testimonial plaques that were sprinkled throughout the room.

"The reason I wanted to talk with you today," Ben began, "is to discuss what we can do to bring up our average daily rate. You've been at the hotel a couple of weeks now and I assume you've learned your way around a bit."

"Yes sir."

Ben's eyes twinkled. "I've told you before, just because my hair is gray and I've been in the hotel business a hundred years, there's no need to call me 'sir.' 'Ben' will do."

Keith smiled and just stopped himself from saying "Yes sir" again.

"I've received word that corporate wants us to raise our ADR ten percent by the end of the quarter, and the front desk has got to do its part." Ben leaned back in his chair and clasped his hands over his vest. He reminded Keith of a kindly, longtime family lawyer getting set to dispense some grandfatherly advice. "I don't want to be insulting, but, since this is your first job as a front office manager—in fact, you're not that long out of college, is that correct?"

"That's right, just a few years," Keith said. "Still 'wet behind the ears,' you might say."

"Well, if you'll indulge me, I'd like to relate a little history of the relationship between the reservations department and the front desk; I think it will help you appreciate how we got to where we are today, and put into perspective what I'll be asking you to do to help us get that extra ten percent."

"Okay." Keith settled back for a long story.

"My first hotel job was in the reservations office. Back then there were no computers. We did have phones, however, in case you were wondering." Keith smiled as Ben chuckled. "People would call in requesting a room, and we would roll an index card into a typewriter and type out a reservation. The caller didn't make special requests, such as 'a room with a desk, please,' or 'a king-size bed, please,' and we didn't ask for any of that information, because we weren't sure what type of room would be available—back then inventory control was all done at the front desk. The card was simply a request that a room be held for the caller on a certain day. The cards would all be gathered up at the end of the shift and taken to the front desk, where they would be filed by the day the reservation was for.

"When the guest arrived at the hotel, the front desk agent would pull the card ('Yes, Mr. Whosis, we have a room for you') and then the selling would begin, based on what types of rooms the agent knew were still available: 'Would you like a king-size bed?' 'We have several rooms with a nice view of the park—would you care for one of those?' and so on. In other words, the front desk agents were the hotel's salespeople, because they had control of the guestroom inventory. They knew which rooms were available and which were not.

"Well, along came computers, and suddenly sales moved from the front desk to the reservations department. Why? Because computers allowed the reservations department to keep track of guestroom inventory. Now when a caller phoned the hotel, the reservationist could look at a computer screen and tell exactly what rooms were still available on the day the caller wanted to stay at the hotel. So the reservationist, instead of merely reserving 'a' room—the old card system could do that much—could now reserve a *particular* room. The reservationist could ask the caller all of the questions the front desk agent used to ask: 'What size bed would you like? 'Would you like a room with a view?' 'For five dollars more I can reserve a room near the pool; would you like that?' and so on. Therefore, once computerized reservations systems arrived and guestroom inventory control shifted from the front desk to the reservations department, the sales function and all of the sales training shifted from the front desk to the reservations department, too."

Ben spread his hands in a gesture of regret. "Consequently, salesmanship was not emphasized at the front desk any more. In fact, many agents saw no need to sell, because most guests had already told the reservationist exactly what types of rooms they wanted. Many front desk agents thought they would be 'bothering' a guest if they suggested a room other than the one called for by the reservation already entered into the computer.

"But—and this is something I could never get your predecessor to understand, or at least to act on," Ben frowned, "front desk agents can still have a tremendous impact on a hotel's bottom line, through upselling. For example, if a guest walks in with his wife, and the front desk agent sees that he has reserved a standard room, the agent should say something like the following: 'Sir, we have a room available that you might enjoy more than the one you've reserved. The room I'm thinking of is a corner room with a great view. It also has a whirlpool tub that's great for relaxing, a sitting area, and a king-size bed—which would be an upgrade from the two double beds in your present room—all for only $15 more. Would you like me to reserve this room for you?'

"Or, if an agent sees a guest come in lugging three sample cases, he can assume that this is a businessperson who probably would like enough space in his room to spread out business papers or samples or what have you. The agent should say something like this: 'Gee, it looks like you're really loaded down, sir. I see that you've reserved a standard guestroom, but I have a bigger room with plenty of desk space for only $10 more.' What's wrong with that?"

Ben stopped talking and looked at Keith expectantly.

"Nothing?" Keith ventured.

"That's right, there's nothing wrong with that!" Ben said enthusiastically. "The agent made a suggestion that might make the guest's stay more pleasant and also increase revenues for the hotel. That's all there is to upselling. But so few agents are trained to do that anymore. Like I said, computers changed everything. In the old days, reservationists were 'order-takers' and the front desk agents were the salespeople; now the roles are completely reversed. And it shouldn't be that way. Front desk agents still have a sales role to play."

Ben chuckled again. "Thank you for letting me climb up on my soapbox. You're probably wondering, 'What does all this have to do with me?' Well, what I want you to do is turn your front desk agents into salespeople again. We've got to teach them how to sell and give them the tools to sell so they'll have the confidence to sell."

"I hope this doesn't sound naive," Keith said, "but, can upselling really make that much difference? I mean, $5 here, $10 there, and not every guest is going to agree to an upgrade." Keith paused. "I guess I'm not sure how much that's really going to add to the bottom line."

"That's the beauty of upselling," Ben replied. "Every extra dollar you bring in through upselling falls to the bottom line. We've already spent the money to get the guest to the hotel—through advertising, the reservationist taking the call, and so on. Now that he's here, anything extra we can entice him into spending is pure gravy."

Ben smiled. "Now, don't get the wrong idea. I don't mean to sound manipulative, because upselling—done properly—is not the art of tricking a guest into buying something he doesn't want. A front desk agent should never pressure a guest. However, there's nothing wrong with pointing out to a guest that, for a few dollars more, his or her experience at the hotel might be enhanced. Usually, guests are unaware that there are rooms available that might better fit their needs. Maybe the reservationist didn't do a great job of selling, who knows? So agents aren't trying to 'gouge' guests when they upsell—they are merely offering a guest some options that the guest might not have thought about, options that might make the guest's experience at the hotel more enjoyable. That's the way you should present upselling to your agents."

"I'll be glad to try," Keith said, "but I'm not sure how to go about it."

"Well, the first thing I'd do is assess the current sales skills of my staff," Ben said. "Is anyone selling right now? You've only been here a couple of weeks and I know you're not fully acquainted with your personnel, so I'd spend some time observing the agents. This might also give you ideas on what types of upselling opportunities the agents are missing. If you discover a pattern, that will give you a plan of attack on good ways to raise the ADR.

"What I suspect you're going to find," Ben continued, "is that few, if any, agents are upselling right now. But don't be discouraged. There are lots of techniques we can use in-house to train them; we may even send them to some outside seminars, or bring a trainer here if we have to. Also, you'll probably want to set up an incentive program to encourage the agents to sell."

Ben stood up to signal an end to the meeting and placed a hand on Keith's shoulder. "Don't worry, I'm confident you can do it. And you're not alone. All we need from the front desk area is an additional five percent; reservations and the sales department have targets to meet, too, and—working together—we'll make our numbers and corporate will be happy. If you run into trouble, don't hesitate to come see me."

"Thank you, Ben."

During the next week, Keith observed the front desk agents as they checked in guests. As Ben predicted, they didn't make any effort to upsell. They were polite and professional, but invariably they sent the guests to whatever room they had previously reserved. Even with walk-in guests there was no salesmanship. The agents always offered the walk-ins one of the hotel's standard guestrooms—the lowest-priced rooms in the house—and almost every walk-in simply accepted them. Keith observed only one walk-in guest who asked if there were better rooms available. The agent said yes, the hotel had some deluxe rooms available, and there was even one club room still available. (The hotel had three basic types of rooms: "standard" guestrooms with either two double beds, two queen-size beds, or one king-size bed; "deluxe" guestrooms with the same bed combinations but with slightly more floor space and better appointments; and "club" rooms that were really mini-suites with king-size beds, sitting areas, and special amenities such as thicker towels, upgraded toiletries, turn-down service, and so on.) When the guest asked the agent to describe the differences in the rooms, Keith was surprised to hear the agent do a terrible job of outlining the different features and amenities that accompanied each type of room. Later, Keith checked with some of the other agents and was shocked to learn that many of them had never seen any of the hotel's guestrooms.

As the week wore on, Keith noticed a pattern that concerned him: most of the hotel's club rooms were given as upgrades to the hotel's business guests. Those rooms were supposed to be real money-makers for the hotel, because the hotel sold them at a higher rate than the standard and deluxe guestrooms, but that was precisely the problem—the rooms were rarely sold. As part of its special corporate rates, the hotel promised business travelers free upgrades to club rooms "subject to availability." And club rooms were always available, because front desk agents weren't selling them! If Keith did nothing more than get his agents to sell more club rooms, that would have a dramatic impact on ADR, because the rooms would be sold rather than given to guests who were already enjoying a discounted corporate rate.

At the end of the week, Keith met with his front desk agents at the beginning of their shifts and explained the situation. "The overall goal of the hotel is to raise ADR by ten percent; our contribution is to increase our numbers by five percent. We can do that by upselling—to all of our guests, but especially to our walk-ins. According to my research, about 12 percent of our guests are walk-ins, and since these guests have no prior reservations, they're not committed to a particular room and should be easier to upsell. If we start out by offering walk-ins our club rooms, rather than our standard rooms, then offer a deluxe room as a compromise if they don't want a club room, I think we can almost make our numbers right there, not even counting upselling to guests who already have reservations.

"Let me give you an example of how a little bit of upselling can make a big difference," Keith continued. "We sold about 1,000 rooms to walk-ins last month. All but 14 of those guests were booked in standard rooms at around $55 per night. If we sell club rooms, which sell for $40 more, to 200 of those walk-ins (that's just one upgraded guest out of five) that brings in an additional $8,800 for the month. Project that over 12 months, and we're bringing in over $100,000 more revenue per year for the hotel. Just moving 200 walk-ins from a standard to a deluxe room at $75 a night would bring in $4,400 more a month. And those dollars fall right to the bottom line.

"If we sell out the club rooms—and that should be our goal every night—they are no longer available as free giveaways to businesspeople, which saves us money and gives us upselling opportunities: 'I'm sorry, Ms. Businessperson, but our club rooms are full tonight. I can go ahead and book you into your standard room, or I can upgrade you to a deluxe guestroom with lots of space and a king-size bed for just $20 more.' Don't save the club rooms so you are sure to have some available to give away as upgrades. What you want to do is sell them out, so we don't have to give them away."

"Isn't that kind of unfair to the business travelers?" asked one agent.

"Not really," Keith replied. "Our deals with business travelers state that we will upgrade them to club rooms if any are available—but we certainly aren't obligated to deliberately not sell club rooms to make sure they're available. That's not good business, and businesspeople don't expect us to do that. The hotel put a lot of money into those club rooms, and it's entitled to try to recoup that investment if it can.

"I know the idea of selling is a new one for many of you," Keith said in conclusion, "but it isn't that difficult, and I'm not going to just shove you out there unprepared. You're going to get some training, and I'm also going to come up with an incentive plan so you can share in the rewards of bringing more revenue to the hotel.

"Upselling can be enjoyable if you approach it the right way, so get ready to have some fun! And here's a slogan I want you to remember from now on: 'Everybody Sells!'"

Discussion Questions

1. What are some ways Keith can train his front desk agents to be salespeople?
2. What types of incentive plans might Keith put in place to encourage his front desk agents to sell?

Case Number: 3325CA
The following industry experts helped generate and develop this case: Richard M. Brooks, CHA, Vice President—Operations, Bridgestreet Accommodations, Inc., Cleveland, Ohio; and S. Kenneth Hiller, Director of Transition, Renaissance Hotels International, Solon, Ohio.

This case also appears in *Case Studies in Lodging Management* (Lansing, Mich.: Educational Institute of the American Hotel & Motel Association, 1998), ISBN 0-86612-184-6.

Chapter 6 Outline

6

Front Office Responsibilities

COMMUNICATION IS VITAL to front office operations because nearly everything that happens in a hotel affects the front office and vice versa. All functions of the front office rely in part on clear communication. Front office staff must communicate effectively with one another, with personnel in other departments and divisions, and with guests. Effective communication is a prerequisite to an efficient front office. This chapter will examine the importance of communication and several ongoing responsibilities of the front office: guest service, guest relations, and security.

Front Office Communications

Communication involves not only memorandums, face-to-face conversations, and messages sent over computer terminals. Effective front office communication also involves the use of log books, information directories, and mail and telephone procedures. The complexity of front office communication tends to be directly related to the number of guestrooms and the size and extent of the hotel's public areas and facilities. The larger the hotel and the more people involved, the more complex the communication network. Even in smaller hotels, communication is not simple or easy.

Log Book

The front desk may keep a **log book** so that front office staff are aware of important events and decisions that occurred during previous workshifts. A typical front office log book is a daily journal which chronicles unusual events, guest complaints or requests, and other relevant information. Front desk agents record in the log book throughout their shift. These notes should be clearly written in a prescribed form so they serve as effective reference material for the next shift.

Before beginning their shift, front desk supervisors and agents should review and initial the log book, noting any current activities, situations that require follow-up, or potential problems. For example, a front desk agent on the morning shift might record that a guest phoned requesting maintenance or housekeeping services. The agent might also note what action was taken to resolve the situation. These notations become an important link in the communication network that informs the subsequent shifts of previous happenings. The front office log book should detail what happened, why, and when. By reviewing these notes, the front desk agent on duty can respond intelligently if the guest contacts the front desk for follow-up.

The front office log book is also important to management. It helps management understand the activity of the front desk and it records any ongoing issues. For example, if there are recurring problems with housekeeping or engineering issues, one of the best ways to identify these problems is in the front office log book. Also, should there be any guest complaints, compliments, or unusual activity, the log book helps management understand what happened and how it was handled.

Information Directory

Front office staff must be able to respond in a knowledgeable way when guests contact the front desk for information. Common guest questions involve:

- Local restaurant recommendations
- Contacting a taxi company
- Directions to local companies
- Directions to the nearest shopping center, drugstore, or gas station
- Directions to the nearest places of worship
- Directions to the nearest bank or automated teller machine
- Directions to a theater, stadium, or ticket agency
- Directions to universities, libraries, museums, or other points of local interest
- Directions to the federal building, capitol, district court, or city hall
- Information about hotel policies (for example, check-out time or pets)
- Information about the hotel's recreational facilities or those near the hotel

Front desk agents may need to access some obscure information to answer guest questions. Some front offices accumulate such data in a bound guide called an **information directory.** The front office information directory may include simplified maps of the area; taxi and airline company telephone numbers; bank, theater, church, and store locations; and special event schedules. Front desk agents should be familiar with the information directory's format and content.

Some hotels have installed computer information terminals in public areas including the lobby area. These terminals are essentially an electronic equivalent of the front office information directory. Computer-based information terminals are easily accessed by guests without front office staff assistance. This ease of access frees front desk agents to attend to other guest needs.

In addition, many hotels provide a printed schedule of daily events or display a daily event board through a closed-circuit television system. A common industry term for displaying daily events is the **reader board.** Printed itineraries may be placed at the front desk, in elevators, and throughout the lobby area. A closed-circuit television system can also reduce the volume of information requests at the front desk. Television monitors may be placed in convenient locations so that guests can review the list of daily events scrolling on the screen.

In convention hotels, it is also common to have a **group résumé** book at the front desk. Each group staying in the hotel has a summary of all its activities, billing instructions, key attendees, recreational arrangements, arrival and departure patterns, and other important information. These summaries are usually stored in a binder at the front desk. Some hotels prefer to store the résumés by group name. Many hotels make the group résumé book required reading for front desk and uniformed staff at the beginning of each work shift. Front desk staff should familiarize themselves with the résumés of all incoming groups to be sure they know what arrangements the front desk is responsible for. In addition, front desk staff should know where the group résumé book is located so that any questions concerning the group can be answered quickly and correctly.

Mail and Package Handling

Registered guests rely on the front office to relay delivered mail and packages quickly and efficiently. Front office managers normally develop policies for mail and package handling based on the policies and regulations supplied by the United States Postal Service.

In general, the front office is expected to time-stamp all guest mail when it arrives at the property. Doing so documents the date and time that the mail was received in case any question arises about when the mail arrived or how quickly the guest was notified of its arrival. When mail and packages arrives, front office records should be checked immediately to verify that the guest is currently registered, due to check in, or has already checked out. Different mail handling procedures should be prescribed for each circumstance.

Usually, mail for a registered guest is held in the appropriate room slot in a mail and message rack or in an alphabetical rack by the guest's last name. Until recently, keys and mail were kept behind the front desk in view of guests and other visitors to the hotel. Because of security issues, keys and mail are now kept out of sight behind the front desk. This approach prevents other people from learning that a particular room is occupied because there is mail in the room slot. The front desk should promptly attempt to notify a guest that mail has been received. Some properties notify guests by switching on an in-room message light on the guestroom telephone; others deliver a printed form to the guestroom. If mail arrives for a guest who has not yet registered, a notation should be made on the guest's reservation record and the mail held until the guest arrives. Guest mail that is not picked up or has arrived for a guest who has already checked out should be time-stamped a second time and returned to its sender or sent to a forwarding address if the guest has provided one.

Guests may also receive registered letters, express mail packages, or other mail requiring a signature on delivery. Some hotels permit the front desk agent to sign for such mail. After doing so, the agent records the item's delivery in the front office mail signature book, and has the guest sign for the mail in the book at the time of pickup or delivery. A sample mail signature book is shown in Exhibit 1. If the sender restricts who can receive the mail, the front office will have to follow other procedures. For example, if the sender stipulates guest signature *only,* the

Exhibit 1 Sample Mail Signature Book

MAIL SIGNATURE BOOK

DATE	Room No.	Registry No.	NAME	WHERE FROM	SIGNATURE	Clerk	DATE	FORWARDED TO	ADDRESS	REMARKS

ORIGAMI INC

Courtesy of Origami, Inc., Memphis, Tennessee

front office cannot sign for the mail. Instead, the front desk agent may page the guest or provide a notice to the guest's room that a delivery attempt was made.

Packages are usually handled as mail. If the package is too large to store at the front desk, it should be taken to a secure room. The package and its location should be recorded in the front office mail signature book.

When mail or packages are received, it is customary to notify the guest immediately. Most hotels will call the guest's room. If no one answers, the message light is turned on and a message is left with the department that customarily answers message requests.

Telephone Services

Most hotels provide in-room local and long-distance telephone service 24 hours a day. Regardless of whether front desk agents or telephone system operators answer incoming calls, all employees answering calls should be courteous and helpful. The telephone is often the first point of contact with the hotel and the way that callers are treated does a lot to create the hotel's image. Front office management may restrict the type of information the front office staff may furnish to callers because of guest privacy and security issues.

Telephone messages recorded by front office staff should be time-stamped and placed in the guest's mail and message rack slot. If guestroom telephones are equipped with a message indicator light, the front desk agent may switch on the in-room message light so that the guest is alerted that a message is waiting at the front desk. In some automated properties, messages can be typed directly into the computer terminal as they are relayed to a switchboard operator or front desk agent. The telephone system may be programmed to automatically turn on the guestroom message light when it receives the message from the front office computer. When the guest returns to the room, the flashing light on the phone informs the guest that mail or a message is waiting at the front desk. The guest can then call the switchboard operator or the front office message center and ask for the mail or message to be delivered. In some hotels, the guest may be able to display recorded messages on the guestroom television screen.

Voice mail is the newest technology in the area of guest mail and message service. **Voice mailboxes** are devices which can record messages for guests. A caller wishing to leave a message for a guest simply speaks into the phone; his or her message is then recorded by the voice mailbox system. To retrieve the message, the guest typically dials a special telephone number which connects him or her with the voice mailbox, and listens to the previously recorded message. A major advantage of voice mail is that the message is captured in the caller's voice. This is especially helpful with foreign callers who may not speak the local language clearly. Voice mail also offers improved confidentiality of messages and eliminates interpretation by the hotel staff.

Facsimiles. Facsimiles—or fax messages—are usually treated like mail, but with special care. Guests are often waiting for these documents. If the incoming fax has special delivery instructions, such as deliver immediately to a specific meeting room, the front desk should dispatch a bellperson with the fax right away. If no special instructions are provided, the hotel may store the fax in the mail rack and turn on the message light in the guestroom. Some hotels deliver the fax in an envelope to the guestroom. Faxes are different from mail in that they do not need to be time stamped and do not come in envelopes. The fax document usually contains the date and time of transmission on it. Confidentiality of the contents is essential. Front desk staff members should never read a facsimile. It is their job simply to deliver the document.

Some front offices maintain a fax log or combined fax and mail log for tracking all received documents. Information recorded in the fax log book may list the recipient, the sender, the time the fax was received, and the total number of fax pages. Front desk agents may also record when the guest was notified, and when the guest picked up the fax. A similar record is kept of outgoing faxes if the property offers public fax service. If a fax is undeliverable, the hotel should immediately notify the party sending the fax. Most hotels charge guests to send faxes, since there are telephone costs involved. Some hotels charge guests for received faxes (to cover costs). Whether there is a charge or not, front desk agents should process and deliver faxes quickly. The guest should be notified as soon as possible that he or she has received a fax. One of the more recent innovations in technology is the in-room fax. Connected to a second telephone line in the room, it offers guests improved convenience and security. Faxes can be received directly in the guestroom instead of at a central hotel fax machine. In addition, in-room fax machines now allow guests to receive newspaper headlines and even copies of their room bills.

Building Telephone Skills

Regardless of whom you talk with over the telephone, it's essential that you make a positive impression. Answering the telephone is an opportunity for you to portray a professional image as well as a positive image for the property.

During any business telephone conversation, you should:

1. **Smile even though you are on the telephone.**
   When you smile, you automatically improve your vocal quality. You'll sound pleasant and interested.
2. **Sit or stand up straight.**
   By sitting or standing up straight, you'll be more alert and pay better attention to what is being said.
3. **Use a low voice pitch.**
   A lower voice pitch will make you sound more mature and authoritative.
4. **Match your speaking rate to the caller's.**
   Let the caller set the tempo of the conversation. For example, he or she may be in a hurry; in that case, you should provide information more quickly.
5. **Avoid extremes in volume.**
   If you speak too loudly, you may sound rude or pushy. If you speak too softly, you may sound timid or uncertain.
6. **Avoid expressions such as "uh-huh" and "yeah."**
   Such expressions make the speaker sound dull, indifferent, and uninterested.

Front office staff often take phone messages for other employees or guests. Most front offices have a standard telephone message form. If you answer the phone, it's important that you listen carefully and take accurate written notes while speaking with the caller. When you take a telephone message, be sure to get the following information:

- Date
- Time of the call
- Name of the person being called
- Caller's full name
- Caller's department (if the call is internal)
- Caller's company (if appropriate)
- Caller's time zone (if out of state)
- Caller's telephone number (and area code, if needed)
- Message (do not abbreviate—provide a full message)

If the message is urgent, mark it as such. It is also a good practice to repeat the telephone number back to the caller for accuracy. Some front offices also recommend that the message also be repeated. Finally, sign your name and follow front office procedures for storing or delivering the message.

Any telephone conversation can be improved by following these simple guidelines. Remember to treat all callers, guests, and employees, with courtesy and respect.

Wake-Up Services. Since a guest may miss an important appointment, a flight, or simply a head start on a vacation by oversleeping, front desk agents must pay special attention to wake-up call requests. Front office mechanical devices or a front office computer system can be used to remind front desk agents to place wake-up calls, or the systems can be programmed to place the calls and play a recorded wake-up message. Despite advances in technology, many hotels still prefer that front desk agents place wake-up calls. For the most part, guests appreciate this personal touch.

Quite often, the clock in the telephone department used for wake-up purposes is called the hotel clock. It is the official time of the hotel. Therefore, the clock should be checked daily to be sure it is correct. Other clocks in the hotel, such as front desk time stamps, should be synchronized with the hotel clock to be sure time accuracy among departments and services is maintained.

Again, technology is providing new services in this area. Instead of calling the hotel operator or service department to place a wake-up call request, guests can simply dial a special hotel extension on their telephone and follow the instructions provided by the system to request a wake-up time. The hotel then has the option of providing an automated wake-up call or prompting the hotel operator to place a personalized wake-up call. Hotels can also combine a wake-up call with room service, allowing the guest to order breakfast upon receiving a wake-up call.

Voice Mail. Voice mail is a message-recording system that allows several guests to receive messages at the same time, thereby freeing the hotel operator for other duties. Voice mail is a service most travelers from large corporations are used to in their own offices and they appreciate the service while traveling. A hotel voice mail system is like a private answering machine for each guestroom. Someone calling a guest can be automatically connected to the voice mail system if the guest doesn't answer the guestroom phone. This enables a guest to receive complete and accurate messages in the caller's own voice and in the privacy of the guestroom. Guests can also call into the system from outside the hotel and retrieve messages by using the keypad of a touch-tone phone. Some voice mail systems allow guest to record a personalized message for callers.

E-Mail. Many hotel business guests have e-mail capability where they work, and an increasing number of hotel guests want to be able to send and receive e-mail at hotels. E-mail allows computer users to create and exchange messages and documents electronically. A hotel guest with a laptop computer can plug into the guestroom's data port (on the phone or wall jack) and communicate with a corporate office, home, other corporate networks, public networks, or with other guests staying a the hotel who are also plugged into the hotel's communication network.

TDDs. A special hotel guest service involves telecommunications devices for hearing- and/or speech-impaired travelers. A TDD is a specially designed piece of equipment for placing and conducting telephone calls. A TDD looks like a small typewriter with a coupler above the keyboard for a telephone receiver. The Americans with Disabilities Act requires that hotels make available, upon request, a TDD for use by an individual who has impaired hearing or a related communication disorder. Similarly, the front desk should have a TDD device to handle in-house calls from hearing- or speech-impaired guests. To us a TDD, the caller turns on the unit, places the telephone receiver into the coupler, dials the telephone number, and begins typing when the other party picks up. There is a small display screen above the typewriter keys that shows what the caller is typing.

Interdepartmental Communications

Many services in a hotel require coordination between the front office and other departments or divisions. The front office generally exchanges most of its information with personnel in the housekeeping and engineering and maintenance departments. Front desk agents should also recognize how influential their advice to guests can be, relative to the hotel's revenue centers.

Housekeeping

The housekeeping department and the front office must keep each other informed of changes in room status to ensure that guests are roomed efficiently and without complication. The more familiar front office staff are with housekeeping procedures, and vice versa, the smoother the relationship will be between the two departments.

Engineering and Maintenance

In many hotels, engineering and maintenance personnel begin each shift by examining the front office log book for repair work orders. Front desk agents use the log book to track maintenance problems reported by guests or staff, such as poor heating or cooling, faulty plumbing, noisy equipment, or broken furniture. The front office log book serves as an excellent reference for the hotel's engineering and maintenance staff.

Many hotels use a multiple-part work order form to report maintenance problems. Exhibit 2 contains a sample maintenance work order form. When the work is completed, the engineering and maintenance staff informs the department that filed the work request order. If a maintenance problem renders a room unsalable, housekeeping must be informed immediately when the problem is resolved so the room can be placed back in the available room inventory. Immediate notification of changes in room status helps minimize lost revenue. To enhance hotel operations, some hotels employ engineering and maintenance staff around the clock.

Revenue Centers

Although hotels enjoy their greatest revenues through guestroom sales, additional services and activities may support or boost overall profitability. In addition to the rooms division, hotel revenue centers may include:

- All-day dining rooms, snack bars, and specialty restaurants
- Bars, lounges, and nightclubs
- Room service
- Laundry/valet service

Exhibit 2 Sample Maintenance Work Order Form

DELTA FORMS - MILWAUKEE U.S.A

(414) 461-0066

HYATT HOTELS®

MAINTENANCE REQUEST

TIME ______ 1345239

BY ______ DATE ______

LOCATION ______

PROBLEM ______

ASSIGNED TO ______

DATE COMPL. ______ TIME SPENT ______

COMPLETED BY ______

REMARKS ______

RPHK-04

HYATT HOTELS MAINTENANCE CHECK LIST

Check (☒) Indicates Unsatisfactory Condition
Explain Check In Remarks Section

BEDROOM - FOYER - CLOSET

☐ WALLS	☐ WOODWORK	☐ DOORS
☐ CEILING	☐ TELEVISION	☐ LIGHTS
☐ FLOORS	☐ A.C. UNIT	☐ BLINDS
☐ WINDOWS		☐ DRAPES

REMARKS: ______

BATHROOM

☐ TRIM	☐ SHOWER
☐ DRAINS	☐ LIGHTS
☐ WALL PAPER	☐ PAINT
☐ TILE OR GLASS	☐ DOOR
☐ ACCESSORIES	☐ WINDOW

REMARKS: ______

Courtesy of Hyatt Corporation, Chicago, Illinois

- Vending machines
- Gift shops, barber shops, and newsstands
- Banquet, meeting, and catering facilities
- Local and long-distance telephone service
- Health clubs, golf courses, and exercise rooms
- Car rentals, limousine services, and tours
- Casinos and gaming activities
- Pay-per-view television movies
- Valet parking and parking garages

Guests frequently learn about these services and facilities through a printed directory placed in each guestroom or through advertising over the guestroom television. Front desk agents must also be familiar with these facilities and services so they can answer guest questions in a positive and knowledgeable way. The transactions charged to room accounts by guests at hotel restaurants, gift shops, and other remote points of sale must be communicated to the front desk in a timely manner to ensure eventual payment.

Marketing and Public Relations

The front office staff should be among the first to know about events the hotel schedules for publicity. In many ways, the effectiveness of a hotel's marketing and public relations effort depends on the participation and enthusiasm of front office staff. Guest receptions, health and fitness programs, family events, and even complimentary coffee in a hotel's lobby may provide settings for guests to socialize and can help promote repeat business. Front office staff may contribute to hotel newsletters, guest history files, and customized registration and check-out processes which can greatly help personalize hotel services for frequent guests.

Guest Services

As the center of front office activity, the front desk is responsible for coordinating guest services. Typical guest services involve providing information and special equipment and supplies. Guest services may also include accommodating guests through special procedures. A guest's satisfaction with the hotel hinges in part on the ability of the front desk to respond to special requests. A request that falls beyond the responsibility of the front office should be directly referred to the appropriate person or department.

A growing number of hotels employ a concierge or other designated staff member to handle guest requests. A concierge should embody the warmth and hospitality of the entire property. As more hotel functions become automated, the concierge may play an even more important role in reinforcing the hotel's personal touch in guest services.

Equipment and Supplies

Guests may request special equipment and supplies while making a reservation, at the time of registration, or during occupancy. Reservations agents should have a reliable method for recording special requests to ensure that they are properly met. After registration, a guest who needs special equipment or supplies will almost always contact a front desk agent. The front desk agent, in turn, follows through by contacting the appropriate service center or hotel department. Equipment and supplies commonly requested by guests include:

- Roll-away beds and cribs
- Additional linens/pillows
- Irons and ironing boards
- Additional clothes hangers

- Audiovisual and office equipment
- Special equipment for visually impaired, hearing impaired, or physically challenged guests

Front desk agents should have alternative ways to meet guest requests when the department that normally provides the equipment or service is closed or inaccessible. Housekeeping, for example, attends to many guest requests, but may not be staffed around the clock. In some hotels, front office staff may have access to linen rooms during late night hours. In others, the housekeeping department may stock a centrally located linen closet and issue a key to appropriate front office staff. Such arrangements enable the front office staff to satisfy requests for additional linens and pillows even when the housekeeping department is closed.

Special Procedures

Guests may ask for special treatment when making a reservation, during registration, at time of check-out, or for that matter, at any point during their stay. Sometimes, special requests represent exceptions to standard front office procedures. Reservations agents should have a reliable method of recording special requests made during the reservations process and communicating such requests to appropriate front office staff. Front desk agents should also have a way to record any procedural requests they encounter or process. In addition, front desk agents should be authorized to use their judgment when attempting to satisfy guest requests. Some requests may be out of procedure, but in the guest's best interest. Therefore, front desk staff should be empowered to handle the request and satisfy the guest if at all possible.

Procedural requests may require more time and effort to fulfill than equipment and supply requests. Typical procedural requests include:

- Split account folios
- Master account folios
- Wake-up calls
- Transportation arrangements
- Entertainment reservations
- Newspaper delivery
- Secretarial services

A knowledgeable front desk agent usually can fulfill a special request involving guest folios. **Split folios** are most often requested by business travelers. Essentially, these folios separate guest charges onto two or more separate folio accounts. One folio account may be set up to record room and tax charges; this part of the folio may be billed to the guest's company or to a group master account. Another folio account may be set up to track incidental charges such as telephone calls, food, and beverages; this part of the folio will most likely be paid directly by the guest.

A convention group meeting in the hotel may request a **master folio.** Typically, only authorized charges incurred by the group are posted to the master folio and subsequently billed to the convention's sponsor. Each group member may be held responsible for other charges posted to his or her individual folio account. The purpose of a master folio is to collect authorized charges which are not appropriately posted elsewhere.

A concierge may handle other procedural requests. Hotels not employing a concierge may have front desk agents update and use the front office information directory as a resource for referrals and outside services.

Some hotels operate a guest service center. Hotels can be confusing places to guests. When guests have a question or special request, they may not know who to call to resolve the issue. Often the call goes to front desk agents, who must then act upon the requests or refer them to the appropriate department. A guest service center makes it easier for guests. For example, some hotels instruct guests to call a single extension number, usually printed in bold numbers on the guestroom telephone. Staff at the service center are specially trained to handle everything—from a room service breakfast request to ordering a guest's car from valet parking. While the process simplifies for the guest, it places a great deal of knowledge responsibility on the guest service staff. For example, when a guest calls to request a bellperson to pick up luggage, the guest service agent must "know" to ask how many pieces of luggage need to be retrieved because this determines the kind of cart the bellperson brings to the guestroom. Also, room service orders can be complicated. Guest service staff must "know" the production capabilities of the kitchen and "know" how to properly communicate special requests.

Guest Relations

Despite front office staff efficiency and attentiveness, guests will occasionally be disappointed or find fault with something or someone at the hotel. The front office should anticipate guest complaints and devise strategies that help staff effectively resolve the situation.

The high visibility of the front office means that front desk agents are frequently the first to learn of guest complaints. Front desk agents should be especially attentive to guests with complaints and seek a timely and satisfactory resolution to the problem. Nothing annoys guests more than having their complaints ignored, discounted, or overlooked. While most front office staff do not enjoy receiving complaints, they should understand that very few guests actually enjoy complaining. Employees should also realize that guests who do not have the opportunity to complain to front office staff often tell their friends, relatives, and business associates instead.

When guests find it easy to express their opinions, both the hotel and the guests benefit. The hotel learns of potential or actual problems and has the opportunity to resolve them. For a guest, this can mean a more satisfying stay. When problems are quickly resolved, a guest often feels that the hotel cares about his or her needs. From this perspective, every complaint should be welcomed as an opportunity to enhance guest relations. Guests who leave a hotel dissatisfied may never return. A popular axiom in the lodging business is that it takes $10 to attract a guest for the first time, but only $1 to keep the guest coming back. By handling guest relations positively, the investment pays off many times.

Complaints

Guest complaints can be separated into four categories of problems: mechanical, attitudinal, service-related, and unusual.

Most guest complaints relate to hotel equipment malfunctions. *Mechanical complaints* usually concern problems with climate control, lighting, electricity, room furnishings, ice machines, vending machines, door keys, plumbing, television sets, elevators, and so on. Even an excellent preventive maintenance program cannot completely eliminate all potential equipment problems. Effective use of a front office log book and maintenance work orders may help reduce the frequency of mechanical complaints. Sometimes, the complaint is not about the mechanical problem, but the speed of response. It is essential, therefore, that the appropriate staff member be dispatched as quickly as possible with the proper tools to fix the problem promptly. Good tracking methods will ensure timely service.

Guests may make *attitudinal complaints* when they feel insulted by rude or tactless hotel staff members. Guests who overhear staff conversations or who receive complaints from hotel staff members may also express attitudinal complaints. Guests should not have to listen to employees arguing or become a sounding board for employee problems. Managers and supervisors (not guests) should listen and attend to the complaints and problems of staff. This can be especially critical to maintaining solid guest relations.

Guests may make *service-related complaints* when they experience a problem with hotel service. Service-related complaints can be wide-ranging and about such things as long waiting time for service, lack of assistance with luggage, untidy rooms, phone difficulties, missed wake-up calls, cold or ill-prepared food, or ignored requests for additional supplies. The front office generally receives more service-related complaints when the hotel is operating at or near full occupancy.

Guests may also complain about the absence of a swimming pool, lack of public transportation, bad weather, and so on. Hotels generally have little or no control over the circumstances surrounding *unusual complaints.* Nonetheless, guests sometimes expect the front office to resolve or at least listen to such situations. Front office management should alert front desk agents that on occasion guests may complain about things the staff can do nothing about. Through such orientation, staff will be better prepared to handle an unusual situation with appropriate guest relations techniques and avoid a potentially difficult encounter.

Identifying Complaints

All guest complaints deserve attention. An excited guest complaining loudly at the front desk requires immediate attention. A guest making a more discreet comment deserves no less attention, although the need for action may be less immediate.

Guest relations stand to improve when the front office systematically identifies its most frequent guest complaints. By reviewing a properly kept front office

Exhibit 3 Guest Perception Detail

Quantitative Details:

1. Name of report and date of survey.
2. The specific department or area the report is detailing.
3. All questions are grouped by the specific departments/categories.
4. Response Option—Guests are given the choice of options from which to mark their opinion.
5. Response Percentages—This number represents the percentage of guest responses per response option.
6. Guest Response—The number of guests who responded to the specific question.
7. Comparison of the overall rating by question for the current month, last month and year-to-date.
8. Response Option Averages—The average of all respondents per response option.
9. Overall Favorability Average—Overall average for all questions compared to current month, last month and year-to-date for the entire department/category.

Sample Hotel
Anywhere, USA

[1] Department \ Guest Perception Detail

[2] Bellman/Valet	Guest Responses [4] % Excellent	% Good	% Fair	% Poor	% N/A	Guest Response	Favorability Rating [7] This Month	Last Month	Yr to Date
How helpful was the Bellman/ Valet in directing you to the Front Desk?	42	13	0	0	45	[6] 53	92	92	89
How did the Bellman handle your luggage?	80	11	0	2	7	54	94	93	92
How would you rate the overall greeting of the Valet/ Doorman? [3]	49	[5] 12	0	0	39	51	94	88	89
Evaluate the frequency with which the Bellman used your name.	79	17	2	2	0	52	91	83	81
How was the manner with which the Bellman promoted the facility?	44	40	2	0	13	45	83	85	82
Averages [8]	59	18	1	1	21	51	91 [9]	88	86

Front Desk	Guest Responses % Excellent	% Good	% Fair	% Poor	% N/A	Guest Response	Favorability Rating This Month	Last Month	Yr to Date
How efficiently was your reservation located at the Front Desk?	70	23	0	0	8	53	92	93	91
At check-in, please evaluate the accuracy of your reservation.	78	19	2	0	2	54	93	92	90
Evaluate the frequency the Front Desk Agent used your name.	55	41	2	0	2	44	85	84	82
Rate the timeliness of your check-in.	75	25	0	0	0	51	92	91	88
Averages	70	26	1	0	3	51	90	90	88

 Data Obtained from Guest Comment Cards

Courtesy of Strategic Quantitative Solutions, Dallas, Texas

log book, management can often identify and address recurring complaints and problems.

Another way to identify complaints involves the evaluation of guest comment cards or questionnaires. Exhibits 3, 4, and 5 demonstrate the level of detail and sophistication that can be expected of a thorough analysis of guest responses to well-designed comment cards. Exhibit 3, "Guest Perception Detail," groups comment card questions by specific hotel departments (in this exhibit, the bellman/valet department and the front desk department are shown). Within each department, the specific questions asked of guests are listed, with their individual responses tabulated. Current month, last month, and year-to-date favorability rating percentages are shown for purposes of comparison. Exhibit 4, "Guest Perception Graph," shows the overall favorability ratings of all hotel departments, in descending order for ease of comparison. The overall hotel average ("Overall Perceptions") is also shown

Exhibit 4 Guest Perception Graph

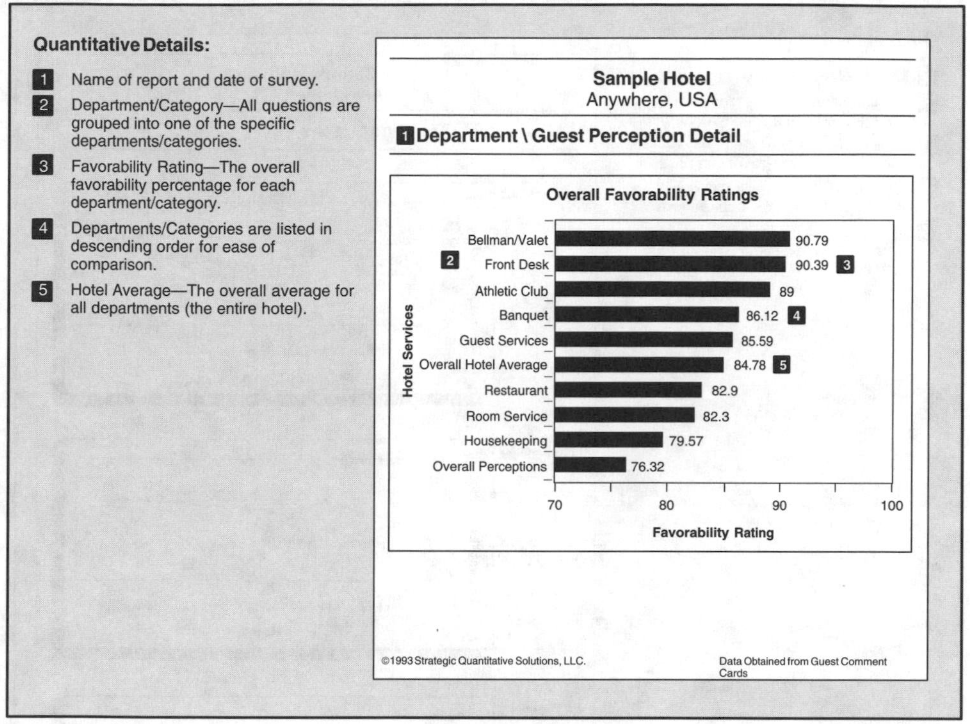

Courtesy of Strategic Quantitative Solutions, Dallas, Texas

on the graph. Departments falling below the overall average generally signal areas that need to be improved. Exhibit 5, "Favorability Trending Graphs," depicts the overall rating trend for all questions asked about specific departments. This exhibit shows the trend graphs for the bellman/valet, front desk, and housekeeping departments. Trend graphs not only help identify areas for improvement, but help measure the success of current and future improvement efforts.

Identifying problems is one of the first steps in taking corrective action. By examining the number and type of complaints received, front office management may gain insight into common and less common problems. Front office staff members may be better equipped to handle frequent complaints courteously and effectively, especially if they are aware the problem may not be immediately corrected.

Handling Complaints

It is usually counterproductive to ignore a guest complaint. In many hotels, front desk agents are instructed to refer complaints to supervisors or managers. But sometimes, front desk agents may not be able to pass the complaint on, especially when the complaint demands immediate attention. The front office should have a contingency plan in place and be empowered to deal with such situations.

Exhibit 5 Favorability Trending Graphs

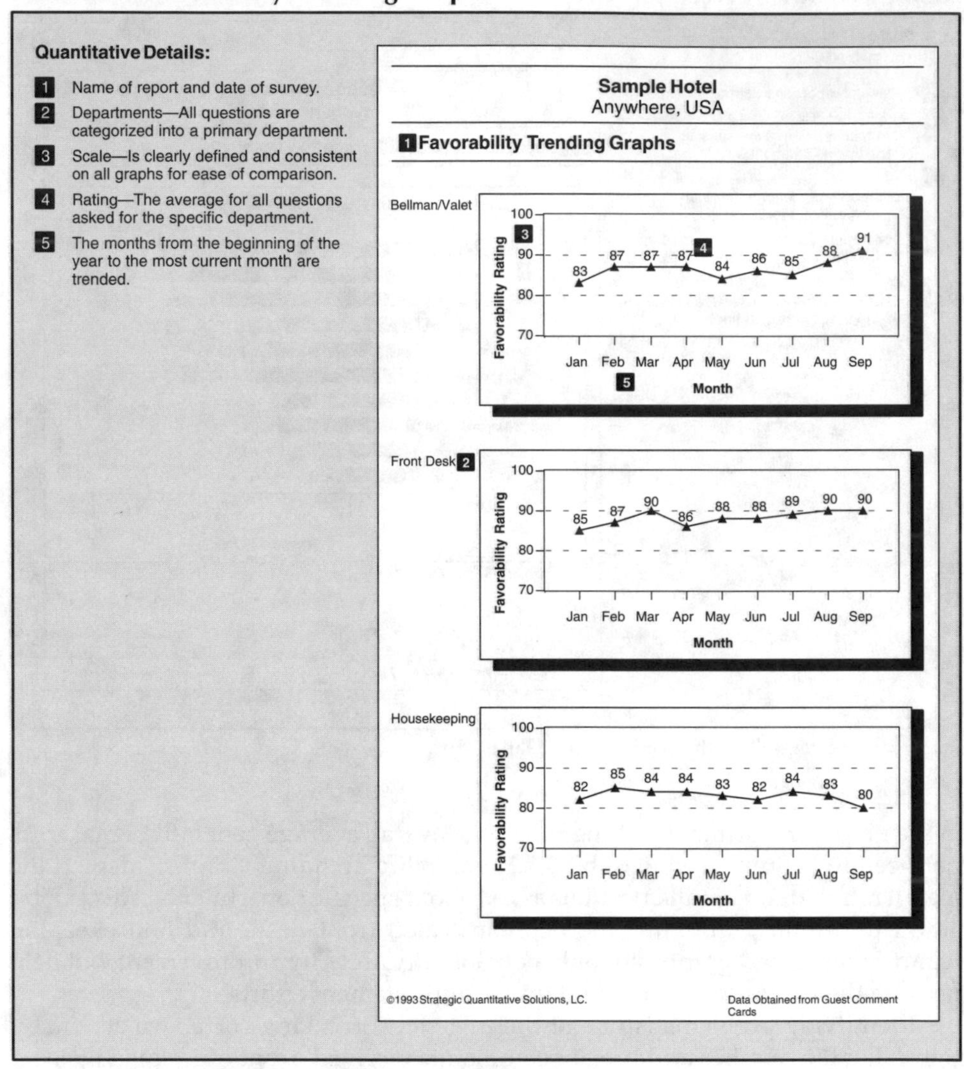

Quantitative Details:
1 Name of report and date of survey.
2 Departments—All questions are categorized into a primary department.
3 Scale—Is clearly defined and consistent on all graphs for ease of comparison.
4 Rating—The average for all questions asked for the specific department.
5 The months from the beginning of the year to the most current month are trended.
Sample Hotel
Anywhere, USA
1 Favorability Trending Graphs
Bellman/Valet
Front Desk 2
Housekeeping
Favorability Rating
Month
Jan Feb Mar Apr May Jun Jul Aug Sep
©1993 Strategic Quantitative Solutions, LC.
Data Obtained from Guest Comment Cards

Courtesy of Strategic Quantitative Solutions, LC, Dallas, Texas

The front office may receive complaints about the hotel's food and beverage operations, regardless of whether those operations are managed by the hotel. Unless the front office and the food and beverage operators establish procedures for referring complaints, guests may continue to be upset and the front office will continue to hear about the problem. The hotel and its revenue outlets should maintain close communications and develop procedures designed to satisfactorily resolve guest complaints.

Front office management and staff should keep the following resolution guidelines in mind when handling guest complaints:

Exhibit 6 Guidelines for Handling Complaints

1. Listen with concern and empathy.
2. Isolate the guest if possible, so that other guests won't overhear.
3. Stay calm. Avoid responding with hostility or defensiveness. Don't argue with the guest.
4. Be aware of the guest's self-esteem. Show a personal interest in the problem. Use the guest's name frequently. Take the complaint seriously.
5. Give the guest your undivided attention. Concentrate on the problem, not on placing blame. Do NOT insult the guest.
6. Take notes. Writing down the key facts saves time if someone else must get involved. Also, guests will tend to slow down when they are speaking faster than you can write. More important, the fact that a front office staff member is concerned enough to write down what they're saying is reassuring to guests.
7. Tell the guest what can be done. Offer choices. Don't promise the impossible, and don't exceed your authority.
8. Set an approximate time for completion of corrective actions. Be specific, but do not underestimate the amount of time it will take to resolve the problem.
9. Monitor the progress of the corrective action.
10. Follow up. Even if the complaint was resolved by someone else, contact the guest to ensure that the problem was resolved satisfactorily. Report the entire event, the actions taken, and the conclusion of the incident.

- When expressing a complaint, the guest may be quite angry. Front office staff members should not go alone to a guestroom to investigate a problem or otherwise risk potential danger.
- Front office staff members should not make promises that exceed their authority.
- If a problem cannot be solved, front office staff should admit this to the guest early on. Honesty is the best policy when dealing with guest complaints.
- Front desk agents should be advised that some guests complain as part of their nature. The front office should develop an approach for dealing with such guests.

Exhibit 6 lists guidelines for handling guest complaints in a professional manner. Learning to deal effectively with guest complaints requires experience. Front office staff members should anticipate how they might resolve some of the hotel's most common complaints. Role playing can be an effective method for learning how to deal with guest complaints. By anticipating complaints, planning and practicing responses, and receiving constructive feedback, front office staff members will be better prepared to deal with actual guest complaints.

Follow-Up Procedures

Front office management may use the front office log book to initiate corrective action, verify that guest complaints have been resolved, and identify recurring problems. This comprehensive written record may also enable management to contact guests who may still be dissatisfied with some aspect of their stay at check-out. After the guest has departed, a letter from the front office manager expressing regret about the incident is usually sufficient to promote goodwill and demonstrate concern for guest satisfaction. It may be good policy for the front office manager to telephone a departed guest to get a more complete description of the incident. Chain hotels may also receive guest complaints channeled through chain headquarters. Cumulative records of guest complaints about hotels in the chain may be compiled and sent to each manager. This method of feedback allows the chain's corporate headquarters to evaluate and compare each hotel's guest relations performance.

Front Office Security Functions

Providing security in a hotel means protecting people (guests, employees, and others) and property. The broad diversity of the lodging industry makes national security standards infeasible. Each lodging property or chain is therefore responsible for developing its own security program. Each hotel's security program should meet its particular needs. The responsibility for developing and maintaining a property's security program lies with its management. The information contained in this section is intended only as an introduction, and focuses on those elements relevant to the front office. Hotel management should consult legal counsel to ensure that the property is in compliance with applicable laws.

The Role of the Front Office

A security program is most effective when *all* employees participate in the hotel's security efforts. Front office staff play a particularly important role. Front desk agents, door attendants, bellpersons, and parking attendants have the opportunity to observe all persons entering or departing the premises. Suspicious activities or circumstances involving a guest or a visitor should be reported to the hotel's security department or a designated staff member.

Several procedures front desk agents should use to protect guests and property have already been mentioned. For example, front desk agents should never give keys, room numbers, messages, or mail to anyone requesting them without first requiring appropriate identification. Similarly, the front desk agent should not announce an arriving guest's room number.

Guests may be further protected if the front office prohibits staff members from providing guest information to callers or visitors. Generally, front desk agents should not mention guestroom numbers. People calling guests at the hotel should be directly connected to the appropriate guestroom without being informed of the room number. Conversely, someone asking for a specific room number over the telephone should never be connected until the caller identifies whom he or she is calling and the hotel employee verifies the identity of the person in the room requested. A person inquiring at the front desk about a guest may be asked to use the house phone to contact the guest. A recent trend in security is to restrict house phones so that they connect only to the hotel operator. The caller can then be properly screened to provide additional security.

Front office staff may also inform guests of personal precautions they may take. For example, front desk agents may suggest that guests hide and secure any valuables left in their cars. Bellpersons accompanying the guest to a room generally provide instructions on the operation of in-room equipment. The bellperson may also review the use of access control devices on the guestroom door and windows, familiarize the guest with pertinent security information, and review any decals or notices in the room relating to guest security. This should always include emergency evacuation paths and procedures. The front office may provide the guests with flyers containing safety tips, such as the example shown in Exhibit 7.

A hotel also helps protect its guests' personal property. The front office may develop a method for ensuring the safety and security of the luggage of arriving guests. Often, luggage and other articles received by a door attendant are moved to a secured area; guests later recover their belongings by presenting a receipt. Other hotel employees can assist in protecting the guests' property. A valet parking attendant, for example, should secure the keys of all parked vehicles so that they cannot be removed by anyone except authorized employees. Procedures for handling guest valuables and providing secured space for additional storage are addressed later in this chapter.

Front office staff are also important to asset protection. Failure to collect payment from guests may represent a more significant loss than, for instance, a guest's theft of towels or ashtrays.

Key Control

For security reasons, most lodging properties use at least three types of guestroom keys: emergency keys, master keys, and individual guestroom keys. An **emergency key** (E-Key) opens all guestroom doors, even when they are double-locked—that is, locked with both a standard door lock and a deadbolt from within the guestroom. Emergency keys should be highly protected. Emergency keys should be stored in a secure place, such as the hotel safe, safe deposit box, or a special cabinet which only the general manager or the hotel security chief control. Authorized staff should use a log book to sign out the key, noting the time, date, and reason for the key's removal. Removal of the key should be witnessed by at least one other authorized staff member, who should also sign the log book. The key should be returned to the secure area as quickly as possible. The return time should be noted in the log and a witness should also sign the log book confirming that the key was returned as recorded. An emergency key should never be removed from the hotel property.

A **master key** opens all guestroom doors that are not double-locked. When not in use, a master key should be secured in a designated place for safekeeping. Only authorized personnel should have access to master keys. Keys are issued to personnel based on their need to use the key, not simply on their rank or status. For

Exhibit 7 Traveler Safety Tips Flyer

TRAVELER SAFETY TIPS

1. Don't answer the door in a hotel or motel room without verifying who it is. If a person claims to be an employee, call the front desk and ask if someone from their staff is supposed to have access to your room and for what purpose.
2. When returning to your hotel or motel late in the evening, use the main entrance of the hotel. Be observant and look around before entering parking lots.
3. Close the door securely whenever you are in your room and use all of the locking devices provided.
4. Don't needlessly display guest room keys in public or carelessly leave them on restaurant tables, at the swimming pool, or other places where they can be easily stolen.
5. Do not draw attention to yourself by displaying large amounts of cash or expensive jewelry.
6. Don't invite strangers to your room.
7. Place all valuables in the hotel or motel's safe deposit box.
8. Do not leave valuables in your vehicle.
9. Check to see that any sliding glass doors or windows and any connecting room doors are locked.
10. If you see any suspicious activity, please report your observations to the management.

We Support the National
Citizens' Crime Prevention Campaign.
TAKE A BITE OUT OF
CRIME®

Printed on recycled paper

Source: American Hotel & Motel Association, Washington, D.C.

example, it would be impractical for all housekeeping room attendants to have one key for each room they service. Therefore, floor or section master keys are provided to them. A written record should be maintained of employees who have been issued master keys. To maintain control over master keys, hotel employees should sign them out at the beginning of their shift in a key log book. At the end of the shift, the keys should be signed back in.

A guestroom key opens a guestroom door so long as it is not double-locked. Front desk agents should not give a guestroom key to anyone not registered to the room. The front desk agent should check appropriate identification to ensure that the person requesting the key is the guest registered to the room. In addition, front desk agents should remind guests to return room keys at check-out. Additional reminders include well-secured key return boxes in the lobby, at hotel exits, and inside courtesy vehicles. Some properties have reduced key loss by requiring a key deposit from each guest at registration. Key deposits also help to bring the guest back to the front desk before departure, which can contribute to the effective settlement of a guest account. The front office should work closely with the engineering and maintenance department to ensure that guestrooms are periodically rekeyed. Hotels have been held liable for the theft of guest belongings taken from guestrooms because the hotel failed to change door locks on a frequent basis. Most mechanical key systems are designed for frequent rekeying.

Some properties do not list the hotel's name, address, or room numbers on guestroom keys. Then, if a guestroom key is lost or misplaced, it cannot be traced to the property for criminal use. A code number representing the room number is typically stamped on the key. A master code list is maintained at the front desk and is used to recycle keys.

One of the major responsibilities of the front desk is to audit the guestroom key inventory several times a week. There are two reasons for this audit. First, front desk agents do not want to assign a guest to a room without an available guestroom key. This is very inconvenient and does not create a good impression with the guest. Second, a key inventory tells the front desk and security staffs how many keys have been put into circulation for any room in the hotel. Key stocks are set with a par inventory. That means a specific number of keys with a certain combination are given for each room. When the inventory drops below hotel limits, the room must be rekeyed. For example, the hotel has a par inventory of four keys per room. If the audit of the keys shows two keys are missing and the room is unoccupied, there are two keys in circulation. Hotel management may choose to rekey the room at that time to prevent the circulating keys from being used again.

Regardless of responsibility or position, front office staff should not remove hotel keys from the property. Keys issued on a temporary basis, to a bellperson for example, should be recorded in a front desk key log. The front office key log should indicate the reason for issue, issue date, time out, time in, recipient's name, and issuer's name. Whenever there is any known or suspected compromise of a key, an unauthorized entry by key, or any loss or theft, every lock affected should be changed (or rotated to another part of the property).

Electronic Locking Systems. An electronic locking system replaces traditional mechanical locks with sophisticated computer-based guestroom access devices.

Exhibit 8 Electronic Guestroom Door Locks

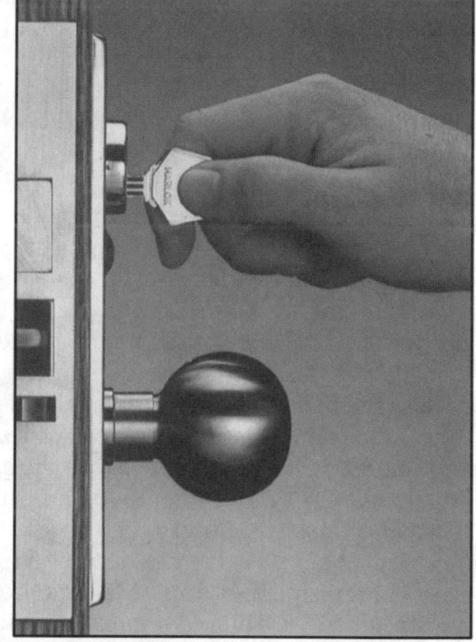

Some electronic door lock systems can be set up for magnetic key cards, guest credit cards, or special keys. (Courtesy of MARLOK, Chicago, Illinois)

Electronic locking systems eliminate the need for emergency and master keys. A **centralized electronic locking system** operates through a master control console at the front desk which is wired to every guestroom door. At registration, a front desk agent inserts a key or card into the appropriate room slot at the front desk console to transmit its code to the guestroom door lock. The key or card, issued to the guest, is the only working guestroom key. Exhibit 8 shows two typical electronic guestroom door locks. These locks can be designed to use a magnetic key card (including the guest's own credit card) or a special high-security key.

Centralized electronic locking systems present an additional opportunity for improved security, and help reduce employee theft. Many of these systems keep track of which keys or cards opened which doors, by date and time. If the hotel staff members know about the system's capability, employees tempted to steal may be discouraged by the fact that an entry record may be used to incriminate them. Report creation and other system functions should be controlled by operator identification and password security codes.

Unlike the centralized system, a **micro-fitted electronic locking system** operates on an individual unit basis. Each guestroom door has its own microprocessor which contains a predetermined sequence of codes. A master console at the front desk contains a record of all code sequences stored within each guestroom door lock. These locks usually contain millions of possible combinations that are chosen at random. This eliminates the possibility that a key can be reused once the guest has checked out. At registration, the front desk agent encodes a key or card with the next code in the sequence stored in the lock on the assigned guestroom. The front desk console and each microprocessor must agree on which code in the sequence is currently valid. Micro-fitted locking systems don't require the extensive wiring and retrofitting that centralized locking systems do, which makes them a comparatively affordable option for smaller properties or existing hotels upgrading their guestroom locking systems.

Most electronic locking systems provide several distinct levels of security, similar to the levels of keying in mechanical systems. Electronic keys can be "time stamped," meaning they are good for only a specific period of time or for a specified number of uses. For example, a hotel engineer could be issued the guestroom key for a specific time period. Once the work is completed and the engineer has left the room, the key cannot be reused. Electronic locking systems may include various guest safety and convenience features, such as a *do not disturb* signal. One form of electronic locking system does not require special keys or cards at all; guests set the locking mechanism by programming a personal four-digit code number, or by using a credit card.

Surveillance and Access Control

Although open to the public, a hotel is a private property. An innkeeper has the responsibility to monitor and, when appropriate, to control the activities of people on the premises. All hotel employees should be trained to recognize suspicious people and situations. Surveillance plays an important role in most aspects of people and property protection. Discouraging or stopping suspicious or unauthorized individuals from entering the property relies in part on procedures for responding to the observations of employees.

Most lobbies are designed so front desk agents can view the property's entrances, elevators, escalators, and stairways. Mirrors may be placed in strategic locations to aid visibility. Observing elevators and escalators is important for both security and safety reasons; front office staff should know how to stop the elevators and escalators in an emergency.

In many hotels, someone is stationed at the front desk at all times. In a smaller property, a front desk agent may be the only staff member on the premises during late night hours. Under such circumstances, some properties limit late night access to the lobby and reception areas, and give the front desk agent the authority to deny admittance. If the front desk agent needs to leave the desk area for any reason, many properties advise the front desk agent to lock the front door. With the front door locked, no one can enter the hotel until the front desk agent returns to the front office area.

Although successful surveillance techniques rely on hotel personnel, proper equipment can enhance the surveillance function. Closed-circuit television cameras and monitors can be an effective surveillance system in multiple-entry properties. Employees are assigned to watch the monitors and respond to incidents picked up by surveillance cameras.

Surveillance equipment is intended to help front office employees, not replace them. An elevator may be equipped and programmed to stop at a certain floor for observation, but it is still up to the staff to actually do the observing. Obviously, a closed-circuit television system is a worthless security device without the staff monitoring it.

Protection of Funds

The accounting division is primarily responsible for the protection of hotel funds. However, other departments, particularly the front office, contribute by protecting certain financial assets.

The front desk cashiering function plays a critical role in the protection of hotel funds. The amount of cash in a cash register should be limited through a **cash bank** system. At the start of a workshift, each cashier is given the smallest amount of cash that will allow him or her to transact a normal business volume. The cashier is responsible for this cash bank and for all changes to it during the workshift. Ideally, only one person should have access to each cash bank, and each cash bank should be in a separate cash drawer.

All front office transactions should be immediately recorded. The front office cashier should take care to close the cash drawer after each transaction. A cashier working with an open cash drawer may fail to record a transaction, either accidentally or deliberately. Front office cashiers should complete a transaction in process before changing currency into different denominations for guests; each request for change should be handled as a new transaction to avoid confusion. A supervisor or a member of the accounting division staff should occasionally conduct an unscheduled audit of front office cash registers.

The front office should have a policy stating where front office cashiers should place cash during a transaction. Generally, the front office cashiers should not place currency on the cash register ledge. This can make it easy for a thief to grab the money and run. Some organizations recommend that the money be placed in the cash drawer, but above the paper money clips, until the transaction is completed. This helps prevent any disputes over what denomination of bills and total was tendered.

Safe Deposit Boxes

Laws in most states limit a property's liability for the loss of a guest's valuables so long as the property has safe deposit boxes or a safe for the storage of guest valuables. Liability is also contingent on whether the hotel notifies the guest that safe deposit boxes or safes are available for their use. The required notice usually takes the form of public postings within guestrooms and in the front desk area. An example of a public posting is shown in Exhibit 9. Front office staff attending to safe deposit boxes should be properly trained and should recognize the importance and seriousness of this responsibility.

Safe deposit boxes should be located in a limited-access area. Unauthorized persons, whether guests or employees, should not be permitted in the safe deposit box area. Such a location may be near the front desk, where the safe deposit boxes may be secured while still visible to guests.

Exhibit 9 Michigan Hotel Liability Notice

Hotel Liability Law

AN ACT

To define the duties and liabilities of hotel keepers and innkeepers with relation to the personal property of their guests, and to provide for the protection of inn and hotel keepers, and to repeal act number two hundred twenty-seven (227) of the Public Acts of eighteen hundred ninety-seven (1897), and act number fifteen (15) of the Public Acts of eighteen hundred seventy-five (1875).

The People of the State of Michigan enact:

SECTION 1. (1) The liability of the keeper of any inn, whether individual, partnership, or corporation, for loss of or injury to personal property of the innkeeper's guest, shall be that of a depository for hire, except that in no case shall such liability exceed the sum of $250.00; and in case of the loss of a trunk or chest, and its contents, it shall not exceed the sum of $150.00; in case of the loss of a traveling bag or dress suit-case, and contents, it shall not exceed the sum of $50.00; and in case of the loss of a box, bundle, or package, and contents, it shall not exceed the sum of $10.00. Nothing in this act shall prohibit an innkeeper from assuming a greater liability than the sum of $250.00 for the personal effects of the innkeeper's quest if the undertaking and agreement is in writing, stating the kind of personal property received and the value thereof, the kind and extent of the liability of the innkeeper, and is signed by the guests and the innkeeper or the innkeeper's clerk. Nothing in this section shall preclude any remedy now existing for the enforcement of the hotel keeper's or innkeeper's lein.

(2) For the purposes of this act,"hotel" or "inn" includes a bed and breakfast as defined in section 12901 of the public health code, Act No. 368 of the Public Acts of 1978, being section 333.12901 of the Michigan Compiled Laws.

SECTION 2. No innkeeper, whether individual, partnership, or corporation, who constantly has in his inn a metal safe or suitable vault in good order, and fit for the custody of money, bank notes, jewelry, articles of gold and silver manufacture, precious stones, personal ornaments, railroad mileage books or tickets, negotiable or valuable papers and bullion, and who keeps on the doors of the sleeping rooms used by his guests suitable locks and bolts, and on the transoms and windows of said rooms suitable fastenings, and who keeps a copy of this section printed in distinct type constantly and conspicuously suspended in the office and in the ladies' parlor or sitting room, barroom, wash-room and in five (5) other conspicuous places in said inn, or in not less than ten (10) conspicuous places in all in said inn, shall be liable for the loss of or injury to any such property belonging to any guest, unless such guest has offered to deliver the same to such innkeeper for custody in such metal safe or vault, and such innkeeper has refused or omitted to take it and deposit it in such safe or vault for custody, and to give such guest a receipt therefor: Provided, however, That the keeper of any inn shall not be obliged to receive from any one guest for deposit in such safe or vault any property hereinbefore described exceeding a total value of two hundred fifty ($250.00) dollars, except under special agreement as hereinbefore provided, and shall not be liable for any excess of such property whether received or not, but every innkeeper shall be liable for any loss of the above enumerated articles of a guest in his inn, caused by the theft or negligence of the innkeeper or any of his servants.

SECTION 292. Any person who shall put up at any hotel, motel, inn, restaurant or cafe as a guest and shall procure any food, entertainment or accommodation without paying therefor, except when credit is given therefor by express agreement, with intent to defraud such keeper thereof out of the pay for the same, or, who, with intent to defraud such keeper out of the pay therefor, shall obtain credit at any hotel, motel, inn, restaurant or cafe for such food, entertainment or accommodation, by means of any false show of baggage or effects brought thereto, is guilty of a misdemeanor. No conviction shall be had under the provisions of this section unless complaint is made within 60 days of the time of the violation hereof.

SECTION 293. Obtaining such food, lodging or accommodation by false pretense, or by false or fictitious show of baggage or other property, or refusal or neglect to pay therefor on demand, or payment thereof with check, draft or order upon a bank or other depository on which payment was refused, or absconding without paying or offering to pay therefor, or surreptitiously removing or attempting to remove baggage, shall be prima facie evidence of such intent to defraud mentioned in the next preceding section of this chapter.

FIRE LAWS

Sec. 496 of Act 328 of Public Acts 1931. Any person who shall carelessly, recklessly or negligently set fire to any hotel, rooming house, lodging house or any place of public abode, or to any bedding, furniture, curtains, drapes, or other furnishings therein so as to endanger life or property in any way, shall be guilty of a misdemeanor.

MEMBER

MICHIGAN LODGING ASSOCIATION

Note: ***Each state's law regarding liability notices is different, and posting requirements may vary.*** (Courtesy of the Michigan Travel and Tourism Association, Lansing, Michigan)

Strict safe deposit box control should include the storage, issuance, and receipt of safe deposit box keys. Only front office staff responsible for safe deposit boxes should have access to unissued keys. These employees should also immediately secure safe deposit box keys when they are returned. Spare safe deposit locks, if any, should be carefully controlled.

Two keys should be required to open any safe deposit box. The front office's *control key* must be used in conjunction with the *guest's key* to open the box. The control key should always be secured. Only those front office staff authorized to provide access to safe deposit boxes should have possession of the control key. The front office control key must be accounted for at each front office shift change.

Under no circumstances should there be more than one guest key for each safe deposit box, even when more than one guest is using the same box. If a guest key is lost, the box should be drilled open in the presence of a witness and a second staff member. The witness could be the assigned guest or the guest's authorized representative.

Access. Controlled access is the most critical of all safe deposit box responsibilities. The front desk agent must verify the identity of the guest before granting the guest access to a safe deposit box. The guest is usually required to sign a form requesting access; the front desk agent should then compare the access request signature with the signature on the safe deposit box record. Often, the front office requests guests to include a piece of personal information (for example, mother's maiden name) on an initial agreement as an additional safeguard. If there is some doubt about the identity of the person requesting access, the agent can request the additional personal information, which an impostor would be unlikely to know. Whatever the control procedure, it should be followed *every time* a safe deposit box is accessed, regardless of how familiar the agent may be with the guest. *No one* should be granted access to a safe deposit box unless that person's signature matches the signature on the safe deposit box record.

After verifying the guest's identity, the agent should accompany the guest to the safe deposit box area. The agent uses the control key and the guest's key to open the box in view of the guest. Front office policies may vary on how to maintain the guest's privacy regarding the contents of the safe deposit box. Only the guest should place items into or remove items from a safe deposit box. The front desk agent should never be alone with the guest's valuables. Once the box has been opened, the front desk agent should leave the area with the control key and the guest should be left alone until he or she summons the front desk agent. When the guest is finished, the front desk agent should lock the box in view of the guest and return the guest's key. The front desk agent should then return the control key to its secured location. When the guest relinquishes the safe deposit box and returns the key, the guest and the front desk agent should both sign the safe deposit box record.

Space limitations often make it impossible to provide a separate safe deposit box for each guest. If guests choose to share a box, each guest's property must be sealed in a container (such as an envelope) to keep it separate from the other guests' property. The guest key to the shared safe deposit box should be maintained at the front desk, in a secure place, and its use recorded.

Unusual Access. If a guest fails to surrender a safe deposit box at check-out, the front office should send the guest a registered letter requesting surrender of the box. If the guest does not respond within the appropriate legal time limit, the front office should dispose of the contents of the box according to state law and the advice of legal counsel. If a guest who failed to surrender a safe deposit box mails the guest key to the front office, the front office should secure the key and ask (by registered letter) the guest to sign a formal safe deposit box release. If that same safe deposit box is opened and found to contain property, the front office should ask the guest to personally remove the contents and surrender the box, or forward a power of attorney form for the guest's representative to do so. Under no circumstances should front office access to a safe deposit box be allowed based solely on telephone or telegram authorization.

Legal challenges related to safe deposit boxes should be referred to front office management. Safe deposit box access may need to be suspended until the front office's rights and obligations are determined.

An in-room safe is another popular option for storing guest valuables. In-room safes are usually located in the guestroom closet; some are larger than a standard safe deposit box. Guest convenience is the main advantage of in-room safes. Several different types of in-room safe systems exist. Some use mechanical keys, while others have electronic locks. In most states, in-room safes are not considered by law to offer the same level of protection for guest valuables as safe deposit boxes. This means that if guest valuables are lost after being placed in an in-room safe, the hotel cannot be held liable since the item was not in the care, custody, or control of the hotel. Claims filed against hotels for articles that are stolen from in-room safes are rare.

Lost and Found

The operation of a lost and found office or area may be assigned to any of several departments. Nevertheless, most guests will contact the front desk when they attempt to locate missing belongings. Clear procedures should be developed for responding to inquiries reaching the front desk concerning lost and found items. All telephone calls about lost or found items should be directed to the department that has been assigned lost and found responsibilities.

To avoid giving conflicting information to the caller, no one but the authorized employee or department should discuss lost and found items with the guest. Employees responsible for the items should ask the caller to provide a description of the item, and to estimate where and when it was lost. The employee should record this information, as well as the guest's name and address. A sample form for reporting lost item information is shown in Exhibit 10.

Responding properly to guest inquiries depends on effective lost and found procedures. When a hotel employee discovers a mislaid article, he or she should immediately bring it to the attention of lost and found staff. Some properties require employees who discover found items to complete a form that describes the item, where it was found, on what date, and by whom. Lost and found personnel should store a found item until it is claimed by the owner or for the length of time

Exhibit 10 Sample Lost and Found Log

LOST AND FOUND LOG

Item No. (optional)	Date and Time Found	Description of Article (include color, size, brand, etc.)	Area/Room No. Where Found	By Whom Found	How Disposed Of (Enter address if mailed)	By Whom	Date

Courtesy of Holiday Inn Worldwide

designated by law. Lost and found items should be secured according to management policy.

Under no circumstances should a found article be mailed to a guest at the address on a registration card without the guest's explicit permission. The front office may send a letter to the guest that asks him or her to contact the hotel to identify a found item. Once ownership of the item is established, the item can be mailed to an address specified by the guest. The department in charge of lost and found should keep records of all such actions. In some states, the hotel has a legal right to sell unclaimed property if the owner does not respond to letters or other appropriate forms of contact within a stipulated length of time. This license to ownership has been questioned in some courts of law, however. The simplest course of action may be to turn over unclaimed property to law enforcement authorities.

Emergency Procedures

Front office management should develop property-specific procedures for responding to emergencies such as fires, floods, earthquakes, tornadoes, and hurricanes. Procedures for medical emergencies and crimes, including robbery within the property, should also be documented. Management should regularly review emergency procedures with front office employees so that they can respond properly to any emergency situation. Front office staff who react quickly and efficiently to an emergency may help avert panic and prevent needless damage, injury, or loss of life.

The front desk usually serves as the command center in the case of an emergency, summoning on-premises security staff, guests, and local police, depending upon management directive. Some properties have a special telephone extension number for guests and staff to call in an emergency. This number is typically monitored by a front office switchboard operator and, in some properties, by security personnel. Properties may also need to develop a communications network by which front office staff responding to an emergency can communicate with other emergency services.

Medical Emergencies. Lodging properties need to be prepared for the possibility of a serious illness, an injury, or even the death of a guest, visitor, or employee. The hotel's management and security staff should be knowledgeable and ready to deal appropriately with such unfortunate incidents. Front office staff usually will perform an important communications function in the event of medical emergencies. Many front offices maintain lists of nearby physicians, dentists, hospitals, ambulance services, and other medical professionals and facilities. These lists are generally located at the front desk or in the switchboard area. When possible, lists of medical and emergency professionals may be presented to guests needing medical attention, thereby allowing them to determine their own medical care. The front office should also develop procedures for advising and referring callers who inquire about a guest's illness, hospitalization, or death.

Robbery. Armed robbery is a possibility at lodging properties since hotels typically maintain large sums of cash on the premises. Front office and revenue center cashiers should comply with a robber's demands and make no sudden movements or attempts to thwart the crime. Unexpected actions or a lack of cooperation by front office staff might prompt the robber to become violent. Front office cashiers should not do anything to jeopardize their lives or the lives of others. They should remain quiet unless directed to talk, keep hands in sight, and should not attempt to disarm the robber or use a weapon.

Front office management may install a silent alarm in the cash drawer that is activated when a certain packet of bills is removed. When complying with a robber's demand for money, the front office cashier is trained to remove this packet of bills with the rest of the money. The front office cashier must not act suspicious or the robber may suspect an alarm is being triggered.

If an alarm cannot be triggered without danger, the front office cashier and other employees who encounter a criminal should observe the person carefully, noting physical characteristics such as height, weight, build, dress, color and style of hair, color of eyes, facial hair, complexion, scars, tattoos, clothing, and anything unusual. Front office staff should note the robber's voice, mannerisms, and the type of weapon he or she is carrying. Front office management may develop a robbery description form that can be completed immediately after the incident.

Again, if it can be done without danger, front office staff should observe the robber's direction of escape and the type and license number of any vehicle used. If the robber leaves behind any evidence such as a robbery note, the front office cashier should not handle it unnecessarily before turning it over to the police. Front office staff should refrain from touching anything the robber may have touched.

Authorities can sometimes gather fingerprints from these sources. Following a criminal incident, the front office should immediately notify the police. While being involved in a robbery is very stressful, front desk staff members should remain as calm as possible and follow established procedures.

Fires and Natural Disasters. The front office is often responsible for monitoring fire alarms and alert systems. The Occupational Safety and Health Administration requires that written plans be formulated for possible fire emergencies. These plans must include:

- Emergency escape procedures and route assignments
- Procedures to identify disabled guests who must be contacted in case of an emergency
- Procedures to protect hotel documents, such as guest folios, voucher, etc.
- Procedures for employees who remain to maintain critical hotel operations until they evacuate
- Procedures to account for all employees after evacuation
- Rescue and first aid duties for those employees qualified to administer aid
- The preferred means of reporting fire and other emergencies
- Names or regular job titles of persons who can be contacted for further information or explanation of duties under the plan

Many cities require the installation of a smoke detector in every hotel guestroom. Some communities require the local fire authority to review and approve emergency fire programs for the property. The local fire department may also assist in training hotel employees in fire emergency procedures.

Summary

Effective communication is essential to an efficient front office. Front office employees must communicate effectively with one another, with personnel in other departments and divisions, and with guests.

The complexity of front office communication tends to be directly related to the number of guestrooms and the size and extent of the hotel's public areas and facilities. The larger the hotel, the larger and more complex the communication network is likely to be. The front desk may maintain a front office log book (typically, a journal that chronicles unusual events, guest complaints or requests, and other relevant information) so that front office staff can be aware of important events and decisions that occurred during previous workshifts. A group résumé book is also helpful in handling group arrangements at the front desk.

In addition, front desk agents may need to access non-hotel information (for example, maps, bank, theater, church, and store locations, and special event schedules) to answer guest inquiries. Some front offices accumulate such data in a bound guide called a front office information directory. Daily hotel activity is communicated to guests and visitors through reader boards placed conveniently in several locations.

Registered guests rely on the front office to quickly deliver mail and messages. Front office staff should time-stamp all guest mail when it arrives. Doing so provides evidence of when the mail was received and helps ensure timely delivery. Guest mail that is not picked up or has arrived for a guest who has already checked out should be time-stamped a second time and returned to its sender.

Front office management may restrict the information persons answering telephones may furnish to callers due to privacy and security issues. Voice mail allows callers to record messages for guests.

Many services in a hotel require coordination between the front office and other departments or divisions. The front office generally exchanges the most information with personnel in the housekeeping and engineering and maintenance departments. For example, housekeeping and the front office must keep each other informed of changes in room status to ensure that guests are roomed efficiently and without complications. In many hotels, the engineering and maintenance staff begin each shift by examining the front office log book for repair work orders.

Front desk agents can influence the performance of the hotel's revenue centers through the use of marketing and public relations skills. Front desk agents must be familiar with these facilities and services so they can answer guest questions. The transactions charged by guests at hotel restaurants, gift shops, and other remote points of sale must be communicated to the front desk to ensure eventual payment.

As the center of front office activity, the front desk is responsible for coordinating guest services. Typical guest services involve providing information and special equipment and supplies. Guest services may also include accommodating guests through special procedures. A request that falls beyond the responsibility of the front office should be referred to the appropriate person or department.

Despite staff efficiency and attentiveness, guests will occasionally be disappointed or find fault with something or someone. The front office should anticipate guest complaints and devise strategies that help staff effectively resolve the situation. Guest complaints can be divided into four categories of problems: mechanical, attitudinal, service-related, and unusual.

Providing security in a hotel means protecting people and property. The responsibility for developing and maintaining a front office security program lies with management. A security program is most effective when all employees participate in the hotel's security efforts. Front office staff play a particularly important role because front desk agents, door attendants, bellpersons, and parking attendants have the opportunity to observe all the people who enter and leave the premises.

For security reasons, most lodging properties use at least three types of guestroom keys: emergency keys, master keys, and individual guestroom keys. Auditing guestroom keys several times a week ensures a sufficient supply of keys and enhances guestroom key security. An electronic locking system replaces traditional mechanical locks with sophisticated computer-based guestroom access devices. There are two types of electronic locking systems: centralized and micro-fitted.

Although open to the public, a hotel is a private property. An innkeeper has the responsibility to monitor and, when appropriate, to control the activities of people on the premises. The accounting division is primarily responsible for the protection of hotel funds. However, other departments, particularly the front office, contribute by protecting certain financial assets.

Front office management should develop property-specific procedures for responding to emergencies such as fires, floods, earthquakes, tornadoes, and hurricanes. Procedures for medical emergencies and crimes should also be considered. Management should regularly review emergency procedures with employees. Staff who react quickly and efficiently to an emergency may help avert panic and prevent needless damage, injury, or loss of life.

Key Terms

cash bank—an amount of money given to a cashier at the start of each workshift so that he or she can handle the various transactions that occur; the cashier is responsible for this cash bank and for all cash, checks, and other negotiable items received during the workshift.

centralized electronic locking system—an electronic locking system that operates through a master control console at the front desk which is wired to every guestroom door.

emergency key—a key that opens all guestroom doors, even when they are double-locked.

group résumé—a summary of all a group's activities, billing instructions, key attendees, recreational arrangements, arrival and departure patterns, and other important information; usually stored in a binder at the front desk.

information directory—a collection of information kept at the front desk for front desk agents to use in responding to guest requests, including simplified maps of the area; taxi and airline company telephone numbers; bank, theater, church, and store locations; and special event schedules.

log book—a journal in which important front office events and decisions are recorded for reference during subsequent shifts.

master folio—a folio used to chart transactions on an account assigned to more than one person or guestroom, usually reserved for group accounts; a master folio collects charges not appropriately posted elsewhere.

master key—a key that opens all guestroom doors which are not double-locked.

micro-fitted electronic locking system—an electronic locking system in which each door has its own microprocessor containing a predetermined sequence of codes; a master console at the front desk stores code sequences for each door.

reader board—a posting or closed-circuit broadcast of daily events at a hotel.

split folio—a folio in which a guest's charges are separated into two or more folios.

voice mailbox—a device capable of storing, recording, and playing back messages for guests through the telephone system.

Review Questions

1. What front desk procedures help ensure the proper delivery of mail, packages, messages, and faxes to guests?
2. How are communications between the front office and the maintenance division handled? What are the functions of the front office log book and maintenance work orders?
3. What are the three main types of requests guests make at the front desk?
4. What is the purpose of the group résumé book? What kind of information is contained on group résumés and how does the front desk use such information?
5. What is the purpose of a front desk information directory? What sort of information might such a directory contain?
6. Why should guest complaints be welcomed by front office staff? How may a property benefit from analyzing the complaints it receives?
7. What are the four major types of complaints? Which is most common? Describe general approaches to handling complaints.
8. What role do front desk agents play in ensuring the safety and security of guests, employees, and assets?
9. What are the typical key control systems? What are three common levels of key security? How is key control affected by electronic locking systems?
10. What are some of the procedures and guidelines related to front office safes and safe deposit boxes?
11. What emergencies at a property might involve front office personnel? What are typical fire protection and natural disaster guidelines?
12. Why is lost and found so important in a hotel? What precautions should be taken to ensure the security of valuables in lost and found?

Internet Sites

For more information, visit the following Internet sites. Remember that Internet addresses can change without notice.

Lodging Publications—Online and Printed

Hospitality Technology News
http://www.hospitalitynet.nl/news/tech.html

Hotel & Motel Management
http://www.innvest.com/hmm

Lodging Magazine Online
http://www.ei-ahma.org/webs/lodging/index.html

Lodging Hospitality
http://www.penton.com/corp/mags/lh.html

Technology Sites

Anasazi, Inc.
http://www.anasazi.com

CSS Hotel Systems
http://www.csshotelsystems.com

Executech Systems, Inc.
http://www.executech.com

Fidelio Products
http://www.micros.com/mktg/html/index.html

First Resort Software
http://www.firstres.com

Hospitality Industry Technology Exposition and Conference
http://www.hitecshow.org

Hospitality Industry Technology Integration Standards
http://www.hitis.org

HOST Group
http://www.hostgroup.com

Lodging Touch International
http://www.lodgingtouch.com

Newmarket Software Systems, Inc.
http://www.newsoft.com

Resort Data Processing, Inc.
http://www.resortdata.com

Western Hospitality Systems—InnSure
http://www.lodgingsystems.com

Electronic Locking Systems

Computerized Security Systems, Inc.
http://www.cssmain.com

ILCO UNICAN
http://www.ilcounican.com

VingCard
http://www.vingcard.com

Case Study

Service Recovery at the Simpson Hotel

"Carrie, what are you doing? It's almost time to go."

"I'm looking for my new book, Mommy. Have you seen it?"

Abraham Nichols's voice echoed up the stairway. "Almost set up there?"

"We'll be a few more minutes, Abe," answered his wife Angela.

"All right, but remember, we'll be getting in late as it is. I'll put the baby in the car."

Two weeks ago, Abe had been asked to attend a two-day conference in a town five hours from his home. He and Angela had decided to make it a weekend getaway for the family. When making reservations at the Simpson Hotel for the family, Abe informed the reservations agent of all their special requirements: their 11:00 P.M. Thursday-night arrival; a clean, nonsmoking double-double with a crib in place for six-month-old Jason and food service available for their eight-year-old daughter; a pool and fitness center; and the group rate for Thursday and Friday nights.

Thursday night before they left, the Nicholses took a quick supper. Carrie didn't eat much, as her parents had expected; she always got excited about vacations. Then they were on their way.

When the Nicholses arrived, everyone was more than ready for bed—everyone except Carrie, who had found the snacks that her parents had packed inadequate. "I'm still hungry, Daddy. Do they have vending machines at this hotel?"

"Well, don't worry, honey. I talked to the people at the hotel ahead of time, and they said we could get food delivered to our room even at 11 at night. You're going to love it here; there's a big pool where you can swim all you want. And here we are," said Abe as they pulled in under the marquee.

Angela pulled the baby out of the car seat while Abe wrestled with the two large suitcases and the baby's bag and Carrie unloaded her day pack. "You'd think a place like this would have a bellperson," Abe grumbled to Angela.

"I know—and valet parking," she answered. "Go ahead and park, we'll bring the luggage inside." Angela grabbed Jason's bag with the hand with which she was holding him, took one suitcase in the other hand, and pushed the last suitcase with her foot.

Carrie yawned. "Can you get the other suitcase for me, honey?" her mother asked.

Once they were inside, the front office agent looked up from what he was doing and said, "Oh, I'm sorry, let me help you with those. There's usually a bellperson to help with luggage, but he was sick and there was no replacement for this shift. Welcome to the Simpson Hotel. Once we get your things over by the front desk, I'll get you checked in right away."

Abe returned a few minutes later and the family checked in. They noticed a vending machine on their way upstairs, but it had nothing that interested Carrie. When they got to their room, they found it clean and smelling fresh. It had two double beds, but no crib. Abe called the front desk right away. "The agent I talked to on the phone when I made the reservation said you'd have a crib for us," he told the front desk agent.

"Oh, I'm very sorry, sir. I'll chase one down for you right away," the agent responded.

"And could you bring us your room service menu?" Abe asked.

"You'll find that in the guest information directory in your room, sir. It's in the blue binder on the desk," the agent answered.

"Oh, OK, thank you," Abe replied.

Carrie went through the menu with her mother, but Carrie wasn't interested in anything on it. "It looks like all they have available right now is two kinds of salad and some cold deli sandwiches," she told her parents. Angela tried to console Carrie. Between the excitement and the hunger, it looked as if Carrie was going to have trouble getting to sleep. Eventually Angela ordered her a small bag of chips, but the room service order-taker told her that they were making an exception for her; usually chips were only available with the sandwiches.

The chips arrived at the same time as the crib. The crib was delivered by a breathless gentleman who had a five-minute explanation of why it had taken him so long. Abe politely thanked him and turned to put Jason down.

"The first session of the conference isn't until 10 tomorrow morning, so let's try to sleep in," Abe told Angela.

"We can try, but we'll see what Jason does. He doesn't know we're on vacation," she answered.

The next morning the family was awakened at 8:30 A.M. by noise. Abe and Angela were both surprised that it was not Jason's crying, but a knock on the door. "Housekeeping," said a voice on the other side. Abe opened the door and blinked at the housekeeper. Jason started crying.

"Very sorry, sir, I didn't mean to wake you," said the housekeeper. "Didn't you see the—never mind, I'll come back later. Very sorry." *It's not my fault they don't use the Do Not Disturb signs,* thought the housekeeper to herself.

The Nicholses had breakfast, then Abe was off to the conference. Carrie was eager to get into the pool, but first Angela had to ask front desk agents where it was. "I'm very sorry, ma'am," the agent said, "Didn't anyone tell you? The pool is closed for repairs." Carrie groaned.

Angela tried to salvage the situation. "Will it be reopened soon? by Sunday?"

"I'm afraid not, ma'am," answered the agent.

"All right, then, there's a museum I read about in a magazine that's supposed to be close by—the Pinkerton Museum of Natural History?"

The front desk agent recognized the name but had no brochures handy. She drew Angela a map on the back of an envelope and gave her directions for how to walk to the museum. The agent couldn't remember all the street names, nor did she know the museum's hours or admission charges. In spite of this, Angela and the children headed out and had a good time that day at the museum. Carrie was so excited that she told the front desk agent all about it when they got back. Angela thanked the agent for her directions.

Abe finished up with the conference meetings late Friday afternoon. He realized that he could have put up a Do Not Disturb sign the night before, but he looked around the room and found none.

After Abe had unwound a bit, Angela left the children with him so she could go work out at the fitness center. She used the treadmill for a while, but when she went to use the rowing machine, she noticed that one of its handles was much looser than the other. She reported it to the front desk on her way back to the room. She also asked the front desk agent about family restaurants in the area. The agent pulled out a phone book and started scanning the yellow pages. "All I see for family restaurants is places across town," the agent told her, "but there's an upscale place just down the road...." Angela thanked him, and the family had their favorite pizza delivered for supper.

That night the Nicholses realized that their room was right over the lounge. They could hear the live music until about 12:00 A.M., but that wasn't too bad, because the singer was singing songs they knew and liked. Saturday night was different; the driving beat seemed to make the whole room vibrate. Somehow the kids managed to fall asleep in spite of the noise; Abe and Angela were still trying to get to sleep at 2:00 A.M. They talked about when they wanted to leave the next day and decided to leave earlier than they had originally planned. After a night like this, they reasoned, they were not going to be in the mood for recreation. Abe began filling out a guest comment card.

The Nicholses learned at check-out the next morning that the hotel had incorrectly billed them the full rack rate for all three nights. "We'll generate a new bill in just a few moments, Mr. Nichols," the front desk agent told him.

Abe was dropping the comment card into the designated slot while he was waiting when Tom Girard, the hotel's general manager, introduced himself. "I'm just taking an informal guest survey today. How was your stay here?"

Abe gave him the whole story—good points and bad points. Tom listened carefully, taking notes on a pad. He thanked Abe for his feedback and apologized for the difficulties the family had. He offered the Nicholses a free lunch at the hotel's restaurant and told Abe that if the family was ever in the area again, they should call Tom's office and he would arrange for a free night's stay.

Three weeks later, the Nicholses received a very thoughtful follow-up letter from Tom Girard. It explained what he and his staff had done to correct the problems the Nicholses had experienced. But Abe reported to Angela that the credit card bill for the hotel stay was $14 higher than their folio had been when they checked out. A call to the Simpson Hotel revealed that the minibar charges were not posted until after the family had left.

Discussion Questions

1. What went right with the Nichols's stay? What went wrong? Was the overall impression they received of the hotel good or bad?
2. How did the general manager do at responding to Mr. Nichols's feedback?
3. How should the GM relay the Nichols's feedback to his department heads and staff? Should a property offer a 100 percent guest-satisfaction guarantee? If so, how should it be implemented?
4. How can the Simpson Hotel's staff develop a process for improving communication, quality control, and accountability—ultimately, for improving guest service?

Case Number: 3326CA
The following industry experts helped generate and develop this case: Richard M. Brooks, CHA, Vice President—Operations, Bridgestreet Accommodations, Inc., Cleveland, Ohio; and S. Kenneth Hiller, Director of Transition, Renaissance Hotels International, Solon, Ohio.

This case also appears in *Case Studies in Lodging Management* (Lansing, Mich.: Educational Institute of the American Hotel & Motel Association, 1998), ISBN 0-86612-184-6.

Chapter 7 Outline

7

Front Office Accounting

WHILE FRONT OFFICE ACCOUNTING may seem intimidating at first, it is actually grounded in straightforward logic and requires only basic math skills. A front office accounting system monitors and charts the transactions of guests and businesses, agencies, and other non-guests using the hotel's services and facilities. The front office's ability to perform accounting tasks in an accurate and complete manner will directly affect the hotel's ability to collect outstanding balances.

This chapter will examine the fundamentals of front office accounting, including creating and maintaining accounts, tracking transactions, following internal control procedures, and settling accounts.

Accounting Fundamentals

An effective guest accounting system consists of tasks performed during each stage of the guest cycle. During the pre-arrival stage, a guest accounting system captures data related to the type of reservation guarantee and tracks prepayments and advance deposits. When a guest arrives at the front desk, the guest accounting system documents the application of room rate and tax at registration. During occupancy, a guest accounting system tracks authorized guest purchases. Finally, a guest accounting system ensures payment for outstanding goods and services at the time of check-out.

The financial transactions of non-guests may also be processed within the parameters of front office accounting. By allowing authorized non-guest transactions, a hotel can promote its services and facilities to local businesses, or track transactions related to conference business. The area of non-guest accounts also includes the accounts of former guests which were not settled at check-out. The responsibility for collecting on non-guest accounts shifts from the front office to the back office accounting division.

In brief, a front office accounting system:

- Creates and maintains an accurate accounting record for each guest or non-guest account.
- Tracks financial transactions throughout the guest cycle.
- Ensures internal control over cash and non-cash transactions.
- Records settlement for all goods and services provided.

While there are generally accepted accounting principles for the lodging industry, front office accounting procedures are often uniquely tailored to each hotel operation. Accounting terminology and report formats often differ from hotel to hotel or chain to chain. The following sections provide a brief review of some general concepts of front office accounting.

Accounts

An **account** is a form on which financial data are accumulated and summarized. An account may be imagined as a bin or container that stores the results of various business transactions. The increases and decreases in an account are calculated and the resulting monetary amount is the **account balance.** Any financial transaction that occurs in a hotel may affect several accounts. Front office accounts are recordkeeping devices to store information about guest and non-guest financial transactions.

In its simplest written form, an account resembles the letter T:

Account Name	
Charges	Payments

This form of recording is called a T-account. The growing use of front office computers has diminished the popularity of T-accounts. However, T-accounts remain a useful tool for teaching bookkeeping principles. For a front office account, *charges* are increases in the account balance and are entered on the left side of the T. *Payments* are decreases in the account balance and are entered on the right side of the T. The *account balance* is the difference between the totals of the entries on the left side and the right side of the T-account.

Front office accounting documents typically use a journal form. In a non-automated or semi-automated recordkeeping system, a journal form might contain the following information:

Description of Account	Charges	Payments	Balance

Similar to a T-account, increases in the account balance are entered under charges, while decreases in the account balance are entered under payments. In a fully automated system, charges and payments may be listed in a single column with the amounts of payments placed within parentheses or noted with minus signs to indicate their effect (a decrease) on the account balance.

In accounting terminology, the left side of an account is called the **debit** side (abbreviated **dr**) and the right side is called the **credit** side (abbreviated **cr**). Despite their prominence in other branches of hospitality accounting, debits and credits play a relatively small role in front office accounting. Debits and credits do not imply anything good or bad about an account. The value of debits and credits results from the use of double-entry bookkeeping, which is the basis for accounting in all modern businesses. In double-entry bookkeeping, every transaction creates entries that affect at least two accounts. The sum of the debit entries created by a transaction must equal the sum of the credit entries created by that transaction. This fact forms the basis for an accounting process called the night audit.

Guest Accounts. A **guest account** is a record of financial transactions which occur between a guest and the hotel. Guest accounts are created when guests guarantee their reservations or when they register at the front desk. During occupancy, the front office is responsible for and records all transactions affecting the balance of a guest account. The front office usually seeks payment for any outstanding guest account balance during the settlement stage of the guest cycle. Certain circumstances may require the guest to make a partial or full payment at other times during the guest cycle. For example, if the front office is to enforce the hotel's house limit, guests who exceed that limit may be asked to settle part or all of the **outstanding balance**. When there is a house limit, account settlement action is initiated when the account balance exceeds a predetermined limit, not at the time of check-out.

Non-Guest Accounts. A hotel may extend in-house charge privileges to local businesses or agencies as a means of promotion, or to groups sponsoring meetings at the hotel. The front office creates **non-guest accounts** to track these transactions. These accounts may also be called *house accounts* or *city accounts.* Non-guest accounts are also created when a former guest fails to settle his or her account at the time of departure. When the guest's status changes to non-guest, the responsibility for account settlement shifts from the front office to the back office. Unlike guest accounts, which are compiled daily, non-guest accounts are normally billed on a monthly basis by the hotel's accounting division.

Folios

Front office transactions are typically charted on account statements called **folios.** A folio is a statement of all transactions (debits and credits) affecting the balance of a single account. When an account is created, it is assigned a folio with a starting balance of zero. All transactions which increase (debits) or decrease (credits) the balance of the account are recorded on the folio. At settlement, a guest folio should be returned to a zero balance by cash payment or by transfer to an approved credit card or direct billing account.

The process of recording transactions on a folio is called **posting.** A transaction is *posted* when it has been recorded on the proper folio in the proper location, and a new balance has been determined. When posting transactions, the front office may rely on handwritten folios (if it is using a non-automated system), machine-posted folios (with a semi-automated system), or computer-based electronic folios (with a fully automated system).

Regardless of the posting technique used, the basic accounting information recorded on a folio remains the same. In a non-automated or semi-automated recordkeeping system, guest folios are maintained (on paper journals) at the front desk. In a fully automated recordkeeping system, electronic folios are stored in a computer and can be retrieved, displayed, or printed on request.

There are basically four types of folios used in front office accounting. They are:

- **Guest folios:** accounts assigned to individual persons or guestrooms
- **Master folios:** accounts assigned to more than one person or guestroom; usually reserved for group accounts

- **Non-guest** or **semi-permanent folios:** accounts assigned to non-guest businesses or agencies with hotel charge purchase privileges

- **Employee folios:** accounts assigned to employees with charge purchase privileges

Additional types of folios are frequently created by front office management to accommodate special circumstances or requests. For example, a business guest may request that his or her charges and payments be split between two personal folios: one to record expenses to be paid by the sponsoring business, and one to record personal expenses to be paid by the guest. In this situation, two folios are created for one guest. If the room and tax portion are to be separated from other charges, the room and tax is posted to the *room folio.* This is sometimes called the *A folio.* Food, beverage, telephone, and other charges are posted to the *incidental folio* or *B folio.*

Every folio should have a unique serial number. Folio serial numbers are needed for many reasons. First, they serve as identification numbers that help ensure that all folios are accounted for during an audit of front office transactions. Second, folio numbers may be used to index information in automated systems. Automated systems frequently create folio numbers when reservations are made. The reservation number is carried forward to the front desk as the folio number. Finally, folio numbers can provide a chain of documentation. In non-automated and semi-automated systems, folios have specific lengths and can hold only a limited number of postings. When a balance must be carried forward to a new folio, the old folio number should be shown as a reference of where the balance originated.

Vouchers

A **voucher** details a transaction to be posted to a front office account. This document lists detailed transaction information gathered at the source of the transaction, such as the hotel dining room or gift shop. The voucher is then sent to the front office for posting. For example, hotel revenue outlets use vouchers to notify the front office of guest charge purchases which require posting. Several types of vouchers are used in front office accounting, including cash vouchers, charge vouchers, transfer vouchers, allowance vouchers, and paid-out vouchers. Most computer systems require few vouchers, since terminals interfaced with a front office computer are capable of electronically transmitting transaction information directly to electronic folios.

Points of Sale

The term point of sale describes the location at which goods or services are purchased. Any hotel department that collects revenues for its goods or services is considered a revenue center and thus, a point of sale. Large hotels typically support many points of sale, including restaurants, lounges, room service, laundry and valet service, parking garages, telephone service, fitness centers, athletic facilities, and shops. The front office accounting system must ensure that all charge purchases at these points of sale are posted to the proper guest or non-guest account.

Some hotels offer guest-operated devices that also function as points of sale. Similar to an actual revenue outlet, these devices result in charges that must be posted to guest folios. Two such devices are in-room movie and in-room vending service systems.

The volume of goods and services purchased at scattered points of sale requires a complex internal accounting system to ensure proper posting and documentation of sales transactions. Exhibit 1 charts the flow of information that results when a guest charges a restaurant purchase to his or her guest account. A computerized **point-of-sale (POS) system** may allow remote terminals at the points of sale to communicate directly with a front office computer system. Automated POS systems may significantly reduce the amount of time required to post charge purchases to guest folios, the number of times each piece of data must be handled, and the number of posting errors and after-departure (late) charges. Overall, automation helps front office staff create a well-documented, legible folio statement with a minimum number of errors.

No matter the location, points of sale must provide some basic information when posting a charge through a remote terminal or submitting a voucher to the front desk. The information includes the voucher or transaction number, the amount of the charge, name of the point of sale outlet, room number and name of the guest, and brief description of the charge. If the charge is being submitted by voucher, the signature of the guest and the identity of the employee submitting the charge are also required. If the charge is posted through a remote terminal, the employee identification is captured by the computer terminal and forwarded to the folio, along with the time of the posting. Posting through an automated terminal still requires a guest signature on a sales slip or voucher for audit purposes or in case there is any dispute regarding the purchase or the amount.

Ledgers

A **ledger** is a summary grouping of accounts. The front office ledger is a collection of front office account folios. The folios represented in the front office are a part of the front office **accounts receivable ledger.** An **account receivable** represents money owed to the hotel. Front office accounting commonly separates accounts receivable into two subsidiary groups: the **guest ledger** (for guest receivables) and the **city ledger** (for non-guest receivables).

Guest Ledger. The guest ledger refers to the set of guest accounts that correspond to registered hotel guests or guests who have sent advance deposits. Guests who make appropriate credit arrangements at registration may be extended privileges to charge purchases to their individual account folios during their stay. Guests may also make payments against their outstanding balance at any time during occupancy. Guests' financial transactions are recorded onto guest ledger accounts to assist in tracking guest account balances. In some front office operations, the guest ledger may be called the *transient ledger, front office ledger,* or *rooms ledger.* When an

Exhibit 1 Restaurant Bill Charged to a Room Account

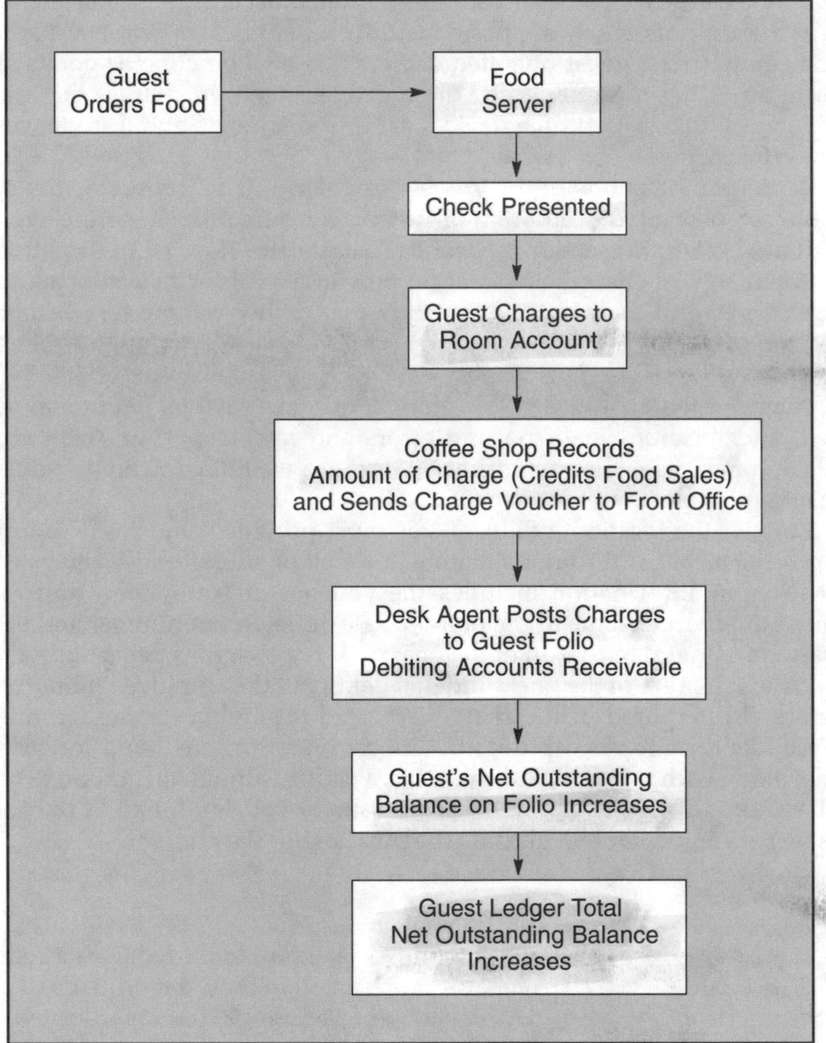

advance deposit is received, it is posted to the guest ledger as a credit balance. When the guest arrives, the amount of the credit balance is diminished throughout the stay by the charges posted to the account. For non-automated and semi-automated hotels, the credit may be posted to the guest's folio immediately or on an advance deposit ledger card. When the guest arrives, the deposit on the ledger card is transferred to the guest's folio.

City Ledger. The city ledger, also called the *non-guest ledger,* is the collection of non-guest accounts. If a guest account is not settled in full by cash payment at check-out, the guest's folio balance is transferred from the guest ledger in the front office to the city ledger in the accounting division for collection. At the time of account transfer, the responsibility for account collection shifts from the front office to the accounting division (back office). The city ledger can contain credit card payment accounts, direct billing accounts, and accounts of past guests due for collection by the hotel.

Creation and Maintenance of Accounts

The task of accurately and completely recording all transactions that affect guest ledger accounts is the responsibility of the front office. The front office also records all transactions which affect non-guest accounts. The back office accounting division is ultimately responsible for collection of non-guest ledger accounts.

Guest folios are created during the reservations process or at the time of registration. To prepare a folio for use, information from the guest's reservation or registration record must be transferred to the folio. Non-automated and semi-automated systems commonly use prenumbered folios for internal control purposes. When prenumbered guest folios are used, the folio number is usually entered onto the guest's registration card for cross-referencing. Manually posted or machine-posted guest folio cards used in non-automated operations are stored in a front desk folio tray. A folio tray may also be referred to as a posting tray, folio well, or bucket.

In a fully automated system, guest information is automatically transferred from an electronic reservation record or captured at registration and entered onto an electronic folio. Electronic folios are automatically cross-referenced with other computer-based records within the front office system. In some systems, a preliminary electronic folio is created automatically and simultaneously with the reservation record. This enables postings to guest accounts before registration. Such items as prepayments and advance deposits can then be accurately monitored through electronic recordkeeping. Since a registration card is also created in a fully automated system, it is stored in the folio tray by room number along with the appropriate pre-stamped credit card voucher. In addition, electronic systems can automatically create the proper number of folios for each guest at the time of registration, and direct charges to each folio as pre-programmed during the reservation process.

At check-in, reservations data are verified and combined with room rate information and the guest's assigned room number to create an in-house electronic folio. For a walk-in guest, equivalent information is captured during registration and entered into a front office computer terminal. Creating an electronic folio within a front office computer system can significantly reduce the possibility of transactional account-entry errors. One of the major advantages of electronic data processing is that captured data need only be handled once. By only having to handle data once, an automated system can significantly reduce errors caused by repetitive data handling.

Recordkeeping Systems

The formats of guest and non-guest account folios may be different, depending upon the front office recordkeeping system.

Exhibit 2 Sample Posting Machine Folio

ROOM	(LAST) NAME (FIRST) (INITIAL)	RATE	FOLIO NUMBER	403131	
STREET ADDRESS		OUT	PHONE READING	OUT	
				IN	
CITY, STATE & ZIP		IN	FROM FOLIO		
NO. PARTY	CREDIT CARD	CLERK	TO FOLIO		

DATE REFERENCE	CHARGES	CREDITS	BALANCE	PREVIOUS BALANCE PICKUP
Jul 27 A RESTR 103	** 14.25		* 14.25	A* 14.25
Jul 27 A ROOM 103	** 60.00		* 74.25	A* 74.25
Jul 27 A LDIST 103	** 6.38		* 80.63	A* 80.63
Jul 27 A MISCCR 103		** 18.38	* 62.25	A* 62.25
Jul 27 A PAID 103		** 62.25	* .00	
			Last Balance Amount Due	

Non-Automated. Guest folios in a manual system contain a series of columns for listing individual debit (charge) and credit (payment) entries accumulated during occupancy. At the end of the business day, each column is totaled and the ending balance is carried forward as the opening folio balance of the following day.

Semi-Automated. Exhibit 2 contains a form of guest folio used in a semi-automated recordkeeping system. Guest transactions are printed sequentially on a machine-posted folio. The information recorded for each transaction includes the date, department or reference number, amount of the transaction, and new balance of the account. The folio's outstanding balance is the amount the guest owes the hotel, or the amount the hotel owes the guest in the event of a credit balance at settlement. The column labeled *previous balance pickup* provides an audit trail within the posting machine framework that helps prove the current outstanding balance is correct. If the semi-automated posting is done by mechanical equipment, it does not retain individual folio balances. This means that each account's previous balance must be re-entered each time an account posting is made to the folio. This process enables

Exhibit 3 Sample Electronic Folio

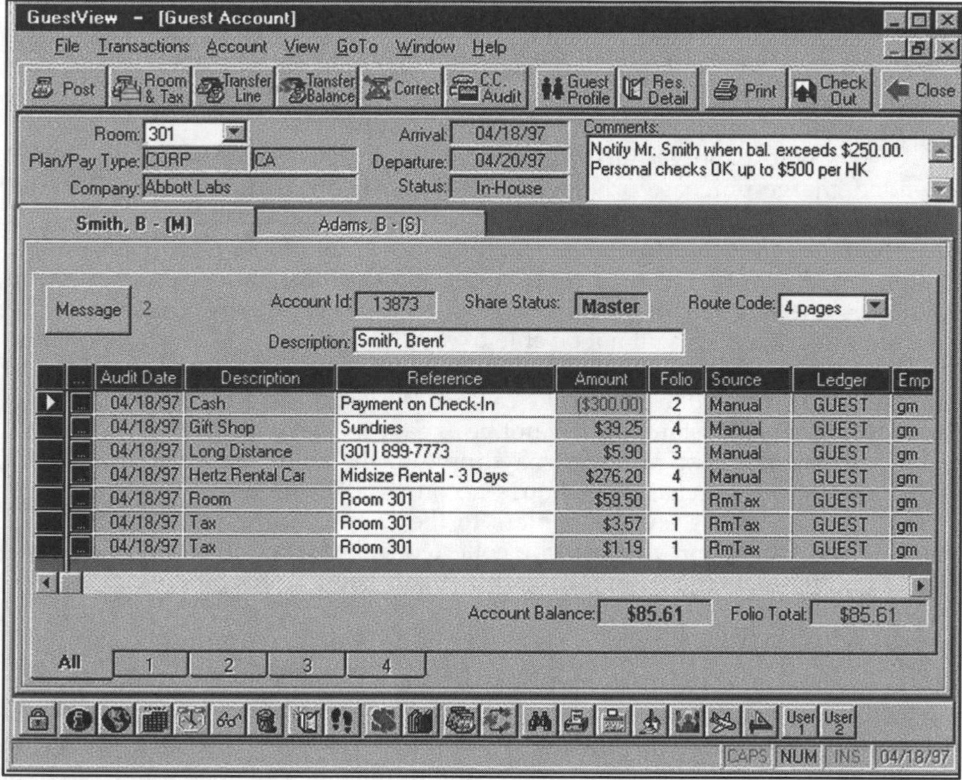

Audit Date	Description	Reference	Amount	Folio	Source	Ledger	Emp
04/18/97	Cash	Payment on Check-In	($300.00)	2	Manual	GUEST	gm
04/18/97	Gift Shop	Sundries	$39.25	4	Manual	GUEST	gm
04/18/97	Long Distance	(301) 899-7773	$5.90	3	Manual	GUEST	gm
04/18/97	Hertz Rental Car	Midsize Rental - 3 Days	$276.20	4	Manual	GUEST	gm
04/18/97	Room	Room 301	$59.50	1	RmTax	GUEST	gm
04/18/97	Tax	Room 301	$3.57	1	RmTax	GUEST	gm
04/18/97	Tax	Room 301	$1.19	1	RmTax	GUEST	gm

This electronic folio is from *GuestView*, a property management system offered by Anasazi, Inc., Phoenix, Arizona. The company's Internet site (http://www.anasazi.com) provides additional selections from its system.

the machine to produce a new current total on the folio card. Electronic posting equipment often does retain folio balances.

Fully Automated. Exhibit 3 contains a form of guest folio used in a fully automated recordkeeping system. Point-of-sale transactions may be automatically posted to an electronic folio. When a printed copy of a folio is needed, debits (charges) and credits (payments) may appear in a single column with payments distinguished by parentheses or a minus sign. Printed folio copies may also be produced in traditional multiple column account format. It is unnecessary to manually maintain an account's previous balance in a fully automated system since computer-based systems maintain current balances for all folios.

Charge Privileges

To establish an in-house line of credit, a guest may be required to present an acceptable credit card or a direct billing authorization at the time of registration. Fully automated hotels allow credit to be established at the time the reservation is made.

This is usually done by obtaining the number and expiration date of the guest's credit card and electronically transmitting this information to the credit card company with a request for an amount guarantee. Once a line of credit has been approved, guests are authorized to make charge purchases. These transactions are communicated manually by vouchers or electronically from remote points of sale locations to the front desk for proper account posting.

Guests who pay cash for accommodations at registration are typically not extended charge purchase privileges. These guests are typically called **paid-in-advance** or **PIA guests.** In a fully automated front office accounting system, PIA accounts are typically set to a *no-post* status. Since point-of-sale terminals throughout the hotel have immediate access to stored account information, a no-post status account is one that cannot accept charge purchase transactions. This means that revenue center cashiers will not be able to post charges to a guest whose account has a no-post status. In non-automated and semi-automated properties, a PIA list is manually distributed to all revenue centers. While this list has the same effect as the computer no-post status, it may not be as easy to use or as current.

Local businesses or residents may apply to the hotel and qualify for house accounts. Charge purchases for house accounts, like those for guest accounts, move from the hotel's revenue centers to the front office for posting. Since all point-of-sale transaction vouchers are collected by the front office every day, it is logical for the front office to audit both guest and non-guest accounts.

Credit Monitoring

The front office must monitor guest and non-guest accounts to ensure they remain within acceptable credit limits. Typically, a line of credit is set for guests who establish charge privileges during the reservations or registration process. Guests who present an acceptable credit card at registration may be extended a line of credit equal to the **floor limit** authorized by the issuing credit card company. This means the front office may not have to seek approval on the credit card as long as the charges do not exceed an amount specified by the credit card company. However, the front office may still need to verify the card's validity. Guest and non-guest accounts with other approved credit arrangements are subject to limitations established by the front office. These internal credit restrictions are called **house limits.**

Front office management may need to be notified when a front office account approaches its credit limit. Such accounts are called **high risk** or **high balance accounts.** The front office manager, or night auditor, is primarily responsible for identifying accounts which have reached or exceeded predetermined credit limits. The front office may deny additional charge purchase privileges to guests with high balance accounts until the situation is resolved. Most front offices periodically review the guest ledger during the day to ensure that guests have not exceeded their approved credit limits. Automated front offices may have a computerized guest list printed on demand that highlights the names of guests whose accounts are near or over their approved credit limits. Front office management may ask the credit card company to authorize additional credit, or request the guest to make a partial payment to reduce the outstanding account balance.

In larger hotels, there may be a full-time credit manager to review high balance accounts. A credit manager may also request additional authorization from credit card companies for guests near or over their floor limits. In addition, it is the credit manager's responsibility to obtain settlement from present and past guests who have not settled their accounts. In smaller hotels, this responsibility is given either to the front desk manager or to the accounting division.

Account Maintenance

A folio is used to record transactions which affect a front office account balance. Guest folios must be accurate, complete, and properly filed since guests may inquire about their account balance or check out of the hotel with little or no advance notice. Transaction postings conform to a basic **front office accounting formula.** The accounting formula is:

Previous Balance	+	Debits	−	Credits	=	Net Outstanding Balance
PB	+	DR	−	CR	=	NOB

Recall that debits increase the balance of an account, while credits decrease the account balance.

This formula can be applied to the folio shown in Exhibit 2. The guest registered on July 27; the first debit—a charge purchase of $14.25—occurred that evening in the hotel's restaurant. Since the front office received no cash payment or credit, the first net outstanding balance on the account is $14.25:

PB	+	DR	−	CR	=	NOB
$0.00	+	$14.25	−	$0.00	=	$14.25

Or, stated another way:

Previous Balance:	$ 0.00
+ Debits:	+ 14.25
− Credits:	− 0.00
= Net Outstanding Balance:	$14.25

Later that evening, the night auditor posted the guest's room and room tax charges ($60) to the account. This transaction, which appears on the second line of the folio, results in a new net outstanding balance:

PB	+	DR	−	CR	=	NOB
$14.25	+	$60.00	−	$0.00	=	$74.25

Next, the guest's long-distance telephone call was posted, resulting in a $6.38 debit posting. The front office later applied a miscellaneous credit (account allowance) of $18.38, and received a cash payment of $62.25 from the guest at check-out. When each of these transactions is applied, the front office posting formula yields a zero net outstanding balance for the account:

PB	+	DR	−	CR	=	NOB
$74.25	+	$6.38	−	$0.00	=	$80.63
$80.63	+	$0.00	−	$18.38	=	$62.25
$62.25	+	$0.00	−	$62.25	=	$ 0.00

At this point, the guest checks out of the hotel and the account is brought to a zero balance and is properly closed.

Tracking Transactions

Charge purchase transactions must be correctly documented in order for the front office to properly maintain accounts. Front office staff rely on accounting vouchers to provide a reliable set of documentation. Even in automated hotels with POS systems communicating directly to the front office system, guests may still question charges when the folio is reviewed. A major concern of the front office accounting process involves the communication of transactional information from remote points of sale to the front office. The night audit is intended to verify transactional data to ensure that the front office collects accounts receivable balances for all goods and services the hotel provides.

A transaction initiates activity within the front office accounting system. From an accounting perspective, nothing happens until a transaction occurs. For this reason, the front office accounting system can be described as a transactional accounting system. Proper posting procedures depend on the nature of the transaction and its monetary value. A transaction can be classified as:

- Cash payment
- Charge purchase
- Account correction
- Account allowance
- Account transfer
- Cash advance

Each type of transaction will have a different effect on the front office accounting system. Each may be communicated to the front office through the use of a different type of voucher, which will help simplify eventual auditing procedures. Most semi-automated front offices require that each voucher be imprinted with transaction information by the front office posting machine. Imprinting provides visual proof that the nature and amount of the voucher were correctly posted to the guest's folio. This procedure also simplifies the night audit routine.

Cash Payment

Cash payments made at the front desk to reduce a guest's net outstanding balance are posted as credits to the guest or non-guest account, thereby decreasing the balance of the account. The front office may use a **cash voucher** to support such transactions. Only cash payment transactions which take place at the front desk will create entries that appear on a front office account folio. Front office account balances are also affected by cash payments made to settle an account or to prepay accommodations. Guests who register and pay cash in advance for their stay may be given a copy of their folio before their stay as proof of payment.

When cash is paid for goods or services at a location other than the front desk, no entry will appear on the account folio. The "account" for this transaction is created, increased, settled, and closed at the point of sale, thereby eliminating the need for front office documentation or posting. For example, a cash payment for a guest's lunch in the hotel's restaurant would not appear on the guest's folio. In addition, some hotels sell items such as newspapers at the front desk. When guests pay for these items with cash, there simply is no charge to post to any account.

Charge Purchase

Charge purchases represent deferred payment transactions. In a deferred payment transaction, the guest (buyer) receives goods and services from the hotel (seller), but does not pay for them at the time they are provided. A charge purchase transaction (debit) increases the outstanding balance of a folio account.

If the transaction occurs somewhere other than at the front desk, it must be communicated to the front desk for proper folio posting. In non-automated and semi-automated properties, this communication is normally accomplished by means of a **charge voucher,** also referred to as an *account receivable voucher.* When the revenue center in which the charge originated uses a form to record the sale (for example, a guest check in the dining room), the form itself is usually considered a source document. To communicate the existence of this transaction, the support document (a voucher) is filled out and sent to the front desk for posting. Many non-automated and semi-automated hotels use a multi-part food and beverage check. When the guest signs the charge to his or her room, a copy of the check goes to the front desk for posting in place of a voucher.

Account Correction

An account correction transaction resolves a posting error on a folio. By definition, an account correction is made on the same day the error is made, *before* the close of business (that is, before the night audit). An account correction can either increase or decrease an account balance, depending on the error. For instance, an account would need to be adjusted if a front desk agent inadvertently posted a lower than normal room rate for a particular guestroom. In this instance, the account correction would increase the guest's folio balance. If a higher than normal room rate had been accidentally posted, then the account correction would decrease the account's balance. A **correction voucher** is used to document an account correction transaction.

Account Allowance

Account allowances involve two types of transactions. One type of account allowance is a decrease in a folio balance for such purposes as compensation for poor service or rebates for coupon discounts. Another type of account allowance corrects a posting error detected *after* the close of business (that is, after the night audit). Such an error will be separately entered into the accounting records of the appropriate revenue centers, thereby also correcting their accounting records.

An account allowance is documented by the use of an **allowance voucher.** Allowance vouchers normally require management approval. Exhibit 4 contains

Exhibit 4 Sample Account Correction and Account Allowance Vouchers

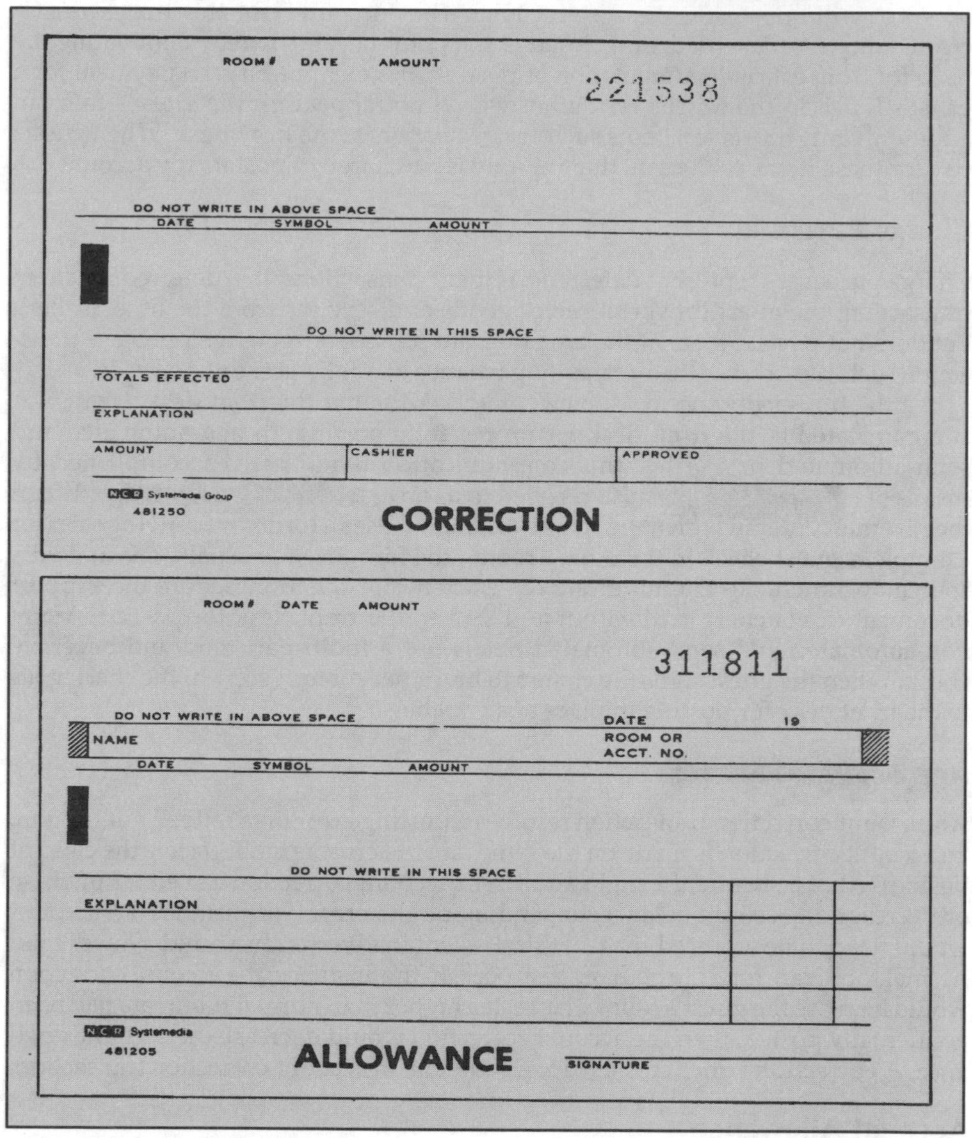
ROOM # DATE AMOUNT

221538

DO NOT WRITE IN ABOVE SPACE

DATE SYMBOL AMOUNT

DO NOT WRITE IN THIS SPACE

TOTALS EFFECTED

EXPLANATION

AMOUNT CASHIER APPROVED

NCR Systemedia Group

481250

CORRECTION

ROOM # DATE AMOUNT

311811

DO NOT WRITE IN ABOVE SPACE

NAME DATE 19

ROOM OR ACCT. NO.

DATE SYMBOL AMOUNT

DO NOT WRITE IN THIS SPACE

EXPLANATION

NCR Systemedia

481205

ALLOWANCE SIGNATURE

sample account correction and account allowance vouchers which may be used in a semi-automated property.

Account Transfer

Account transfers involve two different accounts and tend to have offsetting impacts on subsequent account balances. For example, when one guest offers to pay a charge posted to another guest's folio, the charge will need to be transferred from the first account to a second account. A **transfer voucher** supports the reduction in balance on the originating folio and the increase in balance on the destination folio. An account transfer may also occur when a departing guest uses a credit card to settle his or her account. The guest's outstanding account balance is transferred from a guest account (folio) to a non-guest account (receivable) through the use of a transfer voucher.

Cash Advance

The difference between a cash advance and other types of transactions is that cash advances reflect cash flow out of the hotel, either directly to, or on behalf of, a guest. Cash advance transactions are considered debit transactions since they increase a folio's outstanding balance. Cash advances are supported by **cash advance vouchers.** Cash disbursed by the front office on behalf of a guest (and charged to the guest's account as a cash advance) is typically called a **paid-out.** In some front office operations, a paid-out voucher is used instead of a cash advance voucher.

In the past, front office staff often allowed guests to sign a paid-out slip and receive cash on account; this is no longer common practice. However, a guest who orders a floral delivery, for example, may request that the front desk agent accept the order and pay for the flowers at time of delivery. Since the guest most likely will not leave money at the front desk for this purpose, payment by the front office constitutes a cash advance on the guest's behalf. The front office may pay for the delivery on the presumption that the guest will reimburse the front office. Front office policy should dictate how cash advances are to be handled.

Internal Control

Internal control in the front office involves:

- Tracking transaction documentation.
- Verifying account entries and balances.
- Identifying vulnerabilities in the accounting system.

Auditing is the process of verifying front office accounting records for accuracy and completeness. Each financial interaction produces paperwork which documents the nature and dollar amount of the transaction. For example, consider the transaction that occurs when a guest charges a meal to his or her individual folio. This transaction will likely be supported by the restaurant's guest check, cash register recording, and charge voucher. The charge voucher is prepared in the revenue center and sent to the front office as notification of the transaction. In a semi-automated front office, a front desk agent, in turn, retrieves the guest's folio, posts the charge purchase transaction, refiles the guest folio, and files the charge voucher. Later that day, the front office auditor ensures that all vouchers sent to the front office have been properly posted to the correct accounts. In the case of this example, the auditor will match the front office total of charges from the dining room to the total reported by the dining room. Discrepancies in accounting procedures are easy to resolve when complete documentation is readily available to substantiate account entries.

Front Office Cash Sheet

The front office is responsible for a variety of cash transactions which may affect both guest and non-guest accounts. Proper cash handling procedures and controls must be established, implemented, and enforced.

Most non-automated or semi-automated operations require front office cashiers to complete a **front office cash sheet** that lists each receipt or disbursement of cash. The information contained on a front office cash sheet is used to reconcile cash on hand at the end of a cashier shift with the documented transactions which occurred during the shift. A front office cash sheet provides separate columns to record transactions affecting guest accounts, non-guest (or city ledger) accounts, and miscellaneous transactions. Front office policy may also require the completion of a cash voucher as support documentation for cash transactions affecting front office accounts. A sample front office cash sheet is shown in Exhibit 5.

The most common entry on a front office cash sheet is the money collected from departing guests during check-out. When guests pay on their accounts, the cashier typically records the amount paid, the room number, and the folio number on the front office cash sheet. If a guest has paid for his or her accommodations in advance of check-out, the front desk agent records this payment to offset room and tax charges which are posted subsequently. The front desk agent's cash entries will frequently render a zero folio balance. If a voucher is used in the posting process, some front offices may not require employees to make an entry on the front office cash sheet for cash account settlement. The cash voucher takes the place of the cash sheet in this type of transaction.

The front office cash sheet also provides space for itemizing cash disbursements or paid-outs. When a guest charges a room service purchase to his or her account, for example, he or she may include the server's tip in the total transaction charge. If the front office cashier pays the server his or her tips on the day room service is provided, this transaction will be recorded on the front office cash sheet as a paid-out transaction. Since the amount of cash on hand at the front desk will be lowered by the amount paid to the server, the front office accounting system must be capable of tracking this type of transaction. Similar action is followed if the front office accepts and pays for any delivered item on the guest's behalf. Guest reimbursement is not usually immediate; cash advances tend to be collected at check-out as part of normal folio settlement.

Cash Banks

A second set of front office accounting control procedures involves the use of front office cashier banks. A **cash bank** is an amount of cash assigned to a cashier so that he or she can handle the various transactions that occur during a particular workshift. Good control procedures typically require that cashiers sign for their bank at the beginning of their workshift and that only the person who signed for the bank have access to it during the shift. At the end of a workshift, each front office cashier

Exhibit 5 Sample Front Office Cash Sheet

FRONT OFFICE CASH SHEET

HOTEL______________

FROM ______ A.M. P.M. TO ______ A.M. P.M. __________ 19 ___

__________ CASHIER WATCH

CASH RECEIPTS			ROOM NUMBER			FOLIO NO.	NAME	EXPLANATION	ROOM NO.	CASH DISBURSEMENTS	
MISC'L	CITY LEDGER	GUEST LEDGER	PAID ON ACCOUNT	PAID IN ADVANCE	DEPARTURE					GUEST LEDGER	CITY OR MISC'L

is solely responsible for depositing all cash, checks, and other negotiable instruments received during the workshift.

At the end of the shift, the cashier typically separates out the amount of the initial bank, and then places the remaining cash, checks, and other negotiable items (such as paid-out vouchers) in a specially designed cash voucher or front office cash envelope. The cashier normally itemizes and records the contents of the front office cash envelope on the outside of the envelope before dropping it into the front office vault. From an internal control perspective, at least one other employee should witness this cash banking procedure and both employees should sign a log attesting the drop was actually done and stating the time of the drop.

Monetary differences between the money placed in the front office cash envelope and the cashier's net cash receipts should be noted on the envelope as overages, shortages, or due backs. **Net cash receipts** are the amount of cash, checks, and other negotiable items in the cashier's drawer, minus the amount of the initial cash bank, plus the paid-outs.

For example, assume the front office cashier began the workshift with a $175 cash bank. During the shift, the cashier made paid-outs totaling $49. At the end of the workshift, the amount of cash, checks, and other negotiable items in the cash drawer totals $952.

To determine the amount of net cash receipts, the front office cashier would first add together the value of the cash, checks, and other negotiable items in the cash drawer ($952). The cashier would next subtract the value of the initial cash bank ($175). By adding the amount of paid-outs ($49), the front office cashier will arrive at a net cash receipt position ($826):

$$\$952 - \$175 + \$49 = \$826$$

An **overage** occurs when, after the initial bank is removed, the total of the cash, checks, negotiables, and paid-outs in the cash drawer is greater than the net cash receipts. A **shortage** occurs when the total of the contents of the drawer is less than the net cash receipts. Neither an overage nor a shortage is typically considered "good" by front office management when evaluating the job performance of front office cashiers. Overages and shortages are determined by comparing the cash totals of the cashier's postings against the actual cash, checks, and negotiables in the cashier's bank. Good recordkeeping systems, whether they be non-automated, semi-automated, or fully automated will provide proper cash posting documentation. Since cashiers are dealing with cash, it is essential to have proper procedures to ensure financial integrity at the front desk.

A **due back** occurs when a cashier pays out more than he or she receives; in other words, there is not enough cash in the drawer to restore the initial bank. Due backs are unusual in the front office. A special kind of due back may occur when a cashier accepts many checks and large bills during a shift. This can make it difficult to restore the initial bank without including the checks or large bills. Since checks and large bills are not very useful for processing transactions, they are usually deposited with other receipts. Consequently, the front office deposit may be greater than the cashier's net cash receipts, with the excess *due back* to the front office cashier's bank. Front office due backs are normally replaced with small bills and coins before the cashier's next workshift, thereby restoring the cash bank to its full and correct amount. Due backs do not reflect positively or negatively on the cashier's job performance, and may occur when net cash receipts are in or out of balance.

Audit Controls

A number of front office audit controls ensure that front office staff properly handle cash, guest accounts, and non-guest accounts. Publicly held lodging companies are required to have both their front and back office accounting records audited yearly by independent certified public accountants. In addition, companies with several lodging properties often employ internal auditors to make unannounced visits to individual properties for the purpose of auditing accounting records. In both instances, a report is completed for management and ownership review. Exhibit 6 presents one firm's internal control inspection checklist. The checklist includes items related to standard front office procedures designed to protect the integrity of front office operations.

Settlement of Accounts

The collection of payment for outstanding account balances is called account settlement. Settlement involves bringing an account balance to zero. An account can be brought to a zero balance as a result of a cash payment in full or a transfer to an approved direct billing or credit card account. All guest accounts must be settled at the time of check-out. Transfers to approved deferred payment plans move outstanding guest folio balances from the guest ledger to the city ledger.

Although guest account settlement normally occurs at check-out, guests may make payments against outstanding folio balances at any time. Non-guest folio balances may be initially billed on the day the transaction occurred. Settlement may be due in 15 to 30 days, depending on front office policy. For example, consider the case of a guest who makes a guaranteed reservation but does not show up, often called a *no-show* guest. The account cannot be settled at check-out, since the guest never registered. Instead, the front office sends a statement to the guest for the amount of the guarantee, hoping to collect the account balance in 15 to 30 days. If the guarantee was made by credit card, the hotel may have an agreement with the credit card company to bill it for the no-show guest. The amount of the guarantee is then transferred to the credit card part of the accounts receivable ledger for collection.

Summary

A front office accounting system monitors and charts the transactions of guests and businesses, agencies, and other non-guests using the hotel's services and facilities. The front office's ability to perform accounting tasks in an accurate and complete manner will directly affect the hotel's ability to collect outstanding balances.

A front office accounting system is uniquely tailored to each hotel operation. Accounting system terminology and report formats often differ from hotel to hotel.

Exhibit 6 Sample Internal Control Inspection Checklist

(A) GUEST ACCOUNTS

1. Accounts Receivable per audit:

   a. ______ Sleepers $ ______
   b. ______ After departure charges ______
   c. ______ Prepaid accts. with charges ______
   d. ______ Disputed accounts ______
   e. ______ Delinquent accounts (over 60 days) ______
   f. ______ Skips ______
   g. ______ Tour vouchers ______
   h. ______ Employee accounts ______
   i. ______ Intercompany accounts ______
   j. ______ ______
   k. ______ ______
   l. ______ ______

   SUBTOTAL $ ______

   m. Other direct billing accounts ______

   TOTAL DIRECT BILLING $ ______

   n. Total guest accounts ______

   TOTAL ACCOUNTS RECEIVABLE $ ______

   o. Less advance deposits ______

   BALANCE ACCOUNTS RECEIVABLE $ ______

   p. Variance
      ______ Direct billing accounts
      ______ Accounts confirmed by letter $ ______
      Reset control number per report ______
      Reset control number per machine ______

	Sat.	Unsat.
2. Direct billing accounts signed by guest.	______	______
3. Follow-up on accounts receivable in accordance with company policy.	______	______
4. Only authorized individuals permitted to sign direct billing accounts.	______	______
5. Direct billing accounts have copies of all correspondence and supporting charges pertaining thereto.	______	______
6. Direct billing checks deposited promptly.	______	______
7. Monthly listing of accounts receivable prepared properly.	______	______
8. Direct billing payments, posting, billing, separated and supervised.	______	______
9. Corporate credit authorization on file for direct billings.	______	______

(B) ADVANCE DEPOSITS

	Sat.	Unsat.
1. Folios are complete (date of arrival shown on folios, etc.).	______	______
2. Advance deposit folios are secured.	______	______
3. Revenues or refunds processed promptly on stale dated credit balance accounts.	______	______
4. Advance deposit checks deposited promptly.	______	______

Exhibit 6 *(continued)*

			Sat.	Unsat.
(C)		CREDIT CARD PROCEDURES		
	1.	Credit card imprinters are dated correctly.	______	______
	2.	An examination of all completed credit card vouchers shows:		
		a. Approval where required.	______	______
		b. All cards current (not expired).	______	______
		c. All imprints are legible.	______	______
		d. Clerk's initials and folio number.	______	______
	3.	Credit card transmittals completed correctly (totals correct, non-national credit card charges itemized, adding machine tape included).	______	______
(D)		CHECKS		
	1.	Clerk's initials, folio number, endorsement and payee portion completed properly.	______	______
	2.	Deposit daily.	______	______
	3.	Correct check cashing policies in force.	______	______
	4.	Check register maintained correctly.	______	______
(E)		FRONT OFFICE		
	1.	Reset control number controlled properly.	______	______
	2.	Revenues balanced to D card: (check 3 days)		
		a. Room	______	______
		b. Restaurant	______	______
		c. Long Distance	______	______
		d. Laundry	______	______
		e. Miscellaneous	______	______
	3.	Paid-outs and allowances are completed and approved by management.	______	______
	4.	Corrections controlled and balanced.	______	______
	5.	Copies of all vouchers kept on property.	______	______
	6.	Long-distance calls taxed properly.	______	______
	7.	Long-distance service charges only as permitted by law.	______	______
	8.	Room tax charged correctly.	______	______
(F)		GUEST FOLIOS AND REGISTRATION CARDS		
	1.	Registration cards and folios filled out completely.	______	______
	2.	Folios and registration cards are time stamped in and out.	______	______
	3.	Continuation folios marked to and from.	______	______
	4.	Alphabetical and numerical filing current and in good order.	______	______
	5.	Numerical sequence of unused folios in order.	______	______
	6.	Void folios handled correctly.	______	______
(G)		SECURITY AND SAFETY		
	1.	Drop facilities constructed properly.	______	______
	2.	Deposit witness log used properly.	______	______
	3.	House banks stored properly when not in use.	______	______
	4.	Night Auditor's clearance key secured.	______	______
	5.	Safe deposit boxes:		
		a. Log maintained correctly.	______	______
		b. Keys available for unused boxes.	______	______

(continued)

Exhibit 6 *(continued)*

			Sat.	Unsat.
6.	Vehicle drivers properly licensed.		_______	_______
7.	Cash drawers locked when not in use.		_______	_______
8.	Hotel safe:			
	a.	Safe combinations last changed:_______.	_______	_______
	b.	No terminated employees have safe combinations.	_______	_______
9.	Proper security over keys when not in use.		_______	_______
10.	Adequate security over storerooms.		_______	_______
11.	TV log up to date.		_______	_______
12.	Adequate linen inventory control.		_______	_______

(H) FOLIO ACCOUNTABILITY

1. Unused folios (unopened boxes only):
   Total on hand__________ from number ________ to number________
   Where are unused folios stored: ________________________________
   How long will supply last: ________________________________
   Per attached check sheets, the following folios were not accounted for: ____________
   Total folios checked:________ Period covered from________ to ______
   Total number of folios missing: ________________________________

COMMENTS:____

____

____

____

____

I acknowledge receipt of this inspection and concur that the ratings given my property are factual and accurate (list any exceptions above).

_______________________ ____________ Same Manager present at last audit?
Manager Date Yes______ No______

I hereby certify that on the above date I performed an audit of the above property.

____

Field Auditor, Audit Services Division

In general, an account is a form on which financial data are accumulated and summarized. The increases and decreases in an account are calculated and the resulting monetary amount is the account balance. All the financial transactions that occur in a hotel affect accounts. Front office accounts are recordkeeping devices to store information about guest and non-guest financial transactions. For a front office account, charges are increases in the account balance and are entered on the left side of the T. Payments are decreases in the account balance and are entered on the right side of the T. Front office accounting documents typically use a journal form.

A guest account is a record of financial transactions between a guest and the hotel. Guest accounts are created when guests guarantee their reservations or when they register at the front desk. A hotel may also extend in-house charge privileges to local businesses or agencies as a means of promotion, or to groups sponsoring meetings at the hotel. The front office creates non-guest accounts (also called house accounts or city accounts) to track these transactions.

Front office transactions are typically charted on account statements called folios. A folio is a statement of all transactions (debits and credits) affecting the balance of a single account. All transactions which increase (debits) or decrease (credits) the balance of the account are recorded on the folio. At settlement, a guest folio should be returned to a zero balance by cash payment or by transfer to an approved credit card or direct billing account. The process of recording transactions on a folio is called posting. A transaction is posted when it has been recorded on the proper folio in the proper location, and a new balance has been determined.

There are basically four types of folios used in the front office: guest folios, master folios, non-guest or semi-permanent folios, and employee folios. Additional types of folios are frequently created by front office management to accommodate special circumstances or requests.

A voucher details a transaction to be posted to a front office account. This document lists detailed transaction information gathered at the source of the transaction. The voucher is then sent to the front office. Auditing is the process of verifying front office accounting records for accuracy and completeness.

The term point of sale describes the location at which goods or services are purchased. Any hotel department that collects revenues for its goods or services is considered a revenue center and thus, a point of sale. A computerized point-of-sale (POS) system may allow remote terminals at the points of sale to communicate directly with a front office computer system. Automated POS systems may significantly reduce the amount of time required to post charge purchases to guest folios, the number of times each piece of data must be handled, and the number of posting errors and after-departure (late) charges.

A ledger is a grouping of accounts. The front office ledger is a collection of front office account folios. The folios used in the front office form part of the front office accounts receivable ledger. An account receivable represents money owed to the hotel. Front office accounting commonly separates accounts receivable into two subsidiary groups: the guest ledger (for guest receivables) and the city ledger (for non-guest receivables). The guest ledger is the set of guest accounts that correspond to registered hotel guests. Guests who make appropriate credit arrangements at registration may be extended privileges to charge purchases to their individual account folios. The city ledger, also called the non-guest ledger, is the collection of non-guest accounts. If a guest account is not settled in full by cash payment at check-out, the guest's folio balance is transferred from the guest ledger in the front office to the city ledger in the accounting division for collection.

Most non-automated or semi-automated operations require front office cashiers to complete a front office cash sheet that lists each receipt or disbursement of cash. The information contained on a front office cash sheet is used to reconcile cash on hand at the end of a cashier shift with the documented transactions that occurred during the shift. Front office policy may also require the completion of a cash voucher as support documentation for cash transactions affecting front office accounts.

Establishing and monitoring the credit of guests is often the responsibility of the credit manager. In many cases, these tasks may be part of the front desk manager's duties. The credit manager assists guests in establishing credit as well as reviews the guest and non-guest ledger to ensure that accounts do not exceed established credit limits.

Key Terms

account—a form in which financial data are accumulated and summarized.

account balance—a summary of an account in terms of its resulting monetary amount; specifically, the difference between the total debits and total credits to an account.

account receivable—an amount owed to the hotel.

accounts receivable ledger—a grouping of accounts receivable, including the guest ledger and the city ledger.

allowance voucher—a voucher used to support an account allowance.

cash advance voucher—a voucher used to support cash flow out of the hotel, either directly to or on behalf of a guest.

cash bank—an amount of money given to a cashier at the start of each workshift so that he or she can handle the various transactions that occur; the cashier is responsible for this cash bank and for all cash, checks, and other negotiable items received during the workshift.

cash voucher—a voucher used to support a cash payment transaction at the font desk.

charge voucher—a voucher used to support a charge purchase transaction that takes place somewhere other than the front desk; also referred to as an account receivable voucher.

city ledger—the collection of all non-guest accounts, including house accounts and unsettled departed guest accounts.

correction voucher—a voucher used to support the correction of a posting error which is rectified before the close of business on the day the error was made.

credit (cr)—an entry on the right side of an account.

debit (dr)—an entry on the left side of an account.

due back—a situation that occurs when a cashier pays out more than he or she receives; the difference is due back to the cashier's cash bank; in the front office, due backs usually occur when a cashier accepts so many checks and large bills during a shift that he or she cannot restore the initial bank at the end of the shift without using the checks or large bills.

employee folio—a folio used to chart transactions on an account assigned to an employee with charge purchase privileges.

floor limit—a limit assigned to hotels by credit card companies indicating the maximum amount in credit card charges the hotel is permitted to accept from a card member without special authorization.

folio—a statement of all transactions affecting the balance of a single account.

front office accounting formula—the formula used in posting transactions to front office accounts: Previous Balance + Debits – Credits = Net Outstanding Balance.

front office cash sheet—a form completed by front office cashiers that lists each receipt or disbursement of cash during a workshift; used to reconcile actual cash on hand with the transactions that occurred during the shift.

guest account—a record of the financial transactions that occur between a guest and the hotel.

guest folio—a form (paper or electronic) used to chart transactions on an account assigned to an individual person or guestroom.

guest ledger—the set of accounts for all guests currently registered at the hotel; also called the front office ledger, transient ledger, or rooms ledger.

high balance account—an account that has reached or exceeded a predetermined credit limit; typically identified by the night auditor; also called a high risk account

house limit—a credit limit established by the hotel.

ledger—a grouping of accounts.

master folio—a folio used to chart transactions on an account assigned to more than one person or guestroom, usually reserved for group accounts; collects charges not appropriately posted elsewhere.

net cash receipts—the amount of cash and checks in the cashier's drawer, minus the amount of the initial cash bank.

non-guest account—an account created to track the financial transactions of (1) a local business or agency with charge privileges at the hotel, (2) a group sponsoring a meeting at the hotel, or (3) a former guest with an outstanding account balance.

non-guest folio—a folio used to chart transactions on an account assigned to (1) a local business or agency with charge privileges at the hotel, (2) a group sponsoring a meeting at the hotel, or (3) a former guest with an outstanding account balance.

outstanding balance—the amount the guest owes the hotel—or the amount the hotel owes the guest, in the event of a credit balance at settlement.

overage—an imbalance that occurs when the total of cash and checks in a cash register drawer is greater than the initial bank plus net cash receipts.

paid-in-advance (PIA) guest—a guest who pays his or her room charges in cash during registration; PIA guests are often denied in-house credit.

paid-out—cash disbursed by the hotel on behalf of a guest and charged to the guest's account as a cash advance.

point-of-sale (POS) system—a computer network that allows electronic cash registers at the hotel's points of sale to communicate directly with a front office guest accounting module.

posting—the process of recording transactions on a guest folio.

shortage—an imbalance that occurs when the total of cash and checks in a cash register drawer is less than the initial bank plus net cash receipts.

transfer voucher—a voucher used to support a reduction in balance on one folio and an equal increase in balance on another; used for transfers between guest accounts and for transfers from guest accounts to non-guest accounts when they are settled by the use of credit cards.

voucher—a document detailing a transaction to be posted to a front office account; used to communicate information from a point of sale to the front office.

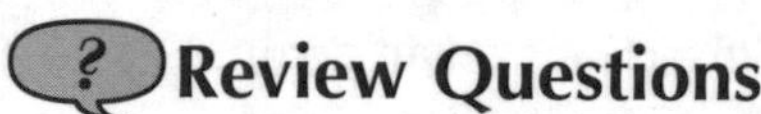

Review Questions

1. What are the specific functions of a front office accounting system? What tasks are performed during each stage of the guest cycle?
2. What is the purpose of an account? How are transactions recorded in an account? How are guest accounts and non-guest accounts different?
3. What are the four types of folios in common use in front office accounting? How is a folio related to an account?
4. What is a point of sale? How can fully automated point-of-sale systems and guest-operated devices streamline the flow of accounting information to the front office?
5. What information is necessary to create a folio? How does the process differ in non-automated, semi-automated, and fully automated front office record-keeping systems?
6. What is the basic front office accounting formula? How is it used in posting transactions?
7. How does accounting for a cash payment differ from accounting for a cash advance at the front desk?
8. What items are recorded on a front office cash sheet? How does a cash sheet help ensure internal control in the front office?
9. What are overages, shortages, and due backs? How might these conditions reflect on a front office cashier's job performance?
10. What is the difference between an account correction and an account allowance? Why is it important to differentiate between the two?

Internet Sites

For more information, visit the following Internet sites. Remember that Internet addresses can change without notice.

Lodging Publications—Online and Printed

Hospitality Technology News
http://www.hospitalitynet.nl/news/tech.html

Hotel & Motel Management
http://www.innvest.com/hmm

Lodging Hospitality
http://www.penton.com/corp/mags/lh.html

Lodging Online
http://www.ei-ahma.org/webs/lodging/index.html

Technology Sites

Anasazi, Inc.
http://www.anasazi.com

CSS Hotel Systems
http://www.csshotelsystems.com

Executech Systems, Inc.
http://www.executech.com

Fidelio
http://www.micros.com

First Resort Software
http://www.firstres.com

Hospitality Industry Technology Exposition and Conference
http://www.hitecshow.org

Hospitality Industry Technology Integration Standards
http://www.hitis.org

HOST Group
http://www.hostgroup.com

Lodging Touch International
http://www.lodgingtouch.com

Newmarket Software Systems, Inc.
http://www.newsoft.com

Resort Data Processing, Inc.
http://www.resortdata.com

Western Hospitality Systems—InnSure
http://www.lodgingsystems.com

Case Study

Front Office Accounting at the Magic Crest Hotel

One of the major problems with front office accounting at the Magic Crest Hotel is monitoring guest and non-guest accounts. For some reason, management has always extended local businesses and government officials charge privileges, the idea being that, with the convenience of deferred payments, local patrons would be more likely to dine and/or host clients at the hotel. This program has proved to be highly successful. The volume of purchases charged to such non-guest accounts now approximates the level of sales incurred by registered guests. Unsure if this is a good or bad situation, Mr. Aerial, the front office manager, requests the front office accounting staff to study the problem and to report its findings at next week's meeting.

At its weekly front office meeting, the front office accountant, Ms. Letsche, reports that there are at least three problems related to the hotel's non-guest charge purchasing policies: its impact on the daily hotel audit, the billing procedures to collect payment, and the number of applications for additional non-guest accounts.

When asked to be more specific, she begins with a review of the daily hotel audit. She states that since the front office receives charge vouchers from the hotel's revenue centers, it is the front desk agent's responsibility to separate guest from non-guest accounts. Since registered guest charges are posted by room number, one would think it easy to sort those charges from the others. Unfortunately, the non-guest account numbers are also three digits, thereby making the sorting more time consuming. Mr. Aerial asks if it is really necessary to separate the charges and Ms. Letsche explains that it is, since the hotel must maintain accurate guest folio balances. She further states that the non-guest vouchers are accumulated and posted on Saturday afternoons, when the hotel's business is less hectic.

The billing procedures to collect non-guest account balances are tricky. Since the hotel bills non-guest accounts on the last day of each month, some charges occurring in a particular month may not be posted in time to appear on that month's bill. In addition, non-guest accounts usually are not paid in a timely fashion. In fact, 47% of last month's non-guest account balances remain unpaid and tomorrow is the date of the next billing cycle. Mr. Aerial explains that the local customers are important to the hotel and suggests that maybe Ms. Letsche is over-sensitive to the billing problems.

Lastly, Ms. Letsche relates the fact that there are at least ten new applications for non-guest accounts. She has instructed her staff not to authorize any new accounts without her written approval. She further states that she is reluctant to authorize any additional non-guest accounts and looks to Mr. Aerial for advice. Convinced of the positive aspects of such business, Mr. Aerial directs her to approve the requests and to assign account numbers effective the first day of next month. Ms. Letsche so instructs her staff.

Discussion Questions

1. What ideas would you suggest to facilitate a more effective processing of guest and non-guest charge vouchers? How might the daily audit be aided by such changes? Is the accumulated postings routine for non-guest accounts an effective plan?
2. What could be done to improve the hotel's billing of non-guest accounts? What could be done to improve collection of outstanding balances?
3. What are the advantages and disadvantages to having a high volume of non-guest accounts? What about the cost of carrying and collecting outstanding balances? How might the hotel's cash flow be affected by such transactions?

Case Number: 3327CA

The following industry experts helped generate and develop this case: Richard M. Brooks, CHA, Vice President—Operations, Bridgestreet Accommodations, Inc.,

Cleveland, Ohio; and S. Kenneth Hiller, Director of Transition, Renaissance Hotels International, Solon, Ohio.

This case also appears in *Case Studies in Lodging Management* (Lansing, Mich.: Educational Institute of the American Hotel & Motel Association, 1998), ISBN 0-86612-184-6.

Chapter 8 Outline

8

Check-Out and Settlement

CHECK-OUT AND SETTLEMENT are part of the final stage of the guest cycle. The services and activities of the departure stage are performed primarily by a member of the front office staff. Before the age of computers in hotels, the workload of the front desk staff in medium and large hotels was great enough that registration and cashier positions were separate. A guest would be checked in by the front desk registration staff and checked out by the front desk cashiering staff. Cross-training of staffs was very rare. Only in smaller hotels did the same person do both jobs. Today, because of front desk automation, most hotels train their front desk personnel on both check-in and check-out procedures. This adds variety to the job, permits more flexible staffing schedules, and provides better service to the guest. Personnel from the front office accounting division may be involved as well. Before departing the hotel, the guest will generally stop at the front desk to review his or her folio, settle any outstanding account balance, receive a receipt of the account statement, and return the room key.

Many guests will forget all the previous courtesy and hard work of the front office staff if check-out and account settlement do not go smoothly. This chapter covers the final phase of the guest cycle by examining the various activities involved in check-out and settlement.

Check-Out and Account Settlement

The front office performs at least three important functions during the check-out and settlement process:

- It resolves outstanding guest account balances.
- It updates room status information.
- It creates guest history records.

Guest account settlement depends on an effective front office accounting system that maintains accurate guest folios, verifies and authorizes a method of settlement, and resolves discrepancies in account balances. Generally, the front office finds it most effective to settle a guest's account while the guest is still in the hotel. A guest can settle an account by paying cash, charging the balance to a credit card, deferring payment to an approved direct billing entity, or using a combination of payment methods.

Most front offices require a guest to specify during registration an eventual method of settlement. This procedure enables the front office to verify or confirm the guest's credit card or direct billing information before he or she arrives at the desk for check-out and account settlement. Pre-settlement verification activities help minimize the guest's check-out time and may significantly improve the front office's ability to collect outstanding account balances. Guests may later change their minds and pay by another form of settlement. However, the pre-settlement verification activities ensure that the hotel will be paid for the accommodations and services it provided during the guest's stay.

Effective front office operations depend on accurate room status information. When a guest checks out and settles his or her account, the front desk agent performs several important tasks. First, the agent changes the guestroom's status from *occupied* to *on-change* on the room status report. *On-change* is a housekeeping term that means that the guest has checked out of the hotel and that the room he or she occupied needs to be cleaned and readied for the next guest. After making the room status change, the front desk agent notifies the housekeeping department that the guest has departed.

In hotels with manual or semi-automated systems, the front desk communicates information to the housekeeping department by telephone or through an electronic room status board or a telewriter. In a fully automated front office, information may be relayed automatically to the housekeeping department when the front desk agent completes the check-out process. Once housekeeping receives the information, a housekeeper cleans and readies the room for inspection and resale. To maximize room sales, the front office must maintain the current occupancy and housekeeping status for all rooms and must exchange room status information with the housekeeping department quickly and accurately.

Check-out and settlement also involves the creation of the *guest history record* that will become part of the *guest history file.* Because a hotel can gain a valuable competitive edge in the hospitality marketplace through the proper analysis of guest history data, guest history files can provide a powerful data base for strategic marketing. Guest history files and records are discussed later in this chapter.

Departure Procedures

Check-out and account settlement can be an efficient process when the front office is well-prepared and organized. The departure stage of the guest cycle involves several procedures designed to simplify check-out and account settlement. These procedures include:

- Inquiring about additional recent charges
- Posting outstanding charges
- Verifying account information
- Presenting the guest folio
- Verifying the method of payment
- Processing the account payment
- Checking for mail, messages, and faxes
- Checking for safe deposit box or in-room safe keys

- Securing the room key
- Updating the room's status

The procedures used will vary among front offices, depending upon the hotel's level of service and degree of automation. The amount of personal contact between the guest and front desk staff may also vary, since some front offices offer automated or express check-out services.

Check-out affords the front office yet another chance to make a positive impression on the guest. A guest approaching the front desk should be greeted promptly and courteously. The front desk agent should check for any messages, faxes, or mail awaiting guest pickup. The front desk agent should also verify that the guest has cleared his or her safe deposit box or in-room safe and returned the key.

To ensure that the guest's folio is accurate and complete, the front desk agent should process any outstanding charges that need posting. In addition, the front desk agent should ask the guest if he or she incurred any recent charges and make the necessary postings to the guest's folio. Before computers became common in hotels, guests used to call the front office before coming to the front desk to check out. This notice allowed the cashier to find any unposted charges and prepare the folio so the guests would not have to stand and wait while the charges were identified and posted. Since most hotels today are automated, guests expect their folios to be accurate and ready for them when they approach the front desk to check out. No matter what degree of automation at a hotel, the guest may leave with a poor impression of the property if the bill is not up-to-date and accurate when he or she is ready to check out.

Traditionally, at check-out the guest is presented a final copy of his or her account folio for review and settlement. During this time, the front desk agent should confirm how the guest intends to settle the account, regardless of which method of settlement the guest specified during the registration process. This request is necessary because many front offices require the guest to establish credit at check-in, regardless of how the guest eventually plans to settle the account. A guest may establish credit by presenting a credit card at check-in, and then decide to settle his or her account balance by cash or check. Guests noted as very important (VIPs) or special guests of a group or corporate account should not be asked for settlement if their account is marked that all charges are to be direct billed.

After determining how the guest will pay, the front desk agent should then bring the guest's account balance to zero. This is typically called **zeroing out** the account. A guest's account balance must be settled in full for an account to be considered zeroed out. As long as the hotel has received full payment or is assured full payment, the account will be settled with a zero balance. For example, if the guest pays cash, the account is brought to a zero balance. If the guest settles using a credit card, the hotel will get an approval from the credit card company for the amount due. The credit card company guarantees payment to the hotel for the amount approved, so the account can also be brought to zero. Hotels are usually paid by credit card companies within a day or two of the settlement transaction. Because of this guarantee, the hotel assumes payment in full and closes the folio. If the account is to be paid through direct billing by the hotel, however, the account is not brought to a zero balance because it must be transferred to the city ledger and billed through the accounts receivable system.

Methods of Settlement

A guest account can be brought to a zero balance in several ways. Methods of settlement include cash payment, credit card or direct billing transfer, or a combined settlement method.

Cash Payment in Full. A cash payment in full at check-out will bring a guest account balance to zero. The front desk agent should mark the folio paid. As mentioned previously, the front office sometimes requires the guest to present a credit card at check-in to gain charge privileges. A guest may have had a credit card imprinted at registration, even though he or she intended to settle the account by cash. The front desk agent should destroy the guest's credit card voucher imprinted at registration when the guest pays the account in full with cash. Guests paying in foreign currency should first convert their money to local currency. Settlements are customarily in local currency only. Hotels often charge a fee to convert currencies, since banks charge hotels fees for currency conversion. Most front desks of major hotels display currency conversion rates for major countries, or have them ready available through the business section of newspapers.

Credit Card Transfer. Even though credit card settlement brings a guest account to zero, the amount of the charge must be tracked until payment is actually received from the credit card company. Therefore, credit card settlement creates a transfer credit on the guest's folio and moves the account balance from the guest ledger to a credit card account in the city (or non-guest) ledger. After the front desk agent swipes the card through a credit card reader, a payment slip is printed by the reader with the proper amount on it. The completed credit card slip is then presented to the guest for signature. The guest's signature completes this transaction. In many locations now, imprinting vouchers is no longer necessary because the hotel computer system sends the settlement transaction directly to the credit card company. In these cases, the guest only signs a voucher printed at the front desk at the time of settlement. When foreign guests present credit cards for payment, the credit card company always provides payment in local currency. Hotels do not have to worry about currency exchange rates or fees.

Direct Billing Transfer. Like credit card settlement, direct billing transfers a guest's account balance from the guest ledger to the city ledger. Unlike credit card settlement, responsibility for billing and collecting a direct billing lies with the hotel, rather than an outside agency. Direct billings are not normally an acceptable method of settlement unless the billing has been arranged and approved by the hotel's credit department before or during guest registration. To complete a direct billing settlement, the front desk agent should have the guest sign the folio to verify that its contents are correct and that the guest accepts responsibility for all charges contained on the folio (should the direct billing account not pay the bill).

Combined Settlement Methods. A guest may elect to use more than one settlement method to bring the folio balance to zero. For example, the guest may make a partial cash payment and charge the remainder of the account balance to an acceptable credit card. Front desk agents must accurately record the combined settlement methods and take care that all required paperwork is properly completed. Properly completed paperwork will help facilitate an effective front office audit.

Once the guest has settled the account, the front desk agent should provide the guest with a copy of the folio and continue to be a goodwill ambassador for the hotel. Check-out and account settlement is one of the last opportunities the front office has to convey hospitality. The front desk agent should take full advantage of this opportunity. For example, the agent should ask if everything at the property met the guest's expectations, especially the room, facilities, and services.

Check-out and account settlement is an excellent time for the agent to let the guest know that the hotel cares about the quality of the guest's experience during his or her stay. Many front offices provide guests with comment cards at check-out, hoping that guests will provide an evaluation of their experience. The front desk agent should always thank guests for staying at the hotel and wish guests a safe trip. The front desk agent should also ask guests to consider returning to the property on any return trip to the area.

As discussed earlier, immediately after the guest has settled his or her account and departed the hotel, the front desk agent must provide updated room status information to the housekeeping department.

Late Check-Out

Guests do not always check out by the hotel's posted check-out time. To minimize **late check-outs,** the front office should post check-out time notices in conspicuous places, such as on the back of all guestroom doors and in a prominent location at the front desk. A reminder of the check-out time can also be included in any predeparture materials distributed to guests expected to depart on the current day. Late check-outs can be a problem for some resorts. Guests may wish to stay the full day and use the recreational facilities of the resort, including their room. It is important to properly communicate and tactfully enforce the check-out time in order to prepare the room for the arriving guests.

Some hotels authorize the front desk to charge **late check-out fees.** A guest will probably be surprised to find such a fee on a folio, especially if he or she is not familiar with the hotel's check-out policy. Whenever a guest calls the front desk inquiring about a late check-out, the front desk agent should inform the guest about the hotel's policy regarding late check-out charges.

Some guests may resent being charged an additional expense and refuse to pay. Front desk agents should approach such situations calmly, offering a well-reasoned explanation for the late check-out fee policy. A front office manager may need to be summoned to discuss the matter with the guest.

Front office staff should not be apologetic about the late check-out fee. The hotel's check-out time is carefully selected and not arbitrarily set. It is not intended to inconvenience guests. Management establishes a check-out time so that the housekeeping department will have sufficient time to prepare rooms for newly arriving guests. Guestrooms should be cleaned and readied for arriving guests before the housekeeping staff completes its workshift. For this reason, the hotel may feel justified in assessing a late check-out fee.

Check-Out Options

Changes in technology and guest needs have prompted front offices to develop alternatives to standard check-out and account settlement procedures. These options combine advances in technology with special guest services to expedite departure activities.

Express Check-Out

Guests may encounter long lines at the front desk when trying to check out between 7:30 A.M. and 9:30 A.M., a prime check-out period for many front offices. To ease front desk volume, some front offices initiate check-out activities before the guest is actually ready to leave. A common pre-departure activity involves producing and distributing guest folios to guests expected to check out. Front office staff, housekeeping staff, or even hotel security staff may quietly slip printed folios under the guestroom doors of expected check-outs before 6 A.M., making sure that the guest's folio can't be seen or reached from outside the room.

Normally, the front office will distribute an **express check-out** form with each pre-departure folio. Express check-out forms may include a note requesting guests to notify the front desk if departure plans change. Otherwise, the front office will assume the guest is leaving by the hotel's posted check-out time. This procedure usually reminds and encourages guests to notify the front desk of any problems in departure before the hotel's check-out time.

A sample express check-out form is shown in Exhibit 1. By completing such a form, the guest authorizes the front office to transfer his or her outstanding folio balance to the credit card voucher that was created during registration. If no credit card imprint was captured or if no credit was established at registration, the front offices generally does not provide express check-out service. Once completing the form, the guest deposits the express check-out form at the front desk when departing. After the guest has left, the front office completes the guest's check-out by transferring the outstanding guest folio balance to a previously authorized method of settlement. Any additional charges the guest makes before leaving the hotel (telephone calls, for example) will be added to his or her folio before the front desk agent brings the account to a zero balance via account transfer. Due to the possible occurrence of late charges, the amount due on the guest's copy of the express check-out folio may not equal the amount applied to the guest's credit card account. This possibility should be clearly stated on the express check-out form to minimize later confusion. When late charges are added to the account, a copy of the updated folio should be mailed to the guest so that he or she has an accurate record of the stay. In this way, the guest is not surprised when his or her credit card billing arrives with a different amount.

For an express check-out procedure to be effective, the front office must have captured accurate guest settlement information during registration. The front desk

Exhibit 1 Sample Express Check-Out Form

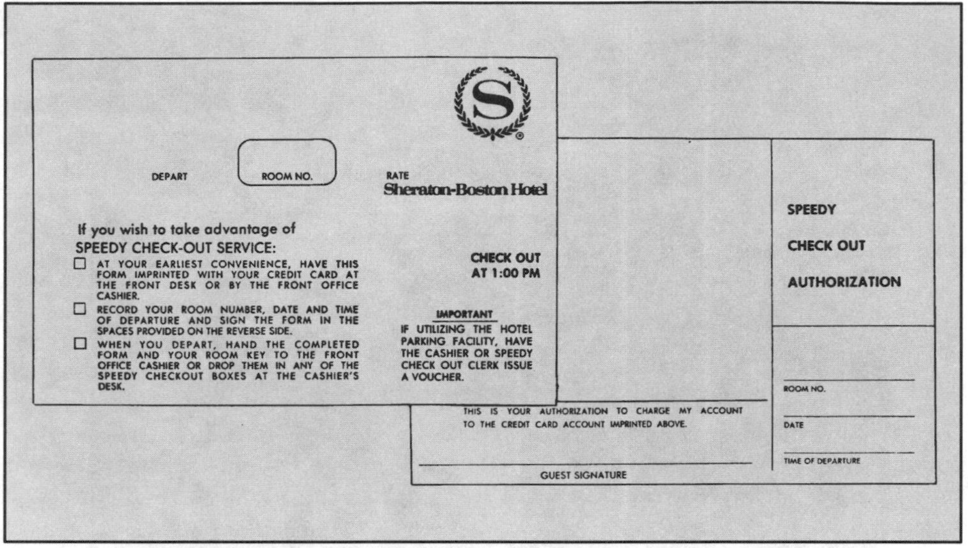

DEPART | ROOM NO. | RATE

Sheraton-Boston Hotel

If you wish to take advantage of
SPEEDY CHECK-OUT SERVICE:

- ☐ AT YOUR EARLIEST CONVENIENCE, HAVE THIS FORM IMPRINTED WITH YOUR CREDIT CARD AT THE FRONT DESK OR BY THE FRONT OFFICE CASHIER.
- ☐ RECORD YOUR ROOM NUMBER, DATE AND TIME OF DEPARTURE AND SIGN THE FORM IN THE SPACES PROVIDED ON THE REVERSE SIDE.
- ☐ WHEN YOU DEPART, HAND THE COMPLETED FORM AND YOUR ROOM KEY TO THE FRONT OFFICE CASHIER OR DROP THEM IN ANY OF THE SPEEDY CHECKOUT BOXES AT THE CASHIER'S DESK.

CHECK OUT
AT 1:00 PM

IMPORTANT
IF UTILIZING THE HOTEL PARKING FACILITY, HAVE THE CASHIER OR SPEEDY CHECK OUT CLERK ISSUE A VOUCHER.

SPEEDY
CHECK OUT
AUTHORIZATION

THIS IS YOUR AUTHORIZATION TO CHARGE MY ACCOUNT TO THE CREDIT CARD ACCOUNT IMPRINTED ABOVE.

GUEST SIGNATURE

ROOM NO.

DATE

TIME OF DEPARTURE

Courtesy of The Sheraton-Boston Hotel, Boston, Massachusetts

agent must be sure to relay room status information to the housekeeping department as soon as an express check-out form is received.

Self Check-Out

In some hotels, guests can check themselves out of the hotel by accessing **self check-out terminals** (see Exhibit 2) in the lobby area or by using an in-room system (see Exhibit 3). Self check-out terminals or in-room systems are interfaced with the front office computer and are intended to reduce check-out time and front desk traffic. Self check-out terminals vary in design. Some resemble automatic bank teller machines, while others possess video and audio capability.

To use a self check-out terminal, the guest accesses the proper folio and reviews its contents. Guests may be required to enter a credit card number by using a keypad or by passing a credit card through a magnetic strip reader attached to the terminal. Settlement can be automatically assigned to an acceptable credit card as long as the guest presented a valid card at registration.

Check-out is complete when the guest's balance is transferred to a credit card account and an itemized account statement is printed and dispensed to the guest. A self check-out system should then automatically communicate updated room status information to the front office computer. The front office system, in turn, relays room status information to the housekeeping department and initiates action to create a guest history record.

In-room folio review and check-out usually relies on an in-room television set with a remote control device or guestroom telephone access via an in-room television set. The guest can confirm a previously approved method of settlement for the account since the in-room television is connected via computer to the front office

Exhibit 2 Self Check-Out Terminal

Courtesy of Hyatt Hotels Corporation

computer system. The front office computer directs the self check-out process. Generally, guests can pick up a printed folio copy at the front desk on their way out. Similar to other self check-out technologies, in-room self check-out automatically updates room status and creates guest history records. Another advantage of in-room folio review is that guests can look at their folios at any time during their stays without having to stop by the front desk.

Unpaid Account Balances

No matter how carefully the front office monitors a guest's stay, there is always the possibility that the guest will leave without settling his or her account. Some guests may leave the hotel and honestly forget to check out. In addition, the front office may discover late charges for a guest who has already checked out. Unfortunately, some guests depart the hotel with no intention of settling their account. These

Exhibit 3 In-Room Check-Out Screens

Room: 1203

Harry Budow

11/28/94	Room Service	$ 21.34
11/28/94	Room	125.00
11/28/94	Room Tax	7.50
11/28/94	Movie	7.95
11/29/94	Room	125.00
	Balance:	**$310.22**

1 Check-out

2 Next Page

Previous Screen

9

Start Over

SERVICES

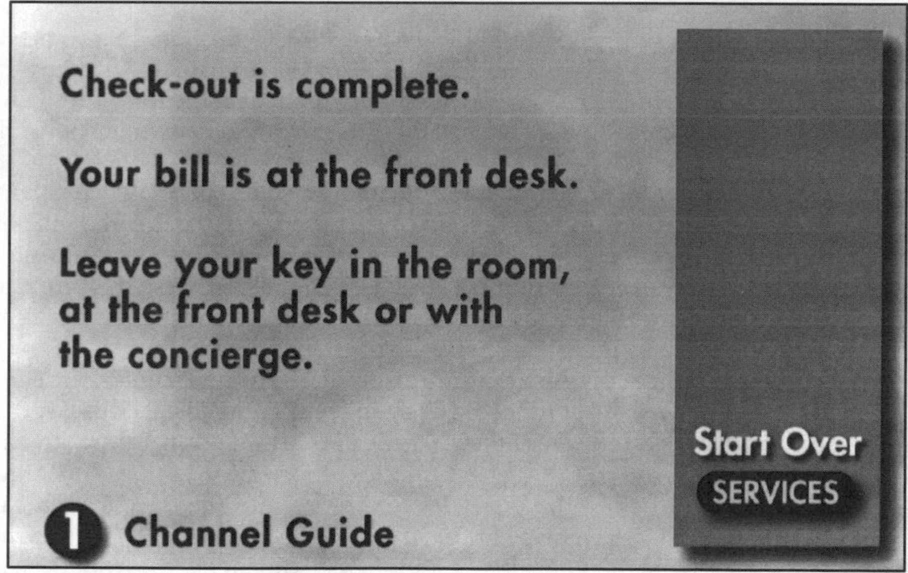
Check-out is complete.
Your bill is at the front desk.
Leave your key in the room, at the front desk or with the concierge.
Start Over
SERVICES
1 Channel Guide

Courtesy of SpectraVision, Richardson, Texas

guests are commonly referred to as *skippers*. Regardless of the reason, after-departure charges or outstanding balances represent **unpaid account balances.**

Late charges may be a major concern in guest account settlement. A late charge is a transaction requiring posting to a guest account that does not reach the front desk for posting until after the guest has checked out and closed his or her account. Restaurant, telephone, and room service charges are examples of potential late charges. Since the guest would not have paid for these purchases before leaving, the hotel may experience problems collecting for after-departure charges.

Even if late charges are eventually paid, the hotel incurs the additional costs involved in after-departure billing. Sometimes, the extra expenses for labor, postage, stationery, and special statements may cost more than the amount of the late charge. Few hotels can easily afford to finance a large volume of late charges. Hence, reducing late charges may be important to maximizing profitability.

At non-automated and semi-automated properties, front desk agents can take several steps to help reduce the occurrence of late charges. Front desk staff can:

- Post transactional vouchers as soon as they arrive at the front desk. This procedure will help minimize the volume of unposted charges prior to and during the check-out period.
- Survey front office equipment and voucher and folio racks for unposted charges before checking a guest out. For example, local telephone traffic and in-room movie charge meters may possess transactional information not recorded on a voucher.
- Ask departing guests whether they have incurred any charge purchases or placed long-distance telephone calls which do not appear on their final folio.

While most guests will respond honestly to a direct question, many guests may not feel obligated to volunteer information about charges not posted to the folio. These guests will simply pay the outstanding balance on the folio and disregard unposted charges. Some guests may be unaware that they remain responsible for paying unposted charges.

Front office management at a non-automated or semi-automated property may establish a system to ensure that revenue outlet charges are delivered quickly to the front desk for posting. This is especially important during peak morning check-out periods. In an effort to minimize late charges, the front desk may employ runners to pick up revenue outlet vouchers, or may exchange voucher information by telephone.

A front office computer system that interfaces with revenue center outlets is often the most effective means of reducing or even eliminating late charges. A restaurant point-of-sale system with a two-way communication interface can instantly verify room account status, check credit authorization, and post charges to the guest's folio, all before the guest leaves the restaurant. Similarly, a call accounting system interface can help eliminate telephone late charges. Guests who make telephone calls from their guestroom and then go directly to the front desk to check out may well find *all* their telephone charges listed on their folio.

Some front offices find that requiring a room key deposit at registration helps reduce unpaid account balances at check-out since guests have to stop at the front desk to reclaim their room key deposit. Eager to retrieve their deposits, guests are more likely to return to the front desk before they leave the hotel. In the process of refunding a deposit, the front office cashier has an opportunity to retrieve the guest's folio, search for any late charges, and complete the settlement process.

Guests who present a credit card at check-in may assume that all charges will automatically be transferred to their credit card account for subsequent billing. Depending on the hotel's legal agreement with a credit card company, the hotel may simply write "signature on file" on the signature line of the credit card voucher and receive payment for the guest's outstanding balance. "Signature on file" means the guest has signed the hotel's registration card at check-in and, by doing so, has agreed to pay the bill in full when he or she departs. Some credit card companies allow after-departure charges to be added to the guest's signed credit card voucher. Front desk agents must be sure that the credit card company will accept additional charges before posting charges to a voucher a guest has already signed. When after-departure charges are posted to a folio and added to a credit card voucher, the hotel should send a copy of the updated folio to the guest so that the guest will understand why additional charges appeared on the account.

Often guests do not intend to depart a hotel without paying. A guest may be in a hurry and actually forget to settle his or her account. In any case, the front desk staff must be sure that the guest has in fact left before changing the room's occupancy status. Usually, either the housekeeping department or a front desk agent must inspect the room.

Account Collection

Late charges that are billed to departed guests should not be classified as uncollectible until the front office has exhausted all billing and collection procedures. A properly completed registration card should contain the guest's signature and his or her home and business addresses and telephone numbers. Procedures for billing late charges may be different for a guest who settled an account in cash and for a guest who settled an account to a credit card. Guests who paid with a credit card will be billed according to the policies and procedures of the credit card company governing late charge collection.

Guest accounts not settled at check-out by cash payment in full—regardless of the credit established or prepayments processed during registration—are transferred from the guest ledger to the city (non-guest) ledger for collection. At that time, the guest account is transferred from the control of the front office to the hotel's accounting division.

Typical city ledger accounts include:

- *Credit card billings* to authorized credit card companies
- *Direct billings* to approved company and individual accounts
- *Travel agency accounts* for authorized tours and groups
- *Bad check accounts* resulting from departed guests whose personal checks were returned unpaid
- *Skipper accounts* for guests who left the hotel without settling their account
- *Disputed bills* for guests who refused to settle their accounts (in part or in full) because of a discrepancy
- *Guaranteed reservations accounts* for billing and tracking no-show guests

Exhibit 4 Billing Scheduling Chart

Schedule	Method	Timing
1st billing	______ Statement with back-up invoice	Mailed no later than ______ hours after the guest's account is transferred to the city ledger.
2nd billing	______ Statement ______ Telephone call ______ Letter	______ Days later
3rd billing	______ Statement ______ Telephone call ______ Letter	______ Days later
4th billing	______ Statement ______ Telephone call ______ Letter	______ Days later
5th billing	______ Statement ______ Telephone call ______ Letter	______ Days later
and so on.		

- *Late charges accounts* for guests who checked out before some charges were posted to their accounts
- *House accounts* for non-guest business and promotional activities

To be effective, the front office must establish a policy for billing departed guests with overdue accounts. Typically, front office management determines the procedures and billing cycle appropriate for account collection. Accounts receivable billing includes determining:

- When outstanding account balances are payable
- The number of days between billings
- How to contact departed guests whose accounts are overdue

The sooner the collection process is started, the sooner the hotel is likely to receive payment on unpaid account balances. Timing is often the key to success in preparing departed guest and non-guest accounts for collection. Each front office needs to develop its own collection schedule. Collection schedules can range from aggressive (short-cycle) to lenient (long-cycle) depending on the hotel's financial needs, clientele profile, history of collection patterns, and so on. Exhibit 4 contains a billing scheduling chart that may be used to develop or outline the methods and timing cycles for collections. Sometimes charges are disputed by guests because they do not remember making the charge. Because of this problem, most hotels keep copies of the charge vouchers or restaurant checks at the front desk until after settlement. These copies will also be helpful in resolving after-departure charges that the guest disputes.

In all collection cases, it is important for hotel staff to be polite but firm in any encounter involving a deferred payment account. Collection activities that violate a consumer's rights may prove to be more costly than the original debt. The Federal Fair Debt Collection Practices Act and the Fair Credit Billing Act clearly state the responsibilities and rights of those involved in collection activities.

Regardless of the collection procedures followed, problems in accounts receivable billing may develop. The hotel should have a documented procedure for collecting overdue accounts. Some hotels appoint a credit committee to examine overdue accounts and decide among collection options.

Just as individual guest accounts must be watched closely, so must meeting and tour master accounts. Credit for tour groups and meetings should be established well before they arrive. Sometimes, the hotel requires a deposit to ensure at least a partial payment. Many hotels prepare a preliminary master account folio before the group's departure and review it with the group leader to answer any questions and expedite the payment process. It is common for the hotels to require individual tour guests to establish credit when checking in, as the tour usually covers only specific expenses, such as room, tax, and certain meals.

From an accounting perspective, some properties attribute uncollectible accounts back to the department that originally accepted the uncollectible charge. For instance, the front office may be assessed the amount of an uncollectible transaction if the post office returns a wrongly addressed billing. Postal returns can happen when a front desk agent fails to request that a guest clarify illegible writing on a registration card. Tracking receivables back to the originating department may help identify departments whose transaction processing procedures regularly result in uncollectible account balances. The credit committee, credit manager, or general manager should then analyze the departments' procedures, or lack thereof, and recommend corrective action. Collection problems may indicate the need for employee retraining or closer supervision.

Account Aging

Credit card billings are normally paid according to the hotel's contractual agreement with the credit card company. The time between billing and payment ranges from immediate to 30 days, and sometimes more. Factors that affect the length of this period include the volume of transactions, frequency of mailing vouchers to the credit card company, electronic transfer of transactions and funds, and any transaction fees levied by the credit card company. Most other city ledger accounts are usually settled within 30 days of billing, which is generally considered satisfactory. Some city ledger accounts, however, may take longer than 30 days to collect. The hotel should establish methods for tracking past due accounts based on the date the charges were incurred. This practice of scheduled billings is normally referred to as **account aging.**

Exhibit 5 Aged Accounts Receivable Report

AGED ACCOUNTS RECEIVABLE

As of ________________, 19___

Name	Balance	Current	Outstanding			
			30–60	60–90	90–120	120+
Elizabeth Penny	$125					$125
Mimi Hendricks	$235			$235		
M/M Phil Damon	$486	$100	$386			
Harrison Taylor	$999			$999		
TOTALS	$1,845	$100	$386	$1,234		$125

Account aging analysis may differ from property to property depending on the variety of hotel credit terms in effect. At large properties, the hotel accounting division typically monitors account aging. At smaller properties, the night auditor may assume this responsibility. An account age analysis sheet identifies which accounts receivable are 30, 60, 90, or more days old. Exhibit 5 shows a simplified aged accounts receivable report. In most hotels, accounts that are less than 30 days old are considered **current.** Accounts that are older than 30 days are considered **overdue.** In some cases, accounts that are older than 90 days are considered **delinquent.**

Front Office Records

After check out, front office records usually consist of the guest's registration card and the account folio. The registration card is usually filed in alphabetical order by departure date. The front office usually makes at least two copies of each guest account folio. One copy serves as the guest's receipt and the other as the hotel's permanent record. Front offices that use a three-part folio usually file the third copy with the guest's credit card voucher or direct billing statement in case the guest later needs a summary of charges, or in case a credit card or sponsoring company disputes portions of a folio.

Non-automated and semi-automated front office operations often maintain storage files for registration cards and guest folio copies. Registration cards are filed alphabetically, while folios tend to be filed numerically by serial number. In a fully automated front office, computer system records may be stored on magnetic disk or magnetic tape or in printed form. Computer records can be used to back up original billings.

Guest Histories

Front office management can better understand its clientele and determine guest trends when it develops and maintains a **guest history file.** This file is a collection of personal and financial data about guests who have stayed at the hotel. An individual **guest history record** within the file normally contains personal and transactional information relevant to the guest's stay. (Guest history records are confidential and proprietary; the front office is obligated to protect guests from invasions of privacy.)

Creating the guest history record is one of the last steps in the check-out and account settlement process. Many front offices build their guest history files from a collection of expired registration cards. Other front offices develop a special form to construct a guest history record. Exhibit 6 contains a sample guest history card. Some front offices use a computer-based system that automatically re-formats guest information into a guest history data base. In most instances, the information needed for a guest history record can be gathered from the guest's registration card and folio.

Guests staying at resort hotels may find themselves filling out a special form that asks for such information as the name of spouses or children, birthdays, hotel room preference, and favorite foods. Having such information on file helps the property provide better guest service.

The hotel's sales and marketing division can use guest history records as a source for mailing lists or to identify guest characteristics important for strategic marketing. This information may help the hotel develop and place advertisements that appeal to the types of clientele the hotel is attempting to attract. Guest history records may also point out the need for new, supplementary, or enhanced services.

A computerized guest history system may be based on special software that allows the hotel to excerpt guest history data for marketing efforts and to measure the effectiveness of past efforts. For instance, a computerized guest history data base may enable the hotel to determine the geographic distribution of its guests' home and business addresses. Hotel advertising may be placed more effectively based upon this type of data.

Exhibit 7 diagrams the computerized guest history system at The Ritz-Carlton Hotel Company. The system enables staff members to use online guest preference information to provide uniquely personal levels of service to returning guests.

Marketing Follow-Through

Just as a hotel's marketing department may rely in part on guest history files to develop new marketing strategies, so too may a property's marketing program

Exhibit 6 Guest History Card

NAME
ADDRESS
FIRM
POSITION
CREDIT / /F/P

	ARRIVED	ROOM	RATE	DEPARTED	AMOUNT		REMARKS
1							
2							
3							
4							
5							
6							
7							
8							
9							
10							
11							

	ARRIVED	ROOM	RATE	DEPARTED	AMOUNT		REMARKS
12							
13							
14							
15							
16							
17							
18							
19							
20							
21							
22							
23							
24							
25							

depend on the front office's performance and follow-through at check-out. For example, if the marketing department creates a program to reward frequent guests with a free stay after a certain number of visits, the front office may be responsible for tracking the number of times a guest stays at the property. Front desk agents may have to validate and record coupons or adapt to some other type of record-keeping system.

Many hotel companies have frequent traveler clubs, designed to encourage brand loyalty. These clubs generally award some type of credit for staying at the property. This credit is usually applied to club membership during check-out. Front desk agents may be responsible for completing a voucher for the guest or for making sure the guest's folio is properly coded to automatically update the guest's club account. Some hotel frequent traveler programs are also co-marketed with airlines, car rental companies, or marketing firms. In these cases, the benefits must also be credited to these co-marketers.

Exhibit 7 The Ritz-Carlton Repeat Guest History Program

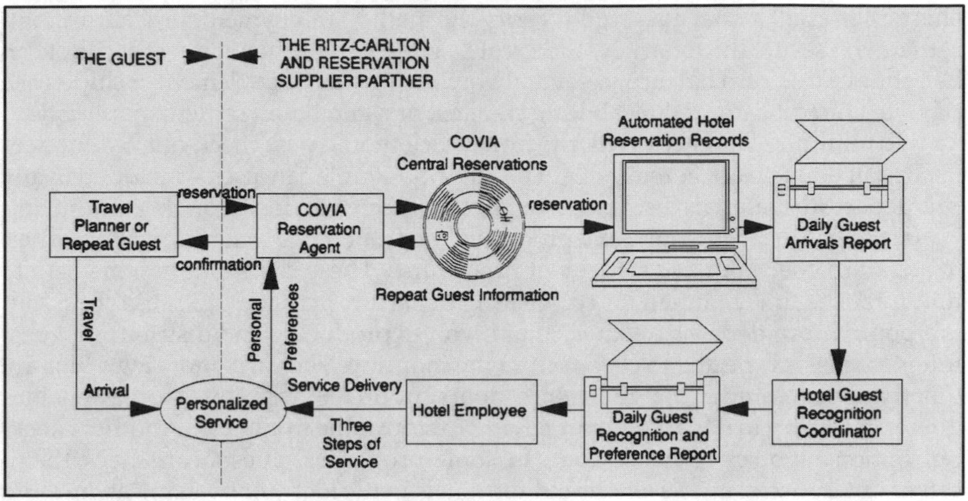

Source: *Application Summary: The Ritz-Carlton Hotel Company.*

If a guest needs a reservation for the next stop on his or her trip, the front office may be helpful in making a reservation at a hotel specified by the guest. A front desk agent can also make a reservation for a guest's return trip to the hotel. Front desk agents should keep in mind that check-out is the last opportunity to offer the hotel's services. Offering to make reservations for guests in transit or to make reservations for a future trip to the hotel often leads to repeat business regardless of whether the guest makes a reservation at that time or not. Guests tend to remember the friendliness, convenience, and special services that help distinguish one property from another.

Summary

Check-out and account settlement are among the final transactions the guest experiences with the front office. Before departing the hotel, the guest will generally stop at the front desk to review his or her folio, pay any outstanding account balance, receive a copy of the account statement, close his or her safe deposit box, and return the room key. During check-out and account settlement, the front office accomplishes several important functions, including reconciliation of the guest account balance, updating of room status information, and initiation of a guest history file. Through the use of pre-settlement verification activities, the front office can reduce the guest's check-out time and improve the front office's ability to collect outstanding account balances.

Effective front office operations also involve the resale of rooms once a guest has checked out. This entails prompt communication of room status information with the housekeeping department.

In addition to collecting any unpaid balances and updating room status information, the front desk agent may check for mail, messages, and faxes, post outstanding charges, verify account information, inquire about additional recent charges, present a final guest folio, verify the method of payment, process account settlement, secure the room key, and create a guest history file. A guest account can be brought to a zero balance in several ways. Methods of settlement include cash payment, credit card or direct billing transfer, or a combined settlement method.

To minimize late check-outs, the front office should post check-out time notices in conspicuous places. A reminder of the check-out time can also be included in any pre-departure materials distributed to guests expected to depart on the current day.

Changes in technology have prompted the front office to develop alternatives to standard check-out and settlement procedures. These check-out options help to minimize the time required for completing departure activities. Express check-out is a popular pre-departure activity that involves producing and distributing guest folios to guests expected to check out in the morning. The early morning folios are quietly slipped under the guestroom doors around 6 A.M. This process enables guests in a hurry to depart without having to stop at the front desk. Another check-out option involves self check-out. In some properties, guests can check themselves out by accessing self check-out terminals in the lobby or by using an in-room system. Self check-out terminals and in-room systems are interfaced with a front office computer and are intended to reduce check-out time and front office traffic.

No matter how carefully the front office monitors the guest's stay, there is always the possibility that a guest will leave without settling his or her account. Some guests may honestly forget to check out, while others may intentionally avoid paying their bill. The front office may also discover late charges after a guest has legitimately checked out. Regardless of the reason, after-departure (late) charges or outstanding account balances represent unpaid account balances. Guest accounts not settled at check-out by cash payment in full, regardless of the credit established or prepayments made during registration, are transferred from the guest ledger to the city (non-guest) ledger for collection. At the time of transfer, responsibility for account settlement is transferred from the control of the front office to the hotel's general accounting division.

Key Terms

account aging—a method for tracking past due accounts according to the date the charges originated.

current account—a city ledger account that is within the current billing period.

delinquent account—a city ledger account that has not been settled within a reasonable collection period, usually 90 days.

express check-out—a pre-departure activity that involves the production and early morning distribution of guest folios for guests expected to check out that morning.

guest history file—a collection of guest history records, constructed from expired registration cards or created through sophisticated computer-based systems, that automatically direct information about departing guests into a guest history database.

guest history record—a record of personal and financial information about hotel guests relevant to marketing and sales that can help the hotel serve the guest on return visits.

late charge—a transaction requiring posting to a guest account that does not reach the front desk for posting until after the guest has checked out and closed his or her account.

late check-out—a room status term indicating that the guest is being allowed to check out later than the hotel's standard check-out time.

late check-out fee—a charge imposed by some hotels on guests who do not check out by the established check-out time.

overdue account—a city ledger account that is unpaid beyond the current billing period, usually between 30 and 90 days.

self check-out terminal—a computerized system, usually located in the hotel lobby, that allows the guest to review his or her folio and settle the account to the credit card used at check-in.

unpaid account balance—charges remaining in a guest account after the guest has left the hotel.

zero out—to settle in full the balance of a folio account as the guest checks out.

Review Questions

1. What are the three functions of the check-out and account settlement process? Why are these functions essential to the hotel's accounting, housekeeping, and marketing functions?
2. What is the definition of *zero out?* What happens to a guest account that is not settled at check-out?
3. What are three methods of guest account settlement at check-out? How are they different from each other? What effect does each have on the guest ledger and city ledger?
4. What difficulties arise from late check-outs? How might these problems be reduced by the use of late check-out fees?
5. How does a typical express check-out procedure work? How does a typical self check-out terminal work? What are the advantages and disadvantages of each?
6. What are late charges? What steps can the front office take to reduce late charges?
7. What types of guest information are useful in collecting payment for late charges and unpaid account balances?
8. What are some elements of an effective billing and collection process? How can tracking uncollectible accounts to the departments responsible improve internal control?

9. What is account aging? Why is it important? Who might be responsible for account aging analysis?
10. What are the uses of guest histories? How can the front office construct a guest history file?

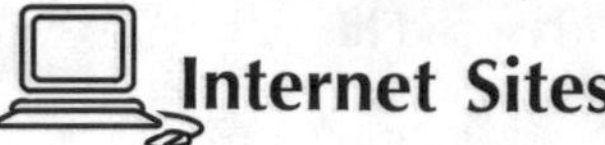

Internet Sites

For more information, visit the following Internet sites. Remember that Internet addresses can change without notice.

Lodging Publications—Online and Printed

Hospitality Technology News
http://www.hospitalitynet.nl/news/tech.html

Hotel & Motel Management
http://www.innvest.com/hmm

Lodging Online
http://www.ei-ahma.org/webs/lodging/index.html

Lodging Hospitality
http://www.penton.com/corp/mags/lh.html

Technology Sites

Anasazi, Inc.
http://www.anasazi.com

CSS Hotel Systems
http://www.csshotelsystems.com

Executech Systems, Inc.
http://www.executech.com

Fidelio
http://www.micros.com

First Resort Software
http://www.firstres.com

Hospitality Industry Technology Exposition and Conference
http://www.hitecshow.org

Hospitality Industry Technology Integration Standards
http://www.hitis.org

HOST Group
http://www.hostgroup.com

Lodging Touch International
http://www.lodgingtouch.com

Newmarket Software Systems, Inc.
http://www.newsoft.com

Resort Data Processing, Inc.
http://www.resortdata.com

Western Hospitality Systems—InnSure
http://www.lodgingsystems.com

Case Study

Accounts Receivable at the Montrose Hotel

For about two months, Kathy Cole, the general manager of the Montrose Hotel, has been noticing a problem with the accounts receivable ledger. It has grown more than it should have, even though occupancy has been improving recently. The total ledger has grown by over 50%, with most of the growth being aged at over 30 days.

Kathy cannot let this condition continue for very long, so she is addressing it with Glenna Danks, the hotel controller. Glenna tells Kathy that they are having trouble collecting on accounts sent to them from the front office.

The front office manager, Russ Fleming, has been on the job for about three months. Russ came to the Montrose Hotel from another of the chain's properties, where he was the assistant front office manager. The hotel Russ came from has a front office computer system, but the Montrose Hotel will not have one until next year. Kathy asks Russ to work with Glenna to find an answer to the issues. Upon researching the problems, Russ and Glenna find the following:

- Registration cards are not being filled in by guests with correct, billable, or readable addresses. Guests are sometimes leaving the space open.
- Credit card vouchers are difficult to read.
- Many credit card vouchers have after-departure charges on them.
- Groups are paying their master accounts more slowly than usual.
- Guest comment cards show many complaints about inaccurate bills and the time it takes to check out of the hotel.

Kathy, Glenna, and Russ must act quickly to bring the accounts receivable ledger back to its usual small amount.

Discussion Questions

1. Identify which departments must be involved in the actual problem resolution.
2. Write an action plan describing what each department must do to resolve the problem. Be sure to include employee training, updating departmental procedures and specific accountabilities for ensuring the work is done properly.
3. Since the front office computer system is not scheduled to be installed for some time, what can hotel management do now, with what they currently have to work with, to resolve the guest comment card complaints?

Case Number: 3328CA

The following industry experts helped generate this case: Richard M. Brooks, CHA, Vice President—Operations, Bridgestreet Accommodations, Inc., Cleveland, Ohio; and Michael L. Kasavana, Professor, The School of Hospitality Business, Michigan State University, East Lansing, Michigan.

This case also appears in *Case Studies in Lodging Management* (Lansing, Mich.: Educational Institute of the American Hotel & Motel Association, 1998), ISBN 0-86612-184-6.

Chapter 9 Outline

9

The Night Audit

SINCE HOTELS OPERATE 24 hours a day, seven days a week, the front office must regularly review and verify the accuracy and completeness of guest and non-guest accounting records. A front office audit process is intended to fulfill this need.

The audit is a daily review of guest account transactions recorded at the front desk against revenue center transactions. This routine helps guarantee the accuracy, reliability, and thoroughness of front office accounting. The front office audit also includes active non-guest accounts. A successful audit will result in balanced guest and non-guest accounts, accurate account statements, appropriate account credit monitoring, and timely reports to management. An effective audit also increases the likelihood of correct account settlement.

The front office audit is usually called the **night audit** because hotels generally perform it during the late evening hours. Before the implementation of automated front office systems, the most convenient time to perform the audit was during the late evening and early morning hours when front office auditors could work with minimal interruption. Most, if not all, hotel outlets are also closed, allowing the night audit to include all revenue departments. Also, most hotels have an *accounting day* or *hotel day* that defines the daily charging period of the hotel. The night audit closes the books on one hotel day and opens the books on another. There is a more detailed description of this later in the chapter.

In a computer-based, fully automated front office, the audit is usually called a **system update** since computer files are electronically updated as part of the audit routine. Most of the manual work performed by night auditors in manual and semi-automated front offices is handled by computers in a fully automated system. The computer can automatically post room revenues with little or no intervention by a front office auditor. In fully automated operations, there is no reason that the night audit must occur at night. Much of the night audit in automated front offices is really creating and distributing system reports, which can be done at any time management desires.

Functions of the Night Audit

The main purpose of the night audit is to verify the accuracy and completeness of guest and non-guest accounts against revenue center transaction reports. Specifically, the night audit is concerned with the following functions:

- Verifying posted entries to guest and non-guest accounts
- Balancing all front office accounts

- Resolving room status and rate discrepancies
- Monitoring guest credit limits
- Producing operational and managerial reports

The Role of the Night Auditor

Performing the night audit requires attention to accounting detail, procedural controls, and guest credit restrictions. The **night auditor** should also be familiar with the nature of cash transactions affecting the front office accounting system. The night auditor typically tracks room revenues, occupancy percentages, and other standard operating statistics. In addition, the auditor prepares a daily summary of the cash, check, and credit card activities that occurred at the front desk. These data reflect the front office's financial performance for the day. The night auditor summarizes and reports the results of operations to front office management. The hotel's accounting division (which is primarily responsible for back office auditing) may also use night audit data in preparing additional statistical analyses.

Establishing an End of Day

The night auditor generally works the night shift, from 11 P.M. to 7 A.M., compiling, balancing, and reviewing the transactions from the previous day. Each front office must decide what time will be considered the end of its accounting (or hotel) day. An **end of day** is simply an arbitrary stopping point for the business day. The front office must establish an end of day so that the audit can be considered complete through a specific, consistent point in time. Usually, the closing time of hotel revenue outlets determines the end of day. For hotels with 24-hour room service, restaurants, or stores, the official end of day is the time when a majority of outlets close or no longer have frequent activity. For casino hotels, with outlets constantly open, the end of day is determined by management as the best time to close the books, generally about 4 A.M., or later.

Typically, the business day ends when the night audit begins, which is usually well after the night shift begins. For example, if a night audit begins at 1:30 A.M., the hotel's business day would end at 1:30 A.M. The period from 1:30 A.M. until the audit is completed is referred to as audit work time. Normally, transactions requiring front office accounting attention that are received during audit work time are not posted until the audit is completed. These transactions are considered part of the next business day.

Cross-Referencing

Hotel departments generate volumes of paperwork in order to document transactions. For each revenue center transaction, the originating revenue center classifies and records the transaction type (cash, charge, or paid-out) and its monetary value. Front office personnel post an entry to the appropriate guest or non-guest folio based on the documentation received. Typically a voucher is used to communicate transactional information.

A front office accounting system depends on transactional documentation to establish accurate records and maintain effective operational controls. Transactional documentation identifies the nature and amount of a transaction, and is the basis for data input into a front office accounting system. This documentation normally consists of charge vouchers and other support documents.

For internal control purposes, an accounting system should provide independent supporting documentation to verify each transaction. In a non-automated or semi-automated operation, supporting documents produced in different departments (for example, a coffee shop guest check and a front office guest folio) provide cross-reference information. Although the night auditor receives information on room revenues from the room rack or folio bucket, the night auditor should also check room rate postings on guest folios against the housekeeping department's report of occupied rooms and the front desk room rack. This is often called a **bucket check.** The bucket check helps ensure that accurate rates have been posted for all occupied rooms and helps reduce the occupancy errors caused when front desk agents do not properly complete check-in and check-out procedures. Similarly, food and beverage postings to guest and non-guest accounts are usually based on vouchers or guest checks sent from the revenue outlet to the front desk. The restaurant's register tape or sales journal can be used as a cross-reference to prove front desk postings.

The night auditor relies on transactional documentation to prove that proper front office accounting procedures have been followed. The auditor's review of daily postings reconciles front office accounts with revenue center and departmental records.

Account Integrity

Sound internal control techniques help ensure the accuracy, completeness, and integrity of front office accounting procedures. Internal control techniques include cash control and the separation of duties. Duties are separated to ensure that no single individual is wholly responsible for accounting for all phases of a transaction.

Proper internal control technique calls for different front office staff to post, verify, and collect for sales transactions at the front desk. If a front desk agent were allowed to sell a guestroom, post the charge, verify the posting, and collect cash for the room, no one else would be able to detect mistakes or possible embezzlement. Instead, duties should be split among employees; a front desk agent may perform the posting, a night auditor the verification, and a cashier the settlement. In many front offices, the night auditor is the only person empowered to post room rates and room tax charges to a guest folio.

The night auditor helps ensure that the front office receives payment for goods and services rendered. The night auditor establishes guest and non-guest account integrity by cross-referencing account postings with departmental source documentation. The audit process is complete when the totals for guest, non-guest, and departmental accounts are **in balance** (that is, proven correct). As long as the audit process presents an **out-of-balance** position, the audit is considered incomplete. In essence, an out-of-balance position exists when the charges and credits posted to guest and non-guest accounts throughout the day do not match the charges and credits posted to the departmental revenue sources. An out-of-balance condition may require a thorough review of all account statements, vouchers, support documents, and departmental source documentation.

Guest Credit Monitoring

Supervising the credit limits of guest and non-guest accounts helps maintain the integrity of a front office accounting system. Establishing lines of credit or credit limits depends on many factors, such as credit card company floor limits, the hotel's house limit, and the guest's status or reputation as a potential credit risk. The night auditor should be familiar with these limits and how they relate to each guest and non-guest account. High account balances should be noted as part of the posting process. At the close of each business day, the night auditor should identify those guest and non-guest accounts that have reached or exceeded assigned credit limits. These accounts are typically called high balance accounts. A report listing high balance accounts, or a **high balance report,** should be prepared for appropriate front office management action.

Audit Posting Formula

Regardless of how the night audit is conducted, the basic account posting formula applies:

$$\text{Previous Balance} + \text{Debits} - \text{Credits} = \text{Net Outstanding Balance}$$

$$PB + DR - CR = NOB$$

The following example clarifies the use of this formula and its role in the night audit. Assume a guest account has a previous balance of $280, departmental charges (debits) of $60, and payments received (credits) of $12.80. During a semi-automated audit, the night auditor enters (picks up) the account balance of $280 into the posting machine, posts the outstanding departmental charge transactions, and computes an account subtotal of $340. Next, the night auditor posts credits (cash payments, checks, and credit card payments) to the account. In this case, credits total $12.80. These credits are subtracted from $340 to yield a net outstanding balance of $327.20. This figure serves as the previous balance (pickup balance) for the next transaction. Using the posting formula, these transactions are:

$$PB + DR - CR = NOB$$

$$\$280 + \$60 - \$12.80 = \$327.20$$

Daily and Supplemental Transcripts

A **daily transcript,** as shown in Exhibit 1, is used in manual and semi-automated hotels as a detailed report of all guest accounts. The daily transcript indicates those guest accounts that had transactional activity on that particular day. A **supplemental transcript** is often used to record the day's transactional activity for non-guest accounts. Together, the daily transcript and a supplemental transcript detail all transactions occurring on a single day.

Exhibit 1 Non-Automated Daily Transcript

TRANSCRIPT OF GUEST LEDGER

HOTEL ______ DATE ______ SHEET NO. ______

Number of: Transient Rooms	Transient Guests	Permanent Rooms	Permanent Guests	Room No.	Balance Brought Forward	Reg. Number	Rooms: Transient	Rooms: Permanent	Telephone: Local	Telephone: Long Distance	Valet	Laundry	Cafe	Sales Tax		Cash Disc.	Transfers	Charges		Cash Receipts	Transfers	Charges	Rebates and/or Allowances	Balance Carried Forward	Room No.
1	2			201	7.50	17650	14.00					2.00	1.50	.27		.73				20.00				6.00	
1	1			202		18321	10.00			1.80			1.00	.21						10.01				3.00	
2	3			203	8.00	17763	16.00		.36				3.00	.36		2.00				29.66				–	
1	2			328		18324	14.00		.20	3.10			2.50	.30						20.10				–	
1	2			329	19.00	17863	15.00		.60		2.00			.30		1.10							2.00	36.00	
1	1			330		18327	10.00			1.50			1.50	.21						13.21				–	
43	49			TOTAL	270.17		249.50		3.75	43.59	5.20	2.39	18.75	8.04		3.75				151.82	19.58		9.79	421.95	

A daily transcript is typically detailed by revenue center, transaction type, and transaction total. The daily transcript and the supplemental transcript form the basis for a consolidated report of front office accounting data against which revenue center totals can be checked. The total of charged purchases reported by the hotel's restaurant, for example, should equal the total amount of restaurant charge purchases posted to guest and non-guest accounts. The equality of these totals is an important concern in the night audit process.

Daily and supplemental transcripts are simply worksheets designed to detect various types of posting errors. They are preliminary screenings of account totals to identify department-level errors. Daily and supplemental transcripts can facilitate the night audit routine by identifying out-of-balance figures in advance of a detailed review. An out-of-balance condition among non-guest accounts, for example, will help the night auditor detect and correct errors without having to review all transactions occurring on that day.

Operating Modes

Night audit procedures may be performed manually, mechanically, or electronically. The following sections briefly explain how each of these three operating modes is used in the night audit routine.

Non-Automated

In a non-automated (manual) system, four forms are typically used to complete the audit process. The system also uses transactional vouchers produced by the hotel's revenue centers and sent to the front desk for processing. The four common night audit forms are:

- Daily and supplemental transcripts
- Guest and non-guest folios
- Front office cash sheets
- Audit recapitulation sheets

The night auditor prepares daily and supplemental transcripts by copying the day's activities from each guest and non-guest account folio to the appropriate line on one of the transcripts. The transcript columns are then summarized to determine the total charge transactions for the day. Information from these two transcripts, along with data from the front office cash sheet, may be transferred to a recapitulation sheet, similar to the one shown in Exhibit 2. The daily account recapitulation sheet provides a one-day, comprehensive summary of front office accounting transactions.

A manual accounting routine simply isn't feasible for a large hotel's front office operation. The night audit routines of non-automated and semi-automated properties tend to be tedious and often involve more bookkeeping and paper-shuffling than actual auditing. Given the abundance of relatively inexpensive front office accounting machinery, it may be inefficient and expensive to hand-post and verify all account entries and to manually compile front office transcripts and recapitulation sheets. Moreover, manual audit forms tend to be cumbersome and lend themselves to errors because of the volume of manual data entries and number of computations required. Manual audit procedures, however, do have a strength: they are an excellent method by which to learn front office posting and auditing concepts.

Semi-Automated

One of the most important developments in the history of front office accounting has been the account posting machine. Posting machines record guest charges on folios and simultaneously perform a number of other activities that simplify the work of front desk agents and night auditors. The first hotel posting machines were actually adapted from banking posting machines, which perform similar functions.

Posting machines may be electromechanical or electronic. Unfortunately, electronic posting machines tend to be merely enhanced versions of the electromechanical machines they were intended to replace. Electronic machines perform basically the same functions as their mechanical forerunners. Mechanical posting machines are capable of producing only a limited number of departmental totals, do not retain individual folio balances, and cannot be connected to other equipment (such as food and beverage point-of-sale systems). Electronic posting

Exhibit 2 Non-Automated Recapitulation Sheet

RECAPITULATION OF GUEST LEDGER TRANSCRIPT

HOTEL ________ DATE ________

Number of: Transient Rooms	Transient Guests	Permanent Rooms	Permanent Guests	Sheet No.	Balance Brought Forward		Rooms Transient	Rooms Permanent	Telephone Local	Telephone Long Distance	Valet	Laundry	Cafe	Sales Tax		Cash Disb.	Transfers	Changes		Cash Receipts	Transfers	Changes	Rebate and/or Allowances	Balance Carried Forward	
43	49			1	270 17		247 50		3 25	43 59	5 20	2 39	18 75	8 04		3 75				151 82	19 58		4 74	421 95	
41	46			2	421 72		233 -		2 40	29 11	5 90	2 06	10 05	7 38		15 50				99 55	8 24			619 33	
38	55			3	463 67		283 75		3 60	46 93	2 60	3 05	32 05	9 68		6 62				142 75	116 55			592 65	
				4																					
				5																					
				6																					
				7																					
				8																					
				9																					
				10																					
122	150				1155 56		764 25		9 75	119 63	13 70	7 50	60 85	25 10		25 87				394 12	144 37		9 79	1633 93	
City					8444 03								8 30	8			144 37			30 51				8566 27	
Totals					9599 59		764 25		9 75	119 63	13 70	7 50	69 15	25 18		25 87	144 37			424 63	144 37		9 79	10200 20	

1,026.65 Dr. Accts. Receivable Guests
152.75 Dr. Accts. Receivable City
10,778.99 Total

Credit Accts. Rec. Guest 548.28
Credit Accts. Rec. City 30.51
Total 10,778.99

DETAILS OF TODAY'S LEDGER ENTRIES

Name	Detail	Debit	Credit
City Ledger			
A.H. Drake	Food Tax	2 30 8	
J.B. Smith Jr.	Food	6 00	
Harry Golden			5 30
Jack Marshall			25 21
Totals		8 38	30 51
General Ledger			
Totals			

RECAPITULATION OF FRONT OFFICE CASH SHEETS

Clerk	Guest	City	Total	Misc'l and/or Gen'l Ledger	Grand Total
Receipts					
Carr	333 78	30 51	364 29	92	365 21
White	41 42		41 42	over 5	41 47
Hansen	19 02		19 02		19 02
Dining Room				391 42	391 42
Totals	394 22	30 51	424 73	392 39	817 12
Disbursements					
Carr	4 45		4 45		4 45
White	21 42		21 42		21 42
Totals	25 87		25 87		25 87
Net	368 35	30 51	398 86	392 39	791 25

Turn-Ins: Name		For'd	Amount
Carr	360 76		
White	20 05		
Hansen	19 02		
Dining Room	391 42		
Sub-Total	791 25	Total	

Transfers: Name	Folio No.	Room No.	Guest Ledger Debit	Guest Ledger Credit	City Ledger Debit	City Ledger Credit
C.A. Smith	18421	706		17 66	17 66	
Walter de Vries	18345	722		66 29	66 29	
James Scofield	18434	523		14 58	14 58	
Mr. and Mrs. H. James	18520	316		8 24	8 24	
Richard Bradford	18514	411		9 28	4 28	
Robert Stern	18451	610		23 32	23 32	
				144 37	144 37	

TURN-INS TO FRONT OFFICE

Name	Detail		Name	Detail	Amount
					391 42
Dining Rm.	Food	366 58	Laundry		92
	Tax	11 79		overage (Carr)	05
	Bar	12 05			
	Tax	1 00			
Sub-Total		391 42	Total		392 39

machines are really computers in many respects. They can be programmed to have more departmental totals than a mechanical machine. In addition, many electronic posting machines can store folio balances in memory and automatically advance the folio to the next blank space for printing. Some have limited abilities to connect to other equipment for posting purposes. Due to the ever decreasing cost of personal computers, mechanical posting machines are no longer manufactured. Electronic posting machines cost almost as much as personal computers, but are much more limited in functionality. Therefore, mechanical and electronic posting machines are quickly being replaced by personal computers with property management system programs.

By comparison, fully automated systems can be linked to point-of-sale terminals in the hotel's revenue centers for more efficient posting and verification of charges. Computer-based systems may retain folio balances to eliminate the need to enter the previous balance (pickup balance) and the errors associated with semi-automated procedures. In addition, the folio is stored electronically until the guest is ready to view it, reducing the need for paper forms.

Even though the posting machine is becoming a part of lodging history, understanding what it does is important. It provides the foundation for what modern property management systems do through computer programming. An overview of basic posting machine operations follows. Typically, front desk agents post charges to guest and non-guest account folios based on charge vouchers received from the hotel's revenue outlets. Machine posting to folios involves locating the folio, removing it from the folio bucket, entering the account's previous balance into the posting machine, posting the charge, balancing the folio, and refiling it in the folio bucket. If the front desk agent enters an incorrect previous balance, it is referred to as a pickup error. Another typical error is entering an incorrect transaction value. Both errors create a new account balance that is in error and the night audit will be out of balance. These problems do not occur with electronic posting machines, which can store previous account balances and thereby eliminate pickup errors.

When an account folio is posted in a semi-automated system, several other actions take place simultaneously:

- The voucher used to initiate the posting is imprinted with the same information posted to the account folio. This procedure provides machine-printed verification that the voucher has been posted to a valid front office account.
- Identical transaction information is printed onto an internal machine paper tape to serve as a permanent journal record and as part of the hotel's internal audit trail. (An **audit trail** is an organized flow of source documents detailing each event in the processing of a transaction.)
- The amount of each posted charge is added to (or subtracted from) the running departmental total for the revenue center originating the posting. Revenue center totals can prove especially helpful in end-of-workshift and end-of-day reporting. In addition, revenue center totals can assist the night auditor in determining whether the audit is in balance and complete.

Forms produced in a semi-automated audit system include a front office cash report and a night audit summary report, sometimes called a **D card.** A sample completed night auditor's report (D card) is shown in Exhibit 3. The D card provides information that enables the night auditor to determine if the front office accounting system is in balance. Essentially, the D card shows the opening balance for the day (which is the previous day's closing balance); provides a running record of all the debits (additions) and credits (subtractions) posted through the machine; and produces a net outstanding balance. If the net outstanding balance proves the total postings entered on guest and non-guest folios equal to the totals of the vouchers posted, the front office accounting system is presumed to be in balance. If the D card ending balance does not match the total folio balance for the day, the system is assumed to be out of balance. The night auditor must then review the revenue center and/or account postings to identify and correct the errors.

Fully Automated

Of the three operating modes, the fully automated audit process is by far the fastest and most efficient and reliable. Fully automated systems can be interfaced with

Exhibit 3 Semi-Automated Night Auditor's Report (D card)

D— NIGHT AUDITOR'S MACHINE BALANCE NO.

DATE Oct. 26

	DATE	TRANS. SYMBOLS	NET TOTALS	CORRECTIONS	MACH. TOTALS
ROOM	Oct 26	ROOM	15.00		* 15.00
RESTAURANT	Oct 26	RESTR	25.10	2.85	* 27.95
TELEPHONE	Oct 26	PHONE	.30	.55	* .85
LONG DISTANCE	Oct 26	LDIST	2.21		* 2.21
LAUN. & DRY CLEAN	Oct 26	LNDRY	2.00		* 2.00
MISCELLANEOUS	Oct 26	MISC	——		* .00
PAID OUT	Oct 26	PDOUT	.50		* .50
TOTAL DEBITS			45.11	3.40	* 48.51
MISCELLANEOUS CR	Oct 26	MISC CR	10.15		* 10.15
PAID	Oct 26	PAID	13.79		* 13.79
TOTAL CREDITS			23.94		* 23.94CR
NET DIFFERENCE			21.17		
OPENING DR. BALANCE			7209.96		
NET OUTSTANDING			7231.13		
TOTAL MCH. DR. BALANCE	Oct 26				*7231.13
LESS CR. BALANCE					——
NET OUTSTANDING					*7231.13

DETECTOR COUNTER READINGS:

AUDITOR'S CONTROL 960

MACH. NUMBER 1

B-6759—K20YY

☒ DATE CHANGED

☒ CONTROL TOTALS AT ZERO

☒ MASTER TAPE LOCKED

☒ AUDIT CONTROL LOCKED

AUDITOR

John Calvin

point-of-sale equipment, call accounting systems, and other revenue center devices for quick, accurate, and automatic postings to electronic guest and non-guest account folios. Extensive audit functions can be performed in a fraction of the time needed in non-automated or semi-automated operating modes. Computer-based systems enable the night auditor to spend more time auditing transactions and analyzing front office activities and less time performing postings and bookkeeping entries. Monitoring account balances and verifying account postings require a simplified procedure that compares guest ledger and non-guest ledger audit data with the front office daily report for balancing. When these documents are out-of-balance, there is usually an internal computer problem or an unusual data handling error.

A computerized front office accounting system retains previous balance information for guest and non-guest accounts, along with appropriate transactional details in its electronic database. Front office staff are guided through a series of steps and may need to input various data elements in response to system-generated directives or commands relative to the night audit routine. These commands can be critical to an effective fully automated audit process.

The computer performs numerous mathematical verifications to ensure postings are correct. For example, a range check will recognize postings of unusual

Exhibit 4 Fully Automated Daily Transaction Report—Selected Local Telephone Department Transactions

LODGISTIX RESORT & CONFERENCE CENTER (90003) PAGE 1

Department Audit Report - JUL12 - All Employees - LO LOCAL JUL12 14:25:03

Folio	Room	Time	Dept	Refer	Chrg/Pymt	Correct	Adjust	Comm Ded	ID
00241	210	0811	LO		.50+				PS
00127	105	0813	LO		.50+				PS
00152	112	0813	LO		.50+				PS
00152	112	0813	LO		.50+				PS
00127	105	0814	LO		.50+				PS
00171	201	0814	LO		.50+				PS
00234	207	0815	LO		.50+				PS
00234	207	0816	LO		.50+				PS
00243	223	0816	LO		.50+T				PS
00243	223	0816	LO		.50+				PS
00002	126	0817	LO		.50+				PS
00002	126	0817	LO		.50+				PS
00226	1000	0817	LO		.50+				PS
00226	1000	0818	LO		.50+				PS
00237	215	0818	LO		.50+				PS
00237	215	0818	LO		.50+				PS
00253	240	0819	LO		.50+				PS
00234	223	0823	LO		.50+				PS
00243	223	0823	LO		.50-T				PS
00085	230	0825	LO	2334			.50-A		PS
00012	107	0826	LO	34455			.50-A		PS
00022	109	0827	LO		.50-T				PS
00023	109	0827	LO		.50+				PS
00001	111	0851	LO			50.00-C			JS
00001	111	0851	LO			50.00+C			JS
00001	111	0852	LO		.50+				JS
00022	109	0852	LO		.50+T				JS
00166	106	0852	LO		.50+				JS
00253	102	1814	LO		6.00+				MD
Total LOCAL					16.00+	.00	1.00-	.00	

End of report

Courtesy of Sulcus, Phoenix, Arizona

size, such as a $15 charge being posted as $1,500. Since most front office accounting systems are capable of tracking each posting by time, shift, employee, folio number, and revenue center, they maintain a detailed audit trail of transactional activity. Exhibit 4 shows a sample page from a daily transaction report listing local telephone calls produced by a fully automated front office accounting system.

Computer systems can also organize, compile, and print records faster than can be done manually. In a night audit, a front office computer can process a large quantity of data, perform numerous computations, and generate accurate account totals. A system update is often used to perform many of these automated functions. System updates are run daily to establish an audited end of day and allow for report production, system file reorganization, and system maintenance.

Computerized front office accounting systems also offer rapid access to information, thereby enabling front office management to more knowledgeably manage operations. Reports detailing revenue data, occupancy statistics, advance deposits, arrivals, no-shows, room status, and other operational information can

Exhibit 5 Computer Generated Revenue Report

Lodgistix Resort & Conference Center (90003)

Daily Report—July 12—Charges

Dept	Net	Gross	Adjust
Room	2301.00+	2301.00+	.00
City Tax	42.68+	42.68+	.00
Occ Tax	85.50+	85.50+	.00
Tax	116.60+	116.60+	.00
Gift Shop	.00	.00	.00
Health Club	.00	.00	.00
Long Distance	38.36+	38.36+	.00
Local	15.00+	16.00+	1.00–
Parking	5.00+	5.00+	.00
Paidout	.00	.00	.00
Deli Food	10.00+	10.00+	.00
Lounge Food	.00	.00	.00
Pool Food	.00	.00	.00
Restaurant Food	301.31+	301.31+	.00
Deli Beverage	.00	.00	.00
Lounge Beverage	21.62+	21.62+	.00
Pool Beverage	.00	.00	.00
Restaurant Beverage	.00	.00	.00
Grand Total	2937.07+	2938.07+	1.00–

Courtesy of Sulcus, Phoenix, Arizona

be generated on request, or as part of the regular system update routine. Exhibit 5 presents a computer-generated revenue center report.

The Night Audit Process

The night audit focuses on two areas: the discovery and correction of front office accounting errors and the creation of accounting and management reports. From an accounting point of view, a night audit ensures the integrity of front office accounts through a cross-referencing process. Guest and non-guest accounts are compared with source documents from revenue centers to prove individual transaction entries and account totals. Discrepancies found during a night audit must be corrected so that the front office accounting system is in balance. From a management reporting point of view, the night audit provides important operating information, such as average rate, occupancy percentage, usage of package plans and other marketing programs, and the number of group rooms and complimentary (no-charge) rooms occupied.

A night audit is conducted on a daily basis due to the transient nature of hotel business. Many computer-based front office accounting systems can perform a nearly continuous system audit routine and provide summary reports at predetermined times as well as on demand. Fully automated systems provide much greater flexibility in front office operations than manual or semi-automated systems.

The degree of scrutiny required during the night audit process depends on the frequency of errors and the volume of transactions to be reviewed. While the first of these factors relates to the quality of front office work, the second correlates with the size and complexity of the hotel. Large, complex hotels typically require closer account scrutiny due to the high volume of transactions posted.

The following steps are common to the sequence of a night audit:

1. Complete outstanding postings.
2. Reconcile room status discrepancies.
3. Verify room rates.
4. Balance all departmental accounts.
5. Verify no-show reservations.
6. Post room rates and taxes.
7. Prepare required reports.
8. Prepare cash receipts for deposit.
9. Clear or back up the system.
10. Distribute reports.

In a computer system update, several of these steps may be condensed or combined. The following sections examine these front office audit procedures from an operational perspective.

Complete Outstanding Postings

One of the primary functions of the night audit is to ensure that all transactions affecting guest and non-guest accounts are posted to appropriate folios before the end of the day. It is important to accurately post and account for all transactions on the day they occur. Charges posted with the wrong date will confuse guests and severely complicate cross-referencing. Posting errors can be problematic and can lead to discrepancies and delays at check-out. This can prove time-consuming since the debated charges will have to be researched for explanation.

Traditionally, the first step of the night audit is to complete all outstanding postings. While sound front office practice dictates that transactions be posted to the proper accounts as they are received, the night auditor must confirm that all transactions received at the front desk have been posted before starting the audit routine. This usually means waiting until all food and beverage outlets, including banquet facilities, are closed. Incomplete postings will result in errors in account balancing and complicate summary reporting.

In addition to completing the posting function, the night auditor verifies that all vouchers for revenue center transactions are posted. If the hotel does not have an interfaced computerized telephone call accounting system, outstanding telephone charges may require manual posting. If the hotel supports point-of-sale or call accounting systems interfaced with a front office accounting system, then the previously posted totals should be verified to ensure that all outlet charges have been posted. This can be done by generating printed posting reports from the interfaced systems and comparing them with the totals reported by the front office accounting system. If the figures are identical, the systems are in balance. If they are not the same, the night auditor begins to compare transactions between the two systems to identify the transactions that have been omitted or improperly posted.

An efficient night auditor may discover some postings that remain from a previous front office workshift. These transactions will also require posting to the appropriate guest or non-guest folio.

Reconcile Room Status Discrepancies

Room status discrepancies must be resolved in a timely manner since imbalances can lead to lost business and cause confusion in the front office. Errors in room status can lead to lost and uncollectible room revenues and omissions in postings. The front office must maintain current and accurate room status information to effectively determine the number and types of rooms available for sale. For example, if a guest checks out but the front desk agent fails to properly complete the check-out procedure, the guest's room may appear occupied when it is really vacant. This error in procedure could prevent the room from being rented until the error is discovered and corrected.

In manual and semi-automated hotels, before the end of the day, the night auditor reconciles discrepancies between the daily housekeeper's report and the front office room status system (the room rack and guest folios in manual and semi-automated hotels). In large hotels, this is sometimes done by the front desk evening shift to give the night auditor more time to do the actual auditing and balancing work. It is also a good time as it may be helpful to call a guest to resolve any questions. To minimize errors, housekeeping departments typically require staff to record the perceived status of all rooms serviced. The auditor must review front office and housekeeping department reports to reconcile and finalize the occupancy status of all rooms for a given night. In fully automated hotels, the night auditor compares the daily housekeeper's report with the room status report of the system and the bucket where the registration cards for in-house guests are kept.

If the housekeeping report indicates that a room is vacant, but the front office believes it is occupied, the auditor should search for an active room folio and registration card. If the folio exists and has a current outstanding balance, there are several possibilities:

- A guest may have departed but forgotten to check out.
- A guest may be a skipper who left with no intention of checking out.
- A front desk agent or cashier may not have properly closed the folio at check-out.

After verifying that the guest has left the hotel, the night auditor should process the check-out and set the folio aside for front office management review and follow-up. If the folio has been settled, the front office room status system should be corrected to show that the room is vacant. The night auditor should verify the guest folio against the housekeeping and the room status reports to ensure that all three are consistent and in balance. In a computerized system, the check-out process is normally linked to a rooms management function that automatically monitors and updates the room's status. Few, if any, room status discrepancies should occur in a computerized front office system, but the night audit process is still necessary to ensure accuracy.

Balance All Departments

The night audit process can become quite complicated when errors are discovered. It is generally considered more efficient to balance all departments first and then look for individual posting errors within an out-of-balance department.

The night auditor typically balances all revenue center departments using source documents that originated in the revenue center. The night auditor seeks to balance all front office accounts against departmental transaction information. Vouchers received at the front desk and other documents are totaled and compared with revenue center summaries. Even fully automated front office accounting systems rely upon source documents to help resolve discrepancies as they arise.

When the front office accounting system is out of balance, the correctness and thoroughness of account postings must be investigated. A detailed department audit (by shift or by cashier) may be conducted and individual postings reviewed until the front office accounting error is corrected.

The process used to balance the revenue center departments is often called the **trial balance.** The night auditor completes the trial balance before verifying the final system balance and creating final night audit reports. The trial balance usually uncovers any corrections or adjustments that need to be made during the night audit process. Night auditors often perform the trial balance before posting room and tax charges. Doing so can simplify the final night audit procedure. If the trial balance was correct and the final balance is wrong, the auditor can deduce that the error must relate to the room and tax posting.

It is important to note that a mathematical balance in guest and non-guest accounts against departmental totals does not necessarily mean that the proper accounts were selected for posting. Posting the correct amount to an incorrect account would still present an in-balance total. This type of error usually goes unnoticed until a guest has a problem with the validity of an entry on his or her statement.

Exhibit 6 presents a sample sequence of night audit procedures useful in departmental balancing.

Verify Room Rates

The night auditor may need to complete a room revenue and count report. This report provides a means for analyzing room revenues since it shows the rack rate (price) for each room and the actual rate at which the room was sold. If a room's rack and actual rates do not match, the night auditor should consider several factors:

- If the room is occupied by a member of a group or by a corporate-rate customer, is the discounted rate correct?

Exhibit 6 Departmental Balancing Sequence

1. Sort vouchers by originating departments.
2. Consider each department's vouchers.
   a) Separate the correction vouchers according to the departments they are to be applied against.
   b) Total the corrections for each department.
3. After verifying each of the corrections with the departments affected, total the correction vouchers. The corrections total must coincide with the correction figures on the front office shift report.
4. Consider the vouchers again.
   a) Total the rest of the outstanding vouchers.
   b) Check individual transaction values on the bottom of the voucher against the figure appearing on the department detail report.
5. The vouchers should agree with the corrected figures of the departments. If the totals do not agree with either figure, the error should be resolved before proceeding.
   a) Verify that the date on the voucher is the current day's date.
   b) Check off each individual posting against its support document (voucher) until the error is found. This can be tedious if there are several errors. However, if the front office uses validating printers, a thorough check of the support document validations will help pinpoint errors.
   c) Post any additional corrections or adjustments.
6. In a computerized system, revised individual shift reports can be printed after the corrections and adjustments have been made. In any operations mode, all of the backup data should be packaged for the accounting office to review.

- If there is only one guest in a room and the actual rate is approximately half the rack rate, is the guest part of a shared reservation? If he or she is, did the second guest register?
- If the room is complimentary, is there appropriate supporting back-up for the rate (for example, a complimentary room authorization form)?

The proper use of room revenue and count information can form a solid basis for room revenue analysis. The night auditor may be required to produce a copy of this report for review by front office management. Some hotels today measure room revenue potential against actual room revenue. The actual room revenue posted is compared with the rack rate of the rooms occupied for the night. The comparison may be shown as a percentage. The night auditor may be responsible for calculating this number and reporting it as part of the night audit or it may be done automatically by the front office computer system.

Verify No-Show Reservations

The night auditor may also be responsible for clearing the reservation rack or filing and posting charges to no-show accounts. In posting no-show charges, the night auditor must be careful to verify that the reservation was guaranteed and the guest never registered with the hotel. Sometimes duplicate reservations may be made for a guest or the guest's name may be misspelled and another record accidentally created by the front office staff. If these are not identified by front office or reservations staff, the guest may actually arrive but appear to be a no-show under the second reservation.

No-show billings must be handled with extreme care. A front desk agent who does not record cancellations properly may cause clients to be billed incorrectly. Incorrect billing may lead the credit card company to reevaluate its legal agreements and relationship with the hotel. Incorrect billing may also cause the hotel to lose the guest's future business and (if applicable) the business of the travel agency that guaranteed the reservation. All front office staff must adhere to established no-show procedures when handling reservation cancellations or modifications.

Post Room Rates and Taxes

Posting room rates and room taxes to all guest folios typically takes place at the end of day. Once room rates and taxes are posted, a room rate and tax report may be generated for front office management review. The ability to electronically post room rates and room taxes on demand is surely one of the most frequently cited advantages of an automated front office system over manual and semi-automated systems. Once the night auditor has verified the room rates to be posted, the computer can auto-post numerous room rate and room tax charges to the appropriate electronic folios in a matter of minutes. With manual or semi-automated systems, the procedure required to post room rate and room tax can be very tedious and time consuming. In addition, automatic charge postings are accurate, with no chance for pickup, tax calculation, or posting errors. This feature can be especially important to hotels located in municipalities that have bed or occupancy taxes in addition to a sales tax. Some automated hotels may pre-set their computer systems to post daily recurring charges, such as valet parking or gratuities. Auto-posting these charges can save night audit time and improve accuracy.

Prepare Reports

The night auditor typically prepares reports that indicate the status of front office activities and operations. Among those prepared for management review are the final department detail and summary reports, the daily operations report, the high balance report, and other reports specific to the property.

Final department detail and summary reports are produced and filed along with their source documents for accounting division review. These reports help prove that all transactions were properly posted and accounted for.

The daily operations report summarizes the day's business and provides insight into revenues, receivables, operating statistics, and cash transactions related to the front office. This report is typically considered the most important outcome of the front office audit. The high balance report identifies guests whose charges are approaching an account credit limit designated by the hotel (the house limit).

In a computerized front office system, the computer may be programmed to produce many management reports on demand. For example, the high balance report may be produced at any time during the day as a continuing check on guest transactions and account balances.

In addition, other reports are usually created at this time by the night audit. A report showing each group in the hotel, the number of rooms occupied by each group, the number of guests for each group, and the revenue generated by each group is common. This report helps the hotel sales department with the group history. The same type of report may be generated for guests on package plans or guests staying in the hotel due to a special promotion or advertising program. Other reports may list guests who stay frequently and guests who are VIPs. In automated hotels, this type of marketing information can be automatically tracked, sorted, and reported.

Deposit Cash

The night auditor frequently prepares a cash deposit voucher as part of the night audit process. If front office cash receipts have not yet been deposited in a bank, the night auditor compares the postings of cash payments and paid-outs (net cash receipts) with actual cash on hand. A copy of the front office cashier shift report may be included in the cash deposit envelope to support any overage, shortage, or due back balances. Since account and departmental balancing often involve cash transactions, accurate cash depositing may depend on an effective audit process.

Clear or Back Up the System

In manual and semi-automated front office operations, totals must be cleared from the system after the night audit is complete. Manual systems are cleared by simply moving the closing balance from the night audit report to the opening balance of the next day's report. In semi-automated operations, the totals in the posting machine must be brought to a zero balance. The night auditor controls this function so that the possibility of fraud is minimized. As each account is reduced to zero, a separate card (sometimes called a *Z card*) is used to verify the zero balance. A Z card is usually submitted with the night audit work to show that all accounts have been properly reset. In semi-automated systems, typically only the ending balance is maintained in the posting machine.

Since a computer system eliminates the need for a room rack, reservation cards, and a variety of other traditional front office forms and devices, front office accounting depends on the continuous functioning of the computer system. A system back-up in the night audit routine is unique to computerized front office systems. Back-up reports must be run and various media duplicated in a timely manner so that the front office can continue to run smoothly.

End-of-day reports can be developed and automatically generated by a front office computer system. Normally, at least two guest lists are printed for back-up and emergency use: one for the front desk and one for the switchboard. A printed

Exhibit 7 Guest Ledger Report

Lodgistix Resort & Conference Center (90003)

Preliminary Audit Report—July 12—Guest Ledger Balances

Status	Open Balance	Room/ Tax	Incdntl	Food	Bever- age	Payment	Close Balance
Canceled-Keep	.00	.00	.00	.00	.00	220.00–	220.00–
Canceled-Return	.00	.00	.00	.00	.00	165.00–	165.00–
No Show	480.00–	.00	.00	.00	.00	.00	480.00–
Checked-out	312.31+	104.55+	.00	.00	.00	104.55–	312.31+
Registered	5485.36+	2441.23+	58.36+	311.31+	21.62+	1440.00–	6877.88+
House Accounts	.00	.00	8.40+	.00	.00	.00	8.40+
Group Master Accounts	.00	.00	15.00+	14.00+	21.00+	.00	50.00+
Total Guest Ledger	5317.67+	2545.78+	81.76+	325.31+	42.62+	1929.55–	6383.59+

Courtesy of Sulcus, Phoenix, Arizona

room status report enables front desk agents to identify vacant and ready rooms should the computer become inoperable. A guest ledger report can be generated, such as the report shown in Exhibit 7. This report contains the opening and closing account balances for all registered guests. A front office activity report can also be generated. Such a report contains expected arrival, stayover, and departure information for several days. A sample activity report is shown in Exhibit 8. In some front office systems, the next day's registration cards are pre-printed as part of the front office activity report. Due to requirements of the Americans with Disabilities Act, hotels must also keep track of guests with disabilities. One reason for this is to ensure that all disabled guests are accounted for in case of an emergency. This report is usually produced at this time and distributed to the various departments needing this information.

Computer-generated front office information should also be copied (backed up) onto magnetic tape or magnetic disk, depending on the system configuration. A system back-up should be conducted after each night audit and stored in a safe place. Many computer systems have two types of system back-up. A daily back-up simply creates a copy of front office electronic files on magnetic tape or magnetic disk. The second type of system back-up is performed once or twice a week. This back-up not only copies daily information, but eliminates account and transaction information deemed to no longer be of value. For example, accounts that have been checked out for over three days and have had no activity during that time can be deleted from active computer memory. Following this procedure will reduce the overall amount of computer storage required for back-up. If any account must be researched in the future, it can be found on previously printed reports or the weekly back-up.

Distribute Reports

Due to the sensitive and confidential nature of front office information, the night auditor must promptly deliver appropriate reports to authorized individuals. The

Exhibit 8 Activity Report

LODGISTIX RESORT & CONFERENCE CENTER (90003) PAGE 1 JUL12 13:14:23

Arrival/Stayover/Departure Activity Report

Date	Avl	Sold		---Arrivals---			---Stayovers--			--Departures--			Rem		
				Gtd	6/4	Shr	Gtd	6/4	Shr	Gtd	6/4	Shr	Blk	Adlts	Kids
JUL12	24	49	Trn	28	5	0	12	0	1	14	0	0		71	16
		67.1%	Grp	2	0	0	0	0	0	0	0	0	3	2	0
JUL13	36	37	Trn	1	0	0	31	5	1	8	0	0		61	14
		50.6%	Grp	0	0	0	0	0	0	2	0	0	0	0	0
JUL14	48	25	Trn	1	0	0	19	5	0	13	0	1		41	8
		34.2%	Grp	0	0	0	0	0	0	0	0	0	0	0	0
JUL15	59	14	Trn	3	0	0	11	0	0	9	5	0		21	4
		19.1%	Grp	0	0	0	0	0	0	0	0	0	0	0	0
JUL16	68	5	Trn	1	0	0	4	0	0	10	0	0		7	2
		6.8%	Grp	0	0	0	0	0	0	0	0	0	0	0	0
JUL17	68	5	Trn	1	1	0	3	0	0	2	0	0		9	2
		6.8%	Grp	0	0	0	0	0	0	0	0	0	0	0	0
JUL18	71	2	Trn	1	0	0	1	0	0	3	1	0		3	0
		2.7%	Grp	0	0	0	0	0	0	0	0	0	0	0	0

	Total	Transient	Group	Rem Blk
Room Nights	511			
Available	374			
Sold	137	132	2	3
Occupancy %	26.8%	96.3%	1.4%	2.1%

End of report

Courtesy of Sulcus, Phoenix, Arizona

distribution of night audit reports is the final step in the night audit routine, and is important to efficient front office operations. Informed managerial decisions can be made if all night audit reports are completed accurately and delivered on time.

Verifying the Night Audit

Numerous types of posting, mathematical, and clerical errors can be identified through an effective night audit. Among the most typical errors are those involving previous balance **pickup**, transpositions, and misplaced folios.

Pickup Errors

In manual and semi-automated front office systems, front desk agents must access the previous balance of an account folio, post the debits and credits, and calculate a new current balance. If the previous balance is entered (picked up) incorrectly, the resulting ending balance will be incorrect. This can happen whenever a posting is made to a folio, not just during the night audit. **Pickup errors** are frequently the most time-consuming errors to locate and correct; it is often necessary to review all previous and ending balances on every folio in order to identify the error.

Transposition Errors

A **transposition error** is one of the easiest to identify. This type of error occurs when numbers related to a transaction are reversed—for example, entering *$523* into a posting machine rather than the actual previous balance of *$532*. A transposition error can usually be identified by subtracting the smaller number from the larger number and dividing by 9. If the result is a whole number (as in the above example), the problem is most likely a transposition error. Transposition errors are sometimes called the Rule of 9's by night auditors.

Missing Folios

Many times, a manual or semi-automated front office system is out of balance because a folio has been filed incorrectly or has been removed from the folio bucket. After check-out, front desk agents move accounts pertaining to check-outs to the forward section of the folio bucket. Sometimes, front desk agents forget to relocate closed folios and the folio is improperly refiled behind the room tab in the bucket. Another example of a missing folio error is closing an "A" folio (room and tax charges), but leaving the "B" folio (incidental charges) in the bucket and unsettled. Other times, a current folio may be filed in the front part of the folio bucket when it should be returned to its proper place elsewhere in the bucket. Sometimes, questions may arise on a particular account, such as a high-balance account. In order to investigate the proper account, the front office credit manager may need to remove the folio from the bucket for review. If this happens, the front desk agent removing the folio should always leave a signed note stating that he or she has temporarily removed the folio, along with the name of the guest on the folio and the folio number. When a folio is missing, the night audit simply will not balance. In automated hotels, where folios are stored electronically, missing folios are not an issue. In addition, front desk staff are alerted when there are multiple folios in a room when guests are checking out, minimizing the occurrence of unpaid, split folios.

Automated System Update

A system update in a computerized front office system accomplishes many of the same functions as a non-computerized night audit routine. System updates are run daily to enable computer system file reorganization, system maintenance, and report production and to provide an end-of-day time frame.

Since many front office computer systems continuously audit transactional postings as they occur, there may be little need for the night auditor to perform account postings. A front office computer system may be connected with remote communications to revenue outlet devices for automatic postings. The front office computer system may support point-of-sale interfaces, call accounting technology, in-room movies and in-room vending, and the like. Its interface capability enables the system to control and monitor charges made at remote revenue outlets throughout the hotel. Management policy usually dictates the extent of system interface application. The night auditor should routinely review interface procedures to ensure the proper handling of automatically posted transactions from revenue outlets.

In the case of guaranteed reservation no-shows, for example, postings may be programmed to flow automatically to a billing file. If a transaction needs to be independently posted, the guest's electronic folio can be displayed on a computer terminal screen for posting. Once complete, the folio can be placed back into electronic storage and/or printed on demand.

Room status discrepancies are somewhat unusual in a fully automated front office environment. Eliminating the room rack and connecting registration and check-out with room status functions decreases the potential for discrepancies. Housekeepers typically report the current occupancy status of a room through the room's telephone before they leave the room. This automatically updates the room's status on the front office computer; if appropriate, a **room variance report** can be programmed to print out automatically. Even in the case of a skipper, a front office computer system may help identify the problem quickly enough so that the hotel can ready the room for resale with minimal loss of room revenue.

In some front office computer systems, the balancing of front office and department accounts is continuously monitored through an on-line accounting system. As a charge purchase is entered at a remote point-of-sale terminal, for example, the charge may be instantaneously posted to an electronic guest folio and an electronic departmental control folio. A **control folio** is a computer-based internal accounting file that supports all account postings recorded by an operating department. To balance departments, the front office computer system tests all non-control folio entries against individual control folio transactions. An imbalance is just as likely to identify a problem in automatic posting techniques as a shortcoming in front office accounting procedures. Detailed departmental reports can be generated and checked against account postings to prove account entries at any time during the day.

Front office computer systems can be programmed to produce a variety of reports of various lengths and content. Since a system update involves computer file reorganization as well as accounting detail, most of a computerized system's output differs significantly from the output of a non-computerized audit routine. Reservation confirmations, revenue center summaries, expected arrival and departure lists, folio production for guests expected to depart, a daily report of operations, and billing statements for non-guest accounts are typically produced as a result of an automated system update.

Front office computer systems may also generate computer-printed copies of several other files as a safeguard against system failure. Activity reports, guest lists, room status reports, account statements, and the like may be printed and held as a hedge against system failure. Since front office computer systems deal with information and not physical inventories, the cash deposit procedures relevant in a non-computerized property are still often maintained.

Summary

Hotels operate 24 hours a day, seven days a week, and the front office must regularly review and verify the accuracy and completeness of its accounting records. A front office audit process is intended to fulfill this need. The audit attempts to balance daily guest and non-guest account transactions against revenue center transactions. A successful audit will result in balanced accounts, accurate account statements, appropriate account credit monitoring, timely reports to management, and increased probability of account settlement. Traditionally, the front office audit has been called the night audit since it is generally performed in the late night and early morning hours. In a fully automated front office, the audit is referred to as a system update since computer files are updated as part of the audit routine.

The chief purpose of the night audit is to verify the accuracy and completeness of guest and non-guest accounts against departmental transaction reports and to provide management reporting. The night auditor must be familiar with the nature and amount of transactions and needs to pay close attention to accounting detail, procedural controls, and guest credit restrictions. The night auditor is usually responsible for tracking room revenues, occupancy percentages, and other standard operating statistics. In addition, the auditor will prepare a daily summary of cash, check, and credit card activities. These data are summarized to reflect the financial performance of the front office on a particular day. In order for the audit to be consistent, the front office must establish an end of day. Finally, the night auditor may be required to provide a variety of marketing reporting helpful to the sales of the hotel. The end of day is simply the end of the business day.

A front office accounting system depends on transactional documentation to establish accurate records and maintain effective operational controls. For internal control purposes, an accounting system must provide independent supporting documentation to verify each transaction. In a non-automated or semi-automated operation, supporting documents produced by different individuals provide cross-reference sources. Although the night auditor receives information on room revenues from a front desk source, the auditor should check room rate postings on guest folios against the housekeeping department's report of occupied rooms and the front desk room rack. This process helps ensure that rates have been posted for all occupied rooms and reduces the occupancy errors caused by front desk agents who do not properly complete check-in and check-out procedures.

Regardless of how the night audit is conducted, the basic posting formula applies. The audit routine is somewhat simplified through the development of a daily transcript, which contains summary information on all guest accounts. In some front office operations, a supplemental transcript may be used to record the transactional activity for non-guest accounts. Together, the daily transcript and a supplemental transcript will detail all transactions occurring on a single day.

A series of ten steps is typically followed when conducting a night audit. These steps include: completing outstanding postings, reconciling room status discrepancies, balancing all departments, verifying room rates, verifying no-show reservations, posting room rates and taxes, preparing reports, depositing cash, clearing or backing up the system, and distributing reports. Many common types of posting errors can occur. Among the most typical errors found in the night audit are those involving previous balance pickup, transpositions, and missing folios.

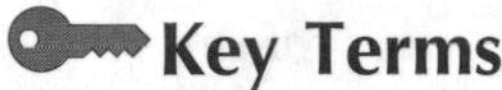

Key Terms

audit trail—an organized flow of source documents detailing each step in the processing of a transaction.

bucket check—the night auditor's check of room rate postings on guest folios against the housekeeping department's report of occupied rooms and the front desk room rack; helps ensure that rates have been posted for all occupied rooms and helps reduce the occupancy errors caused when front desk agents do not properly complete check-in and check-out procedures.

control folio—an accounting department document used internally by a front office computer to support all account postings by department during a system update routine.

daily transcript—a detailed report of all guest accounts that indicates each charge transaction affecting a guest account for the day, used as a worksheet to detect posting errors.

D card—a night auditor's report used in semi-automated front office accounting systems.

end-of-day—an arbitrary stopping point for the business day.

high balance report—a report that identifies guests who are approaching an account credit limit; typically prepared by the night auditor.

in balance—a term used to describe the state of accounts when the totals of debit amounts and credit amounts are equal.

night audit—a daily comparison of guest accounts (and non-guest accounts having activity) with revenue center transaction information.

night auditor—an employee who checks the accuracy of front office accounting records and compiles a daily summary of hotel financial data as part of the night audit; in many hotels, the night auditor is actually an employee of the accounting division.

out-of-balance—a term used to describe the state of accounts when the total of debit amounts and credit amounts are not equal.

pickup error—an error in manual and semi-automated systems that occurs when the user enters an incorrect previous balance or transaction value in the process of posting.

room status report—a report that allows front desk agents to identify vacant and ready rooms, typically prepared as part of the night audit.

room variance report—a report listing any discrepancies between front desk and housekeeping room statuses.

supplemental transcript—a detailed report of all non-guest accounts that indicates each charge transaction that affected a non-guest account that day, used as a worksheet to detect posting errors.

system update—a fully automated audit routine that accomplishes many of the same functions as a non-computerized night audit; daily system updates enable file reorganization, system maintenance, and report production, and provide an end-of-day time frame.

transposition error—an error that occurs when numerals in a figure are reversed; for example, 189 for 198.

trial balance—in the night audit, the process of balancing front office accounts with transaction information by department.

Review Questions

1. What are the two basic purposes of the night audit? Why is it generally performed at night? What is the definition of the term *end of day?*

2. What are the five functions of the night audit process? How does each contribute to the efficiency of the front office accounting system?

3. How do the concepts of cross-referencing and account integrity govern the night audit process? What are the usual source documents for guest account transactions?

4. What information does a daily transcript report? What related purpose does a supplemental transcript have?

5. What differences exist between the night audit processes in the three front office recordkeeping systems? How has the structure of a non-automated night audit affected the development of the automated night audit process?

6. How does the night auditor reconcile room status discrepancies? Why is it important that these reconciliations occur as early as possible?

7. Why does the night auditor verify room rates and no-shows before posting room rates and taxes? Why is it important that these postings occur as late as possible?

8. What accounting, management, and marketing reports are typically generated during the night audit process?

9. What is the purpose of a system back-up for a computerized front office system? What are common elements of an information back-up?

10. What are the differences between an automated front office system update and the traditional night audit? What tasks must still be performed separately in an automated front office?

Internet Sites

For more information, visit the following Internet sites. Remember that Internet addresses can change without notice.

Lodging Publications—Online and Printed

Hospitality Technology News
http://www.hospitalitynet.nl/news/tech.html

Hotel & Motel Management
http://www.innvest.com/hmm

Lodging Online
http://www.ei-ahma.org/webs/lodging/index.html

Lodging Hospitality
http://www.penton.com/corp/mags/lh.html

Lodging Online
http://www.ei-ahma.org/webs/lodging/index.html

Technology Sites

Anasazi, Inc.
http://www.anasazi.com

CSS Hotel Systems
http://www.csshotelsystems.com

Executech Systems, Inc.
http://www.executech.com

Fidelio
http://www.micros.com

First Resort Software
http://www.firstres.com

Hospitality Industry Technology Exposition and Conference
http://www.hitecshow.org

Hospitality Industry Technology Integration Standards
http://www.hitis.org

HOST Group
http://www.hostgroup.com

Lodging Touch International
http://www.lodgingtouch.com

Newmarket Software Systems, Inc.
http://www.newsoft.com

Resort Data Processing, Inc.
http://www.resortdata.com

Western Hospitality Systems—InnSure
http://www.lodgingsystems.com

Case Study

Promoting the Night Auditor at The Macasa DeVille Resort

The Macasa DeVille is a very majestic hotel located in the heart of rodeo country. The hotel until recently had been part of a national reservation system, but it recently canceled its participation and became independent. The Macasa DeVille has 110 guest suites, a formal dining room, two lounges, a health spa, and a horse riding stable. The Macasa DeVille is famous for its backpacking explorations and its fishing expeditions in nearby Lake Gregory. An outstanding view of the valley affords Macasa DeVille guests an excellent location for corporate seminars, executive management meetings, and training seminars.

The Macasa DeVille operates year-round at an average occupancy of 90%. Recently the general manager, Mr. Dailey, and the front office manager, Mr. Nagy, had a disagreement over two important issues. One dealt with discounted room rates, the other with the contents of the daily report of operations Mr. Nagy's department produced for Mr. Dailey's review. Until Mr. Bradley, the front office auditor, brought these two matters to Mr. Dailey's attention, Mr. Dailey was unaware of the fluctuation in assigned room rates and the level of detail the daily report lacked.

Mr. Nagy felt that room rates should be flexible and vary according to the guest's ethnic background and politeness during registration. Each front desk agent was instructed to consult with Mr. Nagy before assigning a room rate during the registration process, regardless of the rate quoted at the time of reservation. In addition, Mr. Nagy believed Mr. Dailey should only be given occupancy statistics and average room rate information on a daily basis. Mr. Dailey did not like this approach and requested that Mr. Nagy resign. When the front office manager refused, Mr. Dailey fired him.

Mr. Dailey, who had not had to recruit or hire a front office manager, was faced with a challenge. He decided that in his search for Mr. Nagy's replacement, he was going to seek someone with night auditing experience. He believed that the information that existed within the confines of the night audit would serve well in formation of the daily report. Further, he believed he could instill a different room rate philosophy into the new front office manager without much trouble.

Mr. Dailey understood the urgency to recruit a new front office manager. He invited Mr. Bradley to apply and hired him two days after Mr. Nagy's departure. Many members of the front office staff were upset, believing the Mr. Bradley had blind-sided Mr. Nagy in hopes of getting his job. Mr. Bradley had to work especially hard to prove to the staff that a former night auditor could manage the department and put to better use much of the front office information.

Discussion Questions

1. Was Mr. Bradley correct in discussing the arbitrary variations in room rates and shortcomings of the hotel's daily report with Mr. Dailey?

2. What information do you think the night auditor most likely relied on to determine the room rate discrepancies? What key information may have been omitted from the daily report of operations?

3. Should a front office manager have night audit experience? What are the advantages and disadvantages of such experience to the front office manager?

4. Develop a daily report format for the Macasa DeVille showing all the information Mr. Dailey should receive.

5. Briefly discuss the front office auditor's role in providing both daily financial information and overall information about the hotel's performance. What makes it so important to management?

Case Number: 3329CA
The following industry experts helped generate this case: Richard M. Brooks, CHA, Vice President—Operations, Bridgestreet Accommodations, Inc., Cleveland, Ohio; and Michael L. Kasavana, Professor, The School of Hospitality Business, Michigan State University, East Lansing, Michigan.

This case also appears in *Case Studies in Lodging Management* (East Lansing, Michigan: Educational Institute of the American Hotel & Motel Association, 1998), ISBN 0-86612-184-6.

Night Audit Problem

This problem is a practical learning experience and a comprehensive review. It takes you step-by-step through an actual front office problem. The Appendix contains the forms that are necessary for completing the problem. Read the instructions and work through the problem, filling in the forms based on the transactions stated below.

Instructions

1. Post the transactions to the guests' folios as they occur.
2. Create a folio for anyone who checks in. Use the following chart to establish the room rates by type of room and number of persons.

Room Type	1-Person Rate	2-Person Rate
Inner hall	$24	$30
Woods	$32	$38
Lake view	$34	$40
Pool	$40	$48
Deluxe	$48	$56
Suite	$60	$70

Extra per person: $6

3. After all transactions have been posted for the day, post the room rate and room sales tax (using four percent as the tax rate) for those guests who are still in the house.
4. Balance the folios.
5. Complete the transcript.
   a. Beginning with the rooms that have checked out:
      - list the room numbers sequentially
      - transfer the room statistics from the folio
      - bring the balance forward
      - enter the various charges and credits
      - carry the balance forward for each guest folio

b. Next, copy the same information for the rooms that are still occupied. List those rooms in numerical sequence.
c. Total all significant columns of the transcript on the House Total line.
d. Copy the City Ledger Control balance forward, the various charges and credits, and forward the balance.
e. Enter the same information for the Advance Payments Control account.
f. Total the significant columns of the House Total, the City Ledger, and the Advance Payments Control account.
g. Balance and check the transcript.

Background

As of April 1, all the rooms on the hotel's first floor are occupied by individuals associated with the "Sunshine" group. The room charge and room sales tax are being picked up by the group; all other charges will be paid by the individuals. Five other rooms are occupied by guests not associated with the "Sunshine" group. The room rates and balances brought forward as of the morning of April 1 are:

Room No.	Name	Room Rate	Balance
101	Sunshine (Master)	$1,330	$(600.00)
245	Brown, Mr. & Mrs. Edwin	48	208.04
302	Jackson, Larry	70	72.80
324	Greenwood, Nelson	24	49.92
440	Foster, Mr. & Mrs. Jack	56	58.24
522	Straight, Mr. & Mrs. Tom	56	97.34

None of the "Incidentals" folios associated with the group guests have a balance. Also, the City Ledger Control Folio has a balance of $50,000 and the Advance Payments control (Deposits) has a credit balance of $2,930.

NOTE: Laundry, although done by an external business, should be treated as a departmental charge.

Transactions

1. Mr. Richard Russell checks in. He desires a "woods" room and is assigned room 206.
2. Mr. Charles McGraw and family (total of four persons) check in. They have a reservation with a deposit of $52. They desire a "lake view" room and are assigned room 409.
3. Mr. Jackson, room 302, checks out, charging his balance to his American Express card.
4. Mr. & Mrs. Carl Anderson arrive without reservations and are assigned to room 455, a suite. Mr. Anderson pays $100 when checking in.
5. Mr. Greenwood, room 324, makes two long distance calls: one to Houston, Texas, for $7.28 and one to Atlanta, Georgia, for $6.24.

6. The room attendant reports that all luggage has been removed from room 522 and that Mr. & Mrs. Straight have disappeared.
7. Mr. & Mrs. Foster, room 440, check out. Mr. Foster charges his bill to the Allied Builders Co., a city ledger account.
8. Flash Cleaners laundry delivers for the Browns. The front desk agent posts the charge of $12 to the Browns' folio.
9. Flash Cleaners also delivers laundry for Mr. Davis, room 100, and Mr. Cotton. Mr. Davis is with the "Sunshine" group; the clerk posts the charge of $9 to his account. Mr. Cotton left his laundry when he departed on March 27 and is expected to return April 3; the charge is $6.
10. The credit manager informs Mr. Brown, room 245, that he has exceeded his credit limit of $200. Mr. Brown pays the cashier $350. He also complains about a lunch he had on March 29 for which he had paid in cash. The manager agrees to give him an allowance of $2.80.
11. Mr. & Mrs. Harry Goodman and their son check in. They are assigned to room 331, a "lake view" room. After checking in, they have lunch in the restaurant and charge the check of $15.60 to their room.
12. Mr. Bob Moose checks into room 401, a suite. After checking in, he spends the afternoon at the bar and charges his bill of $18.72 to his room.
13. Mr. Goodman complains to the restaurant manager about the lunch he had with his family. The manager agrees to make an allowance for the entire amount of the check.
14. Mr. & Mrs. Anderson have lunch in their room (455). They charge the amount of the meal, $8.32, to their room and add a tip of $1.50. The room service waiter collects the tip from the front office cashier.
15. A restaurant check arrives at the front desk for Mr. Foster; the charge is $4.76.
16. Mr. Greenwood, room 324, checks out. He disputes a long-distance charge of $6.24 and the charge is allowed (that is, removed or credited as an allowance). He pays the balance of his bill in full.
17. Mr. Russell, room 206, makes three long-distance calls to Chicago. The charges are $17.25, $14.25, and $6.98.
18. Two charge vouchers from the banquet department arrive at the front office for a dinner party held by the Westside Hospital, a city ledger account. The charges are $250 for food and $120 for beverages.
19. The cashier receives checks for $60 from Mr. Addison and $70 from Mr. Blue as deposits on reservations for April 9.
20. Mr. & Mrs. Brown wine and dine together. Mr. Brown charges the dinner check of $43.68 and the bar check of $15.60 to his room bill.
21. Charges for the "Sunshine" master folio, room 101, are as follows:

Food banquet:	$152.64
Cocktail banquet:	61.68
Cash advance:	43.50
Allowance for rooms:	30.36

22. City Ledger cash received was $1,140.

When you have completed the exercise, using either hand computation, machine posting, or a hotel computer, you will have experienced a night audit in miniature. A particular hotel may have slightly different procedures for handling many of the transactions, but this application illustrates a typical night audit for a small hotel.

Chapter 10 Outline

10

Planning and Evaluating Operations

MOST FRONT OFFICE MANAGERS will readily admit that they rarely have all the resources they feel are necessary. Resources available to managers include people, money, time, materials, energy, and equipment. All these resources are in limited supply. An important part of a front office manager's job involves planning how to apply these limited resources to attain the department's objectives. An equally important part of a front office manager's job is evaluating the success of front office activities in meeting the department's objectives.

Management Functions

The process of front office management can be divided into specific management functions. Exhibit 1 illustrates how management functions fit into the overall process of management. Although specific front office management tasks vary from one hotel to another, fundamental management functions are similar in scope.

Planning

Planning is probably the most important management function performed in any business. Without competent planning, the front office would be chaotic. Without the direction and focus planning provides, the front office manager may become overly involved with tasks that are unrelated to or inconsistent with accomplishing the department's goals. A front office manager's first step in planning what the front office will accomplish is to define the department's goals. The front office manager should use these general goals as a guide to planning more specific, measurable objectives. Planning also includes determining the strategies that will be used to attain the objectives.

Organizing

Using the planned goals as a guide, a front office manager organizes the department by dividing the work among front office staff. Work should be distributed so that everyone gets a fair assignment and all work can be completed in a timely manner. Organizing includes determining the order in which tasks are to be performed and establishing completion deadlines for each group of tasks.

Exhibit 1 Overview of the Management Process

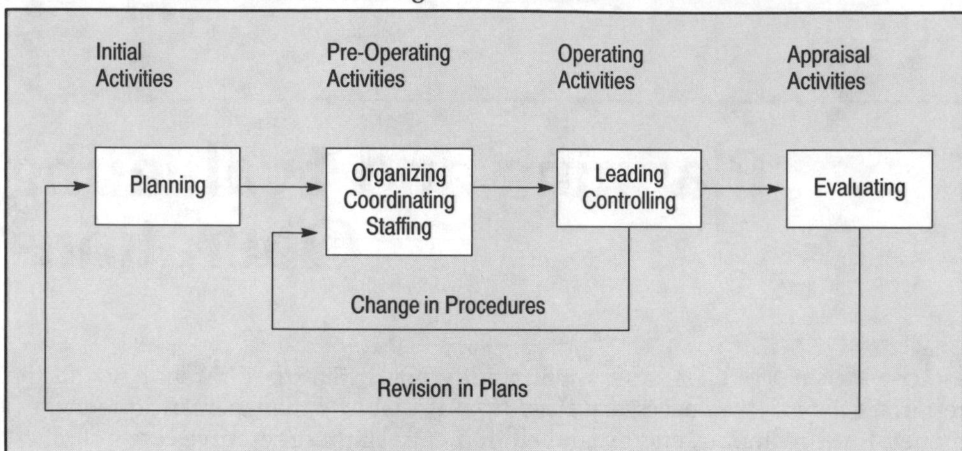

Coordinating

Coordinating involves bringing together and using the available resources to attain planned goals. A front office manager must be able to coordinate the efforts of many individuals to ensure that the work is performed efficiently, effectively, and on time. A manager's ability to coordinate is closely related to his or her other management skills, such as planning and organizing.

Staffing

Staffing involves recruiting applicants and selecting those best qualified for positions. Staffing also involves scheduling employees. Most front office managers develop staffing guidelines. These guidelines are usually based on formulas for calculating the number of employees required to meet guest and operational needs under specified conditions.

Leading

Leading is a complicated management skill that is exercised in a wide variety of situations, and is closely related to other management skills such as organizing, coordinating, and staffing. For a front office manager, leadership involves overseeing, motivating, training, disciplining, and setting an example for the front office staff. For example, to direct the work of others, a front office manager must first analyze the work to be done, organize the tasks in a logical order, and consider the environment in which the tasks will be performed. In addition, if the department is behind in getting the work done, the front office manager steps into the situation and assists until the workload is under control again.

Leading often extends beyond the front office. With so much of the hotel's business activity flowing through the front desk, other department heads count on the front office manager to provide leadership. Senior managers at a hotel often depend on the strong leadership skills of the front office manger to ensure that assignments are completed successfully.

Controlling

Every front office has a system of internal controls for protecting the assets of the hotel. However, internal control systems work only when managers believe in the systems' importance and follow the established procedures for their use. The control process ensures that the actual results of operations closely match planned results. The front office manager also exercises a control function when keeping front office operations on course in attaining planned goals.

Evaluating

Evaluating determines the extent to which planned goals are, in fact, attained. This task is frequently overlooked in many front office operations, or is performed haphazardly. Evaluating also involves reviewing and, when necessary, revising or helping to revise front office goals.

This chapter focuses on elements of two front office management functions: planning and evaluating front office operations. It begins by examining three important front office planning functions:

- Establishing room rates
- Forecasting room availability
- Budgeting for operations

It concludes by examining various methods by which a front office manager may evaluate the effectiveness of front office operations.

Establishing Room Rates

A front office will almost always have more than one room rate category for each of its guestrooms. Room rate categories generally correspond to types of rooms (suites, two beds, one bed, etc.) that are comparable in square footage and furnishings. Differences are based on criteria such as room size, location, view, furnishings, and amenities. Each room rate category is assigned a **rack** (standard or retail) **rate** based on the number of persons occupying the room. The rack rate is the standard price determined by front office management. The rack rate is listed on the room rate schedule to inform front desk agents of the selling price of each guestroom in the hotel. In a fully automated property, front office employees may be able to use a computer terminal to access rack rate data during the reservations or registration process. Often, rack rates must be reported to local and state authorities. Therefore, they must accurately reflect the appropriate accommodation charge for each room rate category.

Front office employees are expected to sell rooms at the rack rate unless a guest qualifies for an alternate room rate. Special rates are often quoted to groups and certain guests for promotional purposes during low occupancy periods. Special room rate categories include:

- *Corporate or commercial rate.* The rate offered to companies that provide frequent business for the hotel or its chain.
- *Group rate.* The rate offered to groups, meetings, and conventions using the hotel for their functions.
- *Promotional rate.* The rate offered to individuals who may belong to an affinity group such as American Automobile Association or American Association of Retired Persons to promote their patronage. The rate may also be extended during special low occupancy periods to any guest to promote occupancy.
- *Incentive rate.* The rate offered to guests in affiliated organizations such as travel agencies and airlines because of potential referral business. The rate may also be offered to promote future business; it is often extended to group leaders, meeting planners, tour operators, and others capable of providing the hotel with additional room sales.
- *Family rate.* A rate reserved for families with children.
- *Package plan rate.* A rate that includes a guestroom in combination with other events or activities.
- *Complimentary rate.* A room rate provided to special guests and/or important industry leaders.

The front office manager must be sure that the sale of rooms at special rates is rigidly controlled. Special rates represent discounts from the rack rate and therefore may adversely affect the average room rate and room revenue. The front office manager should examine the circumstances under which special rates are granted to ensure that front office staff are adhering to prescribed policies. All policies should be clearly explained to front office staff, who should obtain proper approval when applying a special room rate. For example, a complimentary room (provided at no charge) does not increase room revenue, but it may or may not decrease the average room rate, depending upon the front office accounting system. Most hotels require the general manager or other senior member of the management team to approve complimentary rates before guests arrive.

Establishing rack rates for room types and determining discount categories and special rates are major management decisions. To establish room rates that will ensure the hotel's profitability, management should carefully consider such factors as operating costs, inflationary factors, and competition.

Room rates often serve as a market positioning statement since they directly reflect service expectations to the hotel's target market. Room rate positioning can be critical to a hotel's success. For example, a property offering economy facilities and limited guest services will most likely not be successful if its rates are positioned in the mid-price or upscale levels.

The following sections examine three popular approaches to pricing rooms: the **market condition approach**, the **rule-of-thumb approach**, and the **Hubbart Formula.**

Market Condition Approach

This approach is the common sense approach. Management looks at comparable hotels in the geographical market and sees what they are charging for the same product. The thought behind this is that the hotel can charge only what the market will accept, and this is usually dictated by the competition.

There are many problems with this approach, although it is used very often. First, if the property is new, construction costs will most likely be higher than those of the competition. Therefore, the hotel cannot be as profitable as the competition initially. Second, this approach does not take the value of the property into consideration. With the property being new, and perhaps having newer amenities, the value of the property to guests can be greater. The market condition approach is really a marketing approach that allows the local market to determine the rate. It may not take fully into account what a strong sales effort may accomplish. It can, in effect, allow the competition to determine the rates and this could significantly affect the profitability of a hotel's operation.

Hotel's management must not determine the rates of other hotels through direct discussion with competitors. Such discussion would be considered a violation of U.S. anti-trust laws. Rates can be found in many public sources, such as global distribution systems, published rate brochures, directories from the American Automobile Association, and many others.

Rule-of-Thumb Approach

The rule-of-thumb approach sets the rate of a room at $1 for each $1,000 of construction and furnishings cost per room, assuming a 70 percent occupancy. For example, assume that the average construction cost of a hotel room is $80,000. Using the $1 per $1,000 approach results in an average selling price of $80 per room. Singles, doubles, suites, and other room types would be priced differently, but the minimum average room rate would be $80.

The emphasis placed on the hotel's construction cost fails to consider the effects of inflation. For example, a well-maintained hotel worth $100,000 per room today may have been constructed at $20,000 per room 40 years ago. The $1 per $1,000 approach would suggest an average selling price of $20 per room; however, a much higher rate would appear to be appropriate. The suggested rate of $20 per room does not take into account inflation and increased costs of labor, furnishings, and supplies. In these cases, management might consider the current replacement cost of the hotel, rather than its original construction and furnishings cost, as a basis for the rule-of-thumb application. Another way of accounting for inflation would be to index current costs against original costs. For example, if a hotel was built five years ago and inflation has increased at an annual rate of 3 percent, the $1 per $1,000 five years ago would require $1.16 per $1,000 today.

The rule-of-thumb approach to pricing rooms also fails to consider the contribution of other facilities and services toward the hotel's desired profitability. In many hotels, guests pay for services such as food, beverages, telephone, and laundry. If these services contribute to profitability, the hotel may have less pressure to charge higher room rates.

The rule-of-thumb approach should also consider the occupancy level of the hotel. As pointed out, the rule-of-thumb approach assumes 70 percent occupancy when determining the appropriate average room rate. However, if a lower occupancy percentage is expected, the hotel will have to capture a higher average rate to generate the same amount of room revenue. Hotels tend to have a very high level of fixed expenses (especially depreciation and mortgage expenses). For example, a mortgage payment is the same every month, regardless of the hotel's occupancy level. The front office manager must understand the effects of room rate and room occupancy on room revenue to ensure that the hotel meets its revenue goals and financial obligations.

Hubbart Formula Approach

A more recently developed approach to average room rate determination is the Hubbart Formula. To determine the average selling price per room, this approach considers operating costs, desired profits, and expected number of rooms sold. In other words, this approach starts with desired profit, adds income taxes, then adds fixed charges and management fees, followed by operating overhead expenses and direct operating expenses. The Hubbart Formula is considered a *bottom-up* approach to pricing rooms because its initial item—net income (profit)—appears at the bottom of the income statement. The second item—income taxes—is the next item from the bottom of the income statement, and so on. The Hubbart Formula approach involves the following eight steps:

1. Calculate the hotel's desired profit by multiplying the desired rate of return (ROI) by the owners' investment.
2. Calculate pretax profits by dividing desired profit (Step 1) by 1 minus the hotel's tax rate.
3. Calculate fixed charges and management fees. This calculation includes estimating depreciation, interest expense, property taxes, insurance, amortization, building mortgage, land, rent, and management fees.
4. Calculate undistributed operating expenses. This calculation includes estimating administrative and general, data processing, human resources, transportation, marketing, property operation and maintenance, and energy costs.
5. Estimate non-room operated department income or loss, that is, food and beverage department income or loss, telephone department income or loss, and so forth.
6. Calculate the required rooms department income. The sum of pretax profits (Step 2), fixed charges and management fees (Step 3), undistributed operating expenses (Step 4), and other operated department losses less other operated department income (Step 5) equals the required rooms department income. The Hubbart Formula, in essence, places the overall financial burden of the hotel on the rooms department.
7. Determine the rooms department revenue. The required rooms department income (Step 6), plus rooms department direct expenses of payroll and related

expenses, plus other direct operating expenses, equals the required rooms department revenue.

8. Calculate the average room rate by dividing rooms department revenue (Step 7) by the expected number of rooms to be sold.

Illustration of the Hubbart Formula. The Casa Vana Inn, a 200-room property, is projected to cost $9,900,000 inclusive of land, building, equipment, and furniture. An additional $100,000 is needed for working capital, bringing the total cost of construction and opening to $10,000,000. The hotel is financed with a loan of $7,500,000 at 12 percent annual interest and cash of $2,500,000 provided by the owners. The owners desire a 15 percent annual return on their investment. A 75 percent occupancy is estimated; thus, 54,750 rooms will be sold during the year (200 × .75 × 365). The income tax rate is 40 percent. Additional expenses are estimated as follows:

Property tax expenses	$250,000
Insurance expenses	50,000
Depreciation expenses	300,000
Administrative and general expenses	300,000
Data processing expenses	120,000
Human resources expenses	80,000
Transportation expenses	40,000
Marketing expenses	200,000
Property operation and maintenance expenses	200,000
Energy and related expenses	300,000

The other operated departments' income (losses) are estimated as follows:

Food and beverage department	$150,000
Telephone department	(50,000)
Rentals and other departments	100,000

The rooms department estimates direct operating expenses to be $10 per occupied room.

Exhibit 2 contains the calculations used in the Hubbart Formula and reveals an average room rate of $67.81.

Exhibit 3 contains the formula for calculating room rates for single rooms (x) and double rooms ($x + y$), where the price differential between single and double rates is represented by the variable y. Assume that the Casa Vana Inn has a double occupancy rate of 40 percent (that is, two out of every five rooms sold are sold at the double rate) and a room rate differential of $10. Applying the formula from Exhibit 3, single and double rates would be calculated as follows:

$$\text{Doubles Sold Daily} = \text{Doubles Occupancy Rate} \times \text{Number of Rooms} \times \text{Occupancy Percentage}$$

$$= .4(200)(.75)$$

$$= \underline{\underline{60}}$$

Exhibit 2 Calculating Average Room Rate: Hubbart Formula

Item	Calculation	Amount
Desired net income	Owners' Investment ROI $2,500,000 × .15 = $375,000	
	Pretax income $= \frac{\text{net income}}{1 - t}$	
	Pretax income $= \frac{\$375{,}000}{1 - .4}$	
	Pretax income =	$625,000
Plus: Interest expense	Principal × interest rate = interest expense $7,500,000 × .12 =	+ 900,000
Income needed before interest expense and taxes		1,525,000
Plus: Estimated depreciation, property taxes, and insurance		+ 600,000
Income before fixed charges		2,125,000
Plus: Undistributed operating expense		1,240,000
Required operated departments income		$3,365,000
Departmental results excluding rooms		
Less: Food and beverage department income		(150,000)
Rentals and other department income		(100,000)
Plus: Telephone department loss		50,000
Rooms department income		3,165,000
Plus: Rooms department direct expense	54,750 × $10 = $547,500	547,500
Rooms revenue		3,712,500
Number of rooms sold		÷ 54,750
Required average room rate		$ 67.81

Exhibit 3 Determining Single and Double Room Rates from an Average Room Rate

Singles sold (x) + Doubles Sold (x + y) = (Average Rate) (Rooms Sold)

where:

x	=	Price of singles
y	=	Price differential between singles and doubles
x + y	=	Price of doubles

$$\text{Singles Sold Daily} = \text{Rooms Sold Daily} - \text{Doubles Sold Daily}$$
$$= (200 \times .75) - 60$$
$$= \underline{\underline{90}}$$

Using the required average rate of $67.81 calculated in Exhibit 2, the required single and double rates can be determined as follows:

$$\text{Singles Sold } (x) + \left[\begin{array}{c}\text{Doubles Sold } \times \\ (x + \text{Rate Differential})\end{array}\right] = \begin{array}{c}\text{Average} \\ \text{Room Rate}\end{array} \times \begin{array}{c}\text{Daily Number} \\ \text{of Rooms Sold}\end{array}$$

$$\begin{aligned}
90x + 60(x + \$10) &= (\$67.81)(150) \\
90x + 60x + \$600 &= \$10{,}171.50 \\
150x &= \$9{,}571.50 \\
x &= \frac{\$9{,}571.50}{150} \\
x &= \$63.81 \\
\underline{\text{Single Rate}} &= \underline{\underline{\$63.81}} \\
\underline{\text{Double Rate}} &= \$63.81 + \$10.00 \\
&= \underline{\underline{\$73.81}}
\end{aligned}$$

Alternatively, the double rate could be set as a percentage of the single rate. When this is the case, the formula is slightly altered:

$$\text{Singles Sold } (x) + \left[\begin{array}{c}\text{Doubles Sold } (x) \times \\ (1 + \text{Percentage Differential})\end{array}\right] = \begin{array}{c}\text{Average} \\ \text{Room Rate}\end{array} \times \begin{array}{c}\text{Daily Number} \\ \text{of Rooms Sold}\end{array}$$

The percentage differential is simply the percentage difference of the double rate over the single rate. To illustrate this approach, we will call again on the Casa Vana Inn example. Assume a 40 percent double occupancy and a price differential of 15 percent.

$$\text{Singles Sold } (x) + \left[\begin{array}{c}\text{Doubles Sold } (x) \times \\ (1 + \text{Percentage Differential})\end{array}\right] = \begin{array}{c}\text{Average} \\ \text{Room Rate}\end{array} \times \begin{array}{c}\text{Daily Number} \\ \text{of Rooms Sold}\end{array}$$

$$\begin{aligned}
90x + 60(x)(1.15) &= (\$67.81)(150) \\
90x + 69x &= \$10{,}171.50 \\
159x &= \$10{,}171.50 \\
x &= \frac{\$10{,}171.50}{159} \\
x &= \$63.97 \\
\underline{\text{Single Rate}} &= \underline{\underline{\$63.97}} \\
\underline{\text{Double Rate}} &= \$63.97(1.15) \\
&= \underline{\underline{\$73.57}}
\end{aligned}$$

The Hubbart Formula is most useful in setting *target* average prices as opposed to *actual* average prices. It is important to note that the Hubbart Formula generates an average room rate as a target price at the hotel's point of profitability. It relies on management's best estimates of total rooms occupied and the single/double occupancy mix to determine target rates. If these estimates are incorrect, the targets will be incorrect.

Suppose a hotel company is planning to build a new property. Using the Hubbart Formula, management computes an average target room rate of $75. Knowing the current average rate for competing hotels in the area is only $50, management ponders whether the proposed hotel, opening in two years, has too high a targeted room rate.

To evaluate its potential, management assumes the competitor's average price will increase at five percent per year to $55.13 (that is, $50 × 1.05 × 1.05). Since the proposed hotel would be new, management reasons that a price premium may be acceptable. A difference of nearly $20, however, appears to be too great. A more reasonable average room rate might be $65; after three years of successive five percent price increases, the hotel's daily average room rate would be increased to just over $75 as follows:

	Annual increase at 5%	Selling Price
Initial room rate (new hotel)		$65.00
At the end of year 1	$3.25	$68.25
At the end of year 2	$3.41	$71.66
At the end of year 3	$3.58	$75.24

Considering this situation, hotel developers will have to finance the additional deficit in the first year ($75 for the targeted average rate versus $65 expected average rate when the hotel opens). In order to operate, the hotel will need to devise some method of financing the shortfall. As stated before, most hotels do not generate profits during the first few years of operation. In this respect, operating deficits should always be included in the hotel's financing plan.

Forecasting Room Availability

The most important short-term planning performed by front office managers is **forecasting** the number of rooms available for sale on any future date. *Room availability forecasts* are used to help manage the reservations process and to guide front office staff in effective rooms management. Forecasting may be especially important on nights when a full house (100 percent occupancy) is possible.

A room availability forecast can also be used as an *occupancy forecast*. Since there is a fixed number of rooms in the hotel, forecasting the number of rooms available for sale and the number of rooms expected to be occupied forecasts the occupancy percentage expected on a given date. The forecasted availability and occupancy numbers are very important to the daily operations of the hotel. Room occupancy forecasts can be useful to the front office manager attempting to schedule the necessary number of employees for an expected volume of business. These forecasts may be helpful to other hotel department managers as well. For example, the housekeeping department needs to know how many rooms are expected to be occupied to properly schedule room attendants. Restaurant managers need to know the same information to better schedule service staff. The chef needs this figure to determine how much food to order for the restaurants.

Obviously, a forecast is only as reliable as the information on which it is based. Since forecasts can serve as a guide in determining operating costs, every effort should be made to ensure forecasting accuracy.

Forecasting is a difficult skill to develop. The skill is acquired through experience, effective recordkeeping, and accurate counting methods. Experienced front office managers have found that several types of information can be helpful in room availability forecasting:

- A thorough knowledge of the hotel and its surrounding area
- Market profiles of the constituencies the hotel services
- Occupancy data for the past several months and for the same period of the previous year
- Reservation trends and a history of reservation lead times (how far in advance reservations are made)
- A listing of special events scheduled in the surrounding geographic area
- Business profiles of specific groups booked for the forecast dates
- The number of non-guaranteed and guaranteed reservations and an estimate of the number of expected no-shows
- The percentage of rooms already reserved and the cut-off date for room blocks held for the forecast dates
- The impact of city-wide or multi-hotel groups and their potential influence on the forecast dates
- Plans for remodeling or renovating the hotel that would change the number of available rooms
- Construction or renovating plans for competitive hotels in the area

Forecasting Data

The process of forecasting room availability generally relies on historical occupancy data. To facilitate forecasting, the following daily occupancy data should be collected:

- Number of expected room arrivals
- Number of expected room walk-ins
- Number of expected room stayovers (rooms occupied on previous nights that will continue to be occupied for the night in question)

- Number of expected room no-shows
- Number of expected room understays (check-outs occurring before expected departure date)
- Number of expected room check-outs
- Number of expected room overstays (check-outs occurring after the expected departure date)

Some hotels with a very high double occupancy percentage may be as concerned with guest counts as room counts. For example, an all-inclusive resort with a large amount of business from vacationing couples may want to forecast guest as well as room count activity. Convention hotels may often have the same concerns.

Overall, these data are important to room availability forecasting since they are used in calculating various daily operating ratios that help determine the number of available rooms for sale. Ratios are a mathematical expression of a relationship between two numbers that results from dividing one by the other. Most statistical ratios that apply to front office operations are expressed as percentages. The ratios examined in the following sections are percentages of no-shows, walk-ins, understays, and overstays. Occupancy history data from the fictitious property shown in Exhibit 4 (the Holly Hotel) are used to illustrate the calculation for each front office ratio. Managers should look for consistency in ratios. Consistency may be roughly the same ratio every day or identifiable patterns. Without consistency, forecasting ratios and operations performance will be very difficult.

Percentage of No-Shows. The percentage of no-shows indicates the proportion of reserved rooms that the expected guests did not arrive to occupy on the expected arrival date. This ratio helps the front office manager decide when (and if) to sell rooms to walk-in guests.

The percentage of no-shows is calculated by dividing the number of room no-shows for a specific period of time (day, week, month, or year) by the total number of room reservations for the same period. Using figures from Exhibit 4, the percentage of no-shows for the Holly Hotel during the first week of March can be calculated as follows:

$$\text{Percentage of No-Shows} = \frac{\text{Number of Room No-Shows}}{\text{Number of Room Reservations}}$$

$$= \frac{52}{288}$$

$$= .1806 \text{ or } \underline{\underline{18.06\%}} \text{ of Reserved Rooms}$$

Some properties track no-show statistics in relation to guaranteed and non-guaranteed reservations. Non-guaranteed reservations typically have a higher no-show percentage than guaranteed reservations since the potential guest has no obligation to pay if he or she does not register. Properly forecasting no-show rooms also depends on the hotel's mix of business; for example, corporate groups

Exhibit 4 Occupancy History of the Holly Hotel

Occupancy History
First Week of March

Day	Date	Guests	Room Arrivals	Room Walk-Ins	Room Reservations	Room No-Shows
Mon	3/1	118	70	13	63	6
Tues	3/2	145	55	15	48	8
Wed	3/3	176	68	16	56	4
Thurs	3/4	117	53	22	48	17
Fri	3/5	75	35	8	35	8
Sat	3/6	86	28	6	26	4
Sun	3/7	49	17	10	12	5
Totals		766	326	90	288	52

Occupied Rooms	Overstay Rooms	Understay Rooms	Room Check-Outs
90	6	0	30
115	10	3	30
120	12	6	63
95	3	18	78
50	7	0	80
58	6	3	20
30	3	3	45
558	47	33	346

generally have a much lower no-show percentage than other types of group or individual business. A hotel with a large corporate meetings market will most likely have a very low no-show percentage. Conversely, a hotel that does little group business may tend to have a higher no-show percentage overall (except on those occasions when a corporate group stays at the property). Hotels and resorts can control no-shows through a number of policies and procedures, such as requiring a deposit in advance and calling the guest before arrival to confirm arrangements.

Percentage of Walk-Ins. The percentage of walk-ins is calculated by dividing the number of rooms occupied by walk-ins for a period by the total number of room arrivals for the same period. Using figures from Exhibit 4, the percentage of walk-ins for the Holly Hotel during the first week of March can be calculated as follows:

$$\text{Percentage of Walk-Ins} = \frac{\text{Number of Room Walk-Ins}}{\text{Total Number of Room Arrivals}}$$

$$= \frac{90}{326}$$

$$= .2761 \text{ or } \underline{\underline{27.61\%}} \text{ of Room Arrivals}$$

Walk-in guests occupy available rooms that are not held for guests with reservations. Often, hotels can sell rooms to walk-in guests at a higher rate since these guests may have less opportunity to consider alternate properties. Front desk agents are often asked to show a guestroom to a walk-in guest—which is much more effective than trying to sell rooms over the telephone. Walk-in guest sales help improve both occupancy and room revenues. However, from a planning perspective, it is always considered better to have reservations in advance than to count on walk-in traffic.

It should be noted that the walk-in ratio can be dramatically affected by the other ratios. For example, if a hotel has ten no-shows beyond forecast, it may accept more walk-ins than usual to make up for the lost business. When this information is tracked for historical purposes, it is essential that the other ratios also be tracked to show how they affect one another.

Percentage of Overstays. Overstays represent rooms occupied by guests who stay beyond their originally scheduled departure dates. Overstay guests may have arrived with guaranteed or non-guaranteed reservations or as walk-ins. Overstays should not be confused with **stayovers.** Stayover rooms are rooms occupied by guests who arrived to occupy a room before the day in question and whose *scheduled* departure date isn't until after the day in question.

The percentage of overstays is calculated by dividing the number of overstay rooms for a period by the total number of *expected* room check-outs for the same period. The number of expected room check-outs equals the number of actual check-outs on the books minus understays plus overstays. Stated another way, the number of expected room check-outs is the number of rooms shown by the front office computer or the manual count of occupied rooms as due for departure. Using figures from Exhibit 4, the percentage of overstays for the Holly Hotel during the first week of March can be calculated as follows:

$$\text{Percentage of Overstays} = \frac{\text{Number of Overstay Rooms}}{\text{Number of Expected Check-Outs}}$$

$$= \frac{47}{346 - 33 + 47}$$

$$= .1306 \text{ or } \underline{\underline{13.06}}\% \text{ of Expected Check-Outs}$$

To help regulate room overstays, front office agents are trained to verify an arriving guest's departure date at check-in. Such verification can be critical, especially when the hotel is at or near full occupancy and there are no provisions for overstay guests. Overstays may also prove problematic when specific rooms have been blocked for arriving guests. This is especially important for suites or other rooms that may have special importance to an incoming guest.

Percentage of Understays. Understays represent rooms occupied by guests who check out before their scheduled departure dates. Understay guests may have arrived at the hotel with guaranteed or non-guaranteed reservations or as walk-ins.

The percentage of understays is calculated by dividing the number of understay rooms for a period by the total number of expected room check-outs for the same period. Using figures from Exhibit 4, the percentage of understays for the Holly Hotel during the first week of March can be calculated as follows:

$$\text{Percentage of Understays} = \frac{\text{Number of Understay Rooms}}{\text{Number of Expected Check-Outs}}$$

$$= \frac{33}{346 - 33 + 47}$$

$$= .0917 \text{ or } \underline{\underline{9.17\%}} \text{ of Expected Check-Outs}$$

Guests leaving before their stated departure date create empty rooms that typically are difficult to fill. Thus, understay rooms tend to represent permanently lost room revenue. Overstays, on the other hand, are guests staying beyond their stated departure date and may not harm room revenues. When the hotel is not operating at full capacity, overstays result in additional, unexpected room revenues. In an attempt to regulate understay and overstay rooms, front office staff should:

- Confirm or reconfirm each guest's departure date at registration. Some guests may already know of a change in plans, or a mistake may have been made in the original processing of the reservation. The earlier erroneous data are corrected, the greater the chance for improved planning.
- Present an alternate guestroom reservation card to a registered guest explaining that an arriving guest holds a reservation for his or her room. A card may be placed in the guest's room the day before or the morning of the scheduled day of the registered guest's departure.
- Review group history. Many groups, especially associations, hold large closing events for the entire group on the last day of the meeting. Reservations may be made by guests to include attending the event. However, changes in plans or other priorities may require guests to leave early. While it is difficult for the hotel to hold guests to the number of nights they reserved, managers can plan for an early departure, based on the group's history.
- Contact potential overstay guests about their scheduled departure date to confirm their intention to check out. Room occupancy data should be examined each day; rooms with guests expected to check out should be flagged. Guests who have not left by check-out time should be contacted and asked about their departure intentions. This procedure permits an early revised count of overstays and allows sufficient time to modify previous front office planning, if necessary.

Forecast Formula

Once relevant occupancy statistics have been gathered, the number of rooms available for sale on any given date can be determined by the following formula:

	Total Number of Guestrooms
–	Number of Out-of-Order Rooms
–	Number of Room Stayovers
–	Number of Room Reservations
+	Number of Room Reservations × Percentage of No-Shows
+	Number of Room Understays
–	Number of Room Overstays
	Number of Rooms Available for Sale

Note that the above formula does not include walk-ins. They are not included because the number of walk-ins a hotel can accept is determined by the number of rooms available for sale. If a hotel is full due to existing reservations, stayovers, and other factors, it cannot accept walk-ins.

As an example, consider the Holly Hotel, a 120-room property, where on April 1 there are three out-of-order rooms and 55 stayovers. On that day, there are 42 guests with reservations scheduled to arrive. Since the percentage of no-shows has been recently calculated at 18.06 percent, the front office manager calculates that as many as eight guests with reservations may not arrive (42 × .1806 = 7.59, rounded to eight). Based on historical data, six understays and fifteen overstays are also expected. The number of rooms projected to be available for sale on April 1 can be determined as follows:

	Total Number of Guestrooms	120
–	Number of Out-of-Order Rooms	– 3
–	Number of Room Stayovers	– 55
–	Number of Room Reservations	– 42
+	Number of Room Reservations × No-Show Percentage	+ 8
+	Number of Room Understays	+ 6
–	Number of Room Overstays	– 15
	Number of Rooms Available for Sale	19

Therefore, the Holly Hotel is considered to have 19 rooms available for sale on April 1. Once this figure is determined, front office management can decide whether or not to accept more reservations and can determine its level of staffing. Front office planning decisions must remain flexible; they are subject to change as the front office learns of reservation cancellations and modifications. It should also be noted that room availability forecasts are based on assumptions whose validity may vary on any given day.

Sample Forecast Forms

The front office may prepare several different forecasts depending on its needs. Occupancy forecasts are typically developed on a monthly basis and reviewed by food and beverage and rooms division management to forecast revenues, project expenses, and develop labor schedules. A ten-day forecast, for example, may be used to update labor scheduling and cost projections and may later be supplemented by a more current three-day forecast. Together, these forecasts help many hotel departments maintain appropriate staff levels for expected business volumes and thereby help contain costs.

Ten-Day Forecast. The ten-day forecast at most lodging properties is developed jointly by the front office manager and the reservations manager, possibly in conjunction with a forecast committee. A ten-day forecast usually consists of:

- Daily forecasted occupancy figures, including room arrivals, room departures, rooms sold, and number of guests
- The number of group commitments, with a listing of each group's name, arrival and departure dates, number of rooms reserved, number of guests, and perhaps quoted room rates
- A comparison of the previous period's forecasted and actual room counts and occupancy percentages

A special ten-day forecast may also be prepared for food and beverage, banquet, and catering operations. This forecast usually includes the expected number of guests, which is often referred to as the **house count.** Sometimes the house count is divided into group and non-group categories so that the hotel's dining room managers can better understand the nature of their business and their staffing needs.

To help various hotel departments plan their staffing and payroll levels for the upcoming period, the ten-day forecast should be completed and distributed to all department offices by mid-week for the coming period. This forecast can be especially helpful to the housekeeping department. A ten-day forecast form, as shown in Exhibit 5, is typically developed from data collected through several front office sources. (The occupancy multiplier mentioned in section 10 is discussed later in this chapter.)

First, the current number of occupied rooms is reviewed. The estimated number of overstays and expected departures are noted. Next, relevant reservation information is evaluated for each room (and guest) by date of arrival, length of stay, and date of departure. These counts are then reconciled with reservation control data. Then, the actual counts are adjusted to reflect the projected percentage of no-shows, anticipated understays, and expected walk-ins. These projections are based on the hotel's recent history, the seasonality of its business, and the known history of specific groups scheduled to arrive. Finally, conventions and other groups are listed on the forecast to alert various department managers to possible periods of heavy, or light, check-ins and check-outs. The number of rooms assigned each day to each group may also be noted on the sheet.

Most computer systems provide the data on the books in a report format for the front office manager to use. However, most computer systems do not "forecast" business. Programming to successfully analyze historical trends and market conditions has been tried in the past with little success. Therefore, while the computer system can assist in forecasting, it is the knowledge and skill of the front office manager that determines how accurate the forecast is.

Exhibit 5 Sample Ten-Day Forecast Form

Ten-Day Occupancy Forecast

Location ________________ # ____________________ Week Ending ____________

Date Prepared: ______________________ Prepared By: ________________________

To be submitted to all department heads at least one week before the first day listed on forecast.

1. Date and Day (start week and end week the same as the payroll schedule)	Fri.	Sat.	Sun.	Mon.	Tues.	Wed.	Thur.	Fri.	Sat.	Sun.
2. Estimated Departures										
3. Reservation Arrivals—Group (taken from log book)										
4. Reservation Arrivals—Individual (taken from log book)										
5. Future Reservations (estimated reservations received after forecast is completed)										
6. Expected Walk-ins (% of walk-ins based on reservations received and actual occupancy for past two weeks)										
7. Total Arrivals										
8. Stayovers										
9. TOTAL FORECASTED ROOMS										
10. Occupancy Multiplier (based on number of guests per occupied room for average of the same day for last three weeks)										
11. FORECASTED NUMBER OF GUESTS										
12. Actual Rooms Occupied (taken from daily report for actual date to be completed by front office supervisor)										
13. Forecasted Variance (difference between forecast and rooms occupied on daily report)										

14. Explanation (to be completed by front office supervisor and submitted to general manager; attach additional memo if necessary)

APPROVED: __________________________ DATE: ______________________

General Manager's Signature

Three-Day Forecast. A three-day forecast is an updated report that reflects a more current estimate of room availability. It details any significant changes from the ten-day forecast. The three-day forecast is intended to guide management in fine-tuning

Exhibit 6 Sample Three-Day Forecast Form

Three-Day Forecast

Date of Forecast: ____________________ Forecast Completed By: ____________________

Total Rooms in Hotel: ____________________

	Tonight	Tomorrow	3rd Night
Day			
Date			

Previous Night Occupied Rooms[1]			
− Expected Departures			
− Early Departures			
+ Unexpected Stayovers			
+ Unoccupied Rooms[2]			
= Rooms Available For Sale			
+ Expected Arrivals			
+ Walk-ins & Same Day Reservations			
− No-Shows			
= Occupied Rooms			
= Occupancy %			
= Expected House Count[3]			

1 Previous night occupied rooms is determined from either the actual number of rooms occupied last night or the forecasted number of rooms from the previous night.
2 Unoccupied rooms equals the total number of rooms in the hotel less the number of rooms occupied.
3 Expected house count equals the forecasted occupied rooms times the multiple occupancy percentage for the day (found on the computer report).

Distribution: General Manager, Front Desk, Housekeeping, All Food and Beverage, Accounting, Sales, Banquets, Security

labor schedules and adjusting room availability information. Exhibit 6 presents a sample three-day forecast form.

Room Count Considerations. Control books, charts, computer applications, projections, ratios, and formulas can be essential in short- and long-range room count planning. Each day, the front office performs several physical counts of rooms occupied, vacant, reserved, and due to check out, to complete the occupancy statistics for that day. A computerized system may reduce the need for most final counts, since the computer can be programmed to continually update room availability information.

It is important for front desk agents to know *exactly* how many rooms are available, especially if the hotel expects to operate near 100 percent occupancy. Once procedures for gathering room count information are established, planning procedures can be extended to longer periods of time to form a more reliable basis for revenue, expense, and labor forecasting. The checklist in Exhibit 7 may be applicable to non-automated and semi-automated operations alike.

Budgeting for Operations

The most important long-term planning function performed by front office managers is budgeting front office operations. The hotel's annual operations budget is a profit plan that addresses all revenue sources and expense items. Annual budgets are commonly divided into monthly plans which, in turn, are divided into weekly (and sometimes daily) plans. These budget plans become standards against which management can evaluate the actual results of operations. In most hotels, room revenues are greater than food, beverage, banquets, or any other source of revenue. In addition, rooms division profits are usually greater than those of any other department. Therefore, an accurate rooms budget is vital to creating the overall budget of the hotel.

The budget planning process requires the closely coordinated efforts of all management personnel. While the front office manager is responsible for rooms revenue forecasts, the hotel accounting division will be counted on to supply department managers with statistical information essential to the budget preparation process. The hotel accounting division is also responsible for coordinating the budget plans of individual department managers into a comprehensive property-wide operations budget for top management's review. The hotel general manager and controller typically review departmental budget plans and prepare a budget report for approval by the hotel's owners. If the budget is not satisfactory, elements requiring change may be returned to the appropriate division managers for review and revision.

The primary responsibilities of the front office manager in budget planning are forecasting rooms revenue and estimating related expenses. Rooms revenue is forecasted with input from the reservations manager while expenses are estimated with input from all department managers in the rooms division.

Forecasting Rooms Revenue

Historical financial information often serves as the foundation on which front office managers build rooms revenue forecasts. One method of rooms revenue forecasting involves an analysis of rooms revenue from past periods. Dollar and percentage differences are noted and the amount of rooms revenue for the budget year is predicted.

Exhibit 7 Sample Daily Checklist for Accurate Room Counts

- Make counts of the rack and reservations. On tight days, a count should be made at 7:00 A.M., noon, 3:00 P.M., and 6:00 P.M. On normal days, a 7:00 A.M. and 6:00 P.M. count will suffice.
- Check room rack against the folio bucket to catch sleepers and skippers.
- Check housekeeping reports against the room rack to catch sleepers and skippers.
- Check for rooms that are due out, but still have balances on their folios, especially where credit cards are the indicated source of payment.
- Check reservations for any duplications.
- Call the reservations system to make sure all cancellations were transmitted.
- Check the switchboard, telephone rack, and/or alphabetical room rack to make sure that the guest is not already registered.
- Call the local airport for a report on canceled flights.
- Check the weather reports for cities from which a number of guests are expected.
- Check reservations against convention blocks to catch duplications.
- Check with other hotels for duplicate reservations if a housing or convention bureau indicated the reservation was a second choice.
- Check arrival dates on all reservation forms to be sure none were misfiled.
- Check the rooms cancellation list.
- If a reservation was made through the reservations manager, sales manager, or someone in the executive office and the property is close to full, call that staff person. Often, such guests are personal friends and are willing to help out by staying somewhere else.
- Close to the property's cut-off time, consider placing a person-to-person phone call to any guest with a nonguaranteed reservation who hasn't arrived. If the person accepts the call, confirm whether or not he or she will arrive yet that night.
- After the property's cut-off time, if it becomes necessary, pull any reservations that were not guaranteed or prepaid.
- If any rooms are out-of-order or not presently in use, check to see if they can be made up. Let housekeeping know when a tight day is expected, so that all possible rooms are made up.
- Before leaving work, convey in writing all pertinent information to the oncoming staff. Good communication is essential.

For example, Exhibit 8 shows yearly increases in net rooms revenue for the Emily Hotel. For the years 19X1 to 19X4, the amount of rooms revenue increased from $1,000,000 to $1,331,000, reflecting a 10 percent yearly increase. If future

Exhibit 8 Rooms Revenue Summary for the Emily Hotel

Year	Rooms Revenue	Increase Over Dollar	Prior Year Percentage
19X1	$1,000,000	—	—
19X2	1,100,000	$100,000	10%
19X3	1,210,000	110,000	10%
19X4	1,331,000	121,000	10%

Exhibit 9 Rooms Revenue Statistics for the Bradley Hotel

Year	Rooms Sold	Average Daily Rate	Net Rooms Revenue	Occupancy Percentage
19X1	30,660	$50	$1,533,000	70%
19X2	31,974	52	1,662,648	73%
19X3	32,412	54	1,750,248	74%
19X4	32,850	57	1,872,450	75%

conditions appear to be similar to those of the past, the rooms revenue for 19X5 would be budgeted at $1,464,100—a 10 percent increase over the 19X4 amount.

Another approach to forecasting rooms revenue bases the revenue projection on past room sales and average daily room rates. Exhibit 9 presents rooms revenue statistics for the 120-room Bradley Hotel from 19X1 to 19X4. An analysis of these statistics shows that occupancy percentage increased three percentage points from 19X1 to 19X2, one percentage point from 19X2 to 19X3, and one percentage point from 19X3 to 19X4. Average daily room rates increased by $2, $2, and $3 respectively over the same periods. If future conditions are assumed to be similar to those of the past, a rooms revenue forecast for 19X5 may be based on a one percent increase in occupancy percentage (to 76 percent) and a $3 increase in the average daily room rate (to $60). Given these projections, the following formula can be used to forecast rooms revenue for the year 19X5 for the Bradley Hotel:

$$\text{Forecasted Rooms Revenue} = \text{Rooms Available} \times \text{Occupancy Percentage} \times \text{Average Daily Rate}$$

$$= 43{,}800 \times .76 \times \$60$$

$$= \underline{\underline{\$1{,}997{,}280}}$$

The number of rooms available is calculated by multiplying the 120 rooms of the Bradley Hotel by the 365 days of the year. This calculation assumes that all the rooms will be available for sale each day of the year. This will probably not be the case, but it is a reasonable starting point for projection.

Exhibit 10 Expense Categories as Percentages of Rooms Revenue for Bradley Hotel

Year	Payroll and Related Expenses	Laundry Linen and Guest Supplies	Commissions and Reservation Expenses	Other Expenses
19X1	16.5%	2.6%	2.3%	4.2%
19X2	16.9%	2.8%	2.5%	4.5%
19X3	17.2%	3.0%	2.6%	4.5%
19X4	17.4%	3.1%	2.7%	4.6%

This simplified approach to forecasting rooms revenue is intended to illustrate the use of trend data in forecasting. A more detailed approach would consider the variety of different rates corresponding to room types, guest profiles, days of the week, and seasonality of business. These are just a few of the factors that may affect rooms revenue forecasting.

Estimating Expenses

Most expenses for front office operations are *direct expenses* in that they vary in direct proportion to rooms revenue. Historical data can be used to calculate an approximate percentage of rooms revenue that each expense item may represent. These percentage figures can then be applied to the total amount of forecasted rooms revenue, resulting in dollar estimates for each expense category for the budget year.

Typical rooms division expenses are payroll and related expenses; guestroom laundry (terry and linen); guest supplies (bath amenities, toilet tissue, matches); hotel merchandising (in-room guest directory and hotel brochures); travel agent commissions and reservation expenses; and other expenses. When these costs are totaled and divided by the number of occupied rooms, the cost per occupied room is determined. The cost per occupied room is often expressed in dollars and as a percentage. Exhibit 10 presents expense category statistics of the Bradley Hotel from 19X1 to 19X4, expressed as percentages of each year's rooms revenue. Based on this historical information and management's current objectives for the budget year 19X5, the percentage of rooms revenue for each expense category may be projected as follows: payroll and related expenses—17.6 percent; laundry, linen and terry, and guest supplies—3.2 percent; commissions and reservation expenses—2.8 percent; and other expenses—4.7 percent.

Using these percentage figures and the expected rooms revenue calculated previously, the Bradley Hotel's rooms division expenses for the budgeted year are estimated as follows:

- Payroll and related expenses
  $1,997,280 × .176 = $351,521.28
- Laundry, linen, terry, and guest supplies
  $1,997,280 × .032 = $ 63,912.96

- Commissions and reservation expenses
  $1,997,280 × .028 = $ 55,923.84
- Other expenses
  $1,997,280 × .047 = $ 93,872.16

In this example, management should question why costs continue to rise as a percentage of revenue. If costs continue to rise (as a percentage, not in real dollars), profitability will be reduced. Therefore, one of the outcomes of the budget process will be to identify where costs are rising as a percentage of revenue. Then, management can analyze why these costs are increasing disproportionately with revenue and develop a plan to control them.

Since most front office expenses vary proportionately with rooms revenue (and therefore occupancy), another method of estimating these expenses is to estimate variable costs per room sold and then multiply these costs by the number of rooms expected to be sold.

Refining Budget Plans

Departmental budget plans are commonly supported by detailed information gathered in the budget preparation process and recorded on worksheets and summary files. These documents should be saved to provide an explanation of the reasoning behind the decisions made while preparing departmental budget plans. Such records may help resolve issues that arise during the budget review. These support documents may also provide valuable assistance in the preparation of future budget plans.

If no historical data are available for budget planning, other sources of information can be used to develop a budget. For example, corporate headquarters can often supply comparable budget information to its chain-affiliated properties. Also, national accounting and consulting firms usually provide supplemental data for the budget development process.

Many hotels refine expected results of operations and revise operations budgets as they progress through the budget year. Reforecasting is normally suggested when actual operating results start to vary significantly from the operations budget. Such variance may indicate that conditions have changed since the budget was first prepared and that the budget should be brought into line.

Evaluating Front Office Operations

Evaluating the results of front office operations is an important management function. Without thoroughly evaluating the results of operations, managers will not know whether the front office is attaining planned goals. Successful front office managers evaluate the results of department activities on a daily, monthly, quarterly, and yearly basis. The following sections examine important tools that front office managers can use to evaluate the success of front office operations. These tools include:

- Daily operations report
- Occupancy ratios

- Rooms revenue analysis
- Hotel income statement
- Rooms division income statement
- Rooms division budget reports
- Operating ratios and ratio standards

Daily Operations Report

The **daily operations report,** also known as the *manager's report,* the *daily report,* and the *daily revenue report,* contains a summary of the hotel's financial activities during a 24-hour period. The daily operations report provides a means of reconciling cash, bank accounts, revenue, and accounts receivable. The report also serves as a posting reference for various accounting journals and provides important data that must be input to link front and back office computer functions. Daily operations reports are uniquely structured to meet the needs of individual hotel properties.

Exhibit 11 presents a sample daily operations report for a hotel with food and beverage service. Rooms statistics and occupancy ratios form an entire section of a typical daily operations report. Enriched by comments and observations from the accounting staff, statistics shown on the daily operations report may take on more meaning. For example, statistics about the number of guests using the hotel's valet parking services take on added significance when remarks indicate that valet sales are down while occupancy is up. The front office manager may assume that the front office staff is not properly promoting available guest valet parking services.

The information provided by the daily operations report is not restricted to the front office manager or hotel general manager. Copies of the daily operations report are generally distributed to all department and division managers in the hotel.

Occupancy Ratios

Occupancy ratios measure the success of the front office in selling the hotel's primary product: guestrooms. The following rooms statistics must be gathered to calculate basic occupancy ratios:

- Number of rooms available for sale
- Number of rooms sold
- Number of guests
- Number of guests per room
- Net rooms revenue

Generally, these data are contained on the daily operations report. Occupancy ratios that can be computed from these data include **occupancy percentage, average daily rate, revenue per available room (RevPAR), multiple** (or **double**) **occupancy ratio,** and **average rate per guest.** Computed occupancy percentage and

Exhibit 11 Sample Daily Operations Report

DAILY REVENUE REPORT

Day ______ Of ______ Day ______ Date ______ Year ______

Hotel ______________ Completed By ______________

OCCUPANCY SUMMARY	ACTUAL TODAY	%	MONTH TO-DATE	%
SGL Rooms Occupied				
DBL Rooms Occupied				
COMP Rooms Occupied				
TOTAL Rooms Occupied				
O.O.O. Rooms				
Vacant				
TOTAL Available Rooms		100%		100%
House Use				
TOTAL Hotel Rooms				
AVG House Rate (Inc Comps & Perms)	$		$	
AVG Trans Rate (Excl Comp & Perms)	$		$	
TOTAL # GUESTS				
Relocated				
Room Sales Efficiency				
TOTAL ROOMS OCCUPIED				
Forecast				
Budget				

REVENUE SUMMARY	TODAY	MTD	BUDGET MONTH END
Net Rooms			
Food			
Beverage			
Banquet Other			
Long Distance			
Local			
Laundry / Valet			
Garage			
Gift Shop			
Health Club			
Pro Shop (Merchandise)			
Golf Fees			
Tennis Fees			
TOTAL HOTEL			

ROOMS REVENUE ANALYSIS

Type	TODAY # Rooms	%	Ave. Rate	Revenue	MONTH-TO-DATE # Rooms	%	Ave. Rate	Revenue
Rack								
Corporate								
Guaranteed Corporate								
Preferred								
Weekend Rate								
Packages								
Government / Military								
Other								
Total Non Group								
Group								
Total Transient								
Permanents								
Complimentary								
Total		100%				100%		
Club Floor								
Club Express								
RSVP								
Breakations								

COMPLIMENTARY ROOMS

Guest Name	Room No	Company	Check In Date	Check Out Date	Authorized By

REORDER FROM STANDARD REGISTER FORMS SELECTOR R0750

PRINTED BY THE STANDARD REGISTER COMPANY U.S.A.

Exhibit 11 *(continued)*

FOOD & BEVERAGE ANALYSIS

		TODAY			MONTH-TO-DATE		
Outlet		Revenue	# Covers	Ave. Check	Revenue	# Covers	Ave. Check
Room Service	Food						
	Food						
	Food						
	Food						
	Food						
	Food						
	Food						
Banquet	Food						
	Total Food						
Room Service	Bev.						
	Bev.						
	Bev.						
	Bev.						
	Bev.						
	Bev.						
	Bev.						
	Bev.						
	Bev.						
Banquet	Bev.						
	Total Bev.						
Total Food & Bev.							
Room Rental							
Customer Sev. Inc.							
Miscellaneous							
Total Food & Bev. Dept.							

GROUP ANALYSIS

Group	# Rooms	# Guests	Avg. Rate	Revenue
TOTAL				

MARKET SEGMENTS MONTH-TO-DATE

Group	# Rooms	Avg. Rate	Revenue
National Assoc.			
Reg & State Assoc.			
Corporate			
Incentive			
SMERFE			
Tour & Travel			
Total Group			

ARRIVALS	YESTER-DAY	TODAY	ACTUAL MTD
6 PM Resv.			
Guaranteed Resv.			
Walk-ins			
Same Day Cancellations			
6 PM No Show			
Guaranteed No Show			
Relocated			
Total Actual Arrivals			

DEPARTURES	YESTER-DAY	TODAY	ACTUAL MTD
Expected			
Unexpected			
Stayovers			
Total Actual Departures			

Anticipated Occupancy Tonight ______ %

OUT OF ORDER ROOMS

Room No.	Reason	Number of Nights O.O.O.

average daily rate may also appear on a property's daily operations report. These ratios typically are calculated on a daily, weekly, monthly, and yearly basis.

The night auditor typically collects occupied rooms data and calculates occupancy ratios, while the front office manager analyzes the information to identify trends, patterns, or problems. When analyzing the information, the front office manager must consider how a particular condition may produce different effects on occupancy. For example, as multiple occupancy increases, the average daily room rate generally increases. This is because when a room is sold to more than one person, the room rate is usually greater than when the room is sold as a single. However, since the room rate for two people in a room is usually not twice the rate for one person, the average room rate *per guest* decreases.

The following sections examine how daily occupancy ratios are calculated for the Gregory Hotel. Room division data needed for the calculations are as follows:

- The Gregory Hotel has 120 rooms and a rack rate of \$98. (For simplicity, we will assume in this example that this rack rate is applicable to both singles and doubles.)
- Eighty-three rooms were sold at varying rates.
- Eighty-five rooms were occupied by guests. (Rooms sold does not equal rooms occupied by guests because, on this particular day, single guests occupied two rooms at a complimentary room rate, thereby generating no rooms revenue. Note that the handling of complimentary rooms may differ among hotel properties.)
- Ten rooms were occupied by two guests; therefore, a total of 95 guests were in occupancy.
- \$6,960 in rooms revenue were generated.

Occupancy Percentage. The most commonly used operating ratio in the front office is occupancy percentage. Occupancy percentage indicates the proportion of rooms either sold or occupied to number of rooms available during a specific period of time. It is important to note that some hotels use the number of rooms *sold* to calculate this percentage, while other hotels use the number of rooms *occupied* to calculate the number. Including complimentary rooms in the calculation can change certain operating statistics, such as average room rate. Using rooms sold, rooms occupied, or both is valid, depending upon the needs and history of the property. For purposes of this discussion, rooms occupied will be used to illustrate the occupancy percentage calculation.

Sometimes, out-of-order rooms may be included in the number of rooms available. At properties that evaluate management performance partly on the basis of occupancy percentage, including out-of-order rooms in the number of rooms available provides the manager with incentive to get those rooms fixed and recycled more quickly. Including all rooms in the property also provides a consistent base on which to measure occupancy. Conversely, not including out-of-order rooms may allow managers to artificially increase the calculated occupancy percentage simply by improperly classifying unsold rooms as out-of-order. Some properties do not include out-of-order rooms because the rooms are not actually available for sale. Also, to the extent that the occupancy percentage is used to evaluate the performance of front office staff having no control over out-of-order rooms, including those rooms may unfairly penalize staff. Regardless of the approach chosen, it should be used consistently.

The occupancy percentage for the Gregory Hotel is calculated as follows:

$$\text{Occupancy Percentage} = \frac{\text{Number of Rooms Occupied}}{\text{Number of Rooms Available}}$$

$$= \frac{85}{120}$$

$$= .708 \text{ or } \underline{\underline{70.8\%}}$$

Multiple Occupancy Ratios. The multiple occupancy ratio (frequently called the double occupancy ratio, although this phrasing may not always be accurate) is used to forecast food and beverage revenue, to indicate clean linen requirements, and to analyze average daily room rates. Multiple occupancy can be calculated by determining a **multiple occupancy percentage** or by determining the average number of guests per room sold or occupied (also called the *occupancy multiplier* or the *multiple occupancy factor).*

The multiple occupancy percentage for the Gregory Hotel is calculated as follows:

$$\text{Multiple Occupancy Percentage} = \frac{\text{Number of Rooms Occupied by More Than One Guest}}{\text{Number of Rooms Occupied}}$$

$$= \frac{10}{85}$$

$$= .118 \text{ or } \underline{\underline{11.8\%}}$$

The average number of guests per room sold for the Gregory Hotel is calculated as follows:

$$\text{Average Guests per Room Sold} = \frac{\text{Number of Guests}}{\text{Number of Rooms Sold}}$$

$$= \frac{95}{83}$$

$$= \underline{\underline{1.14}}$$

Average Daily Rate. Most front office managers calculate an average daily rate (ADR) even though room rates within a property vary significantly from single rooms to suites, from individual guests to groups and conventions, from weekdays to weekends, and from busy to slack seasons.

The average daily rate for the Gregory Hotel is calculated as follows:

$$\text{Average Daily Rate} = \frac{\text{Rooms Revenue}}{\text{Number of Rooms Sold}}$$

$$= \frac{\$6{,}960}{83}$$

$$= \underline{\underline{\$83.86}}$$

Some hotels include complimentary rooms in the denominator to show the true effect of complimentary rooms on the average daily rate. Sometimes this is called the *average house rate.*

Revenue per Available Room (RevPAR). RevPAR has become one of the most important statistics in recent years. RevPAR divides the total revenue generation of the hotel by the number of available rooms. It measures, in effect, the revenue generating capability of the hotel. Hotels with strong food, beverage, banquet, and recreational facilities have RevPAR well above the average daily rate. Hotels with fewer revenue centers have RevPAR numbers closer to the ADR.

The RevPAR for the Gregory Hotel is calculated as follows:

$$\text{RevPAR} = \frac{\text{Actual Room Revenue}}{\text{Number of Available Rooms}}$$

$$= \frac{\$6{,}960}{120}$$

$$= \underline{\underline{\$58}}$$

Average Rate per Guest. Resort hotels, in particular, are often interested in knowing the average room rate per guest (ARG). This rate is normally based on every guest in the hotel, including children.

The average rate per guest for the Gregory Hotel is calculated as follows:

$$\text{Average Rate per Guest} = \frac{\text{Rooms Revenue}}{\text{Number of Guests}}$$

$$= \frac{\$6{,}960}{95}$$

$$= \underline{\underline{\$73.26}}$$

Rooms Revenue Analysis

Front office staff are expected to sell rooms at the rack rate unless a guest qualifies for an alternate room rate. A **room rate variance report** lists those rooms that have been sold at other than their rack rates. With this report, front office management can review the use of various special rates to determine whether staff have followed all appropriate front office policies and procedures. In a hotel with a computerized front office system, the computer can be programmed to automatically prepare a room rate variance report.

One way for front office managers to evaluate the effectiveness of the front office staff in selling rooms is to look at the **yield statistic,** which is actual rooms revenue as a percentage of potential rooms revenue.

Yield Statistic. Potential rooms revenue is the amount of rooms revenue that can be generated if all the rooms in the hotel are sold at rack rate on a given day, week, month, or year. The ratio of actual to potential rooms revenue is known as the yield statistic. The potential revenue for the Gregory Hotel is $11,760 (all 120 rooms sold at the rack rate of $98). Given actual rooms revenue of $6,960, the yield statistic for the Gregory Hotel can be calculated as follows:

$$\text{Yield Statistic} = \frac{\text{Actual Rooms Revenue}}{\text{Potential Rooms Revenue}}$$

$$= \frac{\$6{,}960}{\$11{,}760}$$

$$= .5918 \text{ or } \underline{\underline{59.18\%}}$$

This result reveals that, for the day in question, actual rooms revenue was 59.18 percent of the amount that could have been generated if all 120 rooms had been sold at the full rack rate of $98.

Hotel Income Statement

The hotel's **income statement** provides important financial information about the results of hotel operations for a given period of time. The period may be one month or longer, but should not exceed one business year. Since a statement of income reveals the amount of net income for a given period, it is one of the most important financial statements used by management to evaluate the overall success of operations. Although front office managers may not directly rely upon the hotel's statement of income, it is an important financial indicator of operational success and profitability. The hotel income statement relies in part on detailed front office information that is supplied through the rooms division income statement. The rooms division income statement is discussed in the next section.

The hotel's statement of income is often called a consolidated income statement because it presents a composite picture of all the hotel's financial operations. Rooms division information appears on the first line, under the category of operated departments. The amount of income generated by the rooms division is determined by subtracting payroll and related expenses and other expenses from the amount of net revenue produced by the rooms division over the period covered by the income statement. Payroll expenses charged to the rooms division may include those associated with the front office manager, front desk agents, reservations agents, housekeepers, and uniformed service staff. Since the rooms division is not

Exhibit 12 Sample Consolidated Statement of Income

Eatonwood Hotel
Summary Statement of Income
For the year ended 12/31/19XX

	Schedule	Net Revenue	Cost of Sales	Payroll & Related Expenses	Other Expenses	Income (Loss)
Operated Departments						
Rooms	1	$ 6,070,356		$ 1,068,383	$ 473,487	$ 4,528,486
Food	2	2,017,928	$ 733,057	617,705	168,794	498,372
Beverage	3	778,971	162,258	205,897	78,783	332,033
Telecommunications	4	213,744	167,298	31,421	17,309	-2,284
Rentals and Other Income	5	188,092				188,092
Total Operated Departments		9,269,091	1,062,613	1,923,406	738,373	5,544,699
Undistributed Operating Expenses						
Administrative and General	6			227,635	331,546	559,181
Marketing	7			116,001	422,295	538,296
Property Operation and Maintenance	8			204,569	163,880	368,449
Utility Costs	9				546,331	546,331
Total Undistributed Operating Expenses				548,205	1,464,052	2,012,257
Totals		$ 9,269,091	$ 1,062,613	$ 2,471,611	$2,202,425	
Income After Undistributed Operating Expenses						3,532,442
Rent, Property Taxes, and Insurance						641,029
Income Before Interest, Depreciation and Amortization, and Income Taxes						2,891,413
Interest Expense						461,347
Income Before Depreciation Amortization, and Income Taxes						2,430,066
Depreciation and Amortization						552,401
Gain on Sale of Property						1,574
Income Before Income Taxes						1,879,239
Income Taxes						469,810
Net Income						$ 1,409,429

a merchandising facility, there is no cost of sales to subtract from the net revenue amount.

Revenue generated by the rooms division is usually the largest single amount produced by revenue centers within a hotel. Based on the figures in Exhibit 12, the amount of income earned by the Eatonwood Hotel's rooms division during the year was $4,528,486—or 81.7 percent of the total operated department income of $5,544,699.

Rooms Division Income Statement

The hotel's statement of income shows only summary information. The separate departmental income statements prepared by each revenue center provide more

Exhibit 13 Sample Rooms Division Income Statement

Rooms—Schedule #1
Eatonwood Hotel
For the year ended 12/31/19XX

	Current Period
REVENUE	$6,124,991
ALLOWANCES	54,635
NET REVENUE	6,070,356
EXPENSES	
Salaries and Wages	855,919
Employee Benefits	212,464
Total Payroll and Related Expenses	1,068,383
Other Expenses	
Cable/Satellite Television	20,100
Commissions	66,775
Complimentary Guest Services	2,420
Contract Services	30,874
Guest Relocation	1,241
Guest Transportation	48,565
Laundry and Dry Cleaning	42,495
Linen	12,140
Operating Supplies	122,600
Reservations	40,908
Telecommunications	12,442
Training	7,122
Uniforms	60,705
Other	5,100
Total Other Expenses	473,487
TOTAL EXPENSES	1,541,870
DEPARTMENTAL INCOME (LOSS)	$4,528,486

detail. Departmental income statements are called schedules and are referenced on the hotel's statement of income.

Exhibit 12 references the rooms division schedule as *1*. The rooms division income statement appears in Exhibit 13. The figures shown in Exhibit 13 for the rooms division net revenue, payroll and related expenses, other expenses, and departmental income are the same amounts that appear for the rooms division under the category of operated departments in Exhibit 12.

The rooms division schedule is generally prepared by the hotel accounting division, not by the front office accounting staff. The figures are derived from several sources, as follows:

Rooms Division Entry	Source Documents
Salaries and wages	Time cards, payroll records
Employee benefits	Payroll records

Commissions . . . . Travel agency billings
Contract cleaning . . . . Supplier invoices
Guest transportation . . . . Invoices
Laundry and dry cleaning . . . . . . Housekeeping and outside laundry/ valet charges for employee uniforms
Linen . . . . Supplier invoices
Operating supplies . . . . Supplier invoices
Reservation expenses (if any) . . . . Reservation system invoices
Other operating expenses . . . . Supplier invoices (such as from equipment rentals, etc.)

(Reservation expenses are fees the hotel pays for central reservation services and reservations made through global distribution systems.)

By carefully reviewing the rooms division income statement, the front office manager may be able to develop action plans to improve the division's financial condition and services. For example, the income statement may indicate that telephone revenue is down due to the application of a long-distance surcharge. This analysis reveals that guests are making fewer telephone calls because the cost per call was increased by the surcharge. Therefore, even though the revenue *per call* may have increased, overall telephone revenues have decreased. In many hotels, there is a surcharge for direct dial long-distance telephone service by the hotel. Yet, there is no surcharge or a minimal charge to use a telephone credit card. Housekeeping provides another example. If a hotel increases the number of rooms a room attendant is assigned to clean per day from 14 to 15, it will likely need fewer attendants. This can produce savings in wages, benefits, and possibly cleaning supplies. Front office managers must note, however, that taking measures to reduce costs may reduce guest service.

Rooms Division Budget Reports

Generally, the hotel's accounting division also prepares monthly budget reports that compare actual revenue and expense figures with budgeted amounts. These reports can provide timely information for evaluating front office operations. Front office performance is often judged according to how favorably the rooms division's monthly income and expense figures compare with budgeted amounts.

A typical budget report format should include both monthly variances and year-to-date variances for all budget items. Front office managers are more likely to focus on the monthly variances since year-to-date variances merely represent the accumulation of monthly variances. Exhibit 14 presents a rooms division budget report for the Gregory Hotel for the month of January. This budget report does not yet contain year-to-date figures since January is the first month of the business year for this particular hotel.

It is important to note that Exhibit 14 presents both dollar and percentage variances. The dollar variances indicate the difference between actual results and budgeted amounts. Dollar variances are generally considered either favorable or unfavorable as follows:

Exhibit 14 Sample Monthly Rooms Division Budget Report

Gregory Hotel
Budget Report—Rooms Division
For January 19XX

	Actual	Budget	Variances $	Variances %
Revenue				
Room Sales	$156,240	$145,080	$11,160	7.69%
Allowances	437	300	(137)	(45.67)
Net Revenue	155,803	144,780	11,023	7.61
Expenses				
Salaries and Wages	20,826	18,821	(2,005)	(10.65)
Employee Benefits	4,015	5,791	1,776	30.67
Total Payroll and Related Expenses	24,841	24,612	(229)	(0.93)
Other Expenses				
Commissions	437	752	315	41.89
Contract Cleaning	921	873	(48)	(5.50)
Guest Transportation	1,750	1,200	(550)	(45.83)
Laundry and Dry Cleaning	1,218	975	(243)	(24.92)
Linen	1,906	1,875	(31)	(1.65)
Operating Supplies	1,937	1,348	(589)	(43.69)
Reservation Expenses	1,734	2,012	278	13.82
Uniforms	374	292	(82)	(28.08)
Other Operating Expenses	515	672	157	23.36
Total Other Expenses	10,792	9,999	(793)	(7.93)
Total Expenses	35,633	34,611	(1,022)	(2.95)
Departmental Income	$120,170	$110,169	$10,001	9.08%

	Favorable Variance	Unfavorable Variance
Revenue	Actual exceeds budget	Budget exceeds actual
Expenses	Budget exceeds actual	Actual exceeds budget

For example, the actual amount of salaries and wages for rooms division personnel in the month of January was $20,826, while the budgeted amount for salaries and wages was $18,821, resulting in an unfavorable variance of $2,005. This dollar variance is bracketed to indicate that it is unfavorable. However, if the revenue variance is very favorable, an unfavorable variance in expenses (such as in payroll) is not necessarily negative. The comparative variance may merely indicate the greater expense associated with serving more guests than were anticipated when the budget was created. One way to verify whether a variance is really unfavorable or favorable is to divide the actual rooms occupied for the period into the actual cost and budgeted cost. If the actual cost is at or below the budgeted cost per room, the variance is actually positive, even though there was more expense.

Percentage variances are determined by dividing the dollar variance by the budgeted amount. For example, the 7.61 percent variance for net revenue shown in Exhibit 14 is the result of dividing the dollar variance figure of $11,023 by the budgeted net revenue amount of $144,780.

The budget report shows both dollar and percentage variances because dollar variances alone or percentage variances alone may not indicate the significance of the variances reported. For example, dollar variances fail to show the magnitude of change from the budgeted base. The monthly budget report for the front office of a large hotel may show that actual net revenue varied from the budgeted amount by $1,000. This may seem to be a significant variance, but if the $1,000 variance is based on a budgeted amount of $500,000, it represents a percentage difference of only 0.2 percent. Most front office managers would not consider this a significant variance. However, if the budget amount for the period was $10,000, a $1,000 dollar variance would represent a percentage variance of 10 percent, a percentage variance most front office managers would consider significant.

Percentage variances alone can also be deceiving. For example, assume that the budgeted amount for an expense item is $10, and the actual expense was $12. The dollar variance of $2 represents a percentage variance of 20 percent. While this percentage difference appears significant, front office management's effort to investigate a $2 variance may not be productive.

The fact that actual results of front office operations differ from budgeted amounts on a budget report shouldn't be surprising. Any budgeting process, no matter how sophisticated, is unlikely to be perfect. Front office managers should not analyze every variance. Only significant variances require management analysis and action. The hotel general manager and controller can provide criteria by which the front office manager can determine which variances are significant.

Operating Ratios

Operating ratios assist managers in evaluating the success of front office operations. Exhibit 15 suggests more than 20 ratios that may be useful to managers in evaluating the success of front office operations.

Payroll and related expenses tends to be the largest single expense item for the rooms division as well as the largest for the entire hotel. For control purposes, labor costs are analyzed on a departmental basis. Dividing the payroll and related expenses of the rooms division by the division's net room revenue yields one of the most frequently analyzed areas of front office operations—labor cost.

Operating ratios should be compared against proper standards—budgeted percentages, for example. Any significant differences between actual and budgeted labor cost percentages must be carefully investigated, since payroll and related expenses represent the largest single expense category.

One method for analyzing payroll and related expenses involves a form similar to the one shown in Exhibit 16.Actual figures for the current and previous periods,

Exhibit 15 Useful Rooms Division Operating Ratios

	Net Revenue	Payroll and Related Expenses	Other Expenses	Departmental Income
% of total hotel revenue	X			
% of departmental revenue		X	X	X
% of departmental total expenses		X	X	
% of total hotel payroll and related expenses		X		
% change from prior period	X	X	X	X
% change from budget	X	X	X	X
per available room	X	X	X	X
per occupied room	X	X	X	X

as well as budgeted amounts, are itemized for comparative analysis. Any significant differences should be highlighted and explained in the remarks section. By conducting a payroll and related expenses analysis, the front office manager demonstrates to general management that he or she attends to the most important controllable expense in the rooms division. Careful attention to staffing as the number of rooms sold fluctuates can guarantee that the percentage of payroll and related expenses to total revenue remains relatively constant from month to month.

Ratio Standards

Operating ratios are meaningful only when compared against useful criteria such as:

- Planned ratio goals
- Corresponding historical ratios
- Industry averages

Ratios are best compared against planned ratio goals. For example, a front office manager may more effectively control labor and related expenses by projecting a goal for the current month's labor cost percentage that is slightly lower than the previous month's. The expectation of a lower labor cost percentage may reflect the front office manager's efforts to improve scheduling procedures and other factors related to the cost of labor. By comparing the actual labor cost percentage with

Exhibit 16 Sample Payroll Analysis Form

Front Office Payroll Analysis

Hotel:______________________________ Period Ending: ________________________

JOB CATEGORY	Amount Last Year	Amount This Year	Amount Budgeted
Front Office	________	________	________
PBX	________	________	________
Head Housekeeper	________	________	________
Asst. Housekeeper, Housekeeping Staff	________	________	________
"Housemen" & Porters	________	________	________
Linen Staff	________	________	________
Laundry Staff	________	________	________
Reservations Staff	________	________	________
Maintenance, Gardener, & Asst. Maintenance	________	________	________
Security, Life Guard, & Uniform Service Staff	________	________	________

	(Last Year)	(This Year)
Payroll and Related Expenses	________	________
Net Revenue	________	________
Labor Cost Percentage	________	________
STATISTICS		
Rooms Rented	________	________
Rooms Cleaned	________	________
Housekeepers Hours Paid	________	________
Number of Rooms Per Housekeeper	________	________
Cost Per Room (Housekeepers)	________	________

REMARKS:

____

____

the planned goal, the manager can measure the success of his or her efforts to control labor costs.

Industry averages may also provide a useful standard against which to compare operating ratios. These industry averages can be found in publications prepared by the national accounting firms and trade associations serving the hospitality industry.

Experienced front office managers realize that operating ratios are only indicators; they do not solve problems or necessarily reveal the source of a problem. At best, when ratios vary significantly from planned goals, previous results, or industry averages, they indicate that problems may exist. Considerably more analysis and investigation are usually necessary to determine appropriate corrective actions.

Summary

Resources available to front office managers include people, money, time, work methods, materials, energy, and equipment, each of which is in limited supply. The front office manager's job involves planning and evaluating the use of such limited resources in meeting the organization's objectives. The process of management can be divided into specific management functions: planning, organizing, coordinating, staffing, leading, and controlling. Although specific front office management tasks vary from hotel to hotel, fundamental management functions are similar in scope.

Planning is probably the most important management function. Without competent planning, productivity may be extremely low. Without the direction and focus planning provides, the front office manager may become overly involved with tasks that are unrelated to or inconsistent with accomplishing the hotel's objectives. Using the planned goals as a guide, a front office manager performs an organizing function when dividing the work among front office staff fairly. Organizing includes determining the order in which tasks are to be performed and when each group of tasks should be completed.

The management function of coordinating involves using resources to attain planned goals. A front office manager must be able to coordinate the efforts of many individuals who are all doing different sets of tasks at the same time. The management function of staffing involves recruiting and selecting applicants and scheduling employees. Staffing guidelines are usually based on formulas for calculating the number of employees required to meet guest and operational needs under specified conditions.

Leading is a complicated management skill that is exercised in a variety of situations and is related to other management skills. For a front office manager, leading involves overseeing, motivating, training, and disciplining employees and making decisions. Every hotel has a system of internal controls for protecting the assets of the business. The control process ensures that the actual results of operations closely match planned results. The management function of evaluating determines the extent to which planned goals are attained. Evaluating also involves reviewing and revising front office goals.

Three important front office planning functions are establishing room rates, forecasting room availability, and budgeting for operations. Hotels will normally have several different room rates. The rack rate is listed on the room rate schedule to inform front desk agents of the standard selling price of each guestroom in the hotel. Front office employees are expected to sell rooms at the rack rate unless a guest qualifies for an alternate room rate. Establishing rack rates for room types and determining discount categories and special rates are major management decisions. To set rates that will ensure the hotel's profitability, management should carefully consider such factors as cost, inflation, and competition.

The rule-of-thumb approach to setting room rates sets the rate at $1 for each $1,000 of construction and furnishings cost per room, assuming a 70 percent occupancy. The Hubbart Formula for determining the average price per room considers costs, desired profits, and expected number of rooms sold. The front office manager must understand the effects of rate and occupancy on room revenue to ensure that the hotel meets its revenue goals.

The most important short-term planning statistic is forecasting the number of rooms available for sale on any future date. Room availability forecasts are used to help manage the reservations process, to guide room sales efforts, and to plan staffing requirements. The process of forecasting room availability generally relies on historical occupancy data. Such statistics as the percentage of no-shows, walk-ins, overstays, and understays can be critical factors in effective forecasting.

The most important long-term planning function performed by front office managers is budgeting. The annual operations budget is a profit plan that addresses revenue sources and expense items and is divided into monthly plans which, in turn, are divided into weekly (and sometimes daily) plans. Budget plans become standards against which management can evaluate the operational results. The primary responsibilities of the front office manager in budget planning are forecasting rooms revenue and estimating related expenses. The process requires the front office manager and the accounting division to coordinate their efforts.

Evaluating the results of front office operations is an important management function. Important management tools used to evaluate front office operations include daily operations reports, occupancy ratios, rooms revenue analysis, the hotel income statement, the rooms division income statement, rooms division budget reports, and operating ratios and ratio standards.

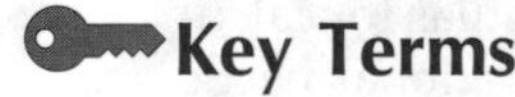

Key Terms

average daily rate—an occupancy ratio derived by dividing net rooms revenue by the number of rooms sold.

average rate per guest—an occupancy ratio derived by dividing net rooms revenue by the number of guests.

daily operations report—a report, typically prepared by the night auditor, that summarizes the hotel's financial activities during a 24-hour period and provides insight into revenues, receivables, operating statistics, and cash transactions related to the front office; also known as the manager's report.

forecasting—the process of predicting events and trends in business; typical forecasts developed for the rooms division include room availability and occupancy.

house count—the forecasted or expected number of guests for a particular period, sometimes broken down into group and non-group business.

Hubbart Formula—a bottom-up approach to pricing rooms; in determining the average price per room, this approach considers costs, desired profits, and expected rooms sold.

income statement—a financial statement that provides important information about the results of hotel operations for a given period of time.

market condition approach—an approach to pricing that bases prices on what comparable hotels in the geographical market are charging for a similar product.

multiple occupancy percentage—the number of rooms occupied by more than one guest divided by the number of rooms occupied by guests.

multiple occupancy ratio—a measurement used to forecast food and beverage revenue, to indicate clean linen requirements, and to analyze daily revenue rate; derived from multiple occupancy percentage or by determining the average number of guests per rooms sold; also called double occupancy ratio.

occupancy percentage—an occupancy ratio that indicates the proportion of rooms sold to rooms available for sale during a specific period of time.

occupancy ratios—a measurement of the success of the hotel in selling rooms; typical occupancy ratios include average daily rate, revenue per available room, average rate per guest, multiple occupancy statistics, and occupancy percentage.

operating ratios—a group of ratios that assist in the analysis of hospitality operations.

overstay—a guest who stays after his or her stated departure date.

rack rate—the standard rate established by the property for a particular category of rooms.

revenue per available room (RevPAR)—a revenue management measurement that focuses on revenue per available room.

room rate variance report—a report listing rooms that have not been sold at rack rates.

rule-of-thumb approach—a cost approach to pricing rooms; using this approach, the room rate is set at $1 for each $1,000 of construction and furnishings cost per room, assuming an occupancy of 70 percent.

stayover—a room status term indicating that the guest is not checking out today and will remain at least one more night; a guest who continues to occupy a room from the time of arrival to the stated date of departure.

understay—a guest who checks out before his or her stated departure date.

yield statistic—the ratio of actual rooms revenue to potential rooms revenue.

Review Questions

1. How do the seven functions of management fit into the overall management process? How do these functions apply to the front office manager's position?
2. What kinds of special room rates might a hotel offer? What are the three common methods of establishing room rates?
3. What information do front office managers require to develop room availability forecasts? Why are these forecasts important? How reliable are such forecasts?
4. What steps can front office employees take to control understays and unwanted overstays?

5. How do ten-day and three-day forecasts help ensure efficiency in front office operations? What is the relationship between these forecasts? What departments in the hotel rely on these forecasts, other than the front office?
6. What are the primary responsibilities of the front office manager in budget planning? How are they performed?
7. What occupancy ratios are commonly calculated by the front office? What is the significance of occupancy ratios?
8. What methods can a front office manager use to evaluate how effectively the front office is selling rooms?
9. How can front office managers use budget reports to analyze operations? Why is reporting of both dollar and percentage variances valuable?
10. Discuss useful standards against which front office managers should compare operating ratios. What is the significance of a variance from standards?

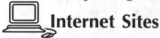

Internet Sites

For more information, visit the following Internet sites. Remember that Internet addresses can change without notice.

Hotels and Hotel Companies

Best Western
http://www.bestwestern.com

Choice Hotels International
http://www.hotelchoice.com

Canadian Pacific Hotels
http://www.cphotels.ca

Days Inn of America, Inc.
http://www.daysinn.com

Hilton Hotels
http://www.hilton.com

Holiday Hospitality Corporation
http://www.holiday-inn.com

Hyatt Hotels Corporation
http://www.hyatt.com

Inter-Continential Hotels
http://www.interconti.com

ITT Sheraton Corporation
http://www.sheraton.com

Marriott Hotels, Resorts, and Suites
http://www.marriott.com/lodging

Opryland Hotel
http://www.opryhotel.com

Radisson Hotels Worldwide
http://www.radisson.com

Ritz Carlton Hotels
http://www.ritzcarlton.com

Walt Disney World Resorts
http://www.disneyworld.com/vacation

Westin Hotels and Resorts
http://www.westin.com

Lodging Publications—Online and Printed

Hospitality Technology News
http://www.hospitalitynet.nl/news/tech.html

Hotel & Motel Management
http://www.innvest.com/hmm

Lodging Hospitality
http://www.penton.com/corp/mags/lh.html

Lodging Online
http://www.ei-ahma.org/webs/lodging/index.html

Technology Sites

Anasazi, Inc.
http://www.anasazi.com

CSS Hotel Systems
http://www.csshotelsystems.com

Executech Systems, Inc.
http://www.executech.com

Fidelio
http://www.micros.com

First Resort Software
http://www.firstres.com

Hospitality Industry Technology Exposition and Conference
http://www.hitecshow.org

Hospitality Industry Technology Integration Standards
http://www.hitis.org

HOST Group
http://www.hostgroup.com

Lodging Touch International
http://www.lodgingtouch.com

Newmarket Software Systems, Inc.
http://www.newsoft.com

Resort Data Processing, Inc.
http://www.resortdata.com

Western Hospitality Systems—InnSure
http://www.lodgingsystems.com

Case Study

Evaluating the Financial Performance of the Clifton Manor Hotel

Five years ago, Cyrus Investments bought the 150-room Clifton Manor Hotel as an investment for its clients. The Clifton Manor Hotel was ten years old at the time and had been profitable for the previous owners. The purchase price for the Clifton Manor Hotel was $6,375,000. This included the land, buildings, and interior furnishings. The previous owner agreed to pay off all outstanding operating expenses. Cyrus Investments paid 25 percent of the purchase price in cash and financed the rest at an annual interest rate of 8 percent for 20 years. The Clifton Manor Hotel is an economy/limited service property with no food and beverage service or meeting space. Food is provided next door at a local restaurant, with a covered walkway to the hotel.

When the hotel was purchased, the owners used the rule-of-thumb approach to set rates. They charged $1 for every $1,000 of cost per room. However, they also reasoned that the rate should help them make future investments in the facility, since a renovation would be necessary within five years. Therefore, they added $3 onto the rate. Cyrus Investments insisted that the hotel not drop its rate during the years of decreasing occupancy. In the first two years (19X1 and 19X2), the rate was held steady. In 19X3, the rate was raised by $1, in 19X4 the rate was raised an additional $2, and in the last year it was raised by another $3.

Selected operating statistics for the Clifton Manor Hotel over the past five years include:

	19X1	19X2	19X3	19X4	19X5
Occupancy	70%	69%	68%	70%	72%
Rooms Division Expense %	22%	23%	24%	21%	20%
Undistributed Operating Expense %	28%	29%	29%	28%	27%

The annual mortgage payment was $486,981 during the period. Fixed charges did not vary by year and were $318,750 per year. Income taxes were 30 percent of profits after the mortgage payment.

As a manager for Cyrus Investments, you have been asked to evaluate the hotel's financial performance for the past five years. The issue at hand is whether the rule-of-thumb approach to setting the hotel's rate was successful.

Discussion Questions

1. Determine the average rate and room revenue per year, with each year being 365 days.
2. Determine the actual rooms division profit, undistributed operating expenses, profit before fixed charges, profit before taxes, and profit after taxes. (Hint: undistributed operating expenses are a percentage of rooms revenue.) What hotel reports could you look at to find the rooms division profit, number of rooms occupied, and occupancy percentage?
3. Determine Cyrus Investment's actual return percentage based upon the cash payment it made when it bought the hotel.
4. Assume Cyrus Investments wanted an annual return on investment of 10 percent for each of the five years. Use the Hubbart Formula to calculate the required average rate in order to meet this goal. Assume no other changes in any of the operating statistics. Was the rule-of-thumb approach successful in meeting the Cyrus Investments return on investment goal?

Case Number: 33210CA

The following industry experts helped generate this case: Richard M. Brooks, CHA, Vice President—Operations, Bridgestreet Accommodations, Inc., Cleveland, Ohio; and Michael L. Kasavana, Professor, The School of Hospitality Business, Michigan State University, East Lansing, Michigan.

This case also appears in *Case Studies in Lodging Management* (Lansing, Mich.: Educational Institute of the American Hotel & Motel Association, 1998), ISBN 0-86612-184-6.

Chapter 11 Outline

- The Concept of Revenue Management
    - Hotel Industry Applications
- Measuring Yield
    - Formula 1: Potential Average Single Rate
    - Formula 2: Potential Average Double Rate
    - Formula 3: Multiple Occupancy Percentage
    - Formula 4: Rate Spread
    - Formula 5: Potential Average Rate
    - Formula 6: Room Rate Achievement Factor
    - Formula 7: Yield Statistic
    - Formula 8: Identical Yields
    - Formula 9: Equivalent Occupancy
    - Formula 10: Required Non-Room Revenue per Guest
- Elements of Revenue Management
    - Group Room Sales
    - Transient Room Sales
    - Food and Beverage Activity
    - Local and Area-Wide Activities
    - Special Events
- Using Revenue Management
    - Potential High and Low Demand Tactics
    - Implementing Revenue Strategies
    - Availability Strategies
- Revenue Management Computer Software
- Summary
- Case Study

11

Revenue Management

HISTORICALLY, A HOTEL'S DAILY PERFORMANCE has typically been evaluated on the basis of either occupancy percentage or average daily rate (ADR). Unfortunately, such one-dimensional analyses fail to capture the relationship between these two factors and the room revenue they produce. For example, a hotel may decrease its room rates, or ADR, in an effort to increase occupancy. This strategy, while helping to improve the occupancy percentage, fails to account for the revenue lost because of lower room rates. In addition, it does not take into account the cost per occupied room, which can reduce overall profitability. Unless occupancy increases can overcome the drop in rate and the relatively stable cost per occupied room, profits may actually go down. Similarly, increases in room rates, or ADR, may be accompanied by a decline in occupancy percentage. This means that some revenue will be lost because rooms that might have been sold at lower rates will remain unsold. Some hotel companies prefer to build occupancy percentage using low room rates to attract business, while others prefer to set a target average room rate and are willing to sacrifice occupancy to achieve it.

Revenue management presents a more precise measure of performance because it combines occupancy percentage and ADR into a single statistic: the *yield statistic*. Simply stated, revenue management is a technique used to maximize room revenues. Revenue management, sometimes called yield management, takes into account as many of the factors influencing business trends as possible. It is also an evaluative tool that allows the front office manager to use potential revenue as the standard against which actual revenue can be compared.

There are various approaches to revenue management. Often, each approach is modeled to meet the needs of an individual hotel. This chapter presents many of the common elements and basic assumptions used in revenue management analysis. Although revenue management analysis can be performed manually, this approach is cumbersome, time-consuming, and error prone. With the use of a computer and appropriate application software, revenue management calculations can be automatically performed very quickly and accurately.

The Concept of Revenue Management

The concept of revenue management originated in the airline industry. Most travelers know that passengers on the same flight often pay different fares. Super-saver discounts, three-day advance-purchase plans, stay-over-Saturday-night packages, and so forth have become the norm for airline pricing. What is not as widely known is the potential application of revenue management to other service industries.

Revenue management has proven successful in the lodging, car rental, cruise line, railroad, and touring industries—basically, in situations where reservations are taken for a perishable commodity. The key to successful implementation appears to be an ability to monitor reservations and to develop reliable forecasts.

Revenue management is based on supply and demand. Prices tend to rise when demand exceeds supply; conversely, prices tend to fall when supply exceeds demand. Proper pricing adjustments, which take existing demand into account and can even influence it, appear to be the key to profitability. To increase revenue, the hotel industry is attempting to develop new forecasting techniques that will enable it to respond to changes in supply and demand with optimal room rates. The hotel industry's focus is shifting from high-*volume* bookings to high-*profit* bookings. By increasing bookings on low-demand days and by selling rooms at higher room rates on high-demand days, the industry improves its profitability. In general, room rates should be higher (in order to maximize rate) when demand exceeds supply and lower (in order to increase occupancy) when supply exceeds demand.

Hotel Industry Applications

All hotel companies have a common problem: they produce a fixed inventory of perishable products that cannot be stored if unsold by a specific time. The commodity that hotels sell is time in a given space. If a room goes unsold on a given night, there is no way to recover the time lost and therefore the revenue lost. Therefore, these products are typically sold for varying prices that depend on the timing of the transaction and the proposed date of delivery.

In the hotel industry, revenue management is composed of a set of demand-forecasting techniques used to determine whether room rates should be raised or lowered, and whether a reservation request should be accepted or rejected in order to maximize revenue. Front office managers have successfully applied such demand-forecasting strategies to room reservation systems, management information systems, room and package pricing, rooms and revenue management, seasonal rate determination, pre-theater dinner specials, and special, group, tour operator, and travel agent rates. Front office managers have identified several benefits, including:

- Improved forecasting
- Improved seasonal pricing and inventory decisions
- Identification of new market segments
- Identification of market segment demands
- Enhanced coordination between the front office and sales divisions
- Determination of discounting activity
- Improved development of business plans

- Establishment of a value-based rate structure
- Initiation of consistent customer-contact scripting (that is, planned responses to customer inquiries or requests regarding reservations)

Revenue management seeks to maximize revenue by controlling forecast information in three ways: capacity management, discount allocation, and duration control.

Capacity Management. Capacity management involves various methods of controlling and limiting room supply. For example, hotels will typically accept a statistically supported number of reservations in excess of the actual number of rooms available in an attempt to offset the potential impact of early check-outs, cancellations, and no-shows. Capacity management (also called selective overbooking) balances the risk of overselling guestrooms against the potential loss of revenue arising from room spoilage (rooms going unoccupied after the hotel stopped taking reservations for a given date).

Other forms of capacity management include determining how many walk-ins to accept on the day of arrival, given projected cancellations, no-shows, and early departures. Capacity management strategies usually vary by room type. That is, it might be economically advantageous to overbook more rooms in lower-priced categories, because upgrading to higher-priced rooms is an acceptable solution to an oversell problem. The amount of such overbooking depends, of course, on the level of demand for the higher-priced rooms. In sophisticated computerized revenue management systems, capacity management may also be influenced by the availability of rooms at neighboring hotels or other competing properties.

Discount Allocation. Discounting involves restricting the time period and product mix (rooms) available at reduced or discounted rates. For each discounted room type, reservations are requested at various available rates, each set below rack rate. The theory is that the sale of a perishable item (the guestroom) at a reduced room rate is often better than no sale at all. The primary objective of discount allocation is to protect enough remaining rooms at a higher rate to satisfy the projected demand for rooms at that rate, while at the same time filling rooms that would otherwise have remained unsold. This process is repeated for each rate level from rack rate on down. Implementing such a scheme requires a reliable mechanism for demand forecasting.

A second objective of limiting discounts by room type is to encourage upselling. In an upselling situation a reservation agent, or front desk agent, attempts to place a guest in a higher rated room. This technique requires a reliable estimate of price elasticity and/or the probability of upgrading. (*Elasticity* refers to the relationship between price and demand. If a small increase in price produces a dramatic drop in demand, the market is said to be price *elastic.* If a small increase in price produces little or no effect on demand, the market is said to be price *inelastic.)*

Duration Control. Duration control places time constraints on accepting reservations in order to protect sufficient space for multi-day requests (representing higher levels of revenue). This means that, under revenue management, a reservation for a one-night stay may be rejected, even though space is available for that night.

For example, if Wednesday is close to selling out but adjacent nights are not, a hotel may want to optimize its revenue potential for the last few remaining rooms on Wednesday by requiring multi-day stays, even at a discounted rate, rather than accepting reservations for Wednesday only. Similarly, if the hotel is projected to be close to capacity Tuesday, Wednesday, and Thursday, then accepting a one-night stay during any of those days may be detrimental to the hotel's overall room revenue since it may block occupancy on the other days. Hotels facing such situations may require that reservations for projected full-occupancy periods must be for more than one night.

These strategies may be combined. For example, duration control may be combined with discount allocation. A three-night stay may be available for discount, while a one-night stay may require the rack rate. It must be cautioned, though, that using these strategies must not be apparent to the guest. It would be difficult to explain to a guest why he or she must stay three nights to get a discounted rate if he or she wants to stay only one night. Proper use of revenue management relies on selling; it never divulges the revenue management strategy being used.

Measuring Yield

Revenue management is designed to measure revenue achievement. One of the principal computations involved in revenue management is the hotel's **yield statistic.** The yield statistic is the ratio of actual revenue to potential revenue. Actual revenue is the revenue generated by the number of rooms sold. Potential revenue is the amount of money that would be received if all rooms were sold at their rack rates (or, as is described below, at the hotel's *potential average rate*).

Potential revenue can be determined in more than one way. Some properties calculate their potential revenue as the amount that would be earned if all rooms were sold at the double occupancy rate. Other properties calculate their potential revenue by taking into account the percentage mix of rooms normally sold at both single and double occupancy. The second method results in a lower total potential revenue figure, since single rooms are assumed to be sold at less than double rooms. In fact, while it is unlikely that a hotel will attain a potential that is based on 100 percent double occupancy (first method), a hotel using the second method may actually be able to exceed its "potential" if demand for double rooms exceeds sales mix projections.

Since the hotel's yield statistic will vary with the method used, once a preferred method has been chosen, it should be used consistently. The second method (using both single and double occupancy) is illustrated in the formulas that follow. For hotels using the first method (based on 100 percent double occupancy), formulas 1, 3, 4, and 5 are not applicable; for such hotels, the potential average double rate (formula 2) will be the same as the potential average rate (formula 5).

The mathematical computations required for revenue management are relatively simple, even though a series of formulas are usually involved. This section is intended to introduce the basic formulations of revenue management calculations.

For the following discussion, assume that the Casa Vana Inn has 300 guestrooms, collects an average of $80 per room, and is currently operating at a 70 percent average occupancy. The hotel offers 100 one-bed and 200 two-bed guestrooms. Management has established single and double rates for each room type. Any one-bed room sold as a single is priced at $90; as a double, it sells for $110. Any two-bed room sold as a single is priced at $100; as a double, it sells for $120.

Formula 1: Potential Average Single Rate

If the hotel had not varied its single rate by room type (for example, if all singles were $90), the potential average single rate would equal its rack rate. When, as in this case, the single rate differs by room type, the potential average single rate is computed as a weighted average. It is found by multiplying the number of rooms in each room type category by its single room rack rate and dividing the sum total by the number of potential single rooms in the hotel. For the Casa Vana Inn, the potential average single rate is computed as follows:

Room Type	Number of Rooms	Single Rack Rate	Revenue at 100% Occupancy Singles
1 bed	100	$ 90	$ 9,000
2 beds	200	100	20,000
	300		$29,000

$$\text{Potential Average Single Rate} = \frac{\text{Single Room Revenues at Rack Rate}}{\text{Number of Rooms Sold as Singles}}$$

$$= \frac{\$29{,}000}{300}$$

$$= \$96.67$$

Formula 2: Potential Average Double Rate

If the hotel had not varied its double rate by room type, the potential average double rate would equal its rack rate. When, as in this case, the double rate differs by room type, the potential average double rate is computed as a weighted average. It is found by multiplying the number of rooms in each room type category by its respective double-room rack rate and dividing the sum total by the number of potential double rooms in the hotel. For the Casa Vana Inn, this computation is as follows:

Room Type	Number of Rooms	Double Rack Rate	Revenue at 100% Occupancy Doubles
1 bed	100	$ 110	$11,000
2 beds	200	120	24,000
	300		$35,000

$$\text{Potential Average Double Rate} = \frac{\text{Double Room Revenues at Rack Rate}}{\text{Number of Rooms Sold as Doubles}}$$

$$= \frac{\$35{,}000}{300}$$

$$= \underline{\underline{\$116.67}}$$

Note: For lodging properties basing potential revenue on 100 percent double occupancy, this step is all that is needed to determine potential average rate(see formula 5).

Formula 3: Multiple Occupancy Percentage

An important element in determining a hotel's yield statistic is the proportion of the hotel's rooms that are occupied by more than one person, that is, the multiple occupancy percentage. This information is important because it indicates sales mix and helps balance room rates with future occupancy demand. In the case of the Casa Vana Inn, if 105 of the 210 rooms sold (at 70 percent occupancy) are normally occupied by more than one person, the multiple occupancy percentage is computed as follows:

$$\text{Multiple Occupancy Percentage} = \frac{105}{210}$$

$$= 0.5 \text{ or } \underline{\underline{50\%}}$$

Formula 4: Rate Spread

In addition to multiple occupancy percentage, another intermediate computation is important to yield statistics. The determination of a room **rate spread** among various room types can be essential to the use of yield decisions in targeting a hotel's specific market. The mathematical difference between the hotel's potential average single rate (formula 1) and potential average double rate (formula 2) is known as the rate spread. For the Casa Vana Inn the rate spread is computed as follows:

$$\text{Rate Spread} = \text{Potential Average Double Rate} - \text{Potential Average Single Rate}$$

$$= \$116.67 - \$96.67$$

$$= \$\ \underline{\underline{20.00}}$$

Formula 5: Potential Average Rate

A very important element in revenue management formulation is the **potential average rate.** A hotel's potential average rate is a collective statistic that effectively combines the potential average rates, multiple occupancy percentage, and rate spread. The potential average rate is determined in two steps. The first step involves multiplying the rate spread by the hotel's multiple occupancy percentage.

The result is added to the hotel's potential average single rate to produce a potential average rate based on demand (sales mix) and room rate information. For the Casa Vana Inn, the potential average rate is computed as follows:

$$\text{Potential Average Rate} = \left(\text{Multiple Occupancy Percentage} \times \text{Rate Spread}\right) + \text{Potential Average Single Rate}$$

$$= (.5 \times \$20) + \$96.67$$

$$= \underline{\underline{\$106.67}}$$

Formula 6: Room Rate Achievement Factor

The percentage of the rack rate that the hotel actually receives is contained in the hotel's **achievement factor (AF),** also called the **rate potential percentage.** When revenue management software is not being used, the achievement factor is generally calculated by dividing the actual average rate the hotel is currently collecting by the potential average rate.[1] The actual average rate equals total rooms revenue divided by either rooms sold or rooms occupied (depending on hotel policy). For the Casa Vana Inn, the room rate achievement factor is computed as follows:

$$\text{Achievement Factor} = \frac{\text{Actual Average Rate}}{\text{Potential Average Rate}}$$

$$= \frac{\$80.00}{\$106.67}$$

$$= 0.750 \text{ or } \underline{\underline{75.0\%}}$$

The achievement factor is also equal to 100 percent minus the discount percentage. By calculating its achievement factor, management discovers how much its actual room rates varied from established rack rates. In this case, the discount percentage is 25 percent.

As is shown below, the achievement factor can be used in one method of determining the yield statistic. It is not *necessary* to calculate the achievement factor, because the yield statistic can be determined without it. Nonetheless, the achievement factor is an important statistic in its own right because it allows management to monitor and therefore better control the hotel's use of discounting. For this reason, many hotels calculate the achievement factor as part of their revenue management efforts.

Formula 7: Yield Statistic

An important element in revenue management is the yield statistic. The yield statistic calculation incorporates several of the previous formulas into a critical index. There are various ways to express and calculate the yield statistic, all of which are equivalent:

$$1.\ \text{Yield} = \frac{\text{Actual Rooms Revenue}}{\text{Potential Rooms Revenue}}$$

$$2.\ \text{Yield} = \frac{\text{Room Nights Sold}}{\text{Room Nights Available}} \times \frac{\text{Actual Average Room Rate}}{\text{Potential Average Rate}}$$

$$3.\ \text{Yield} = \text{Occupancy Percentage} \times \text{Achievement Factor}$$

The first equation is used for a hotel that offers all its rooms at a single rack rate, regardless of occupancy. When (as is far more common) a hotel uses more than one rack rate for different room types and/or occupancies, potential rooms revenue equals total room nights available times the potential average rate.

The self-explanatory second equation is not demonstrated here. The third equation is illustrated below. For the Casa Vana Inn, the calculation is as follows:

$$\begin{aligned}\text{Yield} &= \text{Occupancy Percentage} \times \text{Achievement Factor}\\ &= 0.7 \times 0.75\\ &= 0.525 \text{ or } \underline{\underline{52.5\%}}\end{aligned}$$

Consider another example. Assume that the Cybex Hotel has 150 rooms and a rack rate of $70. On average, the hotel sells 120 rooms per night at an average room rate of $60. What is the yield for this property?

$$\text{Occupancy Percentage} = 120 \div 150 = 0.8 \text{ or } 80\%$$

$$\text{Rate Achievement Factor} = 60 \div 70 = 0.857 \text{ or } 85.7\%$$

$$\text{Yield} = 0.8 \times 0.857 = 0.686 \text{ or } \underline{\underline{68.6\%}}$$

When using this approach to determine the yield statistic, note that complimentary rooms must be treated in the achievement factor the same way that they are treated in the occupancy percentage. That is, if complimentary rooms are included in the occupancy percentage, the actual average room rate used to determine the achievement factor must equal room revenues divided by rooms *occupied,* not rooms *sold.* If complimentary rooms are ignored in the occupancy percentage, they should be ignored in calculating the actual average room rate as well.

Instead of computing yield as a percentage, some lodging operations prefer an alternate statistic that focuses on revenue per available room **(RevPAR).** The RevPAR can be calculated using either of the following equations:

$$\text{RevPAR} = \frac{\text{Actual Room Revenue}}{\text{Number of Available Rooms}}$$

$$\text{RevPAR} = \text{Occupancy Percentage} \times \text{ADR}$$

For example, suppose the 300-room Casa Vana Inn sells 180 rooms for a total of $11,520. What is this hotel's revenue per available room?

$$\text{RevPAR} = \frac{\text{Actual Room Revenue}}{\text{Number of Available Rooms}}$$

$$= \$11{,}520 \div 300 = \$38.40$$

or

$$\text{RevPAR} = \text{Occupancy Percentage} \times \text{ADR}$$

$$= 60\% \times \$64 = \$38.40$$

where occupancy percentage = 180 ÷ 300 = 0.6 or 60%
and ADR = $11,520 ÷ 180 = $64

Formula 8: Identical Yields

Calculations of different combinations of occupancy and actual average room rate may result in identical room revenue and yield statistics. Suppose the Casa Vana Inn is currently operating at 70 percent occupancy with an average rate of $80, but is considering strategies designed to raise its average rate to $100. What occupancy percentage must it achieve to match the yield it currently achieves? The formula for determining identical yield occupancy percentage is as follows:

$$\text{Identical Yield Occupancy Percentage} = \text{Current Occupancy Percentage} \times \frac{\text{Current Average Rate}}{\text{Proposed Average Rate}}$$

$$= 70\% \times \frac{\$80}{\$100}$$

$$= 0.560 \text{ or } 56.0\%$$

Identical yields do *not* generally represent identical operating situations, however. Consider the following three levels of room sales for which the Casa Vana Inn derives identical yield statistics:

Case	Number of Rooms Sold	Occupancy Percentage	Average Room Rate	Room Revenue	Yield
1	190	63.3%	$88.42	$16,800	52.5%
2	200	66.7%	$84.00	$16,800	52.5%
3	210	70.0%	$80.00	$16,800	52.5%

Are these three yield cases identical? Even though all three cases produce identical levels of room revenue and yield statistics, there are some significant differences to note.

Case 1, which represents the smallest number of rooms sold, will most likely have the lowest associated operating costs. Case 1 also generates the highest average room rate, and may appear to be the most profitable of the three cases. Case 3 represents the largest number of rooms sold and hence most likely the highest associated operating costs. This case also presents the lowest average room rate. These facts may be somewhat misleading, however. Often, the more rooms that are sold, the more likely the hotel is to collect greater *non-room* revenue. In other words, a higher occupancy percentage may result in greater total (room and non-room) revenue. Case 2 represents a middle position in terms of both number of rooms sold and average room rate. Some hoteliers may favor this case since an intermediate position is achieved regarding associated operating costs and total revenues collected.

Clearly, identical yields should not be assumed to reveal equivalent operating positions. When identical yields are computed, judging which scenario is best often requires property-specific criteria and management evaluation.

Formula 9: Equivalent Occupancy

Identical yields can be ambiguous because they fail to take direct account of operating costs and non-room revenues. A more effective way of determining whether a change in room rates is justifiable involves calculating an **equivalent occupancy.** The equivalent occupancy formula can be used when management wants to know what other combinations of room rate and occupancy percentage provide equivalent *net* revenue.

The equivalent occupancy formula is very similar to the identical yield occupancy formula, but takes marginal costs into account by incorporating gross profit or contribution margin. The **cost per occupied room** (also called the **marginal cost**) of providing a room is the cost the hotel incurs by selling that room (for example, housekeeping expenses such as cleaning supplies); this cost would not be incurred if the room were not sold (as opposed to **fixed costs,** which are incurred whether the room is sold or not). The **contribution margin** is that portion of the room rate that is left over after the marginal cost of providing that room has been subtracted out.[2]

To find the equivalent occupancy, use either of the following formulas (which are equivalent versions of the same equation):

$$\text{Equivalent Occupancy} = \text{Current Occupancy Percentage} \times \frac{\text{Rack Rate} - \text{Marginal Cost}}{\text{Rack Rate} \times \left(1 - \text{Discount Percentage}\right) - \text{Marginal Cost}}$$

$$\text{Equivalent Occupancy} = \text{Current Occupancy Percentage} \times \frac{\text{Current Contribution Margin}}{\text{New Contribution Margin}}$$

Recall the example discussed under identical yield statistics. Now assume that the Casa Vana Inn is currently operating at 70 percent occupancy with an average rate of \$80, and is considering strategies designed to raise its average rate to \$100. Further assume that the marginal cost of providing a room is \$12. What occupancy percentage must the Casa Vana Inn achieve to match the *net room revenue* it currently receives?

$$\begin{aligned}\text{Equivalent Occupancy} &= \text{Current Occupancy Percentage} \times \frac{\text{Current Contribution Margin}}{\text{New Contribution Margin}} \\ &= 70\% \times \frac{\$80 - \$12}{\$100 - \$12} \\ &= 0.541 \text{ or } \underline{\underline{54.1\%}}\end{aligned}$$

Exhibit 1 Sample Discount Grid

Rack Rate $100.00
Marginal Cost $11.00

Current Occupancy	Equivalent Occupancy Percent Required to Maintain Profitability if Rates Are Discounted by: 5%	10%	15%	20%	25%	30%	35%
100%	106.0%	112.7%	120.3%	129.0%	139.1%	150.8%	164.8%
95%	100.7%	107.0%	114.3%	122.5%	132.1%	143.3%	156.6%
90%	95.4%	101.4%	108.2%	116.1%	125.2%	135.8%	148.3%
85%	90.1%	95.8%	102.2%	109.6%	118.2%	128.2%	140.1%
80%	84.8%	90.1%	96.2%	103.2%	111.3%	120.7%	131.9%
75%	79.5%	84.5%	90.2%	96.7%	104.3%	113.1%	123.6%
70%	74.2%	78.9%	84.2%	90.3%	97.3%	105.6%	115.4%
65%	68.9%	73.2%	78.2%	83.8%	90.4%	98.1%	107.1%
60%	63.6%	67.6%	72.2%	77.4%	83.4%	90.5%	98.9%
55%	58.3%	62.0%	66.1%	70.9%	76.5%	83.0%	90.6%
50%	53.0%	56.3%	60.1%	64.5%	69.5%	75.4%	82.4%
45%	47.7%	50.7%	54.1%	58.0%	62.6%	67.9%	74.2%
40%	42.4%	45.1%	48.1%	51.6%	55.6%	60.3%	65.9%
35%	37.1%	39.4%	42.1%	45.1%	48.7%	52.8%	57.7%
30%	31.8%	33.8%	36.1%	38.7%	41.7%	45.3%	49.4%
25%	26.5%	28.2%	30.1%	32.2%	34.8%	37.7%	41.2%

Recall from the discussion of identical yields that the Casa Vana Inn needs a 56 percent occupancy to produce an identical *yield statistic,* that is, equivalent gross revenue. However, the Casa Vana Inn does not need to match its gross revenue in order to achieve the same net revenue, since by selling fewer rooms (at the higher price), it incurs fewer associated operating costs.

Although rack rates are raised relatively infrequently, discounting is a common practice in the lodging industry. What is the equivalent occupancy to 70 percent with an $80 average room rate if the average room rate is discounted by 20 percent (to $64)?

$$\text{Equivalent Occupancy} = 70\% \times \frac{\$80 - \$12}{\$64 - \$12}$$

$$= 0.915 \text{ or } \underline{\underline{91.5\%}}$$

A **discount grid** can help management to evaluate room rate discounting strategies. For example, if the average room rate of a hotel is $100 and its marginal cost (cost per occupied room) is $11, the grid in Exhibit 1 lists the occupancy percentages needed to achieve equivalent net revenue, given different room rate discount levels. To prepare a discount grid, first calculate the marginal cost of

Exhibit 2 Application of Yield and Equivalent Occupancy Formulas

	Number of Rooms Sold	Occupancy Percentage	Average Room Rate	Gross Room Revenue	Total Contribution Margin*	Yield
Current	210	70.0%	$ 80	$16,800	$14,280	52.5%
Identical	168	56.0%	100	16,800	14,784	52.5%
Equivalent	162**	54.1%	100	16,200	14,280	50.6%
New	150	50.0%	100	15,000	13,200	46.9%
New	165	55.0%	100	16,500	14,520	51.6%

*Based on a marginal cost of $12. Since fixed costs are the same for all situations, the differences between total contribution margins will exactly equal the differences between net room revenues.

**Rounded down from 162.3. Based on this amount, net revenues would be $14,282.

providing a guestroom. Next, integrate this information into the equivalent occupancy formula and perform the calculations to fill in the grid. Completing a discount grid manually is quite time-consuming; spreadsheet programs greatly simplify the process.

Applying the yield and equivalent occupancy formulas to the same data will help illustrate their differences. Suppose once again that the Casa Vana Inn is currently operating at 70 percent occupancy with an average rate of $80 and a marginal cost of $12. Would the Inn be better off with an average rate of $100 and a 50 percent occupancy? What about $100 and 55 percent occupancy? Exhibit 2 presents these data and applies the yield statistic and equivalent occupancy formulas. Note that 50 percent occupancy falls below both the 56 percent needed for identical yield and the 54.1 percent needed to produce equivalent net room revenue. Therefore, according to either approach, the Casa Vana Inn is worse off operating at a 50 percent occupancy and a $100 average room rate.

The second situation, however, finds the two approaches in conflict and illustrates the superiority of the equivalent occupancy formula. At 55 percent occupancy, the Casa Vana Inn falls short of the 56 percent needed to produce an identical yield statistic. When the yield statistic formula is used, the Inn appears to be worse off. However, the 55 percent occupancy level is higher than the 54.1 percent needed to produce equivalent net room revenue. With the equivalent occupancy formula, the Inn would be better off. A close look at the total contribution margin column—which shows that contribution (and therefore net room revenue) would rise—reveals that the equivalent occupancy formula provides more accurate and useful information.

Of course, the net gain in room revenue would have to be weighed against the potential loss of non-room revenue caused by a lower level of occupancy.

Formula 10: Required Non-Room Revenue per Guest

While equivalent occupancy, unlike the yield statistic, accounts for marginal costs, both fail to account for changes in net non-room revenue due to changes in occupancy. A manager wanting some clear indication of whether a change in room rate will render more than an offsetting change in net non-room revenue may find an answer using **breakeven analysis.** This approach involves calculating or estimating a number of elements:

- The net change in room revenue due to room rate changes
- The amount of net non-room revenue needed to offset any reduction in net room revenue (when room rates are discounted) or the amount of net room revenue needed to offset any reduction in net non-room revenue (when room rates are increased)
- The average amount each guest spends in non-room revenue centers
- The change in occupancy likely to result from room rate changes

The breakeven calculation is based on the **weighted average contribution margin ratio** (CMR_W) for all non-room revenue. While a detailed discussion of this topic is beyond the scope of this text, a simple formula for determining the CMR_W for all non-room revenue centers is as follows:[3]

$$CMR_W = \frac{\text{Total Non-Room Revenue} - \text{Total Non-Room Revenue Center Variable Costs}}{\text{Total Non-Room Revenue}}$$

Knowing the CMR_W and the average amount that guests spend in non-room revenue and having estimated the probable change in occupancy (number of guests), the front office manager can then determine whether the net change caused by higher or lower room rates is likely to be more than offset by the net change in non-room revenue.

For example, suppose hotel management is considering room rate discounting in an attempt to increase occupancy and therefore net revenue. The formula used to determine the required non-room revenue per guest follows:

$$\text{Required Non-Room Revenue per Guest} = \frac{\text{Required Increase in Net Non-Room Revenue}}{\text{Number of Additional Guests}} \div CMR_W$$

The front office manager can compare the result of this equation with the actual average non-room spending per guest. If this number is higher than the actual average non-room spending per guest, the hotel is likely to lose net revenue by discounting its room rates; that is, the additional guests brought in through discounting will not spend enough to offset the net loss in room revenue. If the amount needed per additional guest is lower than the actual average amount spent, the hotel is likely to increase its net revenue through discounting.

As another example, assume that the 400-room Bradley Inn has a $144.75 potential average room rate (generating potential room revenue of $57,900) and a $12 marginal cost per room. The Inn currently operates at 60 percent occupancy (240 rooms sold per night) and an average room rate of $137.50. Management believes that it can raise occupancy to 75 percent (300 rooms sold per night) by lowering its average room rate to $110. It also believes it can raise occupancy to 90 percent (360 rooms sold per night) by lowering the average room rate to $91.67. Should management attempt either of these strategies?

It is important to note that since room revenue ($33,000) is the same for all three situations, looking simply at a yield statistic (57 percent) does not offer a solution. Equivalent occupancy calculations offer more useful information. A reduction in average room rate to $110 would require an equivalent occupancy of 76.8 percent (60 percent × $125.50 ÷ $98.00). A reduction to $91.67 would require an equivalent occupancy of 94.5 percent (60 percent × $125.50 ÷ $79.67). Based on management's forecasts of 75 percent and 90 percent occupancies, both average room rate reductions would result in a decrease in net room revenue.

Still, the average room rate reductions may be justifiable on the basis of increased *total* revenue. The first step in determining whether this is the case is calculating the total contribution margin (or, if fixed cost data are available, the net room revenue) of the three options:

Level of Occupancy		Number of Rooms		Room Contribution Margin		Total Revenue Contribution
60%	×	400	×	($137.50 − $12.00)	=	$30,120
75%	×	400	×	($110.00 − $12.00)	=	$29,400
90%	×	400	×	($91.67 − $12.00)	=	$28,681

An average room rate reduction to $110 brings in an additional 60 guests but results in a net room revenue loss of $720. A reduction in average room rate to $91.67 brings in an additional 120 guests but lowers net room revenue by $1,439. In either situation, to offset the loss, the Bradley Inn needs to earn an average net non-room revenue of $12 for each additional guest ($720 ÷ 60 extra guests; $1,439 ÷ 120 extra guests). If the non-room CMR_W is found to be 0.25, the required non-room spending for each additional guest is:

$$\text{Required Non-Room Spending} = \$12 \div 0.25 = \underline{\underline{\$48}}$$

In other words, if the Bradley Inn's guests typically spend an average of more than $48 per day in the Inn's non-room revenue centers, the Inn is likely to increase its total net revenue by offering either room rate discount.

Non-room revenue considerations can become critical factors in a revenue management analysis. Some hotels require that groups receiving discounted room rates contract for hotel food and beverage services to render the total revenue package attractive.

This discussion has thus far approached the breakeven analysis of required non-room revenue by examining a room rate *reduction* that decreases net room revenue and increases occupancy. Breakeven analysis can also be used to examine the net effects of a room rate *increase.* Consider the following situations.

When room rates are increased, occupancy percentage generally falls (unless demand is very inelastic). An increase in price may reduce room sales so much that net room revenue actually falls, despite the higher ADR. Because occupancy has declined, it is likely that non-room revenue will also decline. In this situation, it is clear that the price increase would hurt the hotel's financial position.

However, a room rate increase may in fact lead to higher net room revenue despite the decrease in occupancy it causes. Although higher net room revenue appears to be an outcome that management would desire, such a rate increase should not be implemented without careful analysis because, even if net room revenue goes up, *total* net revenue may still drop. This can occur when the occupancy decline reduces net non-room revenue by an amount greater than the net room revenue increase.

For example, assume that the 400-room Cybex Hotel is considering increasing its room rate from $80 to $90. Current occupancy is 80 percent. Forecasted occupancy after the price increase is estimated to be 75 percent. The marginal cost of selling a guestroom is $14. The average daily non-room spending per guest is $75 and the weighted average contribution margin ratio for all non-room revenue centers is 0.30. Should management implement the rate increase? First, calculate the effect on net room revenue contribution.

Occupancy		Rooms		Room Contribution Margin		Total Contribution
80%	×	400	×	($80 – $14)	=	$21,120
75%	×	400	×	($90 – $14)	=	$22,800

Net room revenue would increase by $1,680 if the room rate were increased. The profit percentage per occupied room would increase from 82.5 percent ($66/$80) to 84.4 percent ($76/$90).

Next, calculate the effect on non-room net revenue.

Net Non-Room Revenue								
At 80% occupancy:	320 guests	×	$75	×	0.30	=	$7,200
At 75% occupancy:	300 guests	×	$75	×	0.30	=	$6,750

Net non-room revenue would decrease by $450 if the room rate were increased.

Finally, subtract the net non-room revenue loss from the net room revenue gain. In this example, total daily net revenue would increase by $1,230 ($1,680 – $450) if the room rate is increased by $10. Given this net gain, management should implement the increase.

Now suppose that the front office manager had forecasted occupancy to be 71 percent after the rate increase rather than 75 percent. This change would lead to a different conclusion, as the following calculations demonstrate.

Occupancy		Rooms		Room Contribution Margin		Total Contribution
80%	×	400	×	($80 – $14)	=	$21,120
71%	×	400	×	($90 – $14)	=	$21,584

Net room revenue would increase by $464 if the room rate were increased.

Net Non-Room Revenue								
At 80% occupancy:	320 guests	×	$75	×	0.30	=	$7,200
At 71% occupancy:	284 guests	×	$75	×	0.30	=	$6,390

Net non-room revenue would decrease by $810 if the room rate were increased.

In this revised example, total daily net revenue would decrease by $346 ($810 – $464). Given such circumstances, management should not implement the room rate increase.

Elements of Revenue Management

The fact that flexible room rates affect both the number of guests and associated revenue transactions helps demonstrate the potential complexities of revenue management. As demonstrated in the previous discussion, focusing attention on only room revenue potential may not present management with a comprehensive overview.

Revenue management becomes even more complex when room rate discounting is granted on a selective rather than general basis, and when it involves selling rooms for which there may be competing buyers. Hotels frequently offer discounts to certain categories of guests (for example, senior citizens, government employees). Hotels must also decide whether to accept or refuse group business at a discounted room rate. This section discusses various situations that can arise when hotels base their booking decisions on revenue management.

The following elements must be included in the development of a successful revenue management strategy:

- Group room sales
- Transient (or FIT) room sales
- Food and beverage activity
- Local and area-wide activities
- Special events

Group Room Sales

In many hotels, groups form the nucleus of room revenue. It is common for hotels to receive reservations for group sales from three months to two years in advance of arrival. Some international business hotels and popular resorts commonly book groups more than two years in advance. Therefore, understanding group booking trends and requirements can be critical to the success of revenue management.

To understand the potential impact of group sales on overall room revenue, the hotel should collect as much group profile information as possible, including:

- Group booking data
- Group booking pace

- Anticipated group business
- Group booking lead time
- Displacement of transient business

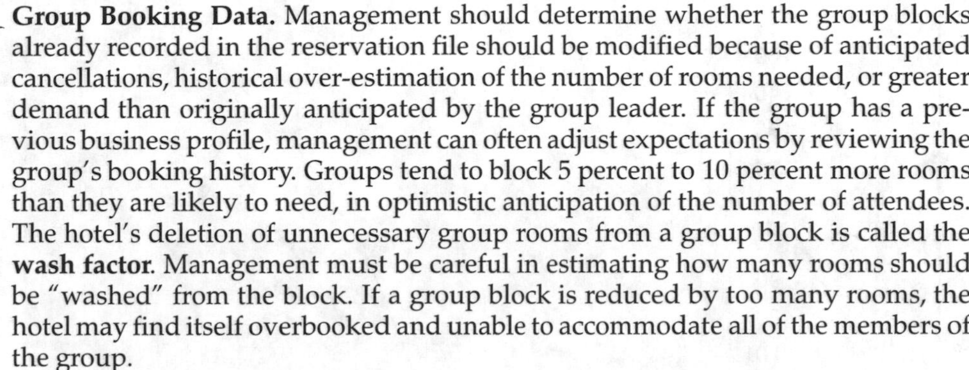

Group Booking Data. Management should determine whether the group blocks already recorded in the reservation file should be modified because of anticipated cancellations, historical over-estimation of the number of rooms needed, or greater demand than originally anticipated by the group leader. If the group has a previous business profile, management can often adjust expectations by reviewing the group's booking history. Groups tend to block 5 percent to 10 percent more rooms than they are likely to need, in optimistic anticipation of the number of attendees. The hotel's deletion of unnecessary group rooms from a group block is called the **wash factor**. Management must be careful in estimating how many rooms should be "washed" from the block. If a group block is reduced by too many rooms, the hotel may find itself overbooked and unable to accommodate all of the members of the group.

Group Booking Pace. The rate at which group business is being booked is called the **group booking pace.** ("Booking" in this context refers to the initial agreement between the group and the hotel, not to the specific assignment of individual rooms in the block to group members.[4]) For example, suppose that in April of a given year a hotel has 300 rooms in group blocks it is holding for a scheduled function in October of the same year. If the hotel had only 250 group rooms booked for October at the same time the year before, the booking pace would be 20 percent ahead of the previous year's pace. Once a hotel has accumulated several years of group booking data, it can often identify a historical trend that reveals a normal booking pace for each month of the year. Although this forecasting process appears simple, it can become very complicated due to unanticipated fluctuations. Management should strive to maintain a straightforward method for tracking group booking pace. Booking pace can be an invaluable forecasting variable.

Anticipated Group Business. Most national, regional, and state associations, as well as some corporations, have policies governing the locations of annual meetings. For example, a group may rotate its meeting location among three cities, returning to each every three years. Although a contract may not yet be signed, hotel management may be correct in feeling confident that the group will return according to the cycle. Of course, a group may not always return to the same hotel in the area. However, even when it goes to other hotels, the group may displace other group and non-group business that will need to find alternate accommodations in the area. The hotel analyzing these data can then forecast the "pressure" in the market and adjust their selling strategies accordingly. In addition, tentative bookings that await final contract negotiations should also be included in the revenue management analysis.

Group Booking Lead Time. Booking lead time measures how far in advance of a stay bookings are made. For many hotels, group bookings are usually made within one year of planned arrival. Management should determine its hotel's lead time

Exhibit 3 Lead Time/Booking Pace for Sample Hotel

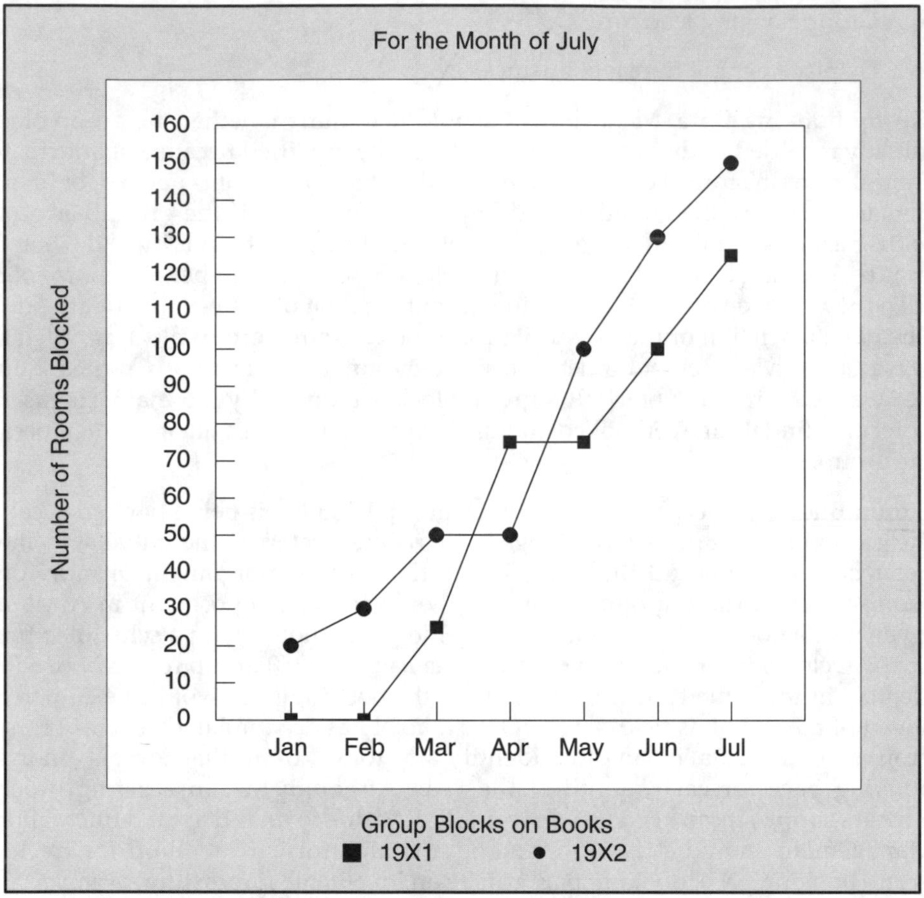

For the Month of July

Number of Rooms Blocked

160
150
140
130
120
110
100
90
80
70
60
50
40
30
20
10
0

Jan Feb Mar Apr May Jun Jul

Group Blocks on Books

■ 19X1 ● 19X2

for group bookings so that booking trends can be charted. Booking trends can be combined with booking pace information to illustrate the rate at which the hotel is booking group business compared with historical trends (see Exhibit 3). This information can be very important when determining whether to accept an additional group and at what room rate to book the new group. If the current booking pace is lower than expected or lags behind the historical trend, it may be necessary to offer a lower room rate to stimulate increased occupancy. On the other hand, if demand is strong and the group booking pace is ahead of anticipated or historical trends, it may not be appropriate to discount room rates.

Displacement of Transient Business. Management should consult its demand forecast when determining whether or not to accept additional group business. **Displacement** occurs when a hotel accepts group business at the expense of transient guests. Since transient guests often pay higher room rates than group members, this situation warrants close scrutiny. Transient rooms are guestrooms sold to

Exhibit 4 Revenue and Yield Calculations

	Tuesday		Wednesday		Thursday		Friday	
	Without Group	With Group	Without Group	With Group	Without Group	With Group	Without Group	With Group
Gross revenue	$24,400	$28,000	$22,800	$26,400	$26,600	$27,800	$25,800	$27,800
Contribution*	19,300	22,000	18,000	20,700	21,050	21,800	20,400	21,800
Yield**	61.0%	70.0%	57.0%	66.0%	66.5%	69.5%	64.5%	69.5%

*Based on a marginal cost of $15.

**Potential revenue = $100 potential average rate × 400 rooms = $40,000.

guests who are not affiliated with a group registered with the hotel. A non-group guest may also be called an FIT (free independent traveler).

Assume that the 400-room Halbrook Lodge has a potential average rate of $100, an actual average transient rate of $80, an actual average group rate of $60, and a marginal cost of $15 per occupied room. Consider the impact of a proposed group block of 60 rooms during an upcoming four-day period:

	Tuesday	Wednesday	Thursday	Friday
Rooms Available	400	400	400	400
Definite Groups Booked	140	140	150	150
Expected Transient Demand	200	180	220	210
Available Rooms	60	80	30	40
Proposed Group Block	60	60	60	60
Transient Displacement	0	0	30	20

If the proposed group block is accepted, no displacement occurs on Tuesday and Wednesday; the hotel clearly benefits on these days because it sells rooms it did not expect to sell (earning an additional $3,600 gross and $2,700 net room revenue each day). On Thursday and Friday, however, 30 and 20 transient guests, respectively, would be displaced. Still, as shown in Exhibit 4, Thursday's room revenue will rise by $1,200 gross and $750 net if the group is accepted. Friday's room revenue will rise by $2,000 gross and $1,400 net if the group is accepted. In other words, accepting the group business will increase the hotel's yield on each of the four days. Since it also raises the hotel's occupancy, this group's business will probably increase non-room revenue as well.

Several factors help determine whether a group reservation should be accepted. As just illustrated, the hotel should first look at revenue factors. A group should probably be accepted only if the expected revenue gain (including that from non-room revenue centers) offsets the transient guest revenue loss. In addition, management must consider what happens to the transient guests who cannot be accommodated. Whether these displaced guests are frequent or first-time guests, they may decide not to return to a hotel that has turned them away. The transient revenue lost may not be confined simply to the nights in question, especially when frequent guests choose not to return. Of course, turning away potential group business may also reduce future business.

Another situation in which the transient revenue lost may not be confined simply to the nights in question occurs when a non-group guest wishing to come in on Tuesday for three nights will be turned away if the group is taken. Even though the group is displacing actual non-group rooms on Thursday because of lack of inventory, it is affecting Tuesday and Wednesday as well.

Deciding whether to accept a group that forces transient displacement is an issue that deserves careful consideration. Management must consider the longer term impact on future business.

Transient Room Sales

As mentioned earlier, transient rooms are those rooms sold to non-group travelers. Transient business is usually booked closer to the date of arrival than group business. A commercial hotel may book a majority of its group business three to six months before arrival, while booking transient business only one to three weeks before arrival. At a resort hotel, group bookings may be established one to two years in advance, while transient business may be booked three months in advance. As with group business, management must monitor the booking pace and lead time of transient business in order to understand how current reservations compare with historical and anticipated rates. This leads to the more complex subject of transient room rate discounting.

In a previous example, room rates were set by bed type and number. However, in today's market there may be many other reasons to price rooms differently. In order to maximize room revenue, front office managers may decide to classify rooms by location, desirability, or size and charge a premium for better rooms. For example, rooms that are smaller, near noisy corridors, or unrenovated or that offer less desirable views are likely to be offered at lower rates. Therefore, these rooms may be classified as standard and be assigned a lower room rate. More desirable rooms may be classified as deluxe and be assigned higher room rates.

In order to build business, hotels may offer deluxe rooms at standard rates to attract guests. This is especially true in times of low demand. Then, as demand improves to a predetermined threshold, any remaining deluxe rooms can then be offered at full rack rate. Under this strategy, management attempts to maximize room revenue, not just average room rate or occupancy percentage. The reasoning is that lower demand creates a more competitive situation for the hotel. Discounting may reduce the amount of business lost because of rate resistance and allows the hotel to sell rooms that might otherwise remain vacant. An astute manager must know when to eliminate room rate discounts. If room rates are increased too soon, occupancy may be lost. If room rates are increased too late, some rooms may be sold for less than they could have been sold for. When discounting a deluxe room to a standard rate, the reservation or front desk agent should tell the guest that he or she is being upgraded. This will add value to the guest's stay. It also reduces the confusion on the part of the guest the next time he or she comes to the hotel and is quoted a higher rate.

Business ethics should be included in any discussion of revenue management. If a guestroom is classified as standard, there is usually a very good reason for it. Therefore, it would appear unethical to sell the room at a rate higher than its rack rate just because someone may be willing to pay the higher rate. Even though demand may provide the opportunity for a higher rate, charging the rate just because the market will accept it for the period is not good business practice. Some hotels have done this and received criticism from the market for doing it. This is one reason many states require room rates to be posted in each room.

Another issue to consider in transient room sales is the discounting offered to certain sources of business. Discounts can be offered to corporate and government travelers, as well as senior citizens, military and airline personnel, travel agents, and others. Quite often, these discounts apply to a substantial portion of a hotel's business. Therefore, controlling discounts is crucial to producing an optimal yield statistic. For example, if a hotel has very few rooms reserved over a holiday period, it may open all discounts to callers just to attract business. As demand builds over the period, the discounts may be selectively closed. When the front office manager believes that rooms can be sold at a higher rate without an offsetting loss in occupancy, the discount should be closed. Some discounts cannot be closed off. Whenever possible, contracts for discounts should provide for flexibility when business conditions warrant.

Food and Beverage Activity

While banquet and catering functions are considered food and beverage revenue generators, they can have an effect on a yield decision. For example, if a banquet with no guestroom requirements is occupying the hotel's ballroom, a group needing 50 guestrooms *and* a ballroom may have to be turned away. In most cases, the group needing both catering and guestroom space will produce more profit for the hotel. Therefore, local food and beverage functions should be viewed in light of the potential for booking groups that need meeting space, food and beverage service, and guestrooms. Cooperation and communication between hotel departments is important to effective revenue management.

Local and Area-Wide Activities

Local and area-wide activities can have dramatic effects on the revenue management strategies of a hotel. Even when a hotel is not in the immediate vicinity of a convention, transient guests and smaller groups displaced by the convention may be referred to the hotel (as an overflow facility). When this occurs, the front office manager should be aware of the convention and the demand for guestrooms it has created. If the demand is substantial, transient and group rates may need to be adjusted.

Convention business may render a trend analysis of group and transient activity invalid. If the booking pace of either group or transient rooms sales is significantly altered, the front office manager should immediately investigate. An increase in demand could indicate a convention in the area or a large booking at another property. A decrease in demand could indicate a major group cancellation at a competing property, which is now reducing its regular pricing to fill its guestrooms.

Ethics and good business practice should play an integral part in a yield strategy or tactic. It is appropriate and legal for competitors to occasionally meet and discuss general business trends. However, it is *not* legal to discuss room rates or the establishment (fixing) of room rates. There may also be additional sources of information that identify what is affecting business in the area. For example, most visitor and convention bureaus publish a list of meetings in their areas. Under no circumstances should employees of two different hotels discuss rate structuring or any other hotel operating issue since such activity might be considered a violation of anti-trust laws in the United States.

Special Events

Quite often, special events such as concerts, festivals, and sporting events are held in or near a hotel. The hotel may be able to take advantage of such demand-enhancing activities by restricting room rate discounts or requiring a minimum length of stay. This is a common practice, for example, during the Christmas holidays at many Southern resorts. Guests wishing to stay over Christmas may be required to guarantee a four- or five-night minimum stay. Similarly, room discounts were eliminated during the 1996 Summer Olympic Games in Atlanta, Georgia, due to high demand and limited availability. Minimum stays were also required. These are all sound revenue management tactics, but they must be managed carefully so the hotel does not alienate frequent travelers.

Using Revenue Management

All elements of revenue management should be viewed together in order to make an appropriate decision. While the process is potentially complex, a failure to include relevant factors may render revenue management efforts less than fully successful.

Yield statistics should be tracked daily. Tracking yield statistics for an extensive period of time can be helpful to trend recognition. However, to use revenue management properly, management must track yield statistics for *future* days. Future period calculations must be done every business day, depending on how far in advance the hotel books its business. If a hotel is currently at 50 percent yield for a day three weeks away, there may be plenty of time to put strategies in place to increase the projected level of yield. Discounts may be opened to raise occupancy or closed to raise average rate. If achieving full potential room revenue is not possible (and it usually is not), the front office manager must decide on the best combination of rate and occupancy.

Each sales contract for group business should be reviewed individually. Contracts should be compared with historical trends as well as with budgets. A hotel usually has a group sales target or budgeted figure for each month. Each group should be examined to see if it will contribute to meeting the budget. If current transient demand is strong and the group will produce only minimal revenue, the hotel may consider not booking it. If demand is weak, the hotel may decide to accept the group simply to create revenue by selling rooms that would not otherwise be sold. Using group booking pace analyses will help management determine whether the hotel is on track to reach its target.

Another factor is the actual group booking pattern already on the books. For example, a hotel may have two days between groups that are not busy. Management may solicit a lower-revenue-generating group to fill the gap. The opposite may also occur. A group may desire space during a period when the hotel is close to filling its group rooms goal. Adding the group may move the hotel group sales above its goal. While this appears to be favorable, it may displace higher-rated transient business. If the group wants the hotel, it may need to be quoted a higher than normal group rate to help make up for the revenue lost through the displacement of transient guests.

The same type of analysis is needed for transient business. For example, due to the discounts offered by the hotel, corporate and government business may be assigned the standard category of rooms. As these standard rooms fill, the hotel may only have deluxe rooms left to sell. If demand is not strong, management may decide to sell the deluxe rooms at the standard rack rate to remain competitive. It is best to look at a combination of group and transient business before making firm occupancy and rate decisions.

Since the objective of revenue management is to maximize revenue, tracking business by revenue source helps determine when to allow discounted room rates. As various sources of business are identified, each should be analyzed to understand its impact on total revenue. Quite often, front office managers will authorize discounted room rates for groups if the group has the potential to generate repeat customers.

Potential High and Low Demand Tactics

Hotels need to determine revenue management strategies for both high and low demand periods. During times of high demand, the normal technique is to increase room revenue by maximizing average room rate. Transient and group business market segments may each require a unique, specific strategy.

Below are some transient business tactics used during high demand periods.

- Try to determine the right mix of market segments in order to sell out at the highest possible room rates. This strategy is highly dependent upon accurate sales mix forecasting.
- Monitor new business bookings and use these changed conditions to reassign room inventory. As occupancy begins to climb, consider closing out low room rates. Management should be prepared to re-open lower room rates should demand begin to slack off. Management must closely monitor demand and be flexible in adjusting room rates.
- Consider establishing a minimum number of nights per stay. For example, a resort that always fills to capacity over Labor Day weekend may require a three-day minimum stay in order to better control occupancy.

A number of group business tactics may be appropriate during high demand periods. When deciding between two or more competing groups, for example, select the group that produces the highest total revenue. Management must rely on its experience with groups to develop sound revenue management policies.

Given the focus on total revenue, it may be wise to sell blocks of guestrooms to groups that also book meeting space, food and beverage service, and hospitality suites. A group that books ancillary space and services is likely to spend more time and money in the hotel. This tactic usually requires restricting access of local patrons to function, meeting, and public spaces; if these spaces are booked by local patrons, potentially more profitable groups needing such space may be forced to go elsewhere.

Another tactic for handling group business during high demand periods is to attempt to move price-sensitive groups to low demand days. In other words, if the hotel forecasts high demand for a time when a price-sensitive group has already booked space, management may try to reschedule the group's business to a period of lower demand. This tactic, which is often easier said than done, allows the hotel to replace the lower room rate group with a group willing to pay higher rates.

The underlying strategy for transient and group business during low demand periods is to increase revenue by maximizing occupancy. Front office managers may find the following business tactics helpful.

- Carefully design a flexible rating system that permits sales agents to offer lower rates in certain situations. Such rates should be determined early in the planning process in anticipation of low demand periods.
- Strive to accurately project expected market mix. The precision of this projection will influence the eventual yield statistic.
- Management should closely monitor group bookings and trends in transient business. Do not close off lower rate categories and market segments arbitrarily.
- As low occupancy periods become inevitable, open lower rate categories, solicit price-sensitive groups, and promote corporate, government, and other special discounts. Consider developing new room rate packages and soliciting business from the local community (for example, weekend getaways for the local transient market).
- Consider maintaining high room rates for walk-in guests. Since these guests have not contacted the hotel prior to arrival, they typically present an opportunity to increase the average rate through top-down upselling techniques.
- A non-financial tactic involves upgrading guests to nicer accommodations than they are entitled to by virtue of their room rate. This technique may lead to increased guest satisfaction and enhanced customer loyalty. The implementation of this policy is strictly a management decision and has some risks. For example, the guest may expect the same upgrade on future stays. This may not be possible and the reservations or front desk staff should take extra care to explain that this is a special, one-time upgrade because the hotel appreciates the guest's business.

This list of suggested tactics is not exhaustive, but it is representative of industry strategies.

Hurdle Rate

Implementing Revenue Strategies

Once all of this has been organized and analyzed, the front office manager must determine what rates will be used on any given day. Rack rates are always left open, whether demand is high or low. Then, the front office manager must set the lowest rate for a given date. Rates that fall below this minimum will not be offered. This is sometimes called the **hurdle rate.** Any room rate that can be sold at a rate above the hurdle rate is acceptable for that date. Any rate below the hurdle rate should not be offered. Some automated revenue management systems will not even display rates below the hurdle rate, thus preventing their use. Hurdle rates can fluctuate from day to day, depending upon the hotel's desired yield and market conditions. The hurdle rate usually reflects the front office manager's pricing strategy to maximize yield.

Sometimes incentives are offered to front desk and reservations agents for selling rooms above the hurdle rate. For example, if the hurdle rate for a given day is $80 and a reservations agent sells a room for $90, he or she might receive 10 promotion points. At the end of the month, all promotion points are totaled. For every 100 points, the reservations agent might receive a monetary reward. Incentives of this kind must be applied carefully, however. Reservations and front desk agents may elect not to offer lower rates that provide fewer incentive points, even though they are above the hurdle rate. While they are building incentive points, they may actually be turning away business.

Incentives may also be provided for longer guest stays. For example, a guest staying three nights may qualify for a lower rate than a guest staying for one night. This is a **stay-sensitive hurdle rate.** Reservations agents may receive incentives for booking a three-night stay, even if it is at a lower rate, because the total revenue generated from the reservation will be greater than the revenue of a one- or two-night stay.

Communicating hurdle rates can be done in various ways. Some hotels post the rate strategies in the reservations office and at the front desk where the agent can see them but the guest cannot. Some computer systems, as stated above, automatically display acceptable rates only. Whatever the communication method, it is essential that reservation information be kept current. Yield strategies can change several times a day and all front desk and reservations agents must know when a change occurs.

Availability Strategies

So far, this chapter has concentrated on maximizing yield by controlling room rates. While this approach can be quite effective, alternative strategies dealing with room availability are also available. Such strategies include *minimum length of stay, close to arrival,* and *sell-through.*

A **minimum length of stay** strategy requires that a reservation must be for at least a specified number of nights in order to be accepted. Examples of this were presented earlier in this chapter. The advantage of this strategy is that it allows the hotel to develop a relatively even occupancy pattern. It is common for resorts to use this approach during peak occupancy periods. It may also be used by hotels during special events or high occupancy periods. The use of minimum length of stay requirements is intended to keep an occupancy peak on one day from reducing occupancy on the days before and after the peak. Minimum length of stay requirements need to be controlled carefully. Because the hotel may be turning down profitable business of shorter duration, the reservations office would be wise to track reservation requests for shorter stays that were denied due to this restriction.

A **close to arrival** strategy allows reservations to be taken for a certain date as long as the guest arrives before that date. For example, if the front office is expecting a 300-room check-in on a given date, the front office manager may decide that more than 300 rooms checking in may be too much of a strain on the front desk and its related departments. Therefore, guests arriving before that date and staying through the date will be acceptable. However, additional arrivals on the peak arrival date will not be accepted. As with a minimum length of stay strategy, the reservations office should track the number of reservation requests denied due to this restriction.

The **sell-through** strategy works like a minimum length of stay requirement except that the required stay can begin before the date the strategy is applied. For example, if a three-night sell-through is applied on Wednesday, the sell-through applies to Monday, Tuesday and Wednesday. Arrivals on each of those days must stay for three nights in order to be acceptable. A sell-through strategy is especially effective when one day has a peak in occupancy and management does not want the peak to adversely affect reservations on either side of the peak day. Hotels use a sell-through strategy as a technique to overbook the peak day. By properly forecasting no-shows, early departures, and reservation cancellations, management may be able to manage the peak day so that the overbooking is reduced and all guests with reservations are accommodated. Without such a strategy, the days before and after the peak may have reduced occupancy because the peak may block extended stays.

Room availability strategies can be used together with room rate strategies. For example, a three-night minimum length of stay can be used in conjunction with a hurdle rate of $90. If the guest desires only a two-night stay, the rack rate of $110 may be quoted to the guest or the reservation may not be accepted.

Revenue Management Computer Software

Although the individual tasks of revenue management can be performed manually, the most efficient means of handling data and generating yield statistics is through a computer. Sophisticated revenue management software is available that can integrate room demand and room price statistics and can simulate high revenue-producing product scenarios.

Revenue management software does not make decisions for managers. It merely provides information and support for managerial decisions. Since revenue management is often quite complex, front office staff will not have the time to process the voluminous data manually. Fortunately, a computer can store, retrieve, and manipulate large amounts of data on a broad range of factors influencing room revenue. Over time, revenue management software can help management create models that produce probable results of decisions. Decision models are based on historical data, forecasts, and booked business.

In those industries where computer-based revenue management has been applied, the following results have been observed:

- Continuous monitoring: a computerized revenue management system can track and analyze business conditions 24 hours a day, seven days a week.
- Consistency: software can be programmed to respond to specific changes in the marketplace with specific corporate or local management rules resident in the software.
- Information availability: revenue management software can provide improved management information which, in turn, may help managers make better decisions more quickly.
- Performance tracking: a computer-based system is capable of analyzing sales and revenue transactions occurring within a business period to determine how well revenue management goals are being achieved.

Revenue management software is also able to generate an assortment of special reports. The following are representative of revenue management software output:

- Market segment report: provides information regarding customer mix. This information is important for effective forecasting by market segment.
- Calendar / booking graph: presents room-night demands and volume of reservations on a daily basis.
- Future arrival dates status report: furnishes demand data for each day of the week. This report contains a variety of forecasting information that enables the discovery of occupancy trends by comparative analysis of weekdays. It can be designed to cover several future periods.
- Single arrival date history report: indicates the hotel's booking patterns (trends in reservations). This report relates to the booking graph by documenting how a specific day was constructed on the graph.
- Weekly recap report: contains the sell rates for rooms and the number of rooms authorized and sold in marketing programs with special and / or discounted rates.
- Room statistics tracking sheet: tracks no-shows, guaranteed no-shows, walk-ins, and turn-aways. This information can be instrumental in accurate forecasting.

Since management is interested in revenue enhancement, computer-based revenue management has become a popular hospitality industry software application.

Summary

Revenue management presents a more precise measure of room revenue and occupancy performance than other historical benchmarks. Revenue management is effective because it combines occupancy percentage and ADR into a single statistic. Revenue management focuses on maximizing room revenues while taking into account factors influencing business trends. It is an evaluative tool that allows front office management to use potential revenue as the standard against which actual revenue is compared.

Revenue management has proven successful in business environments in which reservations are taken for a perishable commodity. The key to successful revenue management appears to be reliable forecasting, since revenue management is based on conditions of supply and demand.

Because revenue management uses a set of demand-forecasting techniques to determine effective prices for a forecasted volume of business, it can be highly successful when applied to the rooms reservation process. Revenue management seeks to maximize revenue by controlling forecast information in three ways: capacity management, discount allocation, and duration control.

Capacity management involves a number of methods of controlling and limiting room supply. Capacity management may be influenced by the availability of rooms at neighboring hotels or competing properties. Discounting involves restricting the time period and product mix (rooms) available at reduced prices. The primary objective of discount allocation is to protect enough remaining rooms at a higher rate to satisfy the projected demand for rooms at that rate, while at the same time filling rooms that would otherwise have remained unsold. Duration control places time constraints on accepting reservations in order to protect sufficient space for multi-day requests (representing higher levels of revenue).

The principal computation involved in revenue management is the yield statistic, which is the ratio of actual revenue to potential revenue. Actual revenue is the revenue generated by the number of rooms sold. Potential revenue is the amount of money that would be received if all rooms were sold at full rack rate or potential average rate. The potential average rate is a collective statistic that combines the hotel's potential average single and double rates, multiple occupancy percentage, and rate spread into a single figure. The achievement factor is found by dividing the hotel's actual average room rate by the potential average rate. Alternatively, some lodging operations prefer the statistic that focuses on revenue per available room (revpar).

Calculations of different combinations of occupancy and actual average room rate may result in identical room revenue and yields. Management must be careful not to assume that identical yields represent identical operating situations with respect to the number of rooms and number of guests in occupancy.

Revenue management becomes even more complex when discounting is granted on a selective rather than general basis, and when it involves selling rooms for which there may be competing buyers. Hotels frequently offer discounts to guests falling into certain categories (for example, senior citizens, government employees). Hotels must also decide whether to accept or refuse group business at a discounted rate. Understanding the impact of group business on the hotel's operating performance may be an important factor in how revenue management should be applied.

Since the objective of revenue management is to maximize revenue, tracking business by revenue source will also help determine when to allow discounted business. Some hotels may decide to allow specific types of discounted business, such as corporate business, because these markets are responsible for many repeat guests. As the various sources of business are determined, each should be analyzed to understand its impact on total revenue. Quite often, managers will take discounted business if it generates frequent customers, since the long-term impact is very positive.

Implementing yield strategies involves setting hurdle rates for rooms. The hurdle rate is the minimum rate that can be offered at a given time. The hurdle rate is sometimes stay-sensitive, meaning lower rates are available to guests who stay a minimum length of time. Sometimes incentives are used to encourage front desk and reservations agents to sell rooms at rates above the hurdle rate. Since hurdle rates change frequently, efficient communication of rates and changes is critical.

Revenue management often focuses on maximizing yield by controlling rates. Other strategies that focus on length of stay and arrival dates are also effective. These other strategies can also be effectively combined with rate control to improve yield.

Endnotes

1. This method does not produce an achievement factor that is as precise as that which can be calculated by revenue management software. This is because the potential average rate is a weighted average of the rack rates of all rooms in the hotel. It is more accurate to use the weighted average of the rack rates of only the rooms that were actually sold (or occupied). Since the sales mix of rooms sold typically changes from day to day, so does the weighted average of those rooms' rack rates. Because it is impractical and cumbersome to manually calculate a weighted average of rack rates for rooms actually sold every day, the potential average rate of *all* rooms is generally used instead. The element of error this introduces may not be significant. Nonetheless, revenue management software is able to calculate the achievement factor more precisely because it can easily and automatically calculate the daily weighted average of the rack rates of rooms sold (or occupied).

2. In theory, and as used in our examples throughout the rest of this chapter, marginal costs are assumed to be constant at a given amount per room. In practice, this is not always the case. For example, certain labor costs may move incrementally; that is, as occupancy goes up, at some point management will have to add another front desk agent to help service the guests. Also, room attendants are usually paid by the shift, not by the room; if a room attendant cleans 12 rooms one day and 15 the next, the marginal cost per room will vary slightly. In addition, some properties are able to shut down wings not in use. If adding a guest means opening up an entire wing, the marginal cost of adding that guest will clearly be much higher than the marginal cost of simply adding a single room. For a more detailed discussion of these issues, see Raymond S. Schmidgall, *Hospitality Industry Managerial Accounting*, 4th ed. (East Lansing, Mich.: Educational Institute of the American Hotel & Motel Association, 1997), chapter 6.

3. For a more detailed discussion of breakeven analysis and contribution margin ratios, see Schmidgall, chapter 7.
4. Group business usually involves the hotel's sales division. The sales division typically *books* the group. It then turns the booking over to the reservations manager, who *blocks* the group. As individual group members contact the hotel, they are *booked* and the size of the block is reduced accordingly.

Key Terms

achievement factor—the percentage of the rack rate that a hotel actually receives; in hotels not using revenue management software, this factor is generally approximated by dividing the actual average room rate by the potential average rate.

booking lead time—a measurement of how far in advance bookings are made.

breakeven analysis—an analysis of the relationships among costs, revenue, and sales volume allowing one to determine the revenue required to cover all costs; also called cost-volume-profit analysis.

close to arrival—a yield management availability strategy that allows reservations to be taken for a certain date as long as the guest arrives before that date; for example, a hotel may accept a reservation for a Wednesday night if the guest's actual stay begins on Tuesday night.

contribution margin—sales less cost of sales for either an entire operating department or for a given product; represents the amount of sales revenue that is contributed toward fixed costs and/or profits.

cost per occupied room—the variable or added cost of selling a product that is incurred only if the room is sold; also called marginal costs.

discount grid—a chart indicating the occupancy percentage needed to achieve equivalent net revenue, given different discount levels.

displacement—the turning away of transient guests for lack of rooms due to the acceptance of group business; also called non-group displacement.

equivalent occupancy—given a contemplated or actual change in the average room rate, the occupancy percentage needed to produce the same net revenue as was produced by the old price and occupancy percentage.

fixed costs—costs that remain constant in the short run even though sales volume varies.

group booking pace—the rate at which group business is being booked.

hurdle rate—in the context of revenue management, the lowest acceptable room rate for a given date.

marginal costs— the variable or added cost of selling a product that is incurred only if the room is sold; also called cost per occupied room.

minimum length of stay—a revenue management availability strategy requiring that a reservation must be for at least a specified number of nights in order to be accepted.

potential average rate—a collective statistic that effectively combines the potential average single and double rates, multiple occupancy percentage, and rate spread to produce the average rate that would be achieved if all rooms were sold at their full rack rates.

rate potential percentage—the percentage of the rack rate that a hotel actually receives, found by dividing the actual average room rate by the potential average rate; also called the achievement factor.

rate spread—the mathematical difference between the hotel's potential average single rate and potential average double rate.

revenue management—a technique based on supply and demand used to maximize revenues by lowering prices to increase sales during periods of low demand and by raising prices during periods of high demand.

revpar—a revenue measurement that focuses on revenue per available room.

sell-through—a revenue management availability strategy that works like a minimum length of stay requirement except that the length of the required stay can begin before the date the strategy is applied.

stay-sensitive hurdle rate—in the context of revenue management, a hurdle rate (or minimum acceptable room rate) that varies with the length of the guest reservation.

wash factor—the deletion of unnecessary group rooms from a group block.

weighted average contribution margin ratio—in a multiple product situation, an average contribution margin for all operated departments that is weighted to reflect the relative contribution of each department to the establishment's ability to pay fixed costs and generate profits.

yield statistic—the ratio of actual rooms revenue to potential rooms revenue.

Review Questions

1. What is the goal of revenue management?
2. Why is communication between the various revenue centers important to the successful implementation of revenue management?
3. What are the importance and limitations of using historical data when planning revenue management strategies?
4. What might be the impact of closing discount rates when business is down?
5. What role does booking pace play in revenue management?
6. What is a wash factor and how does it affect revenue management?
7. Why is transient displacement analysis so important to determining whether to accept a group reservation?
8. What is the difference between marginal cost and fixed cost?

9. What does the equivalent occupancy equation consider that the identical yield equation does not? Why is the difference significant? What important question does neither equation address?
10. Should a group reservation be accepted or rejected solely on the basis of its effect on room revenue? Why or why not?
11. What are several tactics that may be appropriate to take when room demand is low? When room demand is high?
12. What is the hurdle rate? How is it used in revenue management? What availability strategies are there to work with yield management?

Internet Sites

For more information, visit the following Internet sites. Remember that Internet addresses can change without notice.

Hotels and Hotel Companies

Best Western
http://www.bestwestern.com

Choice Hotels International
http://www.hotelchoice.com

Canadian Pacific Hotels
http://www.cphotels.ca

Days Inn of America, Inc.
http://www.daysinn.com

Hilton Hotels
http://www.hilton.com

Holiday Hospitality Corporation
http://www.holiday-inn.com

Hyatt Hotels Corporation
http://www.hyatt.com

Inter-Continental Hotels
http://www.interconti.com

ITT Sheraton Corporation
http://www.sheraton.com

Marriott Hotels, Resorts, and Suites
http://www.marriott.com/lodging

Opryland Hotel
http://www.opryhotel.com

Radisson Hotels Worldwide
http://www.radisson.com

Ritz Carlton Hotels
http://www.ritzcarlton.com

Walt Disney World Resorts
http://www.disneyworld.com/vacation

Westin Hotels and Resorts
http://www.westin.com

Lodging Publications—Online and Printed

Hospitality Technology News
http://www.hospitalitynet.nl/news/tech.html

Hotel & Motel Management
http://www.innvest.com/hmm

Lodging Hospitality
http://www.penton.com/corp/mags/lh.html

Lodging Online
http://www.ei-ahma.org/webs/lodging/index.html

Technology Sites

Anasazi, Inc.
http://www.anasazi.com

CSS Hotel Systems
http://www.csshotelsystems.com

Executech Systems, Inc.
http://www.executech.com

Fidelio
http://www.micros.com

First Resort Software
http://www.firstres.com

Hospitality Industry Technology Exposition and Conference
http://www.hitecshow.org

Hospitality Industry Technology Integration Standards
http://www.hitis.org

HOST Group
http://www.hostgroup.com

Lodging Touch International
http://www.lodgingtouch.com

Newmarket Software Systems, Inc.
http://www.newsoft.com

Resort Data Processing, Inc.
http://www.resortdata.com

Western Hospitality Systems—InnSure
http://www.lodgingsystems.com

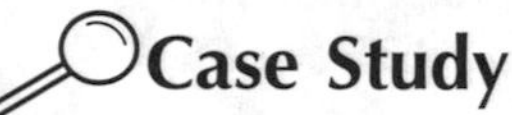

Case Study

Reviving Revenue Management

The Hearthstone Suites Hotel is an all-suite property with 250 rooms. A new property, the Fairmont Hotel, opened near Hearthstone Suites three months ago. Several months before the opening of the Fairmont, Laurie, the GM at the Hearthstone Suites, pushed all her front office and reservations staff to sell as many rooms as possible. As she put it, "Whatever it takes, to stay competitive." The director of sales, Pat, supported the plan from day one, but Jodie, the front office manager, had misgivings from the start. Jodie was concerned that the revenue management program managers implemented a year and a half earlier would be totally useless because of the push for occupancy.

The most recent profit and loss statement indicates that Jodie's fears were fulfilled. Though the occupancy is at budget year-to-date, the average daily rate (ADR) is down by $6. Also, the mix of commercial business is lower than planned—40 percent of guest mix instead of 50 percent. Also, the SMERF segment is higher than it should be—15 percent of guest mix instead of 5 percent. SMERF is a catch-all term for group business at substantially low rates—Social, Military, Educational, Religious, and Fraternal groups.

Jodie, Pat, and Laurie are in a meeting to discuss these latest figures:

Laurie, the general manager, opens the meeting by saying, "Well, we've weathered the storm caused by the opening of the Fairmont. We managed to hold on to our occupancy level. But it looks like we have some regrouping to do. I trust you've each received the profit and loss statement I sent you. I'm concerned about the fact that we've lost so much of our share of the commercial business. And our ADR is much too low."

"I agree," says Jodie, "but I was just following orders when I had my staff focus on selling rooms. Our good occupancy rate has come at the cost of both yield management and revenue. It will take quite awhile to regain our former position."

"We all sat down and agreed months before the Fairmont opened that we should do our best to keep our occupancy numbers, and that's what we've done," says Pat. "You and your staff have worked hard and are to be commended, Jodie."

"Hear, hear," says Laurie, "And now we have some time to re-evaluate our position and start targeting that corporate segment again."

"I just hope it's not too late to win it back from Fairmont," sighs Jodie.

Later that day, Jodie gathers her front desk and reservations team to brief them about re-implementing the revenue management program. "I know you've all been putting a lot of extra effort into filling rooms over the past several months. I'm proud of you; the whole management team is. We've met our occupancy goals. The down side is that our guest mix is off. We've lost some of our commercial segment and gained too much of the SMERF segment. And our ADR is down a full $6. It's time we reviewed the revenue management program we use..."

"The revenue what?" blurts Jack, a fairly new front desk agent. "You never told us about that."

"Now hold on a minute," counters Jodie, "some of you are so new that you haven't been fully trained in this program, but I know I've talked about it to some extent with all of you."

"Sure, you told me a little about it," offers Tracey, a reservationist. "I never have been comfortable with it, to tell the truth. One day I quote a guest $85 and he books a suite. A month later he calls back to book another and I quote $105. Then the guest asks why the rate went up—what am I supposed to say?"

"Well, there are things you can tell guests who ask that, but we're not going to get into that right now," says Jodie.

Bill, the most experienced front desk agent, speaks up. "I've been using the yield management program all along, just like you showed me." He turns to his co-workers. "It's really not unreasonable when you look at the big picture of the hotel's revenue. I just tell inquisitive callers that our rates depend on their arrival dates. Some periods are busier for us than others, and that affects rates."

"Bill, it's good to hear that you continued using the yield management program," Jodie says. We can get into more detail on applying it in formal training. We've had a lot of changes since the push for volume began—changes in personnel and even changes in the yield management program itself. It's clearly time I evaluated training needs in our department in the area of yield management program execution. You can be confident, Tracey—and all of you—when you quote rates that they are competitive for what we offer. That reminds me," and here Jodie pauses a moment, "how many of you have actually been inside some of our suites?"

Three of the six employees raise their hands. "How many have seen rooms at the Fairmont or at any of our other competitors?" continues Jodie. Only Bill raises his hand. "So almost none of you have seen the difference between our suites and the single rooms other properties are offering?"

"There hasn't been time to look at what we're selling," protests Jack.

"...much less to look at what anyone else is selling," adds Linda, another reservationist.

"That's what I was afraid of," says Jodie. "In the next two weeks or so, as I'm re-evaluating training needs, I'm going to have each of you spend time gaining an appreciation of the value we offer—especially in comparison with the value of Fairmont's offerings and those of our other competition."

"Are we still going to be offering the $84 supersaver rate?" asks Tracey. "We've had a lot of repeat business because of that rate."

"I've had callers tell me we're the best deal in town," Linda says.

But Bill cautions, "We won't need to use it next week. The Home Builders convention is in and every room in town will be booked. We can afford to charge more next week."

"That's good thinking, Bill," says Jodie. "I know it's nice to be popular with guests and it's easy to use that discount whenever a potential guest shies away from a quoted rate; but the supersaver rate is intended to be used only as a last resort or in other special cases. We shouldn't be offering it too frequently. We also need to adjust our selling strategies when special events come along like this convention."

"Speaking of selling strategies, when are we going to get to go through that training module on selling skills you were talking about?" inquires Linda. "I've heard about it but I haven't gone through it yet."

Discussion Questions

1. How can the management team address the problem of low ADR?
2. What are some ways Jodie could make employees like Jack and Tracey more familiar and comfortable with a yield management program?
3. What selling skills should training focus on for the Hearthstone Suites Hotel staff?
4. How can the Hearthstone Suites Hotel regain some of the commercial business it has lost?

Case Number: 370CF
This case was developed in cooperation with Lisa Richards of Hospitality Softnet, Inc., a marketing resources and support company (Sixty State Street, Suite 700, Boston, Massachusetts 02109; tel. 617-854-6554).

This case also appears in *Case Studies in Lodging Management* (Lansing, Mich.: Educational Institute of the American Hotel & Motel Association, 1998), ISBN 0-86612-184-6.

Chapter 12 Outline

- Recruiting
  - Internal Recruiting
  - External Recruiting
- Selecting
  - Selection Tools
  - Evaluating Applicants
  - Interviewing
- Hiring
  - Job Offers
  - Processing Personnel Records
- Orienting
- Skills Training
  - Prepare to Train
  - Present the Training
  - Practice Skills
  - Follow Up
- Staff Scheduling
  - Alternative Scheduling Techniques
- Staff Motivation
  - Training
  - Cross-Training
  - Recognition
  - Communication
  - Incentive Programs
  - Performance Appraisals
- Summary
- Case Study

12

Managing Human Resources

FRONT OFFICE MANAGERS face much greater challenges than managers of a generation ago. Labor management has always been a premier issue, but the near future promises to put even more emphasis on this area. Front office managers must be skilled at handling a diverse work force that blends people of varying ages, ethnic backgrounds, cultures, and values. Just as the nature of the work force will change, so will the techniques and incentives that govern its management. This chapter focuses on some of the basic concepts that front office managers need to know in order to effectively manage and develop competent staff.

Recruiting

Employee **recruitment** is the process by which qualified applicants are sought and screened to fill open positions. The process involves announcing or advertising job vacancies through proper sources, and interviewing and evaluating applicants to determine the best person for the job.

The human resources division should assist the front office manager in finding and hiring qualified individuals. Not all hotels, however, have a human resources division. When this is the case, the front office manager may have to conduct the initial interviews, contact applicants' references, and perform other related tasks. Even when the hotel has a human resources division, it is the front office manager's responsibility to identify the skills and qualities needed in the front office job positions and to communicate this information to the human resources division to ensure that it qualifies candidates properly. This is generally done with a job description that identifies the skills, personal qualities, and responsibilities of the position. Regardless of how prospects are identified, the front office manager should personally interview top candidates for front office positions.

Internal Recruiting

Internal recruiting involves the transfer or promotion of current employees. Through this form of recruiting, managers have access to applicants who are familiar with the hotel and possibly the front office and who have proven skills. Internal recruiting may also boost employee morale and productivity. Some hotel employees view internal recruiting as an opportunity to advance and often do their best to prepare for appropriate open positions. Many industry leaders, including company presidents, vice presidents, and general managers, have risen through the ranks as a result of internal recruiting. Exhibit 1 summarizes the advantages and disadvantages of internal recruiting.

Exhibit 1 Advantages and Disadvantages of Internal Recruiting

Advantages

- Improves the morale of the promoted employee.
- Improves the morale of other employees who see future opportunities for themselves.
- Managers can better assess the abilities of internal recruits, since their performances have been observed over time.
- Internal recruiting for supervisory and management positions results in a succession of promotions (one to fill each vacated job), which reinforces the "internal career ladder."
- The cost of internal recruitment is lower than the cost of external recruitment.

Disadvantages

- Internal recruiting promotes "inbreeding."
- Internal recruiting can cause morale problems among those employees who were skipped over for promotion.
- Internal recruiting can have political overtones; some employees attribute internal promotions to friendships with managers and supervisors.
- Filling a gap in one department through internal recruiting may create an even more critical gap in another department.

Internal recruiting includes cross-training, succession planning, posting job openings, paying for performance, and maintaining a call-back list.

Cross-Training. Whenever possible, employees should be trained to perform the duties of more than one job. **Cross-training** makes it easier for the front office manager to develop comprehensive employee schedules that include planned employee vacations and absences. Employees find cross-training beneficial since it diversifies their skills, gives their jobs variety, and makes them more valuable to the hotel. Cross-training may also lead to a wider range of promotion opportunities. One recent innovation developed by a major hotel company is to cross-train front desk agents and bell attendants. In this case, the person who checks the guest in is also the person who carries the guest's bags and escorts the guest to the room. There may be some disadvantages to cross-training, but the overall effects have been very positive.

Succession Planning. In succession planning, the front office manager identifies a key position and targets a particular employee to eventually fill that position. Front office management identifies the employee's training needs and ensures that those needs are met. The manager creates a staffing plan that identifies training dates and times, the trainer or trainers, and the date the employee will be qualified to assume the job.

Posting Job Openings. When the front office posts job openings internally, it gets a known applicant pool. Employees from other departments may want to transfer to the front office or current front office employees may want to advance within their own department. Whatever the case, front office management must make sure that the employee has the skills for the promotion, as well as a good work record.

The front office manager should post each available position as soon as it is officially open. Some hotel companies believe that each position should be open to people on staff before it is announced to outside applicants. Job postings should be placed in a prominent location in the employee lounge or work area. Some hotel properties also find it useful to post entry-level positions. When employees know about these positions, they often encourage qualified friends or acquaintances to apply.

Postings should be comprehensive; they should describe jobs fully and specify minimum qualifications and required skills. The posting should tell applicants whether the job is for a day, night, or weekend shift. Some properties also post the exact wage or salary. In some hotels, employees cannot apply for openings until they have held their current positions for a certain period. When this is the case, the requirement should be clearly stated on the job posting.

Paying for Performance. Employees are more likely to be motivated to excel when they know the hotel has a wage program that rewards hard work and productivity. As employees gain more experience and proficiency, they should be paid accordingly. Giving all employees an identical wage increase, regardless of performance, may be discouraging to those employees who are exceeding expectations.

Maintaining a Call-Back List. While recruiting appears to be an infrequent event, in reality it is ongoing. To assist future staffing efforts, front office management should develop and maintain a call-back list of employees and previous applicants with special skills and interests. Some hotels also maintain a *back-up list*, or waiting list, of former employees who completed their employment in good standing. The front office may hire such individuals as supplemental labor during a peak business period or employee shortage.

External Recruiting

Front office managers may also recruit individuals from outside the hotel to fill open positions. New employees can contribute innovative ideas, unique perspectives, and creative ways of doing things. **External recruiting** includes networking, temporary employment agencies, and employee referral programs. Federal, state, and local government tax credit programs may also provide incentives for management to recruit individuals from designated groups. There are also several programs to encourage the hiring of workers with disabilities. Exhibit 2 summarizes the advantages and disadvantages of external recruiting.

Networking. Networking involves developing personal contacts with friends, acquaintances, colleagues, business associates, educators, and school counselors. These personal contacts can often lead to employment referrals. Companies that provide services or supplies to the hotel may also share leads on possible jobs or

Exhibit 2 Advantages and Disadvantages of External Recruiting

Advantages

- External recruiting brings new blood and new ideas into the company.
- Recruits from the outside can often provide not only new ideas but news about how and what competitors are doing.
- External recruits can provide a fresh look at your company, which sometimes reinforces the reasons current employees work for you. Consider, for example, the value of an external recruit saying such things as "You keep your kitchen much cleaner than they do at XYZ company where I used to work" or "The helpful attitude of employees here certainly makes this a more pleasant place to work than my old job."
- External recruiting sometimes avoids many of the political problems associated with internal recruiting.
- External recruiting serves as a form of advertising for the company (newspaper ads, posters, bulletin board notices, and so on remind the public of your products and services).

Disadvantages

- It is more difficult to find a good fit with the company's culture and management philosophy when recruiting externally.
- Internal morale problems can develop if current employees feel that they have no opportunity to move up in the organization.
- It takes longer to orient external recruits than it does internal recruits.
- External recruiting can lower productivity over the short run because external recruits usually cannot produce as quickly or effectively as internal recruits.
- When employees believe that they could have done the job as well as the external recruit who was hired, political problems and personality conflicts can result.

job candidates. Other network sources may include members of trade or community associations. If a hotel is part of a chain, the front office manager can network with managers of other properties in the area. By working together, they make career advancement better for all employees and make employment with the chain more desirable.

Temporary Employment Agencies. Temporary employment agencies can provide staff to fill a wide range of positions. These agencies often train a pool of employees in specific employment areas. Temporary employment agencies operate for profit and therefore charge a higher hourly rate for temporary employees than the rate generally paid to permanent hourly employees. These higher costs are usually offset in other ways. For example, temporary employment agencies may:

- Reduce overtime, recruitment, and hiring expenses

- Provide screened and trained qualified employees
- Create employee commitment by providing full-time positions and benefits
- Be able to supply complete work crews

On the downside, temporary employees may lack specific training in appropriate procedures. In addition, they will need time to become acquainted with the hotel layout, amenities, facilities, and departmental hours of operation. As a result, temporary workers may be less productive than the front office's own staff, and may require more supervision. Temporary workers are generally considered short-term additions to the permanent work force.

Employee Referral Programs. Some front offices adopt employee referral programs that encourage employees to recommend friends and acquaintances for open positions. An employee referral program usually rewards current employees who refer qualified staff members to the company. The program works best when front office management establishes the size of the referring employee's reward at the outset. The program must also specify which criteria will be applied and how referrals will be credited to the proper source. Usually, the referred employee must work for a specified trial period before the employee who made the referral can claim the reward. This period often ranges from 90 days to 180 days.

Tax Credits. Some government programs, such as the federal Targeted Jobs Tax Credits Program, provide tax incentives to private employers who hire individuals from specified human resource categories. Any front office employee hired under a tax credit program *must* be certified as a member of a targeted category by a local office of the state employment commission *before* being hired. To claim the targeted job tax credit, the hotel must certify that the new employee is not a relative or dependent of the property's owner, and that he or she has not worked for the hotel before.

Workers with Disabilities. Some positions in the front office are well-suited to employees with physical handicaps or disabilities. For example, a wheelchair user may be qualified to work as a telephone operator or reservations agent, since such jobs usually do not require standing or a great deal of moving within a work area. Workers with disabilities are usually highly motivated and may perceive their work as important evidence of their ability, skill, and independence.

In general, employees with disabilities can be recruited through local government job training agencies or with schools that provide training for disabled people. Some communities may also offer tax incentives to companies that employ persons with disabilities. Before hiring such individuals, the front office manager must ensure that work areas are compatible with the employees' needs. A major focus of the Americans with Disabilities Act of 1990 is to make it easier for people with physical and mental disabilities to find jobs and to advance within their careers. Hotels must take appropriate steps to comply with this legislation, particularly in terms of barrier-free design and employment practices. Since the traditional labor market is shrinking, persons with disabilities are becoming an important and growing source of new employees. In addition, job descriptions and specifications must clearly identify any restrictions or requirements that may exclude an employee covered by the ADA. For example, an employee in a wheelchair would not qualify as bell attendant because of the mobility and heavy lifting requirements of the position.

Selecting

Selecting the right person for a front office position should always involve the front office manager. Depending on the policy of the hotel, the front office manager may directly hire an applicant or may be limited to forwarding a hiring recommendation to top management.

Applicants with practical skills, knowledge, and aptitude are likely to become valuable front office employees. Two specific skills frequently required in front office work are mathematical aptitude and keyboard (typing) skills. An employee's mathematical ability will help him or her understand front office accounting and transaction processing; keyboard skills are especially useful for recordkeeping and using a computer.

Since front office work involves a high degree of guest contact, managers usually seek certain personality traits in applicants. These traits include congeniality, flexibility, professional attitude, self-motivation, and a well-groomed appearance. Evaluating applicants in terms of personal qualities is highly subjective. An effective front office selection process usually focuses on a set of skills, attitude, and personal qualities. In addition, since the front office staff members have so much contact with guests, they should reflect the quality of the hotel during that contact. It does not matter whether the contact is by telephone, by letter, or face to face. Guests will create an image of the hotel through employee contact. One hotel company interviews prospective reservations agents by asking a few questions over the telephone. This allows the interviewer to hear the candidate's voice and how the candidate presents himself or herself over the phone. Proper selection of employees will help ensure that the hotel's image and values are upheld in all guest contacts.

Selection Tools

Job descriptions and **job specifications** are important selection tools. A job description lists all the tasks and related information that make up a work position. A job description may also outline reporting relationships, responsibilities, working conditions, equipment and material to be used, and other information specific to the position. Job descriptions are especially helpful in recruiting and selecting employees since they clearly state the duties required to perform a particular job. Job descriptions may also explain how a work position relates to other work positions in the department.

Although each job is unique, some general statements can be made about work requirements in the front office. A job specification usually lists and describes the personal qualities, skills, traits, educational background, and experience a person needs to successfully perform the tasks outlined by a job description. To develop job specifications, managers may draw on the knowledge of other front office staff and any written material related to the job. For example, managers might describe an employee as demonstrating a professional attitude by reporting to work on time. A professional attitude might further be marked by sensitivity to guests, a sense of humor, congeniality, and good listening habits. A flexible employee might be defined as a team player who is willing to work different positions or shifts as necessary. Job specifications may include terminology that relates to the specific needs of the front office. For example, appropriate dress in a resort might mean casual dress, while in a commercial hotel, it is likely to mean business attire. Descriptions of personal qualities must be relevant to the needs of each individual property.

Evaluating Applicants

Generally, front office managers evaluate job applicants by reviewing completed job application forms, checking applicant references, and interviewing selected applicants. A hotel with a human resources division may screen applicants on the basis of front office job descriptions and job specifications. In hotels without a human resources division, the front office manager may be responsible for all aspects of screening and evaluating applicants. A job application form should be easy to complete and should require applicants to provide information that helps determine suitability for the job. Exhibit 3 presents a sample job application form.

Managers should check references to verify an applicant's identity and claims about previous work experiences and skills. Managers should be aware that past employers are often reluctant to provide any information other than the applicant's past job title, dates of employment, and salary. Former employers rarely reveal whether they would rehire the person. Past employer comments, especially if negative, increase the former employer's potential liability for charges of libel, slander, or defamation of character by the former employee. Front office managers must be familiar with their own property's policy on handling calls regarding the work record of current or past employees. Familiarity with such policy positions will allow managers to better understand the comments of job candidates' previous employers. It may also be hotel policy to have a police record check on all job applicants. This may be especially essential for certain positions, such as cashier or hotel van driver. A police check may help uncover an unsafe driving record, a drug record, or a dismissal from another job due to cash handling problems.

Questions contained on a job application form must be carefully structured since federal, state, and local laws prohibit discriminatory hiring practices. Exhibit 4 lists employment questions that may be considered discriminatory and suggests ways to avoid discrimination. Managers may also find this guide helpful when developing interview questions. Since laws, and their interpretation, vary from state to state, a qualified attorney should review job application forms, related personnel forms, and interview procedures to ensure that their contents do not violate antidiscrimination laws.

Interviewing

First impressions do matter. Applicants form impressions of the interviewer, the hotel, the front office, and what it would be like to work there, just as the interviewer forms impressions of how suitable the applicant would be for the job. Often, eventual job satisfaction and productivity is the result of the expectations formed during an interview.

Exhibit 3 Sample Job Application Form

APPLICATION FOR EMPLOYMENT

GENERAL DATA AND AVAILABILITY

Name ______________________________ Social Security # ____/___/____
Last First Middle Initial

Address ______________________________ Phone __________
Street City State Zip

If you are applying for a position which requires you drive, do you have a current Driver's License? Yes ☐ No ☐
If you answered yes, please provide:
License Number __________ Class __________

CITIZENSHIP: If you are not a citizen of the United States of America, do you have a permanent resident visa card, I-94 Form or letter from the Immigration Service indicating that you are legally permitted to work in this country?
Yes ☐ No ☐ If hired, are you able to show proof of status? Yes ☐ No ☐

If you are under 21 years of age: List Age_______ Date of Birth __________

For employment verification, have you used any other name on a previous job? Yes ☐ No ☐

List names ______________________________

Positions Desired: 1st Choice__________ 2nd Choice__________

Wage or Salary Desired:__________per__________ Date available to start work__________

For what job status are you applying? Full Time ☐ Part Time ☐ _______ hours per week . Summer ☐

School Term ☐ Other ☐ Explain:__________

The following conditions may be required at some time in a job assignment. If required would you be willing to work:

A. Shift work? Yes ☐ No ☐ B. Rotational work schedule? Yes ☐ No ☐

C. Work schedule other than Monday through Friday? Yes ☐ No ☐ D. Overtime work ? Yes ☐ No ☐

List any scheduling problems or limitations __________

Is your transportation reliable to meet any work schedule requirement any day of the week? Yes ☐ No ☐

Have you ever been employed at this hotel before? Yes ☐ No ☐ When __________

Reason for leaving__________ Name of Supervisor __________

How did you happen to apply? ☐ Referred by__________ ☐ Ad in paper__________
Which paper

☐ Agency __________ ☐ Sign ☐ Passing by

☐ Friend/Current Employee __________
Name

Do you have any relatives working here? __________
Names

Police Conviction Record: Have you ever been convicted of a felony? Yes ☐ No ☐ If yes, please briefly describe the circumstances of your conviction, indicating the nature and place of the offense and the disposition of the case. A felony conviction does not necessarily bar you from employment since this will be looked upon as only one of the factors considered in the employment decision.

____

____

Page 1

Exhibit 3 *(continued)*

MILITARY EXPERIENCE

Have you ever served in the United States Armed Forces? Yes ☐ No ☐ If so, describe any special training or skills acquired during your service which may be helpful on the job? ______

EDUCATIONAL BACKGROUND

Type of School	Name & Address of School	Years Completed	Graduated	Major Field of Study
High School		9, 10, 11, 12	Yes ☐ No ☐	
College		1, 2, 3, 4	Yes ☐ No ☐	
Other		1, 2, 3, 4	Yes ☐ No ☐	

EMPLOYMENT HISTORY

List the most recent employer first, then follow with the next most recent. We will check all references.

Name and Address of Previous Employer	Dates Worked From Mo Yr / To Mo Yr	Position	Supervisor	Hours Worked Per Week	Rate of Pay
Company					
Address		If currently employed, may we contact this employer for a reference? Yes No			
City State	Why did you leave or are interested in leaving this employer?______				
Phone					

Name and Address of Next Employer	Dates Worked From Mo Yr / To Mo Yr	Position	Supervisor	Hours Worked Per Week	Rate of Pay
Company					
Address					
City State	Why did you leave this employer?______				
Phone					

Include any additional employment history on another sheet of paper.

SPECIAL SKILLS

Typing/Word Processing______ Dictation/Shorthand______ Telephone______ Computers______
Foreign Languages______ Mechanical ______
List List

PERSONAL REFERENCE

The following person knows me and would be able to give a personal reference:

Name Address City State Zip Telephone

APPLICANT, PLEASE READ AND SIGN

I certify that the information contained in this application is correct to the best of my knowledge and understand that falsification of this information is grounds for refusal to hire or, if hired, dismissal. I authorize any of the persons or organizations referenced in this application to give you any and all information concerning my previous employment, education, or any other information they might have, personal or otherwise, with regard to any of the subjects covered by this application and release all such parties from all liability for damage that may result from furnishing such information to you. I authorize you to request and receive such information. I understand this hotel does not discriminate in hiring or employment on the basis of race, color, religious creed, national origin, sex, age, handicap or veteran status.

Signed:______ Date:______

Page 2

Courtesy of Renaissance Hotels & Resorts

Exhibit 4 Pre-Employment Inquiry Guide

SUBJECT	LAWFUL PRE-EMPLOYMENT INQUIRIES	UNLAWFUL PRE-EMPLOYMENT INQUIRIES
NAME:	Applicant's full name. Have you ever worked for this company under a different name? Is any additional information relative to a different name necessary to check work record? If yes, explain.	Original name of an applicant whose name has been changed by court order or otherwise. Applicant's maiden name.
ADDRESS OR DURATION OF RESIDENCE:	How long a resident of this state or city?	
BIRTHPLACE:		Birthplace of applicant. Birthplace of applicant's parents, spouse or other close relatives. Requirement that applicant submit birth certificate, naturalization or baptismal record.
AGE:	*Are you 18 years old or older?	How old are you? What is your date of birth?
RELIGION OR CREED:		Inquiry into an applicant's religious denomination, religious affiliations, church, parish, pastor, or religious holidays observed. An applicant may not be told "This is a Catholic (Protestant or Jewish) organization."
RACE OR COLOR:		Complexion or color of skin.
PHOTOGRAPH:		Requirement that an applicant for employment affix a photograph to an employment application form. Request an applicant, at his or her option, to submit a photograph. Requirement for photograph after interview but before hiring.
HEIGHT:		Inquiry regarding applicant's height.
WEIGHT:		Inquiry regarding applicant's weight.
MARITAL STATUS:		Requirement that an applicant provide any information regarding marital status or children. Are you single or married? Do you have any children? Is your spouse employed? What is your spouse's name?
SEX:		Mr., Miss, Mrs., or an inquiry regarding sex. Inquiry as to the ability to reproduce or advocacy of any form of birth control.
CITIZENSHIP:	Are you a citizen of the United States? If not a citizen of the United States, does applicant intend to become a citizen of the United States? If you are not a United States citizen, have you the legal right to remain permanently in the United States? Do you intend to remain permanently in the United States?	Of what country are you a citizen? Whether an applicant is naturalized or a native-born citizen; the date when the applicant acquired citizenship. Requirement that an applicant produce naturalization papers or first papers. Whether applicant's parents or spouse are naturalized or native born citizens of the United States; the date when such parent or spouse acquired citizenship.
NATIONAL ORIGIN:	Inquiry into languages applicant speaks and writes fluently.	Inquiry into applicant's (a) lineage; (b) ancestry; (c) national origin; (d) descent; (e) parentage, or nationality. Nationality of applicant's parents or spouse. What is your mother tongue? Inquiry into how applicant acquired ability to read, write, or speak a foreign language.
EDUCATION:	Inquiry into the academic vocational or professional education of an applicant and the public and private schools attended.	
EXPERIENCE:	Inquiry into work experience. Inquiry into countries applicant has visited.	
ARRESTS:	Have you ever been convicted of a crime? If so, when, where, and nature of offense? Are there any felony charges pending against you?	Inquiry regarding arrests.
RELATIVES:	Name of applicant's relatives, other than a spouse, already employed by this company.	Address of any relative of applicant, other than address (within the United States) of applicant's father and mother, husband or wife and minor dependent children.
NOTICE IN CASE OF EMERGENCY:	Name and address of person to be notified in case of accident or emergency.	Name and address of nearest relative to be notified in case of accident or emergency.

Exhibit 4 *(continued)*

SUBJECT	LAWFUL PRE-EMPLOYMENT INQUIRIES	UNLAWFUL PRE-EMPLOYMENT INQUIRIES
MILITARY EXPERIENCE:	Inquiry into an applicant's military experience in the Armed Forces of the United States or in a State Militia. Inquiry into applicant's service in particular branch of United States Army, Navy, etc.	Inquiry into an applicant's general military experience.
ORGANIZATIONS:	Inquiry into the organizations of which an applicant is a member—excluding organizations, the name or character of which indicates the race, color, religion, national origin or ancestry of its members.	List all clubs, societies, and lodges to which you belong.
REFERENCES:	Who suggested that you apply for a position here?	

*This question may be asked only for the purpose of determining whether applicants are of legal age for employment.

Source: Michigan Department of Civil Rights, Lansing, Michigan.

In large properties, the human resources division usually handles recruiting (including advertising) and initial screening of all job candidates. After that, the head of each department conducts the main, in-depth interview and decides whom to hire. The front office manager may delegate interviewing and hiring responsibilities to an assistant. Regardless of who does the actual hiring, the front office manager is ultimately responsible for hiring and maintaining a qualified front office staff.

Whoever the interviewer is, he or she should be thoroughly familiar with the job and its duties, benefits, wage scale, and other important factors. The interviewer should be an objective judge of people and their qualifications, a positive role model, and a skillful communicator. Exhibit 5 summarizes common problems associated with interviewing. When managers are aware of factors that can distort an interview, they can better prevent them and increase the probability of a successful interview.

The interview should be held in a comfortable, private setting that allows few, if any, interruptions. Focusing on the applicant shows a sincere interest. Applicants tend to be intimidated by business settings in which they sit in front of a desk and the interviewer sits on the other side of the desk. Interviewers often find it workable and more pleasant for the applicant to hold the interview in or near the actual work area. If the work site is too distracting for a sit-down interview, another location should be chosen. Unless there is an emergency, no telephone calls or other interruptions should be allowed during the interview.

Conducting an Interview. The interview process has at least five objectives:

1. To establish a basis for a working relationship
2. To collect enough accurate information to make an informed hiring decision
3. To provide enough information to help the applicant make a decision
4. To promote the company and the work position to the preferred applicant
5. To create goodwill between the hotel and the applicant

Front office managers should speak in a conversational tone while conducting an interview. Care must be taken so that the applicant doesn't perceive the manager

Exhibit 5 Common Problems Associated with Interviewing

Similarity Error
Many interviewers are predisposed to react positively to candidates who are similar to themselves (in outside interests, personal background, and even appearance) and react negatively to candidates very different from themselves.

Contrast Error
Candidates should be compared to the standards that the club has established for the position, not to each other. Comparing candidates to one another, whether consciously or subconsciously, is particularly troublesome when two poor candidates are followed by a merely average candidate. Because of the contrast between candidates, the average candidate may be viewed as excellent, resulting in a contrast error.

Overweighting Negative Information
It is human nature to notice negative information more than positive information. When we examine a résumé or an application, we tend to look for the negative, not the positive. This also happens in interviews.

First-Impression Error
Many interviewers tend to form a strong first impression of a candidate that they maintain throughout the interview.

Halo Effect
Sometimes an interviewer's favorable impression of a single dimension about a candidate—appearance, background, and so on—can substantially color his or her overall impression. The halo effect occurs when an interviewer views everything that a candidate says or does in this favorable light.

Devil's Horns
The opposite of the halo effect. This phenomenon can often cause interviewers to see everything a candidate says or does in an unfavorable light.

Faulty Listening and Memory
Interviewers do not always hear what is said in the way it was intended, nor do they remember everything that was said.

Recency Errors
An interviewer is likely to remember a candidate's most recent behaviors or responses, rather than behaviors or responses that occurred earlier in the interview.

Nonverbal Factors
Nonverbal factors such as clothing, smiles, speech patterns, and eye contact substantially influence an interviewer's impression of candidates. Some interviewers make up their minds about whom to hire based almost solely on the candidate's attire and demeanor.

as patronizing or condescending. Essentially, managers should treat applicants with the same courtesy and respect they would extend to guests.

Interviewers should allow applicants to set the pace of the interview and should be patient with people who are nervous or shy. Applicants should not be told exactly what the manager is looking for, since some applicants might modify their responses to meet those expectations. Managers should also note the applicant's physical appearance, since many applicants will be groomed according to their highest personal standard.

A well-prepared interviewer has a list of questions already developed before the start of the interview. Interviewers may not ask all the questions, and some questions will evoke answers that lead to additional questions that may not be on the list. Questions should allow applicants to fully express themselves without feeling that they are being interrogated. The use of **closed-ended questions** requiring "Yes" and "No" answers should be limited to verifying information provided on the completed application form or to obtaining additional facts. Asking closed-ended questions such as, "Did you enjoy your previous job?" often do not provoke detailed responses. Also, these types of questions may lead job applicants to respond with answers they feel the interviewer wants to hear. To provoke fuller responses to issues, managers should ask **open-ended questions**, such as, "What did you like most about your previous job?" or "What did you like least about your previous job."

Generally, an interviewer starts the interview with a period of small talk and perhaps humor to put the applicant at ease. Then, he or she moves into the body of the interview by asking the applicant about job expectations—basically, the kind of work and working conditions the applicant is looking for. Interviewers should then focus on one principal area at a time. For example, the interviewer could thoroughly examine the applicant's work experience before talking about education or other areas.

Good interviewers encourage responses by using appropriate gestures and comments. They also listen carefully, noting the applicant's body language. Sudden changes in position or tone of voice, eye movement, facial expressions, and nervous mannerisms may indicate that the applicant feels uneasy with the discussion. When applicants hesitate before answering a question, managers should follow up with related questions to probe for further information. Moreover, when an applicant responds vaguely or changes the subject, it may mean that he or she wants to avoid the topic. Similarly, interviewers can arouse an applicant's suspicions if they try to conceal or avoid topics. When an applicant asks about the work position or aspects of front office operations, the interviewer should respond as directly and honestly as possible.

Providing the applicant a copy of the job description as part of the interview may be a good idea. It will clearly identify what the manager is looking for and the requirements of the job. The front office manager can review the job description with the applicant, identifying the important duties and responsibilities. This enables applicants to form a clearer picture of the job and an informed opinion as to whether they will like the job.

In hotels without a human resources division, the interviewer should determine early in the interview whether the applicant meets the position's basic requirements. This is also the time to mention other hiring prerequisites, such as the federal government's requirement that employees prove their legal right to work in the United States (note, however, that an applicant should not actually be required to provide such proof until after a hiring offer has been made). The person conducting the interview should also determine whether the applicant's personal job requirements may be met with respect to working conditions, scheduled hours, pay rate, type of work, and employment benefits. If it appears as though the job will not be satisfactory or workable for either side, the interview should end. Job offers made or accepted under less-than-ideal conditions are likely to lead to higher rates of employee dissatisfaction and turnover.

Interview Questions. A two-step questioning process is the most common technique used in interviewing. First, the interviewer asks for specific information such as who, what, when, or where. The second, or follow-up, question seeks a more in-depth response—one that will tell the interviewer why or how. For instance, the first question might be, "What did you like most about working at your last hotel?" After the applicant answers, the interviewer might ask, "Why was that your favorite?" Other questioning techniques interviewers can use include:

- Asking the applicant for a list rather than a single response, which allows for more spontaneity. Follow-up questions can be asked that narrow the field.
- Using direct questions to verify facts and cover a lot of information quickly. A direct question is sometimes called a closed question and usually requires a simple answer, such as yes or no.
- Asking indirect or open-ended questions, or asking the applicant to make comparisons. This technique is useful when the interviewer is seeking more than standard responses. An open-ended question is one that the applicant must elaborate on, such as "What were your favorite subjects in school?"
- Pursuing a specific subject in depth when a response seems unreasonable or unrealistic.
- Probing for additional information when the applicant gives a partial response. This is usually done by restating the reply as a question, such as, "So you felt that department was just too big, didn't you?"
- Using short affirmative responses to encourage the applicant to continue talking, such as, "I see," or "Please go on." Sometimes, it may also be helpful to nod your head in agreement.
- Using silence to indicate that the applicant should continue speaking.
- Suggesting sample answers when the applicant does not understand the question.
- Varying applicant responses by making comments rather than always asking questions.

What to ask. All questions must be based on sound business reasoning. Questions asked during an interview should be relevant to the open position. For example, the front office manager is not likely to ask an applicant for a position as a front desk agent the same questions that he or she would ask a person applying for a job as a front office supervisor. Applicants may be asked about their ability to perform specific job functions. Exhibit 6 presents a collection of sample questions that managers may use to develop interviews.

What not to ask. Managers must be careful when phrasing interview questions and when deciding what questions to ask. Generally, managers should avoid asking for information that cannot be legally used in a hiring decision. Discussions should not focus on birthplace, national origin, citizenship, age, sex, race, height and weight, marital status, religion or creed, arrest records, disabilities, and membership in clubs or religious or ethnic organizations. Managers may not ask job applicants about the existence, nature, or severity of a disability.

It is also illegal to ask questions of one sex and not the other. For example, interviewers should not ask only female applicants whether they have children or what plans they may have for child care. If such questions are employment-related and if the front office manager can prove they are, they must be asked of both male and female applicants.

Certain types of information must be obtained *after* an applicant is hired, such as proof of age and proof of the legal right to work in the United States. An appropriate time to obtain such information is while a recruit is completing employment papers. Also, a job offer may be conditioned on the results of a medical examination, drug test, or inquiry, but only if the examination or inquiry is required for all entering employees in the job. Medical examinations or inquiries of employees must be job-related and consistent with the employer's business needs.

Interview Evaluation. The sample interview evaluation form presented in Exhibit 7 lists some key traits for front office staff. Portions of this form should be structured according to front office job specifications. The front office manager can use such a form to evaluate an applicant's strengths and weaknesses. After interviewing an applicant, the front office manager may use the form to compile a score based on the following criteria:

- Applicants score zero if they meet an acceptable level of skill in a given area, or if the skill is not directly job-related.
- Applicants score plus one or plus three according to the degree they surpass the acceptable level of skill in a job-related area.
- Applicants score minus one or minus three according to the degree they fail to meet the acceptable level of skill in a job-related area.

Every applicant possesses strengths and weaknesses. An interview evaluation form ensures that shortcomings in one area do not diminish an applicant's chances for further consideration. After evaluating all applicants, the manager should select and hire the best applicant for the position. Generally, the applicant who scores the highest on the interview evaluation form will probably make the best employee. Once an applicant is selected, the manager should inform other applicants who were interviewed that the position has been filled. Sometimes, an unsuccessful applicant for one position may be qualified for an alternative open position. If so, the manager should encourage the applicant to apply.

Managers should document all employment interviews, especially interviews for applicants who were not hired. These records should contain only job-related

Exhibit 6 Sample Interview Questions

Relevant to Job Background

- Did you regularly work 40 hours a week? How much overtime did you work?
- What were your gross and take-home wages?
- What benefits did you receive? How much did you pay for them?
- What salary/wage do you desire? What is the lowest amount you are likely to accept?
- Which days of the week are best for working?
- Have you ever worked weekends before? Where? How often?
- Which shift do you enjoy working the most? Which shift can't you work? Why?
- How many hours a week would you like to work?
- How will you get to work?
- Is your means of transportation reliable for the shifts you may be working?
- When you started your last job, what position did you hold? What position do you hold now or did you hold when you left?
- What was the starting salary of your present job or the last job you held?
- How often did you get pay increases on your present job or the last job you held?
- What three things do you want to avoid on your next job?
- What qualities do you expect in a supervisor?
- Why did you choose this line of work?
- Why are you interested in working at this hotel?
- Which work experience most influenced your career decisions?

Education and Intelligence

- When you were in school, what subjects did you like the most? Why?
- When you were in school, what subjects did you like the least? Why?
- Do you think your grades are a good indicator of your overall abilities?
- If you had to make the same educational decisions over again, would you make the same choices? Why or why not?
- What is the most important thing you have learned in the past six months?
- What good qualities did you find in your best teachers? Can these apply to work as well?

Personal Traits

Some of the following may be more suitable for people without much work background:

- What do you like to do in your spare time?
- How many times were you absent or late for your present or last job? Is that normal? What were the reasons?
- What does your family think of your working at this hotel?
- On your last job, were the policies concerning being late or absent without cause clearly explained to you? Were these policies fair?
- What was your first supervisor like?
- How did you get your first job? Your most recent job?

Exhibit 6 *(continued)*

For the following questions about personal traits, job titles may be changed to meet the needs of the interview:

- Who has greater responsibilities—a front desk agent or a reservation sales agent? Why?
- Have you ever had to deal with an angry guest who complains about everything? If so, how did you work with the guest to resolve the issues?
- What do you consider the main reason people in the position you are applying for leave their jobs? What would you do to change this?
- What do you consider the most important responsibilities of a good front desk agent?
- Suppose your supervisor insisted you learn a task in a certain way, when you know there is a better way. What would you do?
- Have you ever had a supervisor show favoritism to certain employees? How did you feel about this?
- Of all your job experiences, what did you like the most? Why?
- Of all your job experiences, what did you like the least? Why?
- When you go to a store to purchase something, what qualities do you look for in the sales person?
- What was your biggest accomplishment on your last job?
- What would you have changed about your last job if you had the opportunity?
- If the opportunity was offered to you, would you return to your last employer? Why or why not?
- How much notice did you give your last employer when you decided to leave (or plan to give your current employer)?
- How would your former supervisor and fellow employees describe you?
- What strengths and weaknesses do you bring to this new position?
- What frustrates you on the job? How do you handle this frustration?
- On your last performance review, what areas did your former supervisor mention need to be improved? Why do you think the comment was made?
- What three areas would you most like to improve about yourself?
- What one thing have you done of which you are the proudest? Why?
- What is the funniest thing that has ever happened to you?
- What is important to you about the job you are applying for? Why?

Questions for Managerial Candidates

- What type of training program did you have for your employees? Who set it up and who implemented it?
- What have you done on your last job to improve the performance of the department you supervised? How was this measured?
- What are the most important attributes of a manager?
- What hotels were your biggest competitors? What were their strengths and weaknesses?
- How would your employees describe you as a supervisor?
- How many people did you have to discipline on your last job? Describe the circumstances. How do you feel about terminating employees?
- What did you do to motivate your employees?

Exhibit 7 Sample Interview Evaluation Form

Applicant Name ____________ Position Evaluated ____________ Date ________

	Poor Match		Acceptable	Strong Match	
	–3	–1	0	+1	+3
RELEVANT JOB BACKGROUND					
General background					
Work experience					
Similar companies					
Interest in job					
Salary requirements					
Attendance					
Leadership experience					
EDUCATION/INTELLIGENCE					
Formal schooling					
Intellectual ability					
Additional training					
Social skills					
Verbal and listening skills					
Writing skills					
PHYSICAL FACTORS					
General health					
Physical ability					
Cleanliness, dress, and posture					
Energy level					
PERSONAL TRAITS					
First impression					
Interpersonal skills					
Personality					
Teamwork					
Motivation					
Outlook, humor, and optimism					
Values					
Creativity					
Stress tolerance					
Performing skills					
Service attitude					
Independence					
Planning and organizing					
Problem solving					
Maturity					
Decisiveness					
Self-knowledge					
Flexibility					
Work standards					
Subtotals					

TOTAL POINTS ________

information. The interviewer's personal notes should not become part of a candidate's job application file.

Hiring

The **hiring period** begins when an employer extends an offer to a prospective employee. Hiring involves making all the necessary arrangements to prepare the recruit and current employees for a successful working relationship, including processing personnel records. The hiring period lasts through the recruit's initial on-the-job adjustments.

Job Offers

Since hiring requires a degree of skill and knowledge of complex labor laws, most front office managers rely on the human resources division or someone specifically designated by top management. When only one or two people are authorized to make employment offers, the hotel has greater control over how the job is represented and what pre-employment promises are made. The three steps of making and closing employment offers are extending, negotiating, and concluding.

Extending the Offer. A carefully worded offer can represent the beginning of a potential employee's commitment to the employer. To be sure the terms of the offer are clear and there is no misunderstanding, many hotels require written job offers. Successful employment offers depend on timing. The longer a front office manager waits to extend an offer, the less likely a candidate is to accept. In the interim, the applicant may lose enthusiasm or interest, or may have accepted a job somewhere else. Whenever possible, job offers should be extended in writing. Doing so can eliminate misunderstandings about the job title, job requirements, starting pay, or working schedule.

Negotiating the Offer. During the interview process, the front office manager should become familiar with an applicant's background and expectations. Many of the areas that sometimes become obstacles to job offers (such as pay, starting dates, and employment benefits) should be discussed. Management should negotiate a job offer only when it is reasonably certain the offer will be accepted.

Establishing a reasonable starting date informs recruits that the front office expects its employees to give proper notice before leaving a job. Hotels cannot expect employees to give proper notice when they do not allow potential recruits sufficient time to give proper notice to their current employer.

Completing an Offer. Once an applicant accepts a job offer, the front office manager should assure the applicant that he or she has made the right decision. Recruits should be told that they are not expected to know everything about a job at the outset, but that management believes in their ability to handle the job successfully. Supervisors should immediately begin preparations for the recruit's arrival, including informing other front office staff about the new employee. Current employees should be told the new recruit's name, previous job experience, and starting date. The front office manager should meet with workshift leaders and encourage them to assist with the recruit's training and work relationships.

Processing Personnel Records

Processing new employees' personnel records before they start work helps prepare them for their new positions. Uniforms should be fitted and name tags ordered since these items are needed for the employee's first work day.

The tone of the processing period should be warm, caring, and professional. If it's too light, casual, or hectic, new employees may conclude that the hotel or front office is lax in its policies and procedures. Employees should learn what management expects in the way of service, as well as the goals of the front office and the hotel. Management will find the processing period an excellent time to review goals and expectations with new employees.

At this time, the front office manager or human resources division employee should also discuss time cards, pay procedures, house rules, reporting instructions, and uniforms. Reliance on a checklist will ensure that all important points are covered. Many of these points will be reinforced during employee orientation.

Orienting

New employees should be given an **orientation** when they arrive for their first day of work. A well-planned and organized orientation helps new employees get off to a good start. Usually, the new employee's first days on a job are filled with anxiety. The front office manager should take full responsibility for orienting new front office employees.

Managers should plan to make the employee's transition into the new job as smooth as possible. At the least, the orientation should include information about:

- *The hotel*—its history, reputation for service, names of key management personnel, plans for growth, company policies, and chain information.
- *The benefits*—wages, insurance coverage, employee discounts, vacations, and paid holidays.
- *The working conditions*—applicable training schedules, work schedules, breaks, meal periods, overtime, safety, security, employee bulletin boards and log books, and social activities.
- *The job*—the tasks the job entails, how the job fits within the front office, how the front office fits within the hotel, and what performance standards are expected.
- *The front office team*—introductions to fellow employees, overview of the key responsibilities of each employee, and explanation of reporting structures.
- *The rules and regulations*—regarding, for example, smoking, entry and exit, disciplinary action, and parking privileges.
- *The building*—the layout of the building, the location of the employee entrance, locker room, employee dining room, uniform room, front desk, and other important departments. In addition, front desk, reservations, and bell staff should be shown guestrooms, dining rooms, recreation areas, and meeting rooms to begin to understand the layout of guest areas.

Much of this information should appear in the employee manual or handbook. Time should be set aside during an employee's first day of work to complete all tax withholding, insurance, and similar work-related forms. Uniforms and lockers should be provided if they are part of the job. New employees should also be given a tour of the entire facility, especially the different types of guestrooms and meeting rooms. The tour should include the work area, time clocks, and locations of posted work schedules, supply areas, first aid kits, restrooms, and break areas. A tour of related departments will help reinforce an explanation of the workflow and need for teamwork. During the tour, the front office manager should introduce as many fellow staff members as possible.

Management should ensure that all revenue centers are shown to the recruit. The tour should also point out the locations of housekeeping, laundry, maintenance, accounting, and other important hotel departments. Among the most important features of a tour, however, is the time taken to introduce the new employee to key managers, especially the general manager and the rooms division manager. Such introductions can help make the recruit feel immediately part of the team. It also establishes recognition between management and staff.

Skills Training

Ensuring that employees receive proper training is one of the front office manager's major responsibilities. This does not mean that the manager must necessarily assume the duties and responsibilities of a trainer. The actual training functions may be delegated to trainers, to department supervisors, or even to talented line employees. However, the front office manager should be responsible for ongoing training programs in the department.

Most managers and trainers understand that the goal of training is to help staff members develop skills to do their jobs well. Many managers and trainers, however, are not sure of the best way to train. Often, they need a framework for training. The four-step training method provides that framework. The four steps in the method are:

- Prepare to train.
- Present the traning.
- Practice skills.
- Follow up.

Prepare to Train

Preparation is essential for successful training. Without adequate preparation, the training will lack a logical sequence and key details of the job may be omitted. Before training begins, the job must be analyzed and the staff's training needs must be assessed.

Analyze Jobs. The foundation for training and for preventing performance problems is job analysis. **Job analysis** is determining what knowledge staff members must have, what tasks they need to perform, and the standards at which they must

Exhibit 8 Job Knowledge for Front Office Employees

Knowledge for All Employees

- Quality guest service
- Bloodborne pathogens
- Personal appearance
- Emergency situations
- Lost and found
- Recycling procedures
- Safe work habits
- Manager on duty identification
- Property fact sheet
- Employee policies
- The Americans with Disabilities Act

Knowledge for All Front Office Employees

- Telephone courtesy
- Security
- Guestroom types
- Maintenance needs
- Property policies
- Community information
- Giving directions
- Airport shuttle services
- Elevator courtesy
- Restaurant menus
- OSHA regulations

perform them. Without a complete knowledge of what each staff member is expected to do, you can't train properly. Job analysis involves three steps: identifying job knowledge, creating a task list, and developing a job breakdown for each task performed by front office positions. The knowledge, lists, and breakdowns also form an efficient system for evaluating performance.

Job knowledge identifies what a staff member needs to know to perform his or her job. Job knowledge can be divided into three categories: knowledge for all hotel employees, knowledge for front office employees, and knowledge specific to a position like a front desk agent. Exhibit 8 lists topics that might be covered with all hotel employees and topics relevant for all front office employees. Front desk agents will have knowledge requirements that are specific to operations at the front desk. These topics may include:

- Working as a team with co-workers and other departments

- Target markets
- Overview of responsibilities at the front desk
- Guestroom equipment and amenities
- Telephone system
- Point-of-sale equipment
- Front desk computer system
- Front desk printers
- Room racks
- Types of reservations
- Room inventory and occupancy terms
- Room rate terms
- Room status terms
- Frequent flyer/guest programs
- Check-in/check-out guidelines
- Room forecasts
- Credit card approval procedures
- Credit check report
- Currency exchange
- Par stock system
- VIP procedures

A **task list** should reflect the total job responsibility of a position. Exhibit 9 presents a sample task list for a front desk agent. Note that each line on the sample task list begins with a verb. This format stresses action and clearly indicates to a staff member what he or she will be responsible for doing. Wherever possible, tasks should be listed in an order that reflects the logical sequence of daily responsibilities.

A **job breakdown** includes a list of needed equipment and supplies, steps, how-to's, and tips explaining how to complete a single task. The job breakdown format can vary to suit the needs and requirements of individual operations. Exhibit 10 presents a sample job breakdown for Task #16, Use Effective Sales Techniques, listed in Exhibit 9.

Each member of the front office staff should know the standards that will be used to measure his or her job performance. Therefore, it is important to break down job tasks and document the standards. In order to serve as a performance standard, each task must be observable and measurable. Exhibit 11 shows a sample Training Needs Evaluation for Current Employees form that can be used as a performance evaluation. The front office manager (or the supervising manager) conducting a quarterly performance evaluation should be able to simply check the box matching the staff member's performance.

Exhibit 9 Sample Task List—Front Desk Agent

FRONT DESK AGENT TASK LIST

1. Use the front desk computer system.
2. Use the front desk printers.
3. Use the front desk telephone system.
4. Use the facsimile machine.
5. Use the photocopy machine.
6. Organize the front desk and prepare for check-ins.
7. Use the front office log book.
8. Prepare and use an arrivals list.
9. Block and unblock rooms.
10. Set up preregistrations.
11. Begin guest check-in.
12. Establish the payment method during check-in.
13. Secure authorization for credit cards.
14. Issue and control guestroom keys/key cards.
15. Finish guest check-in.
16. Use effective sales techniques.
17. Preregister and check in group arrivals.
18. Show rooms to potential guests.
19. Use a waiting list when rooms are not ready for check-in.
20. Relocate guests in sold-out situations.
21. Use a manual room rack system.
22. Process room changes.
23. Process safe deposit box transactions for guests.
24. Prepare a cash-only report for outlets.
25. Run and follow up on credit check reports.
26. Process guest mail, packages, telegrams, and faxes.
27. Maintain a guest information directory.
28. Prepare maps and provide directions.
29. Help guests with special requests.
30. Respond to questions about services and events.
31. Handle guest service problems.
32. Cash checks for guests.
33. Pick up, use, and turn in cash bank.
34. Post guest charges and payments.
35. Follow guest privacy and security measures.
36. Process wake-up call requests.
37. Operate the pay movie system.
38. Process guaranteed no-shows.
39. Update room status.
40. Help guests make future reservations.
41. Process guest check-outs.
42. Adjust disputed guest charges.
43. Transfer allowable guest charges.
44. Process automatic check-outs.
45. Handle late guest check-outs.
46. Process late charges.
47. Keep the front desk clean and orderly.

Exhibit 9 *(continued)*

48. Reconcile room status with the p.m. housekeeping report.
49. Prepare a current status report.
50. Perform bucket or tub checks.
51. Inventory and requisition front desk supplies.
52. Complete and turn in the shift checklist.
53. Respond to situations requiring first aid.
54. Respond to emergency alarms.

Source: Hospitality Skills Training Series, *Front Desk Employee Guide* (East Lansing, Mich.: Educational Institute of the American Hotel & Motel Association)

Develop Job Breakdowns. If one person in the front office is assigned the responsibility of writing every job breakdown, the job may never get done, unless the operation is very small with a limited number of tasks. Some of the best job breakdowns are written by those who actually perform the tasks. In properties with large staffs, standards groups can be formed to handle the writing tasks. Group members should include department supervisors and several experienced employees. In smaller properties, experienced staff members might be assigned to write the job breakdowns alone.

Most hotels have a policy and procedures manual. Although this manual rarely contains the detail necessary to set up effective training and evaluation programs, portions of it may be helpful to members of a standards group as they write job breakdowns for each department position. For example, if the procedure sections of the manual include job descriptions and job specifications, they may help a standards group in writing job lists and performance standards. The policy sections may be helpful sources of additional information that can be included in the job breakdowns.

The job breakdowns for tasks that involve the use of equipment may already be written in the operating manuals supplied by vendors. Standards groups should not have to write performance standards for operating the front desk computer system. Instead, the standards group may simply refer to (or even attach) appropriate pages from the operating manual supplied by the vendor for in-house training.

Developing job breakdowns involves breaking down each task on each front office job list by writing the **performance standards** that state the specific observable and measurable steps a staff member must take to accomplish the task. The front office manager should assist the standards group in writing performance standards for at least two or three positions. While assisting the group, the manager should stress that each performance standard must be observable and measurable. The value of each performance standard can be tested by asking whether a supervisor or manager can evaluate a staff member's performance by simply checking a "Yes" or "No" in the quarterly performance review column.

After the standards group has written job breakdowns for two or three tasks, the writing of job breakdowns for the other tasks should be assigned to individual members of the group. Within a specified time, they should submit their work to the front office manager, who then assembles the breakdowns, has them processed

Exhibit 10 Sample Job Breakdown

Use Effective Sales Techniques

***Materials needed:** Promotional programs catalog, promotional materials, brochures, guestroom diagrams, and restaurant and room service menus.*

STEPS	HOW-TO'S	TIPS
1. Upsell guestrooms.	❑ Suggest higher-rate guestrooms when guests check in. ❑ Describe features and benefits of the more expensive rooms. ❑ Show guests room diagrams to help explain features. ❑ If guests have children, suggest a larger room to give them extra space. ❑ Suggest a room with extra amenities to business travelers, or a larger room so they can hold meetings. ❑ If a couple is vacationing, suggest a room with features that will give them a more memorable experience.	*Upselling is a way of selling a more expensive guestroom than the one a guest originally requested.* *It never hurts to offer a guest a better room. You're showing that you want the guest to have a pleasant stay.*
	❑ Be sure to always directly ask guests if they would like to check into a room you describe.	*Don't wait for guests to tell you to book a certain room type. Anticipate what they want and ask if you can book that room type for them.*
2. Suggest the food and beverage outlets.	❑ Suggest ordering from room service if guests say they don't have time to leave their rooms. Tell guests the hours of service. ❑ Use good judgment. Don't recommend heavy dishes on the room service menu late at night.	*Guests usually welcome a positive suggestion.*
	❑ Recommend the property's restaurant if guests ask for a good place to eat. ❑ Show guests the menu to help them decide.	*Remember, you'll be using teamwork when you suggest the property's restaurants.*

Exhibit 10 *(continued)*

Use Effective Sales Techniques (continued)		
STEPS	**HOW-TO'S**	**TIPS**
	❑ Be able to tell guests about reservation and dress code requirements. ❑ Listen to guests. If they specifically ask for a restaurant outside the lodging property, suggest local establishments. ❑ Suggest the lounge if guests are looking for a place to unwind.	
	❑ Stay informed about changes in menus, hours, and entertainment. Guests expect you to be an expert about your property.	*See "Restaurant Menus" in Knowledge for All Front Office Employees.*
3. Suggest property promotions.	❑ Ask your supervisor which promotions are available at your property. ❑ Study the features and benefits of each promotion. ❑ Enthusiastically describe programs that may meet guests' needs. ❑ Give guests any brochures and other promotional materials available.	*Guests like to feel that they are getting "freebies" or "special deals."*

Source: Hospitality Skills Training Series, *Front Desk Employee Guide* (East Lansing, Mich.: Educational Institute of the American Hotel & Motel Association)

into a single format (perhaps similar to that shown in Exhibit 10) and provides copies to all of the group's members. A final meeting can then be held, with the standards group carefully analyzing the breakdowns for each position. After the job breakdowns have been finalized, they should be used immediately to train the front office staff.

Analyze New Employee Training Needs. The task list is an excellent tool with which to plan employee training. Realistically, new staff members cannot be expected to learn all of the tasks before the first day on the job. Before you begin

Exhibit 11 Sample Training Needs Evaluation Form

Training Needs Evaluation for Current Employees

How well are your current employees performing? Use this form to observe and rate their work.

Part 1: Job Knowledge

Rate the employee's knowledge of each of the following topics:	Well Below Standard	Slightly Below Standard	At Standard	Above Standard
Knowledge for All Employees				
Quality Guest Service				
Bloodborne Pathogens				
Personal Appearance				
Emergency Situations				
Lost and Found				
Recycling Procedures				
Safe Work Habits				
Manager on Duty				
Your Property's Fact Sheet				
Employee Policies				
The Americans with Disabilities Act				
Knowledge for All Front Office Employees				
Telephone Courtesy				
Security				
Guestroom Types				
Maintenance Needs				
Property Policies				
Your Community				
Giving Directions				
Transportation to the Airport				
Elevator Courtesy				
Restaurant Menus				
OSHA Regulations				
Knowledge for Front Desk Employees				
What Is a Front Desk Employee?				
Working as a Team With Co-Workers and Other Departments				
Target Markets				

training, study the task list. Then, rate each task according to whether it should be mastered (1) before working alone on the job; (2) within two weeks on the job; or (3) within two months on the job.

Exhibit 11 *(continued)*

Training Needs Evaluation for Current Employees *(continued)*

Part 1: Job Knowledge *(continued)*

Rate the employee's knowledge of each of the following topics:	Well Below Standard	Slightly Below Standard	At Standard	Above Standard
Knowledge for Front Desk Employees *(continued)*				
Using Guestroom Equipment and Amenities				
The Telephone System				
Point-of-Sale Equipment				
The Front Desk Computer System				
Front Desk Printers				
Room Racks				
Types of Reservations				
Room Inventory and Occupancy Terms				
Room Rate Terms				
Room Status Terms				
Frequent Flyer Program				
Check-In and Check-Out Guidelines				
Room Forecasts				
Credit Card Approval Procedures				
Check Approval Procedures				
Credit Check Report				
Currency Exchange				
Par Stock System				
VIPs				

(continued)

Select several of the tasks that you rated as "1" and plan to cover those in the first training session. After the employee understands and can perform these, teach the remaining tasks in subsequent training sessions until the new staff member has learned all of the tasks.

Once you've decided which tasks you'll teach in each training session, turn to the job breakdowns. Think of the job breakdown for each task as a lesson plan for training or as a learning guide for self-directed study. Because the job breakdowns list all the steps staff members must perform, they tell exactly what needs to be done during the training. Job breakdowns can direct the instruction and make sure that critical points or steps are not overlooked.

The knowledge a staff member must know is usually written on a single page. Assign new employees nine or ten knowledge sections or job breakdowns at a time to study. Do not ask an employee to read all the knowledge sections and all the job

Exhibit 11 *(continued)*

Training Needs Evaluation for Current Employees *(continued)*

Part 2: Job Skills

Rate the employee's skills in performing each of the following tasks:	Well Below Standard	Slightly Below Standard	At Standard	Above Standard
Use the Front Desk Computer System				
Use the Front Desk Printers				
Use the Front Desk Telephone System				
Use the Facsimile Machine				
Use the Photocopy Machine				
Organize the Front Desk and Prepare for Check-Ins				
Use the Front Office Logbook				
Prepare and Use an Arrivals List				
Block and Unblock Rooms				
Set Up Preregistrations				
Begin Guest Check-In				
Establish the Payment Method During Check-In				
Secure Authorization for Credit Cards				
Issue and Control Guestroom Keys				
Finish Guest Check-In				
Use Effective Sales Techniques				
Preregister and Check In Group Arrivals				
Show Rooms to Potential Guests				
Use a Waiting List When Rooms Are Not Ready for Check-In				
Relocate Guests in Sold-out Situations				
Use a Manual Room Rack System				
Process Room Changes				
Process Safe-Deposit-Box Transactions for Guests				
Prepare a Cash-Only Report for Outlets				
Run and Follow Up on Credit Check Reports				
Process Guest Mail, Packages, Telegrams, and Faxes				
Maintain a Guest Information Directory				

breakdowns at once. This will overwhelm the employee and he or she won't remember enough information to perform the job well.

Analyze Current Employee Training Needs. Front office managers sometimes feel that there's a problem with an employee's work or with several employees'

Exhibit 11 *(continued)*

Training Needs Evaluation for Current Employees *(continued)*

Part 2: Job Skills *(continued)*

Rate the employee's skills in performing each of the following tasks:	Well Below Standard	Slightly Below Standard	At Standard	Above Standard
Prepare Maps and Provide Directions				
Help Guests With Special Requests				
Respond to Questions About Services and Events				
Handle Guest Service Problems				
Cash Checks for Guests				
Pick Up, Use, and Turn In Your Cash Bank				
Post Guest Charges and Payments				
Follow Guest Privacy and Security Measures				
Process Wake-Up Calls				
Operate the Pay Movie System				
Process Guaranteed No-Shows				
Update Room Status				
Help Guests Make Reservations				
Process Guest Check-Outs at the Desk				
Adjust Disputed Guest Charges				
Transfer Allowable Guest Charges				
Process Automatic Check-Outs				
Handle Late Guest Check-Outs				
Process Late Charges				
Keep the Front Desk Clean and Orderly				
Reconcile Room Status With the P.M. Housekeeping Report				
Prepare a Current Status Report				
Perform Bucket or Tub Checks				
Inventory and Requisition Front Desk Supplies				
Complete and Turn In the Shift Checklist				
Respond to Situations Requiring First Aid				
Respond to Emergency Alarms				

Source: Hospitality Skills Training Series, *Front Desk Employee Guide* (East Lansing, Mich.: Educational Institute of the American Hotel & Motel Association).

work, but they're not exactly sure what it is; or they feel that something's not quite right with the staff, but don't know where to start making improvements. A training needs assessment can help uncover a staff member's weaknesses as well as weaknesses of an entire staff. To conduct a needs assessment of a single employee, observe present performance for two or three days and record it on a copy of a form similar to the one in Exhibit 11. Areas in which the employee scores poorly are those you'll want to target when you plan refresher training.

Develop Department Training Plan. It's a good idea to make a training plan four times a year, every three months or so. And it's best to complete each plan one month before the beginning of each quarter. Follow these steps to prepare for training sessions:

- Carefully review all knowledge sections and job breakdowns that you will use in training.
- Make a copy of each knowledge section and job breakdown for each trainee.
- Establish a training schedule. This will depend on whom you are training and the training method you use. Remember to limit each training session's information to what employees can understand and remember.
- Select a training time and location. When possible, conduct training at the appropriate work stations during slow business hours.
- Notify the employee or employees of the dates and times of the training sessions.
- Practice your presentation.
- Gather all the necessary supplies for demonstrating tasks.

Present the Training

Well-developed job breakdowns provide all the information you need to conduct the "present" step of the four-step training method. Use the job breakdowns as a training guide. Follow the sequence of each step in each job breakdown. For each step, show and tell staff members what to do, how to do it, and why the details are important.

Give them a chance to prepare. Let new employees study the task list to get an overview of all the tasks they will learn to perform. If possible, give the list to them at least one day before the first training session. At least a day before each training session, let new and current employees review the job breakdowns that you plan to cover in that session. Then begin each training session by going over what they will do. Let them know how long activities will take and when their breaks will be.

As you explain the steps, demonstrate them. Make sure staff members can see exactly what you are doing. Encourage them to ask questions whenever they need more information. Be sure to take enough time when presenting your training. Go slowly and carefully. Be patient if staff members don't understand right away. Go over all the steps at least two times. When you show a step a second time, ask them questions to see if they understand. Repeat the steps as many times as necessary. Avoid jargon. Use words that employees who are new to the hospitality industry or your property can understand. They can pick up the jargon later.

Practice Skills

When the trainer and trainees agree that they are familiar with the job and able to complete the steps acceptably, trainees should try to perform the tasks alone. Immediate practice results in good work habits. Have each trainee demonstrate each step of the task presented during the training session. This tells you whether they really do understand. Resist the urge to do the tasks for the employees.

Coaching will help staff members gain the skill and confidence necessary to perform the job. Compliment employees immediately after correct performance. Gently correct them when you observe problems. Bad habits formed at this stage of the training may be very difficult to break later. Be sure that the trainee understands and can explain not only how to perform each step, but also the purpose of each step.

Follow Up

There are a number of things you can do to make it easier for your employees to carry skills over to the workplace after training. Some of these options include:

- Provide opportunities to use and demonstrate new skills during and after training.
- Have employees discuss the training with their co-workers.
- Provide ongoing, open communication on progress and concerns.

Continue Coaching on the Job. While training helps employees learn new knowledge and develop new skills and attitudes, coaching focuses on the actual on-the-job application of what has been learned in the training sessions. As a coach, you challenge, encourage, correct, and positively reinforce the knowledge, skills, and attitudes learned during the training session. On-the-job coaching tips include:

- Observe employees while they work to ensure that they are performing tasks correctly.
- Make casual suggestions to correct minor problems.
- Tactfully correct employees when they make major mistakes. Typically the best way to do his is in a quiet location, when neither of you is busy.
- If an employee is using an unsafe procedure, correct the problem right away.

Give Constant Feedback. Feedback is when you tell employees how well they are performing. Two types of feedback are positive feedback, which recognizes a job well done, and redirective feedback, which recognizes incorrect performance and reviews how the employee can improve. Some tips for giving both types of feedback include:

- Let employees know what they are doing correctly and incorrectly.
- Tell employees when they perform well after training. This will help them remember what they learn. It will also encourage them to use those behaviors and that information on the job.

- If employees are not meeting performance standards, first compliment them for the tasks they are doing correctly. Then, show them how to correct their bad habits, and explain why it's important that they do so.
- Be specific. Describe behavior by stating exactly what the employee said and did.
- Choose your words carefully; you want to sound helpful, not demanding.

  Don't say, "You used quality guest service when you asked the guest who seemed lost if you could help, but you should have known the restaurant's hours of operation. Study your copy of the property's fact sheet."

  Do say, "You used quality guest service when you asked the guest who seemed lost if you could help, and you could give even better service by learning the restaurant's and other facilities' hours of operation. Let me get you another copy of the property's fact sheet."
- Make sure you understand what the employee is saying. Say something such as, "What I'm hearing you say is..."
- Make sure the employee understands your message. Say something such as, "I'm not sure I explained everything clearly. Let me hear what you think I said."
- Always be sincere and tactful with your comments. Employees appreciate an honest compliment about a specific behavior. And no one likes to be embarrassed or put down by criticism.
- Tell employees where to find help when you are not available.

Evaluate. Evaluate employees' progress. Use the task list as a checklist to confirm that all tasks have been mastered. Provide further training and practice for tasks that have not been mastered.

Get Employees' Feedback. Let employees evaluate the training they received. This can help you improve your training efforts for them and other employees. Keep training records for each person who receives training. Track each employee's training history and keep a copy of a training log in that employee's personnel file.

Staff Scheduling

Employee scheduling is one of the most challenging tasks confronting a front office manager. Scheduling can be extremely complex, especially when front office staff have been trained to perform only specific tasks. For example, a front desk agent should not be scheduled as a switchboard operator when he or she has had no switchboard training.

Employee scheduling affects payroll costs, employee productivity, and morale. The more cross-training that occurs within the front office, the fewer staff required to perform front office tasks. Staffing flexibility is the direct result of proper training in several areas. Cross-training provides front office staff with expanded job knowledge and a broader range of skills. Many employees find work more interesting when they are trained to do several tasks. When staff see their skills improving and expanding, they feel more confident; the result for the front office is improved employee morale. Good morale has a way of spreading throughout the entire staff.

Front office managers must be sensitive to the scheduling needs of their staff. For example, hourly staff may request a varied schedule to avoid working hours that conflict with school classes. Some front office staff may ask to work varied shifts to learn the unique challenges posed by each shift. Some front office managers base employee scheduling on seniority. Others base their schedules on other criteria and preferences. Both methods are fair, but the front office manager must be consistent in applying scheduling criteria and attentive to each staff member's needs to determine a workable schedule.

While being sensitive to employee needs, the front office manager must also keep the needs of the front office in mind. Scheduling employees on days when they are available but not needed can be an unnecessary financial burden to the hotel.

Front office managers may find the following tips helpful when developing staffing schedules:

- A schedule should cover a full workweek, typically defined as Sunday through Saturday.
- Schedules should be posted at least three days before the beginning of the next workweek. Some states require schedules be posted five days or more before the beginning of the next work period. It is also essential that the front office manager understand laws pertaining to overtime hours and pay.
- Days off, vacation time, and requested days off should be indicated on the posted work schedule. Employees should be familiar with the required lead time to submit a vacation request.
- The work schedule for the current week should be reviewed daily in relation to anticipated business volume and unanticipated changes in staff availability. If necessary, changes to the schedule should be made.
- Any scheduling changes should be noted directly on the posted work schedule.
- A copy of the posted work schedule can be used to monitor the daily attendance of employees. This copy should be retained as part of the department's permanent records.

Alternative Scheduling Techniques

Alternative scheduling involves a staffing schedule that varies from a typical 9 A.M. to 5 P.M. workday. Variations include part-time and flextime hours, compressed schedules, and job sharing.

Part-Time Scheduling. Part-time staff frequently include students, new or young parents, retirees, and other individuals who choose not to work full-time. Employing part-time staff can provide the front office with extra flexibility in scheduling. It can also help reduce labor costs since expenses attributable to benefits and overtime usually decrease.

Flextime Scheduling. Flextime planning allows employees to vary the time they begin and end workshifts. Each shift has certain hours when all scheduled staff must be present. Staffing needs during the rest of the shift can vary. The front office manager must ensure that each hour of the day is adequately covered. Flextime can enhance staff morale, productivity, and job satisfaction. Moreover, front offices with flextime arrangements can sometimes attract a larger number of high quality employees. Most front office managers use flextime in one form or another to cover the varying workloads of all shifts. For example, traditional shifts at the front desk are from 7 A.M. to 3 P.M. and 3 P.M. until 11 P.M. Due to heavy check-in traffic, however, it may be more beneficial to schedule one or two employees on a noon to 8 P.M. shift. Airport hotels may have a 6 A.M. to 2 P.M. shift to cover early morning departures.

Compressed Schedules. Compressed schedules offer employees the opportunity to work the equivalent of a standard workweek in fewer than the usual number of days. One popular arrangement condenses the 40-hour workweek into four 10-hour days. Compressed schedules tend to be somewhat inflexible. Front office staff members may prefer inflexible hours within a four-day week to flexible hours within a five-day week. Benefits from the employer's point-of-view include enhanced employee morale and reduced absenteeism. Front office managers should be cautious when considering the adoption of compressed schedules. In some states, employees qualify for overtime by working more than eight hours a day, even though their total workweek may not exceed 40 hours.

Job Sharing. In **job sharing,** the combined efforts of two or more part-time employees fulfill the duties and responsibilities of one full-time job. Usually, the staff members who share a job work different hours and often different shift portions. Some overlap is desired so staff can exchange information, solve problems, or simply ensure a smooth workflow. Job sharing can lessen department turnover and absenteeism, as well as increase staff morale. The front office also benefits since even if one job-sharing partner terminates employment, the other may be likely to stay and help train a new partner.

It should be noted that all of the scheduling techniques discussed above must be done with certain restrictions in mind. In hotels where the hourly staff is represented by unions, there may be work scheduling rules that limit the flexibility of schedules or require overtime pay after eight hours are worked on any given day. In other cases, state and federal wage and hour laws may place some limitations on scheduling. Before a front office manager begins scheduling employees, he or she should have a thorough knowledge of these union contract rules and work regulations.

Staff Motivation

Front office managers should strive to create a work environment that fosters the professional development and growth of the staff. To do so, management must provide training, guidance, instruction, discipline, evaluation, direction, and leadership. When the front office lacks these basic elements, staff may become passive, critical, and indifferent to the hotel's objectives. Such feelings may manifest themselves in absenteeism, poor productivity, and high employee turnover.

With the current changes in the labor market and the high cost of employee turnover, the front office must seek ways to retain effective staff. One way to meet this major challenge is to practice strong motivational techniques.

Motivation can mean many different things. For the purpose of this text, motivation means the art of stimulating a front office staff member's interest in a particular job, project, or subject to the extent that he or she is challenged to be continuously attentive, observant, concerned, and committed. Motivation is the result of satisfying human needs associated with personal worth, value, and belonging. In the front office, the outcome of motivation should be that a staff member's sense of worth, value, and belonging has improved from taking part in a particular activity. A front office staff member who receives recognition for contributions he or she makes to the front office's success is typically a highly motivated top performer.

A front office manager can motivate front office staff in a number of ways, including training, cross-training, recognition, communication, and incentive programs.

Training

One of the most effective ways to motivate employees is to train them. Training informs employees that management cares enough to provide the necessary instruction and direction to ensure their success. Successful training includes information not only about the job tasks and duties (the "what to do" on a job), but also about the company culture (the "why tasks are done a certain way" on the job). The what and why must tie together. If the employee does not know why a job is done a certain way, he or she will not really understand the job. This can lead to poor job performance and friction between employees. When employees understand the culture, they become part of it and support it.

Training significantly reduces the frustration front office staff experience when they do not know what is expected of them. Effective training educates staff about performance expectations, required tasks, and equipment. The investment in training pays off because it makes employees more productive and efficient, as well as easier to manage.

Cross-Training

Cross-training simply means teaching an employee job functions other than those he or she was hired to perform. Cross-training has many advantages for both front office management and staff. For the employee, cross-training can offer an opportunity to acquire additional work skills. For the manager, cross-training increases flexibility in scheduling. Cross-trained employees are more valuable since they can perform several job functions. Finally, cross-training can be a valuable motivational tool that removes many of the obstacles associated with professional growth and advancement.

Recognition

When guests make positive comments about a front office staff member or select the hotel for a return stay, it usually reflects guest satisfaction. Front office management should communicate positive feedback to staff as recognition for a job well done.

Graphs and charts which depict improvements in revenues, achievements, occupancy, and guest satisfaction can also be effective motivators.

Guest, managerial, and peer recognition are strong staff motivators. Many hotels solicit guest feedback through comment cards. Comment cards may be handed out at the front desk or placed in guestrooms, dining rooms, or other areas. Comment cards frequently ask guests to mention employees who have provided outstanding service. Completed guest comment cards can be posted on an employee bulletin board, especially those complimenting individual staff efforts.

The front office may offer incentives to staff who are favorably recognized by guests. For example, a front desk agent who is mentioned through guest comment cards, comments to managers, or letters to the front office may receive dinner in the hotel dining room or a gift certificate.

Another popular form of recognition is an employee-of-the-month program. A front office staff member of the month may be selected by front office management or the front office staff. Usually, an employee qualifies for this honor by demonstrating extraordinary commitment to the front office, its standards, and its goals. The front office employee of the month usually receives a prize certificate or a plaque.

Communication

Keeping employees informed about front office operations helps produce positive results. Staff who are informed about upcoming events tend to feel a greater sense of belonging and value.

A front office newsletter or bulletin can be an excellent way to establish and maintain formal communications. Articles included in such a newsletter might be job-related or personal, including such topics as:

- Job opening announcements
- Promotion, transfer, resignation, and retirement announcements
- New recruit announcements
- Performance tips
- Special recognition awards
- Birthday, marriage, engagement, and birth announcements
- Upcoming event information

A front office area bulletin board provides an opportunity to post schedules, memorandums, announcements, VIPs in house or arriving, group functions, regular training reminders, and other pertinent information. Bulletin boards are most effective when they are in an area accessible to all front office staff and when employees regularly review the information. In many hotels, employee bulletin boards may be the only source of day-to-day information employees need to do their job properly.

Incentive Programs

Employees deserve special appreciation for the work they perform. An **incentive program** is one of the most effective ways to acknowledge staff members who excel in their work. Incentive programs vary in structure and design and often are an excellent way to reward exceptional performance. The front office should develop and establish incentive programs that result in a situation which is beneficial to guests, the employees, and the front office. An effective incentive program should challenge the staff and create a spirit of competition.

A well-designed front office incentive program should:

- Recognize and reward exceptional staff performance
- Increase staff productivity
- Demonstrate commitment to guest satisfaction

Front office managers should consider the following basic guidelines when developing an incentive program:

- Develop an incentive program that is appropriate and specific to the front office.
- Outline the specific goals and objectives for the program.
- Define the conditions and requirements which front office staff must meet to receive recognition and rewards.
- Brainstorm a variety of rewards and obtain the necessary approvals for any expenditures.
- Determine the date and time the program will begin. Every staff member should participate. Front office managers should be sure to design a program that is fun, realistic, and creative.

Rewards front office managers typically consider are:

- Commendation letters
- Certificates of appreciation
- Public photo display (with the staff member and general manager and/or front office manager)
- Recognition dinners or events
- Gift certificates
- Complimentary weekend packages
- Special parking privileges
- Recognition plaques

Successful incentive programs also provide staff with feedback about goal attainment. For example, charts posted on the front office bulletin board that show individual progress may be very motivational for a reward-oriented incentive program. Goals should be challenging, but should not be so unrealistic that they appear unachievable. Unrealistic goals can frustrate employees and destroy the motivational value of the incentive program.

Front office incentive programs usually center on enhanced occupancy, room revenue, average rate, and guest satisfaction. Conducting one incentive program at a time will help staff focus on specific goals. For example, the front office manager may develop an incentive program directed at increasing the average daily rate or occupancy. Staff may work toward achieving a specific occupancy percentage or a specific average daily rate. The incentive should last for a specific time period. After this time period elapses, the incentive program should end. During a slow season, for instance, the front office manager may want to concentrate on building occupancy. During peak periods, the front office manager may implement an incentive program to maximize the average daily rate through upselling at the front desk.

Performance Appraisals

Front office staff need to feel secure with respect to their job performance. The interaction between front office staff and management can affect an employee's self-image and job perception. Like the employee evaluations discussed earlier in this chapter, a **performance appraisal** is one of the most effective techniques a manager can use to enhance motivation and morale.

A performance appraisal:

- Provides each front office staff member with formal written feedback on his or her job performance.
- Identifies strengths and weaknesses in performance and provides plans and actions for improvement.
- Gives the manager and each employee the opportunity to develop specific goals and progress dates.
- Recognizes and rewards outstanding performance through possible promotions, wage increases, and additional responsibilities.
- Helps identify employee compatibility with a specific work position.

Front office managers will discover there are many methods and techniques for evaluating staff performance. Each front office manager should tailor an appraisal program to meet the department's goals and objectives. Normally, an effective performance appraisal focuses on an employee's job performance and the steps the employee can follow to improve job skills and performance. Performance appraisals should be fair, objective, informative, and positive. When the appraisal process is complete, the employee should clearly understand what he or she is doing well and where he or she needs to improve. Every employee should receive an appraisal at least once a year.

Many front office managers use written performance appraisal forms and procedures. Written appraisals can be very supportive and beneficial when employee counseling or termination are necessary. Written job evaluations that are acknowledged and signed by the staff member should be placed in the employee's personnel file.

Summary

The nature of the work force has changed, as have the techniques and laws that govern its management. Front office managers must recognize these changes in order to better manage and direct the efforts of the front office staff.

Employee recruitment is the process of seeking and screening qualified applicants to fill positions. The process involves communicating job vacancies and interviewing and evaluating applicants. Internal recruiting—the promotion of current employees—can enhance front office morale and productivity. Internal recruiting includes cross-training, succession planning, posting job openings on the premises, rewarding employees for job performance, and keeping a call-back list. External recruiting includes networking, contacting temporary employment agencies, and following up on employee referrals. Federal, state, and local government programs encourage properties to recruit individuals from designated groups by offering tax benefits.

Job descriptions and job specifications are important selection tools. A job description lists all the tasks and related information that make up a work position. Job specifications list and describe the personal qualities, skills, traits, educational background, and experience needed to successfully perform the tasks outlined by a job description.

A job application form should be simple to fill out and should require applicants to provide only information that determines how suitable the person may be for the job. Front office managers evaluate job applicants by reviewing completed job application forms, checking applicant references, and interviewing selected applicants. Managers should check references to verify an applicant's claims.

A job interviewer should be an objective judge of people, a positive role model, a skillful communicator, and a good salesperson. Managers and interviewers should know what to ask and what not to ask; many types of questions are illegal. After an applicant is interviewed, the applicant should be evaluated. The use of an interview evaluation form will help ensure that shortcomings in one area do not unduly diminish an applicant's chances for further consideration.

Hiring involves making all the necessary arrangements to prepare the new employee and current staff for a successful working relationship. The hiring period lasts throughout the new employee's initial adjustment to the job. Since hiring requires knowledge of complex employment and labor laws, most hotels rely on the human resources division or someone specifically designated by top management.

New employees should be given an orientation when they arrive for their first day of work. The front office manager should take full responsibility for orienting new front office employees.

A critical responsibility of the front office manager is ensuring that employees receive proper training. Training can be guided by job lists, which list the tasks that the person in a position must perform. Job breakdowns specify how each task on a job list should be performed. The job breakdown can serve as a training guide and as a tool for evaluating performance. The front office manager can use performance evaluations based on job breakdowns to identify an employee's training needs.

Scheduling employees is one of the most complex and difficult tasks a front office manager faces. Employee scheduling affects payroll costs, productivity, and morale. Staffing flexibility can be achieved by cross-training employees. Cross-training lowers labor costs and provides employees with expanded job knowledge and a broader range of skills.

Front office management should strive to create a work environment that fosters the professional development and growth of employees. To do so, management should provide training, guidance, instruction, discipline, evaluation, direction, and leadership. When an organization lacks these basic elements, employees may become passive, critical, and indifferent to the company's objectives. Such feelings manifest themselves in absenteeism, poor productivity, and high employee turnover.

Key Terms

closed-ended—questions requiring only "yes" or "no" answers; should be limited to verifying information provided on the application or to obtaining facts.

compressed work schedule—an adaptation of full-time work hours that enables an employee to work the equivalent of a standard workweek in fewer than the traditional five days.

cross-training—teaching employees to fill the requirements of more than one position.

external recruiting—a process in which managers seek outside applicants to fill open positions, perhaps through community activities, internship programs, networking, temporary agencies, or employment agencies.

flextime—a program of flexible work hours that allows employees to vary their times of starting and ending work.

hiring period—the time directly after an employment offer has been made through the new-hire's initial adjustments to the job; this period involves all arrangements necessary to prepare the new-hire and current staff for a successful working relationship.

incentive program—a program offering special recognition and rewards to employees based on their ability to meet certain conditions; programs vary in structure and design and are a way to award exceptional performance.

internal recruiting—a process in which managers recruit job candidates from within a department or property; methods include cross-training, succession planning, posting job openings, and keeping a call-back list.

job analysis—determining what knowledge each position needs, what tasks each position needs to perform, and the standards at which the employee must perform the tasks.

job breakdown—a form that details how the technical duties of a job should be performed.

job description—a detailed list identifying all the key duties of a job as well as reporting relationships, additional responsibilities, working conditions, and any necessary equipment and materials.

job knowledge—information that an employee must understand in order to perform his or her tasks.

job sharing—an arrangement by which two or more part-time employees share the responsibilities of one full-time position.

job specification—a list of the personal qualities, skills, and traits needed to successfully perform the tasks outlined by a job description.

motivation—stimulating a person's interest in a particular job, project, or subject so that the individual is challenged to be continually attentive, observant, concerned, and committed.

open-ended questions—questions requiring more than a "yes" or "no" answer; should lead applicants to move detailed responses.

orientation—the period of time devoted to teaching a new employee the basic elements of the job, including the skills and information required to perform the job.

performance appraisal—the process by which an employee is periodically evaluated by his or her manager or supervisor to assess job performance and to discuss steps the employee can take to improve job skills and performance.

performance standard—a required level of performance that establishes the acceptable quality of work.

recruitment—the process by which qualified applicants are sought and screened to fill currently or soon-to-be-vacant positions; involves announcing or advertising job vacancies and evaluating applicants to determine whom to hire.

task list—a list identifying all the key duties of a job in the order of their importance.

Review Questions

1. How are job descriptions and job specifications used in the selection process?
2. Where can a front office manager look for job applicants? What methods can the manager use to find and recruit employees?
3. What are the steps involved in conducting an interview? What techniques and cautions should an interviewer keep in mind when asking interview questions?
4. What points should be covered in an employee orientation?
5. How does a job breakdown expand on the information contained in a job list? What steps are involved in developing job breakdowns?
6. Why is preparation for training important? How can trainers prepare for training? What guidelines can help trainers effectively train?
7. What are several types of alternative scheduling techniques?
8. The most effective performance appraisals are conducted for what reason(s)?

9. What is motivation? What methods can front office managers use to motivate employees? How could an incentive program be used as a method for motivating front office employees?

Internet Sites

For more information, visit the following Internet sites. Remember that Internet addresses can change without notice.

Hotels and Hotel Companies

Best Western
http://www.bestwestern.com

Choice Hotels International
http://www.hotelchoice.com

Canadian Pacific Hotels
http://www.cphotels.ca

Days Inn of America, Inc.
http://www.daysinn.com

Hilton Hotels
http://www.hilton.com

Holiday Hospitality Corporation
http://www.holiday-inn.com

Hyatt Hotels Corporation
http://www.hyatt.com

Inter-Continential Hotels
http://www.interconti.com

ITT Sheraton Corporation
http://www.sheraton.com

Marriott Hotels, Resorts, and Suites
http://www.marriott.com/lodging

Opryland Hotel
http://www.opryhotel.com

Radisson Hotels Worldwide
http://www.radisson.com

Ritz Carlton Hotels
http://www.ritzcarlton.com

Walt Disney World Resorts
http://www.disneyworld.com/vacation

Westin Hotels and Resorts
http://www.westin.com

Lodging Publications—Online and Printed

Hospitality Technology News
http://www.hospitalitynet.nl/news/tech.html

Hotel & Motel Management
http://www.innvest.com/hmm

Lodging Hospitality
http://www.penton.com/corp/mags/lh.html

Lodging Online
http://www.ei-ahma.org/webs/lodging/index.html

Case Study

Staffing for Ski Season at the Frozen Penguin Resort

As a winter ski destination, the Frozen Penguin Resort encounters many full-occupancy seasonal periods. In fact, the hotel is booked solid for the six weeks in the middle of the ski season (a ten-week season). Anticipating this increase in business, management must develop a plan to staff the resort in both the first two weeks (early) and final two weeks (late) as well as the six-week high point of the season.

Fortunately Mr. Scott, the newly hired front office manager, used to be responsible for staffing the Seaquestered Summer Resort, a property that experienced similar occupancy cycles. The fact that the Frozen Penguin is located in a wilderness region, however, creates a unique challenge to Mr. Scott. He always had the luxury of hiring temporary employees from the community college near the Seaquestered Summer Resort. In the mountains surrounding the Frozen Penguin, there is little availability of temporary staff.

Mr. Scott believes that there are two parts to the solution to the staffing puzzle. First, he figures he must recruit a core staff that will commit itself to working the entire ten weeks. He believes he can pay each staff member a reasonable rate throughout the work period and also offer an incentive bonus, payable at the successful completion of the entire season. Second, Mr. Scott feels that in the past the resort has not sufficiently trained the staff to work at a high level of productivity. He feels that through cross-training and restructuring of front office functions, staff members will be capable of working much more effectively and will maintain good morale.

Discussion Questions

1. What do you think are the strengths and weaknesses of the core staff proposal? Is an incentive bonus for successful completion a sound idea? What else could be done to attract the staff necessary to operate the resort?
2. Provide five questions that Mr. Scott may be wise to ask each candidate during a job interview. Be careful to develop questions that will enable Mr. Scott to evaluate the applicants' potential for the proposed training program.
3. What do you think about Mr. Scott's plan to cross-train and restructure front office functions and responsibilities? What do you believe to be of importance in building morale?
4. How should Mr. Scott communicate the standards to the applicants to ensure that they understand the resort's expectations?

Case Number: 33212CA

The following industry experts helped generate this case: Richard M. Brooks, CHA, Vice President—Operations, Bridgestreet Accommodations, Inc., Cleveland, Ohio; and Michael L. Kasavana, Professor, The School of Hospitality Business, Michigan State University, East Lansing, Michigan.

This case also appears in *Case Studies in Lodging Management* (Lansing, Mich.: Educational Institute of the American Hotel & Motel Association, 1998), ISBN 0-86612-184-6.

Index

D

E

F

G

Q

R

S

T

U

V

W

Y

Z

Appendix

Forms for Night Audit Problem

THE WASHINGTON INN

Name: Sunshine Master Acct. No. ______

Room: 101 Rate: $1330.00 Arrival Date: 3/31

DATE	3/31	4/1					
Balance Fwd.		(600 -)					
Room	1330 -						
Sales Tax	53 20						
Restaurant							
Bar							
Local							
Long Distance	16 80						
Telegrams							
Laundry-Valet							
Cash Disburse							
Transfer							
TOTAL	1400 -						
Less: Cash	2000 -						
: Allowances							
: Transfer							
Carried Fwd.	(600 -)						

THE WASHINGTON INN

Name BROWN, MR. & MRS. EDWIN Acct. No. ______

Room 245 Rate $48.00 Arrival Date 3/28

DATE	3/28	3/29	3/30	3/31	4/1		
Balance Fwd.		1 92	65 84	149 76	208 04		
Room	48 -	48 -	48 -	48 -			
Sales Tax	1 92	1 92	1 92	1 92			
Restaurant		14 -	26 -				
Bar			8 -				
Local							
Long Distance				8 36			
Telegrams							
Laundry-Valet							
Cash Disburse							
Transfer							
TOTAL	49 92	65 84	149 76	208 04			
Less: Cash							
: Allowances							
: Transfer	48 -						
Carried Fwd.	1 92	65 84	149 76	208 04			

THE WASHINGTON INN

Name JACKSON, LARRY Acct. No. ______

Room 302 Rate # 70 Arrival Date 3/31

DATE	3/31	4/1					
Balance Fwd.		72 80					
Room	70 -						
Sales Tax	2 80						
Restaurant							
Bar							
Local							
Long Distance							
Telegrams							
Laundry-Valet							
Cash Disburse							
Transfer							
TOTAL	72 80						
Less: Cash							
: Allowances							
: Transfer							
Carried Fwd.	72 80						

THE WASHINGTON INN

Name GREENWOOD, NELSON Acct. No. ________

Room 324 Rate $24 Arrival Date 3/30

DATE	3/30		3/31		4/1									
Balance Fwd.			21	21	49	92								
Room	24	-	24	-										
Sales Tax		96		96										
Restaurant	13	50												
Bar			3	75										
Local														
Long Distance	6	75												
Telegrams														
Laundry-Valet														
Cash Disburse														
Transfer														
TOTAL	45	21	49	92										
Less: Cash														
: Allowances														
: Transfer	24	-												
Carried Fwd.	21	21	49	92										

THE WASHINGTON INN

Name FOSTER, MR. & MRS. JACK Acct. No. ______________

Room 440 Rate $56.00 Arrival Date 3/31

DATE	3/31		4/1											
Balance Fwd.			58	24										
Room	56	–												
Sales Tax	2	24												
Restaurant														
Bar														
Local														
Long Distance														
Telegrams														
Laundry-Valet														
Cash Disburse														
Transfer														
TOTAL	58	24												
Less: Cash														
: Allowances														
: Transfer														
Carried Fwd.	58	24												

THE WASHINGTON INN

Name STRAIGHT, MR. & MRS. TOM Acct. No. ____________

Room 522 Rate $56.00 Arrival Date 3/31

DATE	3/31	4/1					
Balance Fwd.		97 34					
Room	56 –						
Sales Tax	2 24						
Restaurant							
ROOM SERVICE	28 08						
Bar							
Local							
Long Distance	6 52						
Telegrams							
Laundry-Valet							
Cash Disburse	4 50						
Transfer							
TOTAL	97 34						
Less: Cash							
: Allowances							
: Transfer							
Carried Fwd.	97 34						

THE WASHINGTON INN

Name DAVIS, RONALD Acct. No. ______________

Room 100 Rate INCIDENTALS Arrival Date 3/31

DATE	3/31	4/1					
Balance Fwd.		—					
Room							
Sales Tax							
Restaurant							
Bar							
Local							
Long Distance							
Telegrams							
Laundry-Valet							
Cash Disburse							
Transfer							
TOTAL							
Less: Cash							
: Allowances							
: Transfer							
Carried Fwd.	—						

THE WASHINGTON INN
CITY LEDGER CONTROL

DATE	4/1						
Balance Fwd.	50000 —						
Restaurant							
Bar							
Miscellaneous							
Transfer Debit							
TOTAL							
Cash							
Allowances							
Transfer Credit							
Carried Fwd.							

THE WASHINGTON INN

ADVANCE PAYMENTS CONTROL

DATE	4/1													
Balance Fwd.	(2930	-)												
Transfer Debit														
Refund														
TOTAL														
Cash														
Carried Fwd.														

THE WASHINGTON INN

Name ______________________________ Acct. No. __________

Room ____________ Rate __________ Arrival Date ____________

DATE							
Balance Fwd.							
Room							
Sales Tax							
Restaurant							
Bar							
Local							
Long Distance							
Telegrams							
Laundry-Valet							
Cash Disburse							
Transfer							
TOTAL							
Less: Cash							
: Allowances							
: Transfer							
Carried Fwd.							

THE WASHINGTON INN

Name ________________________________ Acct. No. ____________

Room ________________ Rate __________ Arrival Date ______________

DATE							
Balance Fwd.							
Room							
Sales Tax							
Restaurant							
Bar							
Local							
Long Distance							
Telegrams							
Laundry-Valet							
Cash Disburse							
Transfer							
TOTAL							
Less: Cash							
: Allowances							
: Transfer							
Carried Fwd.							

THE WASHINGTON INN

Name ______________________________________ Acct. No. ______________

Room __________________ Rate _____________ Arrival Date __________________

DATE							
Balance Fwd.							
Room							
Sales Tax							
Restaurant							
Bar							
Local							
Long Distance							
Telegrams							
Laundry-Valet							
Cash Disburse							
Transfer							
TOTAL							
Less: Cash							
: Allowances							
: Transfer							
Carried Fwd.							

THE WASHINGTON INN

Name ______________________________ Acct. No. ______________
Room ______________ Rate ____________ Arrival Date ______________

DATE							
Balance Fwd.							
Room							
Sales Tax							
Restaurant							
Bar							
Local							
Long Distance							
Telegrams							
Laundry-Valet							
Cash Disburse							
Transfer							
TOTAL							
Less: Cash							
: Allowances							
: Transfer							
Carried Fwd.							

THE WASHINGTON INN

Name ______________________________ Acct. No. __________

Room __________ Rate __________ Arrival Date __________

DATE														
Balance Fwd.														
Room														
Sales Tax														
Restaurant														
Bar														
Local														
Long Distance														
Telegrams														
Laundry-Valet														
Cash Disburse														
Transfer														
TOTAL														
Less: Cash														
: Allowances														
: Transfer														
Carried Fwd.														

THE WASHINGTON INN

Name __________________________________ Acct. No. ____________

Room ______________ Rate ___________ Arrival Date ______________

DATE							
Balance Fwd.							
Room							
Sales Tax							
Restaurant							
Bar							
Local							
Long Distance							
Telegrams							
Laundry-Valet							
Cash Disburse							
Transfer							
TOTAL							
Less: Cash							
: Allowances							
: Transfer							
Carried Fwd.							

TRANSCRIPT OF GUEST LEDGER

Hotel ____________________ Date ____________ Sheet No. ______

Room No.	No. Guests	Name	Balance Brought Forward	Room	Tax	Rest.	Bar	Room Service	Telephone		Laundry	Cash Disb.	Trans-fers	Total Charges	Cash	Trans-fers	Allow-ances	Balance Carried Forward
									Local	Long Dist.								
		House Total																
		City Ledger																
		Advance Deposits																
		Accts. Receivable Total																